AMERICAN
LITERATURE
TO 1900

GREAT WRITERS STUDENT LIBRARY

Editor: James Vinson
Associate Editor: D. L. Kirkpatrick

AMERICAN
LITERATURE
TO 1900

INTRODUCTION BY
LEWIS LEARY

First published 1980 by
THE MACMILLAN PRESS LIMITED
London and Basingstoke
Associated companies in New York, Dublin
Melbourne, Johannesburg and Madras

ISBN 0333 28336 8

CONTENTS

EDITOR'S NOTE

The entry for each writer consists of a biography, a complete list of his published books, a selected list of published bibliographies and critical studies on the writer, and a signed critical essay on his work.

In the biographies, details of education, military service, and marriage(s) are generally given before the usual chronological summary of the life of the writer; awards and honours are given last.

The Publications section is meant to include all book publications, though as a rule broadsheets, single sermons and lectures, minor pamphlets, exhibition catalogues, etc. are omitted. Under the heading Collections, we have listed the most recent collections of the complete works and those of individual genres (verse, plays, novels, stories, and letters); only those collections which have some editorial authority and were issued after the writer's death are listed; on-going editions are indicated by a dash after the date of publication; often a general selection from the writer's works or a selection from the works in the individual genres listed above is included.

Titles are given in modern spelling, though the essayists were allowed to use original spelling for titles and quotations; often the titles are "short." The date given is that of the first book publication, which often followed the first periodical or anthology publication by some time; we have listed the actual year of publication, often different from that given on the title-page. No attempt has been made to indicate which works were published anonymously or pseudonymously, or which works of fiction were published in more than one volume. We have listed plays which were produced but not published; librettos and musical plays are listed along with the other plays; no attempt has been made to list lost or unverified plays. Reprints of books (including facsimile editions) and revivals of plays are not listed unless a revision or change of title is involved. The most recent edited version of individual works is included if it supersedes the collected edition cited.

In the essays, short references to critical remarks refer to items cited in the Publications section or in the Reading List. Introductions, memoirs, editorial matter, etc. in works cited in the Publications section are not repeated in the Reading List.

INTRODUCTION

Literature *of* America began with accounts of adventurers who, exploring its coasts, spoke of the perils and possibilities of the new found land. Literature *from* America was written by colonists who described for their countrymen in England their experiences, satisfactions, and hardships in making a home in the wilderness, or, more often than not, attempting to inform or reform people in England whose religious ideas were unlike their own. Literature *in* America, meant for American readers, came later, after Stephen Day had set up a printing press in Cambridge in 1638, but especially almost a century after that when newspapers, and then magazines, provided an outlet for colonial writers.

The various adventures of Captain John Smith, especially his spectacular, self-certified rescue by the Indian Princess Pocahontas, have become part of American lore. William Bradstreet's *History of Plimoth Plantation* (not published until 1886) is admired for its placid homespun simplicity, and Thomas Morton's rakish account of roistering with Indians to the displeasure of his Puritan neighbors has made his *New English Canaan* (1654) a source of continuing delight. Captain Edward Johnson's *The Wonder-Working Providence of Sion's Saviour in New-England* (1654), an epic in prose that rises to rhythms of poetry, is among many a cherished book, as is Nathaniel Ward's whimsical *The Simple Cobler of Agawam* (1647) that grumbles delightfully about, among other matters, the unpredictable silliness of women. But justice prevailed, for it may have been Ward himself who carried to England, without her knowledge, the manuscript of Anne Bradstreet's *The Tenth Muse Lately Sprung Up in America* (1650), a cumbersome and derivative, but effective reminder that inherited culture did survive in the American colonies. When published in Boston (1678), the volume contained later poems presenting scenes and sorrows of the new world, "Contemplations" she called them, and it is on these and on the aphoristic "Meditations" in prose on her spiritual and workaday life that her reputation rests.

Far more popular was Michael Wigglesworth whose jingling and horrendous *The Day of Doom* (1662), the first volume of verse to be published in the colonies and America's first best-seller, remained a reminder to many generations that damnation and hell-fire inevitably await those who succumb to the allure of sin. Equally religious but less condemnatory was Edward Taylor, an inconspicuous clergyman, extracts from whose *Poetical Works* (1939) were not published until more than two centuries after his death. A more comprehensive edition appeared in 1960, and a series of sermons prefaced with preparatory meditations in verse two years later. His *Diary* (1964) and *Metrical History of Christianity* (1962) have been transcribed for publication, but to the delight of scholars who rush to the task, he has not been revealed complete. Here, at last, was a voice rising above the dreary desert of theological dispute to speak with self-abnegating sweetness of the glory of God and the insignificance of man, "a crumb of earth," in such striking imagery that Taylor has been somewhat loosely compared with Richard Crashaw, George Herbert, and Francis Quarles. "God's Determinations Touching His Elect" is a long dramatic poem, speaking with tenderness and compassion of what Wigglesworth had made a nightmare vision. Taylor's "Meditations," though repetitious in theme, are dextrously phrased, and his occasional secular poems are a refreshing proof that in colonial America literary artistry was not moribund.

For colonial Americans wrote busily, and none more so than doughty Cotton Mather whose colossal *Magnalia Christi Americana* (1702), often ridiculed, is now regarded with increasing respect. A multi-faceted man, the bibliography of whose writings requires two large volumes, he straddles, a giant, the tight-minded theological certainty of New England's seventeenth century and her entry into the age of the enlightenment. Mather's *Essays to Do*

Good (1717) provided his young neighbor Benjamin Franklin with title, though not content, for "The Dogood Papers" (1720), contributed to the *Boston Gazette* as America's first series of periodical essays. Franklin was to make a career of being first, in establishing (1741) the first successful magazine in America, in "the Speech of Polly Baker" (1747) presenting what may be thought of as its first short story, and in "Advice to a Young Man in Search of a Mistress" (1745) its first manual of sex. His *Autobiography* (written 1771–89) created the prototype of the self-made, opportunistic, and self-reliant American, and his *The Way to Wealth* (1758) provided a handbook on how others might achieve that end. He was colloquial, iconoclastic, alternately jovial and bitter in satire, warm in praise of conviviality but a champion of frugality, a facile versifier and caustic critic of doggerel. To paraphrase, and perhaps improve, what Ernest Hemingway once said of Mark Twain, all American literature can be thought to have begun with this multi-faceted man.

But not quite all. Among Franklin's eighteenth-century contemporaries were other writers who helped form part of what can be thought of as a distinctively American view. First among them was William Byrd of Virginia, educated in England and familiar with its fashionable spas and London literary circles, who wrote much in the fashionable patois of the time, but, returning to play an inherited role in colonial government, had occasion to survey or inspect backcountry areas that had not been described before. Urbane and witty, with an eye for scene and comic situation, he wrote between 1729 and 1733 accounts of a "History of the Dividing Line," a "Journey to the Land of Eden," and of "Progress to the Mines" that he polished carefully and showed to a few friends, but were not publicly revealed until almost two centuries after his death. A gentle satirist and a stylist of practiced skill, aloof but observant, he represents a kind of writing, patrician but penetrating, that has become another characteristic of literature in America. Of coarser but more ebullient kind was Ebenezer Cooke, first transient, then colonist in Maryland, who in *The Sot-Weed Factor* (1708) and *Sotweed Redivivus* (1730) wrote boisterous doggerel condemning, then damning with faint praise, tobacco (sot-weed) growers and other colonial settlers among whom he found few men honest, or women chaste. His descendants also thrive.

Jonathan Edwards may be thought of as representative of another prominent strand woven to the American pattern. Remembered for such things as his hell-fire sermons, like "Sinners in the Hands of an Angry God" (1741) and his logical masterwork denying *Freedom of the Will* (1754), he is better represented as a person who saw in all physical objects images and shadows of the majesty of God, a concept on which nineteenth-century Transcendentalists would play a variety of changes. His *Treatise Concerning Religious Affections* (1756) is written with charming simplicity and his posthumous *The Nature of True Virtue* (1758) is a rhapsodic celebration of moral beauty upheld by love as a goal for God-directed people. Even with inherited religion in his way, Edwards blazed trails that others would follow – in several directions.

Literature for literature's sake, however, emerged slowly in the American colonies. Richard Lewis, a schoolmaster in Maryland wrote in the 1730's landscape poetry that was printed with approval in London periodicals. During the 1760's there was a brief flurry of activity in Boston, where Mather Byles, Joseph Greene, and other young men amused themselves and honored visiting dignitaries with occasional verse. But the first concerted surge of activity came from young men in Philadelphia under the leadership of William Smith, Provost of its college. Thomas Godfrey presented in *The Prince of Parthia* (written 1759) the first play by an American to be performed on the professional stage. His *Juvenile Poems* (1765) were posthumously edited by his friend Nathaniel Evans, whose *Poems on Several Occasions* (1772) were in turn posthumously edited by their mentor Smith. Thomas Coombe and Jacob Duché, active among the group, when the colonies rose in revolt, fled to England, there to publish writings begun at home. Best remembered among them, however, is Francis Hopkinson, poet, essayist, musician, and lawyer and, until his death in 1791, as graceful and disarming a political satirist as his time produced. His *A Pretty Story* (1774) was an Arbuthnotian satire about a new farm (the colonies) that had trouble in adhering to restrictions set by the nobleman owner of the old farm (Great Britain). In *The Battle of the*

Kegs (1779) he made great fun of British soldiers who fired at floating barrels, thinking them to be filled with armed rebels. During times of stress, Hopkinson's good-natured satire kept his countrymen laughing.

In New England was also gathered a group of young men remembered as the Connecticut Wits. Their leader was John Trumbull, who in *The Progress of Dulness* (1772) told in jovial Hudibrastic couplets of the misadventures of two collegians, Tom Brainless and Dick Hairbrain, and of a local belle, Harriet Simper, who, in choosing between them, chose perforce the duller. Two years before, on graduation from Yale College, Trumbull had in "Prospect of the Future Glory of America" looked to the time when his "land her Steele and Addison shall view" and a "future Shakespeare charm a rising age." To hasten this, he gathered about him a group of young men, students or tutors at the college. Each would engage in large literary activity. Trumbull, again in Hudibrastics, in a mock-epic *M'Fingal* (1775–82) pointed to absurd activities among his countrymen in revolt against or loyal to the Crown. Though his writings long remained popular, Trumbull was too prudent to risk reputation by continued satire, and turned aside from further major literary excursions. But not his friends, Timothy Dwight and Joel Barlow. Each had for years been working over a long poem. Dwight's *The Conquest of Canaan* (1785), celebrating the leading of the Israelites to their promised land, was interpreted as an allegory (though Dwight insisted that it was not) of George Washington leading Americans to freedom. Barlow's *The Vision of Columbus* (1787) tells in cumbrous, often unrelated, detail what the purported discoverer of the new world saw in a dream of its future, in accomplishment and promise. David Humphreys, a soldier, later turned diplomat and successful man of commercial affairs, wrote with more enthusiasm than skill verses that called for industry and frugality among his countrymen. Perhaps more useful than any of these were the spellers and readers put together by Barlow's classmate Noah Webster, so that the new United States, he said, would not have to depend on English texts "to learn our children."

Dwight continued to write, and Barlow also, the first in *The Triumph of Infidelity* (1788), a vitriolic attack on heresies offered by attractive tempters like Voltaire, in *Greenfield Hill* (1794) in which he borrowed English manner and meter to describe the quiet virtues of a New England village, and then in tracts, sermons, and *Travels* (1821–22). Barlow seemed to his friends a traitor to conservative New England ways when, crossing to Europe, he joined Thomas Paine, whose *Rights of Man* (1791–92) and *The Age of Reason* (1794–95) were attacked as heretical, by publishing *Advice to the Privileged Orders* (1792–93) in prose and *The Conspiracy of Kings* (1792) in verse. Best remembered for his charming little homesick poem about a favorite New England dish, *The Hasty-Pudding* (1796), late in life he expanded and revised *The Vision of Columbus* to *The Columbiad* (1807), a handsomely printed book remembered now chiefly by title.

To harass loyalists in Boston, Mercy Warren wrote satirical closet dramas, *The Adulateur* (1773) and *The Group* (1775). Later, she would contribute occasional verse to periodicals, and publish her *Poems, Dramatic and Miscellaneous* (1790). But the principal scourge of the British was Philip Freneau, a young gentleman from Princeton, who on graduating collaborated with his classmate Hugh Henry Brackenridge in writing *A Poem on the Rising Glory of America* (1772) that looked with ebullient optimism to a time when America would discover a new Homer, a new Milton to sing its spacious charms and wondrous prospects. His activities as a patriotic propagandist, notably in *General Gage's Confession* (1775) and *American Liberty* (1775), earned him the title of "the Poet of the American Revolution." But he was more than that. Both early and late he wrote verses of unusual merit, like "The House of Night" (1779), "The Wild Honey Suckle" (1786), and "To a Caty-did" (1815). His *Poems* (1786) reveal him a poet of many facets, whose early aspiring "The Power of Fancy" (written 1770) suggests promise never fully achieved, and his *Miscellaneous Works* (1788) reveals him also deft in prose, humorous, satirical, even philosophical. But much of his active career was spent as a political propagandist, his poetical talent unrealized. Though editions of his *Poems* appeared in 1795, 1809, and 1825, and though he continued to publish verse into the late 1820's, he died in obscurity.

Brackenridge did little better. During the Revolution he wrote patriotic plays for amateur production, *The Battle of Bunkers Hill* (1776) and *The Death of General Montgomery* (1777). Moving after the war to the Pennsylvania frontier where he was unsuccessful as a politician, he wrote his disappointment into *Modern Chivalry* (1792–1805) in which the peripatetic Captain Farrago and various Sancho Panzas, notably an illiterate Irishman named Teague O'Regan, wandered the countryside through a series of quizzical adventures that revealed democratic processes as not always effective. Other instructive novels had now begun to attract attention, many warning of the danger of reading novels because novels render young ladies easy prey to men of evil intention. Often called America's first novel is William Hill Brown's *The Power of Sympathy* (1789), followed in rapid succession by such instructive fictions as Susanna Rowson's *Charlotte Temple: A Tale of Truth* (1791) and Hannah Foster's *The Coquette* (1797), all moral guides. But not until the last years of the decade did America's first respectworthy novelist appear.

Charles Brockden Brown, Quaker born and bred, is often remembered as America's first professional man of letters. From the publication of *The Rhapsodist* (1789), a series of periodical essays, until his death at thirty-nine, he wrote verse, literary criticism, and a substantial number of tales and essays. His career came to an astounding climax as the century ended, with *Alcuin: A Dialogue* (1798), advocating the rights of women, followed in rapid succession by the novels for which he is best remembered: *Wieland* (1798), *Arthur Mervyn* (1799), *Ormond* (1799), and *Edgar Huntly* (1799), gothic tales written under the liberalizing influence of William Godwin, but proudly with American settings. With *Clara Howard* (1801) and *Jane Talbot* (1801) his effective literary career ended. Illness, poverty, and hackwork occupied much of the rest of his brief life. Admired by Shelley and Scott, an influence on Edgar Allan Poe, his *Novels* (1827) were reprinted in Boston, at which time they were read with interest by Henry Wadsworth Longfellow and Nathaniel Hawthorne. In technique, Brown was experimental, often cumbersome, but there is vigor in what he wrote, a sense of scene and situation, and an ability to create characters, often introspective, that certify his writings as more than historical artifacts. *Wieland* explores the sad consequences of religious fanaticism, *Arthur Mervyn* details the adventures of a young man in search of himself, *Ormond* glances at the international conspiracy of Illuminati who would reform the world to their pattern, and *Edgar Huntly* is a murder mystery, brim-filled with terror and suspense, Indians, panthers and backcountry villainy. Together, they contain seeds that, cultivated by surer hands, would later more effectively flower.

Brown's friend and biographer, William Dunlap, also began a career in the 1790's that for him would extend for almost half a century. Painter, dramatist, theatrical manager, novelist, biographer, and historian, brother-in-law of Timothy Dwight, friend and advisor to James Fenimore Cooper, like Franklin he was a jack of many trades. Returning to the United States in the fall of 1787 after three years of study in the London atelier of Benjamin West, he had just missed seeing the production of Royall Tyler's *The Contrast* (1787) in New York that spring, the first play by a citizen of the United States to be produced professionally. Tyler's play, leaning heavily on English sources for much of its dialogue and action, had nonetheless donned native garb in its presentation of Captain Manly, truly a manly veteran of the Revolution who spurned the foppish Chesterfieldian airs of many of his countrymen, urging them to patriotic frugality, but especially in the Captain's servant Jonathan, the ancester of many later native country bumpkins who would continue to fascinate American audiences. Tyler, a young man about town, a soldier, then successful as a jurist, was a better writer of light verse than he was a playwright. He would produce other plays, like *May Day in Town* (1787) and *The Georgia Spec* (1797), and even biblical drama in verse, and a rambling novel, *The Algerine Captive* (1797), but *The Contrast*, by reason of its being an American first, provides the fragile base on which his reputation rests.

Dunlap, not conspicuously successful as a painter, seems to have been sure that as playwright he could do better. *The Father; or, American Shandy-ism* (1789) did well enough to persuade him over the next twenty-some years to write or translate, often to produce as theatrical manager, some fifty more, among the best remembered of which are *André* (1798) and *The Italian Father* (1799). But Dunlap's most lasting contribution is in the reminiscences of people he had known, in his *Diary* (1930), his *Life* (1815) of Brown, his *A History of the American Theatre* (1832), his *History of New York* (1837), and in a remarkably good, usually unnoticed work, *Thirty Years Ago; or, The Memoirs of a Water Drinker* (1836). If he accomplished nothing of primary importance, he was there, he recorded, providing sustenance to every historian of early American literature.

He knew and admired Washington Irving, whom everyone remembers for two stories, "Rip Van Winkle" (1819) and "The Legend of Sleepy Hollow" (1820), both included in *The Sketch Book of Geoffrey Crayon* (1819–20), which appeared as if in reply to Sydney Smith's somewhat surly question, "Who reads an American book?" Though most of the sketches were of English countryside and manners, urbane, witty, in cautiously patterned prose, they seemed to offer proof in plenty that here at last was an American who wrote with skill and grace. But a younger Irving, less cautious, had done better in his sacrilegious burlesque *A History of New York* (1809), supposed to have been the product of a crotchety Dutchman named Diedrich Knickerbocker who wrote boldly, with light flashes of humor, about events of the past that foreshadowed contemporary foolishments. Then, after seventeen years abroad, delightedly a companion of Campbell and Scott, and including a sentimental pilgrimage to Spain that he chronicled in *The Conquest of Granada* (1829) and *The Alhambra* (1832), Irving returned to America and American scenes in *A Tour on the Prairies* (1835) and *Astoria* (1836). Though the effective force of his early writing was diminished, no one of his time wrote more gracefully than he, and his imitators were legion. Among the better were John Pendleton Kennedy in *Swallow Barn* (1832), Nathaniel Parker Willis in *Pencillings by the Way* (1835), and Charles Fenno Hoffman in *A Winter in the West* (1835).

James Fenimore Cooper was of a different sort, a burly man who came to writing late. A former naval officer become country squire, he never achieved dextrous felicity in prose. Author of more than thirty novels, some like *The Spy* (1821) of the American Revolution, some like *The Pilot* (1823) of the sea, others of corrupt European traditions as *The Bravo* (1831) or of corruption in America as *Home as Found* (1838), Cooper was a forthright and contentious man, often embroiled in libel suits brought against his critics, and scolding their kind in *A Letter to His Countrymen* (1834) and *The American Democrat* (1838). Among his better writings is the trilogy *Satanstoe* (1845), *The Chainbearer* (1845), and *The Redskins* (1846) that tells of rent-wars against patroons of the Hudson River Valley. But in his "Leatherstocking Tales" – *The Pioneers* (1823), *The Last of the Mohicans* (1826), *The Prairie* (1827), *The Pathfinder* (1840), and *The Deerslayer* (1841) – he created in the woodsman Natty Bumppo a character who has become in various avatars permanently a part of native lore, the ancestor of many Indian-fighting or Indian-protecting stalwarts in film or fiction.

John Neal also wrote sympathetically of the Indian in *Logan* (1822), of the Revolution in *Seventy-Six* (1823), and of early life in New England in *Brother Jonathan* (1825). In the South William Gilmore Simms wrote romances of frontier life in *Guy Rivers* (1834), of adventure during the American Revolution in *The Partisans* (1835), of Indian warfare in *The Yemassee* (1835), and dozens of other well-wrought volumes. John Pendleton Kennedy's *Horse-Shoe Robinson* (1835) and John Esten Cooke's *Leather Stocking and Silk* (1854) continued the tradition of native romance. Robert Montgomery Bird's *Nick of the Woods* (1837) is a thrilling account of bloodthirsty revenge against bloodthirsty Indian attack. But none of these succeeded, as Cooper did, in setting forth in mythic terms the gradual encroachment of civilization on wilderness.

Irving's friend James Kirke Paulding wrote in verse of the expanding West in *The Backwoodsman* (1818) and William Cullen Bryant of "The Prairies" (1832), but Paulding's later writings would be in fiction of the Hudson River alley, and Bryant, after a brilliant early career that produced "Thanatopsis" (1817) and "To a Waterfowl" (1821), spent much of the rest of a long life as a prominent newspaper editor in New York, respected for the simple dignity of his writings in prose and verse. His early contemporaries, Fitz-Greene Halleck and Joseph Rodman Drake, highly praised in their lifetime, are now virtually forgotten, though the former's *Fanny* (1819) is amusing satire of New York society and his "Alnwick Castle"

(1817) remains a favorite anthology piece. Drake's "The Culprit Fay" (written 1816), a pretty little tale in verse of the adventures of a small elf assigned to deeds of derring-do, was severely criticized by Edgar Allan Poe as he made his distinction between fancy and imagination. America's first prominent bohemian, as dextrous with his pen as clumsy in managing his personal affairs, Poe was also its first complete man of letters. Poet, essayist, editor, a critic so severe that he was called "the tomahawk man," a pioneer in the short story, master of detective fiction and the mystery thriller, he liked cryptograms, puzzles, and bewilderments, so that tales like "Ligeia" (1838) and poems like "Ulalume" (1847) offer a variety of interpretations, and poems like "The Raven" (1845) seem designed to create more of mood than meaning. A runaway boy, troubled through much of his life by misfortunes, many of his own making, Poe's first volume of verse, *Tamerlane* (1827), appeared when he was eighteen, followed by *Al Aaraaf* (1829) and *Poems* (1831), all printed at his own expense. *The Raven and Other Poems* (1845) was his only collection of poetry that found a regular publisher. He had great trouble also in finding someone to underwrite collections of his sketches and stories. *Tales of the Grotesque and Arabesque* (1840) and *Tales* (1845), however, cemented his reputation as a writer as dextrous and devious in prose as in verse. His novel, *The Narrative of Arthur Gordon Pym* (1838), is sometimes read with interest as foreshadowing some elements in Melville's *Moby-Dick*. A nimble writer, of large influence on other writers in his country and abroad, Poe has been considered by many to have fallen short of genuine greatness.

Yet he was overshadowed by writers less talented than he. Perhaps no poet writing in English has been more universally popular during his lifetime than Henry Wadsworth Longfellow from New England, whose simple verse narratives and songs of aspiration or quiet revery were everyone's favorites. He was the great literary educator of his countrymen, introducing them to rhythms and stanzaic forms drawn from many languages, adapting them to simple native situations. *Evangeline* (1847), *Hiawatha* (1855), and *The Courtship of Miles Standish* (1858) were all best-sellers. Such poems as "The Village Blacksmith" (1841), "The Children's Hour" (1860), and "Paul Revere's Ride" (1861) have long remained favorite recitation pieces. But though still remembered with affection, Longfellow is less highly thought of now. With John Greenleaf Whittier, Oliver Wendell Holmes, and James Russell Lowell he is recalled as one of "the schoolroom poets" whose portraits once gracing each classroom are now turned face to the wall.

Everyone remembers that Whittier was a great and good man, who hated slavery, wrote *Snow-Bound* (1866), and verses about childhood and country customs. Holmes, physician, essayist, novelist, witty raconteur, and occasional poet is remembered for a few recitation pieces like "Old Ironsides" (1830), "The Chambered Nautilus" (1858), and "The Deacon's Masterpiece; or, The Wonderful 'One-Hoss Shay'" (1858). His once popular essays collected in *The Autocrat of the Breakfast-Table* (1858) and its sequels are now seldom read. His "medicated novels" like *Elsie Venner* (1861) and *A Mortal Antipathy* (1885) are curious antecedents of "psychological" fiction, seldom removed from the library shelves. Lowell, perhaps the most influential literary person of his generation, ready to supply verse for any occasion, is hardly remembered at all, except perhaps for portions of *The Vision of Sir Launfal* (1848) that ask "what is so rare as a day in June?", and his *Fable for Critics* (1848) that good-naturedly satirizes his literary contemporaries.

Each of these was a genteel man, writing impeccably well in inherited forms, expressing inherited notions. In the South, Henry Timrod and Paul Hamilton Hayne, each fragile, wrote fragile lines, often of infinite sweetness and lingering charm, and later Sidney Lanier, who combined music and poetry, sometimes to the detriment of both, fought courageously against disease to produce dulcet rhythms celebrating scenery and chivalry. Frederick Goddard Tuckerman, who published little during his lifetime, has since the collection of his *Complete Poems* (1965) risen in critical esteem. Skilled craftsmen all, and read with appreciative reverence, they nevertheless look more often to the past than to the workaday world of expanding America.

Sharing center stage with Longfellow, Holmes, and Lowell was Ralph Waldo Emerson who probably had more influence on his and succeeding generations than any writer in America. His was the voice of independence. Rely on yourself, he counselled. Think your own thoughts. Forget the dogma of your fathers. Today is today, and each day can provide its own fresh, new revelation. His "American Scholar" (1837) has been called his country's literary declaration of independence. His essay on "Self Reliance" in *Essays* (1841) seemed to catch up and encourage the buoyant spirit of the United States as it reached toward wealth. But essays like "Experience" in *Essays: Second Series* (1844) and "Fate" in *The Conduct of Life* (1860) showed him to be more than simply an ebullient advocate of confidence as he spoke in them of the terror of living, and of man's fearsome responsibilities. For what purpose, he challenged, are people allowed the privilege of living? And he answered, to be themselves, to realize whatever potential was available. Believing that there was a method of apprehending truth that transcended what senses could apprehend, he was called a Transcendentalist. There was one spirit common to, within, and available to all persons, which, if listened to with care, with knowledge that fate or experience might distort its voice, was a person's best guide. Follow, but with caution, the voice within, confident that what is true for each is true for all. In *Representative Men* (1850) he called on his countrymen to be prepared for the challenge of their time.

And then suddenly, as if in response or rebuttal to what Emerson seemed to have been saying, there appeared in rapid succession four books that stand high among America's masterworks. Nathaniel Hawthorne's *The Scarlet Letter* (1850) and Herman Melville's *Moby-Dick* (1851) dealt with what Emerson had spoken of as the miscmances or terrors of life. Henry David Thoreau's *Walden* (1854) and Walt Whitman's *Leaves of Grass* (1855) have been thought of as extensions or applications of his more ebullient pleas. It has sometimes seemed convenient to capsulize America's writers of the mid-nineteenth century as those of the party of memory – such as Longfellow, Whittier and their kind; those of the party of hope – Emerson, Thoreau, Whitman; and those of the party of doubt – Hawthorne and Melville. But this, however convenient, is a deceptive simplification. Each was in his own degree a Transcendentalist, searching beneath appearances for truths surpassing understanding.

This is why Hawthorne called his fictions romances. They sought below surfaces for what words could not tell – a characteristic, many believe, of that which is best in American, perhaps in any, literature. His *Twice-Told Tales* (1837, enlarged 1842) seemed simple nostalgic narrative sketches, but *Mosses from an Old Manse* (1846) introduced troublesome, ambiguously teasing allegories, defying precise explanation. Until the publication of *The Scarlet Letter*, Hawthorne had been largely a coterie writer, admired by a discriminating few. The popularity of that small book, partly because it seemed a scandalous tale, tempted him to further book-length stories. *The House of the Seven Gables* (1851) owed in externals much to the then pervasive influence of Charles Dickens, but carried within it seeds of symbolic meaning which seem to bear new fruit for each critical generation. With *The Blithedale Romance* (1852), a tale that may in part be sardonic autobiography, Hawthorne's effective career was over. *The Marble Faun* (1860), which tells of Americans abroad, is perhaps more revealing of themes hidden subtly in his earlier writings than successful in its own right. During his later years, his creative powers declined, and the fragments of fiction published posthumously do little to add to his literary stature.

Hawthorne's reputation among his contemporaries came to him after years of apprentice work. Melville's first fiction, however, brought him almost instant fame. After some years footloose at sea, he wrote of exotic escapades in the South Seas in *Typee* (1846) and *Omoo* (1847), books that were well received. But Melville was not satisfied with admiration for his books of adventure. He would be remembered, he hoped, as something more than a man who had lived among savages. So in *Mardi* (1849) he put together a narrative so tangled with emblematic meanings that few in his time or since have been able to unravel them. He followed it with two more simply devised books, *Redburn* (1849) and *White Jacket* (1850), partly winning back some share of popularity. But then he published *Moby-Dick* (1851) and followed it with *Pierre* (1852). A madman certainly, it was thought, had put these books together, each recounting a quest after great emblematic phantoms representing who knows what. A discouraged and apparently seriously distraught Melville retreated then from public exposure with two parting shafts, *The Piazza Tales* (1856), which included such tantalizing gems as "Bartleby, The Scrivener," "Benito Cereno," and "The Encantadas," and *The Confidence-Man* (1857), which anticipated Mark Twain in exposing cupidities of the "damned human race." In retirement, Melville wrote poetry. His *Battle-Pieces* (1866) shares with Whitman's *Drum-Taps* (1865) the distinction of presenting the best verse to emerge from the United States' struggle in the early 1860's to remain united. *Clarel* (1857), a long, musing poem based on travels in the Holy Land, *John Marr and Other Sailors* (1888), and *Timoleon* (1891) were all privately printed. After Melville's death the manuscript of a short narrative, *Billy Budd* (1924), was discovered, seeming to capsulize in some part what he had brilliantly suggested in his earlier, once spurned, great parables of whales and walls. Only then, more than three decades after his death, was he recognized as a writer of whom his countrymen could be, and continue to be proud.

Even less universally appreciated during his lifetime was Henry David Thoreau. Then, as now, people were likely to admire him greatly or think him a pretentious humbug. Thoreau published only two books, *A Week on the Concord and Merrimack Rivers* (1849) and *Walden; or, Life in the Woods* (1854). An adventurer in forest and meadowland, he wandered, notebook in hand, to record what he found valuable. He is often thought of as a hermit who lived in a little house built with his own hands on land owned by Emerson beside Walden Pond. But he was no hermit. He was chanticleer, he said, crowing loudly to wake his neighbors from their daily stupor, so busy were they at being good that they were, he told them, finally good for nothing. Thoreau was a rebel in word and action, and his essay on "Civil Disobedience" (1849) has provided a rallying cry for people in rebellion, in his time, in the time of Mahatma Gandhi, and in ours. All who reverence wildness or wilderness or nature, including the unpredictable nature of man, reverence Thoreau. His posthumously published volumes of travel and his journals remain continuously a delight – to his admirers. (To others, he is self-centered, man-centered, and a bore.)

Much the same must be said of Whitman, that gigantic superman poet who soars in imagination aloft above his country, admiring it, describing it and its people in loving detail, missing nothing, embracing all. His one great work was of America as choreographed by Walt Whitman, and he called it *Leaves of Grass*. From 1855 to 1897 it went through many editions, expanding and rearranging itself as America expanded into new arrangements of land and people. Whitman's outspoken boldness that battered through traditions of form and content attracted many, particularly among the younger persons of his time, but many respectable contemporaries found him far too outspoken about matters of which respectable people do not speak. And yet here, as in Emerson, Thoreau, and Melville also, was the true voice of an emerging new nation. They had their female counterpart in Emily Dickinson, quietly a recluse, who published only a handful of verses during her lifetime, whose *Poems* (1890) appeared posthumously, and were not collected complete until 1955. Dickinson spoke more softly than her male contemporaries, but her brief, often gnomic, lines examine nature and aspiration, and other such mysteries, including death. The critic mistakes his purpose in attempting to explain her. She must be read in order to understand how a person who spoke with such hesitation to her own contemporaries speaks so clearly now to ours.

At midcentury the United States, in politics as in literature, was at a turning point. Civil war loomed on the horizon. Tempers flared, and indignation ran high. Thoreau went to jail rather than pay taxes to support what he thought to be an unjust war against Mexico. Whittier wrote militantly in prose and verse against the injustice of the slavery of blacks. Even mild Emerson was aroused. But none spoke more effectively than Harriet Beecher Stowe whose *Uncle Tom's Cabin* (1852), combining sentiment with realism, exposed the evils of slavery. More than 300,000 copies were sold within a year – no American book had done as well. It was made immediately into a play, and as presented on stage or as story has become part of American lore. Propagandistic and perhaps overwrought, violently attacked and zealously defended, it remains both a sociological and a literary monument.

When in 1865 the Civil War was over, literature in the United States took new directions. Before 1860 it had derived almost entirely from its eastern seaboard. But after the war as the country expanded westward, new voices rose. Though the older poets – Longfellow, Lowell, Whittier, and Whitman, and, though unheard, Emily Dickinson also – still wrote, the new literature of the later decades of the century was largely in prose, much of it about sections of the expanding country seldom written of before. Bret Harte presented in "The Luck of Roaring Camp" (1868) and "The Outcasts of Poker Flat" (1869) frontier types in the mine fields of California. John Hay's *Pike County Ballads* (1871) presented dialect verse accounts of the Illinois frontier, George Washington Cable in *Old Creole Days* (1879) introduced bilingual Louisiana, and Joel Chandler Harris told stories of plantation life in Georgia in *Uncle Remus* (1881) and its popular sequels. Mary Noailles Murfree as Charles Egbert Craddock wrote of people *In the Tennessee Mountains* (1884). Thomas Nelson Page wrote sentimentally of plantation life *In Ole Virginia* (1887). New England rural life was revealed in Harriet Beecher Stowe's *Oldtown Folks* (1869), in Mary E. Wilkins Freeman's *A New England Nun* (1891), and with greater artistry in Sarah Orne Jewett's *The Country of the Pointed Firs* (1896). Lafcadio Hearn, meticulously a stylist, wrote descriptive sketches of urban Ohio, of New Orleans, most effectively in *Chita* (1889), then of the West Indies, and finally of Japan.

These people who revealed uncommon characters in simple, often romantic situations in areas not well known to ordinary readers have been called local colorists. Closely linked to them were novelists often intent on reform like Rebecca Harding Davis, whose *Margaret Houth* (1862) reveals sordidness in the life of a northern mill town, much as Albion W. Tourgée in *A Fool's Errand* (1879) and *Bricks Without Straw* (1880) reveals problems in rebuilding the war-torn south, as do John William De Forest in *Miss Ravenal's Conversion from Secession to Loyalty* (1867) and Constance Fenimore Woolson in *Rodman the Keeper* (1880). Life in the middle west was realistically presented by Edward Eggleston in *The Hoosier School-Master* (1871), by Edgar W. Howe in *The Story of a Country Town* (1883), and with some bitterness by Joseph Kirkland in *Zury, The Meanest Man in Spring County* (1887). Helen Hunt Jackson's *Ramona* (1884) is a romantic tale of Spaniards and Indians in southern California. James Lane Allen in *A Kentucky Cardinal* (1895) and *The Choir Invisible* (1897) wrote of local scenes sentimentally in beautifully cadenced prose. For in spite of what has been called the rise of realism in the late nineteenth century, romance, sentimentality, and optimism stalwartly held their own, in the dozens of exemplary tales by Horatio Alger, each proving that indeed, in America, goodness and diligence inevitably bring success, in Timothy Shay Arthur's horrendous experiences in *Ten Nights in a Bar-Room* (1854), in Margaret Finley's guide to obedience and good manners in *Elsie Dinsmore* (1867), in Louisa May Alcott's happy family accounts in *Little Women* (1868) and its popular sequels, and in Frances Hodgson Burnett's *Little Lord Fauntleroy* (1886) who represented, in contradistinction to Mark Twain's *Huckleberry Finn*, everything that every good boy should be. From the 1880's well into the twentieth century Francis Marion Crawford, Edgar Saltus, and many another provided in romance the thrill and chill of escape to adventure.

Though the theater remained active, not only in larger cities, but increasingly in smaller towns visited by travelling companies, few plays of lasting interest were produced during the nineteenth century. Samuel Woodworth, better known for his song of "The Old Oaken Bucket" (1823), and James Nelson Barker wrote now forgotten plays with native settings, while John Howard Payne, whose major claim to fame is his nostalgic song "Home, Sweet Home" (1823), wrote equally unremembered romantic drama with settings abroad. Everyone flocked to see dramatizations of *Rip Van Winkle* and *Uncle Tom's Cabin*, each done with melodramatic flair. Augustus Daly produced melodramas like *Under the Gaslight* (1867), problem plays like *Divorce* (1871), and romantic dramas of the West, like *Horizon* (1871). Later in the century audiences seemed satisfied with the timely though quite undistinguished society-orientated dramas of Bronson Howard and Clyde Fitch. The slapstick comedy of the minstrel show delighted many audiences.

For native American humor, present since the jocularities of Franklin and Ebenezer Cooke, surged toward popularity at mid-century. Seba Smith had used rustic New England dialect in detailing the adventures of *Major Jack Downing* (1833). Augustus B. Longstreet's sketches in *Georgia Scenes* (1835) had told of raucous backcountry shenanigans, as had James G. Baldwin's in *Flush Times of Alabama and Mississippi* (1853). Johnson Jones Hooper in *Some Adventures of Captain Simon Suggs* (1845) had revealed pecadilloes of a backwoods gambler in the old southwest, and James Russell Lowell had moved beyond conventional verse in *The Biglow Papers* (1848–62) turning dialect and humor to the service of politics and reform. Fabulous tales were told of Mike Fink, the riverboat man, and of Paul Bunyan, the giant lumberjack. Thomas Bangs Thorpe's whopper about "The Big Bear of Arkansas" (1841) became a classic among native tall tales. George Washington Harris had great fun in detailing the often scandalous misadventures of that "nat'ral born durn'd fool" *Sut Lovingood* (1867). David Ross Locke as Petroleum V. Nasby distorted grammar and spelling in presenting the escapades of a renegade clergyman in *The Nasby Papers* (1864). Henry Wheeler Shaw as *Josh Billings* (1865) poked down-to-earth good-natured fun at backsliding in politics, home-life, and morals. None was more popular than Charles Farrar Browne who as Artemus Ward captured the fancy of the public, especially as a lecturer whose laconic humor brought both fame and fortune. It was he who started Mark Twain in the same profitable business.

For dominating the latter years of the nineteenth century were three men beside whom most of these others may seem Lilliputian indeed. Samuel Clemens came roaring in from the west as Mark Twain, to take the country by storm. William Dean Howells, a more precise man from Ohio, moved into New England and then New York to take over from native sons command of their literary establishments. Henry James, born to wealth in the East and largely educated abroad, did most of his writing in England. Clemens and James can be thought to represent extremes, in vulgar terms one proudly plebeian, the other with equal pride patrician. As far as is known, they never met, nor did either comment more than casually on the writings of the other. Howells stood in the middle, friend and counsellor to both. That was characteristic of Howells, to be a middleman, neither too far out nor in too deep. Each of these three continued in activity and influence into the twentieth century when Clemens was an embittered scold and James was read with decreasing enthusiasm, but when Howells was esteemed, except by younger men who thought him to have been too long in office, as the dean of American letters.

Samuel Clemens become Mark Twain, had there ever been another like him? Mountebank and sage, he played a part, and provided himself costume and legend to create an image unique. Journeyman printer, steamboat pilot, speculator, journalist, raconteur, world traveller, a man of few ties and little apparent literary ambition, except as literature secured worldly comfort, he seemed specially favored by fortune. Quite by chance his "The Celebrated Jumping Frog of Calaveras County" (1865), written in California at the suggestion of Artemus Ward, took the East by storm, and when the letters that he wrote as a newspaper correspondent on a cruise ship to the Mediterranean were gathered as *The Innocents Abroad* (1869), his reputation was secure, his profitable career as a public lecturer guaranteed to keep audiences aroar with laughter well underway. He ventured first into the novel in collaboration with Charles Dudley Warner in *The Gilded Age* (1873), a light-handed exposé of political and economic chicanery, which gave name to the era in which Mark Twain, and many another an entrepreneur, flourished. Then he certified himself as a novelist in his own right with *The Adventures of Tom Sawyer* (1876), *The Prince and the Pauper* (1881), and *A Connecticut Yankee in King Arthur's Court* (1889), stories designed to appeal to readers of almost every age. He wrote popular books of travel in humorously peculiar countries like England, Germany, and South Africa, and a nostalgic account of his *Life on the Mississippi* (1883). In *The Tragedy of Pudd'nhead Wilson* (1894) and *The Man That Corrupted Hadleyburg* (1900) he wrote again of varieties of human corruption. But his single masterwork is *The Adventures of Huckleberry Finn* (1884), the book with which Ernest Hemingway was later to testify all American literature begins. This saga of a boy at war with his conscience as he floats down a great river tells much of Samuel Clemens and his time, but even more of conditions that face people, inevitably conscience-ridden, at any time.

Mark Twain's genius was in control of language, colloquial and formal, and in a view of the world as a place roiled by the sometimes well-meaning misdeeds of people. As he grew older, he pointed with increasing despair, less lightened by humor, at the hideous malefactions of what he called, not without affection, the damned human race. To his friend Howells, however, people seemed susceptible to redemption, and he wrote some forty novels to demonstrate that human decency might somehow prevail. There are no large heights nor great depths in Howells's writings, not in the fiction, the plays, the essays, the travel books, or the occasional poems that for more than half a century he diligently produced. He pleaded for realism in literature. Life should be presented as neither worse nor better than it is. He was wholly dedicated, a good man, interested in social causes and, however despairing he may sometimes seem in private correspondence, confident in his public statements that right will prevail.

A generous man, as editor of the *Atlantic Monthly* from 1871 to 1881 Howells encouraged many new young writers, notably the local colorists. His moving to New York when his term of editorship was over provided a visible sign that that city had replaced Boston as the literary capital of the nation. There as elder statesman, he continued as patron and advisor to young men like Stephen Crane, Hamlin Garland, and Frank Norris who ventured even farther than he in realistic detail. His own novels *The Rise of Silas Lapham* (1885) and *A Hazard of New Fortunes* (1889) are worthy of shelfroom beside any of America's best. They are books to which the historian may turn in confidence to learn how people lived and spoke in those late Victorian times.

To some Henry James is without question America's foremost writer of fiction, who in depth of perception and subtle skill with words produced more novels of excellence than any other. They would argue that while Hawthorne, Melville, and even Mark Twain are remembered, each for one superlatively fine book, James is represented by perhaps half a dozen or more of equal excellence. Each admirer will set forth his own favorites, but most will agree that in, at very least, *The Portrait of a Lady* (1881), *The Princess Casamassima* (1886), *The Aspern Papers* (1888), and the three novels representative of what has been called his major phase, *The Wings of the Dove* (1902), *The Ambassadors* (1903), and *The Golden Bowl* (1904), he reached heights unscaled before. Each of these examines Americans in Europe, faced with a culture different from their own, to which they become victims or over which they triumph. Others may prefer his two principal novels with American settings, *Washington Square* (1881) and *The Bostonians* (1886). Still others, however, consider James an unmitigated bore, only to be tolerated in his early, more simply devised stories of *The American* (1877) or *Daisy Miller* (1879).

There is little action, still less of overt adventure in the writings of Henry James. His interest is in the friction of personality on personality, and in the complications that arise when several distinct personalities grope toward understanding of the complex relationships that bind them together or keep them apart. Specifically, his concern was with the culture, the fine things in manners and art, that Europe offered, and how they might be received, assimilated, or rejected by intelligent representatives of the new America where culture, when it existed, was borrowed or bought. Most of his Americans do well, whether trapped within or rising above inherited transatlantic patterns. Decency and honesty override tradition, so that James, for all his foreign settings and subtle discriminations, can be thought of, as much as Walt Whitman, as a champion of the probity and promise of his countrymen.

As the century ended, new writers appeared, some of whom, like Hamlin Garland, who in *Main-Travelled Roads* (1891) began presentation of hardships of Iowa and South Dakota farm life, and Henry Blake Fuller, who in *The Cliff-Dwellers* (1893) told a story of romance and intrigue in a Chicago skyscraper, would write as well into the twentieth century, as would Harold Frederic, who in *The Damnation of Theron Ware* (1896) told of the downfall of a well-intentioned but misguided young clergyman, and S. Weir Mitchell whose historical romances like *Hugh Wynne, Free Quaker* (1897) made him long a popular favorite. Robert Herrick began a novel-writing career that would extend for more than thirty years with *The Man Who Wins* (1897) and *The Gospel of Freedom* (1898), introducing an increasingly pessimistic view of the inevitable influence of capitalism and political corruption on well-meaning people. Ambrose Bierce, newspaper man and iconoclast, leapt to prominence with short narratives of horror and suspense in *Tales of Soldiers and Civilians* (1891), setting a standard that he would not quite reach again. Encouraged by Howells, Norwegian-born H. H. Boyesen in *The Golden Calf* (1892) wrote of the downfall of a young man in search of easy wealth. Needing encouragement from no one, the populist reformer Ignatius Donnelly in *Caesar's Column* (1890) looked with jaundiced eye toward the twentieth century when the rich would get richer and the poor poorer.

These were all respectworthy writers, popular in the best sense. But as the nineteenth century moved toward a close fresh new voices arose, harbingers each of better things. Frank Norris at twenty-one published a long romantic poem, *Yvernelle: A Legend of Feudal France* (1891). But then, first influenced by Emile Zola and later encouraged by Howells, he turned abruptly to realism of the starkest kind. He is sometimes held forth as America's first naturalistic novelist, secured in certainty that people were playthings of fate. His first attempt at fiction of this kind was *Vandover and the Brute*, a gruesome tale of moral disintegration, not published until 1914, twelve years after its author's death. In *Moran of the Lady Letty* (1898) naturalism skirts close to melodrama in a lurid tale of violence and intrigue in adventure at sea. *McTeague* (1899), though tinged with melodrama also, presents a more effective account of how greed and inexperience, and the inexorable hand of fate, can lead to the destruction of people of good intentions. Norris's brief career came to a climax with the publication of *The Octopus* (1901) and then, posthumously, of *The Pit* (1903), novels which he had intended to be part of a trilogy (the final volume to be called *The Wolf*) that would tell of the problems in growing, the chicanery in selling, and, in the third volume, the consumption of American wheat in poverty-stricken Europe. For all his early accomplishment, Norris remains one of the great might-have-beens of American fiction. In *The Responsibilities of the Novelist* (1903), a volume put together after his death the year before, he gives stalwart indication that had he lived he would certainly have seriously contended for success.

Even younger than he, and with a career more brief, was Stephen Crane, who brought a new dimension to the realism of his contemporaries. At twenty-two he borrowed money to pay for the publication of *Maggie, A Girl of the Streets* (1893); it found few readers, but with it modern American fiction was born. With great economy in words, with impressionistic imagery, and with tremendous sympathy Crane presented the fateful circumstances that propelled an attractive innocent toward degradation and destruction. No reinforcement of commentary was necessary. Crane's images created a panoramic backdrop against which characters, often as if in pantomime, moved toward predestined ends. Crane saw with a poet's eye. His own verse as presented in *The Black Riders* (1895) and *War Is Kind* (1899) seemed stark indeed to a generation nourished on Longfellow and Whittier, and responding to the whimsical songs of Eugene Field, the nostalgic sentimentalities of James Whitcomb Riley, and invitations to romantic adventure in Richard Hovey's *Songs from Vagabondia* (1894). Crane's were sharp cryptic poems, stark in imagery, suggesting acquaintance with the poems of Emily Dickinson that had been publicly revealed only five years before, and with them pointing toward the imagist movement that would rise in America a quarter of a century later.

The Red Badge of Courage (1895) is Crane's best known, most often discussed novel. Some critics have placed it beside Hawthorne's *The Scarlet Letter*, Melville's *Moby-Dick*, and James's *The Portrait of a Lady* as among the best produced in America's nineteenth century. It is a story of war, of the advance and retreat of armies, in which a young man faces death, first with terror but finally with assurance that a person can accept and withstand, however briefly, its awesome inevitability. But Crane's health, never robust, broke after service as a war correspondent in Cuba and Greece during the later 1890's, and he spent his later years in Europe, closely associated with Henry James and Joseph Conrad. During the remaining years of his active career, he wrote a dozen further volumes of fiction or reminiscence, none of which was completely a popular or artistic success. But his short stories "The Blue Hotel,"

"The Open Boat," and "The Bride Comes to Yellow Sky" identify him as anticipating Ernest Hemingway in mastery of that form.

Black voices, though often raised in protest by such militant advocates of equal rights as the orator Frederick Douglass, and by autobiographical slave narratives such as those by Nat Turner and William Wells Brown (the latter also, in *Clotel; or, The President's Daughter,* 1853, used fiction to suggest miscegenation in high places), during much of the nineteenth century had been only unobtrusively represented, except as distorted in sentimental song or story most often composed by whites. Booker T. Washington spoke perhaps too optimistically of *The Future of the Negro* (1899) anticipating his biographical *Up from Slavery* that would appear two years later. Paul Laurence Dunbar's *Lyrics of Lowly Life* (1896) and his sketches in *Folks from Dixie* (1898) and *The Strength of Gideon* (1900) combine pathos with humor in picturing the life of blacks in America. More realistic were the stories of blacks in slavery collected in *The Conjure Woman* (1899) by Charles Waddell Chesnutt and the comparison between a black woman enslaved and a black woman free presented in *The Wife of His Youth* (1899).

Women until recently have not fared well in discussion of literature in the United States before 1900. A nod in passing has been directed toward Anne Bradstreet as, curiously, America's first poet, and toward Phillis Wheatley who in the late eighteenth-century somehow miraculously became its first black poet. But many Americans have grumbled as Hawthorne did about the "damned tribe of scribbling women." Margaret Fuller, who never feared to correct Emerson or Thoreau, or anyone else, when convinced, as she often was, that the person, usually male, was wrong, has been largely remembered as a strange woman, perhaps not completely moral, when she was in truth one of the more able literary critics in English of the nineteenth century. Emily Dickinson through her own choosing remained unhonored and unknown, but the posthumous publication of her verse revived interest in poetry that was more than merely metronomically melodious, not only in people like Stephen Crane, but in greater poets – one of whom, Edwin Arlington Robinson, had already begun to publish as the century ended – who during the first decades of the new century would open even more expansive territories for poetry to explore. And Harriet Beecher Stowe, once condescended to as simply a sentimental propagandist, is increasingly recognized as a writer of superior skill, while Sarah Orne Jewett, rising high above others who have sometimes been dismissed as mere local colorists, is almost universally recognized as an artist complete. But not until the twentieth century was almost halfway over did many Americans remember that there had been in their grandparents' time a woman in the United States who had written more candidly than any other about women, their rights and rightful aspirations.

Like *Moby-Dick, Walden,* and *Leaves of Grass,* Kate Chopin's *The Awakening* (1899) was not well received by most readers of its time. Like *The Scarlet Letter,* it spoke of matters that many contemporaries thought indelicate. For more than ten years Chopin had been a popular local colorist, collecting her tales of Creole and Acadian life in Louisiana into *Bayou Folk* (1894) and *A Night in Acadie* (1897). Many of her stories are about spirited girls restive under restrictions of convention. Others, not selected for either volume, tell of married women, tempted toward freedom from bonds imposed by society. *The Awakening* reveals a woman who does break those bonds to search for self-realization unallowed by convention. She fails, as does the ghetto waif in Stephen Crane's *Maggie,* but not for the same reasons. Edna Pontellier of *The Awakening* is not simply a victim. She makes choices, and whether she chooses rightly or wrongly is not subject to authorial comment. Whether Edna's failure to achieve the freedom she seeks is her fault or results from the rigidity of custom is something each reader must determine. In *The Awakening,* Chopin for the first time in the literature of her country presented a candid woman's view of a woman's problem. Beside it, the man's view of a not unsimilar seeking for freedom presented a year later in Theodore Dreiser's *Sister Carrie* has been said to seem shallow indeed. Chopin published nothing further, but with *The Awakening* left testimony that in literature at very least the voice of the woman would increasingly be heard over the land.

READING LIST

1. Bibliographies, handbooks, etc.

Dictionary of American Biography, 20 vols., 1928–37; supplements, 1944, 1958, 1973; concise edition, 1964.

Kunitz, Stanley J., and Howard Haycraft, *American Authors 1600–1900: A Biographical Dictionary of American Literature,* 1938.

Hart, James D., *The Oxford Companion to American Literature,* 1941; 5th edition, 1975.

Spiller, Robert E., and others, editors, *Literary History of the United States: Bibliography,* 1946; 4th edition, 1974.

Wright, Lyle B., *American Fiction: A Contribution Toward a Bibliography, 1774–1850,* 1948; *1851–1875,* 1965; *1876–1900,* 1966.

Dargan, Marion, *Guide to American Biography 1607–1933,* 2 vols., 1949–52.

Leary, Lewis, *Articles on American Literature, 1900–1950,* 1954; *1950–1968,* 1970; *1968–1975,* 1979.

Blanck, Jacob, *Bibliography of American Literature,* 1955—

Holman, C. Hugh, *The American Novel Through Henry James,* 1966.

Rubin, Louis D., Jr., *A Bibliographical Guide to the Study of Southern Literature,* 1969.

Davis, Richard Beale, *American Literature Through Bryant 1585–1830,* 1969.

Ryan, Pat M., *American Drama Bibliography: A Checklist of Publications in English,* 1969.

Gerstenberger, Donna, and George Hendrick, *The American Novel: A Checklist of Criticism of Novels Written since 1789,* 2 vols., 1970.

Nilon, Charles H., *Bibliography of Bibliographies of American Literature,* 1970.

Long, E. Hudson, *American Drama from Its Beginnings to the Present,* 1970.

Clark, Harry Hayden, *American Literature: Poe Through Garland,* 1971.

Stovall, Floyd, editor, *Eight American Authors: A Review of Research and Criticism,* revised by James Woodress, 1971.

Tanselle, G. T., *Guide to the Study of United States Imprints,* 2 vols., 1971.

Cohen, Hennig, *Articles in American Studies, 1954–1968,* 1972.

Kolb, Harold H., Jr., *A Field Guide to the Study of American Literature,* 1976.

Leary, Lewis, *American Literature: A Study and Research Guide,* 1976.

Inge, M. Thomas, editor, *Black American Writers,* 2 vols., 1978.

2. General histories

Quinn, Arthur Hobson, *A History of the American Drama,* 3 vols., 1923–27; revised edition, 2 vols., 1936–43.

Parrington, Vernon Louis, *Main Currents in American Thought: An Interpretation of American Literature from the Beginnings to 1920,* 3 vols., 1927–30.

Pattee, Fred Lewis, *The First Century of American Literature 1770–1870,* 1935.

Quinn, Arthur Hobson, *American Fiction: An Historical and Critical Survey,* 1936.

Brooks, Van Wyck, *Makers and Finders: A History of the Writer in America 1800–1915,* 5 vols., 1936–52.

Jones, Howard Mumford, *The Theory of American Literature,* 1948; revised edition, 1965.

Spiller, Robert E., and others, editors, *Literary History of the United States,* 1946; 4th edition, 1974.

Quinn, Arthur Hobson, editor, *The Literature of the American People: An Historical and Critical Survey*, 1951.
Clark, Harry Hayden, editor, *Transitions in American Literary History*, 1953.
Cunliffe, Marcus, *The Literature of the United States*, 1954; 3rd edition, 1970.
Stovall, Floyd, *The Development of American Literary Criticism*, 1955.
Howard, Leon, *Literature and the American Tradition*, 1960.
Pearce, Roy Harvey, *The Continuity of American Poetry*, 1961.
Peden, William, *The American Short Story*, 1964.
Meserve, Walter J., *An Outline History of American Drama*, 1965.
Waggoner, Hyatt H., *American Poets from the Puritans to the Present*, 1968.
Nye, Russel B., *The Unembarrassed Muse: The Popular Arts in America*, 1970.
Blair, Walter, and Hamlin Hill, *America's Humor: From Poor Richard to Doonesbury*, 1978.

3. Topics, themes, short periods, etc.
Tyler, Moses Coit, *A History of American Literature During the Colonial Period*, 2 vols., 1878; *The Literary History of the American Revolution*, 2 vols., 1897; abridged by Archie H. Jones as *A History of American Literature 1607–1783*, 1967.
Goddard, Harold Clark, *Studies in New England Transcendentalism*, 1908.
Lawrence, D. H., *Studies in Classic American Literature*, 1923.
Rusk, Ralph Leslie, *The Literature of the Middle Western Frontier*, 2 vols., 1925.
Rourke, Constance M., *American Humor: A Study of the National Character*, 1931.
Miller, Perry, *The New England Mind*, 2 vols., 1939–52.
Brown, Herbert Ross, *The Sentimental Novel in America 1789–1860*, 1940.
Matthiessen, F. O., *American Renaissance: Art and Expression in the Age of Emerson and Whitman*, 1941.
Kazin, Alfred, *On Native Grounds: An Interpretation of Modern American Prose Literature*, 1942.
Taylor, Walter Fuller, *The Economic Novel in America*, 1942.
Wilson, Edmund, editor, *The Shock of Recognition: The Development of Literature in the United States Recorded by the Men Who Made It*, 1943; revised edition, 1955.
Cowie, Alexander, *The Rise of the American Novel*, 1948.
Smith, Henry Nash, *Virgin Land: The American West as Symbol and Myth*, 1950.
Westbrook, P. D., *Acres of Flint: Writers of Rural New England*, 1951.
Stafford, John, *The Literary Criticism of "Young America": A Study of the Relationship of Politics and Literature, 1837–1850*, 1952.
Bewley, Marius, *The Complex Fate: Hawthorne, Henry James, and Some Other American Writers*, 1952.
Feidelson, Charles, *Symbolism and American Literature*, 1953.
Hubbell, Jay B., *The South in American Literature 1607–1900*, 1954.
Lewis, R. W. B., *The American Adam: Innocence, Tradition, and Tragedy in the Nineteenth Century*, 1955.
Miller, Perry, *The Raven and the Whale: The War of Words and Wits in the Era of Poe and Whitman*, 1956.
Miller, Perry, *Errand into the Wilderness*, 1956.
Walcutt, Charles Child, *American Literary Naturalism: A Divided Stream*, 1956.
Spencer, Benjamin T., *The Quest for Nationality*, 1957.
Chase, Richard, *The American Novel and Its Tradition*, 1957.
Levin, Harry, *The Power of Blackness*, 1958.
Bode, Carl, *The Anatomy of American Popular Culture 1840–61*, 1959.
Bewley, Marius, *The Eccentric Design: Form in the Classic American Novel*, 1959.
Nye, Russel B., *The Cultural Life of the New Nation 1776–1830*, 1960.
Fiedler, Leslie, *Love and Death in the American Novel*, 1960.
Pizer, Donald G., *Realism and Naturalism in Nineteenth-Century American Fiction*, 1961.
Hoffman, Daniel, *Form and Fable in American Fiction*, 1961.

Martin, Terence, *The Instructed Vision: Scottish Common Sense Philosophy and the Origins of American Fiction,* 1961.

Wilson, Edmund, *Patriotic Gore: Studies in the Literature of the American Civil War,* 1962.

Jones, Howard Mumford, *O Strange New World: American Culture: The Formative Years,* 1964; *Revolution and Romanticism,* 1974; *The Age of Energy: Varieties of American Experience 1865–1915,* 1971.

Marx, Leo, *The Machine and the Garden: Technology and the Pastoral Ideal in America,* 1964.

Tanner, Tony, *The Reign of Wonder: Naivety and Reality in American Literature,* 1965.

Ziff, Larzer, *The American 1890's: Life and Times of a Lost Generation,* 1966.

Martin, Jay, *Harvests of Change: American Literature 1865–1914,* 1967.

Anderson, Quentin, *The Imperial Self: An Essay in American Literary and Cultural History,* 1971.

Cady, Edwin H., *The Light of Common Day: Realism in American Fiction,* 1971.

Petter, Henri, *The Early American Novel,* 1971.

Holman, C. Hugh, *The Roots of Southern Writing: Essays on the Literature of the American South,* 1972.

Aaron, Daniel, *The Unwritten War: American Writers and the Civil War,* 1973.

Rubin, Louis D., Jr., editor, *The Comic Imagination in American Literature,* 1973.

Emerson, Everett, editor, *Major Writers of Early American Literature,* 1975.

Inge, M. Thomas, editor, *The Frontier Humorists: Critical Views,* 1975.

Leary, Lewis, editor, *Soundings: Some Early American Writers,* 1975.

Kolodny, Annette, *The Lay of the Land,* 1975.

Silverman, Kenneth, *A Cultural History of the American Revolution,* 1976.

Davis, Richard Beale, *Intellectual Life in the Colonial South 1585–1763,* 3 vols., 1978.

Smith, Henry Nash, *Democracy and the Novel: Popular Resistance to Classic American Writers,* 1978.

4. Anthologies of primary works

Quinn, Arthur Hobson, editor, *Representative American Plays,* 1917; revised edition, 1930.

Moses, Montrose J., editor, *Representative Plays by American Dramatists,* 3 vols., 1918–25.

Blair, Walter, editor, *Native American Humor,* 1937.

Miller, Perry, and Thomas H. Johnson, editors, *The Puritans,* 1938; revised edition, 1963.

Clark, Barrett H., and others, editors, *America's Lost Plays,* 20 vols., 1940; supplementary vol.: *Satiric Comedies,* edited by William R. Reardon and Walter J. Meserve, 1969.

Warfel, Harry, and G. Harrison Orians, editors, *American Local-Color Stories,* 1941.

Miller, Perry, editor, *The Transcendentalists: An Anthology,* 1950.

Matthiessen, F. O., editor, *The Oxford Book of American Verse,* 1950.

Brown, Clarence Arthur, editor, *The Achievement of American Criticism: Representative Selections from Three Hundred Years of American Criticism,* 1954.

Thorp, Willard, editor, *A Southern Reader,* 1955.

Bradley, Sculley, and others, editors, *The American Tradition in Literature,* 1956; 4th edition, 1974.

Stegner, Wallace, editor, *Selected American Prose 1841–1900: The Realistic Movement,* 1958.

Pearce, Roy Harvey, editor, *Colonial American Writings,* 1960; revised edition, 1969.

Weber, Brom, editor, *An Anthology of American Humor,* 1962.

Brooks, Van Wyck, editor, *A New England Reader,* 1962.

Hoffman, Daniel, editor, *American Poetry and Poetics: Poems and Critical Documents from the Puritans to Robert Frost,* 1962.

Bontemps, Arna, editor, *American Negro Poetry,* 1963; revised edition, 1974.

Cohen, Hennig, and William B. Dillingham, editors, *Humor of the Old Southwest,* 1964; revised edition, 1975.

Allen, Gay Wilson, Walter B. Rideout, and James K. Robinson, editors, *American Poetry*, 1965.

Nye, Russel B., and Norman S. Grabo, editors, *American Thought and Writing*, 2 vols., 1965.

McElderry, Bruce R., Jr., editor, *The Realistic Movement in American Writing*, 1965.

Moody, Richard, editor, *Dramas from the American Theatre 1762–1909*, 1966.

Horner, George F., and Robert A. Bains, editors, *Colonial and Federalist American Writings*, 1966.

Fogle, Richard H., editor, *The Romantic Movement in American Writing*, 1966.

Cady, Edwin, editor, *The American Poets 1800–1900*, 1966.

Spiller, Robert E., editor, *The American Literary Revolution 1783–1837*, 1967.

Meserole, Harrison T., editor, *Seventeenth-Century American Poetry*, 1968.

Silverman, Kenneth, editor, *Colonial American Poetry*, 1968.

Thorp, Willard, editor, *Great Short Works of American Realism*, 1968.

Thorp, Willard, editor, *Great Short Works of the American Renaissance*, 1968.

Turner, Darwin T., editor, *Black American Literature*, 3 vols., 1969.

Howe, Irving, Mark Schorer, and Larzer Ziff, editors, *The Literature of America*, 3 vols., 1970.

Taylor, E. Golden, editor, *The Literature of the American West*, 1971.

Baker, Houston A., Jr., editor, *Black Literature in America*, 1971.

Pizer, Donald, editor, *American Thought and Writing: The 1890's*, 1972.

Brooks, Cleanth, Robert Penn Warren, and R. W. B. Lewis, editors, *American Literature: The Makers and the Making*, 2 vols., 1973.

Litz, A. Walton, editor, *Major American Short Stories*, 1975.

Ellmann, Richard, editor, *The New Oxford Book of American Verse*, 1976.

ADAMS, Henry (Brooks). American. Born in Boston, Massachusetts, 16 February 1838; great grandson of John Adams, grandson of John Quincy Adams, and son of the writer Charles Francis Adams. Educated at Harvard University, Cambridge, Massachusetts, 1854–58, A.B. 1858; studied law at the University of Berlin, 1858–59. Married Marian Hooper in 1872 (died, 1885). Lived in Dresden, 1859–60; travelled in Italy, writing for the *Boston Courier*, 1860; Private Secretary to his father, when Congressman from Massachusetts, in Washington, D.C., 1860–61, and when Minister to the Court of St. James, London, 1861–68; lived in Washington, D.C., and again in London, contributing to various American periodicals, 1869; Editor, *North American Review*, Boston, and Assistant Professor of History, Harvard University, 1870–76; settled in Washington, D.C.; in later life spent six months in each year in France. LL.D.: Western Reserve University, Cleveland, 1892. Member, American Academy of Arts and Letters. *Died 26 March 1918.*

PUBLICATIONS

Collections

Letters, edited by Worthington Chauncey Ford. 2 vols., 1930–38.
A Henry Adams Reader, edited by Elizabeth Stevenson. 1958.
The Education of Henry Adams and Other Selected Writings, edited by Edward N. Saveth. 1965.

Fiction

Democracy: An American Novel. 1880.
Esther. 1884.

Other

Chapters of Erie and Other Essays, with Charles Francis Adams, Jr. 1871.
Essays in Anglo-Saxon Law. 1876.
The Life of Albert Gallatin. 1879.
John Randolph. 1882; revised edition, 1883.
History of the United States of America During the Administration of Jefferson and *Madison.* 9 vols., 1889–91; abridged version edited by Herbert Agar, as *The Formative Years*, 2 vols., 1947.
Historical Essays. 1891.
Memoirs of Marau, Last Queen of Tahiti. 1893; as *Memoirs of Arii*, 1901; edited by Robert E. Spiller, as *Tahiti: Memoirs of Arii Taimai*, 1947.
Recognition of Cuban Independence. 1896.
Mont-Saint-Michel and Chartres. 1904; revised edition, 1912.
The Education of Henry Adams: An Autobiography. 1907; edited by Ernest Samuels, 1974.
A Letter to American Teachers of History. 1910.
The Life of George Cabot Lodge. 1911.
The Degradation of the Democratic Dogma. 1919.
Letters to a Neice and Prayer to the Virgin of Chartres, edited by Worthington Chauncey Ford. 1920.
Henry Adams and His Friends: A Collection of His Unpublished Letters, edited by Harold Dean Cater. 1947.

Selected Letters, edited by Newton Arvin.   1951.
The Great Secession Winter of 1860–61 and Other Essays, edited by George Hochfield.   1958.

Editor, *Documents Relating to New England Federalism 1800–1815.*   1877.
Editor, *The Writings of Albert Gallatin.*   3 vols., 1879.
Editor, with Clara Louise Hay, *Letters of John Hay and Extracts from Diary.*   3 vols., 1908.

Reading List: *The Young Henry Adams, Adams: The Middle Years,* and *Adams: The Major Phase* by Ernest Samuels, 1948–64; *The Mind and Art of Adams* by J. C. Levenson, 1957; *Adams* by George Hochfield, 1962; *The Suspension of Adams: A Study of Manner and Matter* by Vern Wager, 1969; *A Formula of His Own: Adams's Literary Experiment* by John Conder, 1970; *Symbol and Idea in Adams* by Melvin E. Lyon, 1970; *Adams* by Louis Auchincloss, 1971; *Adams* by James G. Murray, 1974; *The Force So Much Closer Home: Adams and the Adams Family* by Earl N. Harbert, 1977.

*   *   *

Standing in much the same relation to American culture in the latter half of the 19th century that Emerson did to the earlier period, Adams might be said to have made a distinguished and melancholy career out of being the right sensibility for the wrong time and place. Dedicated to public service but shunted to the sidelines, genuinely committed to the orderly development of democratic processes but disillusioned by the post-Civil War expansionism that has been called "The Big Barbecue," Adams gradually contracted the sphere of his idealism, his sociality, and the generosity of his responses to a diminished center of bleak pessimism. Even so, this proved to be a sufficient base on which was built a noteworthy career as teacher (Harvard University), editor (*North American Review*), novelist (*Democracy* and *Esther*), and historian. The two novels deal with pressing issues of the period, the growth of business in government and the strength of science in terms of religious dogma. It is, however, in his twin meditations, *Mont-Saint-Michel and Chartres* and *The Education of Henry Adams*, that his erudition and mastery of the ironic mode fuse with a sombre lyricism to produce a pair of eccentric masterpieces that combine autobiography, philosophy of history, and saturnine prophecy.

Respectively subtitled "A Study of Thirteenth-Century Unity" and "A Study of Twentieth-Century Multiplicity," the books establish the figures of the virgin and the dynamo as the historically dominant symbols of forces that shape the values, the social organization, and the concepts of personality in both time-periods. The replacement of the former by the latter, in Adams's view, exemplifies what he believed to be the scientific principle of the acceleration of history. In these terms he attempts to understand and explain the loss of stable certitudes, the increased fragmentation of social groups, and the new burden of impotence and isolation on the individual psyche. Adams doubtless believed that his own shattered private life was an accurate reflection of this larger social and metaphysical explosion, and this personal despair lends a tone of mordant authority to his prose which almost precisely counters the accents of Emerson's optimism. Brilliant, acerbic, and unsparing in its effort to conduct a grim cultural biopsy, Adams's work consummately articulates the outrage of the Genteel Tradition and stands as a major formulation of the ideology that would later be expressed by such alienated writers as Eliot and Pound.

—Earl Rovit

ALCOTT, Louisa May. American.   Born in Germantown, Philadelphia, Pennsylvania, 29 November 1832; daughter of the philosopher Amos Bronson Alcott; grew up in Boston, and later in Concord, Massachusetts. Educated at home by her father, with instruction from Thoreau, Emerson, and Theodore Parker. Began to write for publication, 1848; also worked as a teacher, seamstress, and domestic servant to support her family; army nurse at the Union Hospital, Georgetown, Washington, D.C. during the Civil War, 1861–63; visited Europe, 1865; Editor of the children's magazine *Merry's Museum*, 1867; visited Europe, 1870, then settled in Boston. *Died 6 March 1888.*

Collections

> *Glimpses of Louisa: A Centennial Sampling of the Best Short Stories.* edited by Cornelia
> Meigs. 1968.

Fiction

> *Flower Fables.* 1855.
> *The Rose Family: A Fairy Tale.* 1864.
> *On Picket Duty and Other Tales.* 1864.
> *Moods.* 1865; revised edition, 1882.
> *Morning-Glories and Other Stories.* 1867.
> *The Mysterious Key and What It Opened.* 1867.
> *Three Proverb Stories.* 1868.
> *Kitty's Class Day.* 1868.
> *Aunt Kipp.* 1868.
> *Psyche's Art.* 1868.
> *Little Women; or, Meg, Jo, Beth, and Amy.* 2 vols., 1868–69; as *Little Women and
> Good Wives*, 1871.
> *An Old-Fashioned Girl.* 1870.
> *Will's Wonder Book.* 1870.
> *Little Men: Life at Plumfield with Jo's Boys.* 1871.
> *V.V.; or, Plots and Counterplots.* 1871.
> *Aunt Jo's Scrap-Bag: My Boys, Shawl-Straps, Cupid and Chow-Chow, My Girls,
> Jimmy's Cruise in the Pinafore, An Old-Fashioned Thanksgiving.* 6 vols., 1872–82.
> *Work: A Story of Experience.* 1873.
> *Beginning Again, Being a Continuation of "Work."* 1875.
> *Eight Cousins; or, The Aunt-Hill.* 1875.
> *Silver Pitchers, and Independence: A Centennial Love Story.* 1876; as *Silver Pitchers
> and Other Stories*, 1876.
> *Rose in Bloom: A Sequel to "Eight Cousins."* 1876.
> *A Modern Mephistopheles.* 1877.
> *Under the Lilacs.* 1877.
> *Meadow Blossoms.* 1879.
> *Water Cresses.* 1879.
> *Jack and Jill: A Village Story.* 1880.
> *Proverb Stories.* 1882.
> *Spinning-Wheel Stories.* 1884.
> *Jo's Boys and How They Turned Out.* 1886.

Lulu's Library: A Christmas Dream, The Frost King, Recollections.   3 vols., 1886–89.
A Garland for Girls.   1888.
A Modern Mephistopheles, and A Whisper in the Dark.   1889.
Louisa's Wonder Book: An Unknown Alcott Juvenile, edited by Madeleine B. Stern.   1975.
Behind a Mask: The Unknown Thrillers, edited by Madeleine B. Stern.   1975.
Plots and Counterplots: More Unknown Thrillers, edited by Madeleine B. Stern.   1976.

Plays

Comic Tragedies Written by "Jo" and "Meg" and Acted by the "Little Women," edited by A. B. Pratt.   1893.

Other

Hospital Sketches.   1863; revised edition, as *Hospital Sketches and Camp and Fireside Stories,* 1869.
Nelly's Hospital.   1868.
Something to Do.   1873.
A Glorious Fourth.   1887.
What It Cost.   1887.
Jimmy's Lecture.   1887.
Alcott: Her Life, Letters, and Journals, edited by Ednah D. Cheney.   1889.
Recollections of My Childhood's Days.   1890.
A Sprig of Andromeda: A Letter on the Death of Henry David Thoreau, edited by John L. Cooley.   1962.

Bibliography: in *Bibliography of American Literature* by Jacob Blanck, 1955; in *Louisa's Wonder Book* edited by Madeleine B. Stern, 1975.

Reading List: *Alcott* by Madeleine B. Stern, 1950; *Alcott* by Cathering O. Peare, 1950; *Miss Alcott of Concord* by Marjorie Worthington, 1958; *Alcott and the American Family Story* by Cornelia Meigs, 1970; *Louisa May: A Modern Biography of Alcott* by Martha Saxton, 1977.

*   *   *

Louisa May Alcott's reputation as one of America's best-loved writers is based upon *Little Women,* a domestic novel for girls which is also appealing to adults. *Little Women* reflects the Alcott family background of high-minded idealism while it glosses over the Alcott family problems. Its characters, the four March girls, were drawn from those of the author and her sisters, its scenes from the New England where she had grown up, and many of its episodes from those she and her family had experienced, although the literary influence of Bunyan, Dickens, Carlyle, Hawthorne, Emerson, Theodore Parker, and Thoreau may be traced.

In the creation of *Little Women,* Alcott was something of a pioneer, using her own life as the basis of a juvenile novel, and achieving a realistic but wholesome picture of family life with which readers could readily identify. The Alcott poverty was sentimentalized, the eccentric Alcott father was an adumbrated shadow; yet the core of the domestic drama was apparent. Reported simply and directly in a style that applied her injunction, "Never use a long word, when a short one will do as well," the narrative embodied the simple facts and persons of a family, and so filled a gap in the literature of adolescence and domesticity.

There is no doubt that *Little Women* was the author's masterpiece. It had been preceded by a succession of literary efforts and experiments that gave Alcott a wide range of professional experience before she undertook her domestic novel. Her first published book, *Flower Fables*, consisted of "legends of faery land" and was dedicated to Emerson's daughter Ellen, for whom the tales were originally created. Her first novel, *Moods*, was a narrative of stormy violence, death, and intellectual love in which she attempted to apply Emerson's remark "Life is a train of moods like a string of beads." On and off she worked on an autobiographical, feminist novel, *Success*, subsequently renamed *Work: A Story of Experience*.

The Alcott bibliography encompasses nearly three hundred books, articles, novels, short stories, and poems, many of which appeared in the periodicals of the day. They were written in a variety of literary genres: stories of sweetness and light; dramatic narratives of strong-minded women; realistic episodes of Civil War life based upon her experience as a nurse; pseudonymous blood-and-thunder thrillers of revenge and passion whose leading character was usually a manipulating and vindictive woman. From the exigencies of serialization she developed the skills of cliff-hanger and page-turner. By 1868, when she began *Little Women*, she had produced a broad spectrum of stories from tales of virtue rewarded to tales of vice unpunished.

Little Women was followed by a succession of wholesome domestic narratives, the so-called *Little Women Series*, in which the author continued to supply a persistent demand. More or less autobiographical in origin, perceptive in their characterizations of adolescents, all are in a sense sequels of *Little Women* though none quite rises to its level. *An Old-Fashioned Girl* is a domestic drama in reverse, exposing the fashionable absurdities of one home in contrast with the wholesome domesticity of another. *Eight Cousins* exalts the family hearth again, and *Jack and Jill* enlarges upon the theme of domesticity, describing the home life of a New England village rather than of a single family.

An exception to this preoccupation with domestic life was *A Modern Mephistopheles*. Here Alcott exploited a theme of Goethe in a novel that reverted to the sensationalism of her earlier thrillers. "Enjoyed doing it," she wrote in her journal, "being tired of providing moral pap for the young."

Alcott was a far more complex writer than has been recognized. Drawn to a variety of literary themes and techniques, she eschewed most of them in favor of the domestic novel she had perfected. Motivated by the "inspiration of necessity," she became a victim of her own success. She has inevitably achieved fame as the "Children's Friend" and the author of a single masterpiece. Thanks to its psychological perceptions, its realistic characterizations, and its honest domesticity, *Little Women* has become an embodiment of the American home at its best. As the *Boston Herald* commented after her death: "When the family history, out of which this remarkable authorship grew, shall be told to the public, it will be apparent that few New England homes have ever had closer converse with the great things of human destiny than that of the Alcotts." Imbedded in the domestic novel *Little Women* are "the great things of human destiny," for there the particular has been transmuted into the universal.

—Madeleine B. Stern

ALGER, Horatio (Jr.) American. Born in Revere, Massachusetts, 13 January 1834. Educated at Gates Academy; Harvard University, Cambridge, Massachusetts, graduated 1854; Harvard Divinity School, graduated 1860. Teacher and journalist, 1854–57; lived in Paris, 1860–61; private tutor in Cambridge, Massachusetts, 1861–64; ordained minister, Unitarian church in Brewster, Massachusetts, 1864, but resigned in 1866 and moved to New York City to devote himself to literature; lived in New York, 1866–96: Chaplain, Newsboy's

Lodging House, from 1866; lived in Natick, Massachusetts, 1896 until his death. *Died 18 July 1899.*

PUBLICATIONS

Collections

Alger Street: The Poetry, edited by Gilbert K. Westgard, II.   1964.

Fiction

Bertha's Christmas Vision: An Autumn Sheaf (stories and verse).   1856.
Frank's Campaign; or, What Boys Can Do on the Farm for the Camp.   1864.
Paul Prescott's Charge.   1865.
Helen Ford.   1866.
Timothy Crump's Ward; or, The New Year's Loan, and What Came of It.   1866; revised edition, as *Jack's Ward; or, The Boy Guardian,* 1875.
Charlie Codman's Cruise.   1867; as *Bill Sturdy; or, The Cruise of Shipwrecked Charlie,* 1903(?).
Fame and Fortune; or, The Progress of Richard Hunter.   1868.
Ragged Dick; or, Street Life in New York with the Boot-Blacks.   1868.
Luck and Pluck; or, John Oakley's Inheritance.   1869.
Mark, The Match Boy; or, Richard Hunter's Ward.   1869.
Rough and Ready; or, Life among the New York Newsboys.   1869.
Ben, The Luggage Boy; or, Among the Wharves.   1870.
Rufus and Rose; or, The Fortunes of Rough and Ready.   1870.
Sink or Swim; or, Harry Raymond's Resolve.   1870; as *Paddle Your Own Canoe,* 1903(?).
Paul the Peddler; or, The Adventures of a Young Street Merchant.   1871.
Strong and Steady; or, Paddle Your Own Canoe.   1871.
Tattered Tom; or, The Story of a Street Arab.   1871.
Phil, The Fiddler; or, The Story of a Young Street Musician.   1872.
Slow and Sure; or, From the Street to the Shop.   1872.
Strive and Succeed; or, The Progress of Walter Conrad.   1872.
Bound to Rise; or, Harry Walton's Motto.   1873.
Try and Trust; or, The Story of a Bound Boy.   1873; as *Trials and Adventures of Herbert Mason,* 1903(?).
Brave and Bold; or, The Adventures of a Factory Boy.   1874.
Julius; or, The Street Boy Out West.   1874.
Risen from the Ranks; or, Harry Walton's Success.   1874.
Herbert Carter's Legacy; or, The Inventor's Son.   1875; as *George Carter's Legacy,* 1903(?).
The Young Outlaw; or, Adrift in the Streets.   1875.
Sam's Chance, and How He Improved It.   1876.
Shifting for Himself; or, Gilbert Greyson's Fortunes.   1876.
Wait and Hope; or, Ben Bradford's Motto.   1877.
The Western Boy; or, The Road to Success.   1878; as *Tom, The Bootblack,* 1880.
The Young Adventurer; or, Tom's Trip Across the Plains.   1878.
The Telegraph Boy.   1879; as *The District Telegraph Boy,* N.d.
The Young Explorer; or, Among the Sierras.   1880.

Tony, The Hero. 1880; as *Tony, The Tramp,* 1910(?).
The Train Boy. 1882; revised edition, 1883.
Ben's Nugget; or, A Boy's Search for Fortune: A Story of the Pacific Coast. 1882.
Dan, The Detective. 1883; as *Dan the Newsboy,* 1893; as *Dutiful Dan, The Brave Boy Detective,* 1903(?).
The Young Circus Rider; or, The Mystery of Robert Rudd. 1883.
Do and Dare; or, A Brave Boy's Fight for Fortune. 1884.
Hector's Inheritance; or, The Boys of Smith Institute. 1885.
Helping Himself; or, Grant Thornton's Ambition. 1886.
Joe's Luck; or, A Boy's Adventure in California. 1887.
Frank Fowler, The Cash Boy. 1887.
Number 91; or, The Adventures of a New York Telegraph Boy. 1887.
The Story Boy; or, The Fortunes of Ben Barclay. 1887; as *Ben Barclay's Courage,* 1904.
Bob Burton; or, The Young Ranchman of the Missouri. 1888.
The Errand Boy. 1888.
The Merchant's Crime. 1888; as *Ralph Raymond's Heir,* 1892.
Tom Temple's Career. 1888.
Tom Thatcher's Fortune. 1888.
Tom Tracy. 1888.
The Young Acrobat of the Great North American Circus. 1888.
Luke Walton; or, The Chicago Newsboy. 1889.
Mark Stanton; or, Both Sides of the Continent. 1890.
Ned Newton; or, The Fortunes of a New York Bootblack. 1890.
A New York Boy. 1890.
The Odds Against Him; or, Carl Crawford's Experience. 1890; as *Driven from Home,* n.d.
Struggling Upward; or, Luke Larkin's Luck. 1890.
Dean Dunham. 1890.
The Erie Train Boy. 1890.
$500; or, Jacob Marlowe's Secret. 1890; as *The Five Hundred Dollar Check,* 1891.
Digging for Gold: A Story of California. 1892.
The Young Boatman of Pine Point. 1892.
Facing the World; or, The Haps and Mishaps of Harry Vane. 1893.
In a New World; or, Among the Gold-Fields of Australia. 1893; as *The Nugget Finders,* 1894; as *Val Vane's Victory; or, Well Won,* 1903(?).
Only an Irish Boy; or, Andy Burke's Fortunes and Misfortunes. 1894.
Victor Vane, The Young Secretary. 1894.
Adrift in the City; or, Oliver Conrad's Plucky Fight. 1895.
The Disagreeable Woman: A Social Mystery. 1895.
Frank Hunter's Peril. 1896.
The Young Salesman. 1896.
Walter Sherwood's Probation. 1897.
Frank and Fearless; or, The Fortunes of Jasper Kent. 1897.
The Young Bank Messenger. 1898.
A Boy's Fortune; or, The Strange Adventures of Ben Baker. 1898.
Rupert's Ambition. 1899.
Jed, The Poorhouse Boy. 1899.
Mark Mason's Victory; or, The Trails and Triumphs of a Telegraph Boy. 1899.
A Debt of Honor: The Story of Gerald Lane's Success in the Far West. 1900.
Falling in with Fortune; or, The Experiences of a Young Secretary, completed by Edward Stratemeyer. 1900.
Out for Business; or, Robert Frost's Strange Career, completed by Edward Stratemeyer. 1900.

Ben Bruce: Scenes in the Life of a Bowery Newsboy. 1901.

Lester's Luck. 1901.

Making His Mark. 1901.

Nelson the Newsboy; or, Afloat in New York, completed by Edward Stratemeyer. 1901.

Striving for Fortune; or, Walter Griffith's Trials and Successes. 1901; as *Walter Griffith,* 1901.

Tom Brace: Who He Was and How He Fared. 1901.

Young Captain Jack; or, The Son of a Soldier, completed by Edward Stratemeyer. 1901.

Andy Grant's Pluck. 1902.

A Rolling Stone; or, The Adventures of a Wanderer. 1902; as *Wren Winter's Triumph,* 1902.

Tom Turner's Legacy: The Story of How He Secured It. 1902.

The World Before Him. 1902.

Bernard Brooks' Adventures: The Story of a Brave Boy's Trials. 1903.

Chester Rand; or, A New Path to Fortune. 1903.

Forging Ahead. 1903; as *Andy Gordon,* 1905.

Adrift in New York. 1904.

Finding a Fortune. 1904; as *The Tin Box,* 1905(?).

Jerry, The Backwoods Boy; or, The Parkhurst Treasure, completed by Edward Stratemeyer. 1904.

Lost at Sea; or, Robert Roscoe's Strange Cruise, completed by Edward Stratemeyer. 1904.

From Farm to Fortune; or, Nat Nason's Strange Experience, completed by Edward Stratemeyer. 1905.

Mark Manning's Mission; or, The Story of a Shoe Factory Boy. 1905.

The Young Book Agent; or, Frank Hardy's Road to Success, completed by Edward Stratemeyer. 1905.

Joe the Hotel Boy; or, Winning Out by Pluck, completed by Edward Stratemeyer. 1906.

Randy of the River; or, The Adventures of a Young Deckhand, completed by Edward Stratemeyer. 1906.

The Young Musician. 1906.

In Search of Treasure: The Story of Guy's Eventful Voyage. 1907.

Wait and Win: The Story of Jack Drummond's Pluck. 1908.

Robert Coverdale's Struggle; or, On the Wave of Success. 1910.

Verse

Grand'ther Baldwin's Thanksgiving with Other Ballads and Poems. 1875.

Other

Nothing to Do: A Tilt at Our Best Society. 1857.

From Canal Boy to President; or, The Boyhood and Manhood of James A. Garfield. 1881.

From Farm Boy to Senator, Being the History of the Boyhood and Manhood of Daniel Webster. 1882.

Abraham Lincoln, The Backwoods Boy. 1883.

Bibliography: *Road to Success: The Bibliography of the Works of Alger* by Ralph D. Gardner, 1971.

Reading List: *From Rags to Riches: Alger and the American Dream* by John W. Tebbel, 1963.

*   *   *

In 1867 Horatio Alger, failed preacher and school master, entered upon a literary career which eventually produced more than a hundred so-called boy's novels, thereby becoming one of the most successful writers in history. Indeed, so successful was he that his name has entered the language to signify the rags-to-riches American hero who, though born in dire straits, follows a virtuous and diligent life to a position of wealth and influence.

So prodigious an output necessarily dictated that Alger's characters were little more than caricatures, heroes with faces that "indicated a frank, sincere nature" (as in *The World Before Him*), and villains "with shifty black eyes and thin lips, shaded by a dark moustache" (*Adrift in New York*). His plots also inevitably located an impoverished but ingenuous lad, often an orphan, in a hostile environment, usually the city. There, possessed of those virtues which have become synonymous with the Alger myth – optimism, ambition, thrift, and self-reliance – the lad matured toward an adulthood of power, affluence, and respectability.

This conventional reading of the Alger stories and the myth to which they gave birth is, however, somewhat misleading. For to the more careful reader Alger's novels carry a more ambiguous message. First, it is not simply individual virtue but virtue in the face of good fortune that brings success to Alger's boys. Thus, as the typical story unfolds, the hero chances to save the millionaire's grandson from drowning or to find and return the lost bag of bank notes. In a sense, then, the cultivation of virtue is really a ritual of purification which prepares Alger's hero for the providential moment when he will be tried and found not wanting. Luck, no less than pluck – not to mention virtue – figures deeply in the success of the Alger hero. Second, the Alger hero's virtues are often compromised by their countervailing vices. Thrift, for instance, routinely gives way to a profligate visit to the theater or a spendthrift ride on a ferry boat, and self-reliance is often submerged in the desire for security and dependence.

Alger's heroes, in short, are not of the unalloyed virtue that the myth would have one believe. And virtue itself, compromised as it is, is routinely abetted by dumb luck. Still, Alger's name lives in the language as a synonym for virtue rewarded. And Alger himself, a novelist of admittedly modest abilities, has been eclipsed by his own name in the minds of the millions who have never read his work.

—Bruce A. Lohof

ALLEN, James Lane. American. Born near Lexington, Kentucky, 21 December 1849. Educated at Transylvania Academy, Lexington, 1866–68; Kentucky University, now Transylvania University, Lexington, 1868–72, 1875–77, B.A. (honors) 1872, M.A. 1887. Taught at a district school in Fort Springs, Kentucky, 1872–73, and at a high school in Richmond, Missouri, 1873–74; teacher at his own school in Lexington, Missouri, 1875; Principal, Transylvania Academy, 1878–80; Professor of Latin, Bethany College, West Virginia, 1880–83; opened and taught at a private school in Lexington, Kentucky, 1883–85; thereafter a full-time writer; settled in New York City, 1893; lived in Europe, 1894, 1900, 1909. M.A.: Bethany College, 1880; LL.D.: Kentucky University, 1898. *Died 18 February 1925.*

PUBLICATIONS

Collections

   A Kentucky Cardinal, Aftermath, and Other Selected Works, edited by William K.
      Bottorff.   1967.

Fiction

   Flute and Violin and Other Kentucky Tales and Romances.   1891.
   John Gray: A Kentucky Tale of the Olden Time.   1893.
   A Kentucky Cardinal.   1895.
   Aftermath.   1896.
   Summer in Arcady: A Tale of Nature.   1896.
   The Choir Invisible.   1897; revised edition, 1898.
   The Reign of Law: A Tale of the Kentucky Hemp Fields.   1900; as *The Increasing
      Purpose*, 1900.
   The Mettle of the Pasture.   1903.
   The Bride of the Mistletoe.   1909.
   The Doctor's Christmas Eve.   1910.
   The Heroine in Bronze; or, A Portrait of a Girl: A Pastoral of the City.   1912.
   The Last Christmas Tree: An Idyll of Immortality.   1914.
   The Sword of Youth.   1915.
   A Cathedral Singer.   1916.
   The Kentucky Warbler.   1918.
   The Emblems of Fidelity: A Comedy in Letters.   1919.
   The Alabaster Box (stories).   1923.
   The Landmark (stories).   1925.

Other

   The Blue-Grass Region of Kentucky and Other Kentucky Articles.   1892.
   Chimney Corner Graduates.   1900.

Bibliography: in *Bibliography of American Literature* by Jacob Blanck, 1955.

Reading List: *Allen* by John Wilson Townsend, 1927; *Allen and the Genteel Tradition* by
Grant C. Knight, 1935; *Allen* by William K. Bottorff, 1964.

*   *   *

James Lane Allen was ideally suited to purveying the kind of story and novel demanded by
the popular reading audience of the 1890's. Because of his evangelical religious orthodoxy,
his innate Southern chivalry, and his readings in Hawthorne, Eliot, Thackeray, and Dickens,
he demonstrated the rigorous moral control so often admired by conservative readers of the
fin de siècle.

Although Allen wrote during an era of fiction that is generally regarded as realistic, he
himself is remembered as a Romantic local colorist under the influence of Wordsworth,
Thoreau, and Audubon, who tended to idealize Nature by pointing out the "spiritual
sustenance" nature offers (William K. Bottorff). Allen's settings were often in the central
Kentucky landscape he knew so well.

There are essentially four groups of works in the Allen canon (see H. A. Toulmin, Jr., *Social Historians*). The first group sprang naturally from the disposition of a local colorist: a distinctive, sympathetic treatment of Kentucky life as in *Flute and Violin and Other Kentucky Tales* and *The Blue-Grass Region of Kentucky*. The second group constitutes a limited philosophical growth in its treatment of nature as in *A Kentucky Cardinal* and *Aftermath*. The third group champions the doctrines of evolution and the consequences of circumstance as in *Summer in Arcady, The Reign of Law*, and *The Mettle of the Pasture*. The fourth vein of Allen's writings is the historical problem novel as in *The Choir Invisible*.

It is to *Flute and Violin and Other Kentucky Tales* that the avid Allen reader returns. Three distinct weaknesses, however, become apparent in this early Allen collection – sentimentality, an excessively adorned style, and a Puritanic point of view that weaves, as Grant C. Knight says, "allegories and symbols into the pattern of the narratives." The title story has enjoyed considerable popularity owing to its sentimental portrayal of the Reverend James Moore who communes on his flute with the fatherless waif David, who plays the violin. The Dickensian character complements are marked.

A Kentucky Cardinal is a love story set against the beauties of the rural Kentucky landscape just outside Lexington. The hero, Adam Moss, may well be Allen's finest and most Thoreau-like character. *The Choir Invisible*, a poorly unified work, sought to create a gentleman "in buckskins." The novel, set in Kentucky in 1795, is comparable to Eliot and Thackeray in its morality, humor, and pathos.

Allen's work began a marked decline early in the twentieth century, *The Mettle of the Pasture* had a mixed critical reception. *The Bride of the Mistletoe* and *The Doctor's Christmas Eve* met with indifference and disapproval, and his later works are all but forgotten.

Today's readers and critics will find it difficult to agree with Edmund Gosse's 1888 letter to Joseph B. Gilder that Allen's was "A pen possessed of every accomplishment." The contemporary literary historian will agree, however, that Allen's writings constitute some of the best moments of American local color. Allen may be regarded as the supreme Southern Victorian in his medievalism, in his moral and didactic inclination, in his desire to experiment, and in his eclecticism. As Bottorff notes, from Hawthorne Allen drew his psychology, morality, and complexity, from Thoreau he learned his transcendentalism, and from James the complexity of his psychological probings.

—George C. Longest

ARTHUR, Timothy Shay. American. Born in Newburgh, New York, 6 June 1809; moved with his family to Baltimore, 1817. Briefly attended Baltimore public schools; largely self-educated. Married Ellen Alden in 1836; five sons and two daughters. Watchmaker's apprentice, then worked as a clerk in a Baltimore counting room; Western Agent for a Baltimore bank, 1833; member of the editorial staff of various Baltimore journals, including the *Athenaeum* and *Saturday Visitor*, 1834–38; Co-Editor, *Baltimore Literary Magazine*, 1838–40; Editor, *Baltimore Merchant*, 1840; moved to Philadelphia, 1841, and became a writer for *Saturday Courier, Graham's Magazine*, and *Godey's Lady's Book*; established *Arthur's Ladies' Magazine*, 1845; Founder and Publisher, *Arthur's Home Gazette* (*Arthur's Home Magazine* from 1853), 1852 until his death; published the juvenile periodical *Children's Hour*, from 1867, and *Once a Month*, 1869–70. Member, Executive Committee, Centennial Exhibition, 1876. *Died 6 March 1885.*

Fiction

Insubordination: An American Story of Real Life. 1841.
Tired of Housekeeping. 1842.
Six Nights with the Washingtonians (stories). 1842; as *The Tavern-Keeper's Victims,* 1860.
Bell Martin; or, The Heiress. 1843.
Fanny Dale; or, The First Year after Marriage. 1843.
The Tailor's Apprentice: A Story of Cruelty and Oppression. 1843.
The Little Pilgrims: A Sequel to The Tailor's Apprentice. 1843.
Madeline; or, A Daughter's Love, and Other Tales. 1843.
Making a Sensation and Other Tales. 1843.
The Ruined Family and Other Tales. 1843.
Swearing Off and Other Tales. 1843.
The Seamstress. 1843.
The Stolen Wife. 1843.
Sweethearts and Wives; or, Before and after Marriage. 1843.
The Two Merchants. 1843.
The Village Doctors and Other Tales. 1843.
Cecilia Howard; or, The Young Lady Who Had Finished Her Education. 1844.
Pride or Principle — Which Makes the Lady? 1844.
Family Pride; or, The Palace and the Poor House. 1844.
Hints and Helps for the Home Circle; or, The Mother's Friend. 1844.
Hiram Elwood, The Banker; or, Like Father Like Son. 1844.
The Martyr Wife. 1844.
Prose Fictions Written for the Illustration of True Principles. 1844.
The Ruined Gamester; or, Two Eras in My Life. 1844.
The Two Sisters; or, Life's Changes. 1844.
The Maiden. 1845.
The Wife. 1845.
Anna Milnor, The Young Lady Who Was Not Punctual, and Other Tales. 1845.
The Heiress. 1845.
The Club Room and Other Temperance Tales. 1845.
Married and Single; or, Marriage and Celibacy Contrasted. 1845.
Lovers and Husbands. 1845.
Tales from Real Life. 1845.
The Two Husbands and Other Tales. 1845.
The Mother. 1846.
Random Recollections of an Old Doctor. 1846.
The Beautiful Widow. 1847.
Improving Stories for the Young. 1847.
Keeping Up Appearances. 1847.
Riches Have Wings. 1847.
The Young Lady at Home. 1847.
The Young Music Teacher and Other Tales. 1847.
Agnes; or The Possessed: A Revelation of Mesmerism. 1848.
Debtor and Creditor. 1848.
The Lost Children. 1848.
Retiring from Business; or, The Rich Man's Error. 1848.
Love in a Cottage. 1848.
Rising in the World. 1848.

Lucy Sanford: A Story of the Heart.   1848.
Making Haste to Be Rich.   1848.
The Three Eras of a Woman's Life (includes *The Maiden, The Wife, The Mother).*   1848.
Love in High Life.   1849.
Mary Moreton; or, The Broken Promise.   1849.
Sketches of Life and Character.   1849.
Alice Mellville; or, The Indiscretion; Mary Ellis; or, The Runaway Match.   1850.
All for the Best; or, The Old Peppermint Man.   1850.
The Debtor's Daughter.   1850.
The Divorced Wife.   1850.
Golden Grains from Life's Harvest Field.   1850.
Illustrated Temperance Tales.   1850.
The Lights and Shadows of Real Life.   1850.
The Orphan Children.   1850.
Pride and Prudence; or, The Married Sisters.   1850.
Tales of Domestic Life.   1850.
True Riches and Other Tales.   1850.
The Two Brides.   1850.
The Young Artist; or, The Dream of Italy.   1850.
The Two Wives.   1851.
The Banker's Wife.   1851.
Lessons in Life for All Who Will Read Them.   1851.
Off-Hand Sketches.   1851.
Seed-Time and Harvest (stories).   1851.
Stories for My Young Friends, Parents, Young Housekeepers.   3 vols., 1851.
The Way to Prosper; or, In Union There Is Strength and Other Tales.   1851.
Woman's Trials (stories).   1851.
Words for the Wise (stories).   1851.
Confessions of a House-Keeper.   1852.
Home Scenes and Home Influences.   1852.
The Tried and the Tempted.   1852.
Cedardale.   1852.
Pierre the Organ-Boy and Other Stories.   1852.
The Poor Wood-Cutter and Other Stories.   1852.
Jessie Hampton.   1852.
Uncle Ben's New Year's Gift.   1852.
The Ways of Providence (stories).   1852.
Confessions of a Housekeeper.   1852; revised edition, as *Trials and Confessions of an American Housekeeper,* 1854; as *Ups and Downs,* 1857.
Who Are Happiest? and Other Stories.   1852.
Who Is Greatest? and Other Stories.   1852.
Before and After the Election; or, The Political Experiences of Mr. Patrick Murphy.   1853.
Finger Posts on the Way of Life.   1853.
The Fireside Angel.   1853.
Haven't-Time and Don't-Be-in-a-Hurry and Other Stories.   1853.
Heart-Histories and Life-Pictures.   1853.
Home Lights and Shadows.   1853.
The Home Mission.   1853.
The Iron Rule; or, Tyranny in the Household.   1853.
The Lady at Home.   1853.
The Last Penny and Other Stories.   1853.

Leaves from the Book of Human Life.   1853.
Maggy's Baby and Other Stories.   1853.
Married Life: Its Shadows and Sunshine (stories).   1852.
The Old Man's Bride.   1853.
Sparing to Spend; or, The Loftons and Pinkertons.   1853.
The Wounded Boy and Other Stories.   1853.
Ten Nights in a Bar-Room and What I Saw There.   1854; edited by H. Hugh Holman,
    with *In His Steps* by Charles M. Sheldon, 1966.
The Angel of the Household.   1954.
Shadows and Sunbeams.   1854.
Leaves from the Book of Human Life.   1855.
The Good Time Coming.   1855.
The Hand But Not the Heart.   1855.
What Can Woman Do?   1855.
The Withered Heart.   1857.
The Hand But Not the Heart; or, The Life-Trials of Jessie Loring.   1858.
The Angel and the Demon: A Tale of Modern Spiritualism.   1858.
The Little Bound-Boy.   1858.
Lizzy Glenn; or, The Trials of a Seamstress.   1859.
The Allen House; or, Twenty Years Ago and Now.   1860.
Aunt Mary's Preserving Kettle.   1863.
Nancy Wimble.   1863.
Hidden Wings and Other Stories.   1864.
Light on Shadowed Paths.   1864.
Out in the World.   1864.
Sunshine at Home and Other Stories.   1864.
Sowing the Wind and Other Stories.   1865.
Home-Heroes, Saints, and Martyrs.   1865.
Nothing But Money.   1865.
What Came Afterwards.   1865.
Life's Crosses and How to Meet Them.   1865.
Our Neighbors in the Corner House.   1866.
The Lost Bride; or, The Astrologer's Prophecy Fulfilled.   1866.
Blind Nelly's Boy and Other Stories.   1867.
After the Storm.   1868.
The Peacemaker and Other Stories.   1869.
After a Shadow and Other Stories.   1869.
Not Anything for Peace and Other Stories.   1869.
Heroes of the Household.   1869.
Rainy Day at Home.   1869.
The Seen and the Unseen.   1869.
Anna Lee.   1869.
Beacon Lights.   1869.
Tom Blinn's Temperance Society and Other Tales.   1870.
Idle Hands and Other Stories.   1871.
Orange Blossoms, Fresh and Faded (stories).   1871.
The Wonderful Story of Gentle Hand and Other Stories.   1871.
Grace Myers' Sewing Machine and Other Tales.   1872.
Cast Adrift.   1872.
Three Years in a Man-Trap.   1872.
Comforted.   1873.
Woman to the Rescue: A Story of the New Crusade.   1874.
The Power of Kindness and Other Stories.   1875.
Danger; or, Wounded in the House of a Friend.   1875.

The Latimer Family.   1877.
The Wife's Engagement Ring.   1877.
The Bar-Rooms at Brantley.   1877.
The Mill and the Tavern.   1878.
The Strike at Jivoli Mills and What Came of It.   1879.
Saved as by Fire.   1881.
Death-Dealing Gold.   1890.
The Little Savoyard and Other Stories.   1891.
Two Little Girls and What They Did.   1899.
Won by Waiting.   N.d.

Other

A Christmas Box for the Sons and Daughters of Temperance.   1847.
Advice to Young Men on Their Duties and Conduct in Life.   1847; *Advice to Young Ladies,* 1848.
The Young Wife: A Manual of Moral, Religious, and Domestic Duties.   1847.
Wreaths of Friendship: A Gift for the Young, with Francis Channing Woodworth.   1849.
A Wheat Sheaf, Gathered from Our Own Field, with Francis Channing Woodworth.   1851.
Our Little Harry and Other Poems and Stories.   1852.
The History of Georgia, Illinois, Kentucky, New Jersey, New York, Ohio, Pennsylvania, Vermont, Virginia, with W. H. Carpenter.   10 vols., 1852–54.
The String of Pearls for Boys and Girls, with Francis Channing Woodworth.   1853.
Steps Towards Heaven (sermons).   1858.
Growler's Income Tax.   1864.
Talks with a Philosopher on the Ways of God and Man.   1871.
Strong Drink: The Curse and the Cure.   1877.
Feet and Wings; or, Among the Beasts and Birds.   1880.
Adventures by Sea and Land.   1890.
Sow Well and Reap Well: A Book for the Young.   N.d.
Story Sermons.   N.d.
Talks with a Child on the Beatitudes.   N.d.

Editor, with W. H. Carpenter, *The Baltimore Book.*   1838.
Editor, *The Sons of Temperance Offering.*   2 vols., 1849–50.
Editor, *The Brilliant: A Gift-Book.*   1850.
Editor, *The Crystal Fount for All Seasons.*   1850.
Editor, *The Temperance Gift.*   1854.
Editor, *The Temperance Offering.*   1854.
Editor, *Friends and Neighbors; or, Two Ways of Living in the World.*   1856.
Editor, *The Mother's Rule.*   1856.
Editor, *Our Homes.*   1856.
Editor, *The True Path and How to Walk Therein.*   1856.
Editor, *The Wedding Guest.*   1856.
Editor, *Words of Cheer for the Tempted, The Toiling, and the Sorrowing.*   1856.
Editor, *Orange Blossoms.*   1857.
Editor, *The Boys' and Girls' Treasury.*   1859.
Editor, *Little Gems from the Children's Hour.*   1875.
Editor, *The Prattler.*   1876.
Editor, *The My Books.*   1877.
Editor, *The Budget: A Book for Boys and Girls.*   1877.

Editor, *The Playmate.* 1878.
Editor, *Lucy Grey and Other Stories.*   1880.
Editor, *Sophy and Prince.*   1881.
Editor, *Friendship's Token.*   N.d.

*   *   *

Timothy Shay Arthur is likely to be recalled today as the author of *Ten Nights in a Bar-Room*, the popular melodrama about a small-town miller turned saloon-keeper who brings misfortune upon his family and community, until the killing of his daughter by drunken brawlers saves him and the town for temperance (which to Arthur meant total prohibition). Actually he did not write the play, which was one of the most often performed on the American stage during the late nineteenth century and which still survives, though now it is usually burlesqued; the dramatization was prepared by William W. Pratt from Arthur's novel. Nor did Arthur devote himself before the Civil War exclusively to the temperance cause, although he enjoyed his first success with *Six Nights with the Washingtonians*, tales about the work of this noble band that sought to redeem drunkards through "moral suasion." After gaining experience as a contributor to literary magazines and then as co-editor of several short-lived publications in Baltimore from 1834 to 1840, he moved to Philadelphia, where, after several earlier experiments in finding the profitable format for a journal devoted to "the good, the true, and the beautiful," he founded in 1852 *Arthur's Home Magazine*, which he edited until his death.

During these years he wrote about a hundred novels and uncounted short stories, most of which appeared first either in his magazines or the many gift-books that he edited. Before the Civil War, the majority of these tales were thinly fictionalized guides to young people getting married and setting up a home and business. *The Three Eras of a Woman's Life* was only the most ambitious of about two dozen that advised maiden, wife and mother on the woman's proper "sphere" and duties. *Debtor and Creditor* was one of many that warned against unsound business practices; but Arthur was also one of the first American novelists, even before the age of the Robber Barons, to condemn unscrupulous business practices growing out of a greed for gain in an unexpectedly bleak and cynical novel like *Nothing But Money*. Arthur was also a member of the Church of the New Jerusalem, as the followers of Emmanuel Swedenborg called themselves; and he expounded the doctrines of the church in novels like *The Good Time Coming*, an attempt to dissuade egotistical people from reckless courses. He also, surprisingly, pioneered in fiction dealing with divorce – then a scandalous subject. *The Hand But Not the Heart, After the Storm*, and *Out in the World* castigate hasty marriage and easy divorce, but grant that legal separation may be necessitated by a spouse's philandering or intemperance.

After the Civil War left him disheartened about his fellow Americans, he devoted his fiction largely to the temperance crusade, growing through *Three Years in a Man-Trap, Woman to the Rescue*, and *The Bar-Rooms at Brantley* constantly more hysterical in his denunciation of the evils of drink and shriller in his demands for legal prohibition rather than a reliance upon self-reform. These works in print or on the stage, however, failed to enjoy the success of his earlier writings.

—Warren French

BALDWIN, Joseph G(lover). American. Born in Winchester, Virginia, in January 1815. Received no formal education; self-taught in law. Married Sidney White in 1839; six children. Began practice of law in DeKalb, Mississippi, 1836; moved to Gainesville, Alabama, 1839; Whig Member of the Alabama Legislature, 1844–49; lived in Livingston, Alabama, 1850–53; law partner of Philip Phillips in Mobile, Alabama, 1853–54; moved to San Francisco, 1854, and practised law there; served as Associate Justice, California Supreme Court, 1858–62, then returned to private practice. *Died 30 September 1864.*

PUBLICATIONS

Fiction

    The Flush Times of Alabama and Mississippi: A Series of Sketches.   1853; edited by William A. Owens, 1957.

Other

    Party Leaders: Sketches of Jefferson, Hamilton, Jackson, Clay, Randolph of Roanoke.   1855.

Bibliography: in *Bibliography of American Literature* by Jacob Blanck, 1955.

Reading List: "Baldwin: Humorist or Moralist?" by Eugene Current-Garcia, in *Frontier Humorists: Critical Essays* edited by M. Thomas Inge, 1975.

*   *   *

Although well known to American literary scholars for *The Flush Times of Alabama and Mississippi,* Joseph G. Baldwin has been little studied. As the title itself suggests, *Flush Times* constitutes an attempt to re-create in the *native* American tradition of the Old Southwest humorists a day and age with which Baldwin was well acquainted: an "age of litigation in a lawless country," as Eugene Current-Garcia says. A closer examination both of the author's life and the text of his work, however, suggests that Baldwin, in addition to being frontier humorist, is a serious "moralist" who employs traditional conventions such as satire and irony in his exposure of the vices and weaknesses of mankind, thus bridging the gap between native Southwest humor and the older literary conventions of European art.

While Baldwin's purpose was doubtlessly moral, his generic forte was essays and sketches rather than short stories. His literary models were, in all probability, Lamb and Dickens. His best character types remain self-important Virginians, inexperienced lawyers, and garrulous narrators. Two characters in particular are notable, Ovid Bolus, Esq., a truly artful liar, and Colonel Simon Suggs, Jr., to Current-Garcia the "symbol of his time, the epitome of a lawless, acquisitive society which had raised fraud and corruption to the level of 'super-Spartan roguery.' "

Nineteenth-century sensibilities extended, by contemporary standards, odd shadows. As a practising attorney, Baldwin no doubt felt some sense of embarrassment over his authorship of *Flush Times,* a work which many American Victorians would have considered inconsequential. In order to demonstrate his talents for more "serious" writing, Baldwin published in 1855 *Party Leaders,* which is rarely read today. Containing sketches of political leaders like Jefferson, Hamilton, Jackson, Clay, and Randolph, the book is motivated by the author's biographical and historical impulse and emphasizes moral instruction at the expense of humor.

Had Baldwin not died as suddenly as he did, he might well have become, as his wife believed, the Thucydides of the Civil War. In any event, his accomplishments as frontier humorist, as moralist, and as essayist continue to be admired by readers.

—George C. Longest

BARKER, James Nelson.   American.   Born in Philadelphia, Pennsylvania, 17 June 1784; son of General George Barker. Educated in schools in Philadelphia. Commissioned Captain in the 2nd United States Artillery, 1812; served as Assistant Adjutant-General of the United States Army, rising to the rank of Major, 1814–17. Married Mary Rogers in 1811; one daughter. Began writing for the stage, Philadelphia, 1804–08; lived in Washington, D.C., studying government, 1809–10; returned to Philadelphia, and resumed writing for the stage, 1812; contributed series of articles on "The Drama" to *Dramatic Press*, 1816–17; Alderman of Philadelphia, 1817–29: Mayor, 1819–21; Collector of the Port of Philadelphia, 1829–38; Controller of the United States Department of the Treasury, Washington, 1838–41, and subsequently served various administrations as Clerk in the office of the Chief Clerk of the Treasury, 1841 until his death. *Died 9 March 1858.*

PUBLICATIONS

Plays

    Tears and Smiles (produced 1807).   1808; edited by Paul H. Musser, in *Barker*, 1929.
    The Embargo; or, What News? (produced 1808).
    Travellers; or, Music's Fascination, from a work by Andrew Cherry (produced 1808).
    The Indian Princess; or, La Belle Sauvage, music by John Bray (produced 1808).   1808; revised version, as *Pocahontas* (produced 1820).
    Marmion; or, The Battle of Flodden Field, from the poem by Scott (produced 1812).   1816.
    The Armourer's Escape; or, Three Years at Nootka Sound (produced 1817).
    How to Try a Lover (as *A Court of Love,* produced 1836).   1817.
    Superstition; or, The Fanatic Father (produced 1824).   1826.

Other

    Delaplaine's Repository of the Lives and Portraits of Distinguished American Characters, vol. 1, part 2.   1817.
    Sketches of the Primitive Settlements on the River Delaware.   1827.

Reading List: *Barker* by Paul H. Musser, 1929 (includes bibliography).

*   *   *

James Nelson Barker, Democratic mayor of Federalist Philadelphia and amateur historian, wrote for the Chestnut Street Theatre. The craft of his research and allegorical verse fed best into his politics and plays. His critical articles examined "Tragedy of Character," the problems of adapting and performance, and the social function of drama. Barker intended his earliest, unproduced "mask" (*America*, with "Liberty" singing) to conclude an unfinished dramatization of John Smith's 1624 history of Virginia. Instead, his popular but comically melodramatic opera *The Indian Princess* (John Bray's music) introduced the frequently repeated Pocahontas figure to the stage.

The stage for Barker addressed and shaped the partisan energies that preceded the War of 1812. *Tears and Smiles*, his clever sentimental comedy, marshalled early Yankee types, a patriotic sailor, fops, an Irishman, and mysterious European fugitives to question commercial aristocracy and praise domestic products in fashions, morals, and persons. *The Embargo* supported a comedian's benefit and Jefferson's controversial ban on trade with Britain or France. After the war, Barker's "melo-dramatic sketch" *The Armourer's Escape* let the Indian-captured sailor Jewitt play himself, to capitalize on 1817 interest in the Oregon boundary dispute.

How to Try a Lover, a singularly unpolitical gem in prose, was produced as *A Court of Love*. It celebrates blinding love, from insatiable lust to its most courtly and impractical idealism. Love's confusing possibilities are drawn, with literary parodies ("Almanzor" as hero-lover's pseudonym; conventional allegories of love/honor), through the neoclassically comic dance of a picaresque plot, while carefully described settings develop from dark gothic vault toward brilliant court. Movements and situations belie spoken words. Barker's balancings of characters and antithetical dialogue intensify the skeptical-romantic counterpoint in this "only dream" that "satisfied" him as artist.

Barker's verse tragedies explore what politicians considered resolved. *Marmion* and *Superstition* are historical tragedies of personal and national character. "*The* American playwright" (New York review) and best adaptor of Scott's poem (London critic) re-examined Scott's sources, tightened artistic structure, alternated scenes for deeper psychological effect, and rallied sentiment for war against Britain – though in 1811–12 victory seemed unlikely. *Marmion* poses determining destiny against individual responsibility. In *Superstition* manifest destiny and liberty are susceptible to public hysteria. The inspired leadership of the Puritan Unknown (a fugitive regicide) saves a New England community from Indian attack; but the perverting religious fervor of witch-hunts and narrow-mindedness, part of the colonial heritage, leave a Columbia-figure and the young lovers of a New World dead. Spying courtiers supply objectifying comedy. Behind the play's action loom the New England fathers and the war for independence from the mother country, as well as the current themes of Greek and South American independence, Philadelphia's epidemics and religious riots, and Barker's campaigning for Andrew Jackson (Hero of the People) against New England's Adams ("John the Second"). Though Barker as politician honored "The People," *Superstition* questions their readiness for genuine democracy and implies a vision of rational, tolerant, effective, and affective leadership, fatalistic action, and individual heroism. Allegory becomes symbolic and moving in these tragedies, the finest of early America.

—John G. Kuhn

BARLOW, Joel. American. Born in Reading, Connecticut, 24 March 1754. Educated at Moor's School, Hanover, New Hampshire; Dartmouth College, Hanover; Yale University, New Haven, Connecticut, 1774–78, B.A. 1778; admitted to the Bar, 1786. Served as a

Chaplain with the Massachusetts Brigade, 1780 until the end of the Revolutionary War. Married Ruth Baldwin in 1781. Practiced law after the Revolution, also taught school and was proprietor of a bookshop in Hartford, Connecticut; Founding Editor, with Elisha Babcock, *American Mercury*, 1784; lived in Europe, 1788–1805: European Agent for the Scioto Company, 1788–89; proprietor of La Compagnie du Scioto, 1789; lived in London, a friend of Thomas Paine, 1790–92, and in Paris from 1792: became involved in French radical politics; also served as American Consul in Algiers, 1795; lived in America, at his home Kalorama, near Washington, 1805–11; American Ambassador to France, 1811–12. *Died 24 December 1812.*

PUBLICATIONS

Verse

> *The Prospect of Peace.*   1778.
> *A Poem.*   1781.
> *An Elegy of the Late Titus Hosmer.*   1782.
> *The Vision of Columbus.*   1787; revised edition, as *The Columbiad,* 1807.
> *The Conspiracy of Kings.*   1792.
> *The Hasty-Pudding.*   1796.
> *Doctor Watts's Imitations of the Psalms of David, Corrected and Enlarged.*   1785; supplement, 1785.
> *The Anarchiad: A New England Poem,* with others, edited by Luther G. Riggs.   1861.

Other

> *Advice to the Privileged Orders in the Several States of Europe.*   2 vols., 1792–93.
> *A Letter to the National Convention of France.*   1793(?).
> *The History of England, 1765–95.*   5 vols., 1795.
> *The Political Writings.*   1796.
> *A Letter to the People of Piedmont.*   1798.
> *To His Fellow Citizens.*   2 vols., 1799–1800.

> Editor, *M'Fingal: A Modern Epic Poem,* by John Trumbull.   1792.

> Translator, *New Travels in the United States of America in 1788,* by J. P. Brissot de Warville.   1792; revised edition, 1794.
> Translator, *The Commerce of America with Europe,* by J. P. Brissot de Warville.   1794.
> Translator, with Thomas Jefferson, *Volney's Ruins; or, Meditations on the Revolution of Empires.*   2 vols., 1802.

Reading List: *Life and Letters of Barlow* by Charles Burr Todd, 1886; *The Early Days of Barlow, A Connecticut Wit: His Life and Works from 1754 to 1787* by Theodore Albert Zunder, 1934 (includes bibliography); *The Connecticut Wits* by Leon Howard, 1943 (includes bibliography); *A Yankee's Odyssey: The Life of Barlow* by James Woodress, 1958; *Barlow* by Arthur L. Ford, 1971.

*   *   *

Although Joel Barlow had hoped to be remembered as an epic poet, only one mock-epic poem and a short bitter piece of satiric verse give him what enduring interest he has as a poet. At the same time, however, he holds a secure place as a political pamphleteer in the early national period and as a minor figure in American history. He is a character of considerable interest, for his life touches many of the significant historical events between the Revolution and the War of 1812, and he stands as a representative figure of the American Enlightenment.

Going from a Connecticut farm to Yale on the eve of the Revolution, Barlow versified his way through college, and, after serving as a chaplain in Washington's army, he set about writing his epic, *The Vision of Columbus*, a poem in nine books of heroic couplets celebrating the history of America, past, present, and future. The poem was a considerable success in its day, but it seems unreadable in the 20th century. Twenty years later Barlow brought out an expanded and revised version that he called *The Columbiad*. It appeared as a large quarto, leather bound and handsomely illustrated, the most beautiful book yet produced in America – but still unreadable.

The Hasty-Pudding, on the other hand, is a delightful piece of mock-heroic verse occasioned by Barlow's visit to Savoy in 1793 when he was running unsuccessfully for the French National Assembly. It was inspired by his being served a dish of corn meal mush (polenta, hasty pudding), which reminded him of his Connecticut boyhood. This poem has been reprinted many times and is often anthologized. The other notable piece of verse, "Advice to a Raven in Russia," was occasioned by Barlow's sharp reaction to Napoleon's campaign in Russia in 1812. It was written in the last month of Barlow's life when he had gone to Vilna as American Minister to France in an effort to negotiate a treaty with Napoleon. To a Jeffersonian American the slaughter and carnage all about him evoked bitter criticism, and in a sense Barlow himself some days later was one of Napoleon's victims, for he caught pneumonia on the precipitous return to Paris from Lithuania after Napoleon's debacle.

During the years that Barlow was living in Europe (1788 to 1805), he plunged into political controversy. His tract *Advice to the Privileged Orders* was one of the important answers to Burke's *Reflections on the Revolution in France*, and it was proscribed in England, along with Paine's *The Rights of Man*. He also wrote political polemics in support of France and the Jeffersonians during the contentious days of Adams Administration, and as a result made himself unpopular with the conservative Federalists he had grown up with in Connecticut. Of all that group of writers known as The Connecticut Wits, who flourished in and about Hartford after the Revolution, Barlow was the only one who became a political liberal.

—James Woodress

BELLAMY, Edward.   American.   Born in Chicopee Falls, Massachusetts, 26 March 1850, and lived there for most of his life. Educated at local schools; Union College, Schenectady, New York, 1867–68; travelled and studied in Germany, 1868–69; studied law: admitted to the Massachusetts Bar, 1871, but never practised. Married Emma Sanderson in 1882. Associate Editor, *Union*, Springfield, Massachusetts; Editorial Writer, *Evening Post*, New York, 1878; Founder, with his brother, Springfield *Daily News*, 1880; after 1885 devoted himself to writing and propagation of Socialist ideas: lectured throughout the United States; founded *New Nation*, Boston, 1891. *Died 22 May 1898.*

PUBLICATIONS

Fiction

Six to One: A Nantucket Idyl.   1878.
Dr. Heidenhoff's Process.   1880.
Miss Ludington's Sister: A Romance of Immortality.   1884.
Looking Backward 2000–1887.   1888; edited by John L. Thomas, 1967.
Equality.   1897.
The Blindman's World and Other Stories.   1898.
The Duke of Stockbridge: A Romance of Shays' Rebellion, edited by Francis
   Bellamy.   1900; edited by Joseph Schiffman, 1962.

Other

Bellamy Speaks Again! Articles, Public Addresses, Letters.   1937.
Talks on Nationalism.   1938.
The Religion of Solidarity, edited by Arthur E. Morgan.   1940.
Selected Writings on Religion and Society, edited by Joseph Schiffman.   1955.

Bibliography: in *Bibliography of American Literature* by Jacob Blanck, 1955.

Reading List: *Bellamy,* 1944, and *The Philosophy of Bellamy,* 1945, both by Arthur E.
Morgan; *The Year 2000* by Sylvia E. Bowman, 1958; *Bellamy, Novelist and Reformer* by
Daniel Aaron and Harry Levin, 1968.

*   *   *

Edward Bellamy is known chiefly for his Utopian romance *Looking Backward:
2000–1887,* which within a short time after its publication sold over one million copies. The
purpose of the book was to offer a blueprint of what Bellamy considered to be an ideal
society. To make his presentation more palatable to the general reader, he encased it in a
romantic plot: A young Bostonian after a hypnotic sleep of 113 years awakens in the year
2000 to discover a totally transformed social and economic order. Falling in love with a girl
descended from his fiancée of 1887, he learns from her father, a physician, the details of the
state socialism that has replaced the laissez-faire capitalism that obtained before his long sleep.
Under the new order all commerce, industry and other economic and professional activities
have been nationalized into one vast, interlocking enterprise. All men and women between
the ages of twenty-one and forty-five are required to engage in work suitable to their abilities
and, when possible, to their tastes; and all, no matter what occupation they may be in, receive
the same wages. Superior ability and productivity are rewarded by social recognition and by
assignment to positions of leadership. After the age of forty-five all are retired and are free to
do what they wish.
   Looking Backward is one of a number of books expressing the dissatisfaction of many
Americans with the conditions of labor, the rise of monopolies, and the political corruption
that characterized the second half of the nineteenth century. But Bellamy's book enjoyed a
greater popularity and exerted a stronger influence than any other, with the possible
exception of Henry George's *Progress and Poverty* (1879). Bellamy called his program
Nationalism, and in the 1890's many Nationalist Clubs were formed and began to wield a
political influence, most notably on the newly formed and temporarily quite powerful
Populist Party. As a sequel to *Looking Backward,* Bellamy wrote *Equality,* which he finished

shortly before his death. But by this time the Nationalist movement was losing its momentum, though Bellamy's ideas continued to be an influence on later reform efforts. Bellamy's most lasting contribution, as one critic has put it, was in fostering "an attitude toward social change." For example, many of the innovations of the New Deal had been suggested and made familiar to the public by Bellamy's book.

Bellamy's literary career was not confined solely to reformist writing. He was an able newspaper and magazine editor and the author of unpolitical fiction. Several of his novels, among them *Dr. Heidenhoff's Process* and *Miss Ludington's Sister* received favorable notice in their day; and his *The Duke of Stockbridge* (serialized 1879) has been called, perhaps extravagantly, "one of the greatest historical novels." Dealing with the revolt in 1786 and 1787 of Massachusetts farmers who were overburdened with debt and taxes and ruthlessly exploited by lawyers, merchants, and bankers, this book provides early evidence of Bellamy's concern with social and economic injustice – a concern that doubtless had its origin in his early awareness of the exploitation of workers in the Massachusetts mill town in which he grew up.

—P. D. Westbrook

BIERCE, Ambrose (Gwinnet).   American.   Born in Meigs County, Ohio, 24 June 1842. Educated at high school in Warsaw, Indiana; Kentucky Military Institute, 1859–60. Served in the Ninth Indiana Infantry Regiment of the Union Army during the Civil War, 1861–65; Major. Married Mollie Day in 1871 (divorced, 1905); two sons and one daughter. Printer's Devil, *Northern Indianan* (anti-slavery paper), 1857–59; United States Treasury aide, Alabama, 1865; served on a military expedition, Omaha to San Francisco, 1866–67; worked for the Sub-Treasury, San Francisco, 1867–68; Editor, *News Letter*, San Francisco, 1868–72; in London, 1872–76: member of the staff of *Fun*, 1872–75, and Editor of *The Lantern*, 1875; returned to San Francisco: worked for the United States Mint, from 1875, Columnist for *The Sunday Examiner*, 1876–97; Associate Editor of *The Argonaut*, 1877–79; Agent, Black Hills Placer Mining Company, Rockerville, Dakota Territory, 1880; Editor of *The Wasp*, San Francisco, 1881–86; lived in Washington, D.C., 1900–13: Washington Correspondent for the New York *American* until 1906; member of staff of *The Cosmopolitan*, Washington, 1905–09; travelled in Mexico, 1913–14: served in Villa's forces and was killed in action at the Battle of Ojinaga. *Died (probably 11 January) in 1914.*

PUBLICATIONS

Collections

    Collected Works, edited by Walter Neale.   12 vols., 1909–12.
    The Letters, edited by Bertha Clark Pope.   1921.
    Complete Short Stories, edited by Ernest Jerome Hopkins.   1970.
    Stories and Fables, edited by Edward Wagenknecht.   1977.

Fiction

    The Fiend's Delight.   1873.
    Nuggets and Dust Panned Out in California.   1873.

Cobwebs from an Empty Skull. 1873.
The Dance of Death, with Thomas A. Harcourt. 1877; revised edition, 1877.
Tales of Soldiers and Civilians. 1891; as *In the Midst of Life*, 1892; revised edition, 1898.
The Monk and the Hangman's Daughter, from a translation by Gustav Adolph Danziger of a story by Richard Voss. 1892.
Can Such Things Be? 1893.
Fantastic Fables. 1899.
Battleships and Ghosts. 1931.

Verse

Black Beetles in Amber. 1892.
Shapes of Clay. 1903.

Other

The Cynic's Word Book. 1906; as *The Devil's Dictionary*, 1911; revised edition by Ernest Jerome Hopkins, as *The Enlarged Devil's Dictionary*, 1967.
Write It Right: A Little Black-List of Literary Faults. 1909.
Twenty-One Letters, edited by Samual Loveman. 1922.
Selections from Prattle, edited by Carroll D. Hall. 1936.

Bibliography: *Bierce: A Bibliography* by Vincent Starrett, 1929; in *Bibliography of American Literature* by Jacob Blanck, 1955.

Reading List: *Bierce: A Biography* by Carey McWilliams, 1929; *Bierce, The Devil's Lexicographer*, 1951, and *Bierce and the Black Hills*, 1956, both by Paul Fatout; *Bierce* by Robert A. Wiggins, 1964; *The Short Stories of Bierce: A Study in Polarity* by Stuart C. Woodruff, 1965; *Bierce: A Biography* by Richard O'Connor, 1967; *Bierce* by Mary E. Grenander, 1971.

*   *   *

Though not widely read today, Ambrose Bierce is a familiar name in American letters. After several years of distinguished soldiering in the Civil War, the almost completely self-taught Bierce turned to journalism and ended up being one of the most colourful figures in late 19th- and early 20th-century journalism in America. In San Francisco, where he spent most of his life, he was a newspaper editor and columnist, and delighted in exposing hypocrisy and stupidity in private and public life. Besides his witty and pungent journalistic writing, Bierce produced a sizeable body of short stories and essays, and also some verse, chiefly occasional and satiric. His literary reputation, however, must depend upon the stories collected in *Tales of Soldiers and Civilians*, such as "The Occurrence at Owl Creek Bridge," in which Bierce skilfully uses suspense not as a mere melodramatic devise but logically and calculatingly to wind up the bizarre incidents concerning a young man about to be executed. In other stories, like "One of the Missing," there is perhaps a heavier use of coincidence than most readers would accept unprotestingly.

If young Bierce dealt in the tall-tale and broad Western humour, the older Bierce was a master of sardonic humour and mordant but often sparkling wit. Perhaps the best specimen of these qualities as well as of his life-long cynicism is to be found, outside his journalism, in *The Devil's Dictionary*, a book quoted universally even though many that quote from it may not be aware of the author's identity. As a serious literary writer Bierce belongs to — and has helped perpetuate (in however small a measure) — the tradition of the absurd and grotesque in American writing. There is in him a marked interest in abnormal or intensified psychological states and a persistent hostility to the realistic mode. One will look in vain for a range of emotional experience in his writing and consequently for the depth of serious feeling usually associated with great literature. But for his picturesque personality and his contribution as a committed and hard-hitting journalist, and as a writer of some excellent stories, Bierce is an enduring figure in the history of American literature.

—J. N. Sharma

BILLINGS, Josh.   See **SHAW, Henry Wheeler.**

BIRD, Robert Montgomery.   American.   Born in New Castle, Delaware, 5 February 1806. Educated at Germantown Academy, Philadelphia; University of Pennsylvania, Philadelphia, 1824–27, M.D. 1827. Married Mary Mayer in 1837; one son. Practised as a physician in Philadelphia for one year, then gave up medicine to devote himself to writing; wrote plays for the actor-producer Edwin Forrest, 1831–34, then turned to writing novels, 1835–40; suffered a breakdown and retired to a farm in Maryland, where he subsequently recovered, 1840; Professor of the Institutes of Medicine and Materia Medica, Pennsylvania Medical College, Philadelphia, 1841–43; Literary Editor and Part-Owner, *North American*, Philadelphia, 1847–54. Honorary Member, English Dramatic Authors Society. *Died 23 January 1854.*

PUBLICATIONS

Collections

   The Life and Dramatic Works (includes *Pelopidas, The Gladiator, Oralloossa*), edited by
      Clement E. Foust.   1919.
   The Cowled Lover and Other Plays (includes *Calidorf; or, The Avenger; News of the
      Night; or, A Trip to Niagara; 'Twas All for the Best; or 'Tis All a Notion*), edited by
      Edward O'Neill.   1941.

Plays

   The Gladiator (produced 1831; also produced as *Spartacus*).   In *The Life and Dramatic
      Works*, 1919.

Oralloossa (produced 1832). In *The Life and Dramatic Works*, 1919.
The Broker of Bogota (produced 1834). Edited by Arthur Hobson Quinn, in *Representative American Plays*, 1917.
News of the Night; or, A Trip to Niagara (produced 1929). In *The Cowled Lover and Other Plays*, 1941.
The City Looking Glass: A Philadelphia Comedy, edited by Arthur Hobson Quinn (produced 1933). 1933.

Fiction

Calavar; or, The Knight of the Conquest. 1834; as *Abdalla the Moor and the Spanish Knight*, 1835.
The Infidel; or, The Fall of Mexico. 1835; as *Cortez*, 1835; as *The Infidel's Doom*, 1840.
The Hawks of Hawk-Hollow: A Tradition of Pennsylvania. 1835.
Sheppard Lee. 1836.
Nick of the Woods; or, The Jibbenainosay: A Tale of Kentucky. 1837; edited by Cecil B. Williams, 1939.
Peter Pilgrim; or, A Rambler's Recollections. 1838.
The Adventures of Robin Day. 1839.

Bibliography: in *Bibliography of American Literature* by Jacob Blanck, 1955.

Reading List: *Life of Bird* by Mary Mayer Bird, edited by C. Seymour Thompson, 1945; *Bird* by Curtis Dahl, 1963.

*   *   *

One of the truly remarkable men of his time, Robert Montgomery Bird boasted sufficiently varied interests and equally responsive talents to lead his active mind through the fields of medicine, science, music, art, history, politics, pedagogy, and literature. Early in life he outlined a literary career in which he would begin with poetry and drama, turn next to novels, and finally write history. A scholarly man, widely read in the classics, he was also very much a product of and a part of the Romantic tradition which was being revealed in the idealism of Emerson and Thoreau, the Gothic qualities in Hawthorne and Poe, and the concern for nature which distinguished the novels of Cooper, John P. Kennedy and William G. Simms. Indeed, Bird was a significant force in bringing Romanticism to American literature, particularly the drama.

For his career as a dramatist Bird projected at least fifty-five plays, and in response to the play contests which Edwin Forrest established in 1828 he began to write in earnest. Four of Forrest's nine prize plays were written by Bird – *Pelopidas*, *The Gladiator*, *Oralloossa*, and *The Broker of Bogota* – but it did not prove to be a completely happy arrangement. For his efforts Bird received $1,000 for each play; Forrest, on the other hand, made hundreds of thousands of dollars. When Bird realized that plays such as *The Gladiator* and *The Broker of Bogota* would become permanent in Forrest's repertory, he complained, received no satisfaction, and stopped writing for the stage. "What a fool I was to think of writing plays!" he confided in his *Secret Records*. In all he completed only nine of his projected plays.

As a consequence of the events surrounding his relations with Forrest, Bird turned to politics, journalism, and novels. Two of his most popular novels are *The Hawks of Hawk-Hollow* and *Nick of the Woods*. Bird's loss to American drama, however, must be considered significant. An imaginative man, keenly aware of the forces working upon his culture, he espoused theories of dramaturgy which not only reflected the Romanticism of his day but were ideally suited to the style of acting currently popular. The idealized hero was the central force in his plays. All other dramatic elements – the plot, the dramatic incidents and spectacle, the poetic speech, the passions of the characters, the theme of the play – contributed to the creation of the hero and led to the climax of the play. Bird obviously had the energy and the skill to write good romantic melodrama. An early play, *The City Looking Glass* (written in 1828), also showed considerable potentiality for comedy. Unfortunately, all of this talent was shelved when his indignation was righteously ignited, and the help that copyright laws might have provided was years in the future.

—Walter J. Meserve

BOKER, George Henry.   American.   Born in Philadelphia, Pennsylvania, 6 October 1823. Educated at the College of New Jersey, now Princeton University (one of the founders of the *Nassau Monthly*, 1842), graduated 1842; also studied law. Married Julia Mandeville Riggs in 1844; one son. Devoted himself to writing from 1845, and to writing for the stage from 1848; Founding Member, 1862, Secretary, 1862–71, and President, 1879, Union Club, later Union League, Philadelphia; United States Ambassador to Turkey, 1871–75, and to Russia, 1875–78; President, Fairmount Park Commission, Philadelphia, 1886 until his death. President, Philadelphia Club, 1878. *Died 2 January 1890.*

PUBLICATIONS

Collections

   Glaucus and Other Plays (includes *The World a Mask, The Bankrupt*), edited by Sculley Bradley.   1940.

Plays

   Calaynos (produced 1849).   1848.
   Anne Boleyn (produced 1850).   1850.
   The Betrothal (produced 1850).   In *Plays and Poems*, 1856.
   The World a Mask (produced 1851).   1856; in *Glaucus and Other Plays*, 1940.
   The Widow's Marriage (produced 1852).   In *Plays and Poems*, 1856.
   Leonor de Guzman (produced 1853).   In *Plays and Poems*, 1856.
   Francesca da Rimini (produced 1855).   In *Plays and Poems*, 1856.
   The Bankrupt (produced 1855).   In *Glaucus and Other Plays*, 1940.
   Nydia, edited by Sculley Bradley.   1929; revised version, as *Glaucus*, in *Glaucus and Other Plays*, 1940.

Verse

   The Lesson of Life and Other Poems.   1848.
   The Podesta's Daughter and Other Miscellaneous Poems.   1852.

Poems of the War. 1864.
Our Heroic Themes. 1865.
Königsmark: The Legend of the Hounds and Other Poems. 1869.
The Book of the Dead: Poems. 1882.
Sonnets: A Sequence on Profane Love, edited by Sculley Bradley. 1929.

Other

Plays and Poems. 2 vols., 1856.

Bibliography: in *Bibliography of American Literature* by Jacob Blanck, 1955.

Reading List: *Boker, Poet and Patriot* by Sculley Bradley, 1927.

*   *   *

In keeping with his aspiration to live the life of the poet, George Henry Boker's first publication, *The Lesson of Life,* was a book of verse. The scion of a wealthy and aristocratic family who was classically educated at what would become Princeton University, Boker followed this first book with poems on public affairs, with patriotic verse, and with sonnets – a form with which he enjoyed particular felicity – on love and statesmanship. He subsequently collected many of these pieces into *Plays and Poems,* whose two volumes have been reprinted many times and are today the most accessible source of Boker's verse. Despite his love for poetry, however, Boker is remembered primarily as a dramatist, having written nearly a dozen plays between his first, *Calaynos,* a tragedy in blank verse, and his last, *Nydia,* which he rewrote as *Glaucus* in 1886.

Surely the most famous of Boker's plays is *Francesca da Rimini,* completed in 1853 and first produced in New York two years later. Based on the tragic love story of thirteenth-century Italy which Dante celebrated in *The Inferno* and which had been reworked by so many other authors, Boker's *Francesca* consists of more than 3,500 lines of neo-Elizabethan verse, so befitting its author's poetic urges as well as the day's theatrical tastes. In these lines Boker chronicled once again the unhappy triangle of Francesca, a noblewoman of Ravenna, Paolo, a nobleman of Rimini to whom she had given her heart, and Lanciotto, Paolo's equally noble but sadly deformed brother to whom she had given her hand in marriage. A stirring success, *Francesca* ran on the New York and Philadelphia stage in 1855, and was reproduced for longer runs in 1882–83 and again in 1901–02.

As the corpus of his work reveals, George Henry Boker was a playwright whose sense of the literary matched his sense of the theatrical. Understandably, then, he is among the best remembered of America's nineteenth-century dramatists.

—Bruce A. Lohof

BOYESEN, H(jalmar) H(jorth). American. Born in Frederiksvarn, Norway, 23 September 1848; emigrated to the United States, 1869. Educated at the Latin School, Dramen; Christiania Gymnasium; University of Leipzig; University of Christiania, Ph.D. 1868. Married Elizabeth Keen in 1874. Editor, Norwegian weekly *Fremad* (Forward), Chicago, 1869; Tutor in Greek and Latin, Urbana University, Ohio, 1870–73; Professor of German, Cornell University, Ithaca, New York, 1874–80; Member of the German faculty,

1880–82, Gebhard Professor of German, 1882–90, and Professor of Germanic Languages and Literatures, 1890–95, Columbia University, New York. *Died 4 October 1895.*

PUBLICATIONS

Fiction

> *Gunnar: A Tale of Norse Life.* 1874.
> *A Norseman's Pilgrimage.* 1875.
> *Tales from Two Hemispheres.* 1876.
> *Falconberg.* 1879.
> *Ilka on the Hill-Top and Other Stories.* 1881.
> *Queen Titania* (stories). 1881.
> *A Daughter of the Philistines.* 1883.
> *The Light of Her Countenance.* 1889.
> *Vagabond Tales.* 1889.
> *The Mammon of Unrighteousness.* 1891.
> *The Golden Calf.* 1892.
> *Social Strugglers.* 1893.

Play

> *Alpine Roses,* from his own story *Ilka on the Hill-Top* (produced 1884). 1884.

Verse

> *Idyls of Norway and Other Poems.* 1882.

Other

> *Goethe and Schiller: Their Lives and Works.* 1879.
> *The Story of Norway.* 1886.
> *The Modern Vikings: Stories of Life and Sport in the Norseland* (juvenile). 1887.
> *Against Heavy Odds: A Tale of Norse Heroism* (juvenile). 1890.
> *Essays on German Literature.* 1892.
> *Boyhood in Norway: Stories of Boy-Life in the Land of the Midnight Sun* (juvenile). 1892; as *The Battle of the Rafts and Other Stories,* 1893.
> *Norseland Tales* (juvenile). 1894.
> *A Commentary on the Works of Henrik Ibsen.* 1894.
> *Literary and Social Silhouettes.* 1894.
> *Essays on Scandinavian Literature.* 1894.

Reading List: *Boyesen* by Clarence A. Glasrud, 1963; "Boyesen: Outer Success, Inner Failure" by Per Seyersted, in *Americana Norvegica I* edited by Sigmund Skard and Henry H. Wasser, 1966.

*   *   *

H. H. Boyesen published his first novel, *Gunnar*, in 1874, five years after he came to the United States and mastered English. This romantic Norwegian idyl was influenced by Bjørnstierne Bjørnson's early fiction; Boyesen's success with this first effort was due in large part to his friendship with William Dean Howells, who helped polish the manuscript and serialized the story in the *Atlantic Monthly*. But though he was unquestionably a romantic by nature and early influence, Boyesen became a realist by conviction; with Howells he read and admired Turgenev and Tolstoy. Boyesen met Turgenev in Paris in 1873, with an introduction from a German critic; and Boyesen's second novel, *A Norseman's Pilgrimage*, was dedicated to Turgenev. Howells declined this romantically autobiographical story, warning the author that he was too hungry for publication; ten years elapsed before Turgenev approved one of the realistic stories Boyesen sent him ("A Dangerous Virtue").

Boyesen became one of America's best known teachers and lecturers. His *Goethe and Schiller*, essentially an English re-working of German scholarship and criticism, went into ten editions. His three collections of essays on German and Scandinavian literature published in the 1890's are magazine pieces, usually reprinted without revision. Boyesen was a literary journalist and popularizer, not a scholar and critic. But he was an important European-American liaison man who argued persuasively that Americans were so subservient to British literature that they ignored Goethe and Ibsen.

Boyesen's hundreds of articles, essays, and short stories show that he became "a magazinist" who depended on the income from such writing, but they also reflect his changing experience and convictions. His articles and stories on Norwegian-Americans, including the novel *Falconberg*, are not convincing because he had little contact with his fellow immigrants. But Boyesen lived in New York for fifteen years, on Fifth Avenue and at Southampton; and he was both fascinated and repelled by the social world of the newly rich.

He became sharply critical of American political and financial corruption, arguing that the American novelist was duty-bound to document and criticize American problems; and he tried to do this in such novels as *The Golden Calf* and *Social Strugglers*. For such efforts he was berated as an ungrateful foreigner and blamed for abandoning the idyllic vein of *Gunnar*. But Boyesen was consistent in his views, whether they were expressed in novels, essays, or speeches: when he died suddenly and unexpectedly in 1895, he was arguing vehemently for more realistic and responsible American fiction, citing the "high water mark" of realism established by the new Scandinavian writers.

In his long battle with the "purveyors of romance," Boyesen identified the American girl as the enemy of serious writing. She was "the Iron Madonna" who strangled the American novelist in her fond embrace, because magazine editors and book publishers knew she was the reader and arbiter they must satisfy. The beautiful, vivacious, and independent girls Boyesen found in America had fascinated him from his first arrival. He married one of them, and his subsequent efforts to augment a professor's salary by ceaseless writing and lecturing dissipated his talents and shortened his life. It seems significant that such girls frustrate their Norwegian-born admirers in his earliest fiction, dominate their parents in later stories (*A Daughter of the Philistines*), and victimize their husbands, notably in his most ambitious *Mammon of Unrighteousness*.

—Clarence A. Glasrud

BRACKENRIDGE, Hugh Henry. American. Born in Kintyre, near Campbeltown, Argyll, Scotland, in 1748; emigrated with his family to a farm in York County, Pennsylvania, 1753. Educated at the College of New Jersey, now Princeton University, 1768–71, B.A. 1771, M.A. 1774; studied law under Samuel Chase in Annapolis, Maryland, 1780. Chaplain in Washington's army during the Revolutionary War, 1776–78. Married 1) Miss Montgomery in 1785, one son; 2) Sabina Wolfe in 1790, two sons and one daughter. Teacher in the public school in Gunpowder Falls, Maryland, 1763–67, and at Somerset Academy, Back Creek, Maryland, 1772; Founding Editor, *United States Magazine*, Philadelphia, 1779; moved to Pittsburgh, and practised law there, 1781–99: Founder, *Pittsburgh Gazette*, 1786; Pennsylvania State Assemblyman, 1786–88; established Pittsburgh Academy, 1787, and the first bookshop in Pittsburgh, 1789; Justice of the Pennsylvania Supreme Court, 1799–1816. *Died 25 June 1816.*

PUBLICATIONS

Collections

A Brackenridge Reader, edited by Daniel Marder.   1970.

Fiction

Modern Chivalry.   6 vols., 1792–1805; revised edition, 1815, 1819; edited by Claude Milton Newlin, 1937.

Plays

The Battle of Bunkers Hill.   1776.
The Death of General Montgomery at the Siege of Quebec.   1777.

Verse

A Poem on the Rising Glory of America, with Philip Freneau.   1772.
A Poem on Divine Revelation.   1774.
An Epistle to Walter Scott.   1811(?).

Other

Six Political Discourses Founded on the Scriptures.   1778.
An Eulogium of the Brave Men Who Have Fallen in the Contest with Great Britain.   1779.
Incidents of the Insurrection in the Western Parts of Pennsylvania in 1794.   1795; edited by Daniel Marder, 1972.
The Standard of Liberty.   1802.
Gazette Publications (miscellany).   1806.
Law Miscellanies.   1814.

Editor, *Narratives of a Late Expedition Against the Indians.*   1783.

Bibliography: in *Bibliography of American Literature* by Jacob Blanck, 1955.

Reading List: *The Life and Writings of Brackenridge* by Claude Milton Newlin, 1932; *Brackenridge* by Daniel Marder, 1967.

* * *

Although Hugh Henry Brackenridge wrote in a number of different genres – poetry, drama, and non-fictional prose – his one real claim to our attention today is for the first part of *Modern Chivalry*, an extended piece of satiric fiction published in four volumes between 1792 and 1797. It can hardly be called a novel. The narrative line is thin, merely holding together a series of episodes involving a modern American Quixote, Captain John Farrago, and his Irish servant, Teague O'Regan, as they travel together on the western frontier and later visit the city of Philadelphia. It moves toward no climax in either plot or meaning, but merely illustrates through their adventures various failings of American democracy.

But if *Modern Chivalry* is weak in both narrative and thematic development, it is strong in its realistic pictures of frontier life and manners – exaggerated though they may be for satiric purposes – and in the simple, straightforward style through which both the incidents and the authorial discussions of them are presented. Various kinds of dialect – Irish, Scotch, and Negro – are well reproduced in its pages, and, though the characters may not be fully developed, they are sharply and skillfully sketched through their language and actions. Thus, the book has often been justly praised as an early piece of American realism.

It is also important for what it has to say about the theory and practice of American democracy. Most of the satire is directed against the Teague O'Regans, ignorant and ambitious men who are eager to accept honors and positions for which they are not qualified, and against an electorate that will put such men in office. But the book is not anti-democratic. It attacks as well those men of wealth or inherited position who are no more suited to rule, and members of organizations who admit unqualified persons to their ranks. What the book affirms is the basic principle of democracy: that positions of leadership should be given only to men of ability and integrity, qualities that may appear at any level of society, but which must be developed through education.

Only this first part is wholly successful. Brackenridge published the second in 1804–05 and extended the work yet again in the edition of 1815. His satiric touch was gone, however, and with it much of the charm of the book. The second part even lacks the narrative line of the first and becomes, in effect, an endlessly redundant lecture. It more than doubles the size of *Modern Chivalry*, but it does not add appreciably to what Brackenridge had accomplished in the 1790's.

—Donald A. Ringe

BRADSTREET, Anne (née Dudley). American. Born probably at Northampton, England, on 1612. Educated privately. Married Simon Bradstreet, afterwards Governor of Massachusetts, in 1628 (died, 1697); eight children. Emigrated to America, with the Winthrops, 1630, and lived in Ipswich, 1635–45, and North Andover, 1645–72, both in Massachusetts. *Died 16 September 1672.*

Glasgow University Library
Short Loan Collection

30/09/2004
11:46 am

You have just borrowed or renewed
the following items:

Title :American literature to 1900 / introducti
Please return no later than 07-10-04

4hr & 24hr loan items cannot be renewed

Whenever possible, please return Short
Loan items to the Bookdrop at the Short
Loan Collection entrance gate

Please keep this receipt it is your record of

PUBLICATIONS

Collections

Works, edited by Jeannine Hensley.   1967
Poems, edited by Robert Hutchinson.   1969.

Verse

The Tenth Muse Lately Sprung Up in America.   1650; revised edition, as *Several Poems
Compiled with Great Variety of Wit and Learning,* 1678.

Bibliography: "A List of Editions of the Poems of Bradstreet" by Oscar Wegelin, in *American
Book Collector 4,* 1933; "Bradstreet: An Annotated Checklist" by Ann Stanford, in *Bulletin of
Bibliography 27,* 1970.

Reading List: *Bradstreet and Her Time* by Helen S. Campbell, 1891; *Bradstreet* by Josephine
K. Piercy, 1965; *Bradstreet, The Tenth Muse* by Elizabeth Wade White, 1971; *Bradstreet,
The Worldly Puritan* by Ann Stanford, 1974.

*   *   *

Anne Bradstreet has long been recognized as the first genuine poet to develop in the
English-speaking New World. A recent biographer, Elizabeth Wade White, maintains
further that she "was also the first significant woman poet of England." The one volume that
appeared during her lifetime as *The Tenth Muse Lately Sprung up in America* – published in
England without her knowledge and with a title she did not supply – was the first collection
of poetry to come out of the New England colonies, to which Mrs. Bradstreet had emigrated
as a young wife in 1630.

Paradoxically, Mrs. Bradstreet continues to attract an appreciative audience not for the
poetry in *The Tenth Muse* but for a considerable number of poems that were first published in
1678, six years after her death. Of the thirteen poems in *The Tenth Muse,* only one, the 48-
line "Prologue," appeals to the modern reader; the others are lengthy and tedious exercises in
imitation of various poets – chiefly du Bartas (as rendered into English by Joshua Sylvester),
Spenser, and Sidney. Their works, together with Ralegh's *History of the World,* she first read
as a precocious child in the library of her indulgent father, Thomas Dudley, for many years
steward to the Earl of Lincoln. Mrs. Bradstreet's obvious indebtedness to these authors
suggests that she carried her favorite books aboard the *Arbella* and into the New England
wilderness in 1630.

Life in that wilderness, however – rather than her father's books – prompted the poetry
that has won for her a modest but permanent place in English-American literature. Her
Several Poems contained – in addition to the pieces in *The Tenth Muse* – almost a score of
poems that show her abandoning her old models and striking out with nuances, texture, and
techniques that are her own. One of these is "The Author to Her Book," a well-controlled
sustained metaphor that dramatizes her chagrin on first seeing the poorly printed *The Tenth
Muse.* "Contemplations," often regarded as her best poem, anticipates the romantic view of
nature and hints at her discomfort lest her physical reactions be at odds with her spiritual
convictions. A number of love poems written for her devoted husband, Simon Bradstreet – a
busy colonial official often away from home – reveal a healthy sensuality and suggest that,
although she was a Puritan, she was not puritanical. In other poems to and about her children
and about the fortunes and misfortunes of her family, she avoids sentimentality and brings to

her work the same quiet strength that helped her to survive for forty-two years in remote Massachusetts.

—Thomas F. O'Donnell

BROWN, Charles Brockden. American. Born in Philadelphia, Pennsylvania, 17 January 1771. Educated at the Friends' Latin School, Philadelphia, 1781–86; studied law in the office of Alexander Wilcocks, Philadelphia, 1787–92, but never practised. Married Elizabeth Linn in 1804; three sons and one daughter. Lived in New York, associated with the Friendly Society there, 1798–1801: edited the society's *Monthly Magazine and American Review*, 2 vols., 1799–1800; returned to Philadelphia, and worked in his brother's importing business, 1800–06, and as an independent trader, 1807–10; also Editor of the *Literary Magazine*, 1803–07, and the *American Register*, 1807–10. *Died 22 February 1810*.

PUBLICATIONS

Collections

Novels. 7 vols., 1827.

Fiction

Wieland; or, The Transformation: An American Tale. 1798; edited by Fred Lewis Pattee, with *Memoirs of Carwin*, 1926.
Ormond; or, The Secret Witness. 1799; edited by Ernest Marchand, 1937.
Arthur Mervyn; or, Memoirs of the Year 1793. 2 vols., 1799–1800; edited by Warner Berthoff, 1962.
Edgar Huntly; or, Memoirs of a Sleep-Walker. 1799; edited by David Lee Clark, 1928.
Clara Howard. 1801; as *Philip Stanley; or, The Enthusiasm of Love*, 1807.
Jane Talbot. 1801.
Carwin the Biloquist and Other American Tales and Pieces. 1822.

Other

Alcuin: A Dialogue. 1798; edited by Lee R. Edwards, 1971.
An Address to the Government on the Cession of Louisiana to the French. 1803; revised edition, 1803.
Monroe's Embassy. 1803.
An Address on the Utility and Justice of Restrictions upon Foreign Commerce. 1809.
The Rhapsodist and Other Uncollected Writings, edited by Harry R. Warfel. 1943.

Translator, *A View of the Soil and Climate of the United States of America,* by C. F. Volney.   1804.

Bibliography: in *Bibliography of American Literature* by Jacob Blanck, 1955; "A Census of the Works of Brown" by Sydney J. Krause and Jane Nieset, in *Serif 3*, 1966.

Reading List: *The Life of Brown* by William Dunlap, 2 vols., 1815; *Brown, American Gothic Novelist* by Harry R. Warfel, 1949; *Brown, Pioneer Voice of America* by David Lee Clark, 1952; *Brown* by Donald A. Ringe, 1966.

*   *   *

When Charles Brockden Brown began to write fiction in the latter half of the 1790's, he turned for his models to the popular novels of his time: the Gothic romances of England and Germany, the sentimental tale of seduction, and the novel of purpose. All of these types of fiction had a strong influence on the young American, and each of his six novels can be classified under one or more of these headings. But however much he may have learned from his wide reading, Brown was no mere imitator. He shaped his models to his own artistic ends and turned even such unpromising forms as the Gothic and sentimental romance into vehicles for the development of important themes. He left his indelible mark on everything he wrote.

A major characteristic of Brown's fiction is its intense intellectuality. Though *Wieland* and *Ormond* may both be viewed as tales of seduction, and *Wieland* and *Edgar Huntly* as tales of terror, all three carry a weight of thematic meaning not commonly found in the sentimental or Gothic romance. Sensationalist psychology, theories of education, and the sources of mania are major concerns in *Wieland*; utopian theories, the proper training for women, and the place of religion in education in *Ormond*; and benevolist principles in *Edgar Huntly*. Other of Brown's books are equally intellectual. Benevolist theory also appears in *Arthur Mervyn*, a book modeled on William Godwin's *Caleb Williams*, and Godwinian rationalism clashes with religion in *Jane Talbot*, a sentimental romance.

This is not to say that Brown in a propagandist. He used his fiction, as one critic has observed, not for the exposition, but for the discovery of ideas, which he puts to the test through the actions of his characters. The mistakes that the mad Theodore Wieland, the distraught Clara Wieland, and the rationalistic Henry Pleyel make in attempting to act on the basis of misinterpreted sensations, and the disaster that Edgar Huntly causes by acting on benevolist principles well illustrate Brown's technique. He forces the reader to examine the ideas in the context of the action, but he draws no conclusion himself. Indeed, since all of his books are first-person narrations, told through the voices of one or more characters or through a series of letters, the reader must often penetrate the psychology of the narrator before he can discover the thematic meaning embodied in the action.

In *Ormond*, the point of view causes relatively little trouble, for the story is told in a straightforward manner by a rational character who, throughout most of the book, plays no major role in the action. In other novels, however, where the protagonists tell their own stories, the problem can be difficult. Blessed with an innocent face and a glib tongue, Arthur Mervyn always presents himself in a favorable light, but he exists in a world where appearances are often deceiving, and his actions seem to belie the purity of motive that he consistently attributes to himself. He is, therefore, extremely difficult to penetrate, and critics are divided over the meaning of his experience. The protagonists in *Wieland* and *Edgar Huntly* present a different problem, for both are mentally disturbed. Clara Wieland lapses into madness in the course of her narrative, and Edgar Huntly is driven by strange compulsions from the very first pages of the book. Both narrators are, presumably, brought back to sanity by the close of their stories, but neither is easy for the reader to plumb.

In both of these Gothic tales, however, Brown found effective means for revealing the mental state of his disturbed narrators. Through the use of enclosures in *Wieland* — the temple, the summerhouse, and Clara's room and closet — he suggests the isolation and introspection of all the Wielands, including Clara; through the labyrinthine paths and deep cave in *Edgar Huntly*, he projects his protagonist's mental journey and withdrawal into himself. Other devices, too — Clara's dream, Edgar Huntly's somnambulism, and the appearance of his double, Clithero Edny — help the reader to understand their psychology. All of these were excellent inventions that function well in their respective books. Through them, Brown helped to establish the kind of psychological Gothic that became so popular throughout the nineteenth century in the works of Poe, Hawthorne, and even James.

Brown's position at the head of that tradition accounts for part of the interest he generates among readers today, but his historical importance is not his only claim to attention. Though he never wrote a wholly satisfactory novel — even his best books are marred by structural flaws and a defective style — he achieved so great an intellectual and imaginative intensity in such works as *Wieland*, *Edgar Huntly*, and *Arthur Mervyn* that one can forgive the weaknesses for the strengths. All are told by protagonists whose psychological state fascinates, and the tales they recount appeal to both the intellect and the emotions of the reader. The ideas Brown explores are always interesting, and the means he found to reveal the psychology of the narrators and to advance the action are absorbing. Though a hasty and careless writer — he hurried all six of his novels through the press in about three years — Brown instilled in the best of his books a vitality yet apparent almost two centuries after they were written.

—Donald A. Ringe

BROWN, William Wells. American. Born in Lexington, Kentucky, c. 1816; son of a slave owner, George Higgins, and one of his slaves. Married a free Black woman in 1834; two daughters. Taken to St. Louis as a boy and hired out on a steamboat; subsequently employed in the printshop of the editor of the *St. Louis Times*, then again hired out on a steamboat; escaped from slavery to Ohio and assumed the name of a man who befriended him, 1834; worked as a steward on steamboats on Lake Erie; occasional lecturer for anti-slavery societies in New York and Massachusetts, 1843–49, and associated with various other reform movements in the United States; represented the American Peace Society at the Peace Congress in Paris, 1849; travelled in Europe, 1849–54, and studied medicine abroad. *Died 6 November 1884.*

PUBLICATIONS

Fiction

> *Clotel; or, The President's Daughter: A Narrative of Slave Life in the United States.* 1853; another version published as *Clotelle: A Tale of the Southern States*, 1864; edited by W. Edward Farrison, with *Narrative of Brown*, 1969.

Plays

    Experience; or, How to Give a Northern Man a Backbone.   1856.
    The Escape; or, A Leap for Freedom.   1858.

Other

    Narrative of William Wells Brown, A Fugitive Slave.   1847; revised edition, 1848,
       1849; edited by W. Edward Farrison, with *Clotel,* 1969.
    Three Years in Europe; or, Places I Have Seen and People I Have Met.   1852; revised
       edition, as *The American Fugitive in Europe,* 1855.
    The Black Man: His Antecedents, His Genius, and His Achievements.   1863; revised
       edition, 1863.
    The Negro in the American Rebellion: His Heroism and His Fidelity.   1867.
    The Rising Son: or, The Antecedents and Advancement of the Colored Race.   1874.
    My Southern Home; or, The South and Its People.   1880(?).

    Editor, *The Anti-Slavery Harp: A Collection of Songs for Anti-Slavery Meetings.*   1848.

Reading List: *Brown, Author and Reformer* by W. Edward Farrison, 1969 (includes bibiliography).

*   *   *

Born a slave in Kentucky, William Wells Brown was schooled by the "peculiar institution" for life-long work as a reformer. Within two years of his own escape from bondage in 1834, he was conducting others to freedom on the underground railroad, and by the 1850's he was among the most famous abolitionists in Europe as well as America.

Crusaders then as now employed every medium available to their talents to advance their cause. In this company, Brown was remarkable, for besides oration and documentary reports he also produced a novel, a European travel book, plays, several historical studies, and reflective memoirs. The novel, *Clotel,* the travel book, *Three Years in Europe,* and the five-act drama, *The Escape,* are first examples of their type written by a black American. Together with the range of his own writings they assure Brown a place in American literary history.

Brown's narrative of life in slavery was a best-seller. His novel found a broad audience by virtue of its appearance in several versions, and his histories and recollections went through multiple editions. Their contemporary appeal seems to have been due largely to their reaffimation of standard arguments in their use of familiar literary conventions.

Yet it is the evident redundancy in his work that accounts for Brown's present significance. In his autobiography, Brown's first published book, he describes his master as stealing him as soon as he was born. His mother, he explains, bore seven children by seven different men, including a white relative of the master, who fathered William. Each infant was claimed by the master as his property without regard to lineage or paternal affection. William and his mother tried to escape slavery but were caught, and his mother sold into the Deep South "to die on a ... plantation!" Later, when he made his way alone to freedom on Ohio, he joined the name his mother had given him with that of Wells Brown, his first white friend and surrogate father. These autobiographical facts reveal the terms in which Brown saw destiny. Thus, his fiction centers upon mulatto characters whose very existence images violation and relates incidents where neither blood, race, nor intimacy prevent subjugation. Carried into non-fiction, where he argued the case for equality on the basis of achievement and service, Brown adapts his motifs into a plea for reconciliation within the human family.

It is repeated examination of fate in an America where essential humanity is divided by brutal practice that gives Brown continued inportance. For this first black man of letters established in literature the prevalent Afro-American concern with identity.

—John M. Reilly

BROWNE, Charles Farrar. See **WARD, Artemus.**

BRYANT, William Cullen. American. Born in Cummington, Massachusetts, 3 November 1794. Educated privately, and at Williams College, Williamstown, Massachusetts, 1810–11; studied law under Mr. Howe, Worthington, Massachusetts, 1811–14, and in the office of William Baylies, Bridgewater, Massachusetts, 1814–15; admitted to the Massachusetts Bar, 1815. Married Frances Fairchild in 1821 (died, 1865); two children. Practised law in Great Barrington, Massachusetts, 1816–25; Editor, with Henry J. Anderson, *New York Review and Athenaeum Magazine*, 1825; Assistant Editor, 1826–29, and Editor, and part owner, 1829–78, *Evening Post*, New York. President, American Free Trade League, 1865–69. *Died 12 June 1878.*

PUBLICATIONS

Collections

Poetical Works, Prose Writings, edited by Parke Godwin.   4 vols., 1883–84.
Poetical Works, edited by Henry C. Sturges and Richard Henry Stoddard.   1903.
Selections, edited by Samuel Sillen.   1945.
Letters, edited by William Cullen Bryant II and Thomas G. Voss.   1975–

Verse

The Embargo; or, Sketches of the Times: A Satire.   1808.
The Embargo and Other Poems.   1809.
Poems.   1821.
Poems.   1832; revised edition, 1834, 1836, 1850.
The Fountain and Other Poems.   1842.
The White-Footed Deer and Other Poems.   1844.
Poems.   2 vols., 1855.
Thirty Poems.   1864.
Hymns.   1864; revised edition, 1869.

Poems.   1871.
Poems.   3 vols., 1875.
Poems.   1876.

Other

Letters of a Traveller; or, Notes of Things Seen in Europe and America.   1850; as *The Picturesque Souvenir,* 1851.
Reminiscences of The Evening Post.   1851.
Letters of a Traveller, Second Series.   1859.
A Discourse on the Life, Character, and Genius of Washington Irving.   1860.
Letters from the East.   1869.
Orations and Addresses.   1873.
Bryant and Isaac Henderson: 21 Letters, edited by Theodore Hornberger.   1950.

Editor, *Tales of Glauber-Spa.*   2 vols., 1832.
Editor, *Selections from the American Poets.*   1840.
Editor, *The Berkshire Jubilee.*   1845.
Editor, *A Library of Poetry and Song.*   1871; revised edition, as *A New Library,* 1876(?).
Editor, with Oliver B. Bunce, *Picturesque America; or, The Land We Live In.*   2 vols., 1872–74.
Editor, *A Popular History of the United States,* vols. 1–2, by Sydney Howard Gay.   1876–78.
Editor, with Evert A. Duyckinck, *Complete Works of Shakespeare.*   25 vols., 1888.

Translator, *The Iliad and the Odyssey of Homer.*   4 vols., 1870–72.

Bibliography: in *Bibliography of American Literature* by Jacob Blanck, 1955; *A Bibliography of Bryant and His Critics 1909–1972* by Judith T. Phair, 1975.

Reading List: *A Biography of Bryant* (includes letters) by Parke Godwin, 2 vols., 1883; *Gotham Yankee: A Biography of Bryant* by Harry Houston Peckham, 1950; *Politics and a Belly-Full: The Journalistic Career of Bryant* by Curtiss S. Johnson, 1962; *Bryant* by Albert F. McLean, Jr., 1964; *Bryant* by Charles H. Brown, 1971.

*   *   *

When in his poem "The Poet" William Cullen Bryant urges a writer to eschew the "empty gust/Of passion" but to express "feelings of calm power and mighty sweep,/Like currents journeying through the windless deep," he is making an apt comment on his own best work. For though in "A Fable for Critics" James Russell Lowell goes too far in joking at Bryant for his coldness, his lack of enthusiasm, his "supreme *ice*olation," Bryant's strong points are indeed not passion, not delicacy, not soaring imagination, but dignity and power. Even through his lighter poems sounds a strong didactic note that reminds one that his literary forbears were New England Puritans, his work also has overtones of the sober eighteenth-century neoclassicism of Gray and Collins. He is at his best when with stately force he depicts the grand sweeping cycle of life which carries all away with its resistless current.

Thus his first major poem, "Thanatopsis," written in the tradition of the British Graveyard Poets in grave, resounding lines, pictures man, even new American man, living on the tombs of countless races. When we too join the caravan to the inevitable tomb, Bryant says, may we face our fate with stoic dignity. "The Journey of Life," "The Ages," "The Past," and "The

Flood of Years," though with a more specifically Christian hope of immortality, similarly emphasize with stately resonance and images the cyclical patterns of human existence. The same theme is effectively voiced in such poems as "The Prairies," "Monument Mountain," and "An Indian at the Burial Place of His Fathers," which delineate the successive destruction of America's aboriginal races and remind the white man that he too may disappear. Because of such epic grandeur in his own themes it is not surprising that Bryant was a highly successful translator of Homer.

But the classic dignity of much of Bryant's best work is nicely balanced by his Romantic sense of the soothing power and divinity of nature. Bryant was America's first major Romantic poet. Poems like "A Forest Hymn," "Green River," and "Inscription for the Entrance to a Wood" earnestly inculcate the creed that nature can give solace to the weary heart. Some of these poems verge on pantheism and foreshadow Emerson's doctrine that the divine creation has never ceased. Throughout even the simple nature poems, such as "The Yellow Violet" and "To a Fringed Gentian," Bryant preaches, sometimes somberly, sometimes wittily; his favorite lyric form is a series of descriptive stanzas followed by one or two of moral. Though he is playful in "A Meditation on Rhode Island Coal" and "Robert of Lincoln," he rarely writes for fun. Yet in such a poem as "To a Waterfowl" he can so superbly blend his moralism with telling imagery and restrained emotion that it becomes an integral part of a powerful work of art, indeed one of America's finest lyrics.

Though Bryant was intensely concerned with mutability and nature, he was also acutely awake to American life around him. His first published volume, *The Embargo*, was a satire against the Jeffersonians. Not only was he for many years the writer of powerful liberal editorials in the New York *Evening Post*, of which for many years he was editor, but he also wrote many effective and graceful occasional poems such as his elegy on Lincoln. Like the Hudson River School painters with whom he was closely associated (see "To Cole, The Painter, Departing for Europe"), he patriotically celebrated American landscape, American nature, and American history and legend. He even edited a collection of essays and engravings entitled *Picturesque America*. He wrote on popular causes such as slavery ("The African Chief") and Greek independence ("The Massacre at Scio"). Sometimes, as in "The Death of the Flowers," he verged toward the mawkish sentimentalism that was the bane of America's "Feminine Fifties," but his lack of pretentiousness, quiet integrity, and basic good sense, seen also in his anthologies of American poetry and especially in his first-rate critical essays on poets and poetry, ordinarily saved him from banality. Like so many American authors of his time he also wrote hymns.

With some justice Bryant's poetry has been derogated as bloodless, undramatic, too orotund, too much concerned with death and mutability, out of touch with vivid life, even morbid. To read his verse, Marius Bewley says, is "a little like listening to a harmonium with the pedal stuck," and his poetry gives the impression of "a best parlor filled with marmoreal statuary." But such comment is unfair. Bryant is a significant pioneer in American literature. His best work is also still worthy to be read for what Lowell calls "the grace, strength, and dignity" of his art and for the quiet depth and earnestness of his vision of the ever-flowing stream of nature and human life. His was surely the most powerful poetic voice in America between Edward Taylor and Poe.

—Curtis Dahl

BURNETT, Frances (Eliza) Hodgson. American. Born in Cheetham Hill, Manchester, England, 24 November 1849; emigrated with her parents to Knoxville, Tennessee, 1865; naturalized, 1905. Educated in schools in Manchester. Married 1) Dr. Swan Moses Burnett in 1873 (divorced, 1898), two sons; 2) Stephen Townesend in 1900 (separated, 1901; died, 1914). Full-time writer from 1866; lived in Europe, 1875–77; settled in Washington, D.C.,

1877; lived in England, 1898–1901, then settled near Plandome Park on Long Island. *Died 29 October 1924.*

Fiction

Surly Tim and Other Stories.   1877.
Theo: A Love Story.   1877.
Pretty Polly Pemberton: A Love Story.   1877.
That Lass o' Lowries.   1877.
Dolly: A Love Story.   1877; as *Vagabondia,* 1883.
Kathleen: A Love Story.   1878.
Miss Crespigny: A Love Story.   1878.
Earlier Stories.   1878; second series, 1878.
A Quiet Life, and The Tide on the Moaning Bar.   1878.
Our Neighbour Opposite.   1878.
Jarl's Daughter and Other Stories.   1879.
Natalie and Other Stories.   1879.
Haworth's.   1879.
Louisiana.   1880.
A Fair Barbarian.   1881.
Through One Administration.   1883.
Little Lord Fauntleroy.   1886.
A Woman's Will; or, Miss Defarge.   1887.
Sara Crewe; or, What Happened at Miss Minchin's.   1887.
Editha's Burglar.   1888.
The Fortunes of Philippa Fairfax.   1888.
The Pretty Sister of José.   1889.
Little Saint Elizabeth and Other Stories.   1890.
Children I Have Known.   1892; as *Giovanni and the Other: Children Who Have Made Stories,* 1894.
The Captain's Youngest and Other Stories.   1894; as *Piccino and Other Child Stories,* 1894.
Two Little Pilgrims' Progress: A Story of the City Beautiful.   1895.
A Lady of Quality.   1896.
His Grace of Osmonde.   1897.
In Connection with the De Willoughby Claim.   1899.
The Making of a Marchioness.   1901; revised edition, 1901.
The Methods of Lady Walderhurst.   1901.
In the Closed Room.   1904.
A Little Princess, Being the Whole Story of Sara Crewe Now Told for the First Time.   1905.
Racketty Packetty House.   1905.
The Dawn of a Tomorrow.   1906.
The Troubles of Queen Silver-Bell.   1906.
The Cozy Lion, as Told by Queen Crosspatch.   1907.
The Spring Cleaning, as Told by Queen Crosspatch.   1908.
The Shuttle.   1908.
The Good Wolf.   1908.
Barty Crusoe and His Man Saturday.   1909.

The Land of the Blue Flower.   1909.
The Secret Garden.   1911.
My Robin.   1912.
T. Tembaron.   1913.
The Lost Prince.   1915.
The Way to the House of Santa Claus: A Christmas Story.   1916.
Little Hunchback Zia.   1916.
The White People.   1917.
The Head of the House of Coombe.   1922.
Robin.   1922.

Plays

That Lass o' Lowries, with Julian Magnus, from the novel by Burnett (produced 1878).
Esmeralda, with William Gillette (produced 1881; as *Young Folks' Ways*, produced 1883).   1882.
The Real Little Lord Fauntleroy, from her own novel (produced 1888).
Phyllis, from her own novel *The Fortunes of Philippa Fairfax* (produced 1889).
Editha's Burglar, with Stephen Townesend, from the novel by Burnett (produced 1890; as *Nixie*, produced 1890).
The Showman's Daughter, with Stephen Townesend (produced 1891).
The First Gentleman of Europe, with Constance Fletcher (produced 1897).
A Lady of Quality, with Stephen Townesend, from the novel by Burnett (produced 1897).
A Little Princess, from her own novel *Sara Crewe* (as *A Little Unfairy Princess*, produced 1902; as *A Little Princess*, produced 1903).   In *Treasury of Plays for Children*, edited by Montrose J. Moses, 1921.
The Pretty Sister of José, from her own novel (produced 1903).
That Man and I, from her own novel *In Connection with the De Willoughby Claim* (produced 1903).
The Dawn of a Tomorrow, from her own novel (produced 1909).
Racketty Packetty House, from her own novel (produced 1912).

Other

The Drury Lane Boys' Club.   1892.
The One I Knew Best of All: A Memory of the Mind of a Child (autobiography).   1893.
In the Garden.   1925.

Reading List: *Mrs. Ewing, Mrs. Molesworth, and Mrs. Burnett* by Marghanita Laski, 1950; *Waiting for the Party: The Life of Burnett* by Ann Thwaite, 1974.

*   *   *

When Frances Hodgson Burnett died in 1924, *The Times'* obituary writer praised her work in helping to bring about the 1911 Copyright Act but decided that it was almost solely by her "idyll of child life" *Little Lord Fauntleroy* that Mrs. Burnett would be remembered. *Times* readers rushed to deny that her claims to permanence were so limited. Some of her adult novels were mentioned and, of course, *The Secret Garden*. In fact, since her death, her three major children's books, *Fauntleroy*, *A Little Princess*, and *The Secret Garden*, have never been out of print. *Fauntleroy* made an immediate impact on its first publication. Along with

King Solomon's Mines and *War and Peace* it was one of the best-selling novels of 1886 in America, read by old and young alike. The descriptions of the "handsome, blooming, curly-headed little fellow" may be nauseating to today's taste but it remains an excellent story.

Its wild success changed Mrs. Burnett's career. Up till this time, she had been gradually establishing herself as a serious and important novelist. In 1877 her American publisher, Scribner, wrote to her English publisher, Warne, "She is considered by good judges as the 'Coming Woman' in literature." The *Boston Transcript* wrote of her first full-length novel, *That Lass o' Lowries*: "We know of no more powerful work from a woman's hand in the English language, not even excepting the best of George Eliot." Both this novel and *Haworth's* were set in industrial Lancashire with a liberal use of the dialect which had fascinated her even as a young child in Manchester.

Through One Administration, her last adult novel before *Fauntleroy*, is a considerable achievement, proving that Mrs. Burnett was indeed much more than the romantic middle-brow novelist her later books suggest. It was not the love between Bertha Amory and Tredennis that interested her; it was the lack of love between Bertha and Richard Amory. And the novel's picture of Washington lobbying, of machinations and intrigues, is vivid and convincing. It was at this time (in an article in the July 1883 issue of *The Century*) that Mrs. Burnett was named as one of the five writers in America "who hold the front rank today in general estimation." Then came *Fauntleroy*, a great deal of money and a pattern of writing which had to keep pace with her new way of life – large houses, numerous crossings of the Atlantic, and a constant demand for her talents.

The most interesting of her later adult books are *A Woman's Will*, her autobiography, *The One I Knew the Best of All*, *The Shuttle*, and *The Making of a Marchioness*, In Marghanita Laski's words, the last is a "fairy story diluted with unromantic realism," and it is that realistic treatment of its period which gives it its special appeal today.

Much of the appeal of her children's story *A Little Princess* is its period charm. But its incredible coincidences do not conceal Mrs. Burnett's understanding of children. Sara is real in an unreal story. *The Secret Garden* has real children in a real story. Two unhappy children are convincingly transformed, not by outside intervention but by their own determination. It is a book which made no great impact on publication, but it has steadily established itself as one of the few real classics of children's literature.

—Ann Thwaite

CABLE, George Washington. American. Born in New Orleans, Louisiana, 12 October 1844. Educated in the New Orleans public schools until 1859; largely self-taught. Served in the 4th Mississippi Cavalry during the Civil War, 1863–65. Married 1) Louise Stewart Bartlett in 1869 (died, 1904), six daughters and one son; 2) Eva C. Stevenson in 1906 (died, 1923); 3) Hanna Cowing in 1923. Worked as a state surveyor in Louisiana, 1865–66; incapacitated by malaria, 1866–68; Reporter and Columnist ("Drop Shot") for the New Orleans *Picayune*, 1869; Accountant and Correspondence Clerk for A. C. Black and Company, cotton factors, New Orleans, 1869–79; full-time writer from 1879; settled in Northampton, Massachusetts, 1885; thereafter made yearly tours of the United States, reading his own works; organized the Home-Culture Club in Northampton, 1886, renamed the Northampton People's Institute, 1909; published the journals *The Letter*, 1892–96, and *The Symposium*, 1896. A.M: Yale University, New Haven, Connecticut, 1883; D.Litt.: Washington and Lee University, Lexington, Virginia, 1882; Yale University, 1901; Bowdoin College, Brunswick, Maine, 1904. Member, American Academy of Arts and Letters. *Died 31 January 1925.*

PUBLICATIONS

Collections

    Creoles and Cajuns: Stories of Old Louisiana, edited by Arlin Turner.   1959.

Fiction

    Old Creole Days (stories).   1879.
    The Grandissimes: A Story of Creole Life.   1880.
    Madame Delphine.   1881.
    Dr. Sevier.   1884.
    Madame Delphine, Carancro, Grande Pointe.   1887.
    Bonaventure: A Prose Pastoral of Acadian Louisiana.   1888.
    Strange True Stories of Louisiana.   1889.
    John March, Southerner.   1894.
    Strong Hearts.   1899.
    The Cavalier.   1901.
    Père Raphaël.   1901.
    Bylow Hill.   1902.
    Kincaid's Battery.   1908.
    "Posson Jone' " and Père Raphaël.   1909.
    Gideon's Band: A Tale of the Mississippi.   1914.
    The Amateur Garden.   1914.
    The Flower of the Chapdelaines.   1918.
    Lovers of Louisiana (Today).   1918.

Other

    The Creoles of Louisiana.   1884.
    The Silent South.   1885.
    The Negro Question.   1890.
    A Busy Man's Bible.   1891.
    A Memory of Roswell Smith.   1892.

A Southerner Looks at Negro Discrimination: Selected Writings, edited by Isabel Cable Manes. 1946.
Twins of Genius: Letters of Mark Twain, Cable, and Others, edited by Guy A. Cardwell. 1953.
The Negro Question: A Selection of Writings on Civil Rights in the South, edited by Arlin Turner. 1958.
Mark Twain and Cable: The Record of a Literary Friendship, edited by Arlin Turner. 1960.

Bibliography: in *Bibliography of American Literature* by Jacob Blanck, 1957.

Reading List: *Cable: His Life and Letters* by Lucy Leffingwell Cable Bikle, 1928; *Cable: A Study of His Early Life and Work* by Kjell Ekström, 1950; *Cable: A Biography* by Arlin Turner, 1956; *Cable: The Northampton Years*, 1959, and *Cable*, 1962, both by Philip Butcher; *Cable: The Life and Times of a Southern Heretic* by Louis D. Rubin, Jr., 1969.

*   *   *

George Washington Cable was one of the first progressive writers of the "New South." His father's German background and his mother's New England protestantism contributed to his own sense of isolation in a community whose leaders were primarily French and Catholic. Cable's position as an outsider may have stimulated his interest in sociological problems and made him more sensitive to the needs of minorities, especially Southern blacks. His father's untimely death and the Civil War prevented him from completing his formal education, but he was always an avid reader and enjoyed writing. In his late twenties he took a part-time job on the *New Orleans Picayune*, where his "Drop Shot" column, though occasionally controversial, was well received. At this time Cable began writing a series of short stories, and was discovered by Scribner's Edward King, who was touring Louisiana in search of materials for his "Great South" series. Although Scribner's rejected "Bibi," Cable's story of a tormented slave-prince, on the grounds of its unpleasant subject matter, they published his character sketch of an old Creole, " 'Sieur George," in 1873. Richard Watson Gilder, editor of *Scribner's Monthly* and the *Century*, considered Cable one of his leading local colorists, who would contribute to Gilder's plan for reconciling the North and South through literature. H. H. Boyesen also took an interest in Cable's writing and initiated a correspondence helpful to the latter's career.

In 1879 Cable's *Old Creole Days*, a collection of short stories, was published, and the first installments of *The Grandissimes*, which incorporated the "Bibi" materials, appeared in *Scribner's Monthly*. In 1880 *The Grandissimes* was published in book form, as was *Madame Delphine*, a novella. These two books represent Cable's highest achievement, anticipating the complex drama of Faulkner's works. Each deals with racial injustice, the continuing problems caused by exploitation of the black community, and the Creoles' resistance to social change. He described the lush, exotic world of the deep South unknown to most Americans. Topics considered off limits to the genteel authors of the Tidewater region or the wholesome humorists of the Piedmont are insightfully probed: miscegenation, the cruelties of the *Code Noire*, and the arrogance and indolence of the aristocracy.

By 1882 Cable began a full-time career as a writer, completing *Dr. Sevier*, a serious novel dealing with prison reform, which was followed by a *Century Magazine* exposé, "The Convict Lease System in the Southern States," and a history, *The Creoles of Louisiana*. These three works, openly polemical, offended Gilder and caused tremendous resentment throughout the South. A reading tour with Mark Twain brought Cable some additional income and popularity, but his increasingly fervent publications on the Negro's dilemma, especially "A Freedman's Case in Equity" and *The Silent South*, made him notorious in New

Orleans, and he eventually settled in Northampton, Massachusetts.

There Cable organized the Home-Culture clubs, racially integrated reading groups designed to raise the educational level of average citizens. The success of the movement was due in part to the national atmosphere of self-improvement and upward mobility in the last quarter of the nineteenth century.

When Cable was fifty he published *John March, Southerner,* an ambiguous portrait of a Southern aristocrat during the reconstruction era. As in his earlier fiction he examined outmoded conceptions of chivalry and honor, racial injustice, and anachronistic social and political attitudes. This was his last attempt at social satire. He continued to be an outspoken essayist, but his fiction became unashamedly romantic. The public taste of the period and his editors reinforced his tendency toward sentimentalism. *The Cavalier* was Cable's greatest popular success. He even overcame his Calvinistic distrust of the stage and authorized a dramatic version of the novel, starring Julia Marlowe. Energetic until the end, he wrote three novels in his seventies and shaped an optimistic vision of technological progress in the New South and the eventual integration of the races.

Perhaps because he remained too dependent on the family magazine audience and the taste of his editors, Cable did not live up to his early potential as a major Southern writer. Nevertheless, in his best fiction he transcended the limitations of the local color genre and revealed a daring and prophetic intelligence.

—Kimball King

CAHAN, Abraham.   American.   Born in Vilna, Russia, 7 July 1860; emigrated to the United States, 1882, later naturalized. Educated at the Teachers' Institute, Vilna; later attended a law school in New York. Married Anna Braunstein in 1887. Settled in New York; staff member, *Commercial Advertiser,* New York, 1897–1901; Editor of the Yiddish newspaper *Forverts* (*Jewish Daily Forward*) for more than 40 years. *Died 31 August 1951.*

PUBLICATIONS

Fiction

> *Yekl: A Tale of the New York Ghetto.*   1896.
> *The Imported Bridegroom and Other Stories of the New York Ghetto.*   1898.
> *The White Terror and the Red: A Novel of Revolutionary Russia.*   1905.
> *The Rise of David Levinsky.*   1917.

Other

> *Historye fun die Fereinigte Staaten* (in Yiddish).   2 vols., 1910–12.
> *Bleter fun Mayn Lebn* (in Yiddish).   5 vols., 1926–31; as *The Education of Cahan,* 2 vols., 1969.

> Editor, *Hear the Other Side: A Symposium of Democratic Socialist Opinion.*   1934.

Bibliography: *Cahan: Bibliography* by Ephim H. Jeshurin, 1941.

Reading List: *From the Ghetto: The Fiction of Cahan* by Jules Chametzky, 1977.

*   *   *

Abraham Cahan is perhaps more notable for his leadership in the Yiddish-speaking community of the Lower East Side than he is for any of his English prose. For more than forty years, he was the editor of the popular Yiddish newspaper *Forverts*. As such he guided the immigrant Jewish populace in their Americanization. His editorials, his Yiddish fiction, and his work as a union organizer – all bespoke his socialist, didactic prejudices.

It was not until 1895 that he published his first short story in English. However, at least as early as the 1880's he was contributing non-fiction prose to the *New York World* and the *New York Sun and Press*. In these pieces Cahan introduced the East Side ghetto to non-Jewish America. In the career of Cahan, however, these articles are not as important as the writing he did in the offices of the *Commercial Advertiser* (1897–1901). The relationship between Cahan and his colleagues on the English newspaper was mutually beneficial: Hutchins Hapgood and Lincoln Steffens learned of the intellectual turmoil and excitement of the Lower East Side; Cahan learned more sophisticated techniques of journalism.

Before his tenure on the *Commercial Advertiser*, Cahan had published only two short stories and a novella in English. These three pieces are local-color treatments of immigrant life. Cahan adds a strong moralizing temperament, the socialist criticism of the dehumanization of capitalism.

Cahan never turned from this socialist didacticism. But his later fiction more successfully subsumes this purpose under an aesthetic control. He also became more interested in presenting the dilemma of his old world immigrants in modern America. Their struggles result from the conflict between the teachings and expectations of the past and the realities and threats of the present. In short story form, Cahan's most successful treatment of this conflict is "The Imported Bridegroom," a tale of the repercussions of the modern world vision on Jews in different stages of alienation from their Jewish past.

It is, however, the novel *The Rise of David Levinsky* that assures Cahan a significance in American literature. Past ideals and present desires plague the rise of this Silas Lapham. The title clearly alludes to the famous novel of William Dean Howells, Cahan's favorite American writer and one of his staunchest supporters and mentors in the American literary establishment. The story of David is different from that of Silas: unlike the Protestant version of the rags to riches hero, Cahan's hero never effects a moral rise, never learns to balance his present reality with his past expectations.

Cahan's novel is one of the most powerful about immigrant life in America and one of the most telling portraits of the joylessness of the moneyed life without spiritual fulfilment. After this great success, Cahan seemed to have finished his discourse with English-speaking America. The rest of his career was centered on the *Forverts* and his autobiography in Yiddish.

—Barbara Gitenstein

CHANNING, William Ellery. American. Born in Boston, Massachusetts, 29 November 1818; nephew of the writer William Ellery Channing; raised by a great-aunt in Milton, Massachusetts. Educated at Round Hill School, Northampton, Massachusetts, and Boston

Latin School; attended Harvard University, Cambridge, Massachusetts, 1834. Married Ellen Fuller in 1842. Farmed in Woodstock, Illinois, 1839–40; tutor and newspaper writer, Cincinnati, 1840–41; settled in Concord, Massachusetts, to be near Emerson, 1842, and remained there for the rest of his life; associated with other members of the Concord community, especially Thoreau; lived in New York, writing for the *Tribune*, 1844; visited France and Italy, 1845; Editor, *New Bedford Mercury*, Massachusetts, 1855–58. *Died 23 December 1901.*

PUBLICATIONS

Collections

Poems of Sixty-Five Years, edited by F. B. Sanborn.   1902.

Verse

Poems.   1843; second series, 1847.
Conversations in Rome: Between an Artist, A Catholic, and a Critic.   1847.
The Woodman and Other Poems.   1849.
Near Home.   1858.
The Wanderer: A Colloquial Poem.   1871.
The Burial of John Brown.   1878.
Eliot.   1885.
John Brown and the Heroes of Harper's Ferry.   1886.

Other

Thoreau, The Poet-Naturalist.   1873; revised edition, 1902.

Editor, with Sophia Thoreau, *The Maine Woods*, by Henry David Thoreau.   1864.
Editor, with Sophia Thoreau, *Cape Cod*, by Henry David Thoreau.   1865.
Editor, with Sophia Thoreau, *A Yankee in Canada, with Anti-Slavery and Reform Papers*, by Henry David Thoreau.   1866.

*   *   *

When Emerson helped found *The Dial* in 1840, it was just such a poet as William Ellery Channing for whom he intended the new magazine. Channing was a young man with a talent but with no readily available place for his verses. Under Emerson's sponsorship, Channing went on to publish not only poems in *The Dial*, but two books of lyrics and four book-length poems later in his life. These early lyrics are in many ways most characteristic of him. His themes were beauty, self-reliance, and nature. He was hostile to the development of urban America, and in such poems as "Reverence" and "Walden Spring" he gave voice to his fears and to his longings for a pastoral life which was quickly vanishing in the 1840's. What he wanted was the union of nature and self such as he imaged in "Wachusett":

> It went within my inmost heart,
> The overhanging Arch to see,
> The liquid stream, became a part
> Of my internal Harmony.

Typical of his time and place, he insisted on a union of art and life. To write well was to live well; to *be* a poet was itself a creation of supreme importance.

His increasing awareness of his own loneliness and his isolation was most apparent in two of his book-length poems, *Near Home* and *The Wanderer*. The first of these is a charming hymn to New England as a place of healing power.

> Perpetual newness and the health in things.
> This, is the startling theme, the lovely birth
> Each morn of a new day, so wholly new,
> So absolutely penetrated by itself,
> The fresh, the fair, the ever-living grace....

In *The Wanderer*, Channing completed his journey from the simplicity of his lyrics to a more complex recognition of the tensions between man's love of nature and the forces working against the fulfillment of his pastoral idealism. The poem counterpoises a reverence for the land with a stark awareness of the destructive forces of death and technology. A poetic career beginning in enthusiasm ends in a mature perception of frustration.

Beyond the achievement of his poetry, Channing's career included the first biography of Thoreau, who had been the poet's close friend from 1841. *Thoreau, The Poet-Naturalist* is a narrative built on extensive quotations from Thoreau's journal, which was then unpublished. The book had the virtue of thus putting before the public quite a bit of Thoreau's little-known writing, and it also offered a cogent commentary by Channing who rightly emphasized the ethical strictness and the aesthetic craftsmanship in Thoreau's writing. Appearing at a time when Thoreau was all but unknown, the biography had the virtue of keeping his name alive and making his work more readily accessible.

Finally, it is as a friend that Channing may be best remembered. He was the only close friend of Thoreau; he was a constant companion of Emerson for forty years; he was a frequent visitor in the homes of Alcott and Hawthorne; he was Margaret Fuller's brother-in-law. Ellery Channing was a brilliant talker, full of wit and spontaneity. The universal report from his contemporaries was that he spoke better than he wrote. Emerson was convinced that "In walking with Ellery you shall always see what was never before shown to the eye of man." For his part, Hawthorne wrote in *Mosses from an Old Manse*, "Could he have drawn out that virgin gold [of his conversation] and stamped it with the mint mark that alone gives currency, the world might have had the profit, and he the fame." In a narrow society such as New England was, the vitality of Channing's conversation was not to be ignored. He showed his gifted friends how they might see better; he was a receptive audience, a sympathetic and shrewd critic, one who made it possible for men such as Emerson and Thoreau to act on their talent.

—Robert N. Hudspeth

CHESNUTT, Charles Waddell.   American.   Born in Cleveland, Ohio, 20 June 1858; moved with his family to North Carolina, 1865. Educated privately, and in local schools; largely self-taught. Married Susan U. Perry in 1878; four children. Taught in the North Carolina public schools, 1874–81; Principal, State Normal School, Fayetteville, North Carolina, 1881–83; newspaper reporter in New York, 1884; returned to Cleveland, 1885, and thereafter worked as a court stenographer for the rest of his life; admitted to the Ohio Bar, 1887. Recipient: Spingarn Medal, 1928. *Died 15 November 1932.*

PUBLICATIONS

Collections

The Short Fiction, edited by Sylvia Lyons Render.   1974.

Fiction

The Conjure Woman (stories).   1899.
The Wife of His Youth and Other Stories of the Color Line.   1899.
The House Behind the Cedars.   1900.
The Marrow of Tradition.   1901.
The Colonel's Dream.   1905.

Other

Frederick Douglass.   1899.

Bibliography: "Secondary Studies on the Fiction of Chesnutt" by Joan Cunningham, and "The Works of Chesnutt: A Checklist" by William L. Andrews, both in *Bulletin of Bibliography,* January 1976.

Reading List: *Chesnutt, Pioneer of the Color Line* by Helen M. Chesnutt, 1952; *Chesnutt, America's First Great Black Novelist* by J. Noel Heermance, 1974; *I Choose Black: The Crusade of Chesnutt* by Frances Richardson Keller, 1978.

*   *   *

Charles Waddell Chesnutt, a "voluntary Negro," reflects in his writings major inter- and intraracial tensions of the nineteenth-century United States. Beginning and ending his life in Cleveland, Ohio, and from age seven to twenty-five living in North Carolina, he found the major motivations and materials of his works in his own life and that of contemporaries or immediate forebears on both sides of the Mason-Dixon line. Chesnutt's preoccupations with the problems of powerless blacks and poor whites is doubtless a reflection not only of the trauma which marked his own poverty-stricken youth but also of the resultant resolve to improve the quality of life for all those denied access to the fullness of American life because of color and/or class.

Chesnutt's fiction ranges in form from simple tale to highly plotted novel, in mood from comic to tragic. The subject matter reflects the major contemporary concerns of Afro-Americans. However, the general reading public, primarily white, rejected Chesnutt's increasingly explicit advocacy of equal rights for blacks and other under-privileged citizens. Consequently, after *The Colonel's Dream* in 1905, Chesnutt terminated his writing career.

By that time, however, Chesnutt had won a permanent place in American literary history, especially for his short fiction. His unqualified rating as a conscious, accomplished author by critics such as William Dean Howells and George Washington Cable was unprecedented for an Afro-American prose writer. His works, usually presented from a black perspective, are historically and sociologically accurate as well as aesthetically satisfying and ethically admirable. Chesnutt is recognized as "the first real Negro novelist," "the pioneer of the color line," and the first American writer not only to use the folk tale for social protest but also to extensively characterize Afro-Americans.

Subsequently Chesnutt used his increasing influence otherwise to improve the status of his fellow blacks. In recognition of his achievements, the National Association for the Advancement of Colored People awarded him its annual Spingarn Medal in 1928. Upon Chesnutt's death in 1932, a friend recapitulated accurately: "His great contribution in letters is a monument to our race and ... to our national life."

—Sylvia Lyons Render

CHIVERS, Thomas Holley.   American.   Born in Washington, Georgia, 18 October 1809. Educated at a preparatory school in Georgia, and at Transylvania University, Lexington, Kentucky, M.D. (honors) 1830. Married twice; married second wife, Harriet Hunt, in 1834; two sons, two daughters. Gave up medicine soon after graduation, and thereafter devoted himself to literature, contributing to numerous periodicals throughout his life; settled near Decatur, Georgia, c. 1840; contributed to Poe's *Graham's Magazine*, met Poe, 1845, and was later involved in a controversy about plagiarism of Poe's work. *Died 18 December 1858.*

PUBLICATIONS

Collections

   Chivers: A Selection, edited by Lewis Chase.   1929.
   Correspondence 1838–1858, edited by Emma Lester Chase and Lois Ferry Parks.   1957.

Verse

   The Path of Sorrow; or, The Lament of Youth.   1832.
   Nacoochee; or, The Beautiful Star.   1834.
   The Pleiad and Other Poems.   1845.
   Search after Truth; or, A New Revelation of the Psycho-Physiological Nature of Man.   1848.
   Eonchs of Ruby: A Gift of Love.   1851; revised edition, as *Memoralia; or, Phials of Amber Full of the Tears of Love*, 1853.
   Virginalia; or, Songs of My Summer Nights: A Gift of Love for the Beautiful.   1853.
   Atlanta; or, The True Blessed Island of Poesy: A Paul Epic in Three Lustra.   1853.
   Birth-Day Song of Liberty: A Paean of Glory for the Heroes of Freedom.   1856.

Plays

   Conrad and Eudora; or, The Death of Alonzo.   1834.
   The Sons of Usna: A Tragi-Apotheosis.   1858.

Other

   Life of Poe, edited by Richard Beale Davis.   1952.

Bibliography: in *Bibliography of American Literature* by Jacob Blanck, 1957.

Reading List: *Chivers* (with selections) by S. Foster Damon, 1930; *Chivers: His Literary Career and Poetry* by Charles H. Watts, 1956; "Chivers, Mystic" by Edd W. Parks, in *Ante-Bellum Southern Criticism*, 1962.

*   *   *

Unlike many of his American and Southern contemporaries, Thomas Holley Chivers was free to devote himself to poetry since he had independent means, and, though he could hardly be called a professional man of letters, he took literature seriously and developed a theory of poetry and an aesthetic. Over a period of twenty-five years he published, usually at his own expense, a great deal of verse and a smattering of prose in periodicals in Washington and Decatur, Georgia, as well as occasionally in the *Knickerbocker* and *Graham's*, and in book form in Macon, Georgia, and Franklin, Tennessee, as well as in New York and Philadelphia.

Chivers's theory of poetry as expressed in his prefaces to his collections of poems, especially *Nacoochee*, *Memoralia*, and *Atlanta*, and in his unpublished and incomplete articles and lectures is, according to Edd W. Parks, that true poetry is "divinely inspired" and the poet is "at once the mediator and the revelator of God." "Poets," Chivers says in "The Beauties of Poetry," "are the apostles of divine thought, who are clothed with an authority from the Most High, to work miracles in the minds of men." The poet sees all things with "*internal*, or spiritual eyes," though, admittedly, celestial beauty can only be partially glimpsed on earth. Still, the inspired writer can recognize transcendental truth and can "convey the idea of a heavenly truth by an earthly one."

In his own practice Chivers tried the usual forms – drama, ode, sonnet, narrative – but he gradually became fascinated with rhythm, diction, and sound, and his experimentation with ballad-like forms, refrains, and language in his last three collections led him to a special vocabulary and declamatory style that manifest themselves, among others, in "Lily Adair," "Avalon," "Apollo," and "Rosalie Lee."

The first and last of these poems, to be sure, suggest the work of Poe, and, despite a certain amount of critical attention in the past twenty years, Chivers's work is still largely of interest because of its relationship to Poe's. The thorny problems of precedence and influence have not yet been fully resolved, despite recent efforts by scholars interested in each poet. Even if it is established that Chivers provided Poe with hints concerning rhythm, meter, and refrain, the disinterested critic can only conclude with Jay B. Hubbell in *The South in American Literature* that Poe's supposed "borrowings" are "all assimilated and transformed into something original and Poesque." This, of course, is to say nothing of Chivers's borrowings from Poe, nor to mention that nothing was said of plagiarism until Poe was dead.

Whatever one may say, however, of the Poe-Chivers matter, one must also conclude that Chivers's work, erratic and uneven as it may be, is fascinating in its own right and deserves more critical consideration than it has hitherto received.

—Rayburn S. Moore

CHOPIN, Kate (O'Flaherty).   American.   Born in St. Louis, Missouri, 8 February 1851. Educated at the Sacred Heart Convent, St. Louis, graduated 1868. Married Oscar Chopin in 1870 (died, 1882); five sons and one daughter. Lived in New Orleans, 1870–80, then on her husband's plantation in Cloutierville, Louisiana, 1880–82; returned to St. Louis after her husband's death; began writing in 1888. *Died 22 August 1904.*

PUBLICATIONS

Collections

   Complete Works, edited by Per Seyersted.   1969.
   The Awakening and Other Stories, edited by Lewis Leary.   1970.

Fiction

   At Fault.   1890.
   Bayou Folk (stories).   1894.
   A Night in Acadie.   1897.
   The Awakening.   1899.

Bibliography: in *Bibliography of American Literature* by Jacob Blanck, 1957; *Edith Wharton and Chopin: A Reference Guide* by Marlene Spring, 1976.

Reading List: *Chopin and Her Creole Stories* by Daniel S. Rankin, 1932; *The American 1890's: Life and Times of a Lost Generation* by Larzer Ziff, 1966; *Chopin: A Critical Biography* by Per Seyersted, 1969.

*   *   *

In 1894, when Kate Chopin published *Bayou Folk,* a collection of Louisiana stories, she was greeted as an outstanding local color writer. In 1899, when she brought out *The Awakening,* a novel which in certain respects is an American *Madame Bovary,* she so shocked the public that some libraries banned the book. As a result, her creative spirit was stifled, and, when she died in 1904, she was forgotten. But in 1969, when *The Complete Works of Kate Chopin* appeared, the time was ripe for a reassessment and revival of this writer. Today she is recognized both as a literary artist of the American realist movement and as a particularly significant commentator on the female experience.

   Chopin grew up in the French atmosphere of her mother's family in St. Louis, and she married a Creole, and lived in New Orleans and on a Louisiana plantation for 13 years. Her *oeuvre* consists of two novels and about 100 stories. Nearly all she wrote is set in Louisiana, and she makes the atmosphere of this picturesque state creep into our senses, with the enchanting physical setting and the charming peculiarities of the Creoles, Cajuns, and blacks of the region.

   But she used local color discreetly, and it was never an end in itself to her; rather, her interest was general human nature. As a child she had been taught to face life without fear and embarrassment and to observe people without judging them. She did not believe in idealism, and she disliked moral reformers. In her first novel, *At Fault,* she lets a woman (who has forced a man to remarry his divorced drunkard wife in order to redeem her) come to the conclusion that no one has the right to submit others to the "exacting and ignorant rule of ... moral conventionalities."

   From an early age she was an avid reader, with a particular interest in books dealing with women's position. She was especially influenced by Maupassant, probably because she felt he spoke secretly to her with his frank treatments of the hidden life of women. This fitted in with her own ambition, which was to portray especially the lives of women, as truthfully and openly as America would permit. Her first extant story deals with a "feminine" or traditional heroine who submissively leaves it to the man to decide her fate, and the second with an "emancipated" woman who insists on deciding herself about her own life. Most of her later heroines are variations on these two types. She often wrote about them in pairs, thus keeping up a kind of balanced dialogue between traditional and emancipationist women.

As Chopin gained in self-confidence, she became more daring in her descriptions of unconventional women. When she had just been nationally praised for *Bayou Folk* she wrote "The Story of an Hour," a tale about a woman who, when told that her husband has suddenly died, whispers "free, free, free!" A few weeks later the author in a sense answered this extreme example of the self-assertive woman with an entry in her diary, where she wrote that could she get her husband back, she would have been willing to give up "the past ten years of my growth – my real growth."

Chopin's ultimate examples of the feminine and the emancipated woman are found in *The Awakening*. Adèle Ratignolle strikingly illustrates the patriarchal ideal of the self-forgetting woman. A Creole and a Catholic, she is likened to a "Faultless Madonna" and described as a "mother-woman," that is, one of those who live for and through their family and who consider it "a holy privilege to efface themselves as individuals." She is a perfect foil for Edna Pontellier, an American married to a New Orleans Creole and the mother of two, who says: "I would give up the unessential; I would ... give my life for my children; but I wouldn't give myself." What she means by this becomes clear as she gradually awakens to a self-assertion both in the physical and spiritual field. Like Emma Bovary, she becomes estranged from her husband, neglects her children, has lovers, and finally takes her life. But while Emma acts out roles inherited from romantic literature and gains little self-knowledge, Edna outgrows her romantic notions and learns "to look with her own eyes [and] to apprehend the deeper undercurrents of life."

She realizes that the physical side of love can live apart from the spiritual one, and that sex is a basic force which – in the guise of romantic emotions – drives us blindly on toward procreation. She understands that, for her, a return to the submission and self-delusion of the past is impossible. She refuses to let the children "drag her into the soul's slavery for the rest of her days," but she finally accepts a responsibility not to give them a bad name and takes her life. While defeated by her environment, she is also victorious: finally understanding her own nature and her situation as a woman, she exerts her inner freedom by assuming sole responsibility for her life.

The critics had to concede that, artistically, *The Awakening* is a small masterpiece. But just as with Dreiser's *Sister Carrie* a year later, they could not accept an author who in no way condemns such a heroine. Larzer Ziff has said of Chopin's silence after this setback that it was "a loss to American letters of the order of the untimely deaths of Crane and Norris." Today *The Awakening* is available in some eight editions, and with this novel and her best stories Kate Chopin seems assured a permanent place in American literature.

—Per Seyersted

CLEMENS, Samuel Langhorne. See **TWAIN, Mark.**

COOKE, Ebenezer. American. Born, probably in London, England, c. 1671; emigrated to Maryland after 1711 when he inherited a family estate in Dorchester County. Deputy Receiver-General, Cecil County, Maryland, 1721–23; admitted to the Prince George's County Bar, 1728. *Died in 1732.*

Publications

Verse

The Sot-Weed Factor; or, A Voyage to Maryland.   1708; edited by Brantz Mayer, 1865.
Sotweed Redivivus; or, The Planter's Looking-Glass.   1730.
The Maryland Muse (includes *The Sot-Weed Factor* and *The History of Colonel Nathaniel Bacon's Rebellion in Virginia*).   1731.

Reading List: *Cooke: The Sot-Weed Canon* by Edward H. Cohen, 1975; "Cooke: Satire in the Colonial South" by Robert D. Arner, in *Southern Literary Journal 8*, 1975.

*   *   *

Known as the self-proclaimed "Poet Laureate" of colonial Maryland, Ebenezer Cooke was among the first American poets to write satire about the colonies from the point of view of a disgruntled colonist. He is also recognized as the most popular and successful of America's early Southern poets.

While little is known for certain about Cooke's early life, he is thought to have been born in England, to have spent a brief period of time in Maryland in 1694, and to have migrated there sometime after 1711. His first visit to the "Western Shoars" is thought to have inspired his most famous work, *The Sot-Weed Factor*, published in London in 1708 but believed to have been written much earlier. About the experiences of a British merchant who comes to America to trade with the colonists and is cheated and insulted during the course of his visit, *The Sot-Weed Factor* is a biting satire on the manners and mores of the people who lived in the colony of Maryland at the beginning of the eighteenth century. Written in hudibrastic couplets, the poem burlesques the escapades of drunken lawyers, inept physicians, illiterate and oftentimes dishonest planters, crude and debased women, and even degenerate Indians, all of whom are said to typify the culture in which they lived. Omitted in the American edition of 1731, the final lines of the poem are a "Curse," delivered by the narrator as he departs from America for England, on the "Inhospitable Shoar," which he has just visited, "Where no Man's Faithful, nor a Woman Chast."

A sequel to *The Sot-Weed Factor*, once attributed to an imitator but now correctly attributed to Cooke, was published in Maryland in 1730 by the famous colonial printer William Parks under the title *Sotweed Redivivus*. By the time of the poem's publication, Cooke had permanently established himself in Maryland, where he had become a respected member of the community. As a result, *Sotweed Redivivus* is less a satire of colonial manners than an attempt to write serious didactic poetry on the necessity of remedying the economic woes of Maryland through legislative reform. According to Cooke, the standard of living in Maryland would be greatly improved if its people would endorse legislation to control inflation, limit the production of tobacco for which there was no market, and halt the indiscriminate waste of natural resources, particularly the wanton destruction of forests.

Other poems in the Cooke canon which merit critical analysis are "The History of Colonel Nathaniel Bacon's Rebellion in Virginia," published along with *The Sot-Weed Factor* in a volume entitled *The Maryland Muse* (1731), and a series of elegies on the deaths of public figures with whom Cooke was associated. A mock-heroic epic of the type then popular in England, "The History of Colonel Nathaniel Bacon's Rebellion" reflects Cooke's conservative thinking on the subject of revolution and colonial self-government. Far from praising Nathaniel Bacon, the popular American hero who in 1676 had led the people of frontier Virginia to revolt against the tyrannical administration of Governor William Berkeley, Cooke's stated aim in writing a history of the rebellion was to "Cooke *this* Bacon," whose "dire ... Wars" he considered a threat to civilization and an act of extreme folly. While they lack the clever wit and polished charm of his other poems, Cooke's elegies are among the finest surviving examples of colonial American elegiac verse. Particularly noteworthy is "An Elegy on the Death of the Honourable William Lock" (1732), in which Cooke uses the death of a local dignitary as the occasion for poetic commentary on the inevitability and universality of death.

After 1732 Cooke stopped writing poetry, and because nothing is known about his subsequent activities, scholars have assumed that he died at this time. In recent years, Cooke has attracted the attention of John Barth, whose novel *The Sot-Weed Factor* (1960) has earned Cooke a lasting reputation in tha annals of American literary history.

—James A. Levernier

COOKE, John Esten. American. Born in Winchester, Virginia, 3 November 1830. Educated in schools in Richmond, Virginia; studied law with his father; admitted to the Virginia Bar, 1851. Served as a Captain in the Confederate Army during the Civil War, 1861–65. Married Mary Frances Page in 1867 (died, 1878); three children. Practised law in Richmond, 1851; full-time writer from 1852; moved to an estate near Winchester, 1868, and thereafter devoted himself to both writing and farming. *Died 27 September 1886.*

PUBLICATIONS

Fiction

Leather Stocking and Silk; or, Hunter John Myers and His Times: A Story of the Valley of Virginia. 1854; as *Leather and Silk*, 1892.
The Virginia Comedians; or, Old Days in the Old Dominion. 1854; as *Beatrice Hallam* and *Captain Ralph*, 2 vols., 1892.
Ellie; or, The Human Comedy. 1855.
The Last of the Foresters; or, Humors on the Border: A Story of the Old Virginia Frontier. 1856.
Henry St. John, Gentleman, of "Flower of Hundreds" in the County of Prince George, Virginia: A Tale of 1774–'75. 1859; as *Bonnybel Vane*, 1883; as *Miss Bonnybel*, 1892.
Surry of Eagle's-Nest; or, The Memoirs of a Staff Officer Serving in Virginia. 1866.
Fairfax; or, The Master of Greenway Court: A Chronicle of the Valley of the Shenandoah. 1868; as *Lord Fairfax*, 1888.
Mohun; or, The Last Days of Lee and His Paladins: Final Memories of a Staff Officer Serving in Virginia. 1869.
Hilt to Hilt; or, Days and Nights on the Banks of the Shenandoah in the Autumn of 1864. 1869.
The Heir of Gaymount. 1870.
Hammer and Rapier. 1870.
Out of the Foam. 1871; as *Westbrooke Hall*, 1891.
Doctor Vandyke. 1872.
Her Majesty the Queen. 1873.
Pretty Mrs. Gaston and Other Stories. 1874.
Justin Harley: A Romance of Old Virginia. 1875.
Canolles: The Fortunes of a Partisan of '81. 1877.

Professor Pressensee, Materialist and Inventor. 1878.
Stories of the Old Dominion from the Settlement to the End of the Revolution. 1879.
Mr. Grantley's Idea. 1879.
The Virginia Bohemians. 1880.
Fanchette, by One of Her Admirers. 1883.
My Lady Pokahontas: A True Relation of Virginia. 1885.
The Maurice Mystery. 1885; as *Col. Ross of Piedmont,* 1893.

Other

The Youth of Jefferson; or, A Chronicle of College Scrapes at Williamsburg, in Virginia,
    A.D. 1764. 1854.
The Life of Stonewall Jackson. 1863; revised edition, as *Stonewall Jackson: A Military*
    Biography, 1866.
Wearing of the Gray, Being Personal Portraits, Scenes, and Adventures of the
    War. 1867; edited by Philip Van Doren Stern, 1960.
A Life of Gen. Robert E. Lee. 1871.
Virginia: A History of the People. 1883.
Poe as a Literary Critic, edited by N. Bryllion Fagin. 1946.
Stonewall Jackson and the Old Stonewall Brigade, edited by Richard Barksdale
    Harwell. 1954.
Outlines from the Outpost, edited by Richard Barksdale Harwell. 1961.

Bibliography: *A Bibliography of the Separate Writings of Cooke* by Oscar Wegelin, 1925; in
Bibliography of American Literature by Jacob Blanck, 1957.

Reading List: *Cooke, Virginian* by John O. Beaty, 1932.

*   *   *

Although John Esten Cooke, the younger brother of Philip Pendleton Cooke (1816–1850)
and cousin of John Pendleton Kennedy (1795–1870), was best known in his own time and
afterwards as a writer of long fiction, he was also something of a poet, one of whose fugitive
pieces – "The Band in the Pines" – is still occasionally anthologized; a biographer, whose
lives of Lee and Stonewall Jackson are worthy of attention but more as accounts of battles
than as biography; and a historian, whose *Virginia*, though hardly scholarly according to
modern standards, is a pleasant narrative of the early days of the Commonwealth.

Along with stories, sketches, essays, verse, and other contributions to periodicals, Cooke
produced at least five novels before the Civil War, four of which are actually historical
romances – *Leather Stocking and Silk, The Virginia Comedians, Henry St. John, Gentleman,*
and *Fairfax* (serialized in 1859). The second of these is, according to the author, "intended to
be a picture of our curiously graded Virginia society just before the Revolution" and included
portraits of Patrick Henry and Lewis Hallam's actors in the Williamsburg area. It remains his
best work of historical fiction, despite the fact that many of his numerous books on the war
are based on his own first-hand experience.

Surry of Eagle's-Nest, the most notable of the war novels and his most popular long
fiction, and its sequel, *Mohun,* cover many of the great battles of Lee's army, military actions
in which Cooke participated from the first engagement at Bull Run to Appomattox, and
priceless material for a novelist. Cooke found it difficult, nevertheless, to fuse fact and fiction
in these novels and to refrain, any more than had his predecessors Scott, Cooper, Irving, and
Simms, from introducing extraneous materials into his structure, in these particular instances
Gothic characters, melodrama, and sub-plots in works that are essentially historical or even

realistic. But when, for example, the narrative focuses on Surry and military adventure, it moves swiftly and with eyewitness authority. Though much of Cooke's long fiction now seems romantic and dated, his style remains charming and graceful, his appreciation of the past manifests itself in the ante-bellum work, and his military experience lends authenticity to the best of the Civil War romances.

—Rayburn S. Moore

COOPER, James Fenimore. American. Born in Burlington, New Jersey, 15 September 1789; moved with his family to Cooperstown, New York, 1790. Educated in the village school at Cooperstown; in the household of the rector of St. Peter's, Albany, New York, 1800–02; Yale University, New Haven, Connecticut, 1803–05: dismissed for misconduct; thereafter prepared for a naval career: served on the *Stirling*, 1806–07; commissioned midshipman in the United States Navy, 1808; served on the *Vesuvius*, 1808; for a brief time in command on Lake Champlain, also served on the *Wasp* in the Atlantic, 1809; resigned commission, 1811. Married Susan Augusta DeLancey in 1811; five daughters and two sons. Country gentleman: lived in Mamaroneck, New York, 1811–14, Cooperstown, 1814–17, and Scarsdale, New York, 1817–22; began to write in 1820; lived in New York, 1822–26, and France, 1826–33: United States Consul at Lyons, 1826–29; returned to New York, 1833, and lived in Cooperstown, 1834 until his death. M.A.: Columbia University, New York, 1824. *Died 14 September 1851.*

PUBLICATIONS

Collections

> *Works.* 33 vols., 1895–1900.
> *Representative Selections*, edited by Robert E. Spiller. 1936.
> *Letters and Journals*, edited by James Franklin Beard. 6 vols., 1960–68.

Fiction

> *Precaution.* 1820.
> *The Spy: A Tale of the Neutral Ground.* 1821; edited by Tremaine McDowell, 1931.
> *The Pioneers; or, The Sources of the Susquehanna: A Descriptive Tale.* 1823.
> *Tales for Fifteen; or, Imagination and Heart.* 1823.
> *The Pilot: A Tale of the Sea.* 1823.
> *Lionel Lincoln; or, The Leaguer of Boston.* 1825.
> *The Last of the Mohicans: A Narrative of 1757.* 1826; edited by William Charvat, 1958.
> *The Prairie: A Tale.* 1827.
> *The Red Rover: A Tale.* 1827; edited by Warren S. Walker, 1963.
> *The Borderers: A Tale.* 1829; as *The Wept of Wish Ton-Tish*, 1829; as *The Heathcotes*, 1854.
> *The Water Witch; or, The Skimmer of the Seas: A Tale.* 1830.
> *The Bravo: A Venetian Story.* 1831.
> *The Heidenmauer; or, The Benedictines.* 1832.

The Headsman; or, The Abbaye des Vignersons: A Tale.   1833.
The Monikins: A Tale.   1835.
Homeward Bound; or, The Chase: A Tale of the Sea.   1838.
Home as Found.   1838; as *Eve Effingham; or, Home,* 1838.
The Pathfinder; or, The Inland Sea.   1840.
Mercedes of Castile; or, The Voyage to Cathay.   1840.
The Deerslayer; or, The First War-Path: A Tale.   1841; edited by Gregory Paine, 1927.
The Two Admirals: A Tale of the Sea.   1842.
The Jack O'Lantern (Le Feu-Follet); or, The Privateer.   1842; as *The Wing-and-Wing; or, Le Feu-Follet,* 1842.
Le Mouchoir: An Autobiographical Romance.   1843; as *The French Governess; or, The Embroidered Handkerchief,* 1843; edited by George F. Horner and Raymond Adams, as *Autobiography of a Pocket Handkerchief,* 1949.
Wyandotté; or, The Hutted Knoll.   1843.
Afloat and Ashore; or, The Adventures of Miles Wallingford.   1844.
Lucy Harding: A Second Series of Afloat and Ashore.   1844; as *Afloat and Ashore,* vols. 3–4, 1844.
Satanstoe; or, The Family of Littlepage: A Tale of the Colony.   1845; as *Satanstoe; or, The Littlepage Manuscripts,* 1845; edited by Robert E. Spiller and Joseph D. Coppock, 1937.
The Chainbearer; or, The Littlepage Manuscripts.   1845.
Ravensnest; or, The Redskins.   1846; as *The Redskins; or, Indian and Injin, Being the Conclusion of the Littlepage Manuscripts,* 1846.
Mark's Reef; or, The Crater: A Tale of the Pacific.   1847; as *The Crater; or, Vulcan's Peak,* 1847; edited by Thomas Philbrick, 1962.
Captain Spike; or, The Islets of the Gulf.   1848; as *Jack Tier; or, The Florida Reef,* 1848.
The Bee-Hunter; or, The Oak Openings.   1848; as *The Oak Openings,* 1848.
The Sea Lions; or, The Lost Sealers.   1849; edited by Warren S. Walker, 1965.
The Ways of the Hour: A Tale.   1850.
The Lake Gun, edited by Robert E. Spiller.   1932.

Other

Notions of the Americans, Picked Up by a Travelling Bachelor.   2 vols., 1828; as *America and the Americans,* 1836.
Letter to Gen. Lafayette.   1831.
A Letter to His Countrymen.   1834.
Sketches of Switzerland.   2 vols., 1836; as *Excursions in Switzerland,* 1836.
A Residence in France with a Second Visit to Switzerland.   2 vols., 1836; as *Sketches of Switzerland, Part Second,* 1836.
Recollections of Europe.   2 vols., 1837; as *Gleanings in Europe,* 1837.
England, with Sketches of Society in the Metropolis.   2 vols., 1837; as *Gleanings in Europe: England,* 1837.
Excursions in Italy.   2 vols., 1838; as *Gleanings in Europe: Italy,* 1838.
The American Democrat.   1838; edited by George Dekker and Larry Johnston, 1969.
The Chronicles of Cooperstown.   1838.
The History of the Navy of the United States of America.   2 vols., 1839.
The Battle of Lake Erie.   1843.
Ned Myers; or, A Life Before the Mast.   1843.
Lives of Distinguished American Naval Officers.   2 vols., 1846.
The Works, revised by the author.   12 vols., 1849–51.
New York, edited by Dixon Ryan Fox.   1930.

Reading List: *Cooper, Critic of His Times*, 1931, and *Cooper*, 1965, both by Robert E. Spiller; *Cooper* by James Grossman, 1949; *Cooper* by Donald A. Ringe, 1962; *Cooper: An Introduction and Interpretation* by Warren S. Walker, 1962; *Cooper, The Novelist* by George Dekker, 1967, as *Cooper, The American Scott*, 1967; *Cooper: The Critical Heritage* edited by George Dekker and J. P. McWilliams, 1973; *A World by Itself: The Pastoral Moment in Early Critical Essays 1820–1822*, edited by James Franklin Beard. 1955.

Editor, *Elinor Wyllys*, by Susan A. Fenimore Cooper. 1845.

Bibliography: *A Descriptive Bibliography of the Writings of Cooper* by Robert E. Spiller and Philip C. Blackburn, 1934; in *Bibliography of American Literature* by Jacob Blanck, 1957. *Cooper's Fiction* by H. Daniel Peck, 1977; *Cooper: A Study of His Life and Imagination* by Stephen Railton, 1978.

*　　*　　*

James Fenimore Cooper will always be remembered first for his Leatherstocking tales: *The Pioneers, The Last of the Mohicans, The Prairie, The Pathfinder,* and *The Deerslayer.* These five books recount the experiences of an American frontiersman, variously named Deerslayer, Hawkeye, Pathfinder, Leatherstocking, and the trapper, between the early 1740's, when British America was a line of settlements along the Atlantic coast, and 1805–06, when the Lewis and Clark expedition crossed the continent. Though the books were not written in the order of the events they portray, they form, nonetheless, a kind of American epic, concerned not only with the opening of the West, but also with the costs involved in the process: the cutting of the forests, the killing of the game, and the displacement of the Indian. Leatherstocking, a man of the woods, wants to preserve the natural environment and use it only as needed, but by acting as hunter and scout, he opens the wilderness to the very settlers whose wasteful ways he abhors.

Cooper details both the social and moral consequences of the process, and though he laments the fate of the Indian and warns his countrymen against the destruction of their resources, he does not place his values in Leatherstocking alone. He consistently affirms, rather, the Christian civilization that must supplant the wilderness. The problem America faces, these books seem to say, is to insure that the new society will be a just and democratic one, ruled by the most talented and virtuous men who will not needlessly destroy the bounties of nature. To develop the social aspects of his theme, Cooper includes a wide range of characters, both white and Indian, who illustrate the various attitudes that men have toward God, nature, and society, and he uses his physical setting – both dense woods and desolate prairie – to reveal the moral state of his characters and their relation to a transcendent system of value revealed in the landscape – one that Leatherstocking always recognizes, but which too many of his fellow countrymen fail to perceive.

Cooper uses the physical setting to define the social and moral problems in many of his books. The neutral ground in *The Spy*, where contending irregulars fight during the American Revolution, typifies well a moral world where motives and identities are masked and loyalties are uncertain. The isolated frontier settlements in *The Wept of Wish Ton-Tish* and *Wyandotté* clearly represent the islands of peace and order that the colonists try to establish in a moral chaos. Even the sea in the maritime novels functions in a similar fashion. In the two series of *Afloat and Ashore*, it serves a dual purpose as a testing ground for men. Here the right to rule, by virtue of character, training, and knowledge, may be established in the handling of a ship, but here too the weakness of even the most capable men before the power of God may be starkly revealed. Indeed, in *The Crater*, Cooper uses both the sea and the isolated settlement, some islands in the Pacific, to establish the relation between the moral basis of a society and its ability to survive.

Much of Cooper's success as an artist derives from his ability to project his meaning through setting, whether it be a frontier fort in America, a ship at sea, or a part of the European scene: the city of Venice in *The Bravo*, an isolated valley in Germany in *The Heidenmauer*, or the breathtaking landscape of Switzerland in *The Headsman*. That meaning, moreover, is always both moral and social. At times, of course, one or the other aspect may dominate, and, especially in the social criticism, the moral basis may be muted or unexpressed, but it is never completely absent. His attacks on both aristocracy in his three European novels and on the excesses of American democracy in the books that followed derive from his consistent belief that the evils of society are caused by the fallen nature of men, who must humble themselves before God and act, not from economic, but from moral motives if society is ever to escape the wrongs and injustices that have plagued it in the past.

Cooper detested aristocracy wherever he found it and wrote the European novels not merely to attack it in the abstract, but also to make clear the evils of such societies wherever they might appear. Though Cooper was thinking of contemporary England and of the France of Louis Philippe when he wrote these books, he also wished to warn his countrymen that a similar oligarchy, based on commerce, could develop in the United States and subvert its political principles. When he viewed American democracy, on the other hand, he saw a quite different problem. Though the leveling democrat is impelled by an economic motive no less strong than that of the aristocrat, he wishes to remove all distinctions among men and rule, not through a governing class, but through the manipulation of the electoral process. In place of the aristocrat, there appears the demagogue.

Cooper never found a completely suitable means for presenting his criticism of American democracy, and most of his novels attacking the failings of contemporary America do not succeed as fiction. Yet all of them are interesting. In *The Monikins*, he satirized English, American, and French society through a race of monkeys who live in Antarctica, and in *Homeward Bound* and *Home as Found*, he attempted to depict a cross section of American life through the experience of the Effingham family, descendants of the founder of Templeton in *The Pioneers*, who are returning home after a sojourn in Europe. The device gave him the opportunity to attack the leveling democrats and the social climbers, the Anglophiles and the super-patriots of America, while affirming through the Effinghams what true Americans should be. His major characters are rather wooden, however, and though each book has its interest – the adventure parts of the former are very well done – both are rather weak novels.

Cooper did better in some of his later works: the Littlepage series and his final book, *The Ways of the Hour*. Critics have sometimes set the Littlepage series against the Leatherstocking tales to illustrate a bifurcation in Cooper's fiction, but the two series actually complement each other. The Leatherstocking tales, after all, have much to say about American society, and the first two Littlepage books, *Satanstoe* and *The Chainbearer*, contain major frontier episodes. They portray the rise of the Littlepage family during the eighteenth century and their successful struggle to maintain their possessions against both French and Indian invaders and New England squatters. The third book, *The Redskins*, shows them defending their property against insurgent radical democrats in contemporary New York, but the book is too polemical to work as fiction. *The Ways of the Hour*, focused upon a jury trial for murder, is a far more effective treatment of the failings of American democracy.

Not all of Cooper's novels fit into the two main categories for which he is best known: frontier romance and social criticism. A third major type is one he created, the tale of the sea. Cooper's maritime novels cover a wide range, from delightful romantic fictions, like *The Red Rover* and *The Water Witch*, to serious explorations of moral problems, like *The Two Admirals* and *The Wing-and-Wing*. They include the patriotic *The Pilot*, the grim *Jack Tier*, in which all value seems to have been lost, and the deeply religious *The Sea Lions*, which, like *The Oak Openings*, a late tale of the wilderness, makes a strong affirmation of Christian faith. These tales of the sea may appear diverse in theme and tone, but, seen in the broad pattern of Cooper's thirty-year career as a novelist, their relation to his other work is clear. His successful sailors are men who, like Leatherstocking, submit to the God they perceive in the natural setting. Those who fail to do so cause the many evils and injustices that, Cooper believed, always result when men act from selfish motives in this fallen world.

Cooper also wrote a significant amount of good non-fiction. *Notions of the Americans* and *The American Democrat* are sound statements of American beliefs and principles; his five travel volumes (1836–38) not only describe his sojourn abroad, but also make sharp observations on European society; and *The History of the Navy of the United States of America* and *Lives of Distinguished American Naval Officers* are sound historical works. Though Cooper's claim to our attention must always rest on his fiction, these miscellaneous works made a real contribution to nineteenth-century American thought and are still of interest to serious readers today.

—Donald A. Ringe

CRADDOCK, Charles Egbert.   See MURFREE, Mary Noailles.

CRANE, Stephen.   American. Born in Newark, New Jersey, 1 November 1871. Educated at schools in Port Jervis, New York, 1878–83, and Asbury Park, New Jersey, 1883–84; Pennington Seminary, 1885–87; Hudson River Institute, and Claverack College, New York, 1888–90; Lafayette College, Easton, Pennsylvania, 1890; Syracuse University, New York, 1891. Lived with Cora Taylor from 1897. Began writing in 1891; settled in New York and worked as a journalist: wrote sketches of New York life for the New York *Press*, 1894; travelled in the American West and Mexico, writing for the Bacheller and Johnson Syndicate, 1895; sent by Bacheller to report on the insurrection in Cuba, 1896: shipwrecked on the voyage, 1897; went to Greece to report the Greco-Turkish War for the New York *Journal*, 1897; settled in England, 1897; reported the Spanish-American War in Cuba for the New York *World*, later for the New York *Journal*, 1898. Tubercular: *Died 5 June 1900.*

PUBLICATIONS

Collections

> *Letters*, edited by R. W. Stallman and Lillian Gilkes.   1960.
> *Works*, edited by Fredson Bowers.   10 vols., 1969–75.

Fiction

> *Maggie, A Girl of the Streets (A Story of New York).*   1893.
> *The Red Badge of Courage: An Episode of the American Civil War.*   1895.
> *George's Mother.*   1896.
> *The Little Regiment and Other Episodes of the American Civil War.*   1896.

The Third Violet.   1897.
The Open Boat and Other Tales of Adventure.   1898.
Active Service.   1899.
The Monster and Other Stories.   1899.
Whilomville Stories.   1900.
Wounds in the Rain: War Stories.   1900.
Last Words.   1902.
The O'Ruddy: A Romance, with Robert Barr.   1903.
Sullivan County Sketches, edited by Melvin Schoberlin.   1949; revised edition by R. W. Stallman, as *Sullivan County Tales and Sketches,* 1968.

Play

The Blood of the Martyr.   1940.

Verse

The Black Riders and Other Lines.   1895.
A Souvenir and a Medley: Seven Poems and a Sketch.   1896.
War Is Kind.   1899.

Other

Great Battles of the War.   1901.
Et Cetera: A Collector's Scrap-Book.   1924.
A Battle in Greece.   1936.
Uncollected Writings, edited by Olov W. Fryckstedt.   1963.
The War Despatches, edited by R. W. Stallman and E. R. Hagemann.   1964.
The New York City Sketches and Related Pieces, edited by R. W. Stallman and E. R. Hagemann.   1966.
Notebook, edited by Donald J. and Ellen B. Greiner.   1969.
Crane in the West and Mexico, edited by Joseph Katz.   1970.

Bibliography: *Crane: A Critical Bibliography* by R. W. Stallman, 1972.

Reading List: *Crane* by John Berryman, 1950; *The Poetry of Crane* by Daniel Hoffman, 1957; *Crane* by Edwin H. Cady, 1962; *Crane in England,* 1964, and *Crane, From Parody to Realism,* 1966, both by Eric Solomon; *Crane: A Biography* by R. W. Stallman, 1968; *A Reading of Crane* by Marston LaFrance, 1971; *Crane's Artistry* by Frank Bergon, 1975.

*   *   *

Stephen Crane was a descendant of Methodist ministers and of Revolutionary soldiers. One ancestor was a founder of the city of Newark, New Jersey; a grandfather was a bishop and founder of Syracuse University. His father was a parson, his mother a journalist for religious newspapers. This ancestry of military and civic virtue and literate religious vocation influenced Stephen's responses to experience.

Crane's life was brief; he was dead of tuberculosis before his thirtieth birthday. His career as an author lasted only from 1892 to 1900. Yet he wrote the first naturalistic novel of city life in the United States (*Maggie, A Girl of the Streets*); the greatest novel of the American Civil

War, perhaps the best fictional study in English of fear (*The Red Badge of Courage*); and poems which in their avoidance of debilitated Victorian verse conventions seem heralds of the modernist movement (*The Black Riders, War Is Kind*). He wrote incomparable short stories – of shipwreck and survival ("The Open Boat"), of violence in the American West ("The Bride Comes to Yellow Sky," "The Blue Hotel"); a volume of unsentimental local-color stories of a village childhood (*Whilomville Stories*); and a novella ("The Monster") comparable to Ibsen's *An Enemy of the People* in its treatment of alienation and the callousness of society. In addition to these works he was a prolific journalist whose sketches – of war in the Caribbean and the Balkans, of the underside of New York City life, of travels in the American West and Mexico – are stylistically distinguished and raise journalistic occasions to an imaginative intensity close to that in his fiction. Crane was the doomed boy wonder of American literature.

As varied as his subjects were his fictional modes. Critics still debate whether Crane was an impressionist, a realist, a naturalist. With little formal education – he dropped out of college after two semesters, during which he played on the baseball team, smoked cigarettes, and wrote the draft of *Maggie* – he was a natural writer who absorbed from the literature around him the then dominant methods of writing and transformed these with imaginative energy into the instrument of his own purposes. At the time he wrote *Maggie*, his only literary acquaintance was with the Midwestern realist Hamlin Garland. On its appearance William Dean Howells recognized and encouraged the genius of this youth whose work differed so greatly from his own. *The Red Badge* made Crane famous overnight; he was sent by a newspaper syndicate as a correspondent to the Cuban insurrection and the Spanish-American War; later, he covered the war between Greece and Turkey. He went, he said, to test his knowledge in *The Red Badge*. This novel about a conflict that had ended seven years before Crane's birth had been grounded on his experience on the football field, where "the opposing team is the enemy tribe." After seeing war up close, "*The Red Badge*," Crane concluded, "is all right." In fact there were other models beside football: Crane had read Zola's *The Downfall* (*La Débacle*) and Tolstoi's *Sevastopol*; he had studied the reminiscences and memoirs in *The Century Magazine* series "Battles and Leaders of the Civil War"; and he had absorbed and internalized the creed of aesthetic realism held by the war correspondent in Kipling's *The Light That Failed*.

These influences were welded together by a sensibility that found in war the externalization of its obsessive psychological conflicts. There is war everywhere in Crane's work. *Maggie* shows family life in perpetual conflict, the social environment as hostile there as Nature is to the men adrift in "The Open Boat." In "The Blue Hotel," the immigrant Swede, stranded by a blizzard, brings to a frontier outpost the mental image of the violence he expects to find in the West. Crane encapsulated the theme in a brief poem:

> A man feared that he might find an assassin;
> Another that he might find a victim.
> One was more wise than the other.

One of his ironic war tales is titled "The Mystery of Heroism." Crane was prepossessed by that mystery; he called *The Red Badge of Courage* "a study of fear." His life was such a study, and a conquest of its subject.

He brought to all of his writings a style at once metaphoric, animistic, striated with color, dense with implication. "An artist," he once wrote, "is nothing but a powerful memory that can move itself at will through certain experiences sideways and every artist must be in some things powerless as a dead snake," thus granting his vocation at once freedom from and subjection to necessity. His influence on later American writers is considerable. His theme of grace under pressure in a masculine world of conflict provided Hemingway with a model, while Crane's metaphoric, ironic style anticipates Flannery O'Connor.

As a poet Crane's work was too fragmentary and his career too brief to affect the glib versifiers of the American 1890's, but after 1912, when the Imagist Movement had begun and the conventions Crane avoided were being defied by the new modernists, he was revived and remembered as a forerunner. His theme is the alienation of man in an uncaring universe. He rebels against the pieties of conventional Christianity, overthrows the rule of its vengeful God, proposes a kinder deity. Certain of his poems, such as "War Is Kind" and "A Man Adrift on a Slim Spar," crystallize the themes of his fiction. This one typifies his parabolic brevity:

> A man said to the universe:
> "Sir, I exist!"
> "However," replied the universe,
> "The fact has not created in me
> A sense of obligation."

Crane's personal life in the decade of his authorship was as vivid as any of his fictions. As a reporter he frequented the Bowery in New York City, seeking subjects for his sketches. He befriended a woman whom he saw being entrapped by police on a charge of soliciting; after testifying in her defense he was run out of town by the police department. On his way to Cuba to sail aboard the gun-running tug whose shipwreck led him to write "The Open Boat," he met in Jacksonville, Florida, the undivorced wife of a son of the British Governor General of India. Cora Jackson was then the madame of a pleasure parlor. She and Crane lived together as man and wife until his death. Cora went with Stephen to the Balkans as the first woman war correspondent. While in England, as tenants of Morton Frewen's manor house, Brede Place, in Surrey, they entertained Henry James, Joseph Conrad, H. G. Wells, and other notable writers. The preacher's son Stephen Crane lived in notoriety and scandal. He and Cora were spendthrift, always in need of money. His last two years, while sick and dying, were spent desperately in hack work.

Crane remains the most interesting American writer of the nineties. His work is of lasting value; what is local and dated in it (his struggle against the dour God of his fire-eating, Evangelistic background) is subsumed in what anticipates the spiritual negation of the war-torn twentieth century: his sense of the world as a juggernaut of impersonal force against which the precious values of the individual life must be precariously maintained by heroic struggle.

—Daniel Hoffman

CRAWFORD, F(rancis) Marion.   American.   Born in Bagni di Lucca, Tuscany, Italy, 2 August 1854; son of the sculptor Thomas Crawford. Educated at St. Paul's School, Concord, New Hampshire, 1866–69; Trinity College, Cambridge, 1873; Technische Hochschule, Karlsruhe, Germany, 1874; University of Heidelberg, 1876; Harvard University, Cambridge, Massachusetts, 1881. Married Elizabeth Berdan in 1884; two sons and two daughters. Editor, *Indian Herald*, Allahabad, India, 1879–80; convert to the Roman Catholic Church, 1880; full-time writer from 1882; settled in Sorrento, Italy, 1885, and lived there for the rest of his life. *Died 9 April 1909.*

PUBLICATIONS

Collections

Novels.   30 vols., 1919.

Fiction

Mr. Isaacs: A Tale of Modern India.   1882.
Doctor Claudius: A True Story.   1883.
To Leeward.   1883.
A Roman Singer.   1884.
An American Politician.   1884.
Zoroaster.   1885.
A Tale of a Lonely Parish.   1886.
Saracinesca.   1887.
Marzio's Crucifix.   1887.
Paul Patoff.   1887.
With the Immortals.   1888.
Greifenstein.   1889.
Sant' Ilario.   1889.
A Cigarette-Maker's Romance.   1890.
Khaled: A Tale of Arabia.   1891.
The Witch of Prague.   1891.
The Three Fates.   1892.
Don Orsino.   1892.
The Children of the King: A Tale of Southern Italy.   1893.
Pietro Ghisleri.   1893.
Marion Darche: A Story Without Comment.   1893.
Katharine Lauderdale.   1894.
The Upper Berth (stories).   1894.
Love in Idleness: A Bar Harbour Tale.   1894.
Casa Braccio.   1895.
The Ralstons.   1895.
Taquisara.   1896.
Adam Johnstone's Son.   1896.
A Rose of Yesterday.   1897.
Corleone: A Tale of Sicily.   1897.
Via Crucis: A Romance of the Second Crusade.   1899.
In the Palace of the King: A Love Story of Old Madrid.   1900.
Marietta, A Maid of Venice.   1901.
Cecilia: A Story of Modern Rome.   1902.
Man Overboard!   1903.
The Heart of Rome: A Tale of the "Lost Water."   1903.
Whosoever Shall Offend.   1904.
Soprano: A Portrait.   1905; as *Fair Margaret*, 1905.
A Lady of Rome.   1906.
Arethusa.   1907.
The Little City of Hope: A Christmas Story.   1907.
The Primadonna: A Sequel to Soprano.   1908.
Stradella: An Old Italian Love Tale.   1908.
The Diva's Ruby: A Sequel to Soprano and Primadonna.   1908.

The White Sister. 1909.
The Undesirable Governess. 1910.
Uncanny Tales. 1911; as *Wandering Ghosts,* 1911.

Plays

Doctor Claudius, with Harry St. Maur, from the novel by Crawford (produced 1897).
Francesca Da Rimini (produced 1901). 1902.
The Ideal Wife, from a work by M. Prage (produced 1912).
The White Sister, with Walter Hackett, from the novel by Crawford. 1937.

Other

Our Silver. 1881.
The Novel: What It Is. 1893.
Constaninople. 1895.
Bar Harbor. 1896.
Ave, Roma Immortalis: Studies from the Chronicles of Rome. 2 vols., 1898; revised
  edition, 1902.
The Rulers of the South, Sicily, Calabria, Malta. 2 vols., 1900; as *Southern Italy and
  Sicily and the Rulers of the South,* 1905.
Salve Venetia: Gleanings from Venetian History. 2 vols., 1905; as *Venice, The Place
  and the People,* 1909.

Translator, *The Unknown Life of Christ,* by Nicolai Notovich. 1894.

Reading List: *My Cousin Crawford* by Maud Howe Elliott, 1934; *Crawford* by John
Pilkington, Jr., 1964; *The American 1890's: Life and Times of a Lost Generation* by Larzer
Ziff, 1966.

*   *   *

F. Marion Crawford was America's most successful novelist at the end of the nineteenth
century. He sometimes published three novels a year, simultaneously in New York and
London, and Macmillan paid him $10,000 in advance for each of them in the 1890's. All of
his 42 novels are marred by haste and a kind of contempt for the esthetics of fiction. In *The
Novel: What It Is* Crawford argued that the novel is "an intellectual artistic luxury" that had
one essential ingredient, "a story or romance," and one purpose – to entertain. Crawford
knew both exotic and lowly places in many lands. He could tell a story easily and naturally,
and his fast-moving romances are not impeded by subtleties or significance. He held to
traditional values and opposed social, political, and economic change; he upheld the genteel,
moral, and ideal in literature and the chivalric code of honor of Christian gentlemen.
    The glamor of "the magnificent Marion Crawford," the "Prince of Sorrento," was a factor
in his success. He was born in Rome, son of a New England heiress (the sister of Julia Ward
Howe) and the Irish-American expatriate sculptor Thomas Crawford, whose circle
Hawthorne pictured in *The Marble Faun* (1860). His mother gave her son an international
education, designed for an aristocratic genius: private tutors in Rome, St. Paul's School in
New Hampshire (which he hated), and additional schooling in England and Germany in
preparation for brief periods at Cambridge and Heidelberg. He considered himself both a
Roman and an American. He was a linguistic genius and reputedly knew 16 languages. His
wide travels gave him a "special and accurate knowledge that created a perfect illusion" (Van

Wyck Brooks) of such places as Constantinople (where he was married), St. Petersburg, Munich (where he wrote *A Cigarette-Maker's Romance* and *The Witch of Prague* in 1890), of Iceland and India – as well as Paris, London, and Rome. To a wide audience, many of them attaining great wealth and seeking easy sophistication, Crawford seemed the most cosmopolitan of writers: in a letter to Howells Henry James petulantly called Crawford "a six-penny humbug" – and begged Howells not to betray his jealous outburst!

His first novel *Mr. Isaacs* is the fictional portrait of an enormously wealthy and powerful Persian diamond merchant Crawford had met two years before when he edited a newspaper in Allahabad. With this novel, which anticipated Kipling in its vivid pictures of Indian life, Crawford made himself world famous; Gladstone called it a "literary marvel." Within the same year Crawford published a second semi-biographical novel, *Doctor Claudius*: a Swedish-born Heidelberg Ph.D. inherits an American fortune and marries a Russian countess after saving her inheritance. *A Roman Singer* is based on Crawford's own attempts to become an opera singer. His weakest efforts are the American novels: *An American Politician, Katharine Lauderdale,* and *The Ralstons.* His best are *Saracinesca* and its three sequels, which deal with the Roman social world of his childhood; the others are *Sant' Ilario, Don Orsino,* and *Corleone.* Literary historians exempt these novels from their general condemnation of nineteenth-century melodramatic costume romances and note some other Crawford successes: the English countryside in *A Tale of a Lonely Parish* and the evocation of Phillip II of Spain in *In the Palace of the King.*

—Clarence A. Glasrud

DALY, (John) Augustin. American. Born in Plymouth, North Carolina, 20 July 1838; grew up in New York City. Educated in local schools. Married Mary Dolores Duff in 1869. Drama Critic for the *Sunday Courier*, and writer for the *Times, Sun,* and *Express,* New York, 1859–68; professional playwright from 1862; Manager of the Fifth Avenue Theatre, New York, where he established his own company of actors, 1869 until the theatre burned down in 1873; took over the New York Theatre and reopened it as Daly's Fifth Avenue Theatre, 1873; also formed the first professional organization of theatrical managers in New York, 1873; managed the Grand Opera House, New York, 1873, and the New Fifth Avenue Theatre, 1873–77; visited England, 1878–79; returned to New York and converted the Old Broadway Theatre into Daly's Theatre, where he assembled a new company of actors, and subsequently became internationally known for his productions of Shakespeare: managed the theatre and company, 1879 until his death; toured London, 1884, 1886, 1888, and Paris, 1888, 1891; opened Daly's Theatre, London, 1893. *Died 7 June 1899.*

Publications

Collections

Man and Wife and Other Plays (includes *Divorce, The Big Bonanza, Pique, Needles and Pins*), edited by Catherine Sturtevant. 1942.

Plays

Leah the Forsaken, from a play by S. H. von Mosenthal (produced 1862). 1886.
Taming a Butterfly, with Frank Wood, from a play by Sardou (produced 1864). 1867; revised version, as *Delmonico's; or, Larks up the Hudson* (produced 1871).
Lorlie's Wedding, from a play by C. Birchpfeiffer (produced 1864).
Judith, The Daughter of Merari, with Paul Nicholson (produced 1864).
The Sorceress (produced 1864).
Griffith Gaunt; or, Jealousy, from the novel by Charles Reade (produced 1866). 1868.
Hazardous Ground, from a play by Sardou (produced 1867). 1868.
Under the Gaslight; or, Life and Death in These Times (produced 1867). 1867; revised version (produced 1881); edited by Michael Booth, in *Hiss the Villain: Six English and American Melodramas,* 1964.
A Legend of "Norwood"; or, Village Life in New England, with Joseph W. Howard, from the novel *Norwood* by H. W. Beecher (produced 1867). 1867.
Pickwick Papers, from the novel by Dickens (produced 1868).
A Flash of Lightning, from a play by Sardou (produced 1868). 1885.
The Red Scarf; or, Scenes in Aroostock (produced 1868).
Fernanda, with Hart Jackson, from a play by Sardou (produced 1870).
Man and Wife, from the novel by Wilkie Collins (produced 1870). 1885; in *Man and Wife and Other Plays,* 1942.
The Red Ribbon (produced 1870).
Frou Frou, from a play by Henri Meilhac and Ludovic Halévy (produced 1870). 1870(?).
Come Here; or, The Debutante's Test, from a play by F. von Elsholtz (produced 1870).
Divorce, from the novel *He Knew He Was Right* by Anthony Trollope (produced 1871). 1884; in *Man and Wife and Other Plays,* 1942.
Horizon (produced 1871). 1885.
No Name, from the novel by Wilkie Collins (produced 1871).

Article 47, from a play by Adolphe Belot (produced 1872).

King Carrot, from a play by Sardou, music by Offenbach (produced 1872).

Round the Clock (produced 1872).

Alixe, from a play by Théodore Barrière and A. Régnauld de Prébois (produced 1873).

Roughing It (produced 1873).

Uncle Sam; or, The Flirtation, from a play by Sardou (produced 1873).

Madelaine Morel, from a play by S. H. von Mosenthal (produced 1873).   1884.

The Parricide, from a play by Adolphe Belot (produced 1873).

Folline, from a play by Sardou (produced 1874).

Monsieur Alphonse, from a play by Dumas fils (produced 1874).   1886.

What Should She Do? or, Jealousy, from a novel by E. About (produced 1874).

The Two Widows, from a play by F. Mallefille (produced 1874).

The Critic, from the play by Sheridan (produced 1874; as *Rehearsing the Tragedy*, produced 1888).   1889.

Yorick, from a play by M. Tamayo y Baus (produced 1874).

The Big Bonanza; or, Riches and Matches, from a play by Gustav von Moser (produced 1875).   1884; in *Man and Wife and Other Plays*, 1942.

Pique (produced 1875; as *Only a Woman*, produced 1882; as *Her Own Enemy*, produced 1884).   1884; in *Man and Wife and Other Plays*, 1942.

The School for Scandal, from the play by Sheridan (produced 1874).   1891.

Life (produced 1876).

The American, from a play by Dumas fils (produced 1876).

Lemons; or, Wedlock for Seven, from a play by Julius Rosen (produced 1877).   1877.

Blue Glass, from a play by J. B. von Schweitzer (produced 1877).

The Princess Royal, from a play by J. Adenis and J. Rostaing (produced 1877).

Vesta, from a play by D. A. Parodi (produced 1877).

The Dark City! and Its Bright Side, from a play by T. Cogniard and L. F. Nicolaïe (produced 1877).

The Assommoir, from a novel by Zola (produced 1879).

Love's Young Dream, from a French play (produced 1879).   In *Three Preludes to the Play*, n.d.

An Arabian Night; or, Haroun Al Raschid and His Mother-in-Law, from a play by Gustav von Moser (produced 1879).   1884.

Needles and Pins, from a play by Julius Rosen (produced 1880).   1884; in *Man and Wife and Other Plays*, 1942.

The Royal Middy, with Frederick Williams, from an opera by F. Zell, music by R. Genée (produced 1880).

The Way We Live, from a play by A. L'Arronge (produced 1880).

Tiote; or, A Young Girl's Heart, from a translation by Frederick Williams of a play by M. Drach (produced 1880).

Zanina; or, The Rover of Cambaye, from an opera by A. West and F. Zell, music by R. Genée (produced 1881).

Quits; or, A Game of Tit for Tat (produced 1881).

Royal Youth, from a play by Dumas père and fils (produced 1881).

The Passing Regiment, from a play by Gustav von Moser and Franz von Schönthan (produced 1881).   1884.

Odette, from a play by Sardou (produced 1882).

Mankind, from the play by P. Merritt and G. Conquest (produced 1882).

Our English Friend, from a play by Gustav von Moser (produced 1882).   1884.

She Would and She Would Not, from the play by Colley Cibber (produced 1883).   1884.

Serge Panine, from a play by G. Ohnet (produced 1883).

Seven-Twenty-Eight; or, Casting the Boomerang, from a play by Franz von Schönthan (produced 1883).   1886.

Dollars and Sense; or, The Heedless Ones, from a play by A. L'Arronge (produced 1883). 1885.

The Country Girl, from Garrick's adaptation of the play *The Country Wife* by Wycherley (produced 1884). 1898.

Red Letter Nights; or, Catching a Croesus, from a play by E. Jacobson (produced 1884).

A Woman Won't, from a play by M. Röttinger (produced 1884).

A Wooden Spoon; or, Perdita's Penates, from a play by Franz von Schönthan (produced 1884).

Love on Crutches, from a play by H. Strobitzer (produced 1884). 1885.

Nancy and Company, from a play by Julius Rosen (produced 1886). 1884.

A Night Off; or, A Page from Balzac, from a play by Franz von Schönthan (produced 1885). 1887.

The Recruiting Officer, from the play by Farquhar (produced 1885). 1885.

Denise, from a play by Dumas fils (produced 1885).

Living for Show, from a German play (produced 1885).

The Merry Wives of Windsor, from the play by Shakespeare (produced 1886). 1886.

A Wet Blanket, from a play by P. Bilhaud and J. Lévy (produced 1886). In *Three Preludes to the Play*, n.d.

A Sudden Shower, from a play by F. Beissier (produced 1886). In *Three Preludes to the Play*, n.d.

After Business Hours, from a play by Oscar Blumenthal (produced 1886). 1886.

Love in Harnass; or, Hints to Hymen, from a play by Albin Valabrègue (produced 1886). 1887.

The Taming of the Shrew, from the play by Shakespeare (produced 1887). 1887.

The Railroad of Love, from a play by Franz von Schönthan and G. Kadelburg (produced 1887). 1887.

A Midsummer Night's Dream, from the play by Shakespeare (produced 1888). 1888.

The Lottery of Love, from a play by A. Bisson and A. Mars (produced 1888). 1889.

The Under Current (produced 1888).

The Inconstant; or, The Way to Win Him, from the play by Farquhar (produced 1889). 1889.

An International Match, from a play by Franz von Schönthan (produced 1889). 1890.

Samson and Delilah, from a play by A. Bisson and J. Moineaux (produced 1889).

The Golden Widow, from a play by Sardou (produced 1889).

Roger la Honte; or, A Man's Shadow, from the play by R. Buchanan (produced 1889).

The Great Unknown, from a play by Franz von Schönthan and G. Kadelburg (produced 1889). 1890.

As You Like It, from the play by Shakespeare (produced 1889). 1890.

Miss Hoyden's Husband, from the play *A Trip to Scarborough* by Sheridan (produced 1890).

The Last Word, from a play by Franz von Schönthan (produced 1890). 1891.

The Prodigal Son, from a play by M. Carré, music by A. Wormser (produced 1891).

Love's Labour's Lost, from the play by Shakespeare (produced 1891). 1891.

Love in Tandem, from a play by H. Bocage and C. de Courcy (produced 1892). 1892.

Little Miss Million, from a play by Oscar Blumenthal (produced 1892). 1893.

A Test Case; or, Grass Versus Granite, from a play by Oscar Blumenthal and G. Kadelburg (produced 1892). 1893.

The Hunchback, from the play by J. S. Knowles (produced 1892). 1893.

The Belle's Strategem, from the play by Hannah Cowley (produced 1893). 1892.

Twelfth Night, from the play by Shakespeare (produced 1893). 1893.

The Orient Express, from a play by Oscar Blumenthal and G. Kadelburg (produced 1895).

The Two Gentlemen of Verona, from the play by Shakespeare (produced 1895). 1895.

A Bundle of Lies, from a play by K. Laufs and W. Jacoby (produced 1895).

The Transit of Leo, from a play by B. Köhler and Oscar Blumenthal (produced 1895).
The Countess Gucki, from a play by Franz von Schönthan and F. Koppel-Ellfeld (produced 1896).   1895.
Much Ado about Nothing, from the play by Shakespeare (produced 1896).   1897.
The Wonder! A Woman Keeps a Secret, from the play by Susanna Centlivre (produced 1897).   In *Two Old Comedies*, 1897.
The Tempest, from the play by Shakespeare (produced 1897).   1897.
Number Nine; or, The Lady of Ostend, with F. C. Burnand, from a play by Oscar Blumenthal and G. Kadelburg (produced 1897).
Cyrano de Bergerac, from a translation by G. Thomas and M. F. Guillemard of a play by Rostand (produced 1898).
The Merchant of Venice, from the play by Shakespeare (produced 1898).   1898.

Other

Woffington: A Tribute to the Actress and the Woman.   1888.

Reading List: *The Life of Daly* by Joseph F. Daly, 1917; *Daly's: The Biography of a Theatre* by D. F. Winslow, 1944.

*   *   *

The career of Augustin Daly is particularly difficult to capsulize. A man of tremendous energies and almost total dedication to the theatre, he became the most powerful man in American theatre during his lifetime. A drama critic, theatre manager, playwright, and adapter of foreign plays, he was also the manager of a company of actors that successfully performed Shakespearean drama in England and Europe. In the modern sense of the term he was the first stage director in America, and the strict control he exercised over all aspects of a theatrical production, even the lives of his actors, suggests both his tyranny and his devotion.

The two most important trends in late nineteenth-century American drama were an interest in social comedy and realism. Daly contributed to both, while illustrating in his plays that he was living in the age of spectacular melodrama as well as the rise of realism. Both *Divorce* and *Pique* suggest the slowly developing social comedy. *Under the Gaslight* was his first successful melodrama and boasted such realistic scenes as the Blue Room at Delmonico's, the New York pier, and the famous railroad scene in which the heroine switches the train and saves the life of the hero who is tied to the tracks. His other spectacular melodramas included *A Flash of Lightning* with its water and fire thrills, and *The Red Scarf*, in which the hero was tied to a log and sent to the saw mill.

A strong-minded impresario, Daly was primarily interested in giving audiences what they wanted. Although he tried to encourage playwriting, even tried to work with Mark Twain and William Dean Howells, he was not an innovator. Realism was spectacle to him, not a theory of living and writing. Plays by Shaw and Ibsen were never produced on his stages, and his encouragement to playwrights always involved the limitations which he felt the public dictated. As for his own plays, either original or adaptations, there is still some mystery concerning the part that his brother Joseph Daly contributed to their writing. Because he understood the requirements of the theatre he was able to inject the right ingredients into his plays and meet the demands of commercial theatre. But for this same reason he did not contribute markedly to the development of American drama and, in some ways, considering the force of his standing in theatrical circles, was a negative influence. Mainly he was a contriver of effects, a bold and ingenious creator of theatrical magic from his position as a *regisseur*. But in his best commercial successes, in both the manner of production and the material dramatized, he suggested certain truths about the society that melodrama may reflect.

—Walter J. Meserve

DANA, Richard Henry, Jr. American. Born in Cambridge, Massachusetts, 1 August 1815; son of the writer Richard Henry Dana, Sr. Educated at Harvard University, Cambridge, Massachusetts, 1832–34; worked as a sailor on the brig *Pilgrim*, and on the *Alert*, 1834–36; returned to Harvard, 1836–37, graduated 1837; attended Harvard Law School, 1837–40, and taught elocution at Harvard, 1839–40; admitted to the Massachusetts bar, 1840. Married Sarah Watson in 1841; six children. Practised law, specializing in maritime cases, Boston, 1840–78; a Founder, Free Soil Party, 1848; member of the convention for the revision of the Constitution of Massachusetts, 1853; visited England, 1856; United States District Attorney for Massachusetts, 1861–66; visited England again, 1866; Lecturer, Harvard Law School, 1866–68; Member, Massachusetts House of Representatives, and Counsel for the United States in the proceedings against Jefferson Davis, 1867–68; candidate for United States Congress, 1868; appointed minister to England by President Grant, 1876 (appointment not confirmed by the Senate); Senior Counsel for the United States before the Fisheries Commission at Halifax, 1877; lived in Europe, studying and writing on international law, 1878 until his death. Overseer, Harvard University, 1865–77. LL.D.: Harvard University, 1866. *Died 6 January 1882.*

PUBLICATIONS

Prose

    Two Years Before the Mast: A Personal Narrative of Life at Sea. 1840; revised edition, 1869; edited by John Haskell Kemble, 1964.
    The Seaman's Friend. 1841; as *The Seaman's Manual*, 1841.
    To Cuba and Back: A Vacation Voyage. 1859; edited by C. Harvey Gardiner, 1966.
    Speeches in Stirring Times, and Letters to a Son, edited by Richard Henry Dana, 3rd. 1910.
    An Autobiographical Sketch (1815–1842), edited by Robert F. Metzdorf. 1953.
    The Journal, edited by Robert F. Lucis. 1968.

    Editor, *Lectures on Art, and Poems*, by Washington Allston. 2 vols., 1850.
    Editor, *Elements of International Law*, 8th edition, by Henry Wheaton. 1866.

Bibliography: in *Bibliography of American Literature* by Jacob Blanck, 1957.

Reading List: *Dana* by Samuel Shapiro, 1961; *Dana* by Robert L. Gale, 1969.

*   *   *

Richard Henry Dana, Jr., was the author of the best known of three outstanding 19th-century travel books dealing with what were then largely unexplored sections of the American continent. *Two Years Before the Mast* has won a reputation as an adventure story for boys, while the other books, Francis Parkman's *The Oregon Trail* and Lewis Hector Garrard's *Wah-to-yah and the Taos Trail*, survive principally because of their historical, as well as literary, value. Dana would surely have preferred a similar fate for his book; its popularity among boys was a reputation he neither sought nor welcomed.

The popularity of Dana's book among boys is itself curious, for its often complex, if precise, prose might make it seem less desirable than, in particular, *Wah-to-yah*, characterized as it is by a rather colloquial and flowing style. Undoubtedly the major reason for the popularity of Dana's book is its extensive series of high adventures, vividly and objectively described. Parkman and Garrard lived with Indians – but Dana did that and much more. His realistic narrative deals effectively with a wide range of adventures that include not only life on shipboard but also life in what is today the American southwest, then a seemingly exotic region known to most Americans only through rumor. *Two Years Before the Mast* still makes the author's adventures seem exciting and unique, long after the type of customs and way of life he experienced have vanished.

Dana, after the publication of his book, became a lawyer and was never able to duplicate the success of *Two Years Before the Mast*. He published a travel book based on a trip to Canada, and he was the author of a popular handbook for sailors, *The Seaman's Friend*, but neither book has literary interest for readers today.

—Edward Halsey Foster

DAVIS, Rebecca (Blaine) Harding.   American.   Born in Washington, Pennsylvania, 24 June 1831; moved with her family to Alabama, then to Wheeling, West Virginia. Largely self-educated. Married L. Clarke Davis in 1863 (died, 1904); two sons, including Richard Harding Davis, *q.v.*, and one daughter. Professional writer from 1861; lived in Philadelphia, 1863 until her death; member of the editorial staff of the *New York Tribune* from 1869. *Died 29 September 1910.*

PUBLICATIONS

Fiction

    Margret Howth: A Story of Today.   1862.
    Dallas Galbraith.   1868.
    Waiting for the Verdict.   1868.
    Kitty's Choice (stories).   1874(?).
    John Andross.   1874.
    A Law unto Herself.   1878.
    Natasqua.   1886.
    Kent Hampden (juvenile).   1892.
    Silhouettes of American Life.   1892.
    Dr. Warrick's Daughters.   1896.
    Frances Waldeaux.   1897.

Other

Pro Aris et Focis: A Plea for Our Altars and Hearths.   1870.
Bits of Gossip.   1904.

Reading List: *The Richard Harding Davis Years: A Biography of a Mother and Son* by Gerald Langford, 1961.

*   *   *

When Rebecca Harding Davis died in 1910, she was remembered in the New York *Times* obituary primarily as the mother of Richard Harding Davis, secondarily as a novelist who had, in 1861, written a story about the "grinding life of the working people" that was so stern in its realism that "many thought the author must be a man." Seventy years after her death, aside from an occasional mention of that story, "Life in the Iron Mills," in literary histories, her work is almost entirely unknown, although in recent years feminist critics such as Tillie Olson have sought to reclaim her from obscurity. Mrs. Davis was not a prolific writer – some dozen works, novels, short stories, and improving essays during a writing career of 40 years – and not a particularly good one. Her plots are slipshod, her prose awkward. Her chief gift lies in the creation of character. But having acknowledged her limitations, a critic must recognize her achievement. She lived for her first thirty-two years the proper life of a middle-class spinster in the frontier industrial town of Wheeling, West Virginia, out of touch with literary circles, restricted in her social contacts. Yet she wrought out of this limited life a coherent theory of literary realism that preceded by a quarter of a century the admonition of William Dean Howells that fiction ought to be true to the life of actual men and women.

In her first, and most important, novel, *Margret Howth: A Story of Today*, she attacks her readers' preference for "idylls delicately tinted." She wants them instead to "dig into this commonplace, this vulgar American life and see what is in it." She finds "a new and awful significance" in the grim underlife of the industrial city where workers live thwarted lives amidst the "white leprosy of poverty." Her heroine, Margret, has been deserted by her fiancé and has gone to work as a bookkeeper in a woolen mill to support her ill and aging parents. The novel is a romance, and ultimately her fiancé is restored to his senses and her arms, but in the course of the narrative, as in "Life in the Iron Mills," Mrs. Davis provides a fully realized image of the oppressive noise, stench, and grime of industrial work. In addition, she creates in Margret a new kind of heroine – plain, blunt, occasionally pettish about the sacrifices she is required to make. Margret is the first of a series of Davis heroines who are, as one is described in a later novel, "built for use and not for show."

Mrs. Davis always wrote about contemporary issues – the Civil War, the problem of the free black, and, in *John Andross* (probably her strongest work), political corruption. Contemporary critics were not kind to her. They found her subjects disagreeable, her prose mawkish, her attitude overly didactic. But one critic, writing in *The Nation* in 1878, acknowledged that despite these flaws she contrived in her "grim and powerful etchings" to evoke the American atmosphere, "its vague excitement, its strife of effort, its varying possibilities." That is an apter summary of her contribution to American letters than the *Times* obituary.

—Louise Duus

DAVIS, Richard Harding. American. Born in Philadelphia, Pennsylvania, 18 April 1864; son of Rebecca Harding Davis, *q.v.* Educated at the Episcopal Academy, Swarthmore, Pennsylvania; Ulrich's Preparatory School, Bethlehem, Pennsylvania; Lehigh University, Bethlehem; Johns Hopkins University, Baltimore. Married 1) Cecil Clark in 1899 (divorced, 1910); 2) Elizabeth G. McEvoy in 1912, one daughter. Journalist from 1886: Reporter, *Philadelphia Record*, 1886, Philadelphia *Press*, 1887–88, and the *New York Sun*, 1889–90; Managing Editor, *Harper's Weekly*, New York, 1890; Correspondent for various newspapers and journals, including *Harper's Monthly*, *New York Sun*, and *Collier's Weekly*, from 1890: covered the Queen's Jubilee in London, Spanish War in Cuba, the Greco-Turkish War, Spanish-American War, Boer War, and the First World War: most widely known reporter of his generation. Fellow of the Royal Geographical Society (U.K.). *Died 11 April 1916.*

PUBLICATIONS

Collections

From "Gallegher" to "The Deserter": The Best Stories, edited by Roger Burlinghame. 1927.

Fiction

Gallegher and Other Stories. 1891.
Stories for Boys. 1891.
Van Bibber and Others (stories). 1892.
The Exiles and Other Stories. 1896.
Cinderella and Other Stories. 1896.
Soldiers of Fortune. 1897.
The King's Jackal. 1898.
The Lion and the Unicorn. 1899.
In the Fog. 1901.
Ranson's Folly. 1902.
Captain Macklin, His Memoirs. 1902.
Real Soldiers of Fortune. 1906.
The Scarlet Car. 1907.
Vera the Medium. 1908.
The White Mice. 1909.
Once upon a Time. 1910.
The Man Who Could Not Lose (stories). 1911.
The Red Cross Girl (stories). 1913.
The Lost Road (stories). 1913.
The Boy Scout (stories). 1914.
Somewhere in France (stories). 1915.
Novels and Stories. 12 vols., 1916.

Plays

The Princess Aline. 1895.
The Dictator (produced 1905). In *Farces*, 1906.

Miss Civilization, from a story by James Harvey Smith.   1905.
Farces: The Dictator, The Galloper, Miss Civilization.   1906.
A Yankee Tourist, music by Alfred G. Robyn, lyrics by Wallace Irwin (produced ?).
   Music published 1907.
The Consul.   1911.
Blackmail (produced 1912).
Who's Who.   1913.
Peace Manoeuvres.   1914.
The Zone Police.   1914.

Other

The Adventures of My Freshman.   1884.
The West from a Car-Window.   1892.
The Rulers of the Mediterranean.   1894.
Our English Cousins.   1894.
About Paris.   1895.
Three Gringos in Venezuela and Central America.   1896.
Dr. Jameson's Raiders vs. the Johannesburg Reformers.   1897.
Cuba in War Time.   1897.
A Year from a Reporter's Note-Book.   1898.
The Cuban and Puerto Rican Campaigns.   1898.
With Both Armies in South Africa.   1900.
The Congo and Coasts of Africa.   1907.
Notes of a War Correspondent.   1910.
With the Allies.   1914.
The New Sing Sing.   1915.
With the French in France and Salonika.   1916.
Adventures and Letters, edited by Charles Belmont Davis.   1917.

Bibliography: in *Bibliography of American Literature* by Jacob Blanck, 1957.

Reading List: *Davis: His Day* by Fairfax D. Downey, 1933; *The Davis Years: A Biography of a Mother and Son* by Gerald Langford, 1961.

*   *   *

Although the close connection between journalistic and fictional writing in the late 19th century in America has never been adequately analyzed, critics have often claimed that Richard Harding Davis failed as a writer of fiction because he excelled as a journalist. Such a judgment may be less than accurate, for Davis incorporated in his fiction the best qualities of his journalism – his quick recognition of the picturesque, his unerring selection of interest-arousing features, his keen eye for external detail, his easy phrasing of remarkably lively impressionistic passages, his youthful appreciation of adventure and movement. These qualities explain his immense contemporary popularity.

But beneath the pace and vivid detail and youthful verve of Davis's fiction, a certain emptiness bothered the serious critics. Journalistic superficiality and haste were blamed. "Smart and shallow," Ludwig Lewisohn briefly intoned in *Expression in America* (1932); and others had said much the same thing. Davis wrote too much too rapidly. He never probed beneath the surfaces. Although clever, he was unconvincing; although satisfying, never profound. At his best he exhibited impressive dramatic power, but too often the drama drifted into theatricality. His stories always charmed, but they were rarely memorable. Those who waited for Davis's exceptional promise to be fulfilled, waited in vain. "Like many handsome and idolized American college men," wrote Francis Hackett in the *New Republic* (2 March 1918), Davis "never quite graduated." Although his fiction excited, it did not confront or deal meaningfully with those issues of humanity that contribute timelessness to a literary work.

Despite the reluctant acknowledgment of serious literary critics, however, and despite their occasional condescending tributes to Davis as the best of the journalistic novelists, his work was not without value in his own time, nor is it in ours. He was the very symbol of achievement for the mass of Americans at the turn of the century, and so serves as an index to a cultural state. Not only was he the visible embodiment of the exuberant life style of the Strenuous Age, but he was also a vocal exponent of ideals that for many readers pointed direction in their dreams. Further, in both his journalistic and his fictional work, he, perhaps better than any other writer, preserved "for all ages," as Thomas Beer noted in *Liberty* (October 1924), "the adventurous, expansionist spirit of the decades that ushered in the twentieth century, the world war, and our own times."

—Clayton L. Eichelberger

DE FOREST, John William. American. Born in Humphreysville, now Seymour, Connecticut, 31 March 1826. Educated in local schools. Married Harriet Silliman Shepard in 1856 (died, 1878); one son. Lived in Syria, 1847–50, then in Florence and Paris; writer from 1856; active soldier during the American Civil War: recruited and became Captain of Company I, 12th Connecticut Volunteers; served as Inspector-General, 1st Division, XIX Corps of the United States Army; commissioned Major, United States Volunteers, 1865; also write descriptions of battle scenes for *Harper's Monthly* during the war; Commanding Captain, Veterans Reserve Corps of Company I, 14th Regiment, after the war; Commander of a district of the Freedmen's Bureau in Greenville, South Carolina, 1866 until mustered out of service, 1868; settled in New Haven, Connecticut, 1869, and thereafter devoted himself to writing; invalid, in hospital, from 1903. A.M.: Amherst College, Massachusetts, 1859. *Died 17 July 1906.*

PUBLICATIONS

Fiction

Seacliff; or, The Mystery of the Westervelts. 1859.
Miss Ravenal's Conversion from Secession to Loyalty. 1867.
Overland. 1871.
Kate Beaumont. 1872.
The Wetherel Affair. 1873.
Honest John Vane. 1875.
Playing the Mischief. 1875.
Justine's Lovers. 1878.
Irene the Missionary. 1879.
The Bloody Chasm. 1881; as *The Oddest of Courtships,* 1882.
A Lover's Revolt. 1898.
Witching Times, edited by Alfred Appel, Jr. 1967.

Verse

The Downing Legends: Stories in Rhyme.   1901.
Poem: Medley and Palestina.   1902.

Other

History of the Indians of Connecticut from the Earliest Known Period to 1850.   1851.
Oriental Acquaintance; or, Letters from Syria.   1856.
European Acquaintance.   1858.
The De Forests of Avesnes (and of New Netherland): A Huguenot Thread in American Colonial History.   1900.
"The First Time under Fire" of the 12th Regiment, Connecticut Volunteers.   1907.
A Volunteer's Adventures: A Union Captain's Record of the Civil War, edited by James H. Croushore.   1946.
A Union Officer in the Reconstruction, edited by James H. Croushore and David Morris Potter.   1948.

Bibliography: "De Forest" by James F. Light, in *American Literary Realism 4,* 1968.

Reading List: *Patriotic Gore* by Edmund Wilson, 1962; *De Forest* by James F. Light, 1965.

*   *   *

John William De Forest was in his own day a prolific but little-read author. Despite the praise of William Dean Howells, nineteenth-century readers, with their love for melodrama and romance, could not accept De Forest's realism. Yet unquestionably De Forest deserves the credit as an innovator that literary critics such as Edmund Wilson and Van Wyck Brooks have accorded him. Three of his novels, *Miss Ravenel's Conversion from Secession to Loyalty,* *Kate Beaumont,* and *Playing the Mischief,* are particularly fine examples of realistic fiction.

In his first published work, *History of the Indians of Connecticut from the Earliest Known Period to 1850,* he demonstrated the objectivity and the penchant for debunking romantic myths which characterize his fictional style. By the time the Civil War began he had written two novels. *Witching Times* is set during the hysteria of the Salem witch trials. *Seacliff,* a country-house novel with a mystery theme, presents Mrs. Westervelt, the first of his wealthy, bored, neurotic middle-aged women. The story is told from a limited first-person point of view, a technique later perfected by Henry James. De Forest also published two travel books, *Oriental Acquaintance* and *European Acquaintance,* during this pre-war period.

The author and his family left Charleston, South Carolina just before Fort Sumter was fired on. In 1862 De Forest, a successful author and a family man of 36, became captain of a company of Connecticut volunteers. This Civil War service became the raw material for a series of magazine articles collected and published posthumously under the title *A Volunteer's Adventures,* and for his most famous novel, *Miss Ravenel's Conversion.* His post-war stint in the Freedmen's Bureau gave him local settings for *Kate Beaumont* and *The Bloody Chasm* and the materials for essays in *A Union Officer in the Reconstruction.*

De Forest's descriptions of war are unemotional, graphic and vivid. Perhaps his maturity at the time he had his wartime experience accounts in part for his dispassionate style, but the same objectivity and ironic detachment characterize all his best fiction. Though the fever pitch of the early war years had been lessened by the tragedy of Bull Run, the war was for most Northern readers still the great crusade; the notion that promotions were ruled by political patronage or that generals caused needless deaths through incompetence were unwelcome dashes of cold water. Descriptions of grim field hospitals with amputated limbs and coagulating blood under the operating table or the dead blackening and bloating in the hot Louisiana sun were too strong for the mass audience.

Howells blamed De Forest's lack of success on the female reader. Certainly it is true that De Forest does not romanticize many female figures in his work. Mrs. La Rue of *Miss Ravenel's Conversion* and Mrs. Chester of *Kate Beaumont* are fading flirts still trying to attract young men. Though Mrs. Chester ultimately goes mad, Mrs. La Rue succeeds in captivating Miss Ravenel's first husband and, after his death, finding another influential lover who helps her to recoup her fortunes lost in the war. Josie Murray of *Playing the Mischief* and Olympia Smiles Vane of *Honest John Vane* manipulate men for material gain with complete success; there may be storm clouds in their futures, but they are secure as the novels end. Even the chaste ingenues like Lily Ravenel and Clara Van Dieman of *Overland* respond passionately to the sexual aspects of the men they marry. The Howells theory has, no doubt, an element of truth in it, but other factors enter in as well.

De Forest suffered as Melville, Hawthorne and others did from the unfavorable condition of the American publishing situation. With no international copyright protection from European rivals and the high volume of sales needed to turn a profit, one after another of De Forest's publishers went bankrupt. De Forest approached his work with the detachment of a scientist; even when exposing the scandal and malfeasance of the war and the Grant era, his tone is clinical and detached. His post-war work eschews sermonizing and he either lets the scene speak for itself or comments with ironic indirection. This lack of passion and subtlety of point of view may have been too demanding for his readers. Moreover, the author's cynicism may have disturbed some readers. There are no gods in his pantheon. Democracy is failing in his Washington novels; the Women's Suffrage movement produces humor but no greatness; romantic love is a delusion better buried, as in *A Lover's Revolt*, in more compelling public issues.

Although occasionally he could not resist the lure of popular taste − *Overland* and *The Bloody Chasm* have highly contrived melodramatic plots − at his best he carefully deflates romantic situations. Josie Murray entraps two Congressional lovers, but the man she really admires escapes one romantic embrace after another, coolly appraising the dangers of committment to an enticing but amoral woman. Nelly Armitage, Kate Beaumont's sister, lured by passion into marriage with a handsome drunkard, is praised for her fortitude in staying with him. She replies, "It is mere hardened callousness and want of feeling. I ceased some time ago to be a woman. I am a species of brute." Captain Colburne, the hero of *Miss Ravenel's Conversion*, is bored during the bombardment of Port Hudson and finds his freed servant is no saintly Uncle Tom, but a pilferer who must be constantly watched. His last novel, *A Lover's Revolt*, demonstrates the conflict between the romantic plot elements he knew the mass audience wanted and the realistic passages he wrote so successfully. The book contains the required love story, but the author's prime concern is the military situation in Boston of 1775–76; the love triangle is mechanically and scantily disposed of.

De Forest wrote many fine stories and novels in the years immediately following the war, and he explored new ground with almost every sally, but his books did not sell. He hoped to leave a standard edition of his work as a "little monument," but no publisher would agree to the venture. Finally this accomplished writer gave up in discouragement; he wrote little during the last two decades of his life.

—Barbara M. Perkins

DELAND, Margaret(ta Wade, née Campbell). American. Born near Allegheny, Pennsylvania, 23 February 1857; orphaned; raised by her aunt and uncle in Manchester, Pennsylvania. Educated in local schools, and at Pelham Priory, New Rochelle, New York, 1873–75; studied art and design at Cooper Union, New York City, 1875–76. Married Lorin F. Deland in 1880 (died, 1917). Assistant Instructor of Drawing and Design, Normal College of the City of New York, later Hunter College, 1876–80; settled in Boston, 1880; with her husband created a hostel, in their home, for unmarried mothers, 1880–84; full-time writer from 1886. Honorary degrees: Rutgers University, New Brunswick, New Jersey, 1917; Tufts College, Medford, Massachusetts, 1920; Bates College, Lewiston, Maine, 1920; Bowdoin College, Brunswick, Maine, 1931. Member, National Institute of Arts and Letters, 1926. *Died 13 January 1945.*

PUBLICATIONS

Fiction

John Ward, Preacher. 1888.
A Summer Day. 1889.
Sidney. 1890.
The Story of a Child. 1892.
Mr. Tommy Dove and Other Stories. 1893.
Philip and His Wife. 1894.
The Wisdom of Fools. 1897.
Old Chester Tales. 1898.
Good for the Soul. 1899.
Dr. Lavendar's People. 1903.
The Awakening of Helena Richie. 1906.
An Encore. 1907.
R. J.'s Mother and Some Other People. 1908.
The Way to Peace. 1910.
The Iron Woman. 1911.
The Voice. 1912.
Partners. 1913.
The Hands of Esau. 1914.
Around Old Chester. 1915.
The Rising Tide. 1916.
The Promises of Alice. 1919.
An Old Chester Secret. 1920.
The Vehement Flame. 1922.
New Friends in Old Chester. 1924.
The Kays. 1926.
Captain Archer's Daughter. 1932.
Old Chester Days. 1937.

Play

Screenplay: *Smouldering Fires,* with others, 1925.

Verse

The Old Garden and Other Verses.   1886.

Other

Florida Days.   1889.
The Common Way.   1904.
Small Things.   1919.
If This Be I, As I Suppose It Be (autobiography).   1935.
Golden Yesterdays (autobiography).   1941.

*   *   *

In 1888 Margaret Deland, who had previously written only one book of poetry, *The Old Garden and Other Verses,* published a novel, *John Ward, Preacher.* A complex, thesis-ridden saga of Puritan zealotry gone rigid and perverse, the book became an infamous best-seller and made its author a celebrity. John Ward, an unreconstructed Calvinist, is married to an Episcopalian woman who, as Percy H. Boynton has written (in *America in Contemporary Fiction*) "is so devoted to her husband that she can ignore his bigotry if only he will permit her to. He believes, however, that the salvation of her soul is more imperative than the survival of his home, sends her away, breaks down under the strain, and dies."

In the years that followed the publication of *John Ward,* Deland moved from the infamous and realistic to the conventional and placid. Her Old Chester pieces – many of which were collected in *Old Chester Tales* and *Dr. Lavendar's People* – for which she is best remembered, told of life in the turn-of-the-century village. Old Chester, a fictionalized Manchester, the small Pennsylvania town in which Deland had spent a part of her childhood, was not drawn with the cynicism of Lewis's Gopher Prairie or the grotesquery of Anderson's Winesburg or even with the zeal of Deland's own *John Ward.* Hers, rather, was an image of small-town Americana both peaceful and homiletic.

Reminiscences of her earlier realism were signaled now and again in Old Chester, however. In *The Awakening of Helena Richie,* for instance, the protagonist comes to the village to escape the drunkenness of her husband and her own adulterous past, only to be revealed by Dr. Lavendar and subsequently shown the path of penitence. And in a sequel, *The Iron Woman,* the awakened Helena leads the next generation away from the realistically portrayed pitfalls of adultery and divorce.

Born before the Civil War, Margaret Deland was a sometimes outspoken defender of marriage, family, and community. But by the time of her death in 1945 one could scarcely imagine that so benign a spokesman had ever been thought provocative. Indeed, the very virtues which she had stood for seemed to be in disarray.

—Bruce A. Lohof

DICKINSON, Emily (Elizabeth). American. Born in Amherst, Massachusetts, 10 December 1830. Educated at Amherst Academy; Mount Holyoke Female Seminary, South Hadley, Massachusetts, 1847. Lived a secluded life in Amherst except for brief visits to Washington, Philadelphia, and Boston; semi-invalid, 1884–86. *Died 15 May 1886.*

PUBLICATIONS

Collections

The Poems, edited by Thomas H. Johnson.   3 vols., 1955.
Letters, edited by Thomas H. Johnson and Theodora Ward.   3 vols., 1958; *Selected Letters,* 1971.
Complete Poems (single version of all poems), edited by Thomas H. Johnson.   1960; *Final Harvest* (selections), 1961.

Verse

Poems, edited by Mabel Loomis Todd and T. W. Higginson.   1890; *Second Series,* 1891; *Third Series,* edited by Todd, 1896.
The Single Hound: Poems of a Lifetime, edited by Martha Dickinson Bianchi.   1914.
The Complete Poems, edited by Martha Dickinson Bianchi.   1924.
Further Poems, edited by Martha Dickinson Bianchi and Alfred Leete Hampson.   1929.
Unpublished Poems, edited by Martha Dickinson Bianchi and Alfred Leete Hampson.   1936.
Bolts of Melody: New Poems, edited by Mabel Loomis Todd and Millicent Todd Bingham.   1945.

Other

Letters (includes some poems), edited by Mabel Loomis Todd.   2 vols., 1894.

Bibliography: *Dickinson: An Annotated Bibliography: Writings, Scholarship, Criticism, and Ana 1850–1968* by Willis J. Buckingham, 1970.

Reading List: *The Life and Letters of Dickinson* by Martha Dickinson Bianchi, 1924; *Dickinson* by Richard Chase, 1951; *Dickinson: An Interpretative Biography* by Thomas H. Johnson, 1955; *The Years and Hours of Dickinson* edited by Jay Leyda, 2 vols., 1960; *Dickinson's Poetry: Stairway of Surprise* by Charles R. Anderson, 1960; *Dickinson: A Collection of Critical Essays* edited by Richard B. Sewall, 1963; *The Recognition of Dickinson: Selected Criticism since 1890* edited by Caesar R. Blake and Carlton F. Wells, 1964; *Dickinson: An Introduction and Interpretation* by John B. Pickard, 1967; *The Poetry of Dickinson* by Ruth Miller, 1968; *Dickinson* by Denis Donoghue, 1969; *After Great Pain: The Inner Life of Dickinson* by John J. Cody, 1971; *The Life of Dickinson* by Richard B. Sewall, 2 vols., 1974.

*   *   *

Emily Dickinson's importance as a poet is not in any doubt. Her cause may have been damaged by injudicious partisanship during the 1930's, but a longer retrospect sets her firmly among the major poets who have written in English. She never prepared her poems for publication, and had she done so must in all probability have rejected many of those which are now in print. It follows from this that the general reader is likely to read no more than a selection of her work; and yet nothing that she wrote is without interest, and even the "failures" take their place in an *oeuvre* which is marked by a distinctive union of style and sensibility. In this respect, then, she satisfies T. S. Eliot's criterion (see his "What Is Minor

Poetry?," *On Poetry and Poets*) by which all the work of a major poet should be read. Nor can we deny that her work possesses "significant unity," another of Eliot's desiderata; and if we accept his third point, that a poet's majority does not depend on his having written lengthy works, then Emily Dickinson's status cannot be in doubt.

Even the most enthusiastic appreciations of her work have tended, however, to contain a note of reservation. She has been reproached for faults of technique, and her idiosyncratic sensibility has been criticised on account of the alleged whimsicality of its perceptions. The technical objections fall, insofar as they are not merely general, into three categories. First there is the question of her "bad grammar" (Yvor Winters wrote, in his *Maule's Curse*, of her "habitual carelessness"). The chief issue here is that of her very frequent use of a sort of subjunctive mood, of which the following lines provide an instance:

> Time is a test of trouble
> But not a remedy.
> If such it prove, it prove too
> There was no malady.

The usage here is surely justified, at least in the case of the first "prove," insofar as the subjunctive mood expresses an awareness that the statement is provisional: time may or may not "prove" a remedy. And the second "prove" contains a similar elliptical suggestion: "may prove" or "will prove" are implied. At all events, this feature of Emily Dickinson's poetry occurs far too often to be ascribed to "carelessness," and is better seen as a (largely successful) attempt to express linguistically the poet's tentative and scrupulous searching for the truth, which she could never see as straightforward or self-evident. Nor should we forget that there are, especially during the period of Emily Dickinson's greatest creative power in the early 1860's, many poems of confident assertion, strongly indicative in mood, like "Because I could not stop for Death."

Other critics speak of failings in metre and in rhyme. It is certainly difficult to find any consistent explanation for the irregularities of Emily Dickinson's verse, any principle on which they can be said deliberately to occur. This does not, however, oblige us to consider such irregularities as weaknesses. Emily Dickinson composed by instinct (which is not to say automatically), adapting the basic rhythms of the hymns she had heard from childhood; and her instinct told her that mechanical regularity would make for monotony. Her poems are a great deal more varied than their appearance on the page might suggest. Generalisation is inappropriate in this connection, for her rhythms, considered as personal variations on a rigid pattern, are to be acclaimed or found wanting according to the shapes and sounds of particular poems. To the ear of this author, at least, her rhythmic sense is seldom absolutely deficient, and often inspired.

In the matter of rhyme, it is probably equally misconceived to search for a uniform pattern, although some have tried to show that her use of assonance in place of full rhyme is always deliberate artistry. It would be truer to say that full rhyme usually, though not invariably, accompanies moods of confidence, while assonance implies uncertainty. But there are significant exceptions to this rule. All we can safely assert is that she felt no compulsion to find exact rhymes, and that the use of assonance also helped her to get away from the mechanical jingle of hymn-forms.

Those who object to the quality of Emily Dickinson's sensibility cannot, of course, be answered "in good set terms." This is inevitably a subjective matter; moreover, the idiosyncratic vision of which we are speaking is not evident only intermittently, in this image or that turn of phrase, but informs every line, so that despite their differences Emily Dickinson's poems are always unmistakably hers. One can do no more here than offer a brief sketch of her sensibility, hoping to counter the charge of whimsicality or childishness – as opposed to what might be called child*like*ness, which certainly is present in her work, and helps to account for the immediacy as well as the strangeness of such an image as "Great streets of silence led away/To neighbourhoods of pause." Immediacy of perception; a predominantly spatial (rather than temporal) apprehension; a direct and yet uncanny confrontation with natural phenomena – these qualities, epitomised in poems such as "A narrow fellow in the grass" or "I started early, took my dog" go to make up the distinctive atmosphere of her work. But, although these qualities might in themselves be called childlike or naif, those epithets would quite fail to characterize Emily Dickinson's poetry as a whole. In the following, for instance, we find indeed a physical image, but this is no more than the beginning of the poem, the vivid introduction to the metaphor whose meaning the lines develop:

> It dropped so low in my regard
> I heard it hit the ground
> And go to pieces on the stones
> At bottom of my mind;
>
> Yet blamed the fate that fractured less
> Than I reviled myself
> For entertaining plated wares
> Upon my silver shelf.

This is scarcely the observation of a child. The poem, moreover, is typical in this respect of its author's work. The clarity of physical image serves above all to enforce what we must call the poem's abstract meaning, which in this case is moral and psychological. Similarly, the poem "Presentiment is that long shadow on the lawn" does not describe any particular lawn at dusk so much as it invokes, with wonderful economy, the essential nature of all presentiment and all nightfalls. The same, finally, is true of many of those poems whose theme is death. If we think of the graphic spareness of "There's been a death in the opposite house," of the more exuberant images of "As far from pity as complaint," or of the triumphantly bold conceit which ends "Ample make this bed" ("Let no sunrise' yellow noise/Interrupt this ground"), we recognize that the poet has not only made alive for us an unfamiliar world of the senses, but in doing so has created a new awareness of the experience underlying the phenomena which she has described.

The underlying common quality which especially characterizes Emily Dickinson's poetry is best denoted by her own term "awe." Awe is fear divested of its physical attributes and raised to the status of a mental attitude. It is the spiritual form of fear, or the corporeal form of reverence, and defines the nature of the childlike sensibility's response to the wonder and ecstasy of simple existence. This sense of awe is clearly present in a poem like "I know some lonely houses off the road," but it is also a general presence, found to some degree even in so brief and seemingly impersonal a poem as this:

> How still the bells in steeples stand
> Till swollen with the sky,
> They leap upon their silver feet
> In frantic melody.

The sensibility which perceived bells in this way was not, it goes without saying, "normal" – any more than were the sensibilities of John Clare or Vincent van Gogh. But the intensity of the vision defies the charge of eccentricity, and the perception, although so wholly personal, is at the same time universal. The analogy with van Gogh can be pursued, for in the case of the poet as of the painter an initial sense of strangeness gives way to a recognition that we too have known just such experiences as are being depicted, but could never acknowledge them as ours until they were articulated for us by another's art.

In order further to apprehend, if not to understand, the success of this articulation, we have to consider Emily Dickinson's language. To examine her use of words in constructing the world in which she lived out her poems is a long and rewarding study which cannot be undertaken here. One might usefully begin with a consideration of her undoubted sensitivity to the quality which makes English unique among European languages as a poetic medium, its contrasting and complementary Saxon and Romance elements. Not all poets have recognized the exceptional resources of this vocabulary, but the greatest, of whom Chaucer and Shakespeare are the pre-eminent examples, have undoubtedly done so. Emily Dickinson, as a close reading of her poems will confirm, is to be counted among their number.

—James Reeves

DONNELLY, Ignatius. American. Born in Philadelphia, Pennsylvania, 3 November 1831. Educated at Central High School, Philadelphia, graduated 1849; read law in the office of Benjamin Harris Brewster, Philadelphia: admitted to the Pennsylvania bar, 1852. Married 1) Katharine McCaffrey in 1855 (died, 1894); 2) Marian Hanson in 1898. Moved to Minnesota, 1856: Lieutenant Governor of Minnesota, 1859–63; Republican Member for Minnesota, United States Congress, Washington, D.C., 1863–69; thereafter a liberal Republican, then a Populist: President, National Anti-Monopoly Convention, 1872, and Editor of the *Anti-Monopolist* newspaper, 1874–79; Member of the Minnesota State Senate, 1874–78; Greenback-Democrat candidate for Congress, 1878; thereafter a full-time writer; ran again for Congress, 1884; served as Farmers Alliance Member of the Minnesota State Legislature, 1887, and as President of the State Farmers Alliance of Minnesota; in later years edited *The Representative*, Minneapolis, and again served in the Minnesota Legislature; nominee of the People's Party for Vice-President of the United States, 1898. *Died 1 January 1901.*

PUBLICATIONS

Fiction

> *Caesar's Column: A Story of the Twentieth Century.* 1890; edited by Walter B. Rideout, 1960.
> *Doctor Huguet.* 1891.
> *The Golden Bottle; or, The Story of Ephraim Benezet of Kansas.* 1892.

Verse

> *The Mourner's Vision.* 1850.

Other

> *Nininger City.* 1856.
> *The Sonnets of Shakespeare: An Essay.* 1859.
> *Atlantis: The Antediluvian World.* 1882; edited by Egerton Sykes, 1949.
> *Ragnarok: The Age of Fire and Gravel.* 1883.

The Great Cryptogram: Francis Bacon's Cipher in the So-Called Shakespeare
   Plays. 1888.
In Memoriam Mrs. Katharine Donnelly. 1895.
The American People's Money. 1895; revised edition, as The Bryan Campaign for the
   American People's Money, 1896.
The Cipher in the Plays and on the Tombstone. 1899.

Bibliography: in Bibliography of American Literature by Jacob Blanck, 1957.

Reading List: North Star Sage: The Story of Donnelly by Oscar M. Sullivan, 1953; Donnelly
by Martin Ridge, 1962.

*   *   *

Ignatius Donnelly's works are imaginative, eccentric, and occasionally startling in their
perceptions. Atlantis: The Antediluvian World is an attempt to demonstrate and expand upon
Plato's myth of a great civilization that once supposedly existed near the mouth of the
Mediterranean long before any similarly high culture, an island society suddenly destroyed
by the gods because of its decadence. In his stupifyingly data-crammed book, Donnelly
argued not only that Atlantis actually existed, but that it was "the region where man first rose
from a state of barbarism to civilization." Furthermore, Atlantis was the source of most of the
world's gods, legends, inventions, languages, architectural styles, plants, and animals.
   The book was extremely popular, running through over twenty editions, and it inspired
countless imitators and followers to publish their corroborative findings. Since, as Martin
Gardner says in Fads and Fallacies, there is "not a shred of reliable evidence, geological or
archeological, to support" the myth, this popularity seems a testament to Donnelly's ability to
immerse his readers in an impressively assembled mass of highly interesting but nearly
totally misleading information. Donnelly's argument is dense and the farrago of seemingly
expert testimony he scraped together from a wide variety of library nooks and crannies is
mountainous: his own literary style is far from ornate, however, and though assertive seems
simply the straight-from-the-shoulder truth of a no-nonsense scholar. The work is fun to
read, filled with arcane stories and ingenious, wild yoking of disparate cultural phenomena.
He advances all his evidence quite seriously, including parallel lists showing the similarities
between the Sioux and Danish languages, and hilarious drawings of skulls from Central
America and Egypt artificially deformed in the same fashion. In Ragnarok: The Age of Fire
and Gravel he theorized that long ago the Earth passed through the tail of a giant comet,
producing world-wide catastrophe, "rearings, howlings, ... hissings," and great heat. When
the fires from this heat subsided, an Age of Darkness began, followed by the Ice Age. In The
Great Cryptogram he produced a thousand pages of cipher analyses and lists of parallel
quotations to prove that Francis Bacon wrote Shakespeare's plays. One critic used Donnelly's
de-coding formula to demonstrate that a passage from Hamlet really read "Dou-nill-he, the
author, politician, and mountebanke, will work out the secret of this play. The sage is a
daysie."
   But it would be a distinct mistake to dismiss Donnelly as a crank. He is frequently
fascinating and his forays into scientific theory or literary criticism display impressive if ill-
digested and misguided learning, and sensitivity to literary values. Furthermore, in his fiction
he seriously addressed serious social problems such as the political weakness of the poor (The
Golden Bottle) and racial intolerance (Doctor Huguet). Caesar's Column is a minor anti-
utopian classic predicting class warfare between the economic oppressors and oppressed,
forces equally matched in their brutality. Marred only by two silly love stories, the novel

accurately depicts many technological horrors of the future – such as air raids – and, more importantly, discusses specific social reforms such as an eight-hour work day and socialized medicine. The book's central image is a grotesque symbol of modern civilization: Caesar's column is a gigantic pillar of dead bodies killed in the slaughter of war.

—Jack B. Moore

DRAKE, Joseph Rodman.   American.   Born in New York City, 7 August 1795. Studied medicine at a school in Barclay Street, New York, and qualified 1816. Married Sarah Eckford in 1816. Toured Europe, 1816–19; Partner, with William Langstaff, in a drug store in New York, 1819–20. *Died 21 September 1820.*

PUBLICATIONS

Collections

Life and Works: A Memoir and Complete Text of His Poems and Prose, by Frank Lester Pleadwell.   1935.

Verse

Poems, with Fitz-Greene Halleck.   1819; revised edition, as *The Croakers,* 1860.
The Culprit Fay and Other Poems.   1835.

Bibliography: in *Bibliography of American Literature* by Jacob Blanck, 1957.

*   *   *

Joseph Rodman Drake is an American member of the brotherhood of poets whose small measure of lasting fame depends on one or two popular successes. His fanciful 639-line poem "The Culprit Fay" – written in 1816 but not published until long after his death – continues to please many readers. "The American Flag," written and published pseudonymously in 1819, was widely admired in America and set to music by numerous composers (including Dvorak). His memory also survives because of the monody "On the Death of Joseph Rodman Drake," written by his friend Fitz-Greene Halleck, that opens with the well-known quatrain:

> Green be the turf above thee,
> Friend of my better days!
> None knew thee but to love thee,
> Nor named thee but to praise.

Otherwise, Drake is remembered only by some historical critics who – following the example set by Edgar Allan Poe in the 1830's – are still outraged by the vogue that Drake's work enjoyed in America after his death.

Except for one excursion abroad, Drake lived out his short life in New York City. Trained as a physician, he never aspired to literary fame; he published little during his lifetime, and he reportedly requested on his deathbed that his poetry manuscripts be burned as "valueless." The request was ignored, however, and when his verse appeared in 1835 he was revealed as one of the authors (the other was his friend Halleck) of the "Croaker" poems that had titillated readers of New York newspapers during the summer of 1819. This revelation, together with the appearance of Drake's only long poem, "The Culprit Fay," prompted extravagant praise that Poe deplored (*Southern Literary Messenger*, April 1836), as did later critics. More recently, a biographer of Poe (Vincent Buranelli, *Edgar Allan Poe*, 1961) labeled Drake "a third-rate versifier."

Despite such judgments, Drake's poetry reflects a promising if aborted talent. A number of his "Croaker" poems – "To Ennui," "The National Painting," "To John Minshull, Esquire," to name only a few – poke healthy fun at an America that was already beginning to take itself too seriously. In "The Culprit Fay" – reportedly written in three days – Drake anticipated both Washington Irving and James Kirke Paulding in experimenting with fantasy; the poem tells the story of a Hudson River fairy who, for having fallen in love with "an earthly maid," is sentenced by his "lily-king" to perform herculean tasks in miniature. Derivative as it is, "The Culprit Fay" reflects not only Drake's perceptive reading of great masters – ranging from Shakespeare and Michael Drayton to his own contemporaries Coleridge and Keats – but an exciting young imagination that was too soon stilled by death.

—Thomas F. O'Donnell

DUNBAR, Paul Laurence. American. Born in Dayton, Ohio, 27 June 1872; son of a former slave. Educated at Dayton High School, graduated 1891. Married Alice Ruth Moore in 1898. Elevator operator, Dayton, 1891–93; employed at the Haiti Building, World's Columbian Exposition, Chicago, 1894; encouraged in his writing by prominent Dayton men, and by William Dean Howells, at whose instigation he joined the Pond Lecture Bureau, 1896; attained great popularity throughout the United States as a reader of his own works, and visited England, 1897; Assistant in the Library of Congress, Washington, D.C., 1897–98. Suffered from tuberculosis. *Died 9 February 1906.*

PUBLICATIONS

Collections

Complete Poems. 1913.
The Dunbar Reader, edited by Jay Martin and Gossie H. Hudson. 1975.

Verse

Oak and Ivy. 1893.
Majors and Minors. 1895.
Lyrics of Lowly Life. 1896.

Lyrics of the Hearthside. 1899.
Poems of Cabin and Field. 1899.
Candle-Lightin' Time. 1901.
Lyrics of Love and Laughter. 1903.
When Malindy Sings. 1903.
Li'l' Gal. 1904.
Chris'mus Is A-Comin' and Other Poems. 1905.
Howdy, Honey, Howdy. 1905.
Lyrics of Sunshine and Shadow. 1905.
Joggin' Erlong. 1906.
Speakin' o' Christmas and Other Christmas and Special Poems. 1914.

Plays

The Gambler's Wife, in *Dayton Tattler*, Ohio, 13, 20, and 27 December 1890.
African Romances, music by Samuel Coleridge Taylor. 1897.
Clorindy; or, The Origin of the Cakewalk, music by Will Marion Cook. 1898.
Dream Lovers, music by Samuel Coleridge Taylor. 1898.
Jes Lak White Fo'ks (lyrics only, with others), music by Will Marion Cook. 1900.
Uncle Eph's Christmas, music by Will Marion Cook. 1900.
Plantation Melodies Old and New (lyrics only, with others), music by H. T. Burleigh. 1901.
In Dahomey (lyrics only, with others), music by Will Marion Cook. 1903.
My Lady (lyrics only, with others), music by Will Marion Cook. 1914.

Fiction

The Uncalled. 1898.
Folks from Dixie (stories). 1898.
The Love of Landry. 1900.
The Strength of Gideon and Other Stories. 1900.
The Fanatics. 1901.
The Sport of the Gods. 1902; as *The Jest of Fate*, 1902.
In Old Plantation Days (stories). 1903.
The Heart of Happy Hollow (stories). 1904.

Bibliography: *Dunbar: A Bibliography* by E. W. Metcalf, Jr., 1975.

Reading List: *The Life and Works of Dunbar*, biography by Lida Keck Wiggins, 1907; *Dunbar and His Song* by Virginia Cunningham, 1947; *Oak and Ivy: A Biography of Dunbar* by Addison Gayle, Jr., 1971; *A Singer in the Dawn: Reinterpretations of Dunbar* edited by Jay Martin, 1975.

*   *   *

There were, in truth, two Paul Laurence Dunbars. One was the writer supported by the interest of white Americans because some of his work was sufficiently faithful to black stereotypical images designed and demanded by white Americans. The other, in a sense the more "real" Paul Laurence Dunbar, was the writer of genuine literary talent and dramatic sensibility, whose true literary worth could not be widely assessed until a wide range of his work was gathered and published as late as 1975 in *The Paul Laurence Dunbar Reader*.

In his first manifestation, that of dialect poet, Dunbar was not so much pandering to the demands of white editors and a white reading public as indulging his own natural affinity for the rhythms of common speech and often for comedy; dialect in literature was, after all, very much *à la mode* with the interest in local color in late nineteenth-century America. That he had a gift as a dialect poet is undeniable, but it is rather too bad that his white audience could not accept him as anything more.

Much more he was, as William Dean Howells recognized early. As a writer of fiction and essays, he used the stuff of black lore to greater effect than any black writer had previously, and at least as well as such whites as Joel Chandler Harris had done. Particularly noteworthy in his work is the reflection of religion in black-American life and of the implications of the black migration to American cities. As a poet, Dunbar often superbly starched his ready lyricism with a keen sense of drama. It is a truism to say that while his material was mainly black, his insights were universal.

Dunbar did not choose to be the examplar of the white view of black America in his time, during the adult years of his 33-year life, but he was, and he made a sturdy pivot. He managed to entertain and enlighten whites while helping to imbue fellow blacks with a sense of history and importance that make him a close spiritual ancestor of Countée Cullen, Langston Hughes, James Baldwin, and the host of other powerful twentieth-century black-American voices for pride.

—Alan R. Shucard

DUNLAP, William.   American.   Born in Perth Amboy, New Jersey, 19 February 1766. Educated in local schools until his family moved to New York in 1777; thereafter studied painting with a New York artist. Married Elizabeth Woolsey in 1789; one son and one daughter. Set up as a portraitist in New York, 1782–84; studied art with Benjamin West in London, 1784–86; returned to New York and abandoned painting to write for the New York stage; became a partner in his father's china importing business, c. 1790; Manager and Part-Owner, Old American Company, at the John Street Theatre, later at the Park Theatre, New York, presenting his own plays as well as current French and German plays in translation, 1796 until he went bankrupt, 1805; travelling miniaturist, 1805–06; General Assistant to the new manager of the Park Theatre, 1806–11; established the *Monthly Recorder*, New York, 1813; Assistant Paymaster-General, New York Militia, 1814–16; resumed painting as a livelihood, 1816 until his death. One of the founders, 1826, and Vice-President, 1831–38, of the National Academy of Design. *Died 28 September 1839.*

PUBLICATIONS

Plays

> *The Father; or, American Shandy-ism* (produced 1789).   1789; revised version, as *The Father of an Only Child*, in *Dramatic Works*, 1806.
> *Darby's Return* (produced 1789).   1789; edited by Walter J. Meserve and William R.

Reardon, in *Satiric Comedies*, 1969.

The Miser's Wedding (produced 1793).

Leicester (as *The Fatal Deception; or, The Progress of Guilt*, produced 1794). In *Dramatic Works*, 1806.

Shelty's Travels (produced 1794).

Fountainville Abbey (produced 1795).   In *Dramatic Works*, 1806.

The Archers; or, Mountaineers of Switzerland, music by Benjamin Carr (produced 1796).   1796.

Ribbemont; or, The Feudal Baron (as *The Mysterious Monk*, produced 1796).   1803.

The Knight's Adventure (produced 1797).   1807.

The Man of Fortitude, with John Hodgkinson (produced 1797).   1807.

Tell Truth and Shame the Devil, from a play by A. L. B. Robineau (produced 1797).   1797.

The Stranger, from a play by Kotzebue (produced 1798).   1798.

André (produced 1798).   1798.

False Shame; or, The American Orphan in Germany, from a play by Kotzebue (produced 1798).   Edited by Oral Sumner Coad, with *Thirty Years*, 1940.

The Natural Daughter (produced 1799).

The Temple of Independence (produced 1799).

Don Carlos, from the play by Schiller (produced 1799).

Indians in England, from a play by Kotzebue (produced 1799).

The School for Soldiers, from a play by L. S. Mercier (produced 1799).

The Robbery, from a play by Boutet de Monval (produced 1799).

The Italian Father, from the play *The Honest Whore* by Dekker (produced 1799).   1800.

Graf Benyowsky, from a play by Kotzebue (produced 1799).

Sterne's Maria; or, The Vintage (produced 1799).

Lovers' Vows, from a play by Kotzebue (produced 1799).   1814.

The Force of Calumny, from a play by Kotzebue (produced 1800).

The Stranger's Birthday, from a play by Kotzebue (produced 1800).

The Knight of Guadalquiver (produced 1800).

The Wild-Goose Chase, from a play by Kotzebue (produced 1800).   1800.

The Virgin of the Sun, from a play by Kotzebue (produced 1800).   1800.

Pizarro in Peru; or, The Death of Rolla, from a play by Kotzebue and the version by Sheridan (produced 1800).   1800.

Fraternal Discord, from a play by Kotzebue (produced 1800).   1809.

The Soldier of '76 (produced 1801).

Abbe de l'Epee, from a play by Jean Bouilly (produced 1801).

Where Is He?, from a German play (produced 1801).

Abaelline, The Great Bandit, from a play by J. H. D. Zschokke (produced 1801).   1802.

The Merry Gardener, from a French play (produced 1802).

The Retrospect; or, The American Rovolution (produced 1802).

Peter the Great; or, The Russian Mother, from a play by J. M. Babo (produced 1802).   1814.

The Good Neighbors: An Interlude, from a work by A. W. Iffland (produced 1803).   1814.

Blue Beard: A Dramatic Romance, from the play by George Colman the Younger.   1803.

The Voice of Nature, from a play by L. C. Caigniez (produced 1803).   1803.

The Blind Boy, from a play by Kotzebue (produced 1803).

Bonaparte in England (produced 1803).

The Proverb; or, Conceit Can Cure, Conceit Can Kill (produced 1804).

Lewis of Monte Blanco; or, The Transplanted Irishman (produced 1804).

Nina, from a play by Joseph Marsollier (produced 1804).

Chains of the Heart; or, The Slave of Choice, from a play by Prince Hoare (produced
?). 1804.
The Wife of Two Husbands, from a play by Pixérécourt (produced 1804). 1804.
The Shipwreck, from a play by Samuel James Arnold (produced ?). 1805.
Dramatic Works. 3 vols., 1806–16.
Alberto Albertini; or, The Robber King (produced 1811).
Yankee Chronology; or, Huzza for the Constitution! (produced 1812). 1812.
The Glory of Columbia: Her Yeomanry! (produced 1813). 1817.
The Flying Dutchman (produced 1827).
A Trip to Niagara; or, Travellers in America (produced 1828). 1830.
Thirty Years; or, The Gambler's Fate, from a play by Prosper Goubaux and Victor
Ducange (produced 1828). Edited by Oral Sumner Coad, with *False Shame*, 1940.

Other

Memoirs of the Life of George Frederick Cooke. 2 vols., 1813; revised edition, as *The
Life of Cooke*, 1815.
A Record, Literary and Political, of Five Months in the Year 1813, with others. 1813.
The Life of the Most Noble Arthur, Marquis and Earl of Wellington, with Francis L.
Clarke. 1814.
A Narrative of the Events Which Followed Bonaparte's Campaign in Russia. 1814.
The Life of Charles Brockden Brown, with Selections. 2 vols., 1815; as *Memoirs of
Charles Brockden Brown*, 1822.
A History of the American Theatre. 1832.
A History of the Rise and Progress of the Arts of Design in the United States. 2 vols.,
1834; revised edition, edited by Alexander Wyckoff, 1965.
Thirty Years Ago; or, The Memoirs of a Water Drinker. 2 vols., 1836.
A History of New York, for Schools. 2 vols., 1837.
History of the New Netherlands, Province of New York, and the State of New York. 2
vols., 1840.
*Diary: The Memoirs of a Dramatist, Theatrical Manager, Painter, Critic, Novelist, and
Historian*, edited by Dorothy C. Barck. 3 vols., 1930.

Bibliography: in *False Shame, and Thirty Years*, edited by Oral Sumner Coad, 1940.

Reading List: *Dunlap: A Study of His Life and Works and of His Place in Contemporary
Culture* by Oral Sumner Coad, 1917; *Arts of the Young Republic: The Age of Dunlap* by
Harold E. Dickson, 1968.

*   *   *

"The American Vasari" and "Father of American Theatre" are phrases which honor
William Dunlap as the first historian of United States arts. But his *Rise and Progress of the
Arts*, though richly anecdotal, is a moralistic, opinionated source of biographical sketches. His
American Theatre concentrates on 1787 to 1811 when Dunlap, as playwright and manager,
knew everyone in the business and contributed to its growth from a British "provincial"
company to a theatre bragging of native-born stars and playwrights. Dunlap proposed federal
subsidization, questioned the star-system, and despised the new Scribean play-factories –
despite having translated the lurid *Gambler's Fate*.

The democratic abolitionist and artist saw himself as an anti-partisan reconciler. Because
the best European models required an indefinable purification of "old world vices," Dunlap
was left without dependable aesthetic grounds for resisting commercial standardization. He

became the compromiser who packaged the acceptable best. Over half of his plays introduced fashionable continental dramatists into the American repertory. After successfully adapting *The Stranger*, Dunlap depended particularly upon the popularity of Kotzebue's plays (twelve translations) with their affecting sentimentality coupled with, admittedly, "false philosophy and unsound morals." *False Shame* typically puts all major characters through set-piece confessions of "false shame" before redeeming them by intermarriage or discovering family relationships. It conforms in kind to Dunlap's own sentimental comedies.

Dunlap's first produced play, *The Father*, uses the stock comic doctor and country maidservant to give some savor to its purposeful actions: an American patriot's reunion with his son, an English officer; the redemption of a mildly rakish husband; a pallid literary borrowing from Sterne. Art, politics, and business "now in Virtue's cause engage/And rear that glorious thing, a *Moral Stage*." For stars' benefits or historical occasions Dunlap framed narrative songs. In *Yankee Chronology* a sailor returns to tell and sing of the 1812 victory of the (parable-pun) U.S.S. Constitution. Contradicting the travel-writers, *A Trip to Niagara* frames a moving diorama with interesting American (and British) types to persuade an English snob of some American virtues.

Only an unsophisticated audience could tolerate the ghastliness, disguises, and mistaken identities of the gothic *Mysterious Monk* and the romantic *Fatal Deception* – harmlessly abstract figures justified by much talk in verse about honor. But idea and theme, finally, make *André* a substantial and significant tragedy. General Washington and Major André are its heroic figures, while young Bland tries to be Otway's Pierre. Captain Bland and the other American officers play out their neoclassic alternatives of mind or heart, and the poetic drama gathers relevant force in their debate of the modes, moralities, and reconciliations necessary for an independent country in 1780, or in 1798 (the year of production).

Dunlap refashioned his controversial, unpopular, but finest play into a popular celebration. Incoherent and delightful, *The Glory of Columbia: Her Yeomanry!* wraps pieces of *André* with a despicable Benedict Arnold, some honest Yankee soldiers who capture André, a singing sister Sal in uniform, and a canny Irishman. He changes sides for a final victory pageant at Yorktown and a chorale to "Columbia's Son, Immortal Washington!"

—John G. Kuhn

DUNNE, Finley Peter. American. Born in Chicago, Illinois, 10 July 1867. Educated in Chicago public schools. Married Margaret Abbott in 1902; three sons and one daughter. Journalist from 1885, working for various Chicago newspapers; City Editor, *Chicago Times*, 1891–92; member of the editorial staff of the *Chicago Evening Post* and *Times Herald*, 1892–97; Editor, *Chicago Journal*, 1897–1900; moved to New York, 1900; wrote for *Collier's* and briefly edited the *New York Morning Telegraph*; Editor, with Ida Tarbell and Lincoln Steffens, *The American Magazine*, 1906; edited *Collier's Weekly*, 1918–19. Member, National Institute of Arts and Letters. *Died 24 April 1936.*

PUBLICATIONS

Collections

Mr. Dooley and the Chicago Irish, edited by Charles Fanning.   1976.
Mr. Dooley's Chicago, edited by Barbara C. Schaaf.   1977.

Prose

Mr. Dooley in Peace and in War.   1898.
Mr. Dooley in the Hearts of His Countrymen.   1899.
What Dooley Says.   1899.
Mr. Dooley's Philosophy.   1900.
Mr. Dooley's Opinions.   1901.
Observations by Mr. Dooley.   1902.
Dissertations by Mr. Dooley.   1906.
Mr. Dooley Says.   1910.
New Dooley Book.   1911.
Mr. Dooley on Making a Will and Other Necessary Evils.   1919.
Mr. Dooley Remembers: The Informal Memoirs of Dunne, edited by Philip Dunne.   1963.

Reading List: *Mr. Dooley's America: The Life of Dunne* by Elmer Ellis, 1941; *Dunne and Mr. Dooley: The Chicago Years* by Charles Fanning, 1978.

*   *   *

Finley Peter Dunne is best known for having created Mr. Martin Dooley, an aging Irish saloonkeeper from Chicago, who began appearing in a weekly column in the *Chicago Evening Post* in October 1893. Dunne's own parents had been Irish immigrants to Chicago, and he began his journalistic career there in 1884 at age seventeen. After working on six different newspapers, he settled as precocious editorial chairman at the *Post* in 1892. The last in a series of dialect experiments for his creator, Mr. Dooley succeeded Colonel Malachi McNeery, a downtown Chicago barkeep modeled on a friend of Dunne's, who had become a popular *Post* feature during the World's Fair of 1893. Unlike McNeery, Mr. Dooley was placed on Chicago's South Side, in the Irish working-class neighborhood of Bridgeport. Between 1893 and 1898, 215 Dooley pieces appeared in the *Post*. Taken together, they form a coherent body of work, in which a vivid, detailed world comes into existence — that of Bridgeport, a self-contained immigrant culture, with its own customs and ceremonies and a social structure rooted in family, geography, and occupation. Included are memories of Ireland and emigration, descriptions of the daily round of Bridgeport life, and inside narratives of rough-and-tumble politics in a city ward. In addition, other pieces contain wholly serious treatments of suffering and starvation among the poor, the divisive scramble for middle-class respectability, and conflict between immigrant parents and their American children. In these Bridgeport pieces, Dunne contributed to the development of literary realism in America. In depicting this immigrant community and its working-class inhabitants through the medium of Irish vernacular dialect, he gave Chicagoans a weekly example of the realist's faith in the potentiality for serious fiction of common speech and everyday life.

Dunne's career took a sharp turn in 1898, when Mr. Dooley's satirical coverage of the Spanish-American War brought him to the attention of readers outside Chicago. Beginning with his scoop of "Cousin George" Dewey's victory at Manila, Mr. Dooley's reports of military and political bungling during the "splendid little war" were widely reprinted, and national syndication soon followed. By the time Dunne moved to New York in 1900, Mr. Dooley was the most popular figure in American journalism. From this point until World War I, Dunne's gadfly mind ranged over the spectrum of newsworthy events and characters, both national and international: from Teddy Roosevelt's health fads to Andrew Carnegie's passion for libraries; from the invariable silliness of politics to society doings at Newport; from the Boer and Boxer Rebellions to the Negro, Indian, and immigration "problems." Mr. Dooley's perspective was consistently skeptical and critical. The salutary effect of most pieces was the exposure of affectation and hypocrisy through undercutting humor and common sense. The most frequently quoted Dooleyisms indicate this thrust: Teddy Roosevelt's egocentric account of the Rough Riders is retitled, "Alone in Cubia"; Henry Cabot Lodge's imperialist rationale becomes "Take up th' white man's burden an' hand it to th' coons"; a fanatic is defined as "a man that does what he thinks th' Lord wud do if He knew th' facts iv th' case." Although he joined Ida Tarbell and Lincoln Steffens in taking over *The American Magazine* in 1906, Dunne was not himself a progressive reformer. He viewed the world as irrevocably fallen and unimproveable, and many Dooley pieces reflect their author's tendency toward cynicism, pessimism, and fatalism. More pronounced in the early Chicago work than in the lighter national commentary, Dunne's darker side may be explained by his Irish background and his journalist's education into the realities of nineteenth-century urban life.

Mr. Dooley was the first Irish voice in American literature to transcend the confines of "stage Irish" ethnic humor. Dunne's accomplishment divides (at 1898) into two parts: the Chicago pieces, which contain pioneering realistic sketches of an urban immigrant community, and the pieces written for a national audience, which contain some of the best social and political satire ever penned in America.

—Charles Fanning

DWIGHT, Timothy. American. Born in Northampton, Massachusetts, 14 May 1752. Educated at Yale University, New Haven, Connecticut, 1766–69, 1771–72, B.A. 1769, M.A. 1772. Served as a Chaplain in General Parson's Connecticut Brigade during the Revolutionary War, 1777–79. Married Mary Woolsey in 1777. Headmaster, Hopkins Grammar School, New Haven, Connecticut, 1769–71; Tutor at Yale University, 1771–77; licensed to preach, 1777; Member, Massachusetts Legislature, 1781–82; ordained to the ministry of the Congregational Church, 1783; Pastor, Greenfield Hill Congregational Church, Connecticut, 1783–95; Professor of Divinity, and President, Yale University, 1795–1817 (founder of the medical department). A projector of the Andover Theological Seminary and Missionary Society of Connecticut; Member, American Board of Commissioners for Foreign Missions. LL.D.: Harvard University, Cambridge, Massachusetts, 1810. *Died 11 January 1817.*

PUBLICATIONS

Verse

> *America; or, A Poem on the Settlement of the British Colonies.*   1780(?).
> *The Conquest of Canaan.*   1785.
> *The Triumph of Infidelity.*   1788.
> *Greenfield Hill.*   1794.
> *The Psalms of David,* by Watts, altered by Dwight.   1801.

Other

> *The Nature, and Danger, of Infidel Philosophy.*   1798.
> *Remarks on the Review of Inchiquin's Letters.*   1815.

Theology Explained and Defended in a Series of Sermons.   5 vols., 1818–19; abridged
edition, as *Beauties of Dwight,* 4 vols., 1823.
Travels in New England and New York.   4 vols., 1821–22; edited by Barbara Miller
Solomon, 4 vols., 1969.
An Essay on the Stage.   1824.
Sermons.   2 vols., 1828.

Bibliography: in *Bibliography of American Literature* by Jacob Blanck, 1957.

Reading List: *A Sketch of the Life and Character of Dwight* by Benjamin Silliman, 1817;
Dwight: A Biography by Charles E. Cunningham, 1942; *Dwight* by Kenneth Silverman,
1969.

*   *   *

In his own time Timothy Dwight was a figure of towering significance, president of Yale
University, foremost among the Hartford Wits, educator, and theologian. Today, however,
he is in the main remembered as a staunch advocate of Federalist and Calvinist orthodoxies in
a world of change, and as a poet who made modest if seminal contributions to the growth of
an indigenous American literature.

Dwight's reputation for obstinance originates mostly in his crabbed and dogmatic prose
works. In 1798, for instance, with Deism and Thomas Jefferson on the rise, he announced in
his sermon "The Duty of Americans, at the Present Crisis" that a return to Calvin and to
Federalism was mandatory. In *The Nature, and Danger, of Infidel Philosophy,* published that
same year, he castigated the liberal politics of John Locke, David Hume, and Thomas Paine.
As for his own hero he would go on record two years later with a laudatory *Discourse on The
Character of George Washington.* And his *Theology Explained and Defended,* a five-volume
collection of sermons which he had delivered to his students at Yale, was an apologia for the
theocracy which he sought to maintain.

Dwight's orthodoxy also informed some of his verse. For example, *The Conquest of
Canaan,* an epic in eleven books reminiscent of Milton, was a veiled allegory of the American
War for Independence, with Joshua in the role of Washington. And his most venomous
verse, *The Triumph of Infidelity,* recounted in heroic couplets the sins of Voltaire, Hume, and
other expositors of liberalism. Still other of his poems, however, revealed another, softer, side
of Dwight. In his most famous poem, *Greenfield Hill,* for instance, he spoke in seven different
sections – now as narrator, now as rural mother or clergyman or farmer – of the virtues of
pastoral life in the new nation in ways which are actually Jeffersonian in intonation.

It was also in *Greenfield Hill,* and to a lesser degree in *The Conquest of Canaan,* that
Dwight made an important contribution to the growth of an indigenous literature by
employing landscapes and personalities of an indubitably American nature. Unfortunately,
the more reactionary of Dwight's writings, together with the prevailing view that the setting
of poetry should be other than American, conspired to hide Dwight's attempts at a native
literature. In another generation, however, the authors of the American Renaissance would
build a successfully native literature upon the earlier efforts of poets such as Timothy Dwight.

—Bruce A. Lohof

EGGLESTON, Edward. American. Born in Vevay, Indiana, 10 December 1837. Educated in various Indiana country schools, and at the Amelia Academy, Virginia, 1854–55. Married 1) Lizzie Snider in 1858 (died, 1890), two daughters and one son; 2) Frances E. Goode in 1891. Teacher, Madison, Indiana, 1855; entered the Methodist ministry, 1857: circuit rider in Southeast Indiana, 1856–57; preacher in Minnesota, in Traverse and St. Peter, 1857–58, St. Paul, 1858–60, Stillwater, 1860–61, St. Paul, 1862–63, and Winona, 1864–66; Associate Editor, *The Little Corporal* magazine, and Columnist for the *Evening Journal*, Chicago, 1866–67; Editor, *National Sunday School Teacher*, Chicago, 1867–69; Western (i.e., Chicago) Correspondent, 1867–69, Literary Editor, 1870, and Superintending Editor, 1871, *The Independent*, New York; Editor, *Hearth and Home*, New York, 1871–72; left the Methodist ministry, 1874; Founder and Pastor of the non-sectarian Church of the Christian Endeavor, Brooklyn, New York, 1874 until he retired to devote himself to historical writing, 1879. Co-Founder, Authors' Club, 1882; President, American Historical Association, 1900. D.D.: University of Indiana, Bloomington, 1870; D.H.L.: Allegheny College, Meadville, Pennsylvania, 1893. *Died 2 September 1902.*

PUBLICATIONS

Fiction

Mr. Blake's Walking-Stick: A Christmas Story for Boys and Girls. 1870.
Book of Queer Stories, and Stories Told on a Cellar Door. 1871.
The Hoosier School-Master. 1871; revised edition, 1892.
The End of the World: A Love Story. 1872.
The Mystery of Metropolisville. 1873.
The Circuit Rider: A Tale of the Heroic Age. 1874.
The Schoolmaster's Stories for Boys and Girls. 1874.
Roxy. 1878.
The Hoosier School-Boy. 1882.
Queer Stories for Boys and Girls. 1884.
The Graysons: A Story of Illinois. 1888.
The Faith Doctor: A Story of New York. 1891.
Duffels (collected stories). 1893.

Other

Sunday School Conventions and Institutes. 1867; revised edition, 1870.
The Manual: A Practical Guide to the Sunday-School Work. 1869.
Improved Sunday School Record. 1869.
Tracts for Sunday School Teachers. 1872(?).
Tecumseh and the Shawnee Prophet, with Lillie Eggleston Seelye. 1878.
Pocahontas, with Lillie Eggleston Seelye. 1879; as *The Indian Princess*, 1881.
Brant and Red Jacket, with Lillie Eggleston Seelye. 1879; as *The Rival Warriors, Chiefs of the Five Nations*, 1881.
Montezuma and the Conquest of Mexico, with Lillie Eggleston Seelye. 1880; as *The Mexican Prince*, 1881.
A History of the United States and Its People, for the Use of Schools. 1888.
A First Book in American History. 1889.
Stories of Great Americans for Little Americans: Second Reader Grade.
Stories of American Life and Adventures: Third Reader Grade. 1895.

The Beginners of a Nation.   1896.
The Transit of Civilization from England to America in the Seventeenth Century.   1901.
The New Century History of the United States, edited by G. C. Eggleston.   1904.

Editor, *Christ in Literature.*   1875.
Editor, *Christ in Art.*   1875.
Editor, with Elizabeth Eggleston Seelye, *The Story of Columbus,* 1892.
Editor, with Elizabeth Eggleston Seelye, *The Story of Washington.*   1893.

Bibliography: in *Bibliography of American Literature* by Jacob Blanck, 1959; "Eggleston" by William Peirce Randel, in *American Literary Realism 1,* 1967.

Reading List: *Eggleston, Author of "The Hoosier School-Master,"* 1946, and *Eggleston,* 1963, both by William Peirce Randel.

*   *   *

In 1871 Edward Eggleston, a former Methodist clergyman from Indiana who had become a successful editor of popular magazines for children and adults, published *The Hoosier School-Master,* thereby launching the first of two literary careers for which he is justly famous. In the adventures of a fictional frontier Indiana school-teacher, Eggleston the novelist created a pioneering piece of western dialect fiction, and also contributed seminally to the growth of mid-western realism, a genre which would subsequently be developed by Hamlin Garland.

Written initially for serialization in Eggleston's magazine *Hearth and Home,* with the early installments in print well before the later portions were in outline, *The Hoosier School-Master* has rightly been criticized for its many structural flaws. But Eggleston soon followed with a series of finer though curiously less famous novels in the same realistic vein: *The End of the World,* based upon the Millerite delusion of the 1840's; *The Mystery of Metropolisville,* a poorly constructed but equally realistic saga of boom and bust on the midwestern frontier; *The Circuit Rider,* a novel of remembrance, as the erstwhile preacher Eggleston wrote in its dedication, for his "Comrades of Other Years ... with whom I had the honor to be associate in a frontier ministry"; and *Roxy,* the story of a small-town Ohio girl, thought by some to be Eggleston's best fictional work. Throughout his novels Eggleston sought to portray the commonplace in nineteenth-century American life. As he stated in *The Mystery of Metropolisville,* a novel "needs to be true to human nature in its permanent and essential qualities, and it should truthfully represent ... some form of society."

Given the realistic character of his fiction, it was a short step for Eggleston to his next and final career, that of historian. In 1888 he published his *History of the United States and Its People.* And in 1896 appeared *The Beginners of a Nation,* the first of a projected multi-volume "History of Life in the United States." True to his proclivities as a realist, Eggleston had planned, as he said in 1880, for his history to be "a history of ... the life of the people, the sources of their ideas and habits, the course of their development from beginnings." And had he been able to complete his series he surely would have joined Moses Coit Tyler and John Bach McMaster as one of the great founders of American social history. Unfortunately he came to history too late in life and with too expansive a plan. After publishing the second volume in the series, *The Transit of Civilization,* he died in 1902.

Thus, in history as in literature, Edward Eggleston remains an important but decidedly minor figure.

—Bruce A. Lohof

EMERSON, Ralph Waldo. American. Born in Boston, Massachusetts, 25 May 1803. Educated at Harvard University, Cambridge, Massachusetts, graduated 1821; studied for the ministry. Married 1) Ellen Louisa Tucker in 1829 (died, 1831); 2) Lydia Jackson in 1835, one son. Worked for a time as a schoolmaster; Pastor, Old Second Church of Boston (Unitarian), 1829 until he retired from the ministry, 1832; visited Europe, 1832–33; moved to Concord, Massachusetts, 1834; one of the leaders of the Transcendental Club, and contributor to the club's periodical *The Dial*, from 1840; lectured in England, 1847–48. LL.D.: Harvard University, 1866. *Died 27 April 1882.*

PUBLICATIONS

Collections

Complete Works. 12 vols., 1883–93; edited by Edward Waldo Emerson, 12 vols., 1903–04.
Letters, edited by Ralph L. Rusk. 6 vols., 1939.
The Portable Emerson, edited by Mark Van Doren. 1946.
Collected Works, edited by Alfred R. Ferguson. 1971–

Verse

Poems. 1847.
Selected Poems. 1876.

Other

Nature. 1836; edited by Kenneth W. Cameron, 1940.
Essays. 1841; revised edition, as *Essays: First Series*, 1847; *Second Series*, 1844; revised edition, 1850.
The Young American. 1844.
Nature: An Essay, and Lectures of the Times. 1844.
Orations, Lectures, and Addresses. 1844.
Nature: Addresses and Lectures. 1849.
Representative Men: Seven Lectures. 1850.
English Traits. 1856; edited by Howard Mumford Jones, 1966.
The Conduct of Life. 1860.
Complete Works. 2 vols., 1866.
May-Day and Other Pieces. 1867.
Prose Works. 3 vols., 1868–78(?).
Society and Solitude. 1870.
Letters and Social Aims. 1876.
The Preacher. 1880.
The Correspondence of Carlyle and Emerson 1834–1872, edited by Charles Eliot Norton. 2 vols., 1883; supplement, 1886; edited by Joseph Slater, 1964.
The Senses and the Soul, and Moral Sentiment in Religion: Two Essays. 1884.
Two Unpublished Essays: The Character of Socrates, The Present State of Ethical Philosophy. 1896.
Journals 1820–76, edited by Edward Waldo Emerson and Waldo Emerson Forbes. 10 vols., 1909–14.

Uncollected Writings, edited by Charles C. Bigelow. 1912.
Uncollected Lectures, edited by Clarence Gohdea. 1932.
Young Emerson Speaks: Unpublished Discourses on Many Subjects, edited by Arthur Cushman McGiffert, Jr. 1938.
The Early Lectures, edited by Stephen E. Whicher, Robert E. Spiller, and Wallace E. Williams. 3 vols., 1959–72.
The Journals and Miscellaneous Notebooks, edited by William H. Gilman. 14 vols. (of 16), 1960–78.

Editor, *Essays and Poems*, by Jones Very. 1839.
Editor, with James Freeman Clarke and W. H. Channing, *Memoirs of Margaret Fuller Ossoli*. 2 vols., 1852.
Editor, *Excursions*, by Henry David Thoreau. 1863.
Editor, *Letters to Various Persons*, by Henry David Thoreau. 1865.
Editor, *Parnassus* (verse anthology). 1875.

Translator, *Vita Nuova*, by Dante, edited by J. Chesley Mathews. 1960.

Bibliography: *A Bibliography of Emerson* by George Willis Cooke, 1908; in *Bibliography of American Literature* by Jacob Blanck, 1959.

Reading List: *The Life of Emerson* by Ralph L. Rusk, 1949; *Spires of Form: A Study of Emerson's Aesthetic Theory* by Vivian C. Hopkins, 1951; *Emerson's Angle of Vision: Man and Nature in American Experience* by Sherman Paul, 1952; *Emerson Handbook* by Frederic I. Carpenter, 1953; *Freedom and Fate: An Inner Life of Emerson* by Stephen E. Whicher, 1953; *Emerson: A Collection of Critical Essays*, edited by Milton R. Konvitz and Stephen E. Whicher, 1962; *Emerson: A Portrait* edited by Carl Bode, 1968; *The Recognition of Emerson: Selected Criticism since 1837* edited by Milton R. Konvitz, 1972; *Emerson: Portrait of a Balanced Soul* by Edward Wagenknecht, 1973; *Emerson as Poet* by Hyatt H. Waggoner, 1974; *Emerson: Prophecy, Metamorphosis, and Influence* edited by David Levin, 1975; *The Slender Human Word: Emerson's Artistry in Prose* by William J. Scheick, 1978.

*   *   *

Ralph Waldo Emerson was the most distinguished of the New England Transcendentalists and one of the most brilliant American poets and thinkers of the nineteenth century. Although Transcendentalism as a mode of Romantic thought has been largely discredited by modern scientific theory, Emerson's essays and poems remain remarkably provocative – and much more tough-minded than they have frequently been given credit for being.

Emerson was not a highly systematic philosopher. His thought was an amalgam from a wide variety of sources: (1) New England religious thought and related English writings of the seventeenth and eighteenth centuries; (2) Scottish realism, which he absorbed principally while at Harvard college; (3) French and English skepticism, the lasting effects of which should not be underestimated; (4) Neo-Platonism, the dominant element in his thought, especially as it was interpreted by the English Romantic poets and the German and French Idealists; (5) Oriental mystical writings, even though he never accepted their fatalism or their concept of transmigration; (6) Yankee pragmatism, which was latent in almost all of his work and which muted his Romantic Idealism, especially in his essays on political and economic affairs. In Coleridge's explanation of Platonic dualism Emerson found the ordering principle for these disparate strands of thought. The discovery of Coleridge's distinction between the Reason and the Understanding brought such a surge of confidence in him that it is hardly an exaggeration to say that it transformed Emerson's life. Certainly it transformed his thinking.

Within one great Unity, he came to believe, there are two levels of reality, the supernatural and the natural. The supernatural is essence, spirit, or Oversoul as Emerson most frequently called it. It is an impersonal force that is eternal, moral, harmonious, and beneficent in tendency. The individual soul is a part of the Oversoul, and man has access to it through his intuition (which like Coleridge Emerson called the Reason, thereby confusing his readers then and now). One of the tendencies of the Oversoul is to express itself in form, hence the world of nature as an emanation of the world of spirit. The individual has access to this secondary level of reality through the senses and the understanding (the rational faculty). To explain the relation between the spiritual and physical levels of being Emerson used such oppositions as One and Many, cause and effect, unity and diversity, object and symbol, reality and appearance, truths and hypothesis, being and becoming. Since laws of correspondence relate the two levels of being, the study of physical laws can generate intuitions of spiritual truths. What especially delighted Emerson about this dualism was that it allowed him to entertain both faith and doubt: to accept the promptings of the intuition without question and yet to view the hypotheses of the understanding as only tentative and hence constantly open to question.

In his earlier essays, Emerson particularly stressed the unlimited potential of the individual. The most notable of these, *Nature* (1836), argues that, although nature serves as commodity, beauty, language, and discipline, its most important function is to excite the intuition so that the individual through a mystical experience becomes aware of the power of the Oversoul residing within him. "Nature always speaks of Spirit. It suggests the absolute." "The American Scholar" (1837) warns that books and scholarship can divert one from seeking the spiritual power within, and the "Divinity School Address" (1838) suggests that historical Christianity can do the same. "Self Reliance" (1844), in metaphor after metaphor, challenges the reader to seek the truths of the Reason: "Trust thyself; every heart vibrates to that iron string." In many respects "Self Reliance" is the capstone of American Romanticism. Later essays are more guarded in announcing the individual's limitless potential. In "Experience" (1844), for example, he admits that such this-world elements as health, temperament, and illusion can prevent one from exploiting all of the vast possibilities asserted in *Nature*. The enormous confidence of his earlier essays dwindles to "Patience and Patience, we shall win at last."

On subjects of public interest, Emerson's philosophical liberalism had to contend with his pragmatism. At most he was a cautious liberal. The Democrats, he thought, had the better causes, the Whigs the better men. Following Adam Smith, he believed that "affairs themselves show the best way they should be handled." So he was for *laissez-faire* and free trade, though he was more of an agrarian than Smith. Of the followers of Smith he rejected the utilitarians and the pessimists, and approved of only the optimists, particularly such members of the American school as Daniel Raymond, A. H. Everett, and Henry C. Carey. Emerson had nothing against wealth *per se*, but was against rule by the wealthy because the wealthy were too likely to be nothing more than materialists, persons without intuitive insight. Rule by an upper class, however, was agreeable to him so long as the upper class consisted of persons who are wise, temperate, and cultivated, persons who have the insight and courage necessary to protect the poor and weak against the predatory. Clearly his thinking did not drift far in the direction of Marxism. Nor was he willing to admit that the socialistic experiments of Owen and Fourier, though he admired their objectives, had the magic key to Utopia. Even the Transcendental experiments at Fruitlands and Brook Farm he believed impractical. Bereft of their romance, he said, they were projects that well might make their participants less intuitive and self-reliant rather than more so. Of the other major reforms of his day, Emerson lectured only in favor of child labor legislation, a public land policy, and the abolition of slavery. The passage of the Fugitive Slave Bill in 1850 made him as angry as he probably ever became on a public issue. More practical than most abolitionists, however, he argued that slavery was basically an economic matter, and that if the Northern church people really wanted to emancipate the slaves they should sell their church silver, buy up the slaves, and themselves set them free. He saw the Civil War not only as necessary for liberating the slave but "a hope for the liberation of American culture."

Emerson's aesthetic theory, to the extent that he had one, is a direct outgrowth of his Idealistic philosophy. As he conceived of it, the great work of art is not an imitation of nature but a symbolization of Truth realized intuitively. It is the result of resigning oneself to the "divine *aura* which breathes through forms." In his most quoted statement on the subject he put it this way: "It is not metres, but a metre-making argument that makes a poem – a thought so passionate and alive that like the spirit of a plant or animal it has an architecture of its own, and adorns nature with a new thing." Thus the poet (or any great artist) must first of all be the Seer, intuitively experiencing the absolutes of the Oversoul, and secondly the Sayer, communicating those absolutes so compellingly that readers are stimulated to have intuitions of their own. Emerson was realistic enough to realize that such a process is not easy. Intuitions fade quickly. And words, being but symbols of symbols, are inadequate even at best to convey them. The most that a writer can do is to suggest his intuitions by a series of half-truths. The greatest writing, therefore, must be provocative, not descriptive or explanatory. Such a conviction lies behind Emerson's epigrammatic prose style and the liberties he takes with poetic conventions.

There is a good reason for considering Emerson as primarily a poet even though one must go to his journals and essays to realize the fullness of his thought. His concentration on the concrete image, the simplicity of his symbols and words, and his willingness within limits to let form follow function were practices that profoundly influenced such widely divergent followers as Whitman and Dickinson and through them much of modern poetry. Many of Emerson's best-known poems, such as "Concord Hymn" and "The Snow Storm," celebrate local events. But his more notable ones give expression to elements of his philosophy. Through the voice of the cosmic force, "Brahma" suggests the enclosure of all diversity in the one great Unity; so does "Each and All" in which the beauty and meaning of "each" is seen to be dependent upon its context, or the "all." "The Problem" contrasts the unlimited freedom of the poet's imagination with the stultifying routine of the "cowed churchman." Perhaps Emerson's most poignant poem is "Threnody," written in two periods after the death of his young son Waldo. The first part, composed immediately after Waldo's death, describes the poet's disillusionment with nature, indeed with the cosmic scheme, which he had spent so many years celebrating. The second part, written several years later, asserts his resurgent confidence. Nathaniel Hawthorne probably spoke for some modern readers when he said that he "admired Emerson as a poet of deep beauty and austere tenderness, but sought nothing from him as a philosopher." Yet his philosophy cannot be dismissed so summarily. It resulted in a freedom of spirit, a respect for the individual human being, a sense of awe and wonder before the inexplicable that many modern readers still find stirring and reassuring.

—John C. Gerber

FIELD, Eugene. American. Born in St. Louis, Missouri, 3 September 1850; moved to Amherst, Massachusetts, 1856. Educated at Williams College, Williamstown, Massachusetts, 1868–69; Knox College, Galesburg, Illinois, 1869–70; University of Missouri, Columbia, 1870–71. Married Julia Sutherland Comstock in 1873; eight children. Travelled in Europe, 1872; worked as a reporter for the St. Joseph, Missouri, *Gazette*, St. Louus *Journal*, Kansas City, Missouri, *Times*, and the Denver *Tribune*, 1873–83; Columnist ("Sharps and Flats"), Chicago *Morning News*, later called the Chicago *Record*, 1883–1895. *Died 4 November 1895.*

PUBLICATIONS

Collections

Writings in Prose and Verse. 10 vols., 1896.
Hoosier Lyrics, edited by Charles Walter Brown. 1905.
Poems, Complete Edition. 1910.

Verse

A Little Book of Western Verse. 1889.
Echoes from the Sabine Farm, Being Certain Horatian Lyrics, with Roswell M. Field. 1891; revised edition, 1893.
Second Book of Verse. 1892.
Love-Songs of Childhood. 1894.
Songs and Other Verse. 1896.
A Little Book of Tribune Verse: A Collection of Hitherto Uncollected Poems, Grave and Gay, edited by Joseph G. Brown. 1901.

Fiction

A Little Book of Profitable Tales. 1889.
The Holy-Cross and Other Tales. 1893.
The House: An Episode in the Life of Reuben Baker, Astronomer, and of His Wife Alice. 1896.
Second Book of Tales. 1896.
The Stars: A Slumber Story, edited by Will M. Clemens. 1901.

Other

Tribune Primer. 1881.
The Model Primer. 1882.
Culture's Garland, Being Memoranda of the Gradual Rise of Literature, Art, Music, and Society in Chicago and Other Western Ganglia. 1887.
With Trumpet and Drum. 1892.
The Love Affairs of a Bibliomaniac. 1896.
Field to Francis Wilson: Some Attentions. 1896.
The Eugene Field Book: Verses, Stories, and Letters, edited by Mary E. Burt and Mary B. Cable. 1898.
Sharps and Flats, edited by Slason Thompson. 2 vols., 1900.

Clippings from Denver Tribune 1881–1883, edited by Willard S. Morse.   1909.
Verse and Prose from the George H. Yenowine Collection, edited by Henry H. Harper.
   1917.
Some Love Letters.   1927.

Reading List: *Field's Creative Years* by Charles H. Dennis, 1924; *Life of Field, The Poet of Childhood* by Slason Thompson, 1927; *The Gay Poet: The Story of Field* by Jeannette C. Nolan, 1940; *Field Days: The Life, Times, and Reputation of Field* by Robert Conrow, 1974.

*   *   *

Eugene Field's was a motley genius, for he was a modern jester, the man and his works being a puzzling combination of perverse contrasts. Field is generally remembered as a children's writer of charming if dated bits of verse like "Little Boy Blue" and "Wynken, Blynken, and Nod," yet he still enjoys a sub rosa reputation for off-color lines, his "Little Willie" perhaps the best known of these naughty verses. Field openly professed a dislike for children – other than his own – and his *Tribune Primer,* written in sardonic imitation of grade-school readers, encourages young folks to cultivate the aquaintanceship of wasps and gluepots. While capable of turning out in apparent sincerity the most pious of verses like "The Divine Lullaby," Field was the libidinous originator of pornographic exercises which, like "Bangin' on the Rhine," enjoyed a long underground life even before seeing formal (if surreptitious) print.
   Commencing his career as a newspaper columnist of the humorous one-liner breed, Field, despite his New England birth and education, was fond of identifying himself with the West, hence with the vital western tradition of journalism that produced Mark Twain, Ambrose Bierce, and (closer in generation and region to Field) James Whitcomb Riley. It is a tradition that accommodates Field's many sides, his love of hoaxes, his use of public print to roast friends and enemies alike, his fierce (in all senses) loyalties, his displays of saccharine sentimentality, and his airing of public dislikes and private passions. Most of what he wrote did not outlive him, and he died relatively young, at the height of his career and powers. Though he was a skillfull and witty occasional poet, that alone doomed his work to ephemerality. The best of his writing is the early dialect verse which in its masculine vitality and mining-camp settings anticipates Robert Service and parallels in chronology and spirit Kipling's barracks-room voice.
   Field possessed a genuinely comic sense, which from his inveterate love of practical jokes to his humorous verse and prose, was thoroughly of his times and did not transcend them. He was a classic instance of Victorian madness, in which dilettantism took on a thoroughly middle-class, cigar-smoking, feet-on-desk pose, and self-conscious archaicism gained a popular audience. Born in 1850, he was absolutely in synchronization with his half-century, and died, most timely, five years before it ran out.

—Catherine Seelye

FITCH, (William) Clyde.   American.   Born in Elmira, New York, 2 May 1865; moved with his family to Schenectady, New York, 1869. Educated at a high school in Hartford, Connecticut, and at a college preparatory school in Holderness, New Hampshire; Amherst College, Massachusetts, 1882–86 (Editor, *Student*), B.A. 1886, M.A. 1902. Settled in New

York, 1886; wrote for *Life* and *Puck*, and worked as a tutor; visited Paris and London, and met various writers of the aesthetic movement, 1888; returned to New York, and supported himself by writing children's stories for the *Churchman*, *Independent*, and other magazines; began writing for the stage; full-time playwright and producer/director of his own plays from 1898. *Died 4 September 1909.*

PUBLICATIONS

Collections

> *Plays* (includes *Beau Brummell, Lovers' Lane, Nathan Hale, Barbara Frietchie, Captain Jinks of the Horse Marines, The Climbers, The Stubbornness of Geraldine, The Girl with the Green Eyes, Her Own Way, The Woman in the Case, The Truth, The City*), edited by Montrose Moses and Virginia Gerson.   4 vols., 1915.

Plays

> *Beau Brummell* (produced 1890).   1908; in *Plays*, 1915.
> *Frédéric Lemaître* (produced 1890).   Edited by Oscar Cargill, in *The Social Revolt*, 1933.
> *Betty's Finish* (produced 1890).
> *Pamela's Prodigy* (produced 1891).   1893.
> *A Modern Match* (produced 1892; as *Marriage*, produced 1892).
> *The Masked Ball*, from a play by A. Bisson (produced 1892).
> *The Moth and the Flame* (as *The Harvest*, produced 1893; revised version, as *The Moth and the Flame*, produced 1898).   1908; edited by Montrose Moses, in *Representative Plays*, 1921.
> *April Weather* (produced 1893).
> *A Shattered Idol*, from a novel by Balzac (produced 1893).
> *The Social Swim*, from a play by Sardou (produced 1893).
> *An American Duchess*, from a play by Henri Lavedan (produced 1893).
> *Mrs. Grundy, Jr.*, from a French play (produced 1893).
> *His Grace de Grammont* (produced 1894).
> *Gossip*, with Leo Ditrichstein, from a play by Jules Claretie (produced 1895).
> *Mistress Betty* (produced 1895; revised version, as *The Toast of the Town*, produced 1905).
> *Bohemia*, from a play by Théodore Barrière (produced 1896).
> *The Liar*, from a play by A. Bisson (produced 1896).
> *A Superfluous Husband*, with Leo Ditrichstein, from a play by Ludwig Fulda (produced 1897).
> *The Head of the Family*, with Leo Ditrichstein, from a play by A. L'Arronge (produced 1898).
> *Nathan Hale* (produced 1898).   1899; in *Plays*, 1915.
> *The Merry-Go-Round*, with F. Kinsey Peile (produced 1898).
> *The Cowboy and the Lady* (produced 1899).   1908.
> *Barbara Frietchie, The Frederick Girl* (produced 1899).   1900; in *Plays*, 1915.
> *Sapho*, from the play by Daudet and Belot, based on the story by Daudet (produced 1899).
> *Captain Jinks of the Horse Marines* (produced 1901).   1902; in *Plays*, 1915.
> *The Climbers* (produced 1901).   1905; in *Plays*, 1915.

Lovers' Lane (produced 1901). In *Plays*, 1915.

The Marriage Game, from a play by Emile Augier (produced 1901).

The Last of the Dandies (produced 1901).

The Way of the World (produced 1901).

The Girl and the Judge (produced 1901).

The Stubbornness of Geraldine (produced 1902). 1906; in *Plays*, 1915.

The Girl with the Green Eyes (produced 1902). 1905; in *Plays*, 1915.

The Bird in the Cage, from a play by E. von Wildenbruch (produced 1903).

The Frisky Mrs. Johnson, from a play by Paul Gavault and Georges Beer (produced 1903). 1906.

Her Own Way (produced 1903). 1907; in *Plays*, 1915.

Algy (produced 1903).

Major André (produced 1903).

Glad of It (produced 1903).

The Coronet of a Duchess (produced 1904).

Granny, from a play by Georges Michel (produced 1904).

Cousin Billy, from a play by Labiche and Martin (produced 1905).

The Woman in the Case (produced 1905). In *Plays*, 1915.

Her Great Match (produced 1905). Edited by A. H. Quinn, in *Representative American Plays*, 1917.

Wolfville, with Willis Steell, from a novel by Alfred Henry Lewis (produced 1905).

Toddles, from a play by Godferneaux and Bernard (produced 1906).

The House of Mirth, with Edith Wharton, from the novel by Wharton (produced 1906).

The Girl Who Has Everything (produced 1906).

The Straight Road (produced 1906).

The Truth (produced 1907). 1909; in *Plays*, 1915.

Miss McCobb, Manicurist (produced 1907).

Her Sister, with Cosmo Gordon-Lennox (produced 1907).

The Honor of the Family, from a play by A. Fabre based on a novel by Balzac (produced 1908).

Girls, from a play by Alexander Engel and Julius Horst (produced 1908).

The Blue Mouse, from a play by Alexander Engel and Julius Horst (produced 1908).

A Happy Marriage (produced 1909).

The Bachelor (produced 1909).

The City: A Modern Play of American Life (produced 1909). In *Plays*, 1915.

Fiction

The Knighting of the Twins and Ten Other Tales (juvenile). 1891.

A Wave of Life. 1909.

Other

Some Correspondence and Six Conversations. 1896.

The Smart Set: Correspondence and Conversations. 1897.

Clyde Fitch and His Letters, edited by Montrose Moses and Virginia Gerson. 1924.

*   *   *

No playwright in the history of American drama has been able to match the commercial success of Clyde Fitch and at the same time achieve the international reputation that his work brought him. Many have written better plays; probably some have made more money; but none has equalled his accumulative successes. Clearly aided by the copyright law of 1891 and his membership in the "Syndicate School," Fitch produced a considerable body of work (more than 50 plays, including many adaptations of foreign works), became the first millionaire dramatist in America, and showed himself to be not just an extremely colorful man of the theatre but a dramatist of some sensitivity whose plays were produced in several countries.

His theory of playwriting reflected the prevailing nineteenth-century attitudes toward literature and art. "Try to be truthful," Fitch explained, true to the details of life and environment which he saw, true to every emotion, every motive, every occupation, every class. Fitch himself was most successful in portraying the upper levels of society which in a few plays occasionally reflected the realistic and truthful detail of noteworthy drama. In most instances, however, his concern for truth lacked the necessary perspective, and he simply imitated the popular melodramatic caricature of life with an excess of what became recognized as "Fitchian detail."

As a flamboyant man-about-town Fitch enjoyed the places frequented by New York society. The problems of married life, the peculiarities of individuals, the faults and foibles of a rapidly changing society – these were the aspects of life which appealed to Fitch and which he tried to picture truthfully in his plays. His first full-length social drama was *A Modern Match*, concerned with a selfish woman who refused to assume the responsibilities of marriage. *The Climbers* is one of his better social melodramas, ridiculing the hypocrisy and materialism of New York society. *The Stubbornness of Geraldine* and *Her Great Match* reflect the international social scene. In *The Truth*, concerned with a pathological liar, and *The Girl with the Green Eyes*, which dramatized what he termed an "inherited" jealousy, Fitch was at his melodramatic best, using the particular personal insight which distinguished the plays. In his final play, *The City*, he attempted to present a serious view of city life disintegrating under a weight of moral, economic, and political problems, but the lighter and satiric view of high society was his proper métier.

As one who prepared the way for an established social comedy in America Fitch deserves attention. He was above all a man of that society, and a craftsman of the commercial theatre whose interest in truthfulness in drama helped him create some believable characters and memorable social scenes against a background of melodrama.

—Walter J. Meserve

FOSTER, Hannah (Webster). American. Born in Boston in 1759. Nothing is known about her early life and education. Married the Reverend John Foster in 1785; two daughters. Writer from c. 1780; lived in her husband's parish of Brighton, Massachusetts, until his death, then settled with her daughters in Montreal. *Died 17 April 1840.*

PUBLICATIONS

Fiction

The Coquette; or, The History of Eliza Wharton. 1797.
The Boarding School; or, Lessons of a Preceptress to Her Pupils. 1798.

Bibliography: in *Bibliography of American Literature* by Jacob Blanck, 1959.

*   *   *

Two of the earliest essays into American fiction were designed to "expose the dangerous consequences of seduction." William Hill Brown's *The Power of Sympathy* and Hannah Foster's *The Coquette* are cut from the same Richardsonian pattern. Of the two the more convincing and more durable is the Foster book. Better constructed and more single-minded in its purpose, it can still appeal to readers today.

Moreover, *The Coquette* is based on fact and thus achieves a kind of realism that was more becoming to American rather than English taste. Eliza Wharton, the heroine, was in reality Elizabeth Whitman and her lover was Pierpont Edwards, both of good Massachusetts families. The newspaper accounts tell of her elopement with him and of her death in the Bell Tavern in Danvers, Massachusetts. A secret marriage is hinted at, but that part of the story remains a mystery. These events took place ten years before the appearance of the novel; but even more compelling is the fact that Hannah Foster's husband was the cousin of the wife of Deacon John Whitman of Stow, himself a cousin of Elizabeth Whitman's father. It seems probable that Hannah Foster, through these family connections was in possession of the facts.

The Coquette is an imitation of Richardson's *Clarissa Harlowe*, but it is one of the most successful in a long series of seduction novels written in that period. The characters of Major Peter Sanford, the seducer, and Eliza Wharton are convincing and straightforward. The other characters are skillfully used to build the plot and comment on the unfortunate lovers, so that the reader's attention never moves away from the unfolding tragedy. The motivation is real and the moments of tortured self-revelation raise the novel above the sensationalism and sentimentality of many novels of this genre. Moreover, Foster does not fall into the obvious excesses of the epistolary form; she does not tax the credulity of the reader, nor does she intrude with tedious editorializing.

—Dominic J. Bisignano

FOSTER, Stephen Collins.   American.   Born in Pittsburgh, Pennsylvania, 4 July 1826. Studied privately, Allegheny, Pennsylvania; at Towanda Academy, Pennsylvania, 1841; Athens Academy, Tioga Point, Pennsylvania, 1840–41; Jefferson College, Canonsburg, Pennsylvania, 1841. Married Jane McDowell in 1850; one daughter. Worked as a bookkeeper for his brother, Cincinnati, 1847; thereafter made song writing his life's work: contracted to Firth Pond and Company from 1849. *Died 13 January 1864.*

PUBLICATIONS

Collections

The Melodies.   1909.
Foster's Forgotten Songs, edited by Hamilton A. Gordon. 1941.
A Treasury of Foster.   1946.

Bibliography: *A Pictorial Bibliography of the First Editions* by James J. Fuld, 1957.

Reading List: *Foster, America's Troubadour,* 1935, and *The Literature of Foster,* 1944, both by John T. Howard; *Foster, Boy Minstrel* by Helen B. Higgins, 1944; *The Songs of Foster* by William W. Austin, 1975.

*   *   *

While Stephen Collins Foster's literary output is inextricably linked to the music to which he set it, he must nevertheless be considered as a poet, and more influential in his writing of words than of music. The abstract art of his music surrounds and complements his lyrics in an inimitable Bellinian "simplicity of genius," but his carefully crafted words ultimately reflect and refine the mores of American society in the pre-Civil War period: optimistic, sentimental, patriotic, and proudly unsophisticated.

Foster has been criticised as too sentimental, as having embodied the patronising racism of his time, and of having been not a poet at all but a musician who wrote some of his own lyrics. About a third of Foster's 180-odd songs were, it is true, written to the texts of others, but only two or three of these have survived among the forty and more Foster songs with which most Americans are familiar. As a musician, he responded best to himself as poet.

Of Foster's own lyrics, most, and the most important, form two groups: the sentimental ballad and the Negro dialect song. His few political, patriotic, and non-dialect comic lyrics are neither greatly distinguished in themselves nor sources of memorable musical accompaniments. The sentimental ballads, such as "Beautiful Dreamer," "Come Where My Love Lies Dreaming," and "Jeannie with the Light Brown Hair" are comparable in intensity of emotion to, and less pretentious stylistically than, the sentimental poetry of such contemporaries as Poe and Lanier. At the same time, his lyrics are more metrically and verbally sophisticated than those of his contemporaries who wrote not as poets but only as lyricists.

The Negro-dialect lyrics, or "Etheopian Songs" as they were popularly known, demonstrate Foster's keen ear for the rhythms and patterns of black speech. In his earliest efforts, such as "Oh Susanna" and "Old Folks at Home," some crudities and a tendency to see the black, slave or free, as a happy buffoon, can be traced. But the poet's close observation of blacks for both poetic and musical veracity resulted in a gradual and progressive move away from stereotype to the image of the black person as dignified, sensitive, and empathetic rather than simple and ridiculous. He jettisoned objectionable words commonly descriptive of blacks, leading to later lyrics such as "Old Black Joe" in which dialect disappears entirely, though by then his grasp of it, in "Nelly Bly," "My Old Kentucky Home," and "Massa's in de Cold Ground" demonstrate a command equal to Sidney Lanier's of the contemporary white southerner.

The Civil War, which abolished black servitude and replaced sentimentality with expansionism and urbanism, cut off the possibility of Foster's being an influence on the poetry which followed his death, and froze him into the posture of a spokesman for a vanished age. The strong American sense of nostalgia has thus deified him, and the mythic figure thus created has so far repelled any serious study of his considerable talents as a poet.

—William J. Collins

FREDERIC, Harold. American. Born in Utica, New York, 19 August 1856. Educated at the Advanced School, Utica, graduated 1871. Married Grace Williams in 1877, one daughter and three sons; also had two daughters and one son by Kate Lyon. Worked in Boston, 1873–74; Proofreader, *Utica Morning Herald*, 1875; Reporter, 1875–80, and Editor, 1880–81, *Utica Observer*; Editor, *Evening Journal*, Albany, New York, 1882–84; settled in London, 1884: London Correspondent of the *New York Times*, 1884 until his death. *Died 19 October 1898.*

Publications

Collections

> *Stories of York State*, edited by Thomas F. O'Donnell.   1966.

Fiction

> *Seth's Brother's Wife: A Study of Life in the Greater New York.*   1887.
> *The Lawton Girl.*   1890
> *In the Valley.*   1890.
> *The Return of the O'Mahony.*   1892.
> *The Copperhead.*   1893.
> *The Copperhead and Other Stories of the North During the American War.*   1894.
> *Marsena and Other Stories of the Wartime.*   1894.
> *The Damnation of Theron Ware.*   1896; as *Illumination*, 1896; edited by Everett Carter, 1960.
> *Mrs. Albert Grundy: Observations in Philistia.*   1896.
> *March Hares.*   1896.
> *In the Sixties* (stories).   1897.
> *Gloria Mundi.*   1898; abridged version, as *Pomps and Vanities*, 1913.
> *The Deserter and Other Stories: A Book of Two Wars.*   1898.
> *The Market-Place.*   1899.

Other

> *The Young Emperor William II of Germany: A Study in Character Development on a Throne.*   1891.
> *The New Exodus: A Study of Israel in Russia.*   1892.

Bibliography: *A Bibliography of Writings by and about Frederic* by Thomas F. O'Donnell, Stanton Garner, and Robert H. Woodward, 1975.

Reading List: *Frederic* by Thomas F. O'Donnell and Hoyt C. Franchere, 1961; *The Novels of Frederic* by Austin E. Briggs, 1969; *Frederic* by Stanton Garner, 1969.

*   *   *

Two distinct strains, realistic and romantic, intermix in Harold Frederic's fiction. He regarded Erckmann-Chatrian and Hawthorne as the principal influences on his own work. His reading of popular romance, together with qualities inherent in his temperament and the pattern of his career, manifests itself in certain romantic effects. He lapses into melodrama and sentimentality and recurrently draws central figures who are young, hopeful, naive, and embarked on fairy-tale adventures of personal fulfilment. Frederic's romanticism matures in the brief course of his writing career, however, from an initial school-boy emulation of Erckmann-Chatrian in the earliest stories towards a Hawthorne-like probing of the ambiguities manifest in human character, and of the inner and outer pressures that determine behavior. Frederic's reputation and his distinctive character as a writer depend primarily on his talents as a realist who exploited materials pertaining to the Mohawk Valley region of New York. In the autobiographical derivation of his fiction, in his faithful representation of everyday language, behavior, and scene, and in his dramatic method (i.e., his letting the tale tell itself rather than interpreting it for the reader) Frederic has been compared to William Dean Howells, whom he greatly admired. His essentially comic vision also associates him with Howells and with an underlying American optimism ultimately deriving from Emerson.

Frederic's first novel, *Seth's Brother's Wife*, his masterwork *The Damnation of Theron Ware*, and his best stories are all realistic. They draw upon his childhood experiences in a working-class, Methodist home during the Civil War era and upon his subsequent observations as a photographer's apprentice and a journalist in upstate New York. Seth is a young journalist variously involved with his job, politics, and his brother's wife, his story enacted against the dreary background of a poor upstate farming district. Theron Ware is a small-town Methodist minister whose intellectual, aesthetic, and sexual initiations under the influence of town sophisticates paradoxically result in both *éclaircissement* and moral degeneration. Here as elsewhere Frederic's overt treatment of sexuality and his preoccupation with the type of the modern woman are manifest. The Civil War stories are highly original, dealing with ambivalent attitudes toward the war and with its effects upon civilians at home rather than celebrating military heroics. Written in 1891–92, these have been collected in a modern edition as *Harold Frederic's Stories of York State*. *The Lawton Girl*, a moderately successful sequel to *Seth*, and *In the Valley*, a historical romance of the Revolutionary War, are also set in the Mohawk Valley.

Frederic was a highly successful foreign correspondent, and this activity represented a second career in part motivated by financial objectives. All his fiction except the early stories was written in England, and he initially attempted to assimilate European materials in *The Return of the O'Mahony*. This far-fetched, comical, trivial romance is Frederic's deepest plunge into Irish folk materials, although folklore, legend, and genealogy interested him throughout his career, and his interest in the New York Irish predated his journalistic immersion in Irish politics. *March Hares*, set in London, is believed to be a fictional celebration of Frederic's liaison with Kate Lyon. Its deft, urbane, and comic tone, characteristic of Frederic's mature voice, is reminiscent of that of his bachelor narrator in *Mrs. Albert Grundy*, a series of fictionalized satirical sketches orginally published in the *National Observer* as "Observations in Philistia."

In his last two novels, *Gloria Mundi* and *The Market-Place*, Frederic makes his most serious attempts to discover European materials of sufficient richness to replace the New York regionalist material that he had substantially worked through. Of these *Gloria Mundi*, a Cinderella tale of a young man's coming into a dukedom and an inheritance, is the less successful. Frederic was ill-advised to attempt the depiction of a social milieu inaccessible to him, and the novel lacks the authenticity that characterizes his scene-painting of rural New York. In *The Market-Place*, however, a romance of commercial enterprise dealing with life in the City and with the interaction of political and philanthropic motives, Frederic opens up a vein of material that he might easily have exploited thereafter. Taken together, the central figures of *Theron Ware*, *Gloria Mundi*, and *The Market-Place* manifest a deepening psychological insight and an ever-increasing subtlety and ambiguity in rendering the relationships between character and environment. The peculiar strength of *Theron Ware*, which is generally regarded as a minor classic, may in fact derive from its bringing together the New York regionalist material at which Frederic was a sure hand, with his increasingly subtle probing into the forces that shape and thwart human development.

Frederic's novels reveal curious intermixtures of disparate treatment, material, and attitudes within individual works. Some of the inconsistencies might result from lack of revision, but a sort of intellectual omnivorousness characterizes Frederic. Nonetheless, the diversity of his talents, attitudes, and experiments is in itself remarkable. His novels characteristically reveal multiple perspectives, a tendency to view experience from more than one point of view. The problem of distinguishing between mere inconsistencies and calculated ironies is a crux in assessing individual works fairly and in forming a conclusive judgment of his achievement as a novelist.

—Jean Frantz Blackall

FREEMAN, Mary E(leanor) Wilkins.   American.   Born in Randolph, Massachusetts, 31 October 1852; brought up in Randolph, then in Brattleboro, Vermont; returned to Randolph, 1883. Educated at Brattleboro High School, graduated 1870; Mount Holyoke Female Seminary, South Hadley, Massachusetts, 1870–71; Glenwood Seminary, West Brattleboro, 1871. Married Dr. Charles M. Freeman in 1902 (separated, 1922; died, 1923). Settled in Metuchen, New Jersey, 1902, and remained there for the rest of her life. Recipient: Howells Medal, 1925. Member, National Institue of Arts and Letters, 1926. *Died 13 March 1930.*

PUBLICATIONS

Fiction

   A Humble Romance and Other Stories.   1887; as *A Far-Away Melody and Other Stories,* 1890.
   A New England Nun and Other Stories.   1891.
   Jane Field.   1892.
   Pembroke.   1894; edited by P. D. Westbrook, 1971.
   Madelon.   1896.
   Jerome, A Poor Man.   1897.
   Silence and Other Stories.   1898.
   The People of Our Neighbourhood.   1898; as *Some of Our Neighbours,* 1898.
   The Jamesons.   1899.
   In Colonial Times.   1899.
   The Heart's Highway: A Romance of Virginia in the Seventeenth Century.   1900.
   The Love of Parson Lord and Other Stories.   1900.
   Understudies (stories).   1901.
   The Portion of Labor.   1901.
   Six Trees (stories).   1903.
   The Wind in the Rose-Bush and Other Stories of the Supernatural.   1903.
   The Givers (stories).   1904.
   The Debtor.   1905.
   "Doc" Gordon.   1906.
   By the Light of the Soul.   1907.
   The Fair Lavinia and Others.   1907.
   The Shoulders of Atlas.   1908.
   The Winning Lady and Others.   1909.

The Butterfly House. 1912.
The Yates Pride. 1912.
The Copy-Cat and Other Stories. 1914.
An Alabaster Box, with Florence Morse Kingsley. 1917.
Edgewater People (stories). 1918.
The Best Stories, edited by Henry Wysham Lanier. 1927.

Play

Giles Corey, Yeoman. 1893.

Other

Goody Two-Shoes and Other Famous Nursery Tales, with Clara Doty Bates. 1883.
Decorative Plaques (juvenile verse), designs by George F. Barnes. 1883.
The Cow with Golden Horns and Other Stories (juvenile). 1884(?).
The Adventures of Ann: Stories of Colonial Times (juvenile). 1886.
The Pot of Gold and Other Stories (juvenile). 1892.
Young Lucretia and Other Stories (juvenile). 1892.
Comfort Pease and Her Gold Ring (juvenile). 1895.
Once upon a Time and Other Child-Verses. 1897.
The Green Door (juvenile). 1910.

Bibliography: in *Bibliography of American Literature* by Jacob Blanck, 1959.

Reading List: *Freeman* by Edward Foster, 1956; *Freeman* by P. D. Westbrook, 1967.

*   *   *

Mary E. Wilkins Freeman, who wrote almost exclusively about rural and village life in New England, ranks among the foremost American local colorists or regionalists. Brought up in a family of modest means and station in the small towns of Randolph, Massachusetts, and Brattleboro, Vermont, she drew the material for her fiction from her own experience; and when she started, in her early twenties, to write stories with New England settings she was hailed as an expert in the dialect, customs, and character traits of the people of her region. Thus she won a place among the early realists in American literature, receiving laudatory comments from William Dean Howells, a leader in the realist movement.

Freeman's keenest personal interest and her greatest strength were in the psychological analysis of characters representative of the final phase of Puritanism. In her day the old religion and culture lingered in the back-country, but in an advanced state of decay. This was a period in the rural areas that one literary historian felicitously described as "the terminal moraine of New England Puritanism." Among the people the old Puritan strengths had degenerated into eccentricity, neurosis, and worse; and these warpings of personality are portrayed unforgettably in Freeman's works. Especially fascinating to her was the transformation of the Puritan will – once considered to be under God's direction – into pathological compulsions and obsessions: a man who will not enter his church but sits on its porch for ten years during Sabbath services because of a minor doctrinal difference with the minister ("A Conflict Ended"); a village seamstress who faints from hunger rather than receive payment for two patchwork quilts because she keeps misplacing one rag and forces herself to redo her work twice ("An Honest Soul"); a woman who waits fifteen years for her lover to return from Australia, finds on his return that he is in love with another girl, and lives out the rest of her life in self-imposed solitude ("A New England Nun"); a young farmer who breaks his engagement with his fiancée because of an insignificant political disagreement with her father and postpones reconciliation for ten years (*Pembroke*).

Freeman's best writing is in the form of short fiction, which from the beginning of her career found ready acceptance in periodicals like *Harper's New Monthly*. The best known among the many volumes of her tales were the first two to be published – *A Humble Romance and Other Stories* and *A New England Nun and Other Stories*. Freeman also wrote a number of novels, the most notable of which are *Jane Field* and *Pembroke*, both dealing with New England village life. The latter is a powerful novel, which received the highest praise from Arthur Machen and Conan Doyle. In all her writing Freeman's style is simple and direct, though at times she proves herself adept at using symbols (the chained dog and caged canary in "A New England Nun"). At present, because of her sympathetic and realistic fictional treatment of women, she has aroused considerable interest among feminist critics in America.

—P. D. Westbrook

FRENEAU, Philip (Morin). American. Born in New York City, 2 January 1752. Educated privately, and at the College of New Jersey, now Princeton University, 1768–71. Enlisted in the militia and commanded a privateer in the Revolutionary War: captured by the British, 1780. Married Eleanor Forman in 1789. Teacher on Long Island, and at Somerset Academy, Back Creek, Maryland, 1772; Planter's Secretary, Santa Cruz, West Indies, 1776–79; worked in the Philadelphia Post Office, and helped to edit Jefferson's *Freeman's Journal*, Philadelphia, 1781–84; master of a brig bound for Jamaica, 1784, and lived in the West Indies, serving as an officer on ships in the Caribbean and Atlantic coast trade, 1784–89; Editor, *Daily Advertiser*, New York, 1790–91; Translating Clerk, United States Department of State, and Editor of the *National Gazette*, Philadelphia, 1791–93; Editor of the *Jersey Chronicle*, 1795–96, and of *The Time-Piece*, New York, 1797–98; retired from journalism, and for the rest of his life alternated between the sea and his New Jersey farm. *Died 19 December 1832.*

PUBLICATIONS

Collections

   Poems, edited by Fred Lewis Pattee.   3 vols., 1902–07.
   Poems, edited by Harry Hayden Clark.   1929.
   Prose, edited by Philip M. Marsh.   1955.
   A Freneau Sampler, edited by Philip M. Marsh.   1963.

Verse

   A Poem on the Rising Glory of America, with H. H. Brackenridge.   1772.
   The American Village.   1772.

American Liberty.   1775.
A Voyage to Boston.   1775.
General Gage's Confession.   1775.
The British Prison-Ship.   1781.
Poems.   1786; as *Poems on Various Occasions,* 1861.
A Journey from Philadelphia to New York.   1787; as *A Laughable Poem,* 1809.
The Village Merchant.   1794.
Poems Written Between the Years 1768 and 1794.   1795.
Poems.   2 vols., 1809.
A Collection of Poems on American Affairs.   2 vols., 1815.
Some Account of the Capture of the Ship Aurora, edited by Jay Miller.   1899.
Last Poems, edited by Lewis Leary.   1946.

Other

Miscellaneous Works.   1788.
Letters on Various Interesting and Important Subjects.   1799.
Unpublished Freneauiana, edited by Charles F. Heartman.   1918.
The Writings of Hezekiah Salem, edited by Lewis Leary.   1975.

Editor, *An Historical Sketch of the Life of Silas Talbot.*   1803.

Translator, *New Travels Through North America,* by Abbé Claude Robin.   1783.

Bibliography: *A Bibliography of the Separate and Collected Works of Freneau* by Victor Hugo Paltsits, 1903; in *Bibliography of American Literature* by Jacob Blanck, 1959; *Freneau's Published Prose: A Bibliography* by Philip M. Marsh, 1970.

Reading List: *That Rascal Freneau: A Study in Literary Failure* by Lewis Leary, 1941; *Freneau and the Cosmic Enigma* by Nelson F. Adkins, 1949; *Freneau, Champion of Democracy* by Jacob Axelrod, 1967; *Freneau, Poet and Journalist,* 1967, and *The Works of Freneau: A Critical Study,* 1968, both Philip M. Marsh.

*   *   *

Philip Freneau's poetry and prose reflect his life and times: he gloried in matching the image of the Enlightened gentleman-scholar, one who could be as content administering his estate as intriguing in the latest political uproar, as happy translating the classics as being the master of a ship safely brought into port. Current politics, the latest scientific discovery, the newest philosophy, the recent misfortune of a neighbor, the chance observation of a terrapin: Freneau thought all fit subjects for his pen.

Many of his poems were propaganda, either for political party or for the United States during the two wars against Great Britain. In his poems of the Revolution, he moved from personal attacks on the British ("Cain, Nimrod, Nero – fiends in human guise,/Herod, Domitian – these in judgment rise,/And, envious of his deeds, I hear them say/None but a George could be more vile than they") to calls for greater exertion by the patriots ("Rouse from your sleep, and crush the thievish band,/Defeat, destroy, and sweep them from the land"). But his War of 1812 verse is more urbane: both sides are pictured with wit and humor. Freneau's pen was also lent to other causes: for the Revolution in France, against the American lack of support for poetry ("An age employed in edging steel/Can no poetic raptures feel"), against the dislocation of the Indians, against debtors' prisons. Much of this occasional verse, written in the heat of the moment, deserves to be forgotten, but occasionally, as in "Stanzas to an Alien" or "Stanzas on the Decease of Thomas Paine," he achieves lasting feeling.

The best known of Freneau's prose is that of his essay series. In the early series, the major characters, "The Pilgrim" and "The Philosopher of the Forest," tend to be preachy and fuzzily drawn. The Indian "Tomo-Cheeki" of another series voices the expected noble-savage statements in elegant prose: he is but a device for social criticism through the contrast of cultures. Used somewhat similarly is "Hezekiah Salem," the chief character of a light series that appeared in New York. As a New Englander, Salem is an early progenitor of American humor based on regional differences. But Freneau's greatest prose creation was Robert Slender, spokesman of an electioneering series. Robert Slender is the common man: he speaks as one, he feels as one, his fears are those of one. He views government from the point of view of everyday life, as here where he talks to himself on the way to a tavern:

> Had I, said I, (talking to myself all the while) the disposal of but half the income of the United States, I could at least so order matters, that a man might walk to his next neighbour's without splashing his stockings, or being in danger of breaking his legs in ruts, holes, gutts, and gullies. I do not know, says I to myself, as I moralized on my splash'd stocking, but money might with more profit be laid out in repairing the roads, than in marine establishments, supporting a standing army, useless embassies, exhorbitant salaries, given to many flashy fellows that are no honour to us, or to themselves, and chartering whole ships to carry a single man to another nation.

Freneau's best prose pieces are those in which he speaks in this colloquial, common style.

But the works of Freneau which are read today are not the occasional verse which made him famous, nor his prose, but poems which capture the melancholy so admired by the pre-Romantics. Best known of this type is "The Wild Honeysuckle," which presents the inevitable decay of the flower's beauty: "Smit with those charms, that must decay,/I grieve to see your future doom." The emotion is restrained, is never permitted to become more than a pleasing melancholy:

> From morning suns and evening dews
> At first thy little being came
> If nothing once, you nothing lose,
> For when you die you are the same;
> The space between, is but an hour,
> The frail duration of a flower.

As Freneau revised the last couplet several times, so he revised his best poems frequently, polishing them as a craftsman. One of his best is "Ode to Fancy," a late revision of his very early "The Power of Fancy." The poem begins with Fancy's origin and nature: "Wakeful, vagrant, restless thing,/Ever wandering on the wing,/Who thy wondrous source can find,/Fancy, regent of the mind." The poet then presents the analogy between the creations of man's fancy and the elements of the universe, "Ideas of the Almighty mind!" After a description of Fancy's power, the poem ends with this plea: "Come, O come – perceiv'd by none,/You and I will walk alone." The whole is a unified, satisfying poem. As, later in life, Freneau became a better poet, he also became a more philosophical one, often presenting in verse his views on nature and the universe, still clinging to that most cherished virtue of the Enlightenment – moderation. In one of his last poems, "Winter," he again emphasizes this virtue:

Happy with wine we may indulge an hour;
The noblest beverage of the mildest power.
Happy, with Love, to solace every care,
Happy with sense and wit an hour to share;
These to the mind a thousand pleasures bring
And give to winter's frosts the smiles of spring.

These virtues appear also in Freneau's works: they show wit and sense, and feeling.

—Mary Weatherspoon Bowden

FULLER, Henry Blake. American. Born in Chicago, Illinois, 9 January 1857. Educated at South Division High School, Chicago, 1872, 1875–76, and Allison Classical Academy, Oconomowoc, Wisconsin, 1873–74. Worked at Ovington's Crockery, Chicago, 1876, and the Home National Bank, Chicago, 1877–78; toured Europe and on his return to Chicago became a full-time writer; contributed to the *Chicago Tribune*, 1884, and to the book review section of the *Chicago Evening Post*, 1901–02; editorial writer for the *Chicago Record-Herald*, 1911–13. Member, Advisory Committee, *Poetry*, Chicago, 1912–29. *Died 28 July 1929.*

PUBLICATIONS

Fiction

The Chevalier of Pensieri-Vani (stories). 1890; revised edition, 1892.
The Chatelaine of La Trinité. 1892.
The Cliff-Dwellers. 1893.
With the Procession. 1895.
From the Other Side: Stories of Transatlantic Travel. 1898.
The New Flag: Satires. 1899.
The Last Refuge: A Sicilian Romance. 1900.
Under the Skylights (stories). 1901.
Waldo Trench and Others: Stories of Americans in Italy. 1908.
Lines Long and Short: Biographical Sketches in Various Rhythms (stories). 1917.
On the Stairs. 1918.
Bertram Cope's Year. 1919.
Gardens of This World. 1929.
Not on the Screen. 1930.

Plays

O, That Way Madness Lies: A Play for Marionettes, in *Chapbook 4,* December 1895.
The Puppet-Booth: Twelve Plays. 1896.
The Coffee-House, and *The Fan,* from plays by Goldoni. 2 vols., 1925–26.
The Red Carpet, in *Fuller: A Critical Biography* by Constance Griffin. 1939.

Other

Editor, *The So-Called Human Race,* by Bert Leston Taylor.   1922.

Bibliography: *Fuller and Hamlin Garland: A Reference Guide* by Charles L. P. Silet, 1977.

Reading List: *Fuller: A Critical Biography* by Constance Griffin, 1939; *Fuller* by John Pilkington, 1970; *Fuller of Chicago: The Ordeal of a Genteel Realist in Ungenteel America* by Bernard R. Bowron, Jr., 1974.

*   *   *

An American writer whose work suggests Henry James or William Dean Howells, but without the former's strength and without the latter's variety, Henry Blake Fuller strikes his admirers as subtle and his detractors as dull. In his best novels the style is elegant and spare, distinguished by a dry wit; in verse and drama, and in his last two novels, however, the performance is uncertain and even embarrassing. An "unconquerable reticence," in Harriet Monroe's phrase, and the "deliberate flatness" which Edmund Wilson observed do not encourage many readers to pursue this decorous writer. Three novels and several stories, however, do not deserve their present neglect.

Fuller's fictions pass in Italy or in Chicago. In the first group, somewhat vulgar Americans encounter sophisticated Europeans in a series of books beginning with *The Chevalier of Pensieri-Vani.* An elderly American woman, for example, longs to escape her crass new country for the older, presumably better one; an Italian nobleman is persuaded to alter his family's villa to suit the whims of tasteless Americans; on a train, an American encounters a travelling theatrical troupe and mistakes it for royalty. These ironic miniatures are finely honed and atmospheric, but they are less persuasive than the best of the Chicago novels.

With the Procession traces a middle-class family's pathetic attempts to social climb. An older generation has made the modest family fortune which a younger one wastes. The son is a posturing dilettante, the daughter a fatuous spinster, each aspiring to join Chicago's social "procession." *On the Stairs* follows the equally mediocre lives of two boys, the rise of one and the fall of the other, through two generations that blur the social distinctions which separated them in youth and separate them through economic ones.

Fuller's preoccupation with failures – despite his wry humor – may account, in part, for the indifference with which his best novel was greeted. *Bertram Cope's Year* attempts to overcome Fuller's "unconquerable reticence" in dealing with homosexuals, but in a manner sufficiently elliptical to obscure its intentions. Cope, an androgynous young man of surpassing good looks, attracts everyone despite his seeming diffidence and lack of marked intellect, but the attraction is only superficial. Cope is the *beau ideal* with little to offer, and his catastrophic effect on a variety of people is emotional rather than physical, spun in Fuller's most indirect manner. Critics seem to have misunderstood the novel, and Fuller's friends were embarrassed by it. A decade later he wrote two other novels, but at the time of the failure of *Bertram Cope's Year* he said, "No further novels likely: too much effort and too little return – often none." It deserves attention.

—Bruce Kellner

GARLAND, (Hannibal) Hamlin.   American.   Born near West Salem, Wisconsin, 16 September 1860; as a boy worked with his father on a farm in Iowa. Educated at the Cedar Valley Seminary, Osage, Iowa, graduated 1881. Married Zuline Taft in 1899; two daughters.

Homesteader in the Dakotas, 1883–84; Teacher, Boston School of Oratory, 1884–91; full-time writer from 1891; lived in Chicago, 1893–1916, and in New York City from 1916. Founder/President, Cliff Dwellers, Chicago, 1907. Recipient: Pulitzer Prize, for biography, 1922; Roosevelt Memorial Association Gold Medal for Literature, 1931. Honorary degrees: University of Wisconsin, Madison, 1926; Northwestern University, Evanston, Illinois, 1933. Member, 1918, and Director, 1920, American Academy of Arts and Letters. *Died 4 March 1940.*

PUBLICATIONS

Fiction

Main-Travelled Roads: Six Mississippi Valley Stories. 1891; revised edition, 1907; edited by Thomas A. Bledsoe, 1954.
A Member of the Third House. 1892.
Jason Edwards: An Average Man. 1892.
A Little Norsk; or, Ol' Pap's Flaxen. 1892.
A Spoil of Office. 1892.
Prairie Folks (stories). 1892; revised edition, 1899.
Rose of Dutcher's Coolly. 1895; revised edition, 1899; edited by Donald Pizer, 1969.
Wayside Courtships (stories). 1897.
The Spirit of Sweetwater. 1898; revised edition, as *Witch's Gold*, 1906.
The Eagle's Heart. 1900.
Her Mountain Lover. 1901.
The Captain of the Gray-Horse Troop. 1902.
Hesper. 1903.
The Light of the Star. 1904.
The Tyranny of the Dark. 1905.
Money Magic. 1907; as *Mart Haney's Mate*, 1922.
The Moccasin Ranch. 1909.
Cavanagh, Forest Ranger. 1910.
Other Main-Travelled Roads (includes *Prairie Folks* and *Wayside Courtships*). 1910.
Victor Ollnee's Discipline. 1911.
The Forester's Daughter. 1914.
They of the High Trails (stories). 1916.

Play

Under the Wheel. 1890.

Verse

Prairie Songs. 1893.
Iowa, O Iowa! 1935.

Other

Crumbling Idols: Twelve Essays on Art. 1894; edited by Jane Johnson, 1960.

Ulysses S. Grant: His Life and Character. 1898.
The Trail of the Goldseekers: A Record of Travel in Prose and Verse. 1899.
Boy Life on the Prairie. 1899; revised edition, 1908.
The Long Trail (juvenile). 1907.
The Shadow World. 1908.
A Son of the Middle Border. 1917; edited by Henry M. Christman, 1962.
A Daughter of the Middle Border. 1921.
The Book of the American Indian. 1923.
Trail-Makers of the Middle Border. 1926.
The Westward March of American Settlement. 1927.
Back-Trailers from the Middle Border. 1928.
Roadside Meetings. 1930.
Companions on the Trail: A Literary Chronicle. 1931.
My Friendly Contemporaries: A Literary Log. 1932.
Afternoon Neighbors: Further Excerpts from a Literary Log. 1934.
Joys of the Trail. 1935.
Forty Years of Psychic Research: A Plain Narrative of Fact. 1936.
The Mystery of the Buried Crosses: A Narrative of Psychic Exploration. 1939.
Diaries, edited by Donald Pizer. 1968.

Bibliography: *Henry Blake Fuller and Garland: A Reference Guide* by Charles L. P. Silet, 1977.

Reading List: *Garland: A Biography* by Jean Holloway, 1960; *Garland's Early Work and Career* by Donald Pizer, 1960; *Garland: L'Homme et l'Oeuvre* by Robert Mane, 1968.

*   *   *

Hamlin Garland played an important role in the development of realism in America, but the work of enduring significance that he bequeathed to the last half of the 20th century is modest. One volume of stories, one novel, and his autobiography are all that a contemporary reader need bother about. Garland is one of the most uneven of American writers, for the gulf is wide between the stories in *Main-Travelled Roads* and the popular fiction he later turned out for the *Saturday Evening Post*. His fall from realism into sentimental romance is simply embarrassing.

After Garland left the Midwest and went to Boston to become a writer, he was encouraged by Joseph Kirkland, a realist writer, to make use of his farm background. No authentic farmer yet had appeared in American literature, and the subject was virgin. This advice came in 1887 as Garland was returning from a visit to see his mother, who had had a stroke, and he was burning with indignation over the privations and injustices of farm life. In addition, the 1880's were a period of farm depression, for too much new land had been opened up too fast and the invention of farm machinery had over-stimulated production. Out of this context came the six stories that made up the original edition of *Main-Travelled Roads*. They are "A Branch Road," "Up the Coulé," "Among the Corn Rows," "The Return of a Private," "Under the Lion's Paw," and "Mrs. Ripley's Trip." Some take place in Wisconsin where Garland was born, some in Iowa where the Garlands homesteaded after the Civil War, and one makes use of the Dakotas where Garland homesteaded himself before leaving for Boston to become a writer. The general theme is the hard lot of the farmer, and especially the farm wife, but the stories are not all somber. "Mrs. Ripley's Trip" is bucolic comedy, and "Among the Corn Rows" ends with an elopement and high hopes. All of the stories, however, are filled with closely observed detail that make them good examples of literary realism. There are some naturalistic elements in the victimization of the characters by forces beyond their control, but Garland is not really a naturalist. It is above all the intensity of his feeling that carries these stories.

That Garland's compulsion to write these stories lay mostly in his anger of the moment and not in deeply held convictions is shown by subsequent developments. After he settled his mother in Wisconsin and began to prosper, he lost his zeal for social criticism. He was not dishonest, but he saw the world in terms of himself and later lapsed into a terrible respectability. He continued to write stories, however, and the six stories in *Main-Travelled Roads* eventually grew to twelve, but the later tales are inferior and lapse into sentimentality. He also produced another volume of somber tales, *Prairie Folks*, before his indignation abated, and he wrote four novels worth mentioning. The first, *A Little Norsk*, has something of the hard Dakota farm life in it, but it is marred by sentimentality. His best novel, and one that still can be recommended, is *Rose of Dutcher's Coolly*, the story of a farm girl who goes to the state university and then to Chicago to pursue a career. The detail is good, especially the childhood and adolescence of Rose on the farm, and it deals with feminist problems of the 1890's. *Jason Edwards* is single-tax propaganda written after Garland had met Henry George and become a supporter of the single-tax panacea for economic ills. *A Spoil of Office* is a populist novel attacking political corruption and reminding modern readers who stumble on it that 1892 was the year that James Weaver led the United States' most successful third party movement.

Garland made a literary comeback in 1917 when he wrote his autobiography, *A Son of the Middle Border*. This is a first-rate work that ranks with the best that Garland accomplished in the 1890's. He followed this with three other volumes of family history: *A Daughter of the Middle Border*, *Trail-Makers of the Middle Border* (this one fictionalized), and *Back-Trailers from the Middle Border*, but these are less interesting than the first. Because Garland lived a long time and made a point of meeting writers and public figures, students of literary history will find considerable interest in his literary reminiscences: *Roadside Meetings*, *Companions on the Trail*, *My Friendly Contemporaries*, and *Afternoon Neighbors*. Also noteworthy is Garland's one venture into literary criticism, *Crumbling Idols*, in which he makes a strong defense of realism.

—James Woodress

GILLETTE, William (Hooker). American. Born in Hartford, Connecticut, 24 July 1853. Educated at Hartford High School; Trinity College, Hartford, left without taking a degree. Married Helen Nickles in 1882 (died, 1888). Debut as an actor, New Orleans, later New York and Boston, 1875; appeared with Bernard Macauley's company in Cincinnati and Louisville, 1876–77; returned to New York and from 1881 was one of the most prominent actors of the New York and London stage; appeared in nine of his own plays: especially noted for his portrayal of Sherlock Holmes; retired in 1919 to an estate in Connecticut, but later came out of retirement to appear in various of his early roles in New York and on tour throughout America; retired again in 1936. Awarded honorary degrees by Yale University, New Haven, Connecticut, Columbia University, New York, and Trinity College, all in 1930. Member, American Academy of Arts and Letters, 1913. *Died 29 April 1937.*

PUBLICATIONS

Plays

    Esmeralda, with Frances Hodgson Burnett (produced 1881; as *Young Folks' Ways*, produced 1883). 1882.

The Professor (produced 1881; as *The Professor's Wooing*, produced 1881).
Held by the Enemy (produced 1886).   1898.
A Legal Wreck (produced 1888).
All the Comforts of Home, with H. C. Duckworth, from a German play (produced
    1890).   1897.
Mr. Wilkinson's Widows, from a play by Alexandre Bisson (produced in the 1890's ?).
Too Much Johnson (produced 1894).   1912.
Secret Service (produced 1895).   1898.
Sherlock Holmes, with A. Conan Doyle, from works by Doyle (produced 1899).   1922.
The Painful Predicament of Sherlock Holmes (produced 1905).   1955.
Clarice (produced 1905).
Among Thieves (produced 1909; as *The Robber*, produced 1909).   In *One-Act Plays for
    Stage and Study 2*, 1925.
Electricity (produced 1910).   1913.
The Dream Maker, with Howard E. Morton (produced 1921).
The Red Owl.   1924.
How Well George Does It!   1936.

Fiction

A Legal Wreck.   1888.
The Astounding Crime on Torrington Road.   1927.

Other

The Illusion of the First Time in Acting.   1915.

Editor, *How to Write a Play: Letters from Augier, Banville, Dennery, Dumas, Gondinet,
    Labiche, Legouvé, Pailleron, Sardou, and Zola*, translated by Dudley Miles.   1916.

Reading List: *Sherlock Holmes and Much More* by Doris E. Cook, 1970.

*   *   *

William Gillette's first performance, with an assist from Mark Twain, was in *Faint Heart
Ne'er Won Fair Lady* in 1875. He appeared in several stock companies before opening his
own play, *The Professor*, at Madison Square Garden in 1881. Thereafter he appeared chiefly
in his own plays, except for roles in *Samson, The Admirable Crichton, A Successful Calamity*,
and *Dear Brutus*. Frequently he was at his best in portraying the "cool man of action,"
whether it was the title role in his own *Sherlock Holmes* (he played the part for 30 years) or
Brant in his own *Held by the Enemy* (a melodrama but also the first successful play about the
American Civil War). Notable among his other plays are *A Legal Wreck* (about a coastal New
England town), *Secret Service* (his most popular American Civil War play), and *The Painful
Predicament of Sherlock Holmes*. The last is an hysterically funny mini-play sequel to
Sherlock Holmes featuring a bumbling, loquacious, accident-prone escapee from the nearby
mental hospital, who, while she appeals for help to the always silent Holmes, accidentally
destroys his violin, violin bow, lamp, cocaine pot, crime case notes, and photographs, before
Holmes's servant can summon sanitorium assistance.
    Gillette's best claim to fame today lies in his *Sherlock Holmes*, written in collaboration with
Sir Arthur Conan Doyle, and revived to great acclaim in 1975. Gillette's play bends Doyle's
stories "A Scandal in Bohemia" and "The Final Problem," and not only demonstrates

Holmes's great skill against Moriarity, the Napoleon of Crime, but also shows him falling in love with the heroine, Alice Faulkner, though one sometimes wonders whether he will shoot Moriarity or cocaine. Gillette judiciously and skillfully lifts dialogue directly from Doyle's stories, along with the most dramatic moments, though the melodramatic tension is Gillette's. A good script editor can easily keep the play's many complicated dramatic turns from becoming too intricate, and its melodramatic turns from becoming maudlin. Holmes quickly solves the mystery, foils the thugs, recovers the blackmail papers (50% honestly), and jails Moriarity. Holmes besottedly in love could have provided a deadly melodramatic element, especially when coupled with Alice's innocence and naivety; but, to the audience's delight, the romance spurs interest in the triumph of good, and Alice falls ecstatically into Holmes's arms at the final curtain.

—Louis Charles Stagg

GUINEY, Louise Imogen. American. Born in Roxbury, Boston, Massachusetts, 7 January 1861. Educated at the Convent of the Sacred Heart, Elmhurst, Rhode Island. Worked for a time as a journalist; Postmistress, Auberndale, Massachusetts; worked in the cataloging department, Boston Public Library. Editor, with Alice Brow, *Pilgrim Scrip.* Moved to England, 1895. *Died 2 November 1920.*

PUBLICATIONS

Verse

 Songs at the Start. 1884.
 The White Sail and Other Poems. 1887.
 A Roadside Harp. 1893.
 Nine Sonnets Written at Oxford. 1895.
 England and Yesterday: A Book of Short Poems. 1898.
 The Martyrs' Idyl and Shorter Poems. 1899.
 Happy Ending: Collected Lyrics. 1909; revised edition, 1927.

Fiction

 Lovers', Saint Ruth's, And Three Other Tales. 1895.

Other

 Goose-Quill Papers. 1885.
 Brownies and Bogles (juvenile). 1888.
 Monsieur Henri: A Foot-Note to French History. 1892.
 A Little English Gallery. 1894.
 Three Heroines in New England Romance: Their True Stories, with Harriet Prescott
  Spoffard and Alice Brown. 1894.

Patrins, To Which Is Added an Inquirendo into the Wit and Other Good Parts of His Late Majesty King Charles the Second.   1897.
Robert Emmet: A Survey of His Rebellion and of His Romance.   1904.
Blessed Edmund Campion.   1908.
Letters, edited by Grace Guiney.   2 vols., 1926.
Colonel Guiney and the Ninth Massachusetts: A Filial Appreciation.   1932.

Editor, *James Clarence Mangan: His Selected Poems.*   1897.
Editor, *Sohrab and Rustum and Other Poems,* by Matthew Arnold.   1899.
Editor, *The Mount of Olives and Primitive Holiness,* by Henry Vaughan.   1902.
Editor, *Selected Poems,* by Katherine Philips.   2 vols., 1904–05.
Editor, *Hurrell Froude: Memoranda and Comments.*   1904.
Editor, *Thomas Stanley: His Original Lyrics, Complete.*   1907.
Editor, *Some Poems of Lionel Johnson.*   1912.
Editor, *Arthur Laurie Thomas: A Memoir,* by F. E. Thomas.   1920.
Editor, with Geoffrey Bliss, *Recusant Poets.*   1938.

Translator, *The Sermon to the Birds and the Wolf of Gubbio.*   1898.
Translator, *The Secret of Fougereuse: A Romance of the Fifteenth Century,* by Louise Morvan.   1898.

Bibliography: in *Bibliography of American Literature* by Jacob Blanck, 1959.

Reading List: *Guiney* by Alice Brown, 1921; *Guiney: Her Life and Works* by E. M. Tenison, 1923; *Guiney: Laureate of the Lost* by Henry C. Fairbanks, 1972.

*   *   *

Although she published more than thirty books and a hundred articles, Louise Imogen Guiney is relatively forgotten today. Her best volume of verse, *A Roadside Harp,* brings to maturity the themes and attitudes which she introduced in two previous collections, *Songs at the Start* and *The White Sail and Other Poems,* and which were to preoccupy her throughout her career: an attachment to the past, a fondness for nature, and a love for religion and learning. Technically, Guiney's poetry is conservative and genteel. Its carefully measured rhythms and conventional forms earned her the admiration of the Boston brahmin Oliver Wendell Holmes, who called her his "little golden guinea," and the disapproval of the editor and critic Horace Scudder, who found her work excessively "oblique and allusive."

For her models, Guiney looked toward the classics, in which she was extraordinarily well instructed, and the Renaissance, in which she was an acknowledged expert. Guiney was particularly fond of sonnets and elegies. *Nine Sonnets Written at Oxford* was considered by many to be one of the finest collections of sonnets published during the nineteenth century. So precise was her attention to form and so classical were her tastes that several of Guiney's poems were mistaken for translations of Greek originals. Her narrative poetry, which Guiney herself disparaged for its lack of unity, was less successful. At its best Guiney's poetry sparkles with wit and allusion; at its worst it is imitative and artificial.

Later in life, Guiney found it increasingly more difficult to write poetry, and she turned instead toward scholarship. A poorly written collection of stories, *Lovers', St. Ruth's, and Three Other Tales,* early convinced her that the essay, not fiction, was the form of prose most suited to her talents. Her most famous book of essays, *Patrins,* avoids the stylistic pitfalls of an earlier collection, *Goose-Quill Papers,* which bordered on the precious and even, at times, the euphuistic. In it she summarizes her critical theory, articulated previously in her preface to a translation of Mérimée's *Carmen* and in the introduction to her edition of the poetry of James Clarence Mangan, that literature should be emphatically humanistic and that it should express "joy" rather than what she termed "willful sadness." But Guiney's critical theories, while pronounced, were by no means intolerant. Although she disapproved of realism and naturalism, she was not beyond appreciating the artistry and talent of someone like Harold Frederic, whom she called a "country boy of genius."

Guiney's many biographical works, which include *A Little English Gallery*, *Robert Emmet*, and *Blessed Edmund Campion*, display a painstaking exactitude and a genuine devotion to learning, which characterize nearly everything she wrote. A knowledgeable editor, Guiney published selections from the works of Henry Vaughan, Matthew Arnold, Hurrell Froude, and Lionel Johnson, among others. Many of her essays express her lifelong commitment to Roman Catholicism, and at the time of her death, she was working on a collection, with copious biographical and bibliographical notes, of poetry written by Catholics in England from 1535 to 1735, posthumously published as *Recusant Poets*.

—James A. Levernier

HALLECK, Fitz-Greene. American. Born in Guilford, Connecticut, 8 July 1790. Educated at public schools in Guilford. Worked in a store in Guilford, 1806–11; clerk in the banking house of Jacob Barker, 1812–30, New York; toured Europe, 1822; Confidential Clerk in the banking house of John Jacob Astor, 1832 until his retirement on an annuity left him by Astor, 1849; retired to Guilford. Leading member of the Knickerbocker Group, New York; Vice-President, Authors Club, New York, 1837. *Died 19 November 1867.*

Publications

Collections

Poetical Writings, edited by James Grant Wilson. 1868.

Verse

Poems, with Joseph Rodman Drake. 1819; revised edition, as *The Croakers*, 1860.
Fanny. 1819; revised edition, 1821.
Alnwick Castle with Other Poems. 1817.
The Recorder with Other Poems. 1833.
Fanny with Other Poems. 1839.
Poetical Works. 1847.
Young America. 1865.

Other

A Letter Written to Joel Lewis Griffing in 1814. 1921.

Editor, *The Works of Byron in Verse and Prose.* 1834.
Editor, *Selections from the British Poets.* 2 vols., 1840.

Bibliography: in *Bibliography of American Literature* by Jacob Blanck, 1959.

Reading List: *Life and Letters of Halleck* by James Grant Wilson, 1869; *Some Notices of the Life and Writings of Halleck* by William Cullen Bryant, 1869; *Halleck: An Early Knickerbocker Wit and Poet* by Nelson Frederick Adkins, 1930.

* * *

With the exception of William Cullen Bryant, Fitz-Greene Halleck was, among his contemporaries, the most popular of the Knickerbocker poets, and although such once-famous Knickerbockers as Samuel Woodworth, Robert Sands, and George Pope Morris have long been forgotten by virtually everyone except literary historians, Halleck is still remembered as a minor poet and satirist of New York society in the early nineteenth century.

Poetry was for Halleck, as for other Knickerbockers, an avocation, a pleasant diversion for gentlemen. His poetry is also exceedingly derivative. Campbell, Scott, and Moore are among those who most influenced him, but no poet's influence was greater then Byron's – an influence that Halleck freely acknowledged. (Indeed Halleck repaid the debt in his memoir and collected edition of Bryon's works, the first edition of this sort to be published on either side of the Atlantic.)

Although Halleck published little poetry of consequence, its range was large, including the heroic ("Marco Bozzaris"), the pastoral ("Wyoming"), the sentimental ("Alnwick Castle"), the elegiac ("On the Death of Joseph Rodman Drake"), and the satiric (*Fanny*). His reputation was established in 1819 with the publication of "The Croaker Papers," written jointly with Joseph Rodman Drake. These poems, widely read and praised in their day, satirize prominent figures in the financial, political, and social life of New York. *Fanny*, Halleck's most sustained literary effort and his best, is a pointed but delicate satire of fashionable New York society, a world which Halleck knew well. During the last four decades of his life, Halleck who died in 1867, published little of interest.

Despite his satires of fashionable New York, it was in that New York that Halleck was most at home. As personal secretary to John Jacob Astor, he was assured of access to the social realm he most admired. Here literature was a pastime, a diversion. Astor's world was the ideal setting for the accomplished but amateur poet that Halleck indisputably was.

—Edward Halsey Foster

HARRIGAN, Edward.   American.   Born in New York City, 26 October 1844. Received little schooling; largely self-taught. Married Annie T. Braham in 1876; seven children. Left home for San Francisco, and appeared in vaudeville in the west, 1867–70; returned to New York, and appeared on stage, with Sam Rickey, as a vaudeville comic team, 1870; first appeared with Anthony J. Cannon (stage name: Tony Hart), as Harrigan and Hart, 1871, and with him managed and appeared at the Theatre Comique, New York, 1871 until the theatre was torn down, 1881: during this period wrote more than 80 sketches, music by David Braham, which developed into the complete plays of his later career in which he always acted the leading part; with Hart, opened the New Theatre Comique, 1881, and managed it until it was destroyed by fire, 1884; partnership with Hart ended in 1885; leased Harrigan's Park Theatre, 1884–88; built Harrigan's, later the Garrick, Theatre, 1891-95; retired from the stage in 1908. *Died 6 June 1911.*

PUBLICATIONS

Collections

The Famous Songs of Harrigan and Hart, edited by Edward B. Marks.   1938.

Plays and Sketches

The Mulcahy Twins (produced 1870).   Songs published 1872.
The Little Frauds (produced 1870).   Songs published 1870.
The Mulligan Guards (produced 1873).   Songs published 1873.
The Donovans (produced 1873).
Patrick's Day Parade (produced 1873; revised 1874 and thereafter).   Songs published 1884.
The Absent-Minded Couple (produced 1873).

The Skidmores (produced 1874).
The Invalid Corps (produced 1874).
Going Home Again (produced 1874).
The Night-Clerk's Troubles; or, The Fifth Avenue Hotel (produced 1875).   1875.
The Blue and the Gray (produced 1875).   1875.
Fee Gee (produced 1875).
King Calico's Body Guard (produced 1875).
The Two Awfuls (produced 1875).
Behind the Scenes (produced 1875).
Slavery Days (produced 1875).   Songs published 1875.
Down Broadway; or, From Central Park to the Battery (produced 1875).   Songs
    published 1878.
The Editor's Trouble (produced 1876).   1875.
Christmas Joys and Sorrows (produced 1876).   1877.
Lascaire (produced 1876).
The Telephone (produced 1876).
Ireland vs. Italy (produced 1876).
The Bradys (produced 1876).
The Italian Ballet Master (produced 1876).
Malone's Night Off (produced 1876).
The Bold Hibernian Boys (produced 1876).
S.O.T. (Sons of Temperance) (produced 1876).   Songs published 1876.
The Grand Duke Opera House (produced 1877).
Old Lavender (produced 1877; revised 1878, 1885).   1877.
My Wife's Mother.   1877
Callahan the Detective (produced 1877).
The Crushed Actors (produced 1877).
The Pillsbury Muddle (produced 1877).
Sullivan's Christmas (produced 1877).
The Irish Cousins (produced 1877).
Walking for Dat Cake (produced 1877).   Songs published 1877.
The Two Young Fellows and Her Majesty's Marines (produced 1877).
My Boy Dan (produced 1877).
The Terrible Example (produced 1877).
Love and Insurance (produced 1877).
The Celebrated Hard Case (produced 1878).   1878.
O'Brien, Counsellor-at-Law (produced 1878).
The Great In-Toe-Natural-Walking Match (produced 1878).
The Lorgaire (produced 1878; revised 1888).   1878.
The Mulligan Guard Picnic (produced 1878).   1880.
The Mulligan Guard Ball (produced 1879).   1879.
The Mulligan Guard Chowder (produced 1879).   1879.
The Mulligan Guards' Christmas (produced 1879).   1879.
The Mulligan Guard Nominee (produced 1880).   1880.
The Mulligan Guard Surprise (produced 1880).   1880.
The Major (produced 1881).   1881.
The Mulligans' Silver Wedding (produced 1881).   1881.
Squatter Sovereignty (produced 1882).   1881.
Mordecai Lyons (produced 1882).   1882.
McSorley's Inflation (produced 1882).   1882.
The Muddy Day (produced 1883).   Songs published 1883.
Cordelia's Aspirations (produced 1883).
Dan's Tribulations (produced 1884).   Songs published 1893.
Investigation (produced 1884).   Songs published 1884.

McAllistair's Legacy (produced 1885).
Are You Insured? (produced 1885).
The Grip (produced 1885).
The O'Reagans (produced 1886).
The Leather Patch (produced 1886).   Songs published 1886.
McNooney's Visit (produced 1887).
Pete (produced 1887).
Waddy Googan (produced 1888).   Songs published 1893.
Reilly and the Four Hundred (produced 1890).   Songs published 1890.
The Last of the Hogans (produced 1891; shortened version, as *Sargent Hickey*, produced
    1897).   Songs published 1891.
The Woolen Stocking (produced 1893).   Songs published 1893.
Notoriety (produced 1894).   Songs published 1894.
Marty Malone (produced 1896).
Under Cover (produced 1903).
The Simple Life (produced 1905).

Fiction

The Mulligans.   1901.

Verse

Songs for the Banjo.   1888.
Songs.   1893.

Other

Comique Joker, with Tony Hart.   1870(?).
Pictorial History of the Mulligan Guard Ball.   1879.

Reading List: *The Merry Partners: The Age of Harrigan and Hart* by E. J. Kahn, Jr., 1955.

*   *   *

The enthusiastic comparisons which critics applied to Edward Harrigan's plays would
seem to have assured him an international reputation. William Dean Howells (in *Harper's*,
July 1886) described him as the American Goldoni and a playwright who created "the spring
of a true American Comedy." Others compared him to Hogarth, Balzac, Zola, and Dickens.
At a time when American literature and art were firmly caught up in the rise of realism
Harrigan deserved this critical attention through his successful depiction of Lower East Side
New York life. As a comedian and a playwright he believed in "Holding the Mirror Up to
Nature," as he explained it in an essay in *Pearson's Magazine* (November 1903), and
providing a "series of photographs of life today in the Empire City" (*Harper's Weekly*, 2
February 1889). By using authentic scenes, character types, speech, dress, and gestures he
provided realistic farce-comedy in which he infused his own belief in the kindness and good
nature of the majority of people. As riotous fun, his plays and performances were both a
reflection of the serious artistic and social movements of his generation and an antidote to the
grimness which they frequently unveiled.

Harrigan, after several years in vaudeville, formed a comedy team with Anthony J.

Cannon, who soon changed his name to Hart. As "Harriganandhart" they performed for fourteen years, and Harrigan began writing the sketches, with music by David Braham, that often developed into full-length plays. Many of the most memorable take place in Mulligan's Alley in New York's Sixth Ward. It was a part of New York that Harrigan researched and knew very well – a jumbled population of Germans, Italians, Chinese, Negroes, and Irish who took their ward politics seriously as well as their social activities which seemed always haunted by the "battle of the sexes." There was the Wee Drop Saloon run by Walfingham McSweeny, an Italian junk shop, a Chinese laundry-lodging combination, Lochmuller's butcher shop, and a Negro social club called the Full Moon Union. It was an international community which Harrigan brought to life with elaborate stage-business, meticulous attention to realistic detail, and a comedian's enthusiasm for the "general melee" which characterized his plays.

Harrigan's most famous plays involved the Mulligans – *The Mulligan Guards, The Mulligan Guard Ball, The Mulligan Guard Nominee*, and so on – through which he satirized contemporary military organization, social life on the Lower East Side, and politics. *Cordelia's Aspirations* and *Dan's Tribulations* also involve Dan Mulligan and his wife. His other important plays include *Old Lavender, Waddy Googan,* and *Reilly and the Four Hundred*. The people and their ideas were real if slight, and the spectators came to see something of themselves on stage. Trying always to be "truthful to the laws that govern society," Harrigan also confessed to being provincial and optimistic. Although he did not fulfill the potentiality that some critics saw or stimulate followers for his theory of American comedy, he was a major favorite for a generation or more of New York theatre-goers.

—Walter J. Meserve

HARRIS, George Washington. American. Born in Allegheny City, Pennsylvania, 20 March 1814; grew up in Knoxville, Tennessee. Educated in local schools; apprenticed to a metalworker, Knoxville, 1826–33. Married 1) Mary Emeline Nance in 1835 (died, 1867), six children; 2) Jane E. Pride in 1869. Captain of the *Knoxville*, a Tennessee River boat, 1833–38; wrote for the Knoxville *Argus* in the late 1830's; farmer in Tucaleeche Cove, Tennessee, 1839–43; contributor to the *Spirit of the Times*, New York, 1843; opened a metalworking shop in Knoxville, 1843; Superintendent, Holston Glass Works, 1849; Captain of the steamboat *Alida*, Tennessee River, 1854; coppermine surveyor in Ducktown, Tennessee, 1854; Alderman, Fourth Ward of Knoxville, 1856; Postmaster of Knoxville, 1857; wrote for the *Union and American*, Nashville, Tennessee, 1858–61; moved to Nashville, 1859 until it was occupied by Union troops, 1862, and lived in various parts of the South during the Civil War, 1862–65; worked for the Wills Valley Railroad, 1866–69; contributed to the *Daily American*, Chattanooga, Tennessee, 1867–68. Delegate, Southern Commercial Convention, Savannah, Georgia, 1856; Member, Democratic State Central Committee, Tennessee, 1859. *Died 11 December 1869.*

PUBLICATIONS

Collections

Sut Lovingood's Yarns, and High Times and Hard Times, edited by M. Thomas Inge. 2 vols., 1966–67.

Prose

> *Sut Lovingood: Yarns Spun by a "Nat'ral Born Durn'd Fool: Warped and Wove for Public Wear."* 1867.
> *Interesting Biographical Sketch.* 1867.
> *Sut Lovingood: Travels with Old Abe Lincoln.* 1937.

Bibliography: in *Bibliography of American Literature* by Jacob Blanck, 1959.

Reading List: *Harris* by Milton Rickels, 1966.

*   *   *

George Washington Harris was neither a writer by trade nor a Southerner by birth. Yet he contributed to American literature one of its most distinctively Southern comic figures in Sut Lovingood and brought the American literary vernacular to its highest level of achievement before Mark Twain.

Harris had been brought as a child to Knoxville, Tennessee, by his half-brother from the place of his birth in Allegheny City, Pennsylvania, and he adapted to the attitudes and mores of the ante-bellum South with spirited enthusiasm. With little education in the formal sense, he had a wide cross-section of occupations, including metal working, captaining a steamboat, farming, running a glass works and a sawmill, surveying, running for political office, serving as a postmaster, and working for the railroad. Such diverse experience gave Harris a large reservoir of material from which to draw in his writing.

Writing was a leisure time activity for Harris, who began as an author of political sketches for local newspapers and sporting epistles for the New York *Spirit of the Times.* He quickly developed a facility for local color and dialect and a skill for bringing backwoods scenes and events to life on the printed page. When he contributed the first Sut Lovingood sketch to the *Spirit* (4 November 1854), he outdistanced all the other humorists of the Old Southwest by allowing one central character to tell his own stories in his own vernacular and by granting him (without authorial comment) a lease on life according to the integrity and consistency of that character's independence in thought and action. Mark Twain would learn this lesson well from Harris, whose one collection of stories, *Sut Lovingood: Yarns,* he reviewed, and put it to effective use in *Adventures of Huckleberry Finn.*

While authors and critics such as William Dean Howells and Edmund Wilson have found Sut Lovingood repugnant, others such as Mark Twain, William Faulkner, and F. O. Matthiessen have paid tribute to Harris's genius. What makes Sut distinctive is the combination in his character of such human failings as bigotry, vulgarity, cowardice, brutality, and offensive behavior, along with a steadfast opposition to hypocrisy, dishonesty, and all limitations set on personal and social freedom. Many readers find it difficult to like Sut, but few find it possible to resist the appeal he has, especially those who enjoy seeing hypocritic sins revealed and those who take advantage of innocence appropriately and brutally punished. Sut is a minister of justice in coarse Southern homespun whose wildly funny pranks and incorrigible attitudes make him one of the most intriguing characters in American literary history.

—M. Thomas Inge

HARRIS, Joel Chandler. American. Born near Eatonton, Georgia, 9 December 1848. Educated at local schools. Married Esther LaRose in 1873; three daughters and two sons. Printer's devil and typesetter for *The Countryman* weekly, published at the Turnwold Plantation, 1862–66; member of staff of the *Telegraph*, Macon, Georgia, 1866, the *Crescent Monthly*, New Orleans, 1866–67, the *Monroe Advertiser*, Forsyth, Georgia, 1867–70, the *Morning News*, Savannah, Georgia, 1870–76, and the *Atlanta Constitution*, 1876–1900; Founder, with his son Julian, *Uncle Remus's Magazine* later *Uncle Remus – The Home Magazine*, 1907–08. Member, American Academy of Arts and Letters, 1905. *Died 2 July 1908.*

PUBLICATIONS

Collections

The Complete Tales of Uncle Remus, edited by Richard Chase.   1955.

Fiction

Uncle Remus: His Songs and His Sayings: The Folklore of the Old Plantation.   1881; as *Uncle Remus and His Legends of the Old Plantation*, 1881; as *Uncle Remus; or, Mr. Fox, Mr. Rabbit, and Mr. Terrapin*, 1881; revised edition, 1895.
Nights with Uncle Remus: Myths and Legends of the Old Plantation.   1883.
Mingo and Other Sketches in Black and White.   1884.
Free Joe and Other Georgian Sketches.   1887.
Daddy Jack the Runaway and Short Stories Told after Dark.   1889.
Balaam and His Master and Other Sketches and Stories.   1891.
A Plantation Printer: The Adventures of a Georgia Boy During the War.   1892; as *On the Plantation*, 1892.
Uncle Remus and His Friends: Old Plantation Stories, Songs, and Ballads, with Sketches of Negro Character.   1892.
Little Mr. Thimblefinger and His Queer Country: What the Children Saw and Heard There.   1894.
Mr. Rabbit at Home.   1895.
The Story of Aaron (So Named), The Son of Ben Ali, Told by His Friends and Acquaintances.   1896.
Sister Jane, Her Friends and Acquaintances.   1896.
Stories of Georgia.   1896; revised edition, 1896.
Aaron in the Wildwoods.   1897.
Tales of the Home Folks in Peace and War.   1898.
Plantation Pageants.   1899.
The Chronicles of Aunt Minervy Ann.   1899.
On the Wings of Occasions.   1900.
Gabriel Tolliver: A Story of Reconstruction.   1902.
The Making of a Statesman and Other Stories.   1902.
Wally Wanderoon and His Story-Telling Machine.   1903.
A Little Union Scout: A Tale of Tennessee During the Civil War.   1904.
Told by Uncle Remus: New Stories of the Old Plantation.   1905.
Uncle Remus and Brer Rabbit.   1907.
The Bishop and the Boogerman.   1909.
The Shadow Between His Shoulder-Blades.   1909.

Uncle Remus and the Little Boy.   1910.
Uncle Remus Returns.   1918.
The Witch Wolf: An Uncle Remus Story.   1921.
Qua: A Romance of the Revolution, edited by Thomas H. English.   1946.

Verse

The Tar-Baby and Other Rhymes of Uncle Remus.   1904.

Other

Editor and Essayist: Miscellaneous Literary, Political, and Social Writings, edited by
   Julia C. Harris.   1931.

Editor, *Life of Henry W. Grady, Including His Writings and Speeches: A Memorial
   Volume.*   1890.
Editor, *Theook of Fun and Frolic.*   1901; as *Merrymaker,* 1902.
Editor, *World's Wit and Humor.*   1904.

Translator, *Evening Tales,* by Frederic Ortoli.   1893.

Bibliography: in *Bibliography of American Literature* by Jacob Blanck, 1959.

Reading List: *The Life and Letters of Harris* by Julia C. Harris, 1918; *Harris, Folklorist* by
Stella Brewer Brookes, 1950; *Harris: A Biography* by Paul M. Cousins, 1968.

*   *   *

Joel Chandler Harris's reputation as a writer of the Uncle Remus stories for children is
somewhat misplaced. His first book, though deliberately illustrated and published as a
volume in the publisher's "humorous" catalogue, was introduced by Harris as having a
"perfectly serious" intention. He wanted to preserve the legends in their "original simplicity,
and to wed them permanently to the quaint dialect ... through the medium of which they
have become a part of the domestic history of every Southern family." He had heard them
originally on the Turnwold Plantation from characters similar to Uncle Remus himself, and
he was careful to present the dialect accurately. Indeed, the original publication of the tales in
the Atlanta *Constitution* (and reprinted in northern newspapers) had aroused anthropological
interest even before they were published in book form. Harris's introduction also emphasizes
the universality of the tales, and the African origin of the adventures of the rabbit, terrapin,
fox, tortoise, bear, deer used by Uncle Remus. In a later volume, Harris introduced another
Negro character, African Jack, who sometimes tells the same stories as Uncle Remus has
told, but in different versions and in a different (Gullah) dialect.
   What is often remembered by later readers of the tales is the picture, perhaps overly
sweetened by various illustrators of the stories, of the white-haired 80-year-old ex-slave,
Uncle Remus, and the little 7-year-old white boy (never named) to whom he tells his stories.
Perhaps Uncle Remus is patching his coat, or blowing the ashes off a yam roasted in some hot
coals to share with the boy, as he introduces his story. The stories are often used to point up a
moral lesson for the boy (he shouldn't be stingy, or disturb others' property), but the tales
themselves are always amusing, and often witty, and even the moral lessons are sometimes
tart. Harris, in short, is not merely a transcriber of folk-lore, but an artist. Mark Twain, in
fact, realized the tales' oral potentialities, and successfully used them in his own readings; he
even suggested a joint reading-tour with Harris.

But Harris wrote other things besides the Uncle Remus stories. Though his literary views demanded that proper "American" writing should deal with common people, preferably in a rural setting, he created a wide range of white and black characters, from the mountains and the lowlands. And the story "Free Joe and the Rest of the World" shows something of the harshness of slavery. Free Joe is a free Negro in a small community of slaves and masters, simple and friendless, a misfit, in fact. His wife is a slave, and, once her owner realizes that Joe has been visiting her, she is sold to a distant master. Joe is described as "the embodiment of that vague and mysterious danger that seemed to be forever lurking on the outskirts of slavery, ... a danger always threatening, and yet never assuming shape; intangible, and yet real; impossible, and yet not improbable," suggesting something of the unspoken fears of the southern slave-owner society. Harris also championed a spirit of reconciliation of North and South after the Civil war, suggested in his fiction by the fact that he more than once used the motif of a southern girl marrying a northern man who had fought against the South. These writings, along with the Uncle Remus tales, show Harris as perhaps the first writer to present a comprehensive view of the southern Negro "befo' the war, endurin' the war, en atterwards."

—George Walsh

HARTE, (Francis) Bret. American. Born in Albany, New York, 25 August 1836; lived with his family in various cities in the northeast, then settled in New York City, 1845. Educated in local shcools to age 13. Married Anna Griswold in 1862. Worked in New York in a lawyer's office, then in a merchant's counting room; moved to California, 1854, and taught school, worked as a clerk for an apothecary, and as an expressman in various California towns; writer for the *Northern Californian*, Arcata, 1857–60; settled in San Francisco: typesetter for the *Golden Era*, 1860; clerk in the Surveyor-General's Office, 1861–63; Secretary of the United States branch mint, 1863–69; contributor and, occasionally, Acting Editor, *Californian*, 1864–66; first Editor, *Overland Monthly*, 1868–70; full-time writer from 1870; lived in New York, 1871–78; tried unsuccessfully to establish *Capitol* magazine, 1877; United States Commercial Agent in Krefeld, Germany, 1878–80, and Consul in Glasgow, 1880–85; lived in London, 1885 until his death. *Died 5 May 1902.*

PUBLICATIONS

Collections

> *Works.* 25 vols., 1914.
> *Letters*, edited by Geoffrey Bret Harte. 1926.
> *Representative Selections*, edited by Joseph B. Harrison. 1941.
> *The Best Short Stories*, edited by Robert N. Linscott. 1967.

Fiction

> *Condensed Novels and Other Papers.* 1867; revised edition, 1871.
> *The Lost Galleon and Other Tales.* 1867.
> *The Luck of Roaring Camp and Other Sketches.* 1870; revised edition, 1871.

Stories of the Sierras and Other Sketches. 1872.
The Little Drummer; or, The Christmas Gift That Came to Rupert: A Story for Children. 1872.
Mrs. Skaggs's Husbands and Other Sketches. 1873.
An Episode of Fiddletown and Other Sketches. 1873.
Idyls of the Foothills. 1874.
Tales of the Argonauts and Other Sketches. 1875.
Wan Lee, The Pagan and Other Sketches. 1876.
Gabriel Conroy. 1876.
Thankful Blossom: A Romance of the Jerseys 1779. 1877.
Thankful Blossom and Other Tales. 1877.
My Friend, The Tramp (stories). 1877
The Story of a Mine. 1877.
The Man on the Beach (stories). 1878.
Jinny (stories). 1878.
Drift from Two Shores. 1878; as *The Hoodlum Bard and Other Stories,* 1878.
An Heiress of Red Dog and Other Sketches. 1879.
The Twins of Table Mountain (stories). 1879.
Jeff Briggs's Love Story and Other Sketches. 1880.
Flip and Other Stories. 1882.
In the Carquinez Woods. 1883.
California Stories. 1884.
On the Frontier (stories). 1884.
By Shore and Sedge. 1885.
Maruja. 1885.
Snow-Bound at Eagle's. 1886.
The Queen of the Pirate Isle. 1886.
A Millionaire of Rough-and-Ready, and Devil's Ford. 1887.
The Crusade of the Excelsior. 1887.
A Phyllis of the Sierras, and A Drift from Redwood Camp. 1888.
The Argonauts of North Liberty. 1888.
Cressy. 1889.
Captain Jim's Friend, and The Argonauts of North Liberty. 1889.
The Heritage of Dedlow Marsh and Other Tales. 1889.
A Waif of the Plains. 1890.
A Ward of the Golden Gate. 1890.
A Sappho of Green Springs and Other Tales. 1891.
A First Family of Tasajara. 1891.
Colonel Starbottle's Client and Some Other People. 1892.
Susy: A Story of the Plains. 1893.
Sally Dows, Etc. (stories). 1893.
A Protegee of Jack Hamlin's and Other Stories. 1894.
The Bell-Ringer of Angel's and Other Stories. 1894.
Clarence. 1895.
In a Hollow of the Hills. 1895.
Barker's Luck and Other Stories. 1896.
Three Partners; or, The Big Strike on Heavy Tree Hill. 1897.
The Ancestors of Peter Atherly and Other Tales. 1897.
Tales of Trail and Town. 1898.
Stories in Light and Shadow. 1898.
Mr. Jack Hamlin's Meditation and Other Stories. 1899.
From Sand Hill to Pine. 1900.
Under the Redwoods. 1901.
Openings in the Old Trail. 1902; as *On the Old Trail,* 1902.

Condensed Novels: Second Series: New Burlesques. 1902.
Trent's Trust and Other Stories. 1903.

Plays

Two Men of Sandy Bar, from his own story "Mr. Thompson's Prodigal." 1876.
Ah Sin, with Mark Twain (produced 1877). Edited by Frederick Anderson, 1961.
Sue, with T. Edgar Pemberton, from the story "The Judgment of Bolinas Plain" by Harte (produced 1896). 1902; as *Held Up* (produced 1903).

Verse

The Heathen Chinee. 1870.
Poems. 1871.
That Heathen Chinee and Other Poems, Mostly Humorous. 1871.
East and West Poems. 1871.
Poetical Works. 1872; revised edition, 1896, 1902.
Echoes of the Foot-Hills. 1874.
Some Later Verses. 1898.
Unpublished Limericks and Cartoons. 1933.

Other

Complete Works. 1872.
Prose and Poetry. 2 vols., 1872.
Lectures, edited by Charles Meeker Kozlay. 1909.
Stories and Poems and Other Uncollected Writings, edited by Charles Meeker Kozlay. 1914.
Sketches of the Sixties by Harte and Mark Twain from "The Californian" 1864–67, edited by Charles Meeker Kozlay. 1926; revised edition, 1927.
San Francisco in 1866, Being Letters to the Springfield Republican, edited by George R. Stewart and Edwin S. Fussell. 1951.

Editor, *Outcroppings, Being Selections of California Verse.* 1866.
Editor, *Poems,* by Charles Warren Stoddard. 1867.

Bibliography: in *Bibliography of American Literature* by Jacob Blanck, 1959.

Reading List: *Harte, Argonaut and Exile* by George R. Stewart, 1931; *Mark Twain and Harte* by Margaret Duckett, 1964; *Harte: A Biography* by Richard O'Connor, 1966; *Harte* by Patrick David Morrow, 1972.

*   *   *

Because of the nature of his fiction and the timing of his publication of "The Luck of Roaring Camp" (1868), Bret Harte is often remembered as the earliest of American local colorists. Insofar as his craftsmanship is concerned, however, Harte may be considered the logical extension of earlier Southern humorists like Augustus Baldwin Longstreet, William Tappan Thompson, Johnson Jones Hooper, and Joseph Glover Baldwin, all of whom were realists writing with broad humor of the more primitive moments of Southern frontier life.

Critics have consistently pointed out the influence of Dickens on Harte's work. Joseph B. Harrison in his introduction to *Bret Harte: Representative Selections*, has pinpointed several Dickens influences, e.g., the mixture of humor and sentiment, the exploitation of unique characters in unique situations and environment, the simplification of character to the point of caricature, extravagant dialect and names (Hash, Starbottle, Rats), the love of stupid but good people, opposition to the hypocritical, and satire on injustice.

Harte's literary career lends itself to easy if not simplistic geographic division, i.e., stories composed while the author was in residence in California, in New York, and in Europe. Scholars point out somewhat consistently the gradual deterioration of the artist as he moved further and further from California. In any event, the scholarly consensus is that Harte's literary reputation rests largely on his work completed before the end of 1871 when he returned to the East to write for magazines. Work completed after 1878, when Harte sailed to Europe to be a consul in Prussia, is generally considered hack work and is all but ignored today.

The use of contrast is perhaps the most genuine hallmark of Harte's fiction. Arthur Hobson Quinn, for example, has noted Harte's use of "moral contrast," and John Erskine in *Leading American Novelists* has attributed Harte's successful humor to Harte's perception of contrast in American life itself. "The Outcasts of Poker Flat," which vies with "The Luck of Roaring Camp" for the honor of Harte's best work, centers on use of contrasts: four degenerates are juxtaposed with two innocents, a harlot starves herself to death in order to save a virgin, the gambler Oakhurst gives up his chance for safety to the Innocent and then commits suicide. Erskine notes that Harte perceives the good qualities in the life of the lowly as in "Tennessee's Partner" and that his use of parody in *Condensed Novels*, which satirizes popular sentimental and idealistic novels, is comparable to that of Swinburne.

Local color stories, because of their nature, depend to a large extent upon their fidelity to detail. Harte's stories like "The Outcasts of Poker Flat" or "Miggles," are, therefore, frequently praised for their meaningful use of detail. Some of the best short stories Harte ever wrote were written for *The Overland*: "The Outcasts of Poker Flat," " Miggles," "Tennessee's Partner," "The Idyl of Red Gulch," and "Brown of Calaveras." Scholars generally agree that Harte never again equalled their freshness, spontaneity, compression, and unity.

"Tennessee's Partner" is the third most frequently anthologized Harte story. Here, Harte makes chance, fate, and accident the normal, the customary. The sentimentality in the story satisfied the taste of the reading audience of the late nineteenth century.

Of the more than two hundred poems in the standard edition of Harte, more than one half are narrative, one third humorous or satirical, and one third entirely or partially dialect. Although the great strength of Harte's poetry is his brevity, he fails, on the other hand, to unite brevity and symbolism and emotional implication, a unity necessary to successful poetry. Harte's best poetry is always his satirical and humorous verse. Harte's best two poems and his most frequently reprinted ones are "Plain Language from Truthful James" and "The Society upon the Stanislaus." As a novelist, Harte has generally been judged superficial, for his characters, like many of Dickens' poorer characters, are wooden and puppet-like. The characters, for example, in *Gabriel Conroy, A Waif of the Plains*, and *In the Carquinez Woods* have neither ideas nor passions to be sustained or complicated.

Bret Harte's real achievement, then, is to be found in his local color stories written, for the most part, before 1871, stories which bear his hallmark of brevity, dramatic action reporting, the new morality of the far West, humor, contrast, and uncluttered style. G. K. Chesterton (quoted by Erskine) has observed that Harte's fiction serves, realistically, to remind us that "while it is very rare indeed in the world to find a thoroughly good man, it is rarer still, rare to the point of monstrosity, to find a man who does not either desire to be one or imagine that he is one already."

—George C. Longest

HAWTHORNE, Nathaniel. American. Born Nathaniel Hathorne in Salem, Massachusetts, 4 July 1804. Educated at Samuel Archer's School, Salem, 1819; Bowdoin College, Brunswick, Maine, 1821–25. Married Sophia Peabody in 1842; two daughters and one son. Lived with his mother in Salem, writing and contributing to periodicals, 1825–36; Editor, *American Magazine of Useful and Entertaining Knowledge*, Boston, 1836; weigher and gager in the Boston Customs House, 1839–41; invested in the Brook Farm Commune, West Roxbury, Massachusetts, and lived there, 1841–42; moved to Concord, Massachusetts, 1842–45; Surveyor, Salem Customs House, 1845–49; lived in Lenox, Massachusetts, 1850–51, West Newton, Massachusetts, 1851, and settled again in Concord, 1852; United States Consul in Liverpool, 1853–57; lived in Italy, 1858–59, and London, 1859–60, then returned to Concord. *Died 17 May 1864.*

PUBLICATIONS

Collections

Complete Writings.   22 vols., 1900.
Representative Selections, edited by Austin Warren.   1934
Complete Novels and Selected Tales, edited by Norman Holmes Pearson.   1937.
Works, edited by William Charvat and others.   1963 –
Poems, edited by Richard E. Peck.   1967.

Fiction

Fanshawe: A Tale.   1828; with *The Blithedale Romance*, in *Works*, 1965.
Twice-Told Tales.   1837; revised edition, 1842; in *Works*, 1974.
The Celestial Rail-Road.   1843.
Mosses from an Old Manse.   1846; in *Works*, 1974.
The Scarlet Letter: A Romance.   1850; edited by Sculley Bradley and others, 1962, revised edition, 1978.
The House of the Seven Gables: A Romance.   1851; edited by Seymour L. Gross, 1967.
The Snow-Image and Other Twice-Told Tales.   1851; in *Works*, 1974.
The Blithedale Romance.   1852; edited by Seymour L. Gross and Rosalie Murphy, 1977.
Transformation; or, The Romance of Monte Beni.   1860; as *The Marble Faun*, 1860; edited by Richard H. Rupp, 1971.
Pansie: A Fragment.   1864.
Septimus: A Romance, edited by Una Hawthorne and Robert Browning.   1872; as *Septimus Felton; or, The Elixir of Life*, 1872.
The Dolliver Romance and Other Pieces, edited by Sophia Hawthorne.   1876.
Fanshawe and Other Pieces.   1876.
Dr. Grimshaw's Secret: A Romance, edited by Julian Hawthorne.   1883; edited by Edward H. Davidson, 1954.
The Ghost of Dr. Harris.   1900.

Other

Grandfather's Chair: A History for Youth.   1841; *Famous Old People, Being the Second Epoch of Grandfather's Chair*, 1841; *Liberty Tree, with the Last Words of*

•

Grandfather's Chair, 1841, revised edition, 1842.
Biographical Stories for Children.   1842.
True Stories from History and Biography.   1851.
A Wonder-Book for Girls and Boys.   1851; with *Tanglewood Tales*, in *Works*, 1972.
Life of Franklin Pierce.   1852.
Tanglewood Tales for Girls and Boys, Being a Second Wonder-Book.   1853; with *A Wonder-Book*, in *Works*, 1972.
Our Old Home: A Series of English Sketches.   1863; in *Works*, 1970.
Passages from the American Note-Books, edited by Sophia Hawthorne.   2 vols., 1868.
Passages from the English Note-Books, edited by Sophia Hawthorne.   2 vols., 1870.
Passages from the French and Italian Note-Books, edited by Una Hawthorne.   2 vols., 1871.
Twenty Days with Julian and Little Bunny: A Dairy.   1904.
Love Letters.   2 vols., 1907.
Letters to William D. Ticknor.   2 vols., 1910.
The Heart of Hawthorne's Journal, edited by Newton Arvin.   1929.
The American Notebooks, edited by Randall Stewart.   1932; in *Works*, 1972.
The English Notebook, edited by Randall Stewart.   1941.
Hawthorne as Editor: Selections from His Writings in the American Magazine of Useful and Entertaining Knowledge, edited by Arlin Turner.   1941.

Editor, with Elizabeth Hawthorne, *Peter Parley's Universal History.*   2 vols., 1837; as *Peter Parley's Common School History*, 1838.
Editor, *Journal of an African Cruiser*, by Horatio Bridge.   1845.
Editor, *The Yarn of a Yankee Privateer*, by Benjamin Frederick Browne(?).   1926.

Bibliography: *Hawthorne: A Descriptive Bibliography* by C. E. Frazer Clark, Jr., 1977.

Reading List: *Hawthorne* by Henry James, 1879; *Hawthorne: A Biography* by Randall Stewart, 1948; *Hawthorne's Fiction: The Light and the Dark* by Richard H. Fogle, 1952, revised edition, 1964; *Hawthorne: A Critical Study* by Hyatt A. Waggoner, 1955; *Hawthorne's Tragic Vision* by Roy R. Male, 1957; *Hawthorne, Man and Writer* by Edward Wagenknecht, 1961; *Hawthorne: An Introduction and an Interpretation* by Arlin Turner, 1961; *The Sins of the Fathers: Hawthorne's Psychological Themes* by Frederick Crews, 1966; *Hawthorne, Transcendental Symbolist* by Marjorie Elder, 1969; *The Recognition of Hawthorne: Selected Criticism since 1828* edited by B. Bernard Cohen, 1969; *The Shape of Hawthorne's Career* by Nina Baym, 1976; *Hawthorne: The Poetics of Enchantment* by Edgar A. Dryden, 1977; *Rediscovering Hawthorne* by Kenneth Dauber, 1977.

*   *   *

Nathaniel Hawthorne's fiction is unique in two important respects. He was the first major novelist in English to combine high moral seriousness with transcendent dedication to art. He was also the first major novelist in English to insist upon the basic unreality of his works. An imaginative genius gifted with considerable linguistic skill, he opened a path in literature that few have followed with comparable success. Like all great writers he was original in that fundamental sense in which the work resists duplication because it remains identified with the creative individuality of the author. George Eliot followed Hawthorne in the attempt to wed morality to art, but she attempted the fusion within a framework of realistic verisimilitude. Most writers since Hawthorne who have worked outside of the framework of realism have been less concerned than he with the moral seriousness of their works.

Isolation stands at the heart of his development as an artist. For twelve years after his graduation from Bowdoin College he lived in his mother's house in Salem, publishing

Fanshawe at his own expense and numerous tales and sketches in magazines and gift annuals at rates so low that the income from the twenty-seven tales he published in the *Token* amounted to less than $350. Since all of this early material was published either anonymously or under pseudonyms, he achieved no reputation and acquired no literary friends. In terms of financial success, indeed, it probably would not have mattered much if he had acquired friends and a reputation early. Like other American writers of his time he suffered even during the years of his greatest popularity from the lack of an international copyright law; he could neither compete at home with cheap editions of famous English authors nor reap much income from his sales in England. Although *The Scarlet Letter* made him a name, it earned him a pitifully small income (probably not more than $1,500 from the American sales during his lifetime). Under the circumstances, it is not surprising that he developed a literary aesthetic in which mass appeal had no place. He wrote to please himself and also that occasional isolated reader who would share with him his aesthetic and moral sensibilities.

He early formed the habit of working from the inside outward. Unlike his friend Melville he possessed no well of exotic experience to draw his subject matter from. His material came from his thoughts, his reading, his brooding upon New England and its history. Coming to believe that all truth that matters is inner ("the truth," as he expressed it, "of the human heart"), he considered externalities to be inherently deceptive. Consequently he considered verisimilitude, in the sense of faithfulness to the world of actuality, to be a highly questionable merit in fiction. Much more important to him was the construction of a fictive world that remained faithful to the artist's inmost vision. Hence his insistence that his works were to be judged as romances rather than novels. Hence, too, the considerable drive toward symbol and allegory.

He is a romantic writer, but not because his material is distant in time and place. Among his longer fictions, *The House of the Seven Gables*, *The Blithedale Romance*, and *The Marble Faun* are contemporary with his own time. *The Scarlet Letter* and many of the Tales are set in that Puritan New England that he knew so intimately. He is romantic in the more important sense of considering verifiable fact to be a less important commodity in the world than the unverifiable discoveries of imagination and intuition. He is also romantic in the particularly American sense of possessing a visionary idea of a society in which perfect freedom, equality, and justice might one day prevail, though no such society has yet appeared on earth. It is against such a vision that *The Scarlet Letter* especially must be read; it is the vision that places Hawthorne, for all his idiosyncrasy, in the direct line of American novelists from Cooper through Melville, Twain, and James.

His most frequent themes revolve around the sanctity of the individual, the necessity for warm human relationships, the nature of sin, a distrust of science and the intellect, and a belief in the fundamental ambiguity of earthly phenonema. All are closely related in his work, with an exploration of the nature of sin the tie that binds the others together. Thus the characters of Rappaccini ("Rappaccini's Daughter"), Ethan Brand ("Ethan Brand"), and Roger Chillingworth (*The Scarlet Letter*) mix their sin from the same ingredients: all are coldly intellectual, scientifically detached individuals who possess no effectively warm human relationships, are willing and even eager to intrude upon the privacy of others, and are convinced of the possibility of ultimate triumph over the mysteries of the phenomenal world. The sin of adultery that Hester Prynne of *The Scarlet Letter* has committed is much less sweeping than this. The result of a natural need for human warmth, it is clothed in ambiguity. There are sins and sins. In a more perfect society Hester's act would be no sin. If there exists, however, the unpardonable sin that Ethan Brand seeks it is very close to that attributed to Roger Chillingworth by Arthur Dimmesdale in *The Scarlet Letter*: "He has violated, in cold blood, the sanctity of a human heart."

The terrific "power of blackness" that Melville saw in Hawthorne begins in the isolation of the artist and ends in the ambiguity of his work. As artist he must break through the isolation or remain self-incased and unread. His artistry drives him inward, away from the human contact that is necessary for survival both as a writer and as a man. In his works he must remain true to his deepest vision, including for Hawthorne an abiding sense of the world's unshakeable ambiguities, but he must also make this vision accessible to others. In "The Minister's Black Veil" and "Young Goodman Brown" the touchstones of isolation and ambiguity are given splendid emphasis, but they remain important to the effect of large numbers of other works as well, from deceptively simple sketches such as "Wakefield" or "The Ambitious Guest" through the relative lightness of *The House of the Seven Gables* to the dark complexities of *The Marble Faun*.

In the end, the peculiar conditions of his creative life served him well. Steeped in the New England that he depicted so effectively in the majority of his works, he created masterly short fiction because the form came naturally to him. He probed beneath the surfaces of his subjects because he saw so little in the outward appearances that was of lasting interest. Without the financial support of the British three-decker tradition, he wrote much shorter novels than Dickens or Eliot, but his works gain in impact through compression. Few novelists in English have accomplished so much in so few words as is accomplished in *The Scarlet Letter*. Few have displayed better than Hawthorne does in his best works the power of romance, or, by inference, the limitations of superficial realism. Seldom have the modes of symbol and allegory been so effectively rendered in prose.

—George Perkins

HAY, John (Milton).   American.   Born in Salem, Indiana, 8 October 1838. Educated at Brown University, Providence, Rhode Island, graduated, 1858; studied law in the office of Milton Hay, Springfield, Illinois; admitted to the Illinois Bar, 1861. Served with the Union forces during the Civil War: Colonel. Married Clara Louise Stone in 1874. Secretary to Abraham Lincoln for four years; in the U.S. Diplomatic Service: Secretary of the Legation in Paris, 1865–67; Chargé d'Affaires, Vienna, 1867–68; Secretary of the Legation in Madrid, 1868–70; First Assistant Secretary of State, Washington, D.C., 1879–81; Ambassador to Great Britain, 1897–98; Secretary of State, to President McKinley, 1898–1901, and to President Theodore Roosevelt, 1901–05. Member of the staff, 1870–75, and Editor, 1881, *New York Tribune*. LL.D.: Western Reserve University, Cleveland; Princeton University, New Jersey; Dartmouth College, Hanover, New Hampshire; Yale University, New Haven, Connecticut; Harvard University, Cambridge, Massachusetts. Member, American Academy of Arts and Letters, 1904. *Died 1 July 1905.*

PUBLICATIONS

Collections

Complete Poetical Works, edited by Clarence L. Hay.   1916.

Verse

Jim Bludso of the Prairie Belle, and Little Breeches.   1871.
Pike County Ballads and Other Pieces.   1871; as *Little Breeches and Other Pieces*, 1871.
Poems.   1890.

Fiction

The Bread-Winners: A Social Study.   1884.

Other

Castilian Days.   1871; revised edition, 1890.
Abraham Lincoln: A History, with John G. Nicolay.   10 vols., 1890.
Addresses.   1906.
Letters and Extracts from Diary, edited by Henry Adams and Clara Louise Hay.   3
    vols., 1908.
A Poet in Exile: Early Letters, edited by Caroline Ticknor.   1910.
A College Friendship: A Series of Letters to Hannah Angell.   1938.
Lincoln and the Civil War in the Diaries and Letters of Hay, edited by Tyler
    Dennett.   1939.
Henry James and Hay: The Record of a Friendship, edited by George Monteiro.   1965.

Editor, with John G. Nicolay, *Complete Works,* by Abraham Lincoln.   2 vols., 1894.

Bibliography: in *Bibliography of American Literature* by Jacob Blanck, 1963.

Reading List: *Life and Letters of Hay* by William Roscoe Thayer, 2 vols., 1915; *Hay: The
Gentleman as Diplomat* by Kenton J. Clymer, 1975; *Hay: The Union of Poetry and Politics* by
Howard I. Kushner and Anne Hummel Sherrill, 1977; *Hay* by Robert L. Gale, 1978.

*   *   *

In 1904 John Hay was numbered among the first seven individuals elected to the American
Academy of Arts and Letters. He was so honored as the famous author of *Castilian Days*,
essays on Spain; *Pike County Ballads and Other Pieces*; *Poems*, a collected edition; and
Abraham Lincoln: A History, ten volumes written in collaboration with John G. Nicolay.
Forgotten were the essays and stories he had published in the 1860's and 1870's in *Putnam's*,
Harper's, and the *Atlantic*. It had not yet been established, moreover, that Hay was also the
author of *The Bread-Winners*, an anti-labor novel that so closely reflected Hay's alarm over
the growing threats to society posed by the violent strikes of 1877 and their aftermath, and
one that so obviously drew upon his own sense of himself as a beleaguered member of the
establishment that the prudent author chose to publish his novel anonymously. Its
authorship, a closely guarded secret for decades, was acknowledged only after his death. *The
Bread-Winners* lives today, less for its reactionary argument, than for its sharp portrait of
Maud Matchin, a self-made girl. In this pert and impertinent high-school graduate Hay
created a portrait of American girlhood to stand beside those of James's Daisy Miller and
Howells's Lydia Blood.

Hay's short fiction antedates *The Bread-Winners*, some of it by more than twenty years.
Even though the stories constitute early work, they continue to warrant serious attention,
both for their intrinsic merit and for their surprisingly skilful anticipation of many of the
major technical and thematic interests of the American realists. The principal concerns of his
fiction can be described as the dangers awaiting innocent and not-so-innocent Americans
trying to make their way in Paris ("Shelby Cabell" and "Kane and Abel"), the duties of those
who would be faithful to the Union ("Red, White and Blue"), the wages of love and
miscegenation ("The Foster-Brothers") and the murderous proclivities in the heart of the
midwestern farmer ("The Blood Seedling").

The last of these stories presents the Golyers, a family that figures as well in the Pike County ballads, the first three of which, "Banty Tim," "Jim Bludso, of the Prairie Belle," and "Little Breeches," catapulted Hay to immediate fame. Contemporary arguments over whether Hay or his friend Bret Harte had been the first to exploit the dialects of the American West served both to promote their fame and to delay the assessment of Hay's achievement. If there was no doubt that his poems captured the rhythmic speech of the Pike County Man, the notion that such speech did not provide fit substance for poetry would long plague Hay. It was not immediately recognized that the poems were not primarily attacks on common poetic speech, but rather sly barbs aimed at the conventional morality of his day. In Jim Bludso he presents a hard-talking bigamist who is nevertheless capable of Christian self-sacrifice. This rude practitioner of a religion of humanity, according to the poet, could hardly suffer retribution from a true Christian God. If this poetically unconventional statement did not receive unanimous approval, it did tap a vein of largely unexpressed feelings. With tears in her eyes, George Eliot frequently recited by heart "Jim Bludso," and in *Ulysses* Joyce has Leopold Bloom, on his way to the brothel, ruminate: "I did alla white man could ... Jim Bludso. Hold her nozzle again the bank."

At other times Hay wrote more conventional poems that continue to appeal, among them the political "A Triumph of Order," the skilfully devised "Una," and the witty, self-ironic "A Dream of Bric-à-Brac." But when poets are again permitted to tell stories in verse, Hay's spirited ballads will recover something of the favor they enjoyed in 1897 when, on the occasion of Hay's appointment as Ambassador to the Court of St. James's, English publishers, passing up *Castilian Days* and *Abraham Lincoln*, brought out an edition of Hay's poems, ignoring his properly understated title in 1890 for his collected *Poems* in favor of *Pike County Ballads and Other Poems*, one harking back to his first collection.

—George Monteiro

HAYNE, Paul Hamilton. American. Born in Charleston, South Carolina, 1 January 1830. Educated at Mr. Coates's School, Charleston; Charleston College, graduated 1850; studied law but abandoned his practice for a literary career. Served on Governor Picken's staff during the Civil War. Married Mary Middleton Michel in 1852; one son. Free-lance journalist, and member of the editorial staff of *Southern Literary Gazette*, Charleston, and the Washington *Spectator*, 1850–57; a Founder and Editor, with W. B. Carlisle, *Russell's Magazine*, Charleston, 1857–60; made homeless and bankrupt by the Civil War: moved to Groveton, near Augusta, Georgia, and subsisted on a small farm. LL.D.: Washington and Lee College, Lexington, Virginia, 1882. *Died 6 July 1886.*

PUBLICATIONS

Collections

The Southern Poets, with Lanier and Timrod, edited by J. W. Abernethy. 1904.

Verse

Poems. 1855.
Sonnets and Other Poems. 1857.

*Avolio: A Legend of the Island of Cos, with Poems Lyrical, Miscellaneous, and
   Dramatic.* 1859.
Legends and Lyrics. 1872.
The Mountain of the Lovers, with Poems of Nature and Tradition. 1875.
Poems, Complete Edition. 1882.
The Broken Battalions. 1885.

Other

Lives of Robert Young Hayne and Hugh Swinton Legaré. 1878
A Collection of Hayne Letters, edited by Daniel M. McKeithan. 1944.
The Correspondence of Bayard Taylor and Hayne, edited by Charles Duffy. 1945.

Editor, *The Poems of Henry Timrod.* 1873.

Bibliography: in *Bibliography of American Literature* by Jacob Blanck, 1963.

Reading List: *Hayne: Life and Letters* by Kate Harbes Becker, 1951; *Hayne* by Rayburn S. Moore, 1972.

*   *   *

Paul Hamilton Hayne began publishing poems at the age of fifteen, and by 1861 his poetry had appeared in *Graham's Magazine,* the *Atlantic Monthly,* and the *Southern Literary Messenger* and he had collected three volumes of Romantic verse based chiefly on the examples of Keats, Hunt, Poe, Tennyson, and Longfellow. His work attracted the critical attention of Lowell and Whipple, but the Civil War temporarily interrupted his development.

After the war Hayne's muse continued to develop in the mainstream of the Anglo-American tradition. He became a versatile versifier and employed a wide range of forms, metrical schemes, and techniques. His short poems – sonnets and nature lyrics in particular – demonstrate his work at its best. In fact, as his career progressed, Hayne became a leading American sonneteer, and such pieces as "Aspects of the Pines," "The Voice in the Pines," "To a Bee," "The First Mocking-Bird in Spring," "Hints of Spring," and "Midsummer (on the Farm)" reflect his achievement as a lyricist on nature.

At the same time Hayne could also write successful long poems, narratives like "The Wife of Brittany," an interpretation of Chaucer's "Franklin's Tale" and Hayne's most ambitious and fully realized long poem, and odes like "Muscadines," a sensuous piece whose verbal melody derives from the "liquid magic" of the Southern grape, and "Unveiled," an irregular ode whose tone and view of nature suggest a philosophical kinship with "Tintern Abbey." Even late in his career Hayne continued to write long poems, frequently celebrating occasions or commemorating events such as the centennials of the battles of King's Mountain and Yorktown in 1881 or the sesquicentennial of the founding of Georgia in 1883, among others. The ode on Georgia, it should be noted, and the production of his last four years, including three additional long poems, a fine sonnet on Robert E. Lee, and a handful of lyrics that are among the best he ever wrote on his own locale, were never collected.

After Simms's death in 1870, Hayne became the "representative" poet and literary spokesman for the South. Indeed, in the scope, versatility, and bulk of his production, he remains a substantial minor American poet of the period, even though a sizable proportion of his output is ephemeral magazine verse. Admittedly, few of his poems come near the perfection of, say, Poe's "To Helen," for he lacked Poe's sense of art and critical acumen. Moreover, he accepted without challenge the conventions of the nineteenth-century Anglo-American poetic tradition, and many of his poems embody certain aspects of its weakest features – ornate and artificial language, empty abstractions, unalloyed bookishness and monotonous metrical regularity. But these standards of time and taste cannot change the fact that Hayne's canon reflects the full scope of a striving for expression in a spectrum of poetic types and structures nor should they in any way detract from the devotion he rendered his muse despite discouraging and distressing conditions of poverty and ill health during the last part of his life. His accomplishment was modest, but his dedication to literature was exemplary.

—Rayburn S. Moore

HEARN, (Patricio) Lafcadio (Carlos Tessima).   Japanese.   Born on the island of Santa Maura, Greece, 27 June 1850; raised in Dublin; emigrated to Japan, 1890; naturalized, 1895. Educated at St. Cuthbert's College, Ushaw, County Durham, England, 1863–66; Petits Precepteurs, Yvetot, near Rouen, France, 1867. Married 1) a mulatto c. 1875; 2) Setsu Koizumi in 1891; three sons and one daughter. Settled in the United States, 1869, and worked at various menial jobs in Cincinnati, Ohio; became a proofreader for Robert Clarke Company, then a member of staff of *Trade List* weekly, and a reporter for the *Cincinnati Enquirer*, 1873–75; lost this job because of the miscegenation laws; member of staff of the *Cincinnati Commercial*, 1875–78; Assistant Editor, *New Orleans Item*, 1878–81; member of staff of the *New Orleans Times-Democrat*, 1881–87; lived in Martinique and wrote for *Harper's*, 1887–89, then went to Japan: teacher in the Ordinary Middle School, Matsue, 1890–91, and the Government College, Kumamoto, 1891–94; worked for *Kobe Chronicle*, 1894–95; Professor of English Literature, Imperial University, Tokyo, 1896–1903; English Teacher, Waseda University, 1904. *Died 26 September 1904.*

PUBLICATIONS

i

Collections

Writings.   16 vols., 1922.
Selected Writings, edited by Henry Goodman.   1949.

Fiction

Chita: A Memory of Last Island.   1889.
Youma: The Story of a West-Indian Slave.   1890.
Barbarous Barbers and Other Stories, edited by Ichiro Nishizaki.   1939.

Other

Stray Leaves from Strange Literature.   1884.
Some Chinese Ghosts.   1887.

Two Years in the French West Indies.   1890.
Glimpses of Unfamiliar Japan.   2 vols., 1894.
Out of the East: Reveries and Studies in New Japan.   1895.
Kokoro: Hints and Echoes of Japanese Inner Life.   1896.
Gleanings in Buddha-Fields: Studies of Hand and Soul in the Far East.   1897.
Exotics and Retrospectives.   1898.
In Ghostly Japan.   1899.
Shadowings.   1900.
A Japanese Miscellany.   1901.
Kotto, Being Japanese Curios, with Sundry Cobwebs.   1902.
Kwaidan: Stories and Studies of Strange Things.   1904.
Japan: An Attempt at Interpretation.   1904.
The Romance of the Milky Way and Other Studies and Stories.   1905.
Letters from the Raven, Being the Correspondence of Hearn with Henry Watkin, edited
    by Milton Bronner.   1907.
The Japanese Letters, edited by Elizabeth Bisland.   1910.
Leaves from the Diary of an Impressionist: Early Writings, edited by Ferris
    Greenslet.   1911.
Editorials from the Kobe Chronicle, edited by Merle Johnson.   1913; edited by Makoto
    Sangu, 1960.
Fantastics and Other Fancies, edited by Charles Woodward Hutson.   1914.
Karma, edited by Albert Mordell.   1918.
Essays in European and Oriental Literature, edited by Albert Mordell.   1923.
Creole Sketches, edited by Charles Woodward Hutson.   1924.
An American Miscellany: Articles and Stories Now First Collected, edited by Albert
    Mordell.   2 vols., 1924.
Occidental Gleanings: Sketches and Essays Now First Collected, edited by Albert
    Mordell.   2 vols., 1925.
Some New Letters and Writings, edited by Sanki Ichikawa.   1925.
Editorials, edited by Charles Woodward Hutson.   1926.
Facts and Fancies, edited by R. Tanabé.   1929.
Essays on American Literature, edited by Sanki Ichikawa.   1929.
Gibbeted: Execution of a Youthful Murderer, edited by P. D. Perkins.   1933.
Spirit Photography, edited by P. D. Perkins.   1933.
Letters to a Pagan, edited by R. B. Powers.   1933.
Letters from Shimane and Kyushu.   1935.
American Articles, edited by Ichiro Nishizaki.   4 vols., 1939.
Buying Christmas Toys and Other Essays, edited by Ichiro Nishizaki.   1939.
Literary Essays, edited by Ichiro Nishizaki.   1939.
The New Radiance and Other Scientific Sketches, edited by Ichiro Nishizaki.   1939.
Oriental Articles, edited by Ichiro Nishizaki.   1939.
An Orange Christmas.   1941.
Children of the Levee, edited by O. W. Frost.   1957.
Japan's Religions: Shinto and Buddhism, edited by Kazumitsu Kato.   1966.

Editor, *La Cuisine Creole: A Collection of Recipes.*   1885.

Translator, *One of Cleopatra's Nights,* by Gautier.   1882.
Translator, *Gombo Zhèbes: Little Dictionary of Creole Proverbs.*   1885.
Translator, *The Crime of Sylvestre Bonnard,* by Anatole France.   1890.
Translator, *Japanese Fairy Tale* series.   5 vols., 1898–1922.
Translator, *The Temptation of St. Anthony,* by Flaubert.   1910.
Translator, *Japanese Lyrics.*   1915.

Translator, *Saint Anthony and Other Stories*, by de Maupassant, edited by Albert Mordell.   1924.

Translator, *The Adventures of Walter Schnaffs and Other Stories*, by de Maupassant, edited by Albert Mordell.   1931.

Translator, *Stories*, by Pierre Loti, edited by Albert Mordell.   1933.

Translator, *Stories*, by Zola, edited by Albert Mordell.   1935.

Translator, *Sketches and Tales from the French*, edited by Albert Mordell.   1935.

Lecture notes of Hearn's Japanese students published: *Interpretations of Literature*, 2 vols., 1915, *Appreciations of Poetry*, 1916, *Life and Literature*, 1917, and *Pre-Raphaelite and Other Poets*, 1922, all edited by John Erskine; *A History of English Literature*, 2 vols., 1927, supplement, 1927, revised edition, 1941, *Complete Lectures on Art, Literature, and Philosophy*, 1932, *On Poetry*, 1934, and *On Poets*, 1934, all edited by R. Tanabé; *Lectures on Shakespeare*, edited by Sanki Ichikawa, 1928; *Lectures on Prosody*, 1929; *Victorian Philosophy*, 1930; *Lectures on Tennyson*, edited by Shigetsugu Kishi, 1941.

Bibliography: *Hearn: A Bibliography of His Writings* by F. R. and Ione Perkins, 1934; in *Bibliography of American Literature* by Jacob Blanck, 1963.

Reading List; *Life and Letters* by Elizabeth Bisland, 2 vols., 1906; *Hearn* by Marcel Robert, 2 vols., 1950–51; *Young Hearn* by O. W. Frost, 1958; *Hearn* by Elizabeth Stevenson, 1961; *An Ape of Gods: The Art and Thought of Hearn* by Beongcheon Yu, 1964; *Discoveries: Essays on Hearn* by Albert Mordell, 1964; *Hearn* by Arthur E. Kunst, 1969.

*   *   *

Parental desertion and a rootless, restless childhood left Lafcadio Hearn with a heart "like a bird fluttering impatiently for the migrating season," spurning the "egotistical individualism," "constitutional morality," and scientific positivism of an Anglo-Saxon world from which he "considered [him]self ostracized, tabooed, outlawed." Initially he sought in creole New Orleans ("the paradise of the South") and the tropical Caribbean that "sensuous life ..., the life desire" which would favour "the development of a morbid nervous sensibility to material impressions, ... absolute loss of thinking, ... numbing and clouding of memory." But it was the less languid, more ascetic culture of the Orient which finally offered him the refuge of "feelings, so strangely far away from all the nineteenth century part of me, that the faint blind stirrings of them make one afraid – deliciously afraid."

At his best, Hearn evokes both in form and content an ethos "as gentle as the light of dreams," "the all-temperate world," "soft serenity" and "passionless tenderness" and "the vague but immeasurable emotion of Shinto" of his adoptive homeland. "Depth does not exist in the Japanese soulstream," he observed, and the evocative, picturesque surfaces of his essays seem to gain from his own ocular deficiency: "a landscape necessarily suggests less to the keen-sighted man than to the myope. The keener the view the less depth in the impression produced." His *penchant*, derived from a journalistic training, was for the quick sketch and fleeting *aperçu*; *Two Years in the French West Indies* he described as "simple note-making," "impressions of the moment," a method disclosed by the very titles of his later work: *Glimpses of Unfamiliar Japan*, *Gleanings in Buddha Fields*, *Stray Leaves from Strange Literature*, the latter being "reconstructions of what impressed me as most fantastically beautiful in the most exotic literature." *Some Chinese Ghosts*, *Shadowings*, *In Ghostly Japan* likewise retell a society through its most impalpable manifestations. Herbert Spencer's evolutionary vitalism taught him "a new reverence for all kinds of faith" which Hearn transferred to the cult of ancestor-worship. Seeking to reconcile his western sense of fragmentary but unique identity with oriental quietism and self-abnegation, he came to believe that "We are, each and all, infinite compounds of anterior lives" (*Gleanings*), and that "the thoughts and acts of each being, projected beyond the individual existence, shape other lives unborn" (*Out of the East*). He saw the past as subliminal echoes investing the present, and in the Japanese Festival of the Dead found a ceremonious symbolism of the human condition: "Are we not ourselves as lanterns launched upon a deeper and a dimmer sea, and ever separating further and further one from another as we drift to the inevitable dissolution?" (*In Ghostly Japan*).

Hearn's style, like that he admired in Poe and Gautier, is an "engraved gem-work of words," rich with "voluptuous delicacy" – exquisite, precious, given to elaborate catalogues of isolated details and a self-conscious, sesquipedalian cadence which can overwhelm the sense ("mesmeric lentor," "the stridulous telegraphy of crickets," "a limpid magnificence of light indescribable"). In his sympathy for the intangible and evanescent he can also rise to poignancy and at times a sharp, racy vigour.

—Stan Smith

HERNE, James A.   American.   Born James Ahern in Cohoes, New York, 1 February 1839. Educated in local schools until age 13; largely self-taught. Married 1) Helen Western in 1866 (divorced); 2) the actress Katherine Corcoran in 1878, three daughters. Debut as an actor, in repertory, Troy, New York, 1859; appeared with John Ford's company in Baltimore and Washington, D.C. during the Civil War; leading man in the Lucille Western Company, touring the United States, 1865–67; thereafter managed the Grand Opera House, New York; Stage Director of the Baldwin Theatre, San Francisco, 1875–80: began writing for the stage by collaborating with his associate David Belasco in 1879: starred in *Hearts of Oak* for the next seven years, a success which allowed him to retire to Dorchester, Massachusetts, and devote himself to writing full-time for the stage; dissipated his fortune on his next play: forced to move back to New York and work as a stage manager for Klaw and Erlanger, 1891; appeared in *Shore Acres*, 1892–98, the success of which restored his fortunes; retired to Southampton, Long Island. *Died 2 June 1901.*

PUBLICATIONS

Collections

   Shore Acres and Other Plays (includes *Sag Harbor, Hearts of Oak*), edited by Mrs. James
      A. Herne.   1928.
   The Early Plays (includes *The Minute Men of 1774–1775, Drifting Apart, The Reverend
      Griffith Davenport, Within an Inch of His Life*), edited by Arthur Hobson
      Quinn.   1940.

Plays

   Within an Inch of His Life with David Belasco, from a play by Gaboriau (produced
      1879).   In *The Early Plays*, 1940.

Marriage by Moonlight, with David Belasco, from the play *Camilla's Husband* by Watts Phillips (produced 1879).

Hearts of Oak, with David Belasco (as *Chums*, produced 1879; as *Hearts of Oak*, produced 1879).   In *Shore Acres and Other Plays*, 1928; revised version by Herne, as *Sag Harbor* (produced 1900), in *Shore Acres and Other Plays*, 1928.

The Minute Men of 1774–1775 (produced 1886).   In *The Early Plays*, 1940.

Drifting Apart (produced 1888).   In *The Early Plays*, 1940.

Margaret Fleming (produced 1890).   Edited by Myron Matlaw, in *The Black Crook and Other 19th-Century American Plays*, 1967.

My Colleen (produced 1892).

Shore Acres (produced 1893).   In *Shore Acres and Other Plays*, 1928.

The Reverend Griffith Davenport, from the novel *An Unofficial Patriot* by Helen H. Gardener (produced 1899).   In *The Early Plays*, 1940; Act III edited by Arthur Hobson Quinn, in *American Literature 24*, 1952.

Bibliography: "Selected Bibliography of Herne" by John Perry, in *Bulletin of Bibliography 31*, 1974.

Reading List: *Herne: The Rise of Realism in the American Drama* by Herbert J. Edwards and Julie A. Herne, 1964; *Herne, The American Ibsen* by John Perry, 1978.

*   *   *

Most of the plays by the accomplished actor, James A. Herne, remain in the limbo of strictly minor American drama. *The Minute Men of 1774–1775*, *Drifting Apart*, *My Colleen*, or *The Reverend Griffith Davenport*, and even those written in collaboration with David Belasco, including *Within an Inch of His Life*, *Marriage by Moonlight*, or *Hearts of Oak*, redone by Herne as *Sag Harbor*, are now so obscure as to be virtually unobtainable save in limited library collections. But with *Margaret Fleming* and *Shore Acres* Herne has survived as the most important pivotal American playwright of the late 19th century. In these two plays, particularly the former, Herne took the most significant steps of any American dramatist of his time away from the well-made artificialities of 19th-century romance and melodrama toward the development of effective dramatic realism.

Margaret Fleming abounds in 19th-century conventions and artifices: the wronged young girl who must bear her child in shame and die; the threatened vengeance of the shamed girl's sister, a servant in the home of the seducer; the angelic wife struck blind as she learns of her husband's faithlessness. But the play goes well beyond the surface clichés. The seducer is no caddish rogue, but a successful manufacturer, Philip Fleming, obviously well-respected within the community, and deeply in love with his wife. He is no villain, but neither is he a hero. He is in truth, a "fallen man," and it is his suffering and redemption which motivate a good part of the action, not the fate of the fallen woman who, in life and death, remains offstage, merely a point of reference. The problem of Philip Fleming's infidelity is strictly a domestic matter to be recognized and discussed by husband, wife, and family physician. Margaret Fleming, stunned by her husband's inadequately explained deed, refuses to be martyred and she survives through firmness and conviction evolving out of common sense and rational behavior. Her own behavior as an offended human being, not merely a stereotyped wronged woman, renders her far superior to her husband, whom she permits to return to her but only on her conditions. Reconciliation remains solely a dim hope in the indefinite future.

Thus Herne's skill in giving his central characters the strengths, weaknesses, and motivations of recognizable human individuals well developed within a recognizable contemporary society keeps *Margaret Fleming* from collapse into sentimental bathos. The last act, which survives today through Herne's daughter's reconstruction, refuses to tie up the threads in conventionally neat fashion. There will be a life together for Philip and Margaret Fleming, but the ending, rather than "happy," is believable and eminently satisfactory. The wall remains between husband and wife, but, as Herne acknowledges in this ending (he apparently experimented with several) so shocking to 19th-century audiences, men and women, do, in reality, survive such traumas. They continue their lives; the world does not end; the drama does not conclude with the descent of the final curtain. The "ever after," as in life, is uncertain, possibly dangerous, and even terrifying.

Shore Acres, a lesser play, has too many outdated melodramatics. Still, Herne permits no heroes, no heroines, and no villains. There are logic and sound reason behind the businessman who would foreclose and subdivide the homestead. The love affair and its complications, if we ignore the dark and stormy night syndrome, are understandable. Uncle Nat, the prime mover, talks and acts with reasonable believability. The minor characters, relatively well-developed, enter and depart with clear motivation. For all the frequent transparent arbitrariness, there is a realistic aura in setting, action, and language.

Neither play is a great work of dramatic art. Both, however, are significant. To criticize the creaks and groans of structure is to miss the point of their artistic advances. Though *Margaret Fleming* may have been quite literally driven from the stage by adverse reaction to its daring theme and shocking ending, the courage of the playwright in creating it is recognized for the exceptional deed that it was. The significance of the play, together in a lesser degree with *Shore Acres*, in providing the substantial push behind the American drama's movement toward full-fledged artistic participation in 20th-century world theatre is abundantly apparent.

—Jordan Y. Miller

HERRICK, Robert. American. Born in Cambridge, Massachusetts, 26 April 1868. Educated at Cambridge High School, 1881–85; Harvard University, Cambridge, Massachusetts, 1885–90 (Editor, Harvard *Advocate* and *Monthly*). Married Harriet Emery in 1894 (divorced, 1916); two children. Instructor in Rhetoric, Massachusetts Institute of Technology, Cambridge, 1890–93; joined faculty of the University of Chicago, 1893: Professor of English, 1905–23; Teacher, Rollins College, Winter Park, Florida, 1931; Secretary to the Governor of the Virgin Islands, 1935–38. *Died 23 December 1938.*

PUBLICATIONS

Fiction

Literary Love-Letters and Other Stories.   1897.
The Man Who Wins.   1897.
The Gospel of Freedom.   1898.
Love's Dilemmas (stories).   1898.
The Web of Life.   1900.
The Real World.   1901; as *Jock o' Dreams*, 1908.
Their Child (stories).   1903.
The Common Lot.   1904.

The Memoirs of an American Citizen.   1905; edited by Daniel Aaron, 1963.
The Master of the Inn (stories).   1908.
Together.   1908.
A Life for a Life.   1910.
The Healer.   1911.
His Great Adventure.   1913.
One Woman's Life.   1913.
Clark's Field.   1914.
The Conscript Mother (stories).   1916.
Homely Lilla.   1923.
Waste.   1924.
Wanderings (stories).   1925.
Chimes.   1926.
The End of Desire.   1932.
Sometime.   1933.

Other

Composition and Rhetoric for Schools, with Lindsay Todd Damon.   1899; revised
    edition, 1911.
Teaching English, with May Estelle Cook and Lindsay Todd Damon.   1899.
The World Decision.   1916.
Little Black Dog.   1931.

Reading List: *Herrick: The Development of a Novelist* by Blake Nevius, 1962; *Herrick* by
Louis J. Budd, 1971.

*   *   *

In his first novelette, *The Man Who Wins*, Robert Herrick dealt with the question which
was to be central to his entire work: what is success? A dedicated medical researcher is
diverted into a lucrative practice, but late in life he sees his mistake and encourages young
men not to seek material gain. Similarly, in *The Web of Life* a doctor samples and rejects the
luxurious life of a society physician and refuses to marry the daughter of a capitalist until she
renounces her wealth. *The Master of the Inn* presents a doctor who heals with simple
methods in a rural hospital although he commands a knowledge of modern medicine. *The
Healer* deals with a Canadian doctor who is traduced by his wife into leaving his spiritually
rewarding life in the wild for a financially rewarding practice in Chicago. Disgusted by the
avarice of city doctors, the doctor recommends that the professions all become "great
monastic orders," and returns to his home.
Other novels contrast the proper use of technical knowledge to help mankind with the use
of knowledge for selfish gain. An architect in *The Common Lot* exploits his profession until
his shady practices cause several people to be killed in a fire. Business executives climb to the
top in their fields before realizing the hollowness of their triumphs in *The Real World*, *A Life
for a Life*, and *Waste*. All the executives atone by working for small, struggling businesses
and crusading against trusts. Only the central character of *Memoirs of an American Citizen*, a
meat-packer named Van Harrington who claws his way to a fortune and a seat in the Senate,
seems to have few regrets. Herrick was more proud of this characterization than any other,
and it is doubtless his best. Herrick enlivened these novels with interesting details from the
worlds of business and the professions, freighting them with symbolic weight which
skillfully clarified the conflict between the central figures. However, it is not always clear
why small businesses in the West are more moral and rewarding than large ones in the East.

In all these novels, Herrick buttressed the main plot with a sub-plot contrasting the sordid family relationships of the rich with the more loving and simple ones of the lower classes. In *Together, One Woman's Life, Homely Lilla*, and *The End of Desire*, he placed his main emphasis on the problem of women's rights, sexual liberation, and modern marriage. Advanced for his day in these matters, Herrick recommended that women share men's work and that men relieve women from the drudgery of housework and child-rearing. As with business, Herrick finds greed the enemy of good marriages.

Clark's Field shows why private property should not be allowed to restrict urban growth, while *Chimes* deals with academic life. Herrick's views on many subjects are summarized in his Utopian novel of the future, *Sometime*.

Even if his novels are occasionally resolved by flimsy devices such as earthquakes or fires, Herrick deserves serious attention for his incisive criticism of his culture and his accurate picture of it.

—William Higgins

HOFFMAN, Charles Fenno. American. Born in New York City, 7 February 1806. Educated at Columbia University, New York, 1821–23; studied law with Harmanus Bleecker, Albany, New York; admitted to the New York bar, 1827. Practised law in New York City, 1827–30; Editor, with Charles King, New York *American*, 1830–33; Editor, *Knickerbocker* magazine, New York, 1833; toured the midwest United States, 1833–34; Editor, *American Monthly Magazine*, New York, 1835–37, and New York *Mirror*, 1837; full-time writer, 1838–39; Associate Editor, with Horace Greeley, *New Yorker*, 1840; Third Chief Clerk, 1841–43, and Deputy Surveyor, 1843–44, Office of the Surveyor of Customs of the Port of New York; full-time writer, 1844–47; Editor, *Literary World*, New York, 1847–49; became insane: confined to the Harrisburg, Pennsylvania Insane Asylum, 1849 until his death. A.M.: Columbia University, 1837. *Died 7 June 1884.*

PUBLICATIONS

Verse

The Vigil of Faith and Other Poems. 1842; revised edition, as *Songs and Other Poems*, 1846.
The Echo; or, Borrowed Notes for Home Circulation. 1844.
Love's Calendar, Lays of the Hudson, and Other Poems. 1847.
Poems, edited by Edward F. Hoffman. 1873.

Fiction

Wild Scenes in the Forest and Prairie. 1839.
Greyslaer: A Romance of the Mohawk. 1840.

Other

A Winter in the West.   1835.

Editor, *The New York Book of Poetry.*   1837; as *The Gems of American Poetry,* 1840.

Bibliography: in *Bibliography of American Literature* by Jacob Blanck, 1963.

Reading List: *Hoffman* by Homer F. Barnes, 1930.

*   *   *

During the 1830's and 1840's, Charles Fenno Hoffman was among the more influential of a group of "literati," as Edgar Allan Poe referred to them, who called themselves the "Knickerbockers," a term made famous by Washington Irving's *Knickerbocker History of New York* and by the *Knickerbocker Magazine* (1833–1865), which Hoffman helped to found. This group, which included James Fenimore Cooper, William Cullen Bryant, and Washington Irving, among others, tried to shape the literary tastes of the nation and to make New York the literary center of the day. It especially encouraged the writing of literature on American themes, and it was dedicated to improving the quality and variety of American literature, as it then existed.

Hoffman's works reflect the concerns and preoccupations of the Knickerbocker group. His best poems are those which romanticize the splendor and potentiality of the American landscape. Of these, the most memorable include "To the Hudson River," "The Morning Hymn," "Forest Musings," and "Moonlight on the Hudson." Skilled in the art of prosody, Hoffman injected a lyrical quality into his verse which made many of his poems extremely popular, especially those which were set to music. "Monterey," for example, was for many years one of the most popular ballads written in America, and it is still sung today.

Hoffman's prose, like his verse, was strongly nationalistic in its intentions and themes. His best known novel, *Greyslaer: A Romance of the Mohawk*, was a fictional adaptation of the infamous Beauchamp-Sharp murder case. Critics appreciated *Greyslaer* and for a time the novel competed successfully with the frontier romances of Cooper. The result of an excursion on horseback through Illinois, Michigan, Iowa, and Pennsylvania, *A Winter in the West* provided many Americans with their first detailed account of life on the Western frontier as it existed in the early 1830's. A skilled observer, Hoffman mastered the genre of travel literature. His discrimination and learning allowed him to select and describe incidents and characters which transcend regional particularities and which, even today, provide insight into whatever part of America he visited.

As a critic and editor, Hoffman encouraged the writing and publication of books and literature on American subjects. Hoffman believed that it was the critic's function to encourage excellence rather than to denigrate needlessly. He especially encouraged young writers who he felt might profit from some degree of public recognition, even if undeserved. About *Typee*, Herman Melville's first novel, Hoffman wrote: "One of the most delightful and well written narratives that ever came from an American pen." He was also instrumental in helping such unknown writers as Francis Parkman, whose classic account of overland adventure, *The California and Oregon Trail*, was recommended for publication by Hoffman.

Regrettably, Hoffman's literary career was cut short by illness and financial worries. Unable to support himself by writing, he was forced to take a position in a New York customs office. For several years he had been working on a novel which he hoped would be his greatest literary success but which was accidentally destroyed by his maid, who used it as kindling. This unfortunate mishap proved too much for Hoffman. With nerves already weakened from excessive toil and worry, he began treatment for a mental disorder which eventuated in his incarceration at the state hospital in Harrisburg, Pennsylvania, where he spent the remaining thirty-five years of his life, contented but hopelessly insane.

—James A. Levernier

HOLMES, Oliver Wendell. American. Born in Cambridge, Massachusetts, 29 August 1809. Educated at Phillips Academy, Andover, Massachusetts; studied law at Harvard University, Cambridge, Massachusetts, graduated 1829; studied medicine for two years in Europe, then at Harvard Medical School, M.D. 1836. Married Amelia Lee Jackson in 1840; three children. Practised medicine in Boston; Professor of Anatomy and Physiology, Dartmouth College, Hanover, New Hampshire, 1838–40; discovered that Puerperal Fever was contagious, 1843; Professor of Anatomy, Harvard Medical School, 1847–82. Honorary degrees: Oxford, Cambridge, and Edinburgh universities, 1886. *Died 7 October 1894.*

PUBLICATIONS

Collections

    Complete Poetical Works, edited by Horace E. Scudder. 1895.
    Representative Selections, edited by S. I. Hayakawa and Howard Mumford Jones. 1939.

Verse

    The Harbinger: A May-Gift. 1833.
    Poems. 1836; revised editon, 1846, 1848, 1849.
    Urania: A Rhymed Lesson. 1846.
    Astraea: The Balance of Illusions. 1850.
    Poetical Works. 1852.
    Songs and Poems of the Class of 1829, second edition. 1859; revised edition, 1868.
    Songs in Many Keys. 1861.
    Poems. 1862.
    Humorous Poems. 1865.
    Songs of Many Seasons 1862–1874. 1874.
    Poetical Works. 1877.
    The Iron Gate and Other Poems. 1880.
    Poetical Works. 2 vols., 1881.
    Illustrated Poems. 1885.
    Before the Curfew and Other Poems, Chiefly Occasional. 1888.
    At Dartmouth: The Phi Beta Kappa Poem 1839. 1940.

Fiction

Elsie Venner: A Romance of Destiny.   1861.
The Guardian Angel.   1867.
A Mortal Antipathy: First Opening of the New Portfolio.   1885.

Other

Boylston Prize Dissertations for 1836 and 1837.   1838.
Homoeopathy and Its Kindred Delusions (lectures).   1842.
The Autocrat of the Breakfast-Table.   1858.
The Professor at the Breakfast-Table, with the Story of Iris.   1860.
Currents and Counter-Currents in Medical Science, with Other Addresses and Essays.   1861.
Soundings from the Atlantic.   1863.
The Poet at the Breakfast-Table: His Talks with His Fellow-Boarders and the Reader.   1872.
John Lothrop Motley: A Memoir.   1878.
The School-Boy.   1879.
Poems and Prose Passages, edited by Josephine E. Hodgdon.   1881.
Medical Essays 1842–1882.   1883.
Pages from an Old Volume of Life: A Collection of Essays 1857–1881.   1883.
Ralph Waldo Emerson.   1884.
Our Hundred Days in Europe.   1887.
Over the Teacups.   1890.
Writings.   14 vols., 1891–92.
A Dissertation on Acute Pericarditis.   1937.
The Autocrat's Miscellanies (miscellany), edited by Albert Mordell.   1959.

Editor, with Jacob Bigelow, *Principles of the Theory and Practice of Medicine,* by Marshall Hall.   1839.
Editor, with Donald G. Mitchell, *The Atlantic Almanac 1868.*   1867.

Bibliography: *Bibliography of Holmes* by Thomas Franklin Currier and Eleanor M. Tilton, 1953; in *Bibliography of American Literature* by Jacob Blanck, 1963.

Reading List: *Life and Letters of Holmes* by John T. Morse, Jr., 2 vols., 1896; *Holmes of the Breakfast-Table* by Mark A. De Wolfe Howe, 1936; *Amiable Autocrat: A Biography of Holmes* by Eleanor M. Tilton, 1947; *Holmes* by Miriam R. Small, 1963.

*   *   *

The great popular reputation of Oliver Wendell Holmes in the nineteenth century receded with the eclipse of New England pre-eminence. Except for the rural Whittier, Holmes was the most provincial of the New England writers, and unlike the others he did not espouse causes. The Boston of his occasional verse and genial essays was not (according to the editors of *Representative Selections*) "the rebellious Boston, out of which came the anti-slavery societies, transcendentalism, and the feminist movement." In the opening chapter of his first novel (*Elsie Venner*) Holmes describes and provides a lasting label for cultured, mercantile Bostonians with Bulfinch houses, Beacon Street addresses, and ancestral portraits. He became the spokesman for this "Brahmin Caste of New England" when his *Autocrat of the Breakfast-Table* began to appear in the *Atlantic Monthly* in 1857. Although his public had read his occasional poems ever since he was a Harvard undergraduate, his new image as "the Autocrat" established Holmes's reputation as a major American writer.

There had been little time for writing prose between 1830 and 1857, for Holmes had become an M.D. and held professorships of anatomy at Dartmouth and Harvard. But Holmes was a brilliant and incessant talker, and when he hit upon the scheme of jotting down his own talk, he had the matter for his essay series. Literary historians agree that his personality imposed itself upon and gave unity to his writing – poetry, essays, and fiction alike. There is a consistent mental set in his writing also: he was a clear-headed rationalist who disliked even the "bullying" of science and abhorred the dogmatism of theology. His attacks on Calvinism were his closest approximation to taking up a cause, but it seems strange now that Boston thought of him as an American Voltaire. However, Holmes liked to point out the parallels between his own life and Dr. Johnson's. Johnson was born in 1709, Holmes in 1809; both were urban beings, and Holmes's devotion to Boston matched Johnson's love of London. Both were great talkers and were devoted to common sense; and, though his wit has not survived as well as Johnson's, one, at least, of Holmes's remarks is remembered: "Boston State-House is the hub of the solar system. You couldn't pry that out of a Boston man if you had the tire of all creation straightened out for a crowbar."

The *Atlantic Monthly* version of *The Autocrat of the Breakfast-Table* begins, "I was just going to say, when I was interrupted." After the twelve *Atlantic* installments had become a book in 1858, the author explains that the interruption had lasted a quarter of a century, since two articles entitled "The Autocrat of the Breakfast Table" had appeared in the *New England Magazine* in 1831 and 1832. He had matured and gained confidence in the twenty-five-year interval: along with his medical practice and professorships, he had published important medical essays – and a volume of poems. His Harvard lectures were as celebrated for their wit as for their learning, and from 1841 to 1857 he was a sought-after lyceum lecturer on literary as well as medical subjects. But Dr. Holmes was becoming even better known in Boston and Cambridge as a genial humorist and master of conversation.

His fellow-Brahmin, James Russell Lowell, accepted the editorship of the *Atlantic Monthly* on the condition that Holmes become a regular contributor. Holmes had suggested the name for the new magazine; and there were Holmes's poems, essays, articles, and reviews or installments of novels in the magazine every year until 1893. The *Atlantic* published sixty-five Holmes poems, each of his three novels, three series of *Autocrat* sequels – *The Professor at the Breakfast-Table, The Poet at the Breakfast-Table,* and *Over the Teacups* – and *Our Hundred Days in Europe.*

It is difficult to evaluate Holmes's writing on medical subjects, or determine how his role as a doctor and professor of anatomy related to his literary career. Scientific medicine was just beginning a phenomenal advance in Holmes's day, but it is generally agreed that his own chief claim to medical distinction was his excellence as a teacher. Most interest in recent years has focused on his three "medicated novels" (Holmes accepted the term of a "dear old lady" who refused to read them): *Elsie Venner, The Guardian Angel,* and *A Moral Antipathy.* None of them contributed much to the development of the novel, though they fit into a kind of American novel vacuum – Hawthorne and Melville coming before, Howells and James after. *Elsie Venner* still gets respectful attention, but the plot of *A Moral Antipathy* has been judged "so absurd that it hardly bears repetition." Psychologists and psychiatrists have found validity and importance in the neuroses pictured in these novels, some of them profoundly shocking to Holmes's readers a hundred years ago.

To the twentieth century, Oliver Wendell Holmes was a writer of verse, not poetry – which even his contemporaries might have conceded. Significantly, both "The Deacon's Masterpiece" (or "One Hoss Shay" – sometimes interpreted as an allegory of New England Calvinism) and "The Chambered Nautilus," his acknowledged masterpiece, were both "recited" by the Autocrat of the Breakfast Table.

To the generations growing up in the first half of the twentieth century, the name Oliver Wendell Holmes meant the distinguished jurist whom F. D. Roosevelt had hailed in 1933 as "the greatest living American." This son and namesake, the only member of his family to outlive Dr. Holmes, had his father's clear-headed rationalistic turn of mind – but none of his other traits. Nearly a half century after the son's death, the elder Holmes is again emerging as a distinct figure: the conservative but clear-sighted, talkative Brahmin, who liked mill-owners better than abolitionists and transcendentalists, and who lived long enough to write graceful poetic tributes to nearly all of the nineteenth-century New England worthies.

—Clarence A. Glasrud

HOOPER, Johnson Jones.   American.   Born in Wilmington, North Carolina, 9 June 1815. Educated in local schools. Married a Miss Brantley. Worked on newspapers in Charleston, 1830–35; travelled and lived in the Gulf States of America, 1835–40, read law under his brother in Lafayette, Alabama, 1840–45; writer from 1845; edited the *Dadeville Banner*, and the Wetumpka *Whig*, and helped to edit the Montgomery *Journal*, all Alabama, 1846, then returned to Lafayette; Solicitor, 9th Alabama Judicial Circuit, 1849–53; Editor, *The Mail*, Montgomery, 1853–61; Secretary, Provisional Congress of the Southern States, 1861–62. *Died 7 June 1862.*

PUBLICATIONS

Fiction and Sketches

Some Adventures of Captain Simon Suggs, Late of the Tallapoosa Volunteers, Together with Taking the Census and Other Alabama Sketches.   1845; augmented edition, 1848.
A Ride with Old Kit Kuncher and Other Sketches and Scenes of Alabama.   1849.
The Widow Rugby's Husband, A Night at the Ugly Man's, and Other Tales of Alabama.   1851.
Dog and Gun: A Few Loose Chapters on Shooting.   1856.

Reading List: *The Southern Poor-White from Lubberland to Tobacco Road* by Shields McIlwaine, 1939; *Alias Simon Suggs: The Life and Times of Hooper* by W. Stanley Hoole, 1952; *Hooper: A Critical Study* by Howard Winston Smith, 1963; Introduction by Manly Wade Wellman to *Adventures of Captain Simon Suggs*, 1969.

*   *   *

The achievement of Johnson Jones Hooper is rooted in his contributions to nineteenth-century Southwest humor, a broadly realistic, often satiric, sometimes cold-blooded, oral-vernacular taletelling revealing a near absence of civilized standards of conduct. Some establishment critics of the early twentieth century tended virtually to dismiss Hooper's art as "discomfiture" – an "ancient, primitive, anti-social kind of merry-making" (*Library of Southern Literature*). Despite such narrow judgment, Hooper's work was well received in its own day, appearing in such popular American humor anthologies as *The Big Bear of Arkansas* and *Polly Peablossom's Wedding and Other Tales*. Moreover, within an eighteen-year period twenty-one editions of Hooper's books appeared, eleven editions of his masterpiece, *Some Adventures of Captain Simon Suggs*, appearing between 1845 and 1856.

In form, the work has long been viewed as campaign biography, and hence tied to the political machinations of frontier folk. The work, however, can be taken as a burlesque of campaign biography, with specific events based on Andrew Jackson's military career.

Suggs himself is perhaps the "bad boy" of American literature, a man proficient in the art of drinking, joking, and staying just a step ahead of his creditors. Hooper's biographer, W. Stanley Hoole, cites Bird Young of Tallapoosa County as the historical model for Suggs. As fictional creation, Suggs, however, is the epitome of the poor-white. Shields McIlwaine notes that the adventurer has a "long nose hung above a mouth stained by the filthy weed ...," his family living in "woolhat poverty." As a cultural-sociological phenomenon, Suggs originates perhaps in the Lubberland of William Byrd.

More than any other character from frontier humor, however, Suggs is indebted to the European tradition of the picaresque. As Howard Winston Smith has noted in his helpful critical study, both Suggs and Don Quixote undergo imitation promotions (Suggs to captaincy and Quixote to knighthood), and both works are episodic in nature. The general picaresque trait of the "picaro and the priest," moreover, originating in *Lazarillo de Tormes*, accounts in large part for Hooper's greatest moment in his most frequently anthologized chapter, "The Captain Attends a Camp Meeting." That particular chapter ultimately became the source for chapter twenty of *Huckleberry Finn*. Hooper ties together the many episodes by having each end in the triumph of frontier rascality over both innocence and sophistication.

None of Hooper's later writings has been judged equal to his first book. Both *The Widow Rugby's Husband, A Night at the Ugly Man's, and Other Tales of Alabama* and *Dog and Gun* attest to the author's love of the life he knew, but neither work reveals the real Hooper that Thackeray judged the "most promising writer of his day."

—George C. Longest

HOPKINSON, Francis. American. Born in Philadelphia, Pennsylvania, 2 October 1737. Educated at the Academy of Philadelphia, now the University of Pennsylvania, A.B. 1757, A.M. 1760; admitted to the Pennsylvania Bar and New Jersey Bar, 1775. Married Ann Borden in 1768; one son. Began study of harpsichord, 1754; gave first public performance, 1757, and later set poems and psalms to music: first native American composer of secular songs, 1759; appointed Collector of Customs, Port of Salem, New Jersey, 1763, and New Castle, Delaware, 1772; practised law in Philadelphia and Bordentown, New Jersey, from 1775; Member, New Jersey Governor's Council, 1774, and New Jersey Provincial Congress, 1774–76; Member of the Continental Congress, 1776: signed the Declaration of Independence; subsequently served the new United States Government as Member of the Continental Navy Board, 1776–78, and Treasurer of the Continental Loan Office, 1778–81; Judge of Admiralty for Pennsylvania, 1779–89; Member, Pennsylvania convention to ratify the Constitution, 1787; Judge of the United States District Court for Pennsylvania, 1789–91. A Founder, American Philosophical Society; a designer of the Great Seal of New Jersey, 1776; credited with the design of the American flag, 1777; Secretary of the convention that organized the Protestant Episcopal Church, 1789. *Died 9 May 1791.*

PUBLICATIONS

Collections

The First American Composer, edited by Harold V. Milligan.   1919.

Verse

>*An Exercise.* 1761.
>*Science.* 1762.
>*A Collection of Psalm Tunes.* 1762.
>*A Psalm of Thanksgiving.* 1766.
>*The Psalms of David in Metre.* 1767.
>*The Battle of the Kegs.* 1779.
>*An Ode.* 1788.
>*A Set of Eight Songs.* 1788.
>*Ode from Ossian's Poems.* 1794.

Fiction

>*A Pretty Story.* 1774; as *The Old Farm and the New Farm: A Political Allegory,* 1857.

Other

>*Errata; or, The Art of Printing Incorrectly.* 1763.
>*Account of the Grand Federal Procession.* 1788.
>*Judgments in the Admiralty of Pennsylvania.* 1789.
>*Miscellaneous Essays and Occasional Writings.* 3 vols., 1792.

Reading List: *The Life and Works of Hopkinson* by George E. Hastings, 1926 (includes bibliography); "Hopkinson and Franklin" by Dixon Wecter, in *American Literature 12,* 1940.

*   *   *

Poet, politician, musician, judge, scientist, and artist, Francis Hopkinson excelled in so many activities that his contributions to American culture defy easy classification. More than any other event, the Revolutionary War shaped Hopkinson's interests, and it is with the War that he is associated today. As a member of the Second Continental Congress, Hopkinson signed the Declaration of Independence, an action which alone was enough to guarantee him historical immortality.

Not the least of his accomplishments were the many poems and essays which he wrote in support of his country's decision to separate from Great Britain. His verses, most of which satirized the British and praised the Americans, were light, humorous, and deft. While not the stuff of great poetry, they accomplished what they were intended to do. Easily set to music, they lifted the spirits of American soldiers who sang them at the front, and they helped to demoralize the British by good naturedly ridiculing their cause. Hopkinson's most famous poem, *The Battle of the Kegs,* recounts in ballad form how the British, unfamiliar with explosives, battled relentlessly with a flotilla of mines which American patriots had ingeniously floated in kegs down the Delaware River toward their camp. Other famous poems written by Hopkinson during the Revolutionary War include "A Camp Ballad," "The Toast," and "Tory Medley." Together these poems made Hopkinson one of the most popular American poets of his day.

Equally popular were the prose essays and tracts which Hopkinson directed against the British. From Arbuthnot, Swift, and Addison, Hopkinson developed a fondness for satire, particularly when it was couched in the form of allegory or a fabricated letter. Like his verse, Hopkinson's prose was extremely effective anti-British propaganda. Written in the form of a humorous allegory, *A Pretty Story* describes the events which led the Colonies to declare their independence. In "A Prophecy," also an allegory, Hopkinson uses the persona of a Biblical prophet who predicts the establishment of a new and prosperous government in North America.

Although Hopkinson frequently contributed poems and essays to such periodicals as the *American Magazine*, the *Columbian Magazine*, and the *Pennsylvania Magazine*, his writing before and after the war lacked the vigor which the conflict itself inspired in him. With the possible exception of "My Days Have Been So Wondrous Free" (1759), a work which is thought to be the oldest American song known, his early and late poetry, for the most part dull and uninteresting, is rarely read today. His letters are more profitable because he corresponded with the most important statesmen of his day, including George Washington, Benjamin Franklin, and Thomas Jefferson. *The Miscellaneous Essays and Occasional Writings of Francis Hopkinson*, collected by Hopkinson himself, contains only a small portion of his total literary output. Many of his writings, particularly those written for periodicals, have yet to be collected.

—James A. Levernier

HOVEY, Richard. American. Born in Normal, Illinois, 4 May 1864. Educated at Dartmouth College, Hanover, New Hampshire, 1881–85, B.A. 1885; Episcopal Seminary, New York, 1886. Married Henriette Russell in 1894; one son. Teacher, Thomas Davidson's Summer School of Philosophy, 1888; actor, 1890; lived in England, 1894, and France, 1895–96; Teacher, Barnard College, New York, 1899–1900. *Died 24 February 1900.*

PUBLICATIONS

Verse

Poems. 1880.
The Laurel: An Ode to Mary Day Lanier. 1889.
Harmonics. 1890.
Seaward: An Elegy on the Death of Thomas William Parsons. 1893.
Songs from Vagabondia, with Bliss Carman. 1894; *More Songs*, 1896; *Last Songs*, 1901.
Along the Trail: A Book of Lyrics. 1898.
To the End of the Trail, edited by Mrs. Richard Hovey. 1907.
Dartmouth Lyrics, edited by Edwin Osgood Grover. 1924.
A Poem and Three Letters. 1935.

Plays

> *Launcelot and Guenevere: A Poem in Dramas* (includes *The Quest of Merlin* and *The Marriage of Guenevere*).   1891; revised versions of *The Marriage of Guenevere*, 1895, and of *The Quest of Merlin*, 1898.
> *The Birth of Galahad.*   1898.
> *Taliesin: A Masque.*   1900.
> *The Holy Graal and Other Fragments, Being the Uncompleted Parts of the Arthurian Dramas*, edited by Mrs. Richard Hovey.   1907.

Other

> *Hanover by Gaslight; or, Ways That Are Dark, Being an Exposé of the Sophomoric Career of '85.*   1883(?).
>
> Translator, *The Plays of Maurice Maeterlinck: Princess Maleine, The Intruder, The Blind, The Seven Princesses.*   1894; second series (includes *Alladine and Palomides, Pelleas and Melisande, Home, The Death of Tintagiles*), 1896.

Reading List: *Hovey, Man and Craftsman* by Allan Houston Macdonald, 1957 (includes bibliography by Edward Connery Lathem); *Hovey* by William R. Linnemann, 1976.

*   *   *

Like his contemporary Stephen Crane, Richard Hovey died tragically young, before he could fulfill the artistic promise he demonstrated, before he could make himself felt as a major force in modern poetry. But unlike Crane, Hovey did not seek to confront the turbulence and brutality of his age; yet he rebelled against it in *fin de siècle* aestheticism, in the spirit of Bohemianism, of carefree youth, cheerful pleasures, and hearty fellowship. This spirit ruled his life and his poetry.

After graduating in 1885 from Dartmouth College in New Hampshire, where he was active in campus literary life (Hovey celebrates the college in many poems, including "Men of Dartmouth," "Hanover Winter Song," and "Our Liege Lady, Dartmouth"), he studied to become an Episcopal priest, but left the seminary after one year. In 1887, he met the artist Tom Meteyard and the Canadian poet Bliss Carman, with both of whom he collaborated on the *Vagabondia* books. The dominant theme in these little volumes is that of the bold and energetic young man, "Wandering with the wandering wind,/Vagabond and unconfined!" ("The Wander-Lovers"); these short lyrics describe Hovey's world, one of adventurous, genteel Bohemianism, dedicated to comradeship and a love of Art. Hovey and Carman each wrote about half the number of poems in the books, which were popular, especially among college students, around the turn of the century.

Hovey was also a serious dramatic poet, planning (but never finishing) a series of verse plays of the Arthurian legends (a world popular with much escapist art and literature of the late nineteenth century).

A major influence acknowledged by Hovey is that of the American poet Sidney Lanier. Hovey's ode *The Laurel* (dedicated to Mrs. Lanier) and his serious lyric poetry, notably the elegy *Seaward*, reflect Lanier's rhythms and images. Hovey was also influenced by the French *symbolistes*, and translated Mallarmé and Maeterlinck. But he did not have enough time in which to develop his own lyrical talent into a unique or influential poetic voice.

—Jane S. Gabin

HOWARD, Bronson (Crocker).   American.   Born in Detroit, Michigan, 7 October 1842. Educated at schools in Detroit, and at Russell's Institute, New Haven, Connecticut. Married Alice Wyndham in 1880. Member of the staff of the *Detroit Free Press*; began writing for the stage, 1864; moved to New York, 1865, and worked as a reporter for the *Evening Mail*, *Tribune*, and *Evening Post*, until his first dramatic success, 1870; thereafter a full-time playwright. Founder, 1891, and first President, American Dramatist's Club (later the Society of American Dramatists and Composers). *Died 4 August 1908.*

PUBLICATIONS

Collections

The Banker's Daughter and Other Plays (includes *Old Love Letters, One of Our Girls, Hurricanes, Knave and Queen, Baron Rudolph*), edited by Allan G. Halline.   1941.

Plays

Fantine (produced 1864).
Saratoga; or, Pistols for Seven (produced 1870).   1870.
Ingomar the Idiotic; or, The Miser, The Maid, and the Mangle, with Oswald Allen (produced 1871).
Diamonds (produced 1872).
The Banker's Daughter (as *Lilian's Lost Love,* produced 1873; revised version as *The Banker's Daughter,* produced 1878; as *The Old Love and the New,* produced 1879).   1878; in *The Banker's Daughter and Other Plays,* 1941.
Moorcroft; or, The Double Wedding (produced 1874).
Knave and Queen, with Charles L. Young (as *Ivers Dean,* produced 1877).   In *The Banker's Daughter and Other Plays,* 1941.
Old Love Letters (produced 1878).   1897; in *The Banker's Daughter and Other Plays,* 1941.
Hurricanes (produced 1878; as *Truth,* produced 1878).   In *The Banker's Daughter and Other Plays,* 1941.
Wives, from a play by Molière (produced 1879).
The Amateur Benefit.   1881.
Baron Rudolph (produced 1881; revised version, with David Belasco, produced 1887).   In *The Banker's Daughter and Other Plays,* 1941.
Fun in a Green Room (produced 1882).
Young Mrs. Winthrop (produced 1882).   1899.
One of Our Girls (produced 1885; as *Cousin Kate,* produced 1889).   1897; in *The Banker's Daughter and Other Plays,* 1941.
Camping Out (produced 1886).
Met by Chance (produced 1887).
The Henrietta (produced 1887).   1901; edited by Allan G. Halline, in *American Plays,* 1935.
Shenandoah (produced 1888).   1897; edited by A. H. Quinn, in *Representative American Plays,* 1917.
Aristocracy (produced 1892).   1898.
Peter Stuyvesant, with Brander Matthews (produced 1899).

Fiction

Kate. 1906.

Other

The Autobiography of a Play (on *The Banker's Daughter*). 1914.

Reading List: *In Memoriam Bronson Howard* (addresses), 1910.

*   *   *

The contribution to American drama which inspired some critics to describe Bronson Howard as the "Dean of American Drama" derives largely from his ability to support himself as a dramatist, the first American to achieve this distinction. As a professional dramatist he founded the American Dramatist's Club in 1891, lectured at Harvard on what he termed "The Laws of Dramatic Composition," established himself firmly as the major playwright to deal with the American businessman, and brought to American drama the international social scene which was then being exploited in fiction with considerable success by Henry James and William Dean Howells.

The fact that Howard could make a career as a playwright suggests something about his abilities. As a good craftsman of the stage, he understood and accepted the commercially oriented conventions and limiting requirements of the late nineteenth-century American theatre. Although he was markedly more farsighted than his contemporaries in terms of his chosen themes and materials, he carefully adhered to his own outline of a well-constructed play which must be "satisfactory" to an audience and reach a properly moral and happy conclusion. Toward the end of his career he weakened his position as a man of independent thought by joining the stable of playwrights of the Theatrical Syndicate. He was always a man of the theatre, sometimes belligerently so, and it was never his intention to pull together the established rift in America between theatre and drama. Indeed, his expressed antagonism toward dramatic literature and literary people probably further delayed a developing American drama.

A major characteristic of his playwriting was the carefully crafted and commercially successful work which suggested a direction for future dramatists whose careers among theatre managers would be more secure after Howard's efforts. His first success was a play called *Saratoga*, for which he embroidered the usual farce action with better than average farce dialogue and used a favorite American resort as his scene. The fact that the play was transferred successfully to English circumstances by Frank Marshall as *Brighton* (1874) suggests something of his style. More significant are his business plays. *Young Mrs. Winthrop* showed the difficulties which the demands of the business world may bring to married life. *The Henrietta* satirized life on the New York Stock Exchange. *Aristocracy* combined Howard's interest in the American businessman and the socially intriguing international scene by revealing that the obvious route by which new wealth of the American west may unite with New York traditional society was through London aristocracy. In an earlier play, *One of Our Girls*, Howard contrasted American and French social conventions. His single play – a very successful one – which remains outside his usual society-oriented work is *Shenandoah*, a romantic tale of the Civil War.

Basically a transitional dramatist in American theatre, Howard helped to diminish the popularity of foreign plays on the American stage and give the American dramatist greater importance in the theatre. This is his real contribution. Otherwise, he was a generally skillful dramatist for his time who could write entertaining and sentimental social melodrama.

—Walter J. Meserve

HOWE, E(dgar) W(atson).   American.   Born in Treaty, Indiana, 3 May 1853. Educated in local schools; apprenticed, as a printer, to his father, 1865–68. Married Clara L. Frank in 1875 (divorced, 1901); two sons and one daughter. Worked as a printer in Indiana, Missouri, Iowa, Nebraska, and Utah, 1868–72; Publisher, *Globe*, Golden, Colorado, 1872; Founder, with his brother James, and Editor, *Daily Globe*, Atchison, Kansas, 1877–1911; Editor and Publisher of *E. W. Howe's Monthly*, Atchison, 1911–33. Litt.D.: Rollins College, Winter Park, Florida, 1926; Washburn College, Topeka, Kansas, 1927. *Died 3 October 1937.*

PUBLICATIONS

Fiction

The Story of a Country Town.   1883; edited by Brom Weber, 1964.
The Mystery of The Locks.   1885.
A Moonlight Boy.   1886.
A Man Story.   1889.
An Ante-Mortem Statement.   1891.
The Confessions of John Whitlock, Late Preacher of the Gospel.   1891.
Dying Like a Gentleman and Other Stories.   1926.
The Covered Wagon and the West (stories).   1928.
Her Fifth Marriage and Other Stories.   1928.
When a Woman Enjoys Herself and Other Tales of a Small Town.   1928.

Other

Mark Antony De Wolfe Howe 1808–1895: A Brief Record of a Long Life.   1897.
Daily Notes on a Trip Around the World.   2 vols., 1907.
A Trip to the West Indies.   1910.
Country Town Sayings: A Collection of Paragraphs from the Atchison Globe.   1911.
Travel Letters from New Zealand, Australia, and Africa.   1913.
Success Easier Than Failure.   1917.
The Blessing of Business.   1918.
Ventures in Common Sense, edited by H. L. Mencken.   1919.
The Anthology of Another Town.   1920.
Adventures in Common Sense.   1922.
Notes for My Biographer: Terse Paragraphs on Life and Letters.   1926.
Preaching from the Audience: Candid Comments on Life.   1926.
Sinner Sermons: A Selection of the Best Paragraphs of Howe.   1926.
Plain People (autobiography).   1929.
The Indignation of Howe.   1933.

Reading List: *Howe, Country Town Philosopher* by Calder M. Rickett, 1968; *Howe* by S. J. Sackett, 1972.

*   *   *

"I come of a long line of plain people," E. W. Howe writes at the beginning of his autobiography *Plain People*, but as a famous editor in the days of personal journalism and as a minor novelist of the late 19th century, Howe achieved a measure of distinction in his own day and a small niche in the history of American life and culture. He is the author of one novel that continues to be reprinted and read, and his autobiography, long out of print, deserves to be better known. Howe is an authentic bit of Americana woven into the fabric of national experience – a figure to be compared in this respect with Benjamin Franklin, Horatio Alger, H. L. Mencken, and Will Rogers.

After establishing himself as a newspaper editor, Howe turned toward literature. For months in the early 1880's he worked over the manuscript of *The Story of a Country Town* at the kitchen table after finishing a long day in the newspaper office. When commercial publishers turned down his book, he published it himself. The novel was an immediate success and encouraged him to write several more, all of which were failures and never have been reprinted. Eventually he resigned himself to filling his newspaper columns with aphoristic paragraphs that attracted national attention. He published additional books during the rest of his life, but they are mostly forgotten travel letters, tracts on business, and collections of his newspaper and magazine paragraphs. One other, however, is worth reading: *The Anthology of Another Town*, a prose version of and answer to Edgar Lee Masters's *Spoon River Anthology*.

The Story of a Country Town draws on the life of Howe's father and his own experience growing up in northwest Missouri where the novel takes place. It's basically a melodramatic tragedy of a backwoods Othello who becomes insanely jealous when he discovers that his wife once was in love with another man. As a work of art, it is full of crudities, but the story is told with such a passionate intensity by Howe's persona, young Ned Westlake, who observes the action, that readers are swept along by it.

Both Howells and Twain, who received copies from the author, wrote flattering letters about the novel. Howells thought it a "very remarkable piece of realism" and praised the fidelity of the country town setting, although he objected to the sentimentality of the tragic romance. The novel generally has been classed with early examples of realism, but it is only partly realistic, and Howe's later novels demonstrated that he was really a sentimental romancer at heart. *The Story of a Country Town* can be seen, with its bitter memories of the narrator's youth, as a forerunner of the revolt-from-the-village literature of Sinclair Lewis, Sherwood Anderson, and Masters, but Howe during his later years filled his newspaper columns with the most blatant Chamber-of-Commerce puffery and really believed that all virtue resided in the small town and rural life.

—James Woodress

HOWELLS, William Dean. American. Born in Martin's Ferry, Ohio, 1 March 1837. Largely self-educated. Married Elinor Mead in 1862 (died, 1910); one son and two daughters. Compositor, 1851–58, Reporter, 1858–60, and News Editor, 1860–61, *Ohio State Journal*, Columbus; also correspondent, in Columbus, for the Cincinnati *Gazette*, 1857; contributor to his father's newspaper, *The Sentinel*, Jefferson, Ohio, from 1852, and wrote for various national magazines from 1860; United States Consul in Venice, 1861–65; Assistant Editor, 1866–71, and Editor-in-Chief, 1871–81, *Atlantic Monthly*, Boston; Professor of Modern Languages, Harvard University, Cambridge, Massachusetts, 1869–71; wrote the "Editor's Study" column for *Harper's* magazine, 1886–92; Co-Editor, *Cosmopolitan* magazine, 1892. Recipient: American Academy of Arts and Letters Gold Medal, 1915. M.A.: Harvard University, Cambridge, Massachusetts, 1867; Litt.D.: Yale University, New Haven,

Connecticut, 1901; Oxford University, 1904; Columbia University, New York, 1905; L.H.D.: Princeton University, New Jersey, 1912. President, American Academy of Arts and Letters, 1908–20. *Died 11 May 1920.*

PUBLICATIONS

Collections

> *Representative Selections*, edited by Clara Marburg Kirk and Rudolf Kirk. 1950.
> *Selected Writings*, edited by Henry Steele Commager. 1950.
> *Complete Plays*, edited by Walter J. Meserve. 1960.
> *Selected Edition*, edited by Ronald Gottesman. 1968—

Fiction

> *Their Wedding Journey.* 1872; edited by John K. Reeves, in *Selected Edition*, 1968.
> *A Chance Acquaintance.* 1873; edited by Ronald Gottesman, David J. Nordloh, and Jonathan Thomas, in *Selected Edition*, 1971.
> *A Foregone Conclusion.* 1874.
> *The Lady of the Aroostook.* 1879.
> *The Undiscovered Country.* 1880.
> *A Fearful Responsibility and Other Stories.* 1881.
> *Doctor Breen's Practice.* 1881.
> *A Modern Instance.* 1882; edited by David J. Nordloh and David Kleinman, in *Selected Edition*, 1978.
> *A Woman's Reason.* 1883.
> *The Rise of Silas Lapham.* 1885; edited by Walter J. Meserve and David J. Nordloh, in *Selected Edition*, 1971.
> *Indian Summer.* 1886; edited by Scott Bennett and David J. Nordloh, in *Selected Edition*, 1971.
> *The Minister's Charge; or, The Apprenticeship of Lemuel Barker.* 1886; edited by David J. Nordloh and David Kleinman, in *Selected Edition*, 1968.
> *April Hopes.* 1888.
> *Annie Kilburn.* 1888.
> *A Hazard of New Fortunes.* 1889; edited by David J. Nordloh, in *Selected Edition*, 1976.
> *The Shadow of a Dream.* 1890; with *An Imperative Duty*, edited by Martha Banta, Ronald Gottesman, and David J. Nordloh, in *Selected Edition*, 1970.
> *An Imperative Duty.* 1891; with *The Shadow of a Dream*, edited by Martha Banta, Ronald Gottesman, and Divad J. Nordloh, in *Selected Edition*, 1970.
> *Mercy.* 1892; as *The Quality of Mercy*, 1892.
> *The World of Chance.* 1893.
> *The Coast of Bohemia.* 1893.
> *A Traveler from Altruria.* 1894; complete edition, edited by Clara Marburg Kirk and Rudolf Kirk, as *Letters of an Altrurian Traveller (1893–1894)*, 1961; with *Between the Dark and the Daylight*, in *Selected Edition*, 1968.
> *The Day of Their Wedding.* 1896.
> *A Parting and a Meeting.* 1896; with *The Day of Their Wedding*, as *Idyls in Drab*, 1896.
> *The Landlord at Lion's Head.* 1897.

An Open-Eyed Conspiracy: An Idyl of Saratoga.   1897.
The Story of a Play.   1898.
Ragged Lady.   1899.
Their Silver Wedding Journey.   1899.
A Pair of Patient Lovers (stories).   1901.
The Kentons.   1902; in *Selected Edition*, 1971.
The Flight of Pony Baker: A Boy's Town Story.   1902.
Questionable Shapes.   1903.
Letters Home.   1903.
The Son of Royal Langbrith.   1904; edited by David Burrows, Ronald Gottesman, and
   David J. Nordloh, in *Selected Edition*, 1969.
Miss Bellard's Inspiration.   1905.
Through the Eye of a Needle.   1907.
Between the Dark and the Daylight: Romances.   1907; with *A Traveler from Altruria*,
   in *Selected Edition*, 1968.
Fennel and Rue.   1908.
New Leaf Mills: A Chronicle.   1913.
The Daughter of the Storage and Other Things in Prose and Verse.   1916.
The Leatherwood God.   1916; in *Selected Edition*, 1976.
The Vacation of the Kelwyns: An Idyl of the Middle Eighteen-Seventies.   1920.
Mrs. Farrell.   1921.

Plays

Samson, from the play by Ippolito d'Este (produced 1874).   1889.
The Parlor Car.   1876.
Out of the Question.   1877.
A Counterfeit Presentment.   1877.
Yorick's Love (produced 1878).   In *Complete Plays*, 1960.
The Sleeping-Car (produced 1887).   1883.
The Register.   1884.
The Elevator (produced 1885).   1885.
The Garroters (produced 1886).   1886.
A Foregone Conclusion, with William Poel, from the novel by Howells (produced
   1886).   In *Complete Plays*, 1960.
Colonel Sellers as a Scientist, with Mark Twain, from the novel *The Gilded Age* by
   Twain and Charles Dudley Warner (produced 1887).   In *Complete Plays*, 1960.
A Sea Change; or, Love's Stowaway: A Lyricated Farce, music by George
   Henschel.   1887.
The Mouse Trap (produced 1887–88?).   In *The Mouse Trap and Other Farces*, 1889.
The Mouse Trap and Other Farces (includes *A Likely Story, Five O'Clock Tea, The
   Garroters*).   1889.
The Sleeping-Car and Other Farces.   1889.
The Albany Depot.   1892.
A Letter of Introduction.   1892.
The Unexpected Guests.   1893.
Evening Dress (produced 1894).   1893.
Bride Roses (produced 1894).   1900.
A Previous Engagement.   1897.
Room Forty-Five.   1900.
The Smoking Car.   1900.
An Indian Giver.   1900.

Minor Dramas (includes *A Masterpiece of Diplomacy* and *Her Opinion of His Story*).   2
  vols., 1907.
The Mother and the Father.   1909.
Parting Friends.   1911.

Verse

Poems of Two Friends, with John J. Piatt.   1860.
No Love Lost: A Romance of Travel.   1869.
Poems.   1873.
Stops of Various Quills.   1895.

Other

Lives and Speeches of Abraham Lincoln and Hannibal Hamlin.   1860.
Venetian Life.   1866; revised edition, 1872, 1907.
Italian Journeys.   1867; revised edition, 1872, 1901.
Suburban Sketches.   1871; revised edition, 1872; as *A Day's Pleasure and Other
  Sketches*, 1876.
Sketch of the Life and Character of Rutherford B. Hayes.   1876.
A Little Girl among the Old Masters.   1884.
Three Villages.   1884.
Tuscan Cities.   1886.
Modern Italian Poets: Essays and Versions.   1887.
A Boy's Town (juvenile).   1890.
Criticism and Fiction.   1891.
A Little Swiss Sojourn.   1892.
Christmas Every Day and Other Stories Told for Children.   1892.
My Year in a Log Cabin.   1893.
My Literary Passions.   1895.
Impressions and Experiences.   1896.
Stories of Ohio.   1897.
Doorstep Acquaintance and Other Sketches.   1900.
*Literary Friends and Acquaintance: A Personal Retrospect of American
  Authorship.*   1900; edited by David F. Hiatt and Edwin H. Cady, in *Selected Edition*,
  1968.
Heroines of Fiction.   2 vols., 1901.
Literature and Life: Studies.   1902.
London Films.   1905.
Certain Delightful English Towns.   1906.
Roman Holidays and Others.   1908.
Seven English Cities.   1909.
My Mark Twain: Reminiscences and Criticisms.   1910; edited by Marilyn Austin
  Baldwin, 1967.
Imaginary Interviews.   1910.
Familiar Spanish Travels.   1913.
The Seen and Unseen at Stratford-on-Avon: A Fantasy.   1914.
Years of My Youth (autobiography).   1916; in *Selected Edition*, 1975.
Life in Letters, edited by Mildred Howells.   2 vols., 1928.
Prefaces to Contemporaries (1882–1920), edited by George Arms, William M. Gibson,
  and Frederick C. Marston, Jr., 1957.

Criticism and Fiction and Other Essays, edited by Clara Marburg Kirk and Rudolf Kirk.   1959.
The Mark Twain–Howells Letters 1872–1910, edited by Henry Nash Smith and William M. Gibson.   2 vols., 1960.
Discovery of a Genius: Howells and Henry James, edited by Albert Mordell.   1961.
Howells as Critic, edited by Edwin H. Cady.   1973.

Editor, *Three Years in Chili*, by Mrs. C. B. Merwin.   1861; as *Chili Through American Spectacles*, n.d.
Editor, *Choice Autobiographies*.   8 vols., 1877–78.
Editor, with Thomas Sergeant Perry, *Library of Universal Adventure by Sea and Land*.   1888.
Editor, *Mark Twain's Library of Humor*.   1888.
Editor, *The Poems of George Pellew*.   1892.
Editor, *Recollections of Life in Ohio from 1813 to 1840*, by William Cooper Howells.   1895.
Editor, with Russell Sturgis, *Florence in Art and Literature*.   1901.
Editor, with Henry Mills Alden, *Southern Lights and Shadows* (stories).   1907.
Editor, *The Great Modern American Short Stories: An Anthology*.   1920.
Editor, *Don Quixote by Cervantes*, translated by Charles Jarvis.   1923.

Translator, *Venice, Her Art Treasures and Historical Associations: A Guide*, by Adalbert Müller.   1864.

Bibliography: *A Bibliography of Howells* by William M. Gibson and George Arms, 1948; in *Bibliography of American Literature* by Jacob Blanck, 1963.

Reading List: *The Road to Realism*, 1956, and *The Realist at War*, 1958, both by Edwin H. Cady; *Howells: His Life and World* by Van Wyck Brooks, 1959; *Howells: A Century of Criticism* edited by Kenneth E. Eble, 1962; *Howells and the Art of His Times* by Clara Marburg Kirk, 1965; *The Immense Complex Drama: The World and Art of the Howells Novel*, by George C. Carrington, Jr., 1966; *The Literary Realism of Howells* by William McMurray, 1967; *Howells* by William M. Gibson, 1967; *The Achievement of Howells* by Kermit Vanderbilt, 1968; *Howells: The Friendly Eye* by Edward Wagenknecht, 1969; *Howells: An American Life* by Kenneth S. Lynn, 1971; *The Realism of Howells* by George N. Bennett, 1973.

*   *   *

William Dean Howells's literary career was remarkable not only for its length and variousness but for its continuous and conscientious productivity. For more than fifty years, extending from the nineteenth well into the twentieth century, Howells appeared in print as a journalist, a poet, a sensitively observant but unsentimental traveler, a novelist, a playwright, a critic and a polemicist in the cause of realism (these last two functions merging in *Criticism and Fiction*), a publicist and explicator of foreign writers for an ill-informed American public, and the educator of that same public to the greatness of its own writers like James and Twain.

The experience behind this writing was also rich and varied, directly furnishing much of the material for the immense productivity. Moreover, it was an experience that had its public occasions, most notably Howells's outspoken opposition to the treatment of the Chicago anarchists in the Haymarket affair. Beneath the surface of a life that moved from midwestern printshops and newspapers through the consulship at Venice and the editorship of the *Atlantic* to the new center of literary activity in New York, and brought varied relationships with the literary giants of New England and deep literary and personal friendships with the new giants of American literature, James and Twain, there was profound personal experience: the challenge of Darwinian science to religious faith, and an increasing awareness of cultural dislocations, political corruptions, and economic inequities. Thus, Howells's writing became a permanently valuable record of a broad spectrum of the American literary, social, economic, religious, and moral experience. Even more importantly, in an impressive number of his fictions Howells achieved the transmutation of actual and vicarious experience into realistic art, met his own criterion of "dispersing the conventional acceptations by which men live on easy terms with themselves" without falling into the error of claiming thereby to have solved "the riddle of the painful earth."

Howells's relatively late decision to become a novelist kept him close to his own experience and to the unsophisticated literary devices in the early novels. The tentatively novelistic *Their Wedding Journey* stated his intention to deal with "poor Real life," but the pronouncement stemmed more from his distrust of his ability to manage a sustained narrative and his desire to employ the methods of the travel book than from a theory of realism. *A Chance Acquaintance* also employed the narrative structure of the journey, but it also developed a situation in which the moral spontaneity of an unsophisticated American girl (a portrait highly praised by James) served to reveal the stultifying snobbishness of a proper Bostonian, and, to the dissatisfaction of many, chose the "realistic" mode of an "unhappy" ending in which the girl rejected the ungentlemanly gentleman. Throughout this apprenticeship period, Howells continued to exploit the kind of confrontation labelled by Edwin H. Cady the "conventional-unconventional formula." He also put to use his own experience in summer boarding houses in *Mrs. Farrell* (serialized as *Private Theatricals*) and in pre-Jamesian versions of the international novel in *A Foregone Conclusion* and *The Lady of the Aroostook*. The former is often cited as a benchmark in the terrain of Howells's early novels because of its skillful dramatic development (a lesson learned from Turgenev) of a "tragic" involvement of an Italian priest and another of Howells's radically innocent American girls.

Beginning in 1880 with *The Undiscovered Country*, Howells's fiction began to take account of issues not easily confined within the limits of the novel of manners (the terminology most frequently applied to the pre- and post-"economic" fiction). That novel has begun to receive deserved attention as an original transformation of Hawthornian themes into a probing study of the problem of religious faith and as Howells's first major attempt to achieve a reconciliation of the American present with its past through a pastoral vision. It was followed by *A Modern Instance*, in any accounting, including Howells's own, one of his most penetrating studies of American life. In spite of general contemporary misunderstanding, it was a contemporary reviewer who noted that the novel was not an anti-divorce tract but "a demonstration of a state of society of which divorce was the index." As the novel expands from a brilliant study of the disintegration of a marriage through a failure of moral discipline, that state of society is depicted as one marked by the decay of vital religious faith, of family solidarity as the nexus of social stability, of the social ethic which is being displaced by purely commercial principles. *The Rise of Silas Lapham* also involves a questioning of American commercial society as Lapham's moral rise is achieved by the sacrifice of the materialistic success for which he very nearly sold his soul. It was so far, moreover, from being a mere comedy of manners – as many readers have termed it because of Lapham's attempts to gain entrance into Boston society and because of the apparent submergence of the moral issue to the romantic sub-plot (the relationship of the plots is a point of extensive critical debate) – that Howells suffered some kind of psychic breakdown in being confronted with the issues it raised: the degree and nature of his commitment to a democracy which included the Irish and Jews; his own relationship with proper Bostonians and New England literati, most of whom had little appreciation for the realistic art to which he had committed himself. The increasing doubts about the America about which he had once been thoroughly optimistic but which he came to feel, as he told James, was "coming out all wrong in the end" made him ripe for the reading of Tolstoy (begun in 1885) and for the expression of a newly open radicalism in the novels of the 1890's which Everett Carter has distinguished as works of "critical realism."

The most important of these was *A Hazard of New Fortunes*. It was preceded by *Annie Kilburn*, a demonstration of the Tolstoyan lesson of the necessity for "*justice* not *alms*" as the corrective for the economic and social ills of the polity. It was followed by *The Quality of Mercy*, an accusation of a system of which embezzlers were merely symptomatic, and *The World of Chance*, an examination of the malfunctioning or absence of causality in not only the business world but in all human involvements. Howells then abandoned the realistic novel as the vehicle of his socialistic ideas and turned to an openly dialectical form in two Altrurian (Utopian) romances.

The recovery of a "usable" Howells after a period in which he was the largely unread touchstone of timid gentility and Victorian morality for writers and critics like Sinclair Lewis and H. L. Mencken was directly due to the rediscovery of these two Utopias, with their socio-economic criticisms of American life. Critical debate continues today concerning their artistic quality and their significance to the totality of Howells's career: they have often been seen, even in approaches modified from the doctrinaire criticism of the 1930's, as marking the limit of Howells's artistic growth, and as evidencing a "tragic vision" absent from his other work (and shaped not only by Tolstoy but a number of profound personal experiences, including the hazard of his career in defense of the Haymarket anarchists and the protracted illness and agonizing death of his daughter). Consequently, his career has been seen as a growth through the comedy of manners to social realism to a unique critical realism and then a falling away. That falling away has been variously explained as simply an exhaustion of the creative impulse; as a failure of nerve in questioning the values and value of American society; as a recognition of his inability to provide solutions to the problems he examined; as a deliberate return to the intellectually and financially safe fiction of his earlier career. The complications of Howells's reputation can be seen in the various interpretations of *A Hazard of New Fortunes*, a key novel. It has been seen variously as a comedy of manners, a symbolic myth of Christian atonement, a realistic tragedy, a treatise on aesthetics, and a combined "psychological" and "economic" novel.

After 1893, Howells still had twenty-seven years of productive life during which he published a dozen or so novels. Of these, almost half – *The Landlord at Lion's Head*, *The Kentons*, *The Son of Royal Langbrith*, *The Leatherwood God*, and the posthumous *The Vacation of the Kelwyns* – have, from various critical perspectives, been judged worthy to be included in the permanent Howells canon. If that canon is initiated by *A Modern Instance* – indeed, a case may be made for the earlier *A Foregone Conclusion* or *The Undiscovered Country* – the continuous excellence of Howells's realistic fiction throughout his career assures him an important place in the history of the development of American fiction. And, if there is added to that assessment his also continuous and influential role in his associations with the *Atlantic*, *Harper's*, and other journals, his importance as a *force* in American literature is difficult to overstate.

—George N. Bennett

INGRAHAM, Joseph Holt. American. Born in Portland, Maine, 25 January 1809. Possibly educated at Bowdoin College, Brunswick, Maine. Married Mary Brooks in 1849; three daughters and one son, the writer Prentiss Ingraham. Teacher at Jefferson College, Washington, Mississippi; writer of romances from 1835; established a girls school at Nashville, Tennessee, 1849; began theological studies: ordained deacon, 1851, and priest, 1852, in the Protestant Episcopal Church, and thereafter wrote only books with religious themes; missionary in Aberdeen, Mississippi, 1852–54; Rector, St. John's Church, Mobile, Alabama, 1855–58, and Christ Church, Holly Springs, Mississippi, 1859 until his death. *Died 18 December 1860.*

PUBLICATIONS

Fiction

Lafitte, The Pirate of the Gulf. 1836; as *The Pirate,* 1839.
Burton; or, The Sieges. 1838; as *Quebec and New York; or, The Three Beauties,* 1839.
Captain Kyd; or, The Wizard of the Sea. 1839; as *Kyd the Buccaneer,* 1839.
The American Lounger; or, Tales, Sketches, and Legends Gathered in Sundry Journeyings. 1839.
The Quadroone; or, St. Michael's Day. 1840.
The Dancing Feather; or, The Amateur Freebooters: A Romance of New York. 1842; as *The Pirate Schooner,* 1877.
Edward Austin; or, The Hunting Flask: A Tale of the Forest and Town. 1842.
The Gipsy of the Highlands; or, The Jew and the Heir. 1843.
Jemmy Daily; or, The Little News Vender. 1843.
Morris Graeme; or, The Cruise of the Sea-Slipper: A Sequel to The Dancing Feather. 1843.
Fanny H—; or, The Hunchback and the Roué. 1843.
Mark Manly; or, The Skipper's Lad: A Tale of Boston in the Olden Times. 1843.
Frank Rivers; or, The Dangers of the Town. 1843.
The Young Genius; or, Trials and Triumphs. 1843.
Howard; or, The Mysterious Disappearance: A Romance of the Tripolitanian War. 1843.
Black Ralph; or, The Helmsman of Hurlgate. 1844.
Theodore; or, The Child of the Sea, Being a Sequel to Lafitte. 1844.
Rodolphe in Boston! 1844.
Billy Woodhull; or, The Pretty Haymaker. 1844.
The Corsair of Casco Bay; or, The Pilot's Daughter. 1844.
Ellen Hart; or, The Forger's Daughter. 1844.
The Miseries of New York; or, The Burglar and Counsellor. 1844.
Steel Belt; or, The Three Masted Goleta: A Tale of Boston Bay. 1844.
Arnold; or, The British Spy! (includes *The Bold Insurgent*). 1844; as *The Treason of Arnold,* 1847.
The Midshipman; or, The Corvette and Brigantine. 1844.
La Bonita Cigarera; or, The Beautiful Cigar Vendor: A Tale of New York. 1844.
The Spanish Galleon; or, The Pirate of the Mediterranean: A Romance of the Corsair Kidd. 1844.
Estelle; or, The Conspirator of the Isle: A Tale of the West Indian Seas. 1844.
The Silver Bottle; or, The Adventures of Little Marlboro in Search of His Father. 1844.
Herman de Ruyter; or, The Mystery Unveiled: A Sequel to The Beautiful Cigar Vendor. 1844.
The Diary of a Hackney Coachman. 1844.

Santa Claus; or, The Merry King of Christmas.   1844.

Caroline Archer; or, The Milliner's Apprentice.   1844.

Eleanor Sherwood, The Beautiful Temptress!   1844.

The Clipper-Yacht; or, Moloch the Money-Lender: A Tale of London and the Thames.   1845.

Marie; or, The Fugitive: A Romance of Mount Benedict.   1845.

Freemantle; or, The Privateersman! A Nautical Romance of the Last War.   1845.

Scarlet Feather; or, The Young Chief of the Abenaquies: A Romance of the Wilderness of Maine.   1845.

Forrestal; or, The Light of the Reef.   1845.

Rafael.   1845.

The Knights of Seven Lands.   1845; as *The Seven Knights,* 1845.

Montezuma, The Serf; or, The Revolt of the Mexitili: A Tale of the Last Days of the Aztec Dynasty.   1845.

Will Terril; or, The Adventures of a Young Gentleman Born in a Cellar.   1845.

Norman; or, The Privateersman's Bride: A Sequel to Freemantle.   1845.

Neal Nelson; or, The Siege of Boston: A Tale of the Revolution.   1845; as *Sons of Liberty,* 1887.

A Romance of the Sunny South; or, Feathers from a Traveller's Wing.   1845.

Paul Deverell; or, Two Judgments for One Crime: A Tale of the Present Day.   1845.

Paul Perril, The Merchant's Son; or, The Adventures of a New-England Boy Launched upon Life.   2 vols., 1845–46(?).

The Adventures of Will Wizard! Corporal of the Saccarapa Volunteers.   1845.

Alice May, and Bruising Bill (stories).   1845.

Bertrand; or, The Story of Marie de Heywode, Being a Sequel to Marie.   1845.

Charles Blackford; or, The Adventures of a Student in Search of a Profession.   1845.

The Cruiser of the Mist.   1845.

Fleming Field; or, The Young Artisan: A Tale of the Days of the Stamp Act.   1845.

Grace Weldon; or, Frederica the Bonnet-Girl: A Tale of Boston and Its Bay.   1845.

Harry Harefoot; or, The Three Temptations: A Story of City Scenes.   1845.

Henry Howard; or, Two Noes Make One Yes (includes *Trout-Fishing*).   1845.

Mary Wilbur; or, The Deacon and the Widow's Daughter.   1845.

The Mast-Ship; or, The Bombardment of Falmouth.   1845.

The Wing of the Wind.   1845.

Arthur Denwood; or, The Maiden of the Inn: A Tale of the War of 1812.   1846.

The Lady of the Gulf.   1846; as *Josephene,* 1853(?).

Leisler; or, The Rebel and the King's Man: A Tale of the Rebellion of 1689.   1846.

Ramero; or, The Prince and the Prisoner!   1846.

Bonfield; or, The Outlaw of the Bermudas.   1846.

The Silver Ship of Mexico.   1846.

Berkeley; or, The Lost and Redeemed.   1846.

Mate Burke; or, The Foundlings of the Sea.   1846.

The Mysterious State-Room: A Tale of the Mississippi.   1846.

The Odd Fellow; or, The Secret Association, and Foraging Peter (stories).   1846.

Pierce Fenning; or, The Lugger's Chase.   1846; as *The Rebel Coaster,* 1867.

The Ringdove; or, The Privateer and the Cutter.   1846(?); as *A Yankee Blue-Jacket,* 1888.

The Slave King; or, The Triumph of Liberty.   1846.

The Spectre Steamer and Other Tales.   1846.

The Young Artist, and The Bold Insurgent (stories).   1846.

The Surf Skiff; or, The Heroines of the Kennebec (includes *Captain Velasco*).   1847.

The Truce; or, On and Off Soundings: A Tale of the Coast of Maine.   1847.

Blanche Talbot; or, The Maiden's Hand: A Romance of the War of 1812 (includes *Henry Temple*).   1847.

The Brigantine; or, Guitierro and the Castilian: A Tale Both of Boston and Cuba (includes *The Old Bean*).   1847.
Edward Manning; or, The Bride and the Maiden.   1847.
Beatrice, The Goldsmith's Daughter: A Story of the Reign of the Last Charles.   1847.
Ringold Griffitt; or, The Raftsman of the Susquehannah: A Tale of Pennsylvania.   1847.
The Free-Trader; or, The Cruiser of Narragansett Bay.   1847.
The Texan Ranger; or, The Maid of Matamoras (includes *Alice Brandon*).   1847.
Wildash; or, The Cruiser of the Capes.   1847.
Jennette Alison; or, The Young Strawberry Girl.   1848.
Nobody's Son; or, The Life and Adventures of Percival Mayberry.   1851.
The Arrow of Gold; or, The Shell Gatherer.   1854(?).
The Prince of the House of David; or, Three Years in the Holy City.   1855.
Rivingstone; or, The Young Ranger Hussar: A Romance of the Revolution.   1855.
The Pillar of Fire; or, Israel in Bondage.   1859.
The Throne of David: From the Consecration of the Shepherd of Bethlehem to the Rebellion of Prince Absalom.   1860.
The Sunny South; or, The Southerner at Home.   1860; as *Not "A Fool's Errand,"* 1880; as *Kate's Experiences,* 1880.
Mortimer; or, The Bankrupt's Heiress.   1865.
Wildbird; or, The Three Chances.   1869.
The Avenging Brother; or, The Two Maidens.   1869.
The Pirate Chief; or, The Cutter of the Ocean.   N.d.

Other

The South-West.   1835.
Pamphlets for the People, in Illustration of the Claims of the Church and Methodism.   1854.

Bibliography: in *Bibliography of American Literature* by Jacob Blanck, 1963.

Reading List: *Ingraham* by Robert W. Weatherby II, 1978.

*   *   *

Joseph Holt Ingraham was one of the first Americans to try to make a living by writing fiction, and his career provides a paradigm of the forms to which early would-be professionals turned in their efforts to meet the destructive competition from imported works in the days before international copyright.

After achieving success with his non-fiction account of his travels in Louisiana and Mississippi (*The South-West*), he turned to the then favorite two-volume historical novel after the manner of Scott and Cooper. His first, *Lafitte, The Pirate of the Gulf*, a conventional romance about a patriotic Louisiana pirate who turns out to have been highborn, was his most successful and remained in print well into the twentieth century. *Burton* (which is about the Canadian campaign of Aaron Burr during the American Revolution) and *Captain Kyd* (another fantasy about a famous pirate) were less successful; despite the appeal of the subjects, the stories were too preposterous and chaotically constructed even for readers accustomed to Gothic fiction. A fourth double-decker, *The Quadroone*, another tale of baby-switching during the Spanish occupation of New Orleans in the eighteenth century, was coldly received; and a projected fifth, *The Dancing Feather*, an unlikely tale of contemporary piracy in New York harbor, had to be ended abruptly after the tenth chapter of a planned fifty and published as a cheap paperback.

During the next five years, Ingraham led in productivity a pack of hungry writers churning out the hundred-page pamphlets that new high-speed printing presses made it possible to sell for a quarter. Ingraham wrote at least sixty; most were stories of pirates and other nautical adventurers, though some were early tales of the shady side of big city life. Typical and most interesting are *The Beautiful Cigar Vendor* and its sequel *Herman de Ruyter*, in which Ingraham provides his own solution to the mystery of the disappearance of Mary Cecilia Rogers, a New York girl who inspired also Poe's "The Mystery of Marie Roget."

When Ingraham entered the work of the Protestant Episcopal church in 1847, what the *Knickerbocker* magazine called his "cheap and nasty," "immoral" stories ceased to flow from his pen, although in 1851 he produced a final short work, *Nobody's Son*, protesting the mistreatment of orphans in the manner of Dickens' popular fictions.

Ingraham's greatest success and major contribution to literature came late in his life, however, when, as he was engaged in the ministry, he began to write a life of Christ in the form of a series of letters from an impressionable young Egyptian girl visiting the Holy Lands in Christ's time. These developed into *The Prince of the House of David*, the first religious best-seller, and the prototype of a vein that has flourished through the works of Lew Wallace, Lloyd Douglas, and others to the present day. Further attempts, however, to tell the story of Moses (*The Pillar of Fire*) and the founding of the Hebrew kingdom (*The Throne of David*) were less successful because the novels became too long-winded and clumsily constructed. He failed to find a publisher for a projected fourth novel, *St. Paul, The Roman Citizen*, before his sudden and still mysterious death.

—Warren French

IRVING, Washington.   American.   Born in New York City, 3 April 1783. Educated in local schools; studied law in the offices of Henry Masterton, 1799, of Brockholst Livingstone, 1801, and of Josiah Ogden Hoffman, 1802; admitted to the New York Bar, 1806, but never practised. Served as a Staff Colonel in the United States Army during the war of 1812. Travelled in Europe, 1804–06; became partner, with his brothers, in family hardware business, New York and Liverpool, 1810: representative of the business in England, 1815 until the firm collapsed, 1818; thereafter a full-time writer: lived in Dresden, 1822–23, London, 1824, Paris, 1825, and Madrid, as member of the United States Legation, 1826–29; Secretary, United States Legation in London, 1829–32; returned to New York, then toured the southern and western United States, 1832; lived at the manor house "Sunnyside," Tarrytown-on-Hudson, New York, 1836–42; United States Ambassador to Spain, 1842–45, then returned to Tarrytown. Recipient: Royal Society of Literature medal, 1830. D.C.L.: Oxford University, 1831. *Died 28 November 1859.*

PUBLICATIONS

Collections

> *Works* (Author's Revised Edition).   21 vols., 1860–61.
> *Representative Selections*, edited by Henry A. Pochmann.   1934.
> *Complete Works*, edited by Henry A. Pochmann.   1969–.
> *Complete Tales*, edited by Charles Neider.   1975.

Fiction and Sketches

> Salmagundi; or, The Whim-Whams and Opinions of Launcelot Langstaff, Esq., and Others, with James Kirke Paulding and William Irving.   2 vols., 1807–08.
> The Sketch Book of Geoffrey Crayon, Gent.   7 vols., 1819–20; revised edition, 2 vols., 1820.
> Bracebridge Hall; or, The Humourists: A Medley.   1822; edited by J. D. Colclough, 1898.
> Letters of Jonathan Oldstyle, Gent.   1824; edited by Stanley T. Williams, 1941.
> Tales of a Traveller.   1824.
> The Alhambra: A Series of Tales and Sketches of the Moors and Spaniards.   1832.
> Essays and Sketches.   1837.
> Chronicles of Wolfert's Roost and Other Papers.   1855.

Plays

> Charles the Second; or, The Merry Monarch, with John Howard Payne, from a play by A. V. P. Duval (produced 1824).   1824; edited by A. H. Quinn, in Representative American Plays, 1917.
> Richelieu: A Domestic Comedy, with John Howard Payne, from a play by A. V. P. Duval (produced 1826; as The French Libertine, produced 1826).   1826.
> Abu Hassan.   1924.
> The Wild Huntsman, from a play by Friedrich Kind.   1924.
> An Unwritten Play of Lord Byron.   1925.

Verse

> The Poems, edited by William R. Langfeld.   1931.

Other

> A History of New York from the Beginning of the World to the End of the Dutch Dynasty.   2 vols., 1809; revised edition, 1812, 1848; edited by Edwin T. Bowden, 1964.
> A History of the Life and Voyages of Christopher Columbus.   4 vols., 1828; edited by Winifred Hulbert, as The Voyages of Columbus, 1931.
> A Chronicle of the Conquest of Granada.   2 vols., 1829.
> Voyages and Discoveries of the Companions of Columbus.   1831.
> Miscellanies (A Tour on the Prairies, Abbotsford and Newstead Abbey, Legends of the Conquest of Spain).   3 vols., 1835; A Tour of the Prairies edited by John Francis McDermott, 1956.
> Astoria; or, Anecdotes of an Enterprise Beyond the Rocky Mountains.   2 vols., 1836; edited by Edgeley W. Todd, 1964.
> Adventures of Captain Bonneville; or, Scenes Beyond the Rocky Mountains of the Far West, based on journals of B. L. E. Bonneville.   1837; as The Rocky Mountains, 1837; edited by Edgeley W. Todd, 1961.
> The Life of Oliver Goldsmith, with Selections from His Writings.   2 vols., 1840; edited by G. S. Blakely, 1916.
> Biography and Poetical Remains of the Late Margaret Miller Davidson.   1841.
> A Book of the Hudson.   1849.
> Mahomet and His Successors, in Works.   2 vols., 1850; in Works, 1970.

Life of George Washington.   5 vols., 1855–59; abridged and edited by Charles Neider, 1976.

Spanish Papers and Other Miscellanies, edited by Pierre M. Irving.   2 vols., 1866.

Letters to Mrs. William Renwick and to Her Son James Renwick.   1915.

Letters to Henry Brevoort, edited by George S. Hellman.   2 vols., 1915.

Journals (Hitherto Unpublished), edited by William P. Trent and George S. Hellman.   3 vols., 1920.

Notes and Journals of Travel in Europe 1804–1805.   3 vols., 1921.

Diary: Spain 1828–1829, edited by Clara Louisa Penney.   1926.

Notes While Preparing Sketch Book 1817, edited by Stanley T. Williams.   1927.

Tour in Scotland 1817, and Other Manuscript Notes, edited by Stanley T. Williams.   1927.

Letters from Sunnyside and Spain, edited by Stanley T. Williams.   1929.

Journal (1823–1824), edited by Stanley T. Williams.   1931.

Irving and the Storrows: Letters from England and the Continent 1821–1828, edited by Stanley T. Williams.   1933.

Journal 1803, edited by Stanley T. Williams.   1934.

Journal 1828, and Miscellaneous Notes on Moorish Legend and History, edited by Stanley T. Williams.   1937.

The Western Journals, edited by John Francis McDermott.   1944.

Contributions to the Corrector, edited by Martin Roth.   1968.

Irving and the House of Murray (letters), edited by Ben Harris McClary.   1969.

Editor, *The Miscellaneous Works of Goldsmith.*   4 vols., 1825.
Editor, *Poems,* by William Cullen Bryant.   1832.
Editor, *Harvey's Scenes of the Primitive Forest of America.*   1841.

Translator, with Peter Irving and Georges Caines, *A Voyage to the Eastern Part of Terra Firma; or, The Spanish Main,* by F. Depons.   3 vols., 1806.

Bibliography: *A Bibliography of the Writings of Irving* by Stanley T. Williams and Mary Allen Edge, 1936; in *Bibliography of American Literature* by Jacob Blanck, 1963.

Reading List: *Life and Letters of Irving* by Pierre M. Irving, 4 vols., 1862–64 *The Life of Irving* by Stanley T. Williams, 2 vols., 1935; *The World of Irving* by Van Wyck Brooks, 1944; *Irving and Germany* by Walter A. Reichart, 1957; *Irving: Moderation Displayed* by Edward Wagenknecht, 1962; *Irving* by Lewis Leary, 1963; *Irving: An American Study* by William L. Hedges, 1965; *Irving Reconsidered: A Symposium* edited by Ralph Aderman, 1969; *Irving: A Tribute,* 1972, and *A Century of Commentary on the Works of Irving,* 1976, both edited by Andrew B. Myers.

*   *   *

Born in 1783, the year in which the American Revolution ended, Washington Irving, son of a prosperous New York hardware merchant, became the first author of the new country to be acclaimed in England. Although he never wrote a novel – indeed, his chief achievement resides in perhaps a dozen sketches and short stories – he must be acknowledged as the first man of letters in the United States. He lived until 1859, much admired by Poe and Hawthorne, whose grapplings with the darker side of human nature were as foreign to his own sanguine temperament as were their respective interests in ideas and in the extended development of plot and character. Yet Irving had managed to win not only their admiration but also that of Scott, Coleridge, and Byron. By the time he published *The Sketch Book of Geoffrey Crayon, Gent.* in 1819–20, his best work had been done. In the succeeding forty years he, like his contemporary William Cullen Bryant, became enshrined as a living figurehead of literary culture in America, though the conditions of American life rapidly outstripped his preparation or inclination to treat them in his writing.

In the event, however, Irving did bring to his vocation a belletristic sensibility, and a style that combined grace and poise with an inimitable pictorial quality. This style seems a fusion of Augustan balance with the sentiments of early Romanticism; it is among the first purely literary artifacts in the culture of the new republic. Irving's stylistic influence is visible in Hawthorne, in the tales of Bret Harte set in Spanish California, and even in Henry James (e.g., the description of Gardencourt in *The Portrait of a Lady*). But a decade before achieving the grace and strength of this style in *The Sketch Book*, Irving had scored a literary triumph of a different stripe with *A History of New York* (as the pseudonymous Diedrich Knickerbocker). This burlesque, Hudibrastic in its energy, is a satiric debunking of the Colonial history of Dutch New York, published in 1809, its author's and its country's twenty-sixth year. Although Irving was not to be so boldly satirical again, this youthful extravagance exhibits also another aspect of his sensibility which stayed with him to the end: his fascination with the past.

Never one to stay tied to the family hardware business, he served in the War of 1812 as a staff colonel, and in 1815 returned to Europe (he had taken a grand tour in 1804) – little knowing that he would not see New York again for seventeen years. Arriving in England, he sought out Scott, who had admired his *History*. Irving quickly became Scott's disciple, and, as is seen in *The Sketch Book*, he turned, in his most memorable stories, to the local settings and legends of the same Dutch ancestors whose political figures he had, as Diedrich Knickerbocker, lampooned a decade earlier. But Irving, although he anticipates by half a century the local color movement in fiction, was not merely a local colorist. He used the color of his native locale, the Hudson Valley, to impart the tinge of native realism to fables he deftly appropriated from European literature. "Rip Van Winkle," the tale which would bring Irving world-wide fame, is in part a nearly literal rendering from Otmar's *Volkssagen*. "The Legend of Sleepy Hollow," Irving's other masterpiece, is similarly based on Bürger's *Der Wilde Jäger* and one of the Rübezahl tales. Yet Irving did more than give these Germanic folk motifs a local habitation and a name. He infused them with subliminal universal significance, and at the same time, by an authorial alchemy no doubt unconscious on his part, expressed in them the very spirit of his nation and of his time.

In "Rip Van Winkle" the localization of the ancient German tale is perfect. Rip, a shrew-bedevilled husband, is a stock comic figure seeking regressive freedom in his bottle and in the wilderness of the mountaintop. There, encountering the ghosts of Hendrik Hudson's crew, he drinks their magical draught – and awakens as an old man, his fowling gun rusted beside him. In the meantime, however, life had gone on in the village below: that life included the American Revolution. So Rip's return from the blessed otherworld of the irretrievable past is to a new, busy, bustling nation he cannot understand, or enter. Irving's pervasive theme of nostalgia for the unrecoverable past is here at once mythologized and made unforgettable.

In "The Legend of Sleepy Hollow" Irving again appropriates a comic stereotype, for his Ichabod Crane, the Yankee schoolmaster, is akin to satirical versions of the Puritan character – calculating, narrow-gauged, lacking in spontaneity – found in the popular culture of the time. With intuitive prescience Irving puts Ichabod in opposition to Brom Bones, a brawny, forthright Dutchman whose character resembles that of such frontier folk heroes yet to come as Mike Fink or Davy Crockett. Thus at the beginning of American literature Irving anticipates the regional conflict between East and West, between the Puritan, urban, prudential character and the freedom of the natural man. He further imbeds this story in the expressive energies of popular culture by making the plot hinge on a tall tale that is also the frontiersman's hoax. Ichabod, known to be superstitious, is run out of town by the headless horseman. Brom Bones, in the saddle with the pumpkinhead in his lap, stays in Kinderhook to marry the girl. Thus Irving bestows his favor on an American of the coming century. In his own life, however, Irving was not as lucky as Brom Bones. His fiancée, Matilda Hoffman, daughter of a judge, died, and it may be that this early loss colored Irving's Romantic nostalgia.

Elsewhere in *The Sketch Book* Irving wrote at lower levels of intensity, exploring the folk customs of English Christmas, describing "A Country Church," "A Sunday in London," and the like. These at best are gentle impressionistic evocations of nostalgic moods. In *Bracebridge Hall* and *Tales of a Traveller* he reiterated similar subjects; *Chronicles of Wolfert's Roost* draws on Irving's travels in Germany and Spain, but the best tales are "Kidd the Pirate" and "The Devil and Tom Walker," the one an American legend, the other a native adaptation of the Faustian theme. Little in these books has lived, though in their time they doubtless enriched American literature with an antiquarian's love of the vanished or vanishing folkways of Europe.

Irving spent the winter of 1825 in Dresden, the next three years in Madrid, and then served from 1829 until his return in 1832 as Secretary of the American legation in London. His Spanish sojourn led to his writing the tales in *The Alhambra* and to his lengthy biographies of Mahomet and Columbus. These, as Stanley Williams has observed, are really romances rather than factual accounts of their subjects. After returning to the States, Irving, aware of the public's desire for fictional treatments of the West, took a tour of the wilds and provided them with *A Tour of the Prairies*, *Astoria* (an account of John Jacob Astor's success in the fur trade) and *Adventures of Captain Bonneville*. Thus the famous writer tried to obviate suspicion of his long exile, but these writings bring to the West only the pictorialist's eye trained in London and Madrid. Irving could not romanticize such subjects.

It was characteristic of this genial author's temperament that he chose as his private vehicle the sketch during the decades when the short story was supplanting it in popularity. In fact his own tales served as models for Poe, Hawthorne, and other authors whose fictions hurried the genre of the sketch into oblivion. If Irving's works of lasting value are but few and those few brief, his career is nonetheless significant; not only did he write some incomparable tales, and prove that authorship was a possible profession in a new country, but at the very moment when American literary consciousness was first developing he enriched his nation's culture with his cosmopolitan reflection of the themes and modes of British and continental Romanticism.

—Daniel Hoffman

JACKSON, Helen (Maria) Hunt (née Fiske). American. Born in Amherst, Massachusetts, 15 October 1830. Educated at Ipswich Female Seminary, Massachusetts, and at Abbott Brothers School, New York City. Married 1) Edward Bissell Hunt in 1852 (died, 1863), two sons; 2) William Sharpless Jackson in 1875. Neighbor and schoolmate of Emily Dickinson, who remained her life-long friend; after her first marriage, travelled throughout the United States with her husband, an officer in the Army Corps of Engineers; after his death, settled in Newport, Rhode Island, 1866, and thereafter became a full-time writer; travelled in Europe, 1868–70; moved to Colorado Springs, 1875; became interested in Indian affairs: appointed United States Special Commissioner to investigate conditions of the Mission Indians of California, 1882–83. *Died 12 August 1885.*

PUBLICATIONS

Fiction

Saxe Holm's Stories. 2 vols., 1874–78.
The Story of Boon. 1874.
Mercy Philbrick's Choice. 1876.
Hetty's Strange History. 1877.
Nelly's Silver Mine: A Story of Colorado Life. 1878.
The Hunter Cats of Connorloa. 1884.
Ramona. 1884.
Zeph: A Posthumous Story. 1885.
Pansy Billings and Popsy: Two Stories of Girl Life. 1898.

Verse

Verses. 1870; revised edition, 1871, 1874.
Easter Bells. 1884.
Pansies and Orchids, edited by Susie B. Skelding. 1884.
Sonnets and Lyrics. 1886.

Other

Bits of Travel. 1872.
Bits of Talk about Home Matters. 1873.
Bits of Talk, in Verse and Prose, for Young Folks. 1876.
Bits of Travel at Home. 1878.
A Century of Dishonor: A Sketch of the United States Government's Dealings with Some of the Indian Tribes. 1881; edited by Andrew F. Rolle, 1965.
Mammy Tittleback and Family: A True Story of Seventeen Cats. 1881.
The Training of Children. 1882.
Report on the Condition and Needs of the Mission Indians of California, with Abbot Kinney. 1883; *Father Junipero and His Work* edited by Richard B. Yale, 1966.
Glimpses of Three Coasts. 1886.
Between Whiles. 1887.

Editor, *Letters from a Cat,* by Deborah Fiske. 1879.

Translator, *Bathmendi*, by J. P. C. de Florian.   1867.

Bibliography: in *Bibliography of American Literature* by Jacob Blanck, 1963.

Reading List: *Jackson* by Ruth Odell, 1939; by Allan Nevins, in *American Scholar*, 1941; *Jackson* by Evelyn I. Banning, 1973.

*   *   *

When Helen Hunt Jackson died in 1885 Emily Dickinson promised her immortality: "Helen of Troy will die, but Helen of Colorado, never." At the time of her death her reputation was at its height as the result of two works, *A Century of Dishonor* and *Ramona*, both produced partly in consequence of Mrs. Jackson's move to Colorado and the West after her second marriage in 1875. Thomas Wentworth Higginson compared her to George Eliot; another critic thought her verse in some respects superior to that of Elizabeth Barrett Browning. *A Century of Dishonor* went out of print in 1885 and remained so until 1965 but *Ramona* went through over three hundred printings in the intervening years and was transferred to both stage and screen.

Paradoxically these two works alone do not give much understanding of either the writer's background or of her cultural and literary drives. In essence she was a New Englander whose closest friends and influences included not only Emily Dickinson and Higginson but Nathaniel Hawthorne, Horace Greeley, and the sculptors Horace Greenough and William Wetmore Story. Much of her verse and prose was filled by preoccupations with sin and morality, with the evil in man and the need for moral struggle. Allan Nevins had argued in *American Scholar* (1941) that *A Century of Dishonor* is too sentimental, and he is correct in that its purpose was polemical rather than literary or historical. But there is far less sentimentality in the main body of her work. Though her descriptions are often close to cosy, her sympathies are defined by a rationalism and an individualism that make her characters in the end fully responsible for their own fates, and she does not bring excess emotion to the telling of their destinies. Her characters survive and struggle on after what in other novelists of the day would have been the final and crippling climax, as can be seen in both *Hetty's Strange History* and *Mercy Philbrick's Choice*.

Such a modern sounding quality is linked to what some of her contemporary critics felt needed apology: a devaluing of narrative in some of her work. At times the results are anti-climactic, for it is difficult to sustain the dramatic tension once the central focus of the plot has been passed. The difference in the characters' lives before and after this point is described is often too extremely presented, but the great advantage is escape from dénouement. It is possible that the emphasis on the continuity of life was one aspect of an outlook that was partly formed by a vigorous and intelligent sense of humour, though this quality is to be found more in her ephemeral writings like *Bits of Travel at Home* than in the more formal works.

Modern readers would be attracted not only by her sympathy for the Native American but also by her strong feminism. Her heroines are the prime movers of her plots; the men revolve about them. Her women tend to be socially committed, fulfilling themselves through the exercise of their talents in the world, and, if introspective, only in a way that strengthens them when in contact with others. The women she describes would not have been at home among the New England mill-workers; their freedom of action depended on their freedom from poverty. Her lack of interest in this connection prevented her being swamped by naturalism and has deprived her of readers in a century that demands it.

In life Helen Hunt Jackson was vivacious, articulate, intelligent, and active. Her work deserves respect as that of a modern woman in the thirty years after the Civil War.

—R. A. Burchell

JAMES, Henry. English. Born in New York City, 15 April 1843; brother of the philosopher William James; emigrated to England; naturalized, 1915. Educated at the Richard Pulling Jenks School, New York; travelled, with his family, in Europe from an early age: studied with tutors in Geneva, London, Paris, and Boulogne, 1855–58, Geneva, 1859, and Bonn, 1860; lived with his family in Newport, Rhode Island, 1860–62; attended Harvard Law School, Cambridge, Massachusetts, 1862–65. Settled with his family in Cambridge, 1866, and wrote for the *Nation* and *Atlantic Monthly*, 1866–69; toured Europe, 1869; returned to Cambridge, 1870–72: wrote art criticism for the *Atlantic Monthly*, 1871–72; lived in Europe, 1872–74, Cambridge, 1875, and Paris, 1875–76: writer for the *New York Tribune*, Paris, 1875–76; settled in London, 1876, and lived in England for the rest of his life; settled in Rye, Sussex, 1896; travelled throughout the United States, 1904–05. L.H.D.: Harvard University, 1911; Oxford University, 1912. Order of Merit, 1916. *Died 28 February 1916.*

PUBLICATIONS

Collections

    Novels and Stories, edited by Percy Lubbock.   35 vols., 1921–24.
    Complete Plays, edited by Leon Edel.   1949.
    Complete Tales, edited by Leon Edel.   12 vols., 1962–65.
    Representative Selections, revised edition, edited by Lyon N. Richardson.   1966.
    Letters, edited by Leon Edel.   1974–

Fiction

    A Passionate Pilgrim and Other Tales.   1875.
    Roderick Hudson.   1875; edited by Leon Edel, 1960.
    The American.   1877; edited by James W. Tuttleton, 1978.
    Watch and Ward.   1878; edited by Leon Edel, 1960.
    The Europeans: A Sketch.   1878; edited by Leon Edel, with *Washington Square*, 1967.
    Daisy Miller: A Study.   1879.
    An International Episode.   1879.
    The Madonna of the Future and Other Tales.   1879.
    Confidence.   1880; edited by Herbert Ruhm, 1962.
    A Bundle of Letters.   1880.
    The Diary of a Man of Fifty, and A Bundle of Letters.   1880.
    Washington Square.   1881; edited by Gerald Willen, 1970.
    The Portrait of a Lady.   1881; edited by Robert D. Bamberg, 1975.
    The Siege of London, The Pension Beaurepas, and The Point of View.   1883; revised
       edition, 1884.
    Novels and Tales.   14 vols., 1883.
    Tales of Three Cities.   1884.
    *The Author of Beltraffio, Pandora, Georgina's Reasons, The Path of Duty, Four
       Meetings.*   1885.
    Stories Revived.   1885.
    The Bostonians.   1886; edited by Leon Edel, 1967.
    The Princess Casamassima.   1886.
    The Reverberator.   1888.
    The Aspern Papers, Louisa Pallant, The Modern Warning.   1888.
    A London Life, The Patagonia, The Liar, Mrs. Temperly.   1889.
    The Tragic Muse.   1890.

The Lesson of the Master, The Marriages, The Pupil, Brooksmith, The Solution, Sir Edmund Orme. 1892.
The Real Thing and Other Tales. 1893.
The Private Life, The Wheel of Time, Lord Beaupre, The Visits, Collaboration, Owen Wingrave. 1893.
Terminations, The Death of the Lion, The Coxon Fund, The Middle Years, The Altar of the Dead. 1895.
Embarrassments, The Figure in the Carpet, Glasses, The Next Time, The Way It Came. 1896.
The Other House. 1896.
The Spoils of Poynton. 1897; edited by Leon Edel, 1967.
What Maisie Knew. 1897; edited by Douglas Jefferson, 1966.
In the Cage. 1898; edited by Morton Dauwen Zabel, 1958.
The Two Magics, The Turn of the Screw, Covering End. 1898; *The Turn of the Screw* edited by Robert Kimbrough, 1966.
The Awkward Age. 1899; edited by Leon Edel, 1967.
The Soft Side (stories). 1900.
The Sacred Fount. 1901; edited by Leon Edel, 1953.
The Wings of the Dove. 1902; edited by J. Donald Crowley and Richard A. Hocks, 1978.
The Better Sort (stories). 1903.
The Ambassadors. 1903; edited by S. P. Rosenbaum, 1966.
The Golden Bowl. 1904.
Novels and Tales (New York Edition), revised by James. 24 vols., 1907–09.
Julia Bride. 1909.
The Finer Grain. 1910.
The Outcry. 1911.
The Ivory Tower, edited by Percy Lubbock. 1917.
The Sense of the Past, edited by Percy Lubbock. 1917.
Gabrielle de Bergerac, edited by Albert Mordell. 1918.
Travelling Companions (stories). 1919.
A Landscape Painter (stories). 1919.
Master Eustace (stories). 1920.
Eight Uncollected Tales, edited by Edna Kenton. 1950.

Plays

Daisy Miller, from his own story. 1883.
The American, from his own novel (produced 1891). 1891.
Guy Domville (produced 1895). 1894.
Theatricals (includes *Tenants, Disengaged*) (produced 1909). 1894.
Theatricals: Second Series (includes *The Album, The Reprobate*) (produced 1919). 1894.
The High Bid (produced 1908). In *Complete Plays,* 1949.
The Saloon (produced 1911). In *Complete Plays,* 1949.
The Outcry (produced 1917). In *Complete Plays,* 1949.

Other

Transatlantic Sketches. 1875; revised edition, as *Foreign Parts,* 1883.
French Poets and Novelists. 1878; revised edition, 1883; edited by Leon Edel, 1964.
Hawthorne. 1879; edited by William M. Sale, Jr., 1956.

Portraits of Places. 1883.
Notes on a Collection of Drawings by George du Maurier. 1884.
A Little Tour in France. 1884.
The Art of Fiction, with Walter Besant.   1885; edited by Leon Edel, in *The House of Fiction,* 1957.
Partial Portraits. 1888.
Picture and Text. 1893.
Essays in London and Elsewhere. 1893.
William Wetmore Story and His Friends. 2 vols., 1903.
The Question of Our Speech, The Lesson of Balzac: Two Lectures.   1905.
English Hours. 1905; edited by Alma Louise Lowe, 1960.
The American Scene. 1907; edited by Leon Edel, 1968.
Views and Reviews. 1908.
Italian Hours. 1909.
The Henry James Year Book, edited by Evelyn Garnaut Smalley.   1911.
A Small Boy and Others (autobiography).   1913.
Notes of a Son and Brother (autobiography).   1914.
Notes on Novelists and Some Other Notes.   1914.
Letters to an Editor. 1916.
Within the Rim and Other Essays 1914–1915.   1919.
The Middle Years (autobiography), edited by Percy Lubbock.   1917.
Letters, edited by Percy Lubbock.   2 vols., 1920.
Notes and Reviews. 1921.
A Most Unholy Trade, Being Letters on the Drama.   1923.
Three Letters to Joseph Conrad, edited by Gerard Jean-Aubry.   1926.
Letters to Walter Berry. 1928.
Letters to A. C. Benson and Auguste Monod, edited by E. F. Benson.   1930.
Theatre and Friendship: Some James Letters, edited by Elizabeth Robins.   1932.
The Art of the Novel: Critical Prefaces, edited by R. P. Blackmur.   1934.
Notebooks, edited by F. O. Matthiessen and Kenneth B. Murdock.   1947.
The Art of Fiction and Other Essays, edited by Morris Roberts.   1948.
James and Robert Louis Stevenson: A Record of Friendship and Criticism, edited by Janet Adam Smith.   1948.
The Scenic Art: Notes on Acting and the Drama 1872–1901, edited by Allan Wade.   1948.
Daumier, Caricaturist. 1954.
Selected Letters, edited by Leon Edel, 1955.
The American Essays, edited by Leon Edel.   1956.
The Future of the Novel: Essays on the Art of the Novel, edited by Leon Edel.   1956; as *The House of Fiction,* 1957.
The Painter's Eye: Notes and Essays on the Pictorial Arts, edited by John L. Sweeney.   1956.
Parisian Sketches: Letters to the New York Tribune 1875–1876, edited by Leon Edel and Ilse Dusoir Lind.   1957.
Literary Reviews and Essays on American, English, and French Literature, edited by Albert Mordell.   1957.
James and H. G. Wells: A Record of Their Friendship, Their Debate on the Art of Fiction, and Their Quarrel, edited by Leon Edel and Gordon N. Ray.   1958.
French Writers and American Women: Essays, edited by Peter Buitenhuis.   1960.
James and John Hay: The Record of a Friendship, edited by George Monteiro.   1965.
Switzerland in the Life and Work of James: The Clare Benedict Collection of Letters from James, edited by Jörg Hasler.   1966.

Translator, *Port Tarascon,* by Alphonse Daudet.   1891.

Bibliography: *A Bibliography of James* by Leon Edel and D. H. Laurence, 1957; revised edition, 1961; in *Bibliography of American Literature* by Jacob Blanck, 1968.

Reading List: *James: The Major Phase* by F. O. Matthiessen, 1944; *James* (biography) by Leon Edel, 5 vols., 1953–72, revised edition, 2 vols., 1978; *The American James* by Quentin Anderson, 1957; *The Comic Sense of James* by Richard Poirier, 1960; *The Novels of James* by Oscar Cargill, 1961; *The Ordeal of Consciousness in James* by Dorothea Crook, 1962; *The Expanse of Vision: Essays on the Craft of James* by Lawrence B. Holland, 1964; *The Imagination of Loving: James's Legacy to the Novel* by Naomi Lebowitz, 1965; *James: A Reader's Guide* by S. Gorley Putt, 1966; *James: The Critical Heritage* edited by Roger Gard, 1968; *James* by Tony Tanner, 1968; *The Negative Imagination: Form and Perspective in the Novels of James* by Sallie Sears, 1969; *Reading James* by Louis Auchincloss, 1975; *Language and Knowledge in the Late Novels of James* by Ruth Bernard Yeazell, 1976.

*   *   *

Few who accord the novels and short stories of Henry James the attention they deserve come away from the experience unmoved by the subject matter and unenlightened by the artistry, yet it is probably true that James would be little read today if it were not for the continuing enthusiasm of individuals who discover him first as a reading assignment in a college or university course. More than almost any other great novelist, James is a writer whose best works require a sympathetic power of attention that the casual reader is not disposed to give. For most people James is an acquired taste. Unless they approach him in the right spirit they never acquire the taste at all. Yet he is certainly one of the great writers in English, one of those artists of another era who nevertheless seems most perennially modern.

His dedication to literature for fifty years from the Civil War until his death in 1916 produced a body of work of monumental scope. He never married, never carried on anything resembling a conventional courtship. His friendships were virtually all rooted in shared literary or artistic enthusiasms. He travelled – often, it seems, merely to reinvigorate himself for a new assault upon his artistic problems. With less talent and similar dedication he might have produced novels and tales that consisted mainly of the same stories retold, the same techniques exploited again and again in order to recapture prior successes. Something of this tendency resides in his work, as it does in the work of all masters, but there is also an extraordinary continual development that reaches its peak in three late masterpieces: *The Wings of the Dove*, *The Ambassadors*, and *The Golden Bowl*. The late work of some poets can best be read largely in the light of the education gained by studying their earlier efforts: James is one of a relatively few novelists whose work cries out to be approached in a similar manner.

"It's a complex fate being an American," James once wrote, "and one of the responsibilities it entails is fighting against a superstitious valuation of Europe." Herein is expressed the essence of the "international theme" that runs through much of his work. In a time when more than a few novelists were making capital out of the social complications that arise when individuals from one side of the Atlantic confront the natives of the other side upon their home ground, James made this subject peculiarly his own by returning to it in work after work. So doing, he lifted it outside the confines of drawing room comedy and placed it squarely at the crossroads of the two great traditions of the nineteenth-century novel in English. Among the best of James's international novels and tales are *The American*, *The Europeans*, *Daisy Miller*, *The Portrait of a Lady*, *The Wings of the Dove*, *The Ambassadors*, and *The Golden Bowl*. In these works the central concerns of previous novelists in English come together in a confrontation almost mythic in its implications. Simply expressed, the central concern of English novelists from Austen through Scott, Dickens, and Eliot was the accommodation of individual aspirations within the sheltering embrace of the social framework; both their social view and their art were shaped by a realistic vision of compromise. Just as simply expressed, the central concern of American novelists from

Cooper through Hawthorne, Melville, and Twain, was with those individual aspirations that are incapable of accommodation within any social framework except the as-yet-unrealized American dream of perfect freedom, equality, and justice; their social view and their art were shaped by a vision that looked toward a world considerably more ideal than the world they lived in. James brought these visions together in an amalgamation inherently tragic. His best works express in metaphor how much the condition of modern man hangs continually in the balance between the European dream of social accommodation and the American dream of perfect freedom.

Closely related to the international theme is James's continual emphasis upon partial perspectives. Human knowledge, he insists, and consequently human action, is sharply limited by inescapable conditions of time and place. From Christopher Newman to Lambert Strether his Americans achieve their destiny because the perspectives forced upon them by birth and education allow them no choices except the ones they inevitably make. From Madame de Cintré to Madame de Vionnet his Europeans are similarly limited. This at least is the theory: the novel is realistic, as James most often intended it should be, when the fates of the characters follow inevitably from the conditions that surround them; it is romantic, as James sometimes allowed, when the fates evolve from conditions imposed by the author that are quite distinct from the facts of observable reality. The realistic effect that he intended for most of his novels derives from the success with which he developed techniques for objectifying the partial perspectives from which humans direct their lives.

An important part of his work is also the theme of awareness that comes too late. His people are concerned above all with the question of how to live, but most of them have not any clear idea of how to begin. Sometimes they are wealthy, like Christopher Newman in *The American*, Milly Theale in *The Wings of the Dove*, and Maggie Verver in *The Golden Bowl*. Sometimes they become wealthy, like Isabel Archer in *The Portrait of a Lady*. Sometimes they live in expectation of wealth, like Kate Croy in *The Wings of the Dove*. In most instances they have at least, like Lambert Strether in *The Ambassadors*, enough to enable them to live comfortably, though it is often true of the less attractive figures that they suppose themselves in need of more than they possess. In any event they are mostly free of the more mundane cares of life and have nearly total leisure in which to pursue happiness through courtship, marriage, liaisons, social activity, travel, the search for culture: whatever, in short, seems most attractive to them. To live most fully, James makes clear in a number of places, is to be most fully aware of one's possibilities so that one may make the best of them. Since, however, the most interesting possibilities come from human relationships which are inherently a tissue of subtle complexities, to be most fully aware is to possess a depth of sympathetic insight that comes to few people until it is too late to take advantage of it. Total freedom for James's characters involves the freedom to make social commitments different from those that all too often they make, wrongly, in bondage to some mistaken understanding, or do not make at all because, sadly, they fail to perceive the opportunity that lies before them.

A great critic, James is also a great technical experimenter. The best of his criticism is preserved in individual essays such as "The Art of Fiction" and in his *Notebooks* and the prefaces that he wrote for the New York edition of his works. All are read most profitably in conjunction with the example of his fiction. His technical experiments are most readily approached through those many fictions in which he enforces the theme of partial perspectives by contriving severely limited perspectives from which to narrate. Some of the easier works in which this theme and this method are important are the early *Daisy Miller* and the late "The Beast in the Jungle." Because Daisy is never seen except from the partial view that Winterbourne enjoys, the reader remains in danger of sharing Winterbourne's misunderstanding of her character. Because May Bartram, in "The Beast in the Jungle," is never seen except in a view accessible to Marcher, the same potential problem exists. Fundamentally simple in these works, both theme and technique become more complex in "The Aspern Papers," *The Turn of the Screw*, and *The Sacred Fount*. In all three the careful reader is aware that there may be some aspect of the truth that remains dark to the central character. In "The Aspern Papers" most readers believe they can see beyond the limited vision of the narrator; in *The Turn of the Screw* there are good reasons to suppose both that the ghosts do and do not exist; in *The Sacred Fount* the puzzle that begins the novel becomes not less but more of a puzzle as it ends. In *The Portrait of a Lady*, *The Wings of the Dove*, *The Ambassadors*, and *The Golden Bowl* the theme of partial perspectives (which involves often the theme of too late awareness) merges with the international theme to provide the substance of James's most lasting achievement.

Many of James's fictions conclude upon a sense of loss. In his deepest vision human life is fundamentally tragic because of the eternal tension between the individual's sense of his vast human opportunities and his frequently inadequate awareness of his personal limitations. Like Isabel Archer or Lambert Strether, twentieth-century readers, too, are possessed by dreams of boundless freedom. Like both, they make in the end the choices that they *can* make – which are often not at all the choices that they would make if they lived in a world in which a just and equal perfect freedom came less insistently into conflict with the requirements of social accommodation.

—George Perkins

JEWETT, Sarah Orne. American. Born in South Berwick, Maine, 3 September 1849, and lived there for all of her life. Educated at Miss Rayne's School, 1855, and the Berwick Academy, 1861–65, graduated 1865. Full-time writer from 1865; contributed to the *Atlantic Monthly* from 1869; through association with the editor, William Dean Howells, came to know the Boston literary circle of Lowell and Whittier; later travelled abroad and met Tennyson, Christina Rossetti, and Henry James. Litt.D.: Bowdoin College, Brunswick, Maine, 1901. *Died 24 June 1909.*

PUBLICATIONS

Collections

Stories and Tales. 7 vols., 1910.
Letters, edited by Richard Cary. 1956; revised edition, 1967.
The Country of the Pointed Firs and Other Stories, edited by Mary Ellen Chase. 1968.

Fiction

Deephaven. 1877; edited by Richard Cary, with other stories, 1966.
Old Friends and New (stories). 1879.
Country By-Ways. 1881.
The Mate of the Daylight and Friends Ashore (stories). 1883.
A Country Doctor. 1884.
A Marsh Island. 1885.
A White Heron and Other Stories. 1886.
The King of Folly Island and Other People. 1888.

Strangers and Wayfarers. 1890.
Tales of New England. 1890.
A Native of Winby and Other Tales. 1893.
The Life of Nancy (stories). 1895.
The Country of the Pointed Firs. 1896.
The Queen's Twin and Other Stories. 1899.
The Tory Lover. 1901.
An Empty Purse: A Christmas Story. 1905.
Uncollected Short Stories, edited by Richard Cary. 1971.

Verse

Verses, edited by M. A. DeWolfe Howe. 1916.

Other

Play Days: A Book of Stories for Children. 1878.
The Story of the Normans (juvenile). 1887.
Betty Leicester: A Story for Girls. 1890.
Betty Leicester's English Xmas (juvenile). 1894; as *Betty Leicester's Christmas,* 1899.
Letters, edited by Annie Fields. 1911.
Letters Now in Colby College Library, edited by Carl J. Weber. 1947.

Editor, *Stories and Poems for Children,* by Celia Thaxter. 1895.
Editor, *The Poems of Celia Thaxter.* 1896.
Editor, *Letters of Sarah Wyman Whitman.* 1907.

Bibliography: *A Bibliography of the Published Writings of Jewett* by Clara Carter Weber and Carl J. Weber, 1949; in *Bibliography of American Literature* by Jacob Blanck, 1969.

Reading List: *Jewett* by F. O. Matthiessen, 1929; *Jewett* by John Eldridge Frost, 1960; *Jewett* by Richard Cary, 1962; *Jewett* by Margaret Farrand Thorp, 1966.

*　　*　　*

The American novelist Willa Cather ranked Sarah Orne Jewett's *The Country of the Pointed Firs* with Nathaniel Hawthorne's *The Scarlet Letter* and Mark Twain's *Huckleberry Finn* as one of the three American prose literary works most likely to endure. The estimate is probably overenthusiastic; yet *The Country of the Pointed Firs*, a loosely constructed episodic novel laid on the Maine Coast in America, is at least a minor classic and will continue to be read for many years to come. Jewett was an eminently successful literary regionalist – a depicter of setting and character in the area where she had been born and brought up in a patrician family whose sympathies had been Tory during the Revolutionary War. Yet her somewhat aristocratic viewpoint – she was inordinately proud of her Anglo-Norman ancestry – in no way affected her understanding and admiration of the fishing and farming people about whom she wrote in her best work.

Her first book, *Deephaven*, fashioned from sketches that had previously appeared in the *Atlantic Monthly*, deals with life among all classes in a typical Maine seaport, with emphasis upon social and economic decay as commerce and shipping became more and more concentrated in the larger ports like Boston and New York. Jewett's tone in this volume, as in much of her writing, is one of nostalgia for a time when her region had figured vitally in the maritime life of the nation and had nurtured a population of hardy seafarers who sailed their vessels to all the great ports of the world. These days, regrettably, were past, but Jewett still found much to praise among the Maine folk of her time. *The Country of the Pointed Firs* is her major tribute to these quiet, resourceful, hard-working people, the significance of whose lives, now that the adventurous sea-faring days were gone, Jewett found to be in the success with which they had adjusted to a harsh environment. The women especially (and most of Jewett's strong characters are women) had learned to live in harmony with their native region — a rocky, island-studded coast with steep pastures and forested mountains rising close back from the water. The most notable of these women, the widow Elmira Todd, subsisted as an herbalist, thus personifying the Maine folks' ability to draw life-giving strength from a seemingly sterile land.

Jewett, in her Preface to *Deephaven*, stated that she considered one of her functions as a regional writer was to make the rest of the nation acquainted with the lives and characteristics of a little-known segment of the population. But more important, taking her cue from a statement by George Sand regarding the French peasantry, Jewett believed that the scrutiny to which she, as a writer, subjected her Maine neighbors would reveal a human worth and gentle heroism rarely found elsewhere. Jewett, indeed, saw a physical resemblance between the Maine Coast and the coast and isles of Greece, and she saw classical qualities in her Maine characters. Thus Mrs. Todd, standing on an Atlantic headland and mourning her husband drowned in shipwreck, reminds Jewett of Antigone "alone on the Theban plain." Elsewhere Mrs. Todd as an herbalist reminds Jewett of the enchantress Medea. Such allusions, inserted in passing, underline Jewett's point in this and other books: that the simplest persons can attain a dignity, even a tragic grandeur, essentially the same as that found in the literary records of the classic ages. She did not always find these qualities only among maritime people. The persons in her fiction include up-country farmers, elderly ladies in elm-shaded inland towns, and Irish maid-servants, and almost invariably she presents them as possessing, and exhibiting, a potential for the full range of human experience from tragedy to ecstasy.

Jewett's prose is notable for its purity and variety. Her descriptions of land and sea are lyrically evocative. Her narrative style is direct and flowing. In her dialogue she succeeds better than any other New England writer in reproducing the accents and, especially, the rhythms of the speech of her region. Unlike many local-colorists, she does not strive for phonetic renderings of dialect — efforts that usually result in grotesque and nearly unintelligible manglings of spelling. Jewett emphasizes regional diction, idiom, and cadence with only minor alterations of spelling. The result is not only readable but authentic.

Jewett in her lifetime was an admired and popular writer, publishing a sizable number of novels and collections of tales and sketches. Among the novels *A Country Doctor*, which draws from her experiences in accompanying her physician father on his rounds, deserves mention, as does *A Marsh Island*, an idyllic celebration of life on a coastal farm. Among her volumes of short fiction and sketches three of the richest are *Country By-Ways*, *A White Heron and Other Stories* (the title piece being her most famous story), and *The King of Folly Island and Other People*, containing the superb story "Miss Tempy's Watchers."

Though born and brought up in a small Maine town and always fiercely loyal to the place of her birth, Jewett was very much in touch with, and an influence in, the literary life of her times. A close friend of Mrs. James Fields, wife of the prominent Boston publisher, she was active in Boston literary circles and met many of the nation's and world's great writers as they visited the publisher's home. Eventually she became recognized as the author who carried local color, or regionalism, to the highest artistic level it has attained in America. Her writing has served as a model for other American authors, not all of them local-colorists, especially women of her and later generations. For example, Willa Cather, following Jewett's example and personal advice, redirected her early efforts from rather mediocre fiction in the manner of Henry James to the writing of highly successful competent novels based on life in the midwestern farmlands where she had been brought up. Jewett always held that an author's chief source of material should be his or her own locale and personal experience. To this conviction she remained faithful throughout her writing career.

—P. D. Westbrook

KENNEDY, John Pendleton. American. Born in Baltimore, Maryland, 25 October 1795. Educated at the Sinclair Academy, Baltimore, and Baltimore College, graduated 1812; studied law: admitted to the Maryland bar, 1816. Served in the United States Army during the War of 1812. Married 1) Mary Tennant in 1824 (died, 1825); 2) Elizabeth Gray in 1829. Practised law in Baltimore from 1816; Member, Maryland House of Delegates, 1820–23; inherited large income from an uncle c. 1830 and increasingly gave up the law for literature and politics; Member from Maryland, United States House of Representatives, 1838, 1840–44: Chairman of the Congressional Committee on Commerce; Member of the Maryland House of Delegates, and Speaker of the House, 1846–48; Secretary of the Navy, under President Fillmore, 1852–53: organized Commodore Perry's expedition to Japan, 1852. Provost, University of Maryland; President, Board of Trustees, Peabody Institute, Baltimore. *Died 18 August 1870.*

PUBLICATIONS

Collections

Collected Works.   10 vols., 1871–72.

Fiction

Swallow Barn; or, A Sojourn in the Old Dominion.   1832; edited by Ernest E. Leisy, 1937.
Horse Shoe Robinson: A Tale of the Tory Ascendency.   1835; edited by Ernest E. Leisy, 1937.
Rob of the Bowl: A Legend of St. Inigoe's.   1838; edited by William S. Osborne, 1965.
Quodlibet, Containing Some Annals Thereof.   1840.

Other

The Red Book, with Peter Hoffman Cruse.   2 vols., 1820–21.
Defense of the Whigs.   1843.
Memoirs of the Life of William Wirt, Attorney General of the United States.   1849.
The Border States.   1860.
Mr. Ambrose's Letters on the Rebellion.   1865.

Editor, with Alexander Bliss, *Autograph Leaves of Our Country's Authors.*   1864.

Bibliography: in *Bibliography of American Literature* by Jacob Blanck, 1969.

Reading List: *The Life of Kennedy* by Henry T. Tuckerman, in *Collected Works,* 1871; *Kennedy, Gentleman from Baltimore* by Charles H. Bohner, 1961; *Kennedy* by Joseph V. Ridgely, 1966.

*   *   *

Only two of John Pendleton Kennedy's four works of fiction can really be called novels. Much like Washington Irving's *Bracebridge Hall,* which it both resembles and satirizes, *Swallow Barn* is hardly more than a series of sketches loosely held together by common characters and a pair of shadowy plot lines, and *Quodlibet* is a satire on Jacksonian politics and policies of the 1830's projected through a history of the imaginary borough of Quodlibet. *Horse Shoe Robinson* and *Rob of the Bowl* are thus his only true novels. Both are historical romances of the kind made popular by Scott and Cooper.

Swallow Barn is in many ways his most attractive book. Hardly the realistic work it has sometimes been called, it makes good-natured fun of a group of Virginia planters in the early nineteenth century, burlesques their chivalric ideals and pretensions, yet also treats with respect many of the gentlemanly values they attempt to preserve. *Quodlibet*, by contrast, attacks the leveling democrats through one of their number. Solomon Secondthoughts recounts the history of Quodlibet in such a way as to damn the very policies and practices he thinks he is upholding. The work is thus a clever, if dated, piece of satire.

Horse Shoe Robinson and *Rob of the Bowl*, on the other hand, develop their themes through the use of history. Kennedy sought to maintain historical accuracy in both, but like other historical romances, the books are concerned not so much with demonstrable fact as with the meaning to be found in the events of the past. Thus, *Horse Shoe Robinson* portrays the American Revolution as a desperate struggle by young patrician leaders and their yeoman supporters to establish a free society, and *Rob of the Bowl* depicts the successful defense of seventeenth-century Maryland against both Puritan rebels and lawless buccaneers as the maintenance of established order against the threat of disruption.

Kennedy's four books would thus seem to work at cross purposes: *Horse Shoe Robinson* affirming the need for progressive social change, and *Rob of the Bowl* upholding the value of social stability; *Swallow Barn* satirizing Virginia aristocrats, and *Quodlibet* attacking leveling democrats. Yet the books are not so diverse in meaning as they may seem. The issues they present are those that troubled thinking Americans during the 1830's, and Kennedy seems to suggest that some kind of balance among the conflicting ideas should be maintained: though American society must progress, it should not change so radically as to destroy the important personal and social values that had come to it from the past. Taken together, then, his four works of fiction indicate the skill with which Kennedy, who did not think of himself as a professional man of letters, was able to develop a complex social theme.

—Donald A. Ringe

KIRKLAND, Joseph. American. Born in Geneva, New York, 7 January 1830; grew up in Michigan and Illinois. Received little formal education; studied law, 1873–80: admitted to the Illinois bar, 1880. Served in the American Civil War, in the Illinois 12th Regiment, 1861, as Aide-de-Camp, Adjutant-General's Department, Washington, D.C., 1861, and on the staff of Generals Fitz-John Porter and McClellan, 1862–63: Major. Married Theodosia Burr Wilkinson in 1863; four children. Sailor on a packet ship, 1847; Clerk and Reader, *Putnam's Monthly*, 1852; Auditor, Illinois Central Railroad, Chicago, 1856–58; Supervisor, Carbon Coal Company, Tilton, Illinois, 1858; established coal mining business, in Tilton, 1863, and a retail coal business, in Chicago, 1868: bankrupt, 1877; worked for the United States Revenue Service, 1875–80; practised law, in partnership with Mark Bangs, Chicago, 1880–90; Special Correspondent and Literary Editor, *Chicago Tribune*, 1889 until his death. Member, Committee on the World Exposition in Chicago, 1893. *Died 29 April 1894.*

PUBLICATIONS

Fiction

Zury, The Meanest Man in Spring County: A Novel of Western Life.   1887.
The McVeys (An Episode).   1888.
The Captain of Company K.   1891.

Play

Sidonie, The Married Flirt, with James B. Runnion, from a novel by Daudet (produced
1877).

Other

The Story of Chicago, completed by Caroline Kirkland.   2 vols., 1892–94.
The Chicago Massacre of 1812.   1893.

Editor, *Lily Pearl and the Mistress of Rosedale,* by Ida Glenwood.   1892.
Editor, with John Moses, *The History of Chicago.*   2 vols., 1895.

Bibliography: in *Bibliography of American Literature* by Jacob Blanck, 1969.

Reading List: *Kirkland* by Clyde E. Henson, 1962.

*   *   *

Joseph Kirkland's claim to fame rests entirely on one book, *Zury*, and a superficial reading
of it is likely to be misleading. Literary historians have been too quick to classify Kirkland
with other "agrarian realists" and "protest novelists." It is true that *Zury* contains many
details conveying the narrowness, brutality, and deprivation of midwestern farm life in the
middle of the nineteenth century. Zury (the name is short for Usury) has a beloved sister who
dies as a result of the primitive conditions on the farm, and the family has no coins with
which to weight her eyelids. Since she dies in mid-winter, the family has no choice but to let
the body freeze and wait for the spring thaw to bury her.

The novel also forcefully describes the cruelty and niggardliness Zury must possess to
accumulate his modest fortune. Having been made selfish by his environment, he seeks to
avoid his responsibility for making pregnant the young and innocent school teacher from the
East, Anne Sparrow. He arranges to marry her to a local idler, John McVey.

However, to emphasize these details is to neglect the end of *Zury* and the entirety of the
sequel, *The McVeys*. The second volume followed soon after the first, and in it Zury sees his
error and takes an interest in his and Anne's twin children (McVey has conveniently died).
Although she at first rejects him, Zury and Anne eventually marry and symbolically combine
the vitality and toughness of Zury's West with the culture and refinement of Anne's East,
and the last scene of *The McVeys* finds them cozy and happy in a prosperous farmhouse. One

might suggest that Kirkland was ultimately more "realistic" than some of his more bitter contemporaries, and certainly more entertaining.

After writing *The Captain of Company K*, an episodic but vivid story of the Civil War, Kirkland showed little interest in artistic creation, and devoted himself to editorial and historical work.

—William Higgins

LANIER, Sidney. American. Born in Macon, Georgia, 3 February 1842. Educated at a private academy in Macon, and at Oglethorpe University, near Milledgeville, Georgia, 1857–60, graduated 1860. Served with the Macon Volunteers in the Confederate forces during the Civil War, 1861–65: prisoner-of-war, 1864–65. Married Mary Day in 1867; four sons. Worked in his father's law office, and as a hotel clerk, and teacher, Macon, 1865–73; musician from an early age: flute player in the Peabody Orchestra, Baltimore, from 1873; Lecturer in English Literature, Johns Hopkins University, Baltimore, 1879–81. *Died 7 September 1881.*

<small>PUBLICATIONS</small>

Collections

> *The Works* (includes letters), edited by Charles R. Anderson and others.   10 vols., 1945.
> *Selected Poems*, edited by Stark Young.   1947.

Verse

> *The Centennial Meditation of Columbia,* music by Dudley Buck.   1876.
> *Poems.*   1877.
> *Poems,* edited by Mary Day Lanier.   1884; revised edition, 1891, 1916.
> *Poem Outlines.*   1908.

Fiction

> *Tiger-Lilies.*   1867.

Other

> *Florida: Its Scenery, Climate, and History.*   1875.
> *Some Highways and Byways of American Travel,* with others.   1878.
> *The Science of English Verse.*   1880.
> *The English Novel and the Principle of Its Development,* edited by William Hand Browne.   1883; edited by Mary Day Lanier, 1897.
> *Music and Poetry: Essays upon Some Aspects and Inter-Relations of the Two Arts,* edited by Henry Wysham Lanier.   1898.
> *Retrospects and Prospects: Descriptive and Historical Essays,* edited by Henry Wysham Lanier.   1899.
> *Letters of Lanier: Selections from His Correspondence 1866–1881,* edited by Henry Wysham Lanier.   1899.
> *Bob: The Story of Our Mocking-Bird,* edited by Henry Wysham Lanier.   1899.
> *Shakespeare and His Forerunners: Studies in Elizabethan Poetry and Its Development from Early English,* edited by Henry Wysham Lanier.   2 vols., 1902.

Editor, *The Boy's Froissart, Being Sir John's Froissart's Chronicles.*   1879.
Editor, *The Boy's King Arthur, Being Sir Thomas Malory's History of King Arthur and His Knights of the Round Table.*   1880.
Editor, *The Boy's Mabinogion.*   1881.
Editor, *The Boy's Percy, Being Old Ballads of War, Adventure, and Love.*   1882.

Bibliography: in *Bibliography of American Literature* by Jacob Blanck, 1969.

Reading List: *Lanier: A Biographical and Critical Study* by Aubrey H. Starke, 1933; *Lanier, Poet and Prosodist* by Richard Webb and Edwin R. Coulson, 1941; *Lanier: The Man, The Poet, The Critic* by Edd Winfield Parks, 1968; *Lanier* by Jack De Bellis, 1972.

*   *   *

The life of Sidney Lanier is an odyssey from a small Southern city to the great cultural centers of America; from a law desk in a Georgia office to a prominent place in a major professional orchestra; from an aesthetically restrictive tradition to an existence totally imbued with the arts. Throughout his career, from the time he was deciding whether to defy Southern tradition in favor of art, through the period in which he was totally devoted to art, music seems to have been in competition with poetry for his time and attention. But there was never any conflict in the negative sense, for without his musical experiences Lanier could never have arrived at the type of poetry he was finally to create.

The story of Sidney Lanier is both inspiring and pathetic. It is a series of thwarted plans, shattered hopes, incomplete projects. Lanier spent most of his life dreaming of entering artistic circles, but when he finally decided to devote himself body and spirit to attaining this end he was able to reach only slightly beyond the periphery. He was forever not quite reaching his goals. He aimed for the *Atlantic Monthly*, the country's arbiter of literary taste, but reached *Lippincott's*; he vowed to play only for Theodore Thomas' orchestra in New York, but instead worked with Asger Hamerik at the Peabody Conservatory; he craved acclaim in New York City, but had to find it in Baltimore. True, what he did accomplish was of no little consequence – *Lippincott's* was also one of the nation's leading publications, Hamerik a conductor of international reputation, and Baltimore a thriving and respected center of culture. But they were all second choices for Lanier, and represent the disappointment that underlay all his successes.

Yet considering Lanier's background, he accomplished miracles. He came from a genteel Southern tradition which scorned the arts as a profession. His education was removed from the main currents of American academic life, and he had very little formal musical training. Constantly hounded by poverty after the war, he was forced to write pot-boilers in order to support his family, wasting precious creative energy. Tuberculosis had attacked him when he was twenty-two; by the time he finally determined to pursue an artistic career, he had only seven years to live, and of this time had to spend weeks and months away from his work in desperate search of a cure.

It is remarkable that Lanier managed to do so much in so little time. He played first flute in a conservatory orchestra; delivered successful and popular lectures on Shakespeare and on the English novel; wrote numerous essays on music and about literature; wrote editions for children of legendary classics; produced a guide-book to Florida which is still popular in that state; composed numerous musical works; wrote one of the best studies of English prosody (*The Science of English Verse* is a musical analysis of poetry); and in the midst of all these activities wrote dozens of poems, some of which are the most beautifully original in American literature.

His poetic style is a unique result of an attempt to convey musical impression in verse; this stems from his lifelong interest in the unity of poetry and music. His creative technique is original, and Lanier arrived at it through music. One has only to compare the early, naive, and sentimental lyrics of his 1868 song "Little Ella" and the intricately-textured poem of 1880, "Sunrise," to see the drastic and revolutionary development of Lanier's verse. This change was brought about by music, and it is therefore music which made Lanier a poet. Without it, his verse would have remained pretty and lyrical, but simple in structure, texturally unimaginative, and tied to the limiting song-concept. But Lanier's best works, his later poems, reflect the influence of larger musical forms, the blending of voices, lines, and timbre characteristic of the symphony. Without his experience of sophisticated orchestral music, Lanier never could have developed as a poet; if he had never played Berlioz' *Symphonie Fantastique*, he might never have written his best poem, "The Marshes of Glynn." To Lanier, music and poetry were two different, but intimately related, media through which he expressed one ideal. This ideal is most notably expressed at the end of the poem "The Symphony": "Music is Love in search of a word." Lanier believed that man could come to terms with the problems of his civilization only through the redeeming powers of faith and love of art.

The most creative periods of Lanier's life – and the happiest – were those in which he was musically most active. Lanier's friends were, in the main, musical, not literary. He found enthusiastic applause for his flute-playing – which is supposed to have been astonishingly good – a compensation for the rejection-slips he received for his poetry. His writing, because it was so original, often came under harsh attack, but his performances never earned an unfavorable review.

Lanier is a unique figure – or rather a phenomenon – in American literature; and since he is one of the rare American poets who was also a professional musician, his poetry's qualities are determined by practical experience. Lanier was an innovator whose possible further accomplishments can only be wistfully speculated; but he is generally acknowledged by today's critics to be a significant figure in early modern literature.

—Jane S. Gabin

LOCKE, David Ross.   See **NASBY, Petroleum V.**

LONGFELLOW, Henry Wadsworth.   American.   Born in Portland, Maine, 17 February 1807. Educated at Bowdoin College, Brunswick, Maine, 1822. Married 1) Mary Potter in 1831 (died, 1835); 2) Frances Appleton in 1843 (died, 1861). After graduation appointed to the new Chair of Modern Languages, Bowdoin College, on condition he study abroad for a further three years: sent by trustees to Spain, 1826–29; Smith Professor of Modern Languages, Harvard University, Cambridge, Massachusetts, 1836–54; visited Europe, 1842, 1868–69. *Died 24 March 1882.*

PUBLICATIONS

Collections

The Works and *Final Memorials*, edited by Samuel Longfellow.   14 vols., 1886–87.
Works.   10 vols., 1909.
The Essential Longfellow, edited by Lewis Leary.   1963.
The Letters, edited by Andrew Hilen.   4 vols., 1966–72.

Verse

Hyperion: A Romance.   2 vols., 1839.
Voices of the Night.   1839.

Ballads and Other Poems. 1842.
Poems on Slavery. 1842.
Poems. 1845.
The Belfry of Bruges and Other Poems. 1845.
Evangeline: A Tale of Acadie. 1847.
Poems, Lyrical and Dramatic. 1848.
The Seaside and the Fireside. 1849.
The Golden Legend. 1851.
The Song of Hiawatha. 1855.
Poetical Works. 1858.
The Courtship of Miles Standish and Other Poems. 1858.
Tales of a Wayside Inn. 1863.
Noël (in French). 1864.
Household Poems. 1865.
Flower-de-Luce. 1867.
The New-England Tragedies. 1868.
Poetical Works. 1868.
The Divine Tragedy. 1871.
Three Books of Song. 1872.
Christus: A Mystery (includes *The Divine Tragedy, The Golden Legend, The New-England Tragedies*). 1872.
Poetical Works. 1872; revised edition, 1875, 1880, 1883.
Aftermath. 1873.
The Hanging of the Crane. 1874.
The Masque of Pandora and Other Poems. 1875.
Kéramos and Other Poems. 1878.
The Early Poems, edited by Richard Herne Shepherd. 1878.
Ultima Thule. 1880; *In the Harbor: Ultima Thule – Part II,* 1882.
Michael Angelo. 3 vols., 1882–83.
Boyhood Poems, edited by Ray W. Pettengill. 1925.

Play

The Spanish Student (produced 1895). 1843.

Fiction

Kavanagh: A Tale. 1849.

Other

Syllabus de la Grammaire Italienne. 1832.
Outre-Mer: A Pilgrimage Beyond the Sea, numbers 1–2. 2 vols., 1833–34; vol. 2, 1835; revised edition, 1851.
Prose Works. 2 vols., 1857.
Complete Works, revised edition. 7 vols., 1866.

Editor, *Manuel de Proverbes Dramatiques.* 1830; revised edition, 1830, 1832.
Editor and Translator, *Elements of French Grammar,* by Lhomond. 1830.
Editor, *French Exercises.* 1830.
Editor, *Novelas Españolas.* 1830.

Editor, *Le Ministre de Wakefield,* by Oliver Goldsmith, translated by T. E. G. Hennequin. 1831.
Editor, *Saggi de' Novellieri Italiani d'Ogni Secolo.* 1832.
Editor, *The Waif: A Collection of Poems.* 1845.
Editor, *The Poets and Poetry of Europe.* 1845; revised edition, 1871.
Editor, *The Estray: A Collection of Poems.* 1846.
Editor, with George Nichols and John Owen, *The Works of Charles Sumner.* 10 vols., 1870–83.
Editor, *Poems of Places: England,* 4 vols.; *Ireland,* 1 vol.; *Scotland,* 3 vols.; *France,* 2 vols.; *Italy,* 3 vols.; *Spain,* 2 vols.; *Switzerland,* 1 vol.; *Germany,* 2 vols.; *Greece,* 1 vol.; *Russia,* 1 vol.; *Asia,* 3 vols.; *Africa,* 1 vol.; *America,* 6 vols.; *Oceanica,* 1 vol. 31 vols., 1876–79.

Translator, *Coplas de Don Jorge Manrique.* 1833.
Translator, *The Divine Comedy,* by Dante. 3 vols., 1867.

Bibliography: in *Bibliography of American Literature* by Jacob Blanck, 1969.

Reading List: *The Life of Longfellow, with Extracts from His Journals and Correspondence* by Samuel Longfellow, 2 vols., 1886; *Longfellow and Scandinavia: A Study of the Poet's Relationship with the Northern Languages and Literature* by Andrew Hilen, 1947; *Longfellow: A Full-Length Portrait,* 1955, and *Longfellow: Portrait of an American Humanist,* 1966, both by Edward Wagenknecht; *Longfellow: His Life and Work* by Newton Arvin, 1963; *Longfellow* by Cecil B. Williams, 1964; *Longfellow* by E. L. Hirsch, 1964; *Life of Longfellow* by Eric S. Robertson, 1972.

*   *   *

Some writers survive for the wrong reasons, like nostalgia or derision; some survive despite their defects, like prolixity or sentimentality; some survive – or deserve to – because of a small body of modest work culled long after the fact of popularity. Henry Wadsworth Longfellow belongs in all three categories.

No American writer was so admired, even revered, during his life; no writer has been so ridiculed subsequently. From 1839, when "A Psalm of Life" first moved his readers – as heavily influenced as the poem itself by Victorian and Puritan attitudes – to embrace its homilies ("Heart within, and God o'erhead!"), until his death in 1882, the decorous optimism of Longfellow's lyrics and the monotonous drone of his narrative poems stood him in high esteem. Oliver Wendell Holmes may have best defined Longfellow's appeal to his contemporaries: "a soft voice, a sweet and cheerful temper, a receptive rather than aggressive intelligence...." This may, however, be a more damning indictment of the limitations of popular taste than of the poet's achievement. Longfellow's sympathetic biographer, Newton Arvin, proposed that we "agree, once for all, that he was a minor writer." Still, in the classroom at least, the myth of Longfellow's significance persists, and probably rather more than fewer students have turned away from poetry because of some educators' insistence on perpetuating the lie.

Longfellow's lack of variety and seeming inability either to escape conventional metrics or to bring any originality to them always hampered him; moreover, he did not easily judge the prosody best suited to his materials. At the age of thirteen, he had published his first poem in the *Portland Gazette,* "The Battle of Lovell Pond," hammered out in anapestic couplets with mathematical regularity. He never really advanced far in technical proficiency after that. His earliest successes – "The Skeleton in Armour," "The Wreck of the Hesperus," and the quintessential "Excelsior" suffer from this limitation. When, as in the last poem, the subject is "inspirational," he invites derision; and "higher" in its Latin comparative form is easily translated into shredded packing material – and not only by schoolboys who do not know their Latin. Longfellow was technically endowed to write light verse, had he possessed the sense of humor to do so, for he is not without extraordinary invention in manipulating syntax to suit his rhythms; and his inexhaustible command of rhyme, if employed for amusement, might not so easily undermine the content. At the zenith of his career, Longfellow beat his *Evangeline* into submission in jiggling dactyllic hexameters. This popular narrative traces the wanderings of a girl from Acadia (Nova Scotia) in search of her lost lover. Finally, after many remarkable adventures, she becomes a kind of nun in Pennsylvania in her old age, only to meet her lover on his death bed. This "first genuine ... fount which burst from the soil of America," called by one critic "one of the decisive poems of the world," sold 36,000 copies in its first ten years. *Hiawatha* did even better: 30,000 copies in six months. This pseudo-epic traces the development of an American Indian from birth to immortality: fathered by the West Wind; educated by nature and animals; loved by the beautiful Minnehaha; given mythic significance in his killing of an underwater monster, with the assistance of a helpful squirrel; sobered and matured by the deaths of Minnehaha (for whom he mourns seven days and seven nights) and his best friend (for whom he mourns seven times longer); and, finally, brought to a kind of metaphysical suicide – he simply gets in his canoe and starts paddling west – by the inevitable coming of the white race. Longfellow cramped this really promising material into 164 pages of four-trochee lines, likened by Oliver Wendell Holmes to the "normal rhythm of breathing" and by more than one high school student to tom-toms. At least *Hiawatha* didn't rhyme.

Longfellow wrote two inferior novels, *Hyperion* and *Kavanaugh*, which offer some insight into his private life and attitudes toward religion, politics, and literature. His single play, *The Spanish Student*, about a gypsy dancer named Preciosa (who turns out to be the long-lost daughter of a wealthy nobleman) and her chaste beau, suffers all the usual limitations of 19th-century melodrama. Although Longfellow had a successful career in education – he was one of the first modern language teachers, first at Bowdoin, then for 18 years at Harvard – his critical prose is distinguished by clarity rather than ingenuity or originality.

In spite of these several reservations, however, Longfellow wrote a number of valuable poems. In the sparse landscape of 19th-century American poetry, they grow sturdily. "Mezzo Camin," written in 1842 but not published until after his death, is a fine sonnet in which he laments his lack of significant poetic accomplishment. "The Cross of Snow," also unpublished during his life, and also a sonnet, is a touching tribute to his wife after her early death. Despite an insufferable circuitous dependent clause taking up all of its octet, the sonnet "Nature" ends superbly. A mother puts her child to bed: "So nature deals with us, and takes away/Our playthings one by one, and by the hand/Leads us to rest so gently, that we go/Scarce knowing if we wish to go or stay,/Being too full of sleep to understand/How far the unknown transcends the what we know." Its sustained imagery invites comparison with Whitman's "Goodbye, My Fancy," Emerson's "Terminus," and other epitaphic poems of the period. His ode to old age, "Morituri Salutamus," is especially valuable during the recent movement in America to recognize the oldest generation. "The Tide Rises, The Tide Falls" clearly anticipates Robert Frost's "Stopping by Woods on a Snowy Evening," even if less powerful a poem. Finally, his less well-known "The Jewish Cemetery at Newport" deserves attention. Its inhabitants, "Taught in the school of patience to endure/The Life of anguish and the death of fire," now abide in American soil, "not neglected; for a hand unseen,/Scattering its bounty, like a summer rain,/Still keeps their graves and their remembrance green." Probably there are other poems as well by this mild man which reflect, not without some distinction, the age of restraint and decorum for which they were written. Further, a skeleton in armour, a village smithy, a midnight ride by Paul Revere, even an arrow shot into the air, may introduce some beginning readers to some of the pleasures in poetry.

—Bruce Kellner

LONGSTREET, Augustus Baldwin. American. Born in Augusta, Georgia, 22 September 1790. Educated at the Waddell Academy, Willington, South Carolina, 1808–11; Yale University, New Haven, Connecticut, 1811–13, graduated 1813; Litchfield, Connecticut Law School, 1813–14; admitted to the Georgia bar, 1815. Married Frances Eliza Parke in 1816. Practised law in Greensboro, Georgia, from 1816; Member, Georgia Legislature, 1821; Circuit Judge, Superior Court of Georgia, 1822–25; settled in Augusta, 1827; contributed to the *Southern Recorder*, Milledgeville, Georgia, and various other newspapers, 1827–30; Founding Editor, *The Sentinel*, Augusta, 1834–36; ordained Methodist minister, 1838; President, Emory College, Oxford, Georgia, 1839–48, Centenary College, Jackson, Louisiana, 1849, University of Mississippi, 1849–56, and the University of South Carolina, Columbia, 1857–65; settled in Mississippi, 1865. *Died 9 July 1870.*

PUBLICATIONS

Fiction and Sketches

Georgia Scenes, Characters, and Incidents, etc. 1835.
Master William Mitten; or, A Youth of Brilliant Talents Who Was Ruined by Bad Luck. 1864.
Stories with a Moral, Humorous and Descriptive of Southern Life a Century Ago, edited by Fitz. R. Longstreet. 1912.

Other

A Voice from the South. 1847.

Bibliography: in *Bibliography of American Literature* by Jacob Blanck, 1973.

Reading List: *Judge Longstreet: A Life Sketch* by O. P. Fitzgerald, 1891 (includes letters and unpublished material); *Longstreet: A Study of the Development of Culture in the South* by John Donald Wade, 1924, edited by M. Thomas Inge, 1969.

*   *   *

Augustus Baldwin Longstreet's reputation rests primarily on *Georgia Scenes*, a collection of sketches and tales about life in Middle Georgia in the early nineteenth century. *Georgia Scenes* contrasted with the plantation literary tradition which focused on wealthy slaveholding landowners. As a circuit-court judge, Longstreet visited many rural communities and collected humorous stories and anecdotes of rough but colorful country people. Their simple amusements such as barn dances, horse-swapping, and shooting matches are affectionately recorded, along with a slightly more brutal side of life (gander-pulling, fights, and political disputes). Overt cruelty and violence are generally overlooked. For example, in "The Fight" the maiming of the combatants is treated in an almost slapstick vein. In his close attention to physical details and settings and in his attempts to write colloquial dialogue, Longstreet anticipated the local color writers of the post-civil war period. His best works, such as "Turn-Out," in which unruly country boys playfully "force" their schoolmaster to give them a day's vacation, are based on folk traditions and rituals and possess an archetypal power. Poe praised Longstreet because he was anxious to see American writers use native materials in their stories.

Longstreet was forty before he turned his hand to fiction. First his legal career, then his work as newspaper owner and editor, and later his ministry in the Methodist Church took precedence over authorship. He sometimes feared his comic sketches were undignified; in fact, everything he wrote expressed firm religious beliefs and conservative political views. In *Georgia Scenes* his narrator, Hall, describes rural escapades, while the character Baldwin ridicules the affectations of newly rich townspeople. Both are aloof and frequently disapproving, like the author. Blacks, although they seldom appear in the stories, are treated comically or with contempt. Later essays, such as those collected in *A Voice from the South*, were devoted to defending slavery.

In his own day Longstreet was best known as the president of four different Southern universities. Some of his experiences with students are included in his only novel, *William Mitten*. As a record of the times this neglected work is as informative as *Georgia Scenes*; and the author's characterizations of William and William's mother and uncle reveal a surer sense of satire and of the dynamics of family life than one finds in the earlier work. His essays on religious and political subjects and the posthumously collected tales in *Stories with a Moral* are elegantly phrased but discursive and tedious. He eventually considered himself more of a moral guide or social historian than a story-teller. Although some critics consider Longstreet a frontier humorist, he is primarily a Southern writer, highly didactic, constructing a value system unique to his region.

—Kimball King

LOWELL, James Russell.   American.   Born in Cambridge, Massachusetts, 22 February 1819. Educated at Harvard College, Cambridge, 1834–38, B.A. 1838, and Harvard Law School, 1838–40, LL.B. 1840; admitted to the Massachusetts Bar, 1840. Married 1) Maria White in 1844 (died, 1853), three daughters, one son; 2) Frances Dunlap in 1857 (died, 1885). Editor, with Robert Carter, *The Pioneer: A Literary and Critical Magazine*, Boston, 1843; Editorial Writer, *Pennsylvania Freeman*, Philadelphia, 1845; Corresponding Editor, *National Anti-Slavery Standard*, 1848; lived in Europe, 1851–52; delivered Lowell lectures, Boston, 1855; Smith Professor of the French and Spanish Languages and Literatures, 1855–86, and Professor Emeritus, 1886–91, Harvard University; first Editor, *Atlantic Monthly*, Boston, 1857–61; Editor, with Charles Eliot Norton, *North American Review*, Boston, 1864–72; visited Europe, 1872–75; Delegate to the Republican National Convention, and Member of the Electoral College, 1876; American Ambassador to Spain, 1877–80, and to Great Britain, 1880–85. D.C.L.: Oxford University, 1872; LL.D.: Cambridge University, 1874; University of Edinburgh, 1884. *Died 12 August 1891.*

PUBLICATIONS

Collections

Poetical Works, edited by Horace E. Scudder.   1896; revised edition, edited by Marjorie P. Kaufman, 1978.
The Complete Writings, edited by Charles Eliot Norton.   16 vols., 1904.
Essays, Poems, and Letters, edited by William Smith Clark II.   1948.

Verse

Class Poem. 1838.
A Year's Life and Other Poems. 1841.
Poems. 1844.
Poems: Second Series. 1848.
A Fable for Critics. 1848.
The Biglow Papers. 1848; edited by Thomas Wortham, 1977.
The Vision of Sir Launfal. 1848.
Poems. 2 vols., 1849.
The Biglow Papers, Second Series. 3 vols., 1862.
Ode Recited at the Commemoration of the Living and Dead Soldiers of Harvard
    University. 1865.
Under the Willows and Other Poems. 1869.
Poetical Works. 1869.
The Cathedral. 1870.
Three Memorial Poems. 1877.
Under the Old Elm and Other Poems. 1885.
Heartsease and Rue. 1888.
Last Poems, edited by Charles Eliot Norton. 1895.
Four Poems. 1906.
Uncollected Poems, edited by Thelma M. Smith. 1950.
Undergraduate Verses: Rhymed Minutes of the Hasty Pudding Club, edited by Kenneth
    Walter Cameron. 1956.

Play

Il Pesceballo: Opera Seria, with Francis J. Child. 1862; edited by Charles Eliot
    Norton, 1899.

Other

Conversations on Some of the Old Poets. 1845.
Fireside Travels. 1864.
Among My Books. 2 vols., 1870–76.
My Study Windows. 1871.
Democracy and Other Addresses. 1887.
Political Essays. 1888.
The English Poets, Lessing, Rousseau: Essays. 1888.
Books and Libraries and Other Papers. 1889.
The Writings. 10 vols., 1890; 2 additional vols. edited by Charled Eliot Norton,
    1891–92.
American Ideas for English Readers (lectures). 1892.
Letters, edited by Charles Eliot Norton. 2 vols., 1894.
Lectures on English Poets, edited by S. A. Jones. 1897.
Impressions of Spain, edited by Joseph B. Gilder. 1899.
Early Prose Writings. 1902.
The Anti-Slavery Papers, edited by William Belmont Parker. 2 vols., 1902.
The Round Table. 1913.
The Function of the Poet and Other Essays, edited by Albert Mordell. 1920.
New Letters, edited by M. A. De Wolfe Howe. 1932.
The Pioneer (magazine), edited by Sculley Bradley. 1947.

The Scholar-Friends: Letters of Francis James Child and Lowell, edited by M. A. De
   Wolfe Howe and G. W. Cottrell, Jr.   1952.
Literary Criticism, edited by Herbert F. Smith.   1969.

Editor, *The Poems of Maria Lowell*.   1855.
Editor, *The Poetical Works of Dr. John Donne*.   1855.
Editor, *The Poetical Works of Andrew Marvell*.   1857.

Bibliography: in *Bibliography of American Literature* by Jacob Blanck, 1973.

Reading List: *Lowell: A Biography* by Horace E. Scudder, 2 vols., 1901; *Lowell* by Richmond
C. Beatty, 1942; *Victorian Knight-Errant: A Study of the Early Literary Career of Lowell* by
Leon Howard, 1952; *Lowell* by Martin B. Duberman, 1966; *Lowell* by Claire McGlinchee
1967; *Lowell: Portrait of a Many-Sided Man* by Edward C. Wagenknecht, 1971.

*   *   *

Of all the schoolroom poets James Russell Lowell was easily the most talented, clearly the
most versatile, and probably the one who strove hardest to achieve poetic excellence. Yet
today his poetry is less critically valued and read than the verses of his contemporaries
Holmes, Longfellow, and Whittier. Some explanation for the disparity between his ability
and accomplishments resides in the very nature of his life and talents. Among other things he
was poet, essayist, journalist, editor, critic, linguist, teacher, reformer and diplomat. In 1848,
before his thirtieth birthday, he published *A Fable for Critics*, *The Biglow Papers*, and *The
Vision of Sir Launfal* to secure his poetic reputation. Ten years later he assumed the first
editorship of the *Atlantic Monthly* and by his critical judgment and taste made it into the finest
literary journal in America. In his later years he became Minister to Spain, and from 1880–85
he served as the American Minister to England. To highlight these few achievements from so
many illustrates part of Lowell's problem: his brilliance, erudition, and versatility constantly
led him to new tasks and dissipated the control and self-discipline needed for artistic
excellence. In addition his responsiveness to the tradition of public oratory and imitations of
older writers made his serious verse declamatory and derivative. Dated by now forgotten
issues and lacking a significant form, much of his longer poetry remains unreadable today.
   Despite these critical problems, Lowell wrote good poetry and in selected pieces well
deserves his place among American poets. His *A Fable for Critics* occupies a central place
among the few critical pronouncements written by nineteenth-century American authors. Its
mocking, casual humor perfectly balances shrewd critical insights, while its taut epigrams
still surprise and delight. Lowell called Poe "two-fifths sheer fudge," depicted Byrant as
"quiet, as cool, and as dignified,/As a smooth, silent iceberg, that never is ignified," and noted
that Cooper's females were "All sappy as maples and flat as a prairie." Even his shortcomings
were catalogued: "There is Lowell, who's striving Parnassus to climb/With a whole bale of
isms tied together with rhyme." Both series of his Biglow Papers display a mastery of Down
East Humor, Yankee dialect and caricature. Though their contemporary subject matter and
grotesque mixture of moral aphorisms with political observations render them uneven,
individual pieces like "The Courtin'" and "Sumthin' in the Pastoral Line" demonstrate
Lowell's rare gift for native idiom and folk humor. His exploration of these New England
materials produced his finest poem, "Fitz Adam's Story," a 632-line saga about the essential
traits of a Yankee world. Though its central story concerns the attempts of a crusty Deacon
Bitters to outsmart the devil, the poem's rich digressions on religion, back-country types, and
rural descriptions constitute its main pleasure.
   Among his longer, more serious poems, "Agassiz," *Ode Recited at the Harvard
Commemoration*, *The Cathedral*, and a few others deserve continued reading and
examination. In these poems Lowell's deeply felt thoughts were elaborately and skillfully

presented, while the form, that of the familiar verse essay, perfectly suited his penchant for rhymed declamation and long digressions. "Agassiz," a moving tribute to the great Harvard scientist, cleverly blends the tradition of the pastoral elegy with contemporary images as the telegraph wire announces Agassiz's death. Throughout the poem Lowell balances his personal sorrow with a tenuous, yet affirmative, hope that such a nature as Agassiz's must exist somewhere "perfected and conscious." In the *Ode* Lowell uses the occasion of the Civil War to present a rhymed meditation on the complex oppositions of song and deed, war and truth, death and the ideal. The poem's conclusion and didactic tone prove acceptable because of the poem's careful development of basic images and firm structure. Perhaps Lowell's most successful longer poem is *The Cathedral*. Like Tennyson's *In Memoriam* it deals with a quest for religious certainty by a man imbued with his age's disbelief. The magnificent stone monument of Chartres Cathedral serves as the focus for the poem's imagery and structure. Its four main sections examine natural, religious, and even democratic responses to the spiritual, and build to the hesitant but honest suggestion that the commonplace of miracles is available for every age.

What Lowell achieved is best seen in a poem like *The Cathedral*. If his verse lacked the mightly choral power of Whitman and only fitfully imitated Emerson's grandeur, it deserves its own place among the American traditions of vernacular poetry, satiric verse, and rhymed public oratory. As Henry James once noted upon rereading Lowell: "He looms, in such a renewed impression, very large and ripe and sane.... He was strong without narrowness; he was wise without bitterness and bright without folly. That appears for the most part the clearest ideal of those who handle the English form, and he was altogether in the straight tradition."

—John B. Pickard

MARKHAM, Edwin. American. Born Charles Edward Anson Markham in Oregon City, Oregon, 23 April 1852. Educated at San Jose Normal School, California; Christian College, Santa Rosa, California. Married 1) Annie Cox in 1875 (divorced, 1884); 2) Carolyn E. Bailey in 1887; 3) Anna Catherine Murphy in 1898; one son. Schoolteacher: Headmaster, University Observation School, Oakland, California, for 10 years. Lived in New York and New Jersey from c. 1900: lecturer and editor. Recipient: Academy of American Poets Prize. Honorary Degrees: Baylor University, Waco, Texas; Syracuse University, New York; New York University. Honorary President, Poetry Society of America. Member, American Institute of Arts and Letters, 1930. *Died 7 March 1940.*

PUBLICATIONS

Collections

Poems, edited by Charles L. Wallis.   1950.

Verse

The Man with the Hoe and Other Poems.   1899.
Lincoln and Other Poems.   1901.
The Shoes of Happiness and Other Poems.   1915.
Gates of Paradise and Other Poems.   1920.
Funeral of Adam Willis Wagnalls.   1924.
New Poems: Eighty Songs at Eighty.   1932.
The Star of Araby.   1937.

Other

Modern Poets and Christian Teaching, with Richard Watson Gilder and E. R. Sill.   1906.
The Burt-Markham Primer: The Nature Method, with Mary Burt.   1907.
Children in Bondage: A Presentation of the Anxious Problem of Child Labor, with Benjamin B. Lindsey and George Creel.   1914.
California the Wonderful.   1914.
Archibald Henderson: An Appreciation of the Man.   1918.
Campbell Meeker.   1925.

Editor, *The Real America in Romance.*   15 vols., 1909–27.
Editor, *Foundation Stones of Success.*   10 vols., 1917.
Editor, *The Book of Poetry.*   3 vols., 1926.
Editor, *Songs and Stories of California.*   1931.
Editor, *The Book of English Poetry.*   1934.
Editor, *Poetry of Youth.*   1935.

Reading List: *Markham* by William L. Stidger, 1933; *The Unknown Markham: His Mystery and Its Significance* by Louis Filler, 1966.

*   *   *

Edwin Markham, best known for a single poem, "The Man with the Hoe," produced five published collections of verse in his lifetime, as well as a few other poetic attempts, and in addition a series of articles on the injustices of child labour and on various other Progressive/ Reform causes. As a poet he was an unsophisticated traditionalist (hence, a mainstream writer, as Dickinson, Whitman, Wallace Stevens, E. E. Cummings, and W. C. Williams could never be). He strove, generally with the aid of regular rhythms and conventional rhymes, to promote brotherhood, love, and all the other standard virtues. A strong sense of Christian "awareness" runs throughout his work, which reflects not only his sensitive conscience in the face of man's inhumanity to man, but his spiritual commitment: an ongoing manifesto of the need for *good works* and the security of *faith*.

A series of unlikely circumstances combined to make "The Man with the Hoe" (based on the painting by the Barbizon artist Jean-François Millet) one of America's most famous poems of all time: deeper and more suggestive than its subject, in almost a subliminal, inexpressible way. Millet's painting of course must be kept in mind here; then the opening lines of the poem: "Bowed by the weight of centuries he leans/Upon his hoe and gazes on the ground,/The emptiness of ages in his face,/And on his back the burden of the world." That the above poem and no other quite like it could profoundly affect an entire nation, was proven by the general neglect accorded Markham's comparable poem (likewise predicated on a Millet painting of a poor peasant), "The Sower" (in *Lincoln and Other Poems*): "He is the stone rejected, yet the stone/Whereon is built metropolis and throne."

Markham's "Lincoln, The Man of the People" was well received, with its image of the fallen President suggesting the fall of "a lordly cedar," leaving "a lonesome place against the sky." A good deal of comment and speculation were provoked by his poem "Virgilia" (in *The Shoes of Happiness and Other Poems*). With its companion-piece, "The Crowning Hour," it spoke of a mysterious lost love and the poet's determination to undertake a cosmic quest in order to find her; here again one can sense, despite all the changes in fashion and style since the poem was written, the basis for strong reader identification: "Our ways go wide and I know not whither,/But my song will search through the worlds for you,/Till the Seven Seas waste and the Seven Stars wither/And the dream of the heart comes true."

Staid, ultra-conventional though Markham's poems were, he himself was a deeply passionate man and a much more complicated person than generally regarded. School superintendent and principal, writer of popular poems and verses, public lecturer and anthologist of popular verse – these job designations do not begin to explain him, any more than do the facts of his unhappy childhood and his tormented relationship with his neurotic mother, or his being a product of the Oregon-California coastal region. A restless, driven man, he lived an inner life quite at variance with his outward appearance of majestic, assured, bearded dignity; this is borne out, for example, by the nightmare poem "The Ballad of the Gallows Bird" (printed originally in 1926).

—Samuel Irving Bellman

MELVILLE, Herman. American. Born in New York City, 1 August 1819. Educated at the Albany Academy to age 13. Married Elizabeth Shaw in 1847; two sons and two daughters. Worked from age 15 as a clerk, farmhand, and schoolteacher; went to sea as a cabin boy on the *Highlander*, bound for Liverpool, 1839–40; served on the whaler *Acushnet*,

1841 until he jumped ship in the Marquesas, 1842; left the island on the Sydney schooner *Lucy Ann*, and jumped ship in Tahiti, 1842; sailed to Honolulu, and worked as a clerk and bookkeeper, 1843; shipped back to Boston on the frigate *United States*, 1843–44; devoted himself to writing from 1844; lived in New York, 1847–50, and Pittsfield, Massachusetts, 1850–63; travelled in the Near East and Europe, 1856–57; lectured in the United States, 1857–60; returned to New York, and served as District Inspector of Customs, 1866–85. *Died 28 September 1891.*

PUBLICATIONS

Collections

Works. 16 vols., 1922–24.
Representative Selections, edited by Willard Thorp.   1938.
Collected Poems, edited by Howard P. Vincent.   1947.
The Portable Melville, edited by Jay Leyda.   1952.
Letters, edited by Merrill R. Davis and William H. Gilman.   1960.
Selected Poems, edited by Hennig Cohen.   1964.
Great Short Works, edited by Warner Berthoff.   1966.
Writings, edited by Harrison Hayford, Hershel Parker, and G. Thomas Tanselle.   1968–

Fiction

Narrative of Four Months' Residence among the Natives of a Valley in the Marquesas Islands; or, A Peep at Polynesian Life.   1846; as *Typee*, 1846; revised edition, 1846; in *Writings*, 1968; edited by George Woodcock, 1972.
Omoo: A Narrative of Adventures in the South Seas.   1847; in *Writings*, 1968.
Mardi, and a Voyage Thither.   1849; in *Writings*, 1970.
Redburn, His First Voyage.   1849; in *Writngs*, 1969.
White Jacket; or, The World in a Man-of-War.   1850; edited by Hennig Cohen, 1967; in *Writings*, 1970.
The Whale.   1851; as *Moby-Dick; or, The Whale*, 1851; edited by Harrison Hayford and Hershel Parker, 1967.
Pierre; or, The Ambiguities.   1852; edited by H. A. Murray, 1957.
Israel Potter, His First Fifty Years of Exile.   1855; as *The Refuge*, 1865.
The Piazza Tales.   1856; edited by Egbert S. Oliver, 1948.
The Confidence-Man, His Masquerade.   1857; edited by Hershel Parker, 1971.
The Apple-Tree Table and Other Sketches.   1922.
Billy Budd and Other Prose Pieces, edited by Raymond M. Weaver, in *Works.*   1924; *Billy Budd* edited by Harrison Hayford and Merton M. Sealts, Jr., 1962.

Verse

Battle-Pieces and Aspects of War.   1866; edited by Hennig Cohen, 1963.
Clarel: A Poem, and Pilgrimage in the Holy Land.   1876; edited by Walter E. Bezanson, 1960.
John Marr and Other Sailors, with Some Sea-Pieces.   1888.
Timoleon.   1891.

Other

Journal up the Straits October 11, 1856–May 5, 1857, edited by Raymond M. Weaver. 1935; edited by Howard C. Horsford, as *Journal of a Visit to Europe and the Levant,* 1955.

Journal of a Visit to London and the Continent 1848–1850, edited by Eleanor Melville Metcalf. 1948.

Bibliography: *The Merrill Checklist of Melville* by Howard P. Vincent, 1969; in *Bibliography of American Literature* by Jacob Blanck, 1973.

Reading List: *Melville: The Tragedy of Mind* by William E. Sedgwick, 1944; *Melville* by Richard Chase, 1949; *Melville* by Newton Arvin, 1950; *The Melville Log: A Documentary Life of the Melvilles* by Jay Leyda, 2 vols., 1951, revised edition, 1969; *Melville* by Leon Howard, 1951; *Melville's Quarrel with God* by Lawrance Thompson, 1952; *The Fine-Hammered Steel of Melville* by Milton R. Stern, 1957; *The Example of Melville* by Warner Berthoff, 1962; *Melville: The Ironic Diagram* by John D. Seelye, 1970; *An Artist in the Rigging: The Early Work of Melville,* 1972, and *Melville's Short Fiction,* 1977, both by William Dillingham; *Melville: The Critical Heritage* edited by Watson G. Branch, 1974; *Melville* (biography) by Edwin Haviland Miller, 1975.

*   *   *

What characterizes Herman Melville's novels from *Typee* through *Moby-Dick* is the sense of an immanent personality, the author through his narrator, examining himself, his experiences, and the world about him. This personality seeks categorical answers and finds none, and, when his quest fails, seeks ways to survive in an inscrutable universe. In these novels, the theme of the autobiographical quest is signalled by the presence of a first person narrator and by the easy identification of setting and events with the facts of Melville's life as a sailor. If the writings after *Moby-Dick* seem less autobiographical, it is because Melville places more distance between himself and his stories. Their subjects are more obviously interior, spiritual voyages to less romantic places, and an omniscient author, skeptical though compassionate, has displaced the roving, questing youth who spins high-spirited tales of his travels.

Soon after he returned from his voyage to the Pacific, Melville began to write. His first books, *Typee* and *Omoo,* are sailor's yarns based on his adventures in the Marquesas Islands and Tahiti after he jumped ship to sojourn with cannibals, to comb the beaches, and, when his Polynesian paradise began to pall, to go back to the sea. Hindsight reveals hints of themes which were to preoccupy him later, such as man's capacity for evil, appearance and reality, or the dubious blessings of both civilization and its opposite, primitivism; for it was typical of Melville to present another side of the question as a way of stating the complexity and uncertainty of things. They also show a capacity for quiet comedy, delight in word play, and penchant for social criticism. But in the main these books are light-hearted, colorful adventure, mildly fictionalized. Actually, *Typee* follows the facts closely, exploiting the potentiality for suspense in the uncertainty of the Typee's eating habits, the temptations of the narrator's situation as their petted prisoner, and the accumulating pressure to escape from being culturally if not physically consumed by them. An Australian whaler in need of hands rescues him, and he sails off toward the horizon. At this point the sequel, *Omoo* (the name means "wanderer"), begins. The captain proves incompetent and the mate a drunkard, so the sailors refuse duty. They are confined to a casually kept jail in Tahiti from which the young narrator wanders to a nearby island. After more wanderings of a picaresque sort, he goes back to sea.

Such open-endedness suggests uncertainty, or at least open-mindedness, and it encourages sequels. By this time Melville had been taken up by Evert and George Duyckinck, influential New York editors. He began to imbibe their ideas on literary nationalism and liberal politics and to borrow from their extensive collection of Renaissance books, reading Rabelais, Montaigne, Burton, Browne, and the British dramatists. This was heady stuff, and along with the chagrin he felt because publishers and critics questioned the authenticity of his realistic narratives, it caused him to try another tack. His third narrative, *Mardi*, begins realistically. On board a whaler in the South Seas two sailors contemplate desertion. However, theirs soon becomes "a chartless voyage" among allegorical islands of a mythical archipelago. The sailor-narrator rescues a symbolically provocative white captive, loves her, loses her, and pursues her beyond the ends of the earth. He is as relentless as Ahab in quest of the white whale and as self-destructive, but the search is put aside from time to time for intervals of philosophizing, rhapsodizing, and satirizing on topics of contemporary political, theological, artistic and scientific interest. *Mardi* is a thing of patches, some of which presage the bravura passages of *Moby-Dick* and *The Confidence-Man*. Melville's family and friends advised that he forego his mental travelling, and to the accompaniment of grumbling about financial necessities, he restrained himself in *Redburn* and *White Jacket*.

Redburn recalls Melville's first voyage, a summer's service on a trader carrying cotton to Liverpool. *White Jacket* reflects his experiences as an ordinary seaman on a "homeward bound" American frigate. They contributed to his bank account and reputation. In *Redburn* the titular narrator is a callow lad who grows up, discarding his social pretension, encountering misery and evil about which he can do little, yet learning to stand on his own. *White Jacket* is likewise an initiation story but more. Its titular character is named for a non-regulation pea jacket he is issued, which distinguishes him in a way that he first finds flattering yet proves so disadvantageous that the plot concerns his efforts to rid himself of it. His ship is treated as a microcosm of his nation, a professedly democratic state but one sustained by an authoritarian hierarchy which abuses "the people," as the ratings are called, and which is corrupt or inept. Despite this irony, *White Jacket*, with its emphasis on the brotherhood of the common seaman and the prospect that "Our Lord Admiral" above will right earthly wrongs, is Melville's most optimistic book.

Apparently *Moby-Dick* was conceived in the pattern of its predecessors – a sailor recalling, in a realistic and casual way, his experiences aboard a whaler on a Pacific cruise. But it grew from narrative to novel, encompassing drama and epic and a number of lesser genres (e.g., sermon, natural history, tall tale, technical manual); expanding its tonal range to include low comedy, high wit, and lofty tragedy; and posing questions both metaphysical and pragmatic. If the theme of this leviathanic book must be simplistically stated, one could say that it is a quest for a way to live with dignity in a world in which the only certainty is uncertainty. Superficially, it is the melodramatic tale of the search for an albino whale by a mad sea captain whom it had maimed, but the book is so rich that it encourages many interpretations. Indeed this seems the intention of the author, supporting its essential nature as an epistemological quest.

Pierre is a departure from Melville's six sea narratives. It opposes an Edenic countryside and a postlapsarian city, settings in which Pierre, an idealistic young patrician, attempts to attack the evil he discovers, the sin of his father, with the weapons of Christian rectitude. In a memorable analogy, Melville suggests that clocks on earth are only relatively accurate because they must be made applicable to earthly contours. Absolutely perfect time obtains in heaven alone. Pierre's attempt to apply celestial time to earth is disastrously out of joint. Badly received, *Pierre* compels, in the words of its subtitle, for "the ambiguities" laid bare through its psychological and ethical probing.

Melville now turned magazinist. *Israel Potter*, the fictionalized biography of a soldier during the Revolutionary War and later adrift in London, explores the endurance of the common man. *Piazza Tales* is distinguished for "Bartleby," an account of the response of a worldly lawyer whose copyist gently declines to exist; "Benito Cereno," the gothic adventure of a goodnatured American sea captain who encounters a ship deviously controlled by its cargo of slaves; and "The Encantadas," sketches of the Galapagos Islands, a volcanic waste in the thrall of an evil spell. The last prose fiction Melville published, *The Confidence-Man*, is a darkly comic work of such originality of concept, technique, and verbal dexterity that it seems a prototype of the modern American novel. The setting is a Mississippi River steamboat on April Fool's Day. The action is a series of confidence men (though perhaps only one, variously guised) in ritualistic confrontation with their marks who are vulnerable because of their faith, hope, and charity. The book satirizes American types and deflates American beliefs through the device of the confidence man who preaches trust apparently for some selfish reason. But one is never sure. This, Melville's most ingenious book, was a failure. Thereafter he never attempted to write for a popular audience.

Always self-taught, Melville studied poetry. Near the end of the Civil War he undertook a verse sequence, *Battle-Pieces*, which sought to comprehend this national tragedy. It begins with "The Portent," on the hanging of the abolitionist firebrand John Brown, and ends with elegies to the dead of both sides. Walt Whitman's "Drum-Taps" is the only comparable body of verse. A decade later he published *Clarel*, an ambitious narrative poem about a party of "pilgrims" of diverse background and persuasion who tour the Holy Land. The framework permits discussions of science, religion, and the future of the New World. While on the whole they do not lift the spirits and the tetrameter couplets grow wearisome, the poem has a stony integrity and curious, digressive cantos on such subjects as Piranesi's prison etchings and the Hindu god Rama. His shorter verses, issued privately, draw from his early life as a sailor, his travels in Europe and the Levant, and his literary explorations. They are uneven, but the most flawed are not without interest for their tensions, juxtapositions, and sense of tragedy, for what they attempt rather than what they achieve.

Melville's last work is a short novel, *Billy Budd*. A handsome sailor on a warship strikes down a petty officer. There are mitigating circumstances, but he is hanged so that the discipline of the crew might be secured. The tale is sensitive to every complexity and delicately controlled, but as always with Melville its emphasis is on questions rather than answers.

—Hennig Cohen

MILLER, Joaquin. Pseudonym for Cincinnatus Hiner Miller. American. Born in Liberty, Indiana, 10 March 1839; moved with his parents to Oregon, 1850. Studied law in Oregon; admitted to the Oregon Bar, 1861. Messenger in the gold mining district of Idaho, 1856–59; Manager, *Democratic Register* newspaper, Eugene, Oregon, 1863; practised law in Canon City, Oregon, 1863–66; County Court Judge, Grant County, Oregon, 1866–70; lived in London and gained notoriety as the "frontier poet," 1870–71; returned to the United States and subsequently became a fruit grower: lived on his estate in Oakland, California, 1887 until the end of his life; Correspondent in the Klondike for the New York *Journal*, 1897–98. *Died 17 February 1913.*

PUBLICATIONS

Collections

Poetical Works, edited by Stuart P. Sherman.   1923.
Selections (verse), edited by Juanita Joaquina Miller.   1945.
Selected Writings, edited by Allen Rosenus.   1976.

Verse

Specimens. 1868.
Joaquin, et al. 1869.
Pacific Poems. 1871.
Songs of the Sierras. (produced 1880), 1871.
Songs of the Sun-Lands. 1873.
The Ship in the Desert. 1875.
Songs of Italy. 1878.
Songs of Far-Away Lands. 1878.
Songs of the Mexican Seas. 1887.
In Classic Shades and Other Poems. 1890.
Songs of the Soul. 1896.
Complete Poetical Works. 1897; revised edition, 1902.
Chants for the Boer. 1900.
As It Was in the Beginning: A Poem Dedicated to the Mothers of Men. 1903.
Light: A Narrative Poem. 1907.
Panama: Union of the Oceans. 1912.

Plays

The Baroness of New York. 1877.
Forty-Nine: A California Drama. 1882.
First Fam'lies in the Sierras. 1875; revised version, as The Danites in the
    Sierras, 1882.
The Silent Man. 1883.
Tally-Ho!, music by John Philip Sousa. 1883.
An Oregon Idyll, in Collected Works. 1910.

Fiction

The One Fair Woman. 1876.
Shadows of Shasta. 1881.
'49: The Gold-Seeker of the Sierras. 1884.
The Destruction of Gotham. 1886.

Other

Life Amongst the Modocs: Unwritten History. 1873; as Paquita, The Indian Heroine,
    1881; revised edition, as My Own Story, 1890; as Romantic Life Amongst the Red
    Indians: An Autobiography, 1890.
The Danites and Other Choice Selections, edited by A. V. D. Honeyman. 1878.
Memory and Rime. 1884.
The Building of the City Beautiful. 1893.
An Illustrated History of the State of Montana. 2 vols., 1894.
The Battle of Castle Crags. 1894.
True Bear Stories. 1900.
Japan of Sword and Love, with Yone Noguchi. 1905.
Collected Works. 6 vols., 1909–10.
Trelawney with Shelley and Byron. 1922.
California Diary, 1855–1857, edited by John S. Richards. 1936.

Overland in a Covered Wagon: An Autobiography, edited by Sidney G. Firman (based on Introduction to *Collected Works*). 1930.

Bibliography: in *Bibliography of American Literature* by Jacob Blanck, 1973.

Reading List: *Miller: Literary Frontiersman* by Martin S. Peterson, 1937; *Splendid Poseur: Miller, American Poet* by M. Marion Marberry, 1953; *Miller* by O. W. Frost, 1967.

*   *   *

Were it not for the outlandish image of himself which he deliberately cultivated, Cincinnatus Hiner Miller, better known as Joaquin Miller, after the Mexican bandit Joaquin Murietta, whose exploits he helped to popularize, would probably be forgotten today. Dressed in Western sombrero, boots, and buckskin britches, Joaquin Miller proclaimed himself the poetic spokesman for the American West, and during his lifetime he came to symbolize, both in America and abroad, the spirit of freedom, adventure, and bravado which characterized the West in the popular imagination.

Ironically, Miller rose to fame not in America but in England, where he went to find a publisher for his book, *Pacific Poems*, and to make his presence felt in more sophisticated literary circles than those which America offered him. His earlier collections of poetry, *Specimens* and *Joaquin et al.*, had received scant recognition in America, and Miller shrewdly understood that he and his works might best appeal to a foreign audience unfamiliar with the stereotypes which he projected. Although Americans simply refused to take him seriously, Miller became something of a celebrity in Britain, where his rustic dress and primitive manners endeared him with the public and brought him to the attention of the leading literary figures of the day. From Britain, Miller's fame spread to America. His most famous book, *Songs of the Sierras*, first published in London, was issued the same year in Boston.

Most of Miller's works are vaguely autobiographical. He drew his themes from his own experiences, which he embellished or exaggerated according to the effects which he wished to achieve. Nearly all of Miller's works are about the West. *Life Amongst the Modocs* and *Memorie and Rime* are prose accounts of his early adventures in the mines and among the Indians of California. *Shadows of Shasta*, Miller's most successful novel, draws attention to the injustices done to the Indians, with whom Miller greatly sympathized. When he writes about the West, Miller was generally passionate and bold. He possessed the ability to make legend seem real and the real seem legendary. As a playwright, Miller, who possessed a flare for the dramatic, was especially effective. His most popular play, *The Danites in the Sierras*, was acted before packed audiences, much to the chagrin of Bret Harte and Mark Twain, who envied Miller's dramatic talents. When he departed from Western themes, however, as he did in the novels *The One Fair Woman* and *The Destruction of Gotham*, Miller's writing becomes forced and unconvincing.

Miller's poetry, while lacking in intrinsic merit, had a profound effect on the development of Western American Literature. For forms and techniques, Miller studied the British romantics and the American fireside poets. Like Longfellow, Miller was especially fond of rhymed iambic pentameter, and his Western heroes bear a marked resemblance to those of Byron. In those poems where form matches content, Miller's verse possesses a haunting, rhythmic quality, reminiscent of Indian chants, which captures the spirit and vitality of his Western themes. Miller is especially noted for his attempts to write poetry in the American vernacular. His most famous poem, "Columbus," has become a classic in its own right and is still recited by American schoolchildren, who see in it a primitive expression of the American Dream.

—James A. Levernier

MITCHELL, Donald Grant. Pseudonym: Ik Marvel.   American.   Born in Norwich, Connecticut, 12 April 1822. Educated at John Hall's School, Ellington, Connecticut, 1830–37; Yale University, New Haven, Connecticut (Editor, *Yale Literary Magazine*), 1837–41, graduated 1841. Married Mary Frances Pringle in 1853. Settled on the family farm in New London County, Connecticut, 1841, and devoted himself to farming and writing; clerk to the United States Consul in Liverpool, 1844–45; toured Europe, 1845–46; wrote for the *Morning Courier and New York Enquirer*, also studied law in the offices of John Osborne Sargent, New York, 1846–50; Editor, *Lorgnette*, New York, 1850; full-time writer from 1850; served as United States Consul in Venice, 1853–54; lived in Paris, 1855; returned to the United States, and settled on a farm, later called Edgewood, near New Haven, Connecticut. Recipient: New York Agricultural Society silver medal, 1843; New England Association of Park Superintendents silver cup, 1904. *Died 15 December 1908.*

PUBLICATIONS

Fiction

The Lorgnette; or, Studies of the Town by an Opera Lover.   1850; as *The Opera Goer*, 1852.
Reveries of a Bachelor; or, A Book of the Heart.   1850.
Dream Life: A Fable of the Seasons.   1851.
Fudge Doings, Being Tony Fudge's Record of the Same.   1855.
Seven Stories, with Basement and Attic.   1864.
Dr. Johns, Being a Narrative of Certain Events in the Life of an Orthodox Minister of Connecticut.   1866.

Other

Fresh Gleanings; or, A New Sheaf from the Old Fields of Continental Europe.   2 vols., 1847.
The Battle Summer, Being Transcripts from Personal Observation in Paris 1848.   1849.
My Farm of Edgewood: A Country Book.   1863.
Wet Days at Edgewood, with Old Farmers, Old Gardeners, and Old Pastorals.   1865.
Rural Studies, with Hints for Country Places.   1867; as *Out-of-Town Places*, 1884.
Pictures of Edgewood, photographs by Rockwood.   1868.
About Old Story-Tellers, of How and When They Lived, and What Stories They Told.   1878.
A Report to the Commissioners on Lay-Out of East Rock Park.   1882.
Bound Together: A Sheaf of Papers.   1884.
English Lands, Letters, and Kings.   4 vols., 1889–97.
American Lands and Letters.   2 vols., 1897–99.
Looking Back at Boyhood.   1906.
Works.   15 vols., 1907.
Louis Mitchell: A Sketch, edited by Waldo H. Dunn.   1947.

Editor, with Oliver Wendell Holmes, *The Atlantic Almanac 1868.*   1867.
Editor, *The Atlantic Almanac 1869.*   1868.
Editor, with Alfred Mitchell, *The Woodbridge Record, Being an Account of the Descendants of the Rev. John Woodbridge.*   1883.
Editor, *Daniel Tyler: A Memorial Volume.*   1883.

Bibliography: in *Bibliography of American Literature* by Jacob Blanck, 1973.

Reading List: *The Life of Mitchell* by Waldo H. Dunn, 1922.

*   *   *

There was perhaps no writer in nineteenth-century America who could more appropriately be labelled "genteel" than Donald Grant Mitchell. There was also perhaps no writer who more fully expressed the ambitions and mores of middle-class Americans. Like his contemporaries Richard Watson Gilder, Thomas Bailey Aldrich, and Richard Henry Stoddard, Mitchell addressed a middle-class audience that in both public and private life gave priority to "respectability," and nowhere was respectability more firmly entrenched than in the home. In a series of "country books" that included *My Farm of Edgewood*, *Wet Days at Edgewood*, and *Rural Studies*, Mitchell detailed an ideal respectable domestic life based on his own life at Edgewood, his home in rural Connecticut. The "country books" are long out of print, but for half a century they were highly regarded. At the time of Mitchell's death in 1908, surely few of his readers could have guessed that within a generation both Edgewood and its genial master would be forgotten.

Mitchell established his reputation in 1849 with the publication of *Reveries of a Bachelor* – a book utterly without original ideas but with a wealth of sentimental observations that gave it especial appeal for young women. Mitchell never disappointed his original audience; in book after book, they (and their husbands) found abundant sentiment and gentle advice. The formula extended even to his literary criticism, collected in, among other volumes, *American Lands and Letters*. Strictly speaking, it was not literary criticism but literary appreciation that he wrote.

Mitchell's genial, invariably pleasing writings deserve greater attention than they usually receive. As literature, they are of minor interest, yet as expositions of the aspirations and values of the genteel American they are invaluable. If a reader wishes to discover the ideal perimeters of life in middle-class America a century ago, Mitchell's books can show him.

—Edward Halsey Foster

MITCHELL, Langdon (Elwyn). American. Born in Philadelphia, Pennsylvania, 17 February 1862; son of S. Weir Mitchell, *q.v.* Educated at St. Paul's School, Concord, New Hampshire; studied abroad for three years in Dresden and Paris, then studied law at the Harvard Law School, Cambridge, Massachusetts, and Columbia University, New York; admitted to the New York Bar, 1886, but did not practice. Married the actress Marion Lea in 1892; one son and two daughters. Playwright and author from the mid-1880's; Lecturer in English Literature, George Washington University, Washington, D.C., 1918–20; Professor of Playwriting, University of Pennsylvania, Philadelphia, 1928–30. Member, National Institute of Arts and Letters. *Died 21 October 1935.*

Plays

Sylvian, in *Sylvian and Poems.*   1885.
George Cameron (produced 1891).
In the Season (produced 1892).   1898.
Ruth Underwood (produced 1892).
Deborah (produced 1892; as *The Slave Girl,* produced 1893).
Don Pedro (produced 1892).
Becky Sharp, from the novel *Vanity Fair* by Thackeray (produced 1899).   Edited by J.
     B. Russak, in *Monte Cristo and Other Plays,* 1940.
The Adventures of Françoise, from a novel by S. Weir Mitchell (produced 1900).
The Kreutzer Sonata, from a work by Jacob Gordin (produced 1906).   1907.
The New York Idea (produced 1906).   1908.
The New Marriage (produced 1911).
Major Pendennis, from the novel by Thackeray (produced 1916).

Fiction

Love in the Backwoods (stories).   1897.

Verse

Sylvian: A Tragedy, and Poems.   1885.
Poems.   1894.

Other

Understanding America.   1897.

*   *   *

Langdon Mitchell's reputation in American theatre rests almost completely on one play –
The New York Idea. His first published play, *Sylvian,* a tragedy written partly in verse and
more for the closet than the stage, appeared in a volume of verse in 1885. Among his ten
other plays, *Becky Sharp,* a dramatization of Thackeray's *Vanity Fair,* was a successful
vehicle for the American actress Minnie Madden Fiske. But only *The New York Idea* which
Arthur Hobson Quinn, the drama historian, termed a "sterling comedy," could be considered
a contribution to the developing American drama. It also helped spread the work of
American dramatists abroad where it played in London, was produced in Germany as
Jonathans Tochter under the direction of Max Reinhardt, and was translated into other
European languages.
     Something of a landmark in the progress of social comedy in America, *The New York Idea*
– "New York is bounded on the North, South, East and West by the state of Divorce" –
mixes farce-comedy with melodrama in delightful portions while Mitchell reveals his rather
probing insights into the "state of Divorce" through witty and satirical comments. As a satire
on marriage in New York society, the play defines marriage as "three parts love and seven
parts forgiveness of sin." The fast-moving plot is determined by two divorced women who
plan to marry each other's ex-husband until one of them decides she really loves the man she
had just divorced. Most of the characters are one-dimensional foils for the author's quick wit

– the stuffy husband, the insipid clergyman, the English fop intriguer. Contrived situations such as the wedding scene and the club-house episode make the play successful and show Mitchell's particular skills as a dramatist. With wit, irony, and carefully created incongruities, the play treats a serious issue with a modern touch that provides some distinction to early twentieth-century American drama.

Mitchell never repeated his success and, in fact, made only two more attempts to write for the theatre, neither one successful. In related work he became, in 1928, the first occupant of the Chair of Playwriting founded by the Mask and Wig Club at the University of Pennsylvania, a position he held for two years. For the student or historian of American drama he remains primarily the author of a single memorable play.

—Walter J. Meserve

MITCHELL, S(ilas) Weir. American. Born in Philadelphia, Pennsylvania, 15 February 1829; son of the physician John Kearsley Mitchell. Educated at the University Grammar School, Philadelphia; University of Pennsylvania, Philadelphia, 1844–48, left because of illness without taking a degree, subsequently awarded a B.A. as of Class of 1848, 1906; Jefferson Medical College, Philadelphia, M.D. 1850; studied medicine in Europe, 1850–51. Served as a Surgeon with the Union Army during the Civil War. Married 1) Mary Middleton Elwyn in 1858 (died, 1862), two sons, including Langdon Mitchell, *q.v.*; 2) Mary Cadwalader in 1875. Practised medicine in Philadelphia, initially as an assistant to his father, from 1851; member of staff of the Philadelphia Orthopaedic Hospital and Infirmary for Nervous Diseases for forty years, and Professor at the Philadelphia Polyclinic and College for Graduates in Medicine; also a researcher: published extensively on pharmacological, physiological, and toxicological subjects, and, most notably, on his research into nervous diseases: pioneered the application of psychology to medicine; renowned for developing the theory of the "rest cure" as treatment for various mental diseases; devoted himself increasingly to writing during the last decades of his life. Trustee, University of Pennsylvania, from 1875; Trustee, Carnegie Institution, Washington, D.C.; first President, Franklin Inn (writer's club of Philadelphia), 1902–14. M.D.: University of Bologna, 1888; LL.D.: Harvard University, Cambridge, Massachusetts, 1886; University of Edinburgh, 1895; Princeton University, New Jersey, 1896; University of Toronto, 1906; Jefferson Medical College, 1910. Fellow, American Academy of Arts and Sciences. *Died 4 January 1914.*

PUBLICATIONS

Fiction

The Children's Hour (juvenile), with Elizabeth Stevenson. 1864.
The Wonderful Stories of Fuz-Buz and Mother Grabem the Spider (juvenile). 1867.
Hephzibah Guinness, Thee and You, and A Draft on the Banks of Spain. 1880.
In War Time. 1885.
Roland Blake. 1886.
Prince Little Boy and Other Tales Out of Fairy-Land. 1888.

Far in the Forest. 1889.
Characteristics. 1892.
Mr. Kris Kringle: A Christmas Tale. 1893.
When All the Woods Are Green. 1894.
Philip Vernon: A Tale in Prose and Verse. 1895.
A Madeira Party. 1895.
Hugh Wynne, Free Quaker. 1897.
The Adventures of François, Foundling, Thief, Juggler, and Fencing-Master During the French Revolution. 1898.
The Autobiography of a Quack, and The Case of George Dedlow. 1900.
Dr. North and His Friends. 1900.
Circumstance. 1901.
The Autobiography of a Quack and Other Stories. 1901.
A Comedy of Conscience. 1903.
Little Stories. 1903.
New Samaria, and The Summer of St. Martin. 1904.
The Youth of Washington, Told in the Form of an Autobiography. 1904.
Constance Trescot. 1905.
A Diplomatic Adventure. 1906.
A Venture in 1777 (juvenile). 1908.
The Red City: A Novel of the Second Administration of President Washington. 1908.
The Guillotine Club and Other Stories. 1910.
John Sherwood's Ironmaster. 1911.
Westways: A Village Chronicle. 1913.

Play

Francis Drake: A Tragedy of the Sea. 1893.

Verse

The Hill of Stones and Other Poems. 1883.
A Masque and Other Poems. 1888.
The Cup of Youth and Other Poems. 1889.
A Psalm of Deaths and Other Poems. 1891.
The Mother. 1891.
The Mother and Other Poems. 1893.
Collected Poems. 1896.
Ode on a Lycian Tomb. 1899.
The Wager and Other Poems. 1900.
Selections from the Poems. 1901.
Pearl, Rendered into Modern English Verse. 1906.
The Comfort of the Hills. 1909.
The Comfort of the Hills and Other Poems. 1910.
Complete Poems. 1914.

Other

Researches upon the Venom of the Rattlesnake. 1861.
Gunshot Wounds and Other Injuries of Nerves, with George R. Morehouse and William W. Keen. 1864.

Wear and Tear; or, Hints for the Overworked. 1871.
Injuries of Nerves and Their Consequences. 1872.
Fat and Blood, and How to Make Them. 1877; revised edition, 1878, 1884.
Lectures on Diseases of the Nervous System, Especially in Women. 1881; revised
  edition, 1885.
Researches upon the Venom of Poisonous Serpents, with Edward T. Reichert. 1886.
Doctor and Patient. 1888.
Two Lectures on the Conduct of the Medical Life. 1893.
The Composition of Expired Air and Its Effects upon Animal Life, with J. S. Billings and
  D. H. Bergey. 1895.
Clinical Lessons on Nervous Diseases. 1897.
*A Brief History of Two Families: The Mitchells of Ayrshire and the Symons of
  Cornwall.* 1912.
Some Recently Discovered Letters of William Harvey, with Other Miscellanea. 1912.
Works. 13 vols., 1913.

Editor, *Five Essays,* by John Kearsley Mitchell. 1859.

Bibliography: in *Bibliography of American Literature* by Jacob Blanck, 1973.

Reading List: *Mitchell: His Life and Letters* by Anna Robeson Burr, 1929; *Mitchell: Novelist
and Physician* by Ernest Earnest, 1950; *Mitchell as a Psychiatric Novelist* by David M. Rein,
1952; *Mitchell, M.D. – Neurologist: A Medical Biography* by Richard D. Walker, 1970.

                              *   *   *

    S. Weir Mitchell enjoyed during his lifetime almost as wide an acclaim for his work as a
physician as for his writing. The hand that produced hundreds of scientific medical treatises
was no less prolific in this *other* imaginative area, as Mitchell viewed it, and he voluminously
turned out novels, short fiction, and poetry. "He's a world-doctor for sure," but "I can't say
that he's a world-author," said Walt Whitman. Contemporary praise that ranked one
Mitchell novel with *The Scarlet Letter,* two others as superior to *Henry Esmond* and *A Tale of
Two Cities,* and one of his poems as finer than "Lycidas" was sincere but excessive.
    Preceding and then accompanying his novel writing, Mitchell's short fiction is noteworthy
mainly for its foreshadowing and typifying. The tales of fantasy, a few O. Henryish pieces,
and several Poe-esque stories of supernatural mystery are more distinctive, but traditional
trappings prevail in others. Probably most memorable is "The Case of George Dedlow," the
autobiography of a quadruple amputee whose legs return during a climactic seance.
    Mitchell's primary success as a storyteller came from his "summer-born books," the
thirteen novels which were largely vacation products of his last thirty years. More accurately
labeled romances, these works reveal a pioneer physician but a literary conservative during
the rise of American Realism. Mitchell made three distinct contributions to American fiction,
each with important realistic implications but none with significant realistic achievement.
Characterization grounded in the psychological knowledge of his clinical experience was first
in time and remains first in import. His coup here, the obsessed, neurotic woman with a
marked capacity for evil, is best seen in *Roland Blake, Circumstance,* and *Constance Trescot.*
Mitchell chose his names carefully: Octopia Darnell is octopus-like in her demanding hold
upon the Wynnes, Lucretia Hunter is an unscrupulous seeker of lucre, and Constance
Trescot is relentless in driving her husband's killer to suicide. Mitchell rightly thought
Constance Trescot the best of his novels. A second contribution was the creation of a
convincing atmosphere of a definite past. His long works of historical fiction – *Hugh Wynne,
Free Quaker,* a best-seller about the American Revolution; *The Adventures of François,* set
during the French Revolution; and *The Red City,* a novel of Philadelphia in Washington's

second administration – manifest the extensive research and historical immersion with which Mitchell prepared himself for their writing. His third contribution, like his first, is more suggestive than fully realized. *Characteristics* and its sequel, *Dr. North and His Friends*, have been called "conversation novels" and lauded for their experimental originality. Plainly autobiographical, they continue the tradition of Oliver Wendell Holmes's autocratic *Breakfast-Table* series but look toward the more sophisticated use of conversation and complex interpersonal relationships in more serious fiction.

Mitchell was always serious about his poetry, but the judgment he hoped it would be given by time has not been forthcoming. His own nomination for immortality was the "Ode on a Lycian Tomb," inspired by the *Les Pleureuses* monument and his deep grief for the death of a daughter.

—Bert Hitchcock

MOWATT, Anna Cora (née Ogden).   American.   Born in Bordeaux, France, 5 March 1819, to American parents; lived in or near Bordeaux as a child; settled with her family in New York City, 1826. Educated at Mrs. Okill's School, New York, 1826–28, and at a school in New Rochelle, New York, 1828–31. Married 1) James Mowatt in 1834 (died, 1851), three adopted children; 2) William Foushee Ritchie in 1854. Travelled abroad for her health, 1837–38; returned to New York and began writing for the stage, 1839; appeared in recitals of poetry, New York and Boston, 1841–42, and thereafter wrote under the pseudonym Helen Berkley for *Godey's Lady's Book*, *Graham's*, and other magazines, and compiled books on cooking, etiquette, etc. for various publishers; made debut as actress, New York, 1845, and appeared, with E. L. Davenport as leading man, in New York and other major American cities, London, and Dublin, 1846 until she retired in 1854; full-time writer from 1854; lived abroad after 1861, mainly in Florence. Active in the campaign to preserve Mount Vernon: Vice-Regent, Mount Vernon Ladies Association of the Union, 1858–66. *Died 21 July 1870.*

PUBLICATIONS

Plays

    Gulzara; or, The Persian Slave (produced 1840).   In *The New World*, 1840.
    Fashion; or, Life in New York (produced 1845).   1849.
    Armand; or, The Peer and the Peasant (produced 1847).   1849.

Fiction

    The Fortune Hunter; or, The Adventures of a Man about Town: A Novel of New York Society.   1842.
    Evelyn; or, A Heart Unmasked.   1845.
    Mimic Life; or, Before and Behind the Curtain (stories).   1856.
    Twin Roses.   1857.
    Fairy Fingers.   1865.
    The Mute Singer.   1866.
    The Clergyman's Wife and Other Sketches.   1867.

Verse

Pelayo; or, The Cavern of Covadonga. 1836.
Reviewers Reviewed: A Satire. 1837.

Other

Life of Goethe. 1844.
Etiquette of Courtship and Marriage. 1844.
The Management of the Sick Room. 1844.
The Memoirs of Madame d'Arblay. 1844.
Autobiography of an Actress; or, Eight Years on the Stage. 1853.
Italian Life and Legends. 1870.

Reading List: *Life and Letters* by Marius Blesi, 1952; *Anna Cora: The Life and Theatre of Anna Cora Mowatt* by Eric Wollencott Barnes, 1954, as *The Lady of Fashion,* 1955.

*   *   *

Mid-nineteenth-century American stage history records no more engaging figure than author-actress Anna Cora Mowatt, whose performances in her own and others' plays delighted audiences throughout the United States and Great Britain. Though known today chiefly for her comedy, *Fashion,* an amusing satire on middle-class pretentiousness, Mrs. Mowatt's popularity during the 1850's derived from numerous other writings, but primarily from the many successful roles she brought to life in both English and American theatres. Her dual career marked a turning point, demonstrating that an American woman of genteel birth, given talent, perseverance, family support, and hard work, could achieve professional recognition in theatrical circles without sacrificing social respectability.

As her autobiography reveals, the story of Mrs. Mowatt's dramatic experiences is still fascinating. Born in Bordeaux, the ninth of sixteen children of wealthy Americans, she enjoyed from early childhood such cultural advantages as extensive European travel; entrée into the world of art, literature, and theatre; familial stimulus and encouragement toward creative effort; and, above all, the guidance and support of her husband, James Mowatt, whom she married at fifteen. At sixteen she published a juvenile poetic romance entitled *Pelayo; or, The Cavern of Covadonga,* and then wrote an operetta, "The Gypsy Wanderer." These youthful effusions led to more mature essays, stories, and sketches appearing in leading American periodicals, and to her three plays, *Gulzara; or, The Persian Slave, Fashion,* and *Armand.* Other publications included three novels, two romantic tales of theatrical life under the title *Mimic Life; or, Before and Behind the Curtain,* and the detailed account of her experiences in *Autobiography of an Actress* – in all, an impressive collection, written mainly between frequent illnesses and extended theatrical engagements.

Although Anna Mowatt's stage performances were more widely heralded than her writings in the 1850's, throughout ensuing decades her reputation as the author of *Fashion* superseded that of her acting career. For the play not only scored immediate hits and enjoyed repeated, long-run performances in both England and America; it has continued, even within recent times, to attract more attention from producing groups than any other nineteenth century American play except *Uncle Tom's Cabin.* Its enduring appeal is well deserved because no other play of its period captured so accurately or spoofed with such buoyant, satiric humor, characterization, and sprightly dialogue, the bourgeois aspirations of mid-century New York society.

—Eugene Current-Garcia

MURFREE, Mary Noailles. Pseudonym: Charles Egbert Craddock.   American.   Born
at Grantlands, the family estate near Murfreesboro, Tennessee, 24 January 1850; became
lame as a child; moved with her family to Nashville, Tennessee, 1856. Educated at a school
in Nashville and, after the Civil War, at boarding school in Philadelphia. Writer from 1874.
Died 31 July 1922.

PUBLICATIONS

Fiction

In the Tennessee Mountains (stories).   1884.
Where the Battle Was Fought.   1884.
Down the Ravine.   1885.
The Prophet of the Great Smoky Mountains.   1885.
In the Clouds.   1886.
The Story of Keedon Bluffs.   1887.
The Despot of Broomsedge Cove.   1889.
In the "Stranger People's" Country.   1891.
His Vanished Star.   1894.
The Phantoms of the Foot-Bridge and Other Stories.   1895.
The Mystery of Witch-Face Mountain and Other Stories.   1895.
The Young Mountaineers: Short Stories.   1897.
The Juggler.   1897.
The Story of Old Fort Loudon.   1899.
The Bushwhackers and Other Stories.   1899.
The Champion.   1902.
A Spectre of Power.   1903.
The Frontiersmen (stories).   1904.
The Storm Centre.   1905.
The Amulet.   1906.
The Windfall.   1907.
The Fair Mississippian.   1908.
The Raid of the Guerilla and Other Stories.   1912.
The Ordeal: A Mountain Romance of Tennessee.   1912.
The Story of Duciehurst: A Tale of the Mississippi.   1914.

Bibliography: in *Bibliography of American Literature* by Jacob Blanck, 1973; "Murfree: An
Annotated Bibliography" by Reese M. Carleton, in *American Literary Realism 1870–1910,*
Autumn 1974.

Reading List: *Charles Egbert Craddock (Mary Noailles Murfree)* by Edd Winfield Parks,
1941; *Murfree* by Richard Cary, 1967.

*   *   *

Mary Noailles Murfree gained a deserved reputation in her day as an accurate and graphic
local colorist. Her short stories and novels set in the mountains of Tennessee are distinguished
for their accurate transcription of dialect and their vivid depictions of scenery. "I love to be
particular," she frequently quoted, and in her attention to the detail of mountain background
and speech she was indeed "particular."

The eight stories of *In the Tennessee Mountains*, published under the pseudonym of Charles Egbert Craddock, won immediate popularity and came to be regarded as significant contributions to the short story genre. In the books that followed, notably *Where the Battle Was Fought*, *The Prophet of the Great Smoky Mountains*, and *In the "Stranger People's" Country*, the meticulous portrayal of landscape and local color continued to be her forte.

Murfree's characterizations were sometimes stylized, and her lengthy descriptions occasionally impeded the flow of the narrative, especially in her novels. Her themes were in general restricted to a handful of set situations involving the legal tussles of mountainfolk and townspeople, the impact of the sophisticated stranger upon the mountain girl and her jealous lover, the complications that follow in the wake of the superstitious religious fanatic. None the less, many of her characters achieved a high degree of verisimilitude: her beauties and crones, her fugitives from justice, her blacksmiths and preachers. In narrating their frustrated lives against the picturesque setting of the Tennessee Mountains, Murfree captured the public imagination and gained for herself a niche in regional literature.

Her style matched her vigorous themes. It was straightforward, forceful, and robust. Thus the revelation that Charles Egbert Craddock was the pseudonym of a woman astounded not merely her readers but her editor, Thomas Bailey Aldrich of *The Atlantic Monthly*.

Although Murfree experimented with other literary genres, including the historical novel and the romance, she is remembered primarily for her local color stories of the Tennessee Mountains. Her work has been compared, in respect to its general portrayal of scenery and people, with that of other regional writers such as Bret Harte, George Washington Cable, and Sarah Orne Jewett.

—Madeleine B. Stern

NASBY, Petroleum V(esuvius).   Pseudonym for David Ross Locke.   American.   Born in Vestal, near Binghamton, New York, 20 September 1833. Educated in local schools to age 10; apprentice printer at the *Democrat*, Cortland, New York, 1843–50. Married Martha H. Bodine; three sons. Itinerant printer in various American cities, 1850–52; Founding Editor, with James G. Robinson, *Plymouth Advertiser*, Ohio, 1852–56; subsequently worked for various Ohio newpapers; Editor, *Jeffersonian*, Findlay, Ohio, 1861–65 (wrote first Nasby letter for the paper, 1861); Editor and Proprietor of the *Toledo Blade*, 1865 until his death (wrote Nasby letters for the paper until 1887); Managing Editor, *Evening Mail*, New York, 1871; served as Alderman from the third ward, Toledo. *Died 15 February 1888.*

PUBLICATIONS

Collections

   Let's Laugh (selections), edited by Lloyd E. Smith.   1924.

Fiction and Sketches

   The Nasby Papers: Letters and Papers Containing Views on the Topics of the Day.   1864.
   Nasby: Divers Views, Opinions and Prophecies of Yoors Trooly.   1866.
   Swinging round the Circle; or, Andy's Trip to the West, Together with a Life of Its Hero.   1866.
   Swingin round the Cirkle.   1867.
   Ekkoes from Kentucky.   1867.
   The Impendin Crisis uv the Dimocracy.   1868.
   The Struggles (Social, Financial and Political) of Petroleum V. Nasby.   1873; as *The Moral History of America's Life Struggle*, 1874; abridged edition, edited by Joseph Jones, 1963.
   Eastern Fruit on Western Dishes: The Morals of Abou Ben Adhem.   1875.
   Inflation at the Cross Roads.   1875; as *Nasby on Inflation*, 1876.
   The President's Policy.   1877.
   A Paper City (novel).   1878.
   The Democratic John Bunyan, Being Eleven Dreams.   1880.
   The Diary of an Office Seeker.   1881.
   Nasby in Exile; or, Six Months of Travel in England, Ireland, Scotland, France, Germany, Switzerland, and Belgium.   1882.
   Beer and the Body.   1884.
   Prohibition.   1886.
   The Demagogue: A Political Novel.   1891.
   The Nasby Letters.   1893.

Plays

   Inflation, with Charles Gayler (produced 1876).
   Widow Bedott (produced 1879).

Verse

Hannah Jane. 1881.

Other

Civil War Letters, edited by Harvey S. Ford. 1962.

Reading List: *Nasby* by James C. Austin, 1965; *The Man Who Made Nasby, David Ross Locke* by John M. Harrison, 1969.

*   *   *

Petroleum V. Nasby was the creation of David Ross Locke, one of America's greatest newspaper men. Beginning as a printer at the age of twelve and progressing successfully as writer, editor, and publisher of several New York and Ohio newspapers, he took over the Toledo, Ohio, *Blade* in 1865, and made it one of the most widely read papers in the midwest. He had very little schooling, but he developed a rough but powerful editorial style that contributed to the course of American history. He supported the Republican Party from its beginnings. His opposition to the Confederacy during the Civil War encouraged the Union cause and President Lincoln personally. His insistence on the rights of Negroes helped lead public opinion toward the Emancipation Proclamation and the Thirteenth, Fourteenth, and Fifteenth Amendments to the Constitution. His attacks on political corruption promoted Civil Service reform and the exposure of political fraud in the Gilded Age. He aided the causes of prohibition and women's rights which led long after his death to the Eighteenth and Nineteenth Amendments.

But his greatest and most lasting fame came from the Nasby letters – a series of newspaper columns written from 1862 until Locke's death in 1888. Petroleum Vesuvius Nasby, the fictitious writer of the letters, stood for everything that Locke was against. Nasby was an illiterate, drunken, bigoted, racist Democrat. The Nasby letters are considered part of the American tradition of crackerbox humor – journalistic humor expressed in a lowbrow, rustic dialect and with a common-sense philosophy. But they are not humorous in a strict sense of the term; they are bitterly satirical, violently partisan, grossly concrete pictures of the American political scene. With the exception of Benjamin Franklin, Locke was probably America's greatest political satirist.

The best-known Nasby letters were collected in various books beginning in 1864. The best of these is *Divers Views,* which exposed blatantly the pro-Southern views of the Ohio Copperhead, Nasby, during the Civil War. But each collection included parts of the earlier material, and *The Nasby Letters* is the most complete, comprising a panorama of Republican thought and action during the most critical quarter-century of United States history.

The Nasby letters were but a part of Locke's literary activities. He was one of the most popular lecturers in America in an age when public lecturing was as important as television is today. His three famous lectures, delivered throughout the country under the pseudonym of Nasby, were small masterpieces on the issues of civil rights for Negroes, women's rights, and political corruption. He was the author of two excellent political novels, *A Paper City* and *The Demagogue*; two plays, *Inflation* and *Widow Bedott*, the latter being performed continually into the twentieth century; a very popular, very sentimental poem, *Hannah Jane*; a number of quite creditable hymns; and an untold number of articles, editorials, stories, novels, verses, and essays in newspapers, magazines, and pamphlets.

Locke did not pretend to be a literary artist. He wrote for his times, and he believed that politics was the most important concern of a democracy. He was a significant editor and publisher. And his Nasby letters and his lectures deserve continued attention.

—James C. Austin

NEAL, John. American. Born in Falmouth, now Portland, Maine, 25 August 1793. Educated for a brief period in local schools. Married Eleanor Hall in 1828; five children. Clerk in a succession of shops in Portland, then worked as an itinerant teacher of penmanship and drawing in various towns along the Kennebec River; settled in Baltimore: kept a dry goods store, with John Pierpont, 1814 until the business failed, 1816; studied law, while writing for a living (briefly edited the *Baltimore Telegraph*; contributed to *Portico*; assisted Paul Allen in compiling *A History of the American Revolution*; published novels), 1816–23; lived in England, contributing to the most prominent English periodicals, particularly *Blackwood's Magazine*, 1823–27; returned to America, 1827, settled in Portland, and practised law there; edited the *Yankee*, Portland, 1828–29; later briefly edited the *New England Galaxy*, Boston, and a Portland newspaper; Editor, *Brother Jonathan*, New York, 1843; active contributor to the *North American Review*, *Harper's*, and the *Atlantic Monthly*, from 1850. M.A.: Bowdoin College, Brunswick, Maine, 1836. *Died 20 June 1876.*

PUBLICATIONS

Collections

  Observations on American Art: Selections from the Writings, edited by Harold Edward Dickson. 1943.

Fiction

  Keep Cool: A Novel, Written in Hot Weather. 1817.
  Logan: A Family History. 1822.
  Errata; or, The Works of Will Adams. 1823.
  Randolph. 1823.
  Seventy-Six. 1823.
  Brother Jonathan; or The New Englanders. 1825.
  Rachel Dyer: A North American Story. 1828.
  Authorship: A Tale. 1830.
  The Down-Easters. 1833.
  True Womanhood: A Tale. 1859.
  The White-Faced Pacer; or, Before and After the Battle. 1863.
  The Moose-Hunter; or, Life in the Maine Woods. 1864.
  Little Mocassin; or, Along the Madawaska: A Story of Life and Love in the Lumber Region. 1866.

Play

Otho.   1819.

Verse

The Battle of Niagara.   1818; revised edition, 1819.

Other

> *One Word More: Intended for the Reasoning and Thoughtful among Unbelievers.*   1854.
> *Account of the Great Conflagration in Portland.*   1866.
> *Wandering Recollections of a Somewhat Busy Life: An Autobiography.*   1869.
> *Great Mysteries and Little Plagues.*   1870.
> *Portland Illustrated.*   1874.
> *American Writers*, edited by Fred Lewis Pattee.   1937.
> *Critical Essays and Stories,* edited by Hans-Joachim Lang, in *Jahrbuch für Amerikastudien*, 1962.

Bibliography: in *Bibliography of American Literature* by Jacob Blanck, 1973.

Reading List: *A Down-East Yankee from the District of Maine* by Windsor Pratt Daggett, 1920; *That Wild Fellow Neal and the American Literary Revolution* by Benjamin Lease, 1972.

*   *   *

Strongly influenced by American nationalism following the War of 1812, John Neal developed a theory of literature that, put into practice in a series of unusual novels, has helped to win him a minor place in American literary history. Concerned that American writers like Charles Brockden Brown, Washington Irving, and James Fenimore Cooper were not sufficiently "American" in their writing, Neal sought to create an original body of fiction that would imitate no foreign models, that would accurately depict American persons and places, and that would faithfully reproduce the American language. He constructed his works, moreover, on a psychological theory that placed great stress on the "heart" and the "blood," as opposed to the mind, a theory that led him to write rather formless fictions that frequently lapse into incoherence.

He turned to the American past for some of his novels – Indian conflicts in *Logan*, the American Revolution in *Seventy-Six* and *Brother Jonathan*, and the Salem witch trials in *Rachel Dyer* – and he drew American characters and reproduced American speech with considerable skill. At his best, Neal achieved a degree of realism uncommon in his time and occasionally reached a depth of psychological penetration suggestive of Poe. At his worst, however, he strained too much for effect, descended to Byronic posturing, indulged in both Gothic and sentimental absurdities, and fell into melodrama. All of Neal's books suffer to some degree from his excesses, and from his unwillingness – or inability – to give form to his novels. Only *Rachel Dyer*, perhaps his best book, exhibits a sustained authorial control, but even it has a long and digressive passage in one of the courtroom scenes.

Neal's one significant contribution to American fiction is his style. Derived from the cadences of American speech, it ranges from local dialect through the more general vernacular to the Biblical or prophetic. At its best, it gives a sense of immediacy to his work, whether the story is told, like *Seventy-Six*, by a common man who uses his natural language, or, like *Rachel Dyer*, by a narrative voice appropriately attuned to the seriousness of the action and theme. Neal was especially skillful in moving his story forward through the speech of his characters, and in some of his works, the reader will find page after page containing little more than conversation. In both style and technique of narration, therefore, John Neal stands near the head of the vernacular tradition in American literature and dimly foreshadows the language of Mark Twain.

—Donald A. Ringe

NORRIS, (Benjamin) Frank(lin).   American.   Born in Chicago, Illinois, 5 March 1870; moved with his family to San Francisco, 1884. Educated at a school in Belmont, California, 1885–87; studied art at the Atelier Julien, Paris, 1887–89; studied English literature at the University of California, Berkeley, 1890–94, and writing at Harvard University, Cambridge, Massachusetts, 1894–95. Married Jeanette Black in 1900; one daughter. War Correspondent for the *San Francisco Chronicle* in South Africa during the Uitlander insurrection, 1895–96; member of the editorial staff of the *Wave*, San Francisco, 1896–97; War Correspondent, in Cuba, for *McClure's Magazine*, New York, 1898; Reader for Doubleday, publishers, New York, 1899–1902; settled on a ranch near Gilroy, California, 1902. *Died 25 October 1902*

PUBLICATIONS

Collections

(*Complete Works*).   10 vols., 1928.
The Letters, edited by Franklin Walker.   1956.

Fiction

Moran of the Lady Letty: A Story of Adventure off the California Coast.   1898; as *Shanghaied*, 1899.
McTeague: A Story of San Francisco.   1899; edited by Donald Pizer, 1977.
Blix.   1899.
A Man's Woman.   1900.
The Epic of Wheat: The Octopus: A Story of California.   1901; edited by Kenneth S. Lynn, 1958; *The Pit: A Story of Chicago*, 1903.
A Deal in Wheat and Other Stories of the New and Old West.   1903.
The Joyous Miracle.   1906.
The Third Circle.   1909.
Vandover and the Brute, edited by Charles G. Norris.   1914.

Verse

Yvernelle: A Legend of Feudal France.   1891.

Other

> *The Responsibilities of the Novelist and Other Literary Essays.* 1903.
> *The Surrender of Santiago: An Account of the Historic Surrender of Santiago to General Shafter, July 17, 1898.* 1917.
> *Two Poems and "Kim" Reviewed.* 1930.
> *Norris of "The Wave": Stories and Sketches from the San Francisco Weekly, 1893 to 1897,* edited by Oscar Lewis. 1931.
> *The Literary Criticism,* edited by Donald Pizer. 1964.
> *A Novelist in the Making: A Collection of Student Themes and the Novels Blix and Vandover and the Brute,* edited by James D. Hart. 1971.

Bibliography: *Norris: A Bibliography* by Kenneth A. Lohf and Eugene P. Sheehy, 1959; *The Merrill Checklist of Norris* by John S. Hill, 1970; in *Bibliography of American Literature* by Jacob Blanck, 1973.

Reading List: *Norris: A Study* by Ernest Marchand, 1942; *Norris* by Warren French, 1962; *The Novels of Norris* by Donald Pizer, 1966; *Norris: Instinct and Art* by William D. Dillingham, 1969.

*   *   *

Although Frank Norris never wrote a work that could be considered a masterpiece, he occupies an important place in American literary history. He is an early practitioner of naturalism, along with his contemporaries Crane and Dreiser; he is an example of the French influence on American letters; and he is a noteworthy creator of the fictional landscape of California. Norris was a very uneven writer and capable of writing both popular magazine romance as well as serious fiction in the realistic/naturalistic tradition. Only two or three of his novels have demonstrated survival power.

As a young man Norris studied art in Paris, but there is no evidence that he read the French realists/naturalists at that time. He then was interested in romance, and his first work was a narrative poem, *Yvernelle: A Legend of Feudal France,* published while he was a student at the University of California. In 1894, when he entered Harvard as a special student of writing under Lewis Gates, he discovered Balzac, Flaubert, and especially Zola. He worked on his first novel *McTeague* during that year but didn't finish it until later after returning to California.

McTeague is a remarkable first novel, the most important piece of naturalism produced in America up to that time. It shows a strong Zola influence but is thoroughly naturalized in the United States. It is the story of a San Francisco dentist who is victimized by his inability to cope with marriage and complex social relationships. McTeague is a man of great strength but under the influence of alcohol loses his self-control. He is too stupid to cope with his wife, who becomes a miser, and a former friend, who causes him to lose his dental practice. The San Francisco locale is well done, and the disintegration of McTeague under the impact of forces he cannot control makes this a powerful naturalistic novel. The ending, unfortunately, is melodramatic and the symbolism far too obvious.

The Octopus, however, is a more mature work and is generally regarded as Norris's best achievement. It was the first of a projected trilogy to be called *The Epic of Wheat.* *The Octopus* deals with the growing of the wheat and is laid in the San Joaquin Valley of California. The ranching scenes, especially the planting of the wheat, are rendered with a good eye for the local color. Although there are many characters and several sub-plots, the story basically concerns the struggle between the ranchers and the railroad (the octopus) over shipping rates and land prices. It is an unequal battle because the railroad holds all the trump cards, and in the climactic episode of the novel the ranchers are defeated in an armed confrontation with the railroad deputies. There are a good many romantic elements in the novel and it ends on a note of cosmic optimism, but the work falls mainly in the category of naturalism. After the railroad has won the struggle, the President of the company argues that the railroad is a "force born out of certain conditions." No man can stop or control it any more than anyone can stop the wheat from growing.

The second novel in the trilogy was *The Pit*, completed before Norris's fatal appendectomy and published posthumously. It depicts the trading of the wheat on the Chicago grain exchange, and, while it is inferior to *The Octopus*, it tells an absorbing story of the protagonist's unsuccessful efforts to corner the wheat market. The third volume in the trilogy, which was to be called *The Wolf* and was to deal with the distribution of the wheat in a famine-stricken Europe, was never written.

Another of Norris's novels that also deserves attention is *Vandover and the Brute*, a work that he wrote before *McTeague* but never could get published. It was issued with some cuts, and perhaps some additions by his brother Charles, in 1914. The novel, a powerful study of disintegrating character, was too advanced for Doubleday, McClure and Co. in 1899. Vandover is weak-willed, indolent, badly brought up, and after his father dies, leaving him a handsome legacy, he squanders his money, is victimized by a friend, and ends in abject degradation.

Norris is perhaps the most notable disciple of Zola in American literature. He praised Zola passionately and often reread his favorite novels, *L'Assommoir*, *La Terre*, *Germinal*, *La Bête Humaine*. He researched his novels as Zola did, studying a manual of dentistry before writing *McTeague*, visiting a wheat farm while planning *The Octopus*. So pervasive was the influence that he joked about it in the inscription he wrote in the flyleaf of his wife's copy of *The Octopus*: "To my boss, Jeanette Norris, most respectfully ... Mr. Norris (The Boy Zola)."

Although he was influenced by Zola, Norris never got over the original impulse towards romance. His critical views as outlined in *The Responsibilities of the Novelist* favor the spontaneous, improvising story-teller. He cites Dumas as an excellent example. He also believed that all good novels must have some significant pivotal event – such as the battle between the ranchers and the railroad deputies in *The Octopus*. It is no wonder that Norris is not a thorough-going naturalist. In addition, Norris never took himself very seriously. He wrote too fast and between *McTeague* and *The Octopus* there is much trash. He was torn between the Kipling-Richard Harding Davis tradition and Zola.

—James Woodress

O'BRIEN, (Michael) Fitz-James. Irish.   Born in Ireland, probably in County Limerick, in 1828; emigrated to the United States, 1852. Served in the American Civil War in the 7th New York   Regiment,   1861–62:   Aide-de-Camp   to   General   Lander;   commissioned Lieutenant, 1862; died of wounds. Left Ireland for London, 1849: Editor of *The Parlour Magazine*, 1851; settled in New York, 1852: Staff Member, *New York Daily Times*, 1852–53; regular contributor to *Harper's Monthly*, 1853–62, and Assistant Editor and Columnist ("Man about Town"), *Harper's Weekly*, 1857; Drama Critic, *New York Saturday Press*, 1858–59; press agent for actress Matilda Heron, 1859; Columnist ("Here and There"), *Vanity Fair*, 1860. *Died 6 April 1862.*

PUBLICATIONS

Collections

> *The Poems and Stories*, edited by William Winter.   1881.
> *The Golden Ingot, The Diamond Lens, A Terrible Night, What Was It?*   1921.
> *The Fantastic Tales*, edited by Michael Hayes.   1977.

Plays

> *My Christmas Dinner* (produced 1852).
> *A Gentleman from Ireland* (produced 1854).
> *The Sisters*, from a French play (produced 1854).
> *Duke Humphrey's Dinner* (produced 1856).
> *The Tycoon; or, Young America in Japan*, with Charles G. Rosenberg (produced 1860).

Verse

> *Sir Brasil's Falcon.*   1853.

Bibliography: in *Bibliography of American Literature* by Jacob Blanck, 1973.

Reading List: *O'Brien: A Literary Bohemian of the Eighteen-Fifties* by Francis Wolle, 1944 (includes bibliography).

*   *   *

After education in Ireland, and a short stint in London on the literary fringes, Fitz-James O'Brien emigrated to the United States and soon became a prominent member of New York's literary Bohemia that frequented Pfaff's, the old Hone House, and Windust's. O'Brien contributed lavishly to a number of American periodicals over the next six years among them the *American Whig Review, Putnam's Magazine, Harper's Weekly* and *Monthly, Vanity Fair, The Atlantic Monthly*, the *New York Times*. O'Brien was also the author of several plays, one, *A Gentleman from Ireland*, being presented successfully as late as 1895. His most imaginative story, "The Diamond Lens," appeared in 1858, winning him some fame, but at that point O'Brien's career as dandy author and bohemian faltered. He had acted as literary agent to M. L. Bateman, a theatrical director, and became involved with Matilda Heron, who appears to have had some responsibility for the collapse of O'Brien's fortunes. His splendid clothes, extensive library, elegant furnishings, soon disappeared; even his attractive personal appearance suffered a change for the worse with a broken nose from a professional pugilist. But he retained all his ebullience, and his end was brilliant. When the Civil War broke out, he joined the 7th Regiment of the National Guard of New York and won special mention for gallantry at the Battle of Bloomery Gap. A few days later he was wounded in the shoulder, indifferently nursed, and died of tetanus in 1862.

The general judgment on O'Brien is that he is more significant as personality than as author. Certainly, he wrote with unfortunate facility, and his verse is jaunty and negligible. Several of his stories, however, suggest a minor Poe with a dash of Hoffman. O'Brien had an undisciplined but powerful Gothic imagination that ranged over such topics as abnormal psychology, mesmerism, magic, alchemy, revenants, along with sharp flashes of prophetic imagination. "The Diamond Lens," a study of a mad microscopist, "The Wondersmith," with its aggressive manikin robots, and the ectoplasmic visitor of "What Was It?" retain some power to "electrify" the reader.

—Ian Fletcher

PAGE, Thomas Nelson. American. Born in Oakland Plantation, Hanover County, Virginia, 23 April 1853. Educated in local schools, and at Washington College, later Washington and Lee University, Lexington, Virginia, 1869–72; read law with his father, 1872–73; studied law at the University of Virginia, Charlottesville, 1873–74, LL.B. 1874. Married 1) Annie Seddon Bruce in 1886 (died, 1888); 2) Florence Lathrop Field in 1893 (died, 1921). Practiced law in Richmond, Virginia, 1875–93; writer, 1884–1910; settled in Washington, D.C., 1893; United States Ambassador to Italy, 1913–19. Litt.D.: Washington and Lee University, 1887; Yale University, New Haven, Connecticut, 1901; Harvard University, Cambridge, Massachusetts, 1913; LL.D.: Tulane University, New Orleans, 1899; College of William and Mary, Williamsburg, Virginia, 1906; Washington and Lee University, 1907. Member, American Academy of Arts and Letters. *Died 1 November 1922.*

PUBLICATIONS

Fiction

In Ole Virginia; or, Marse Chan and Other Stories.   1887.
Two Little Confederates.   1888.
On Newfound River.   1891.
Among the Camps; or, Young People's Stories of the War.   1891.
Elsket and Other Stories.   1891.
The Burial of the Guns.   1894.
Pastime Stories.   1894.
Unc' Edinburg: A Plantation Echo.   1895.
The Old Gentleman of the Black Stock.   1897.
Two Prisoners.   1898.
Red Rock: A Chronicle of Reconstruction.   1898.
Santa Claus's Partner.   1899.
Gordon Keith.   1903.
Bred in the Bone (stories).   1904.
Under the Crust (stories).   1907.
Tommy Trot's Visit to Santa Claus.   1908.
John Marvel, Assistant.   1909.
The Land of the Spirit (stories).   1913.
The Stranger's Pew (story).   1914.
The Red Riders.   1924.

Verse

Befo' de War: Echoes in Negro Dialect, with A. C. Gordon.   1888.
The Coast of Bohemia.   1906.

Other

The Old South: Essays Social and Political.   1892.
Social Life in Old Virginia Before the War.   1897.
The Negro: The Southerner's Problem.   1904.
The Novels, Stories, Sketches, and Poems.   18 vols., 1906–18.
Robert E. Lee: The Southerner.   1908; as *General Lee,* 1909.

The Old Dominion: Her Making and Her Manners.   1908.
Mount Vernon and Its Preservation.   1910.
Robert E. Lee: Man and Soldier.   1911.
Italy and the World War.   1920.
Dante and His Influence.   1922.
Washington and Its Romance.   1923.

Editor, *The Old Virginia Gentleman and Other Sketches,* by George W. Bagby.   1910.

Bibliography: by Theodore L. Gross, in *American Literary Realism 1,* 1967.

Reading List: *Page: A Memoir of a Virginia Gentleman* by Roswell Page, 1923; *Page* by Theodore L. Gross, 1967.

*   *   *

Thomas Nelson Page owed his popularity to the local color movement, the interest of Northern readers in the defeated South following the Civil War, and the growth of the family magazine. Although there were writers in the deep South and the mountain areas, the dominant literary image of the region was provided by accounts of life in the tidewater. Page and other writers in the plantation literary tradition increased the Southerner's pride in his past and dramatized his sense of victimization and self-sacrifice. Page's essays and dialect stories, published first in such magazines as *Scribner's* and *Century,* eulogized a civilization in which landlords abided by an almost medieval sense of *gentilesse,* women were exalted, and all the chivalric virtues prevailed. Sir Walter Scott's romances and stories by the Virginia writers George Bagby and Armistead Gordon had influenced Page's style and themes. His protagonists were typically those who had survived the war and were faced with the task of adjusting to a new and alien culture. He attempted to evoke a world that lived only in memory, and nostalgia was, therefore, the dominant mood of his most successful work.

The favorable reception in both North and South of "Marse Chan," "Meh Lady," and the other stories of *In Ole Virginia* convinced Page that authorship would prove a surer path to fame than the legal profession. Consequently, after his first wife died and he married a wealthy widow, Page devoted himself to full-time writing. He wrote several novels in which he experimented with urban settings and satirical dialogue. Even in these works, however, Page described the impact of Southern values on the rest of the nation. Each of the major novels written in his middle years (*Red Rock, Gordon Keith,* and *John Marvel, Assistant*) concerns Southern "missionaries," Virginia gentlemen who preach their Southern ideals and convert Yankees in the process. Part of their doctrine was a distrust of industrialization, a belief that aristocratic paternalism could still combat the grosser aspects of democracy, and a wistful agrarianism. It was the first decade of the new century that brought Page to the peak of his literary fame. After 1910 he all but retired from writing and devoted his time to political affairs in Washington, D.C.; he was a personal friend of Theodore Roosevelt, and eventually became ambassador to Italy.

Few writers after Page described Southern institutions so uncritically. Of the later writers Margaret Mitchell came closer than most to sharing the elegant Virginian's views, while Glasgow, Cabell, Faulkner, and their contemporaries perceived the ironies and injustices of the system Page had defended. At his best Page epitomized the plantation literary tradition, and the strengths and weaknesses of his prose provide an excellent illustration of a once popular literary genre.

—Kimball King

PAULDING, James Kirke. American. Born in Great Nine Partners, now Putnam County, New York, 22 August 1778; grew up in Tarrytown, New York. Educated for a brief period in a local school. Married Gertrude Kemble in 1818 (died, 1841); several children. Settled in New York City c. 1796, worked in a public office, and continued his studies on his own; writer from c. 1805; wrote for the *Analectic Magazine*, 1812; Secretary of the Board of Navy Commissioners, Washington, D.C., 1815–23; Naval Agent in New York City, 1823–38; Secretary of the Navy, in the administration of Martin Van Buren, 1838–41; returned to a country estate near Hyde Park, New York, 1846. *Died 6 April 1860.*

PUBLICATIONS

Collections

> *Collected Works*, edited by William I. Paulding.   4 vols., 1867–68.
> *The Letters*, edited by Ralph M. Aderman.   1962.

Fiction

> *Salmagundi; or, The Whim-Whams and Opinions of Launcelot Langstaff, Esq., and Others*, with Washington and William Irving.   2 vols., 1807–08: *Second Series* (by Paulding only), 2 vols., 1819–20.
> *The Diverting History of John Bull and Brother Jonathan.*   1812.
> *Koningsmarke: The Long Finne: A Story of the New World.*   1823.
> *John Bull in America; or, The New Munchausen.*   1825.
> *The Merry Tales of the Three Wise Men of Gotham.*   1826.
> *Tales of the Good Woman.*   1829.
> *Chronicles of the City of Gotham from the Papers of a Retired Common Councilman.*   1830.
> *The Dutchman's Fireside: A Tale.*   1831.
> *Westward Ho!*   1832; as *The Banks of the Ohio*, 1833.
> *The Book of Saint Nicholas.*   1836.
> *A Gift from Fairy-Land.*   1838; as *A Christmas Gift from Fairy Land*, 1838.
> *The Old Continental; or, The Price of Liberty.*   1846.
> *The Puritan and His Daughter.*   1849.
> *A Book of Vagaries* (selections), edited by William I. Paulding.   1868.

Plays

> *The Lion of the West*, revised by John Augustus Stone and William Bayle Bernard (produced 1831; as *The Kentuckian; or, A Trip to New York,* produced 1833).   Edited by James N. Tidwell, 1954.
> *The Bucktails; or, Americans in England.*   1847.
> *American Comedies* (includes *The Bucktails; The Noble Exile; Madmen All, or, The Cure of Love; Antipathies, or, The Enthusiasts by Ear*).   1847.

Verse

> *The Lay of the Scottish Fiddle: A Tale of Havre de Grace, Supposed to Be Written by Walter Scott, Esq.*   1813.
> *The Backwoodsman.*   1818.

Other

Naval Biography.   1815.
The United States and England.   1815.
Letters from the South.   1817.
A Sketch of Old New England.   1822.
The New Mirror for Travellers, and a Guide to the Springs.   1828.
Works.   7 vols., 1834–37.
A Life of Washington.   2 vols., 1835.
Slavery in the United States.   1836.

Bibliography: "A Bibliography of the Separate Publications of Paulding" by Oscar Wegelin, in Papers of the Bibliographical Society of America 12, 1918.

Reading List: The Literary Life of Paulding by William I. Paulding, 1867; Paulding: Versatile American by Amos L. Herold, 1926 (includes bibliography).

*   *   *

Through the 1830's, James Kirke Paulding's popularity with American readers rivalled that of his somewhat younger contemporaries Irving and Cooper. His name was also well known not only in Britain, but on the continent, where two of his novels – The Dutchman's Fireside and Westward Ho! – appeared in numerous translations. Although his audience dwindled sharply after 1845, he is still remembered as perhaps the most versatile, if not the most graceful, American author of the generation that matured between the two wars with England. During his long career Paulding won fame as a poet, novelist, essayist, biographer, playwright, and critic. He also wrote scores of short stories and sketches for both American and British periodicals. Most of his writing was done while he followed another career as public servant that culminated with his appointment in 1838 as Secretary of the Navy by President Martin Van Buren, a long-time friend whose ancestral roots were, like Paulding's, in the Dutch-American Hudson River valley.

Paulding was always more concerned with ideas than with art. Unlike his friend Irving (to whom he was related by marriage and with whom he collaborated on Salmagundi) he never made peace with either England or the romantic movement, which he scorned as a British conspiracy designed to sap the fiber of sturdy new-world republicanism. In a series of satires, commencing with The Diverting History of John Bull and Brother Jonathan and concluding with John Bull in America, he vigorously defended his young country against printed attacks by British travelers and reviewers. During the same period he wrote The Lay of the Scottish Fiddle, a book-length parody of The Lay of the Last Minstrel, burlesquing not only Scott's verse but his copious notes, and The Backwoodsman, another lengthy, often clumsy poem in heroic couplets designed, according to Paulding, to inform young American writers of the "rich poetic resources" available to them on their native ground. His call for American literary independence continued in his best-remembered essay, "National Literature," which appeared in Salmagundi, Second Series.

Prompted by the success of Cooper's The Spy and The Pioneers, Paulding turned to the novel in 1823, with Koningsmarke. Here he continued his satirical attack on Scott and what he considered to be the excesses of romanticism. In this first novel, Paulding hoped to demonstrate that Fielding, rather than Scott, was the proper model for American novelists. When Koningsmarke was misread and praised for the wrong reasons, Paulding abandoned satire and modified his attitude toward romanticism. The Dutchman's Fireside, set in the 1750's and in an area (upstate New York) that Cooper had already celebrated, was widely praised – not only by Cooper himself but by British readers, including an anonymous critic for The Westminster Review who praised Paulding for being "neither too elaborate like

Irving, nor too diffuse like Cooper." Paulding's third novel, *Westward Ho!*, captured the sense of adventure that urged many of his contemporaries to move from a settled east to an unsettled and still dangerous west. A fourth novel, *The Old Continental*, is based on the Benedict Arnold episode of the American Revolution. This and *The Puritan and His Daughter* were poorly planned and awkwardly written; they deserve the neglect they received even in Paulding's time.

Although Paulding had great ambitions as a playwright, he wrote only two plays of note, both comedies that dramatized social tensions between the England and America of his time. The second of them, *The Lion of the West*, won him a national prize, and was successfully produced in America and in London. It is most memorable for the character of Nimrod Wildfire, who closely resembles the American frontier hero, Davy Crockett.

Paulding's greatest success as a biographer came with his *Life of Washington*, a work that appeared in numerous editions until it was superseded by Washington Irving's.

—Thomas F. O'Donnell

PAYNE, John Howard. American. Born in New York City, 9 June 1791. Educated at a school in Boston to 1805, and at Union College, Schenectady, New York, 1806–08. Clerk in the counting house of Grant and Bennet Forbes, New York, 1805–06; Editor, *Thespian Mirror*, 1805–06, and *The Pastime*, 1807–08; began writing for the stage, 1806; made debut as an actor in New York in 1809 and enjoyed an immediate success; settled in England, 1813; acted in the provinces, 1814; thereafter earned his living in London by dramatic hackwork; acted as a secretary at Covent Garden, 1818–19; leased Sadler's Wells Theatre, 1820, but went bankrupt: imprisoned for debt, Fleet Prison, 1820–21; settled in Paris, 1821; wrote the lyrics for "Home Sweet Home" (in his *Clari*, 1823); collaborated with Washington Irving in writing plays, 1823–26; lived in London, 1823–25, and resettled there, 1826; Editor and Publisher of the weekly theatrical paper *Opera Glass*, 1826–27; returned to America, 1832; United States Consul in Tunis, 1842–45, 1851–52. *Died 9 April 1852.*

PUBLICATIONS

Collections

> *Trial Without Jury and Other Plays* (includes *Mount Savage, The Boarding Schools, The Two Sons-in-Law, Mazeppa, The Spanish Husband*), edited by Codman Hislop and W. R. Richardson. 1940.
> *The Last Duel in Spain and Other Plays* (includes *Woman's Revenge, The Italian Bride, Romulus the Shepherd King, The Black Man*), edited by Codman Hislop and W. R. Richardson. 1940.

Plays

> *Julia; or, The Wanderer* (as *The Wanderer*, produced 1806). 1806.
> *Lover's Vows*, from versions by Mrs. Inchbald and Benjamin Thompson of a play by Kotzebue (produced 1809?). 1809.

Trial Without Jury; or, The Magpie and the Maid, from a play by L. C. Caigniez and Théodore Baudouin (as *The Maid and the Magpie,* produced 1815?). In *Trial Without Jury and Other Plays,* 1940.

Accusation; or, The Family of D'Anglade, from a play by Frédéric du Petit-Méré (produced 1816). 1817.

The Tragedy of Brutus; or, The Fall of Tarquin, music by Hayward (produced 1818). 1818.

Thérèse, The Orphan of Geneva, from a play by Victor Ducange (produced 1821). 1821.

Adeline; or, The Victim of Seduction, from a play by Pixérécourt (produced 1822). 1822.

Love in Humble Life, from a play by Scribe and Dupin (produced 1822). 1823(?).

Ali Pacha; or, The Signet-Ring, adapted by J. R. Planché (produced 1822). 1822.

Peter Smink; or, The Armistice (produced 1822; revised version, produced 1826). 1826(?).

The Two Galley Slaves; or, The Mill of St. Aldervon, music by Tom Cooke and C. E. Horn (produced 1822). 1823(?).

Mount Savage, from a play by Pixérécourt (as *The Solitary of Mount Savage; or, The Fate of Charles the Bold,* produced 1822). In *Trial Without Jury and Other Plays,* 1940.

Clari; or, The Maid of Milan, music by Henry Bishop (produced 1823). 1823.

Mrs. Smith; or, The Wife and the Widow (produced 1823). 1823.

Charles the Second; or, The Merry Monarch, with Washington Irving, from a play by A. V. P. Duval (produced 1824). 1824; edited by A. H. Quinn, in *Representative American Plays,* 1917.

'Twas I; or, The Truth a Lie, from a French play (produced 1825). 1827.

The Fall of Algiers, music by Henry Bishop (produced 1825). 1825.

Richelieu: A Domestic Comedy, with Washington Irving, from a play by A. V. P. Duval (produced 1826; as *The French Libertine,* produced 1826). 1826.

The White Maid, from a play by Scribe, music by Adrien Boieldieu (produced 1827; also produced as *The White Lady*).

The Lancers (produced 1827). 1828(?).

Procrastination (produced 1829).

The Spanish Husband; or, First and Last Love, from a play by La Beaumelle (produced 1830). In *Trial Without Jury and Other Plays,* 1940.

Fricandeau; or, The Coronet and the Cook (produced 1831).

Oswali at Athens (produced 1831).

Woman's Revenge (produced 1832). In *The Last Duel in Spain and Other Plays,* 1940.

Virginia (produced 1834).

Fiction

Essays of Howard; or, Tales of the Prison. 1811.

Verse

Juvenile Poems. 1813; selections published as *Lispings of the Muse,* 1815.

Other

Indian Justice: A Cherokee Murder Trial, edited by Grant Foreman. 1934.

Payne to His Countrymen, edited by Clemens de Baillou. 1961.

Bibliography: "Payne: A Bibliography" by Charles F. Heartman and Harry B. Weiss, in *American Book Collector 3* and *4*, 1933.

Reading List: *The Early Life of Payne* by W. T. Hanson, 1913; *Payne* by Rosa P. Chiles, 1930; *America's First Hamlet* by Grace Overmyer, 1957.

* * *

During the first half of the nineteenth century, theatre audiences in both England and America enjoyed the strong, romantic rhetoric of poetic drama. In America the earliest dramatist to achieve success in this genre, and the most prolific, was John Howard Payne. A youthful prodigy, he attracted attention as an actor, a critic, and an editor of the *Thespian Mirror*, and a playwright whose first work, *Julia; or, The Wanderer*, was performed at New York's Park Theatre in 1806. When his career as an actor did not reach the success he anticipated, however, he embarked in 1813 for what he felt would be the greener theatrical fields of England. In this he was seriously mistaken for his acting engagements were few and soon relegated him to the provinces. But chance and necessity offered him a new career.

In 1809 before going to England Payne had published a version of August von Kotzebue's *Das Kind der Liebe* which he had adapted from two English translations. Six years later while in Paris he translated the current French hit, *La Pie Voleuse* by L. C. Caigniez and Théodore Baudouin as *The Maid and the Magpie* for the Drury Lane management. This was the beginning of a career – adapting and translating comedy, melodrama, and romantic tragedy – in which his particular forte was his ability to recognize dramatic material and create a successful play from various sources. Like other prolific dramatists of his time, his talent was not in writing original plays, but he soon became the first American dramatist to enjoy a substantial reputation abroad.

Among his best works is *The Tragedy of Brutus; or, The Fall of Tarquin*. Using five major sources he created a major acting vehicle for Edmund Kean, whereas the subsequent cry of plagiarism was particularly ironic at a time when play pirating was a common sport. Another popular adaptation was *Clari; or, The Maid of Milan*, which contains the song for which most Americans will, if at all, remember Payne – "Home, Sweet Home." They would, however, readily recognize the name of his collaborator in his most successful comedy, *Charles the Second; or, The Merry Monarch* – Washington Irving. Before Irving tired of the drama they worked on six plays together.

Returning to America in 1832 Payne epitomized the plight of the dramatist during America's formative years. With considerable skill and abundant energy, he had created many successful plays and made money for everyone – actors, managers – but himself. Recognized by theatre-goers and critics as a major contributor to American drama, he was never financially secure and became increasingly bitter over the treatment of American dramatists during the final years of his life which were separated from the theatre. His position in the history of American drama is unquestionably secure.

—Walter J. Meserve

POE, Edgar Allan. American. Born in Boston, Massachusetts, 19 January 1809; orphaned, and given a home by John Allan, 1812. Educated at the Dubourg sisters' boarding school, Chelsea, London, 1816–17; Manor House School, Stoke Newington, London, 1817–20; Joseph H. Clarke's School, Richmond, 1820–23; William Burke's School, Richmond, 1823–25; University of Virginia, Charlottesville, 1826; United States Military

Academy, West Point, New York, 1830–31. Served in the United States Army, 1827–29; Sergeant-Major. Married his 13-year-old cousin Virginia Clemm in 1836 (died, 1847). Journalist and editor: Assistant Editor, 1835, and Editor, 1836–37, *Southern Literary Messenger*, Richmond; Assistant Editor, *Gentleman's Magazine*, Philadelphia, 1839–40; Editor, *Graham's Lady's and Gentleman's Magazine*, Philadelphia, 1841–42; Sub-Editor, *New York Evening Mirror*, 1844; Co-Editor, *Broadway Journal*, 1845–46, New York. Lecturer after 1844. *Died 7 October 1849.*

PUBLICATIONS

Collections

    Complete Works, edited by James A. Harrison. 17 vols., 1902.
    The Letters, edited by John Ward Ostrom. 1948; revised edition, 2 vols., 1966.
    Poems, edited by Floyd Stovall. 1965.
    Collected Works, edited by Thomas O. Mabbott. 1969–

Verse

    Tamerlane and Other Poems. 1827.
    Al Aaraaf, Tamerlane, and Minor Poems. 1829.
    Poems. 1831.
    The Raven and Other Poems. 1845.

Play

    Politian: An Unfinished Tragedy, edited by Thomas O. Mabbott. 1923.

Fiction

    The Narrative of Arthur Gordon Pym of Nantucket. 1838.
    Tales of the Grotesque and Arabesque. 1840.
    The Murders in the Rue Morgue, and The Man That Was Used Up. 1843.
    Tales. 1845.
    The Literati. 1850.

Other

    The Conchologist's First Book (revised by Poe). 1839.
    Eureka: A Prose Poem. 1848; edited by Richard P. Benton, 1973.
    Literary Criticism, edited by Robert L. Hough. 1965.

Bibliography: *Bibliography of the Writings of Poe* by John W. Robertson, 1934; *A Bibliography of First Printings of the Writings of Poe* by C. F. Heartman and J. R. Canny, 1941; *Poe: A Bibliography of Criticism 1827–1967* by J. Lesley Dameron and Irby B. Cauthen, Jr., 1974.

Reading List: *Poe: A Critical Biography* by Arthur H. Quinn, 1941; *Poe: A Critical Study* by Edward H. Davidson, 1957; *The French Face of Poe* by Patrick F. Quinn, 1957; *Poe the Poet: Essays New and Old on the Man and His Work* by Floyd Stovall, 1959; *Poe* by Vincent Buranelli, 1961; *Poe* by Geoffrey Rans, 1965; *The Recognition of Poe: Selected Criticism since 1829* edited by Eric W. Carlson, 1966; *Poe: A Collection of Critical Essays* edited by Robert Regan, 1967; *Poe, Journalist and Critic* by Robert D. Jacobs, 1969; *Poe Poe Poe Poe Poe Poe Poe* by Daniel Hoffman, 1972; *Poe's Fiction: Romantic Irony in the Gothic Tales* by G. R. Thompson, 1973; *Poe* by David Sinclair, 1977; *The Tell-Tale Heart: The Life and Works of Poe* by Julian Symons, 1978.

*   *   *

Although Edgar Allan Poe wrote that for him "poetry has been not a purpose but a passion," he wrote only some fifty poems (excluding his album verses, jingles, and acrostics). Obliged to work at drudging journalism, he never realized his dream of founding a literary magazine of his own. While grinding out scores of reviews of some of the most forgettable books of the nineteenth century he wrote the tales, poems, and essays on which his posthumous renown is based. Aiming his work "not above the popular, nor below the critical, taste," he made use, as a professional magazinist must, of the fictional conventions of his day, turning to his own obsessive needs the Gothic horror story ("Ligeia," "The Fall of the House of Usher," "Berenice") and the tale of exploration ("A Descent into the Maelstrom," *Narrative of Arthur Gordon Pym*). In "The Gold Bug," "The Murders in the Rue Morgue," and "The Purloined Letter" he virtually invented the modern detective story, and he set the mold upon science fiction with "Mesmeric Revelations," "The Facts in the Case of Monsieur Valdemar," and "The Balloon Hoax." He also wrote dozens of satirical sketches. His critical writings were the most systematic and intelligent produced in America until his time.

Despite the paucity of his productions as a poet, he proved a major influence upon Baudelaire, who translated several of his tales and wrote that if Poe had not existed, he would have had to invent him. Through Baudelaire, Poe's critical theories influenced the entire French Symbolist movement. Although Poe believed, with Tennyson, that imprecision of meaning was necessary for the creation of beauty, he also believed that the poet is a deliberate maker who devises all of his effects to contribute to the single aim of his poem. "The Philosophy of Composition," an essay purporting to demonstrate how Poe wrote "The Raven," presents the creative process as an interlocked series of conscious choices. Although this would seem the opposite of the Romantic view of the poet as inspired seer, Poe's systematic process is in fact determined by Romantic necessity and is derived from Coleridge's aesthetic. That necessity is the excitation of the soul through the contemplation of the most melancholy of subjects – the death of a beautiful woman. The complex interaction in this theory between obsessive emotional need and what Poe is his detective stories called "ratiocination" is characteristic of all of his best work.

It seems ironic and cruel that a writer whose tales of guilt and terror won him the admiration of Dostoevsky had to live a hand-to-mouth existence and, after his death, was defamed by a hostile editor and reviled by readers who took as autobiographical the characters in his tales who were opium fiends and necrophiliacs. Allen Tate (in his essay "The Angelic Imagination") identifies what it is in Poe's work that really set on edge Victorian sensibility: the lack of any God save impersonal force, a fictive world without Christian morality. Far more evocatively than in the naturalistic novels of fifty years later, Poe imagined the nightmare of a universe without the consolations of faith.

This visionary author's life was unmitigatedly wretched. His parents were itinerant actors; the alcoholic father deserted, leaving Elizabeth Arnold Poe with three infant children. A brother and sister of Edgar's were adopted by connections in Baltimore but she kept young Eddie by her as she acted the heroine in plays no more melodramatic than his life would be. Stricken by tuberculosis, she died a lingering death in Richmond, Virginia, attended by kindly local matrons, when Edgar was only three. The boy was taken into the home of John Allan, a prosperous tobacco factor who brought Edgar to England when his business took him there and sent the boy to the school so vividly remembered in "William Wilson." Allan sent Poe to the new University of Virginia where, on a niggardly allowance among the scions of wealthy families, he ran up gambling debts and was expelled. Mrs. Allan, like Poe's natural mother, died of tuberculosis, and Poe, who had no inclination for the tobacco business, quarreled with his "Pa" (he had discovered Allan's infidelities while his wife was still alive). Allan withheld love from Edgar, never adopted him, and so Poe was cast adrift penniless to make his way as an author. Not even a hitch in the army or a later enlistment in the military academy at West Point mollified Allan. Poe, deciding to leave West Point, could not persuade "Pa" to intercede for his release and had to feign illness until he was expelled. By this time he had published two volumes of poems. One is dedicated to the Corps of Cadets.

Poe's career henceforth was as assistant or principal editor on several magazines in Richmond, Philadelphia, and New York. While so engaged, he wrote nearly 90 tales and sketches, countless critical columns and reviews, two novellas, and an astrophysical treatise on the nature of the universe, entitled *Eureka*, which he described as a poem.

Poe married his first cousin Virginia Clemm when she was thirteen and lived with her and her mother (his aunt) until Virginia, too, died of tuberculosis at twenty-three. Thereafter Poe conducted frenzied courtships of several poetesses; at this time he well may have been mad with grief. He died in delirium, under unexplained circumstances, on a trip to Baltimore. Poe's biographers agree that he idealized women, and that sexual desire seems not to have had an overt part in any of his relationships.

Poe classified his own fiction into the categories of "Tales of the Grotesque and Arabesque." Borrowing these terms from Scott, Poe meant by them to describe satirical, bizarre, jocose writings on the one hand, and on the other the fictional equivalents of poems. These were his prose efforts to excite his readers' souls by the contemplation of beauty and terror. His review of Hawthorne outlines his theory of fiction. The tale, like the poem, must be all of a piece, each detail contributing to the desired unity of effect; symbolism (Poe in the nomenclature of the day calls it allegory) must be present as a "profound undercurrent" in the tale. His fiction will work by indirection.

In Poe's work there is a mysterious interpenetrability of the soul's excitation with subterranean dread. A *frisson* of horror runs through his most impassioned tales. The clue of Poe's contradictions may be in his sketch "The Imp of the Perverse," for the fiction frequently dramatizes its theme of man's irresistible urge toward self-destruction (a man is driven to commit a terrible crime, then to reveal his guilt). This connects also with the theme of double identity ("William Wilson," "The Cask of Amontillado") and Poe's strain of hoaxing, not entirely confined to his jocular productions. Poe delighted in tricking his readers. He would make them believe that his mesmerizer had really hypnotized a dying man so that the soul lingered and answered questions for months after the death of the body; or that his balloonists had actually crossed the Atlantic in three days, arriving in South Carolina. So too with fantastic descents into the maelstrom and journeys to the end of the earth and back. "The Philosophy of Composition" is in one respect such a hoax. Like his detective genius Monsieur Dupin, Poe demonstrates his intuitive intellectual superiority.

Although only in *Pym* did he write a successful fiction of more than thirty pages, Poe's significance is multifold. He is a systematic critic and theorist predictive of the Symbolist movement. His best poems and fictions embody his aesthetic intention that every part of the literary artifact must contribute to the unifying effect of the whole. His mastery of popular genres made him the unwitting godfather of much popular literature in the present century, as well as a major influence on films. His poetic theory passed from the Symbolists back into American poetry through T. S. Eliot and its influence continues in Allen Tate and Richard Wilbur, among others. His fiction is widely translated and widely read. Poe's work indeed has reached both the popular and the critical taste.

—Daniel Hoffman

RILEY, James Whitcomb. American. Born in Greenfield, Indiana, 7 October 1849. Educated at local schools, and at Greenfield Academy, 1870. Worked as a house- and sign-painter, 1870–71; itinerant entertainer, giving readings and lectures, 1872–75, 1876; worked in his father's law office, 1875–76; lived in Indianapolis from 1879; Journalist, *Indianapolis Journal*, 1879–88; gave annual reading tour of the United States, 1882–1903. Recipient: American Academy of Arts and Letters Gold Medal, 1911. M.A.: Yale University, New Haven, Connecticut, 1902; D.Litt.: University of Philadelphia, 1904; D.L.: Indiana University, Bloomington, 1907. Member, American Academy of Arts and Letters, 1911. *Died 22 July 1916.*

PUBLICATIONS

Collections

> *Letters*, edited by William Lyon Phelps. 1930.

Verse

> *The Old Swimmin'-Hole and 'leven More Poems.* 1883; revised edition, as *Neghborly Poems*, 1891.
> *Afterwhiles.* 1887.
> *Nye and Riley's Railway Guide*, with Edgar Watson Nye. 1888; as *Nye and Riley's Wit and Humor: Poems and Yarns*, 1900.
> *Old-Fashioned Roses.* 1888.
> *Pipes o' Pan at Zekesbury.* 1888.
> *Rhymes of Childhood.* 1890.
> *The Flying Islands of the Night.* 1891.
> *Green Fields and Running Brooks.* 1892.
> *Poems Here at Home.* 1893.
> *Armazindy.* 1894.
> *The Days Gone By and Other Poems.* 1895.
> *A Tinkle of Bells and Other Poems.* 1895.
> *A Child-World.* 1896.
> *Rubáiyát of Doc Sifers.* 1897.
> *The Golden Year*, edited by Clara E. Laughlin. 1898.
> *Riley Love-Lyrics.* 1899.
> *Home-Folks.* 1900.
> *The Book of Joyous Children.* 1902.
> *His Pa's Romance.* 1903.
> *A Defective Santa Claus.* 1904.
> *Riley Songs o' Cheer.* 1905.
> *While the Heart Beats Young.* 1906.
> *Morning.* 1907.
> *The Boys of the Old Glee Club.* 1907.
> *The Riley Baby Book.* 1913; as *Baby Ballads*, 1914.

Fiction

> *The Boss Girl, A Christmas Story, and Other Sketches.* 1885; revised edition, as *Sketches in Prose and Occasional Verses, 1891.*

Other

Poems and Prose Sketches. 16 vols., 1897–1914.
Complete Works, edited by Edmund Henry Eitel. 6 vols., 1913.

Bibliography: *A Bibliography of Riley* by Anthony J. and Dorothy R. Russo, 1944.

Reading List: *Riley, Hoosier Poet* by Jeannette Covert Nolan, 1941; *Hoosier Boy: Riley* by Minnie B. Mitchell, 1942; *Poet of the People: An Evaluation of Riley* by Jeannette Covert Nolan, Horace Gregory, and James T. Farrell, 1951; *Those Innocent Years: The Legacy and Inheritance of a Hero of the Victorian Era, Riley* by Richard Crowder, 1957; *Riley* by Peter Revell, 1970.

* * *

Although James Whitcomb Riley occasionally committed prose, he was pre-eminently a poet – one of the most famous in turn-of-the-century America. Not exactly the household word he once was, Riley remains an important figure in American popular culture; school children continued to learn "Little Orphant Annie" and "The Raggedy Man" well through the 1930's and more than sixty years after his death his work stays in print. He began to write verse in the 1870's, contributing primarily to Indiana newspapers, particularly the Indianapolis *Journal,* on the staff of which he served for years. His verse was widely reprinted and, as his reputation spread, new poems began to appear in newspapers and magazines far from his Indiana base. His first book *The Old Swimmin'-Hole and 'leven More Poems* was published in 1883 and new collections of his periodical verse quickly followed. He issued book-length poems only twice – *The Flying Islands of the Night,* a verse drama so uncharacteristic that his readers rejected it, and the more acceptable *Rubáiyát of Doc Sifers,* written in the Hoosier dialect used in his most popular poems.

He occasionally tried set forms – sonnets, for instance – but he ordinarily worked in rhymed couplets or quatrains, and the subject matter dictated the length of the poems. The stanza forms sometimes vary, and the meter is sometimes irregular, but in most cases these are designed to fit the speaking voice. Riley was as much performer as poet, traveling the country to give readings, and his admirers have always known that his verse fits better in the mouth than on the page. His dialect poems are much more effective than his other verse, which too easily succumbs to conventional poetic diction, as a comparison of "Knee-deep in June" with the sonnet beginning "O queenly month of indolent repose!" will show.

Riley wrote many happy poems – evocations of nature and recollections of childhood – but popular taste has always been as lugubrious as it is sentimental, and Riley, whose own despondency found an answering chord in his audience, fills his work with broken toys and broken hearts, dead children and cheerful cripples, lost days, lost joys, "lost sunshine/Of youth." He offers the consolation of Heaven or of time which lets one taste "the sweet/Of honey in the saltest tear." It is pain not comfort, however, that gives Riley his best images, as in the old man who wants to "strip to the soul,/And dive off in my grave like the old swimmin'-hole" or the speaker in "A Summer's Day" who longs to "spread/Out like molasses on the bed,/And jest drip off the aidges in/The dreams that never comes ag'in." Riley's triumph as a popular poet is that he gave a great deal of pleasure to a great many people over a great many years, but all his readers know, as they wink back the happy tears, that

> the Gobble-uns'll git you
> Ef you
> Don't
> Watch
> Out!

—Gerald Weales

ROWSON, Susanna (née Haswell).   English.   Born in Portsmouth, Hampshire, in 1762;
grew up in Massachusetts where her father, a naval officer, was stationed; returned with her
family to England, 1778. Educated privately. Married William Rowson in 1786. Full-time
writer, 1786 until her husband went bankrupt, 1792; appeared with him on the stage, in
Edinburgh, 1792–93, and with the Philadelphia Company, for which she also wrote, in
Philadelphia, Baltimore, and Annapolis, Maryland, 1793–96; wrote and acted for the Federal
Street Theatre Company, Boston, 1796–97; Founder and teacher at a young ladies' academy
in Boston, 1797–1822; Editor, *Boston Weekly Magazine*, 1802–05. President, Boston
Fatherless and Widows Association. *Died 2 March 1824.*

Fiction

Victoria.   1786.
The Inquisitor; or, Invisible Rambler.   1788.
The Test of Honour.   1789.
Charlotte: A Tale of Truth.   1791; as *Charlotte Temple*, 1794; edited by Clara M. and
    Rudolf Kirk, 1964; edited by William S. Kable, in *Three Early American Novels*,
    1970.
Mentoria; or, The Young Lady's Friend.   1791.
Rebecca; or, The Fille de Chambre.   1792; as *The Fille de Chambre*, 1793.
Trials of the Human Heart.   1795.
Reuben and Rachel; or, Tales of Old Times.   1798.
Sarah; or, The Exemplary Wife.   1813.
Charlotte's Daughter; or, The Three Orphans.   1828; as *Lucy Temple: One of the Three
    Orphans*, 1842 (?).
Love and Romance: Charlotte and Lucy Temple.   1854.

Plays

Slaves in Algiers; or, A Struggle for Freedom, music by Alexander Reinagle.   1794.
The Female Patriot; or, Nature's Rights, from the play *The Bondman* by Philip
    Massinger (produced 1795).
The Volunteers: A Musical Entertainment, music by Alexander Reinagle (produced
    1795).   1795.
Americans in England; or, Lessons for Daughters (produced 1797).   1796; as *The
    Columbian Daughters; or, Americans in England* (produced 1800).
The American Tar (produced 1796).
Hearts of Oak, from the work by John Till Allingham (produced 1810–11?).

Verse

Poems on Various Subjects.   1788.
*A Trip to Parnassus; or, The Judgment of Apollo on Dramatic Authors and
    Performers.*   1788.
The Standard of Liberty: A Poetical Address.   1795.
Miscellaneous Poems.   1804.

Other

An Abridgement of Universal Geography, Together with Sketches of History.   1805.
A Spelling Dictionary.   1807.
A Present for Young Ladies (miscellany).   1811.
Youth's First Step in Geography.   1818.
Biblical Dialogues Between a Father and His Family.   1822.
Exercises in History, Chronology, and Biography, in Question and Answer.   1822.

Bibliography: "Rowson, The Author of *Charlotte Temple*: A Bibliographical Study" by R. W. G. Vail, in *Proceedings of the American Antiquarian Society 42*, April–October 1932.

Reading List: *Rowson, America's First Best-Selling Novelist* by Ellen B. Brandt, 1975; *In Defense of Women: Rowson* by Dorothy Weil, 1976.

*   *   *

Because of the popularity, variety, and number of Susanna Rowson's books, she may properly be considered the foremost woman of letters of her generation in the United States. The phenomenal success on both sides of the Atlantic of her novel *Charlotte Temple* has tended to obscure her other considerable accomplishments, but she also wrote other novels and a large number of plays, poetry, textbooks, and miscellanies which defy classification. Her literary career is even more remarkable in light of her prominence in her other occupations, those of actress and educator. She has the distinction of being not only one of America's first professional women but also one of the first advocates of women's rights in the United States.

Charlotte: A Tale of Truth has gone through over 200 editions since it was first published in 1791 and was, according to R. W. G. Vail, "the most popular of all early American novels." While detractors have dismissed it as being sentimental and formulaic, supporters have accounted for its popularity by insisting on its forthright realism within the sentimental convention. Rowson herself claimed that the story of seduction and betrayal is an actual one, and in the early 1800's the gravestone of the purported model, Charlotte Stanley, was changed to "Charlotte Temple." It still may be seen in Trinity Churchyard in New York City. No other novel by Rowson can approach the popularity of this best seller, but others were highly regarded, notably *The Fille de Chambre* and *Reuben and Rachel.*

One of her few extant plays, *Slaves in Algiers* is the first successfully produced play by a woman in America. A musical comedy, written in collaboration with Alexander Reinagle, it is of topical interest in that it was a protest against the capture of American ships off the Barbary coast from 1785 to 1794. The play is notable for its fervent nationalism and the insistence upon the equality of women in the new nation. Although it was well-received by play-goers, William Cobbett roundly attacked it for its feminist sentiments.

Rowson's poems and songs were not critically well-received, and today they seem florid and derivative. Nevertheless many of them were immensely popular, especially "America, Commerce, and Freedom." Her textbooks and miscellanies are of only historical interest today. In spite of her significant contributions to American letters, little critical attention has been paid her until quite recently, but two new studies of her career suggest that her work is worthy of serious consideration.

—Nancy C. Joyner

SALTUS, Edgar (Evertson). American. Born in New York City, 8 October 1855. Educated at St. Paul's School, Concord, New Hampshire; studied briefly at Yale University, New Haven, Connecticut, the Sorbonne, Paris, University of Heidelberg, and University of Munich, 1872–76; Columbia University Law School, New York, 1876–80, LL.B. 1880, but never practiced law. Married 1) Helen Sturgis Read in 1883 (divorced, 1891); 2) Elsie Welsh Smith in 1895 (separated, 1901; died, 1911), one daughter; 3) Marie Giles in 1911. Settled in New York; writer from 1884; worked as an editor and compiler for P. F. Collier and Son, publishers, in the late 1890's. *Died 31 July 1921.*

PUBLICATIONS

Fiction

Mr. Incoul's Misadventure. 1887.
The Truth about Tristrem Varick. 1888.
Eden. 1888.
A Transaction in Hearts. 1889.
A Transient Guest and Other Episodes. 1889.
The Pace That Kills. 1889.
Mary Magdalen. 1891.
Imperial Purple. 1892.
The Facts in the Curious Case of H. Hyrtl, Esq. 1892.
Madame Sapphira: A Fifth Avenue Story. 1893.
Enthralled: A Story of International Life. 1894.
When Dreams Come True: A Story of Emotional Life. 1894.
Purple and Fine Women. 1903.
The Perfume of Eros: A Fifth Avenue Incident. 1905.
Vanity Square: A Story of Fifth Avenue Life. 1906.
Daughters of the Rich. 1909.
The Monster. 1912.
The Paliser Case. 1919.
The Ghost Girl, edited by Marie Saltus. 1922.

Verse

Poppies and Mandragora, edited by Marie Saltus. 1926.

Other

Balzac. 1884.
The Philosophy of Disenchantment. 1885.
The Anatomy of Negation. 1886.
Love and Lore. 1890.
The Pomps of Satan (essays). 1904.
Historia Amoris, A History of Love. 1906.
The Lords of the Ghostland: A History of the Ideal. 1907.
Oscar Wilde: An Idler's Impression. 1917.
The Gardens of Aphrodite. 1920.
The Imperial Orgy: An Account of the Tsars from the First to the Last. 1920.

Parnassians Personally Encountered, edited by Marie Saltus.   1923.
The Uplands of Dream (essays and poems), edited by Charles Honce.   1925.
Victor Hugo, and Golgotha: Two Essays, edited by Marie Saltus.   1925.

Editor, *The Lovers of the World*.   3 vols., n.d.

Translator, *After-Dinner Stories from Balzac*.   1886.
Translator, *Tales Before Supper from Gautier and Merimée*.   1887.

Reading List: *Saltus, The Man* by Marie Saltus, 1925; *Saltus* by Claire Sprague, 1968.

*   *   *

In 1884 Edgar Saltus began his literary career with *Balzac*, an introductory study which witnesses to his predominantly European culture. This was followed by his elegant popularisations of German contemporary pessimists, Schopenhauer and Hartmann, in *The Philosophy of Disenchantment* and *The Anatomy of Negation*. His first novel, *Mr. Incoul's Misadventure*, inaugurates the first, most successful phase of his fiction.

In 1891 Saltus published *Mary Magdalen*, reportedly originating in conversations with Oscar Wilde, the first of his impressionist quasi-histories. *Imperial Purple*, high-coloured portraits of the Roman emperors from Caesar to Heliogabalus, was deservedly popular, but the attempted emulation in *Imperial Orgy*, which presented the Russian Czars from Ivan the Terrible to Nicholas "the last," is considerably less achieved.

Mr. Incoul's Misadventure, in fact, is typical of Saltus's novels, with its pessimism, self-conscious style, occasional authentic glimpses of upper class life, melodramatic themes, and loose plotting: a millionaire coldly and ingeniously revenges himself on his wife and the man who loves her. *The Truth about Tristram Varick*, is more lucid in structure, with a "point of view" presented by the hero, though the incidents are hardly less melodramatic. *Eden* is less successful, but introduces us to what was to become Saltus's standard types of women: blonde Eve and darkly passionate, "fatal" Lilith. *A Transaction in Hearts* has an interesting "new" woman and a powerful story line. *The Pace That Kills* has a suicidal villain-hero who is a less attractive version of Incoul, while *Enthralled* is an extravaganza owing something to Hugo and Wilde's *The Picture of Dorian Gray*. In *When Dreams Come True*, a *bildungsroman* of sorts, Saltus breaks through his own sterotypes – the "fatal woman" emerges as a witty and balanced wife – and produces his best novel. The relationship with his first wife, from whom he was divorced in 1891, underlies his virulent novel *Madame Sapphira*.

The later novels are less satisfying. *The Perfume of Eros*, the best of them, memorably portrays a slum child for whom the wages of sin are success; a charming flapper is killed off when her moral situation threatens to become too complex. *Vanity Square* promises that critique of a cultured and bored society Saltus was well endowed to write, but, though embodying entertaining discussion of ideas, disentegrates into fable. In *Daughters of the Rich* Saltus moves from New York to Southern California, but it is inhabited by the familiar Saltus types and situations: "new" women, murder, and misunderstandings in love. Incest, duels, two unconsummated marriages, theosophy, and mildly Wildean wit hardly redeem *The Monster*. *The Paliser Case* is a faded version of *The Perfume of Eros*, and *The Ghost Girl* a mediocre Gothic novel.

Saltus's sometimes amusing short stories were written largely for popular consumption and are more melodramatic in plot and exotic in setting than the novels. The poetry was collected in *Poppies and Mandragora*; chiselled in a Parnassian manner, it faintly recalls Hérédia. The brief essay *The Gardens of Aphrodite*, which discusses the god of love as Eros-Don Juan, is interesting in itself and for the light it casts on Saltus's fiction. *Lords of the Ghostland* examines the major religions of the world, introducing theosophy for the first time. *Oscar Wilde: An Idler's Impression* agreeably records a friendship, mainly through reported conversations. French literature is the subject of *Parnassians Personally Encountered* and *Victor Hugo and Golgotha*; Saltus also translated Balzac, Mérimée, and Gautier.

Saltus's importance is largely that of populariser of European *fin de siècle* modes and topics in the United States. He produced no masterpiece, but his pessimism, determinism, use of fable, allegory, and paradox suggest a poor man's Oscar Wilde, a Wilde without the drama, but a dweller in a high, slightly flashy Bohemia.

—Ian Fletcher

SEDGWICK, Catharine Maria. American. Born in Stockbridge, Massachusetts, 28 December 1789. Educated at the district school, and at boarding schools in Boston and Albany, New York; also received private instruction in several languages. Lived in Albany and New York City, 1807–13; returned to Stockbridge, 1813; later lived in Lenox, Massachusetts, and New York; writer from 1822; travelled in Europe, 1839–40, and in the American Midwest, 1854. Active in the work of the Unitarian Church, and the Women's Prison Association of New York. *Died 31 July 1867.*

PUBLICATIONS

Fiction

A New-England Tale; or, Sketches of New England Character and Manners. 1822; revised edition, as *A New England Tale, and Miscellanies,* 1852.
Redwood. 1824.
The Travellers. 1825.
Hope Leslie; or, Early Times in the Massachusetts. 1827.
Clarence; or, A Tale of Our Own Times. 1830.
The Linwoods; or, "Sixty Years Since" in America. 1835.
Home. 1835.
Tales and Sketches. 2 vols., 1835–44.
Live and Let Live; or, Domestic Service Illustrated. 1837.
Wilton Harvey. 1845.
The Boy of Mount Rhigi (juvenile). 1848.
Married or Single? 1857.
The Poor Rich Man and the Rich Poor Man. 1864.

Other

Means and Ends; or, Self-Training. 1839.
Letters from Abroad to Kindred at Home. 1841.
Morals of Manners; or, Hints for Our Young People. 1846.
Facts and Manners for School-Day Reading. 1848.
The Works. 3 vols., 1849.
Memoir of Joseph Curtis, A Model Man. 1858.

Reading List: *Life and Letters* edited by Mary E. Dewey, 1871.

*   *   *

The novels of Catharine Maria Sedgwick, the best of which include *Redwood* and *Hope Leslie*, are distinguished by close attention to realistic detail, especially regional customs and manners. They utilize American scenery, manners, customs, and materials, and are usually centered on moral circumstances of especially American interest. *Redwood*, for example, contrasts a Northern and a Southern family. *Hope Leslie* is set in Puritan New England, and aspects of New England history, scenery, and manners are finely detailed. In *The Linwoods*, the tensions that resulted in the American Revolution are dramatized in the conflicts between a family of colonists and a family of royalists. *Clarence* demonstrates the value of a natural aristocracy, an aristocracy of talent and virtue such as projected by Thomas Jefferson, over an aristocracy based solely on birth and wealth. *A New-England Tale*, the first of Sedgwick's novels, is partially a religious tract attacking the remnants of Calvinism in New England, and *Married or Single?* is one of the earliest feminist American pleas for socially equitable treatment of women.

Sedgwick's moral preoccupations are largely tied to social and political concerns of her day, and while these moral concerns are in many instances now of little interest (as well as obscure to readers without training in American social and political history), her novels have continuing literary value among the earliest and the best examples of regionalism in American writing. Sedgwick had an acute ear for American dialect and a fine sense of regional customs and manners. As a literary stylist, she was not especially remarkable, although superior to most of her contemporary American writers, but she was capable of detailing with precision regional characteristics, landscapes, and dialect. Furthermore, alone among her contemporary American novelists, she was capable of creating credible women in fiction. While it was common for American novelists to portray women as ideally (if improbably) passive and unambitious, Sedgwick portrayed heroines who were morally superior; all of her novels center on women whose superior moral judgment places them far above others – particularly men.

—Edward Halsey Foster

SHAW, Henry Wheeler. Pseudonym: Josh Billings.   American.   Born in Lanesboro, Massachusetts, 21 April 1818. Educated at the Lenox Preparatory School, Massachusetts; Hamilton College, Clinton, New York, 1833–34. Married Zilpha Bradford in 1845. Worked at odd jobs in the Midwest, 1835–45, and in the East, 1845–54; settled in Poughkeepsie, New York, 1854; auctioneer and realtor in Poughkeepsie, 1854–66; Alderman, 1858; writer from 1859; contributed to the *Poughkeepsie Daily Press* from 1860; lecturer from 1863; contributed to the *New York Weekly*, 1867–85, and *Century Magazine*, 1884–85. *Died 14 October 1885.*

PUBLICATIONS

Collections

Complete Works.   1888.
Uncle Sam's Uncle Josh, edited by Donald Day.   1953.

Prose

Josh Billings, Hiz Sayings.   1865.
Josh Billings on Ice, and Other Things.   1868.
Josh Billings' Farmers' Allminax for the Year 1870.   1870 (and later volumes to 1879);
    1870–79 sequence published in 1 vol., 1902.
*Everybody's Friend; or, Josh Billings's Encyclopedia and Proverbial Philosophy of Wit
    and Humor.*   1874.
Josh Billings, His Works Complete.   1876.
Josh Billings' Trump Kards: Blue Grass Philosophy.   1877.
Complete Comical Writings.   1877.
Old Probability: Perhaps Rain − Perhaps Not.   1879.
Josh Billings' Cook Book and Piktorial Proverbs.   1880.
Josh Billings Struggling with Things.   1881.
Josh Billings' Spice Box.   1881.

Reading List: *Shaw (Billings)* by David B. Kesterson, 1973.

*   *   *

Farmer, boatman, explorer, real-estate salesman, auctioneer, Henry Wheeler Shaw turned
to writing in his middle age and leapt into national prominence in America with an "Essa on
the Muel bi Josh Billings" ("The Muel is haf hoss and haf Jackass, and then kums to a full
stop, natur diskovering her mistake"). He took a pen name but avoided the topical subjects of
his contemporaries. Unfortunately for the modern reader, he did adopt the comic device of
atrocious spelling, then considered in America to be a sure-fire laugh-getter. As with the Irish
dialect of Finley Peter Dunne's "Mr. Dooley," however, it is often worth the extra effort in
reading, for Josh Billings's cracker-barrel philosophy and "trump-kard" aphorisms are
frequently hilarious. It's worth the trouble to meet characters such as Mehitable Saffron, "the
virgin-hero ov wimmins' rights ... she spoke without notes, at arms' length."
    Max Eastman declared that Josh Billings was "the father of imagism" and found nothing
in New England poetry before Billings's time "quite comparable to his statement that goats
'know the way up a rock as natural as woodbine,' which is Homeric." Certainly Billings is a
primitive La Bruyère, a rustic La Rochefoucauld, and an aphorist with a moralistic rather
than a cynical streak. "Most people repent ov their sins bi thanking God they aint so wicked
as their nabers." He stressed that "yu hav tew be wise before yu kan be witty" and there is
plenty of wisdom in such comments as "There may cum a time when the Lion and the Lamb
will lie down together − i shall be as glad to see it as enny body − but i am still betting on the
Lion."

—Leonard R. N. Ashley

SIMMS, William Gilmore.   American.   Born in Charleston, South Carolina, 17 April
1806. Educated in public and private schools in Charleston; apprenticed to a druggist, then
studied law; admitted to the South Carolina bar, 1827. Married 1) Anna Malcolm Giles in
1826 (died, 1832); 2) Chevillette Roach in 1836 (died, 1863); at least 15 children. Practiced
law in Charleston from 1827, but subsequently gave up law for literature; Editor, *Charleston
City Gazette*, 1830–32; visited the North and formed friendship with William Cullen Bryant;

settled in New Haven, 1833; returned to Charleston, 1835; divided his time between his wife's family home, Woodlands Plantation, Barnwell County, and Charleston, from 1836; Editor, *Southern Quarterly Review*, 1849–54; advocate of slavery: lectured in New York, 1856; after the Civil War wrote serials for magazines in New York and Philadelphia. *Died 11 June 1870.*

PUBLICATIONS

Collections

The Letters, edited by Mary C. Simms Oliphant, Alfred Taylor Odell, and T. C. Duncan Eaves. 5 vols., 1952–56; supplement, 1977.
Writings, edited by John C. Guilds. 1969–

Fiction

The Book of My Lady: A Melange (stories). 1833.
Martin Faber: The Story of a Criminal. 1833; in *Writings 5,* 1974.
Guy Rivers: A Tale of Georgia. 1834.
The Yemassee: A Romance of Carolina. 1835; edited by C. Hugh Holman, 1961.
The Partisan: A Tale of the Revolution. 1835.
Mellichampe: A Legend of the Santee. 1836.
Richard Hurdis; or, The Avenger of Blood. 1838.
Pelayo: A Story of the Goth. 1838.
Carl Werner: An Imaginative Story, with Other Tales. 1838; in *Writings 5,* 1974.
The Damsel of Darien. 1839.
Border Beagles: A Tale of Mississippi. 1840.
The Kinsmen; or, The Black Riders of Congaree. 1841; as *The Scout,* 1854.
Confession; or, The Blind Heart: A Domestic Story. 1841.
Beauchampe; or, The Kentucky Tragedy. 1842; portion revised, as *Charlemont; or, The Pride of the Village,* 1856.
Castle Dismal; or, The Bachelor's Christmas: A Dramatic Legend. 1844.
The Prima Donna: A Passage from City Life. 1844; in *Writings 5,* 1974.
Helen Halsey; or, The Swamp State of Conelachita: A Tale of the Borders. 1845; as *The Island Bride,* 1869.
Count Julian; or, The Last Days of the Goth. 1845.
The Wigwam and the Cabin (stories). 2 vols., 1845–46; as *Life in America,* 1848.
The Lily and the Totem; or, The Huguenots in Florida. 1850.
Flirtation at the Moultrie House. 1850; in *Writings 5,* 1974.
Katharine Walton; or, The Rebel of Dorchester. 1851.
The Golden Christmas: A Chronicle of St. John's, Berkeley. 1852.
The Sword and the Distaff; or, "Fair, Fat, and Forty." 1852; revised edition, as *Woodcraft; or, Hawks about the Dovecote,* 1854.
As Good as a Comedy; or, The Tennesseean's Story. 1852; in *Writings 3,* 1972.
Marie De Berniere (stories). 1853; as *The Maroon: A Legend of the Caribbees, and Other Stories,* 1855.
Vasconselos: A Romance of the New World. 1853.
Southward Ho! A Spell of Sunshine. 1854.
The Forayers; or, The Raid of the Dog-Days. 1855.
Eutaw. 1856.

The Cassique of Kiawah.   1859.
Cavalier of Old South Carolina: Simms's Captain Porgy, edited by Hugh W. Hetherington, 1966.
Voltmeier; or, The Mountain Men, edited by James B. Meriwether, in *Writings 1.*   1969.
Joscelyn: A Tale of the Revolution, edited by Keen Butterworth, in *Writings 16.*   1975.

Verse

Monody on the Death of General Charles Cotesworth Pinckney.   1825.
Lyrical and Other Poems.   1827.
Early Lays.   1827.
The Vision of Cortes, Cain, and Other Poems.   1829.
The Tri-Color; or, The Three Days of Blood in Paris.   1830.
Atalantis: A Story of the Sea.   1832.
Southern Passages and Pictures.   1839.
Donna Florida.   1843.
Grouped Thoughts and Scattered Fancies.   1845.
Areytos; or, Songs of the South.   1846.
Lays of the Palmetto.   1848.
Charleston and Her Satirists: A Scribblement.   1848.
The Cassique of Accabee, A Tale of Ashley River, with Other Pieces.   1849.
Sabbath Lyrics; or, Songs from Scripture.   1849.
The City of the Silent.   1850.
Norman Maurice; or, The Man of the People.   1851.
Michael Bonham; or, The Fall of Bexar.   1852.
Poems: Descriptive, Dramatic, Legendary, and Contemplative.   1853.

Other

The Remains of Maynard Davis Richardson.   1833.
Slavery in America.   1838.
The History of South Carolina.   1840.
The Geography of South Carolina.   1843.
The Life of Francis Marion.   1844.
Views and Reviews in American Literature, History, and Fiction.   1845; edited by C. Hugh Holman, 1962.
The Life of Captain John Smith.   1846.
The Life of the Chevalier Bayard.   1847.
The Life of Nathanael Greene.   1849.
Father Abbott; or, The Home Tourist.   1849.
South Carolina in the Revolutionary War.   1853.
Egeria; or, Voices of Thought and Counsel for the Woods and Wayside.   1853.
Works.   20 vols., 1853–66.
Sack and Destruction of the City of Columbia, S.C.   1865; edited by A. S. Salley, 1937.

Editor, *The Charleston Book: A Miscellany in Prose and Verse.*   1845.
Editor, *War Poetry of the South.*   1867.

Bibliography: *A Bibliography of the Separate Writings of Simms* by Oscar Wegelin, 1941.

Reading List: *Simms* by William P. Trent, 1892; *Simms as Literary Critic* by Edd Winfield Parks, 1961; *Simms* by Joseph V. Ridgely, 1962.

The most versatile and representative Southern writer of the 19th century and one of the more talented American writers of the period, William Gilmore Simms tried his hand at many literary forms and tasks. He published at least four biographies, the best of which, *The Life of Francis Marion*, is a consideration of sources and materials also used in several of his long fictions on the Revolution. He also wrote books on the geography and history of South Carolina.

Simms was early and late a journalist. He edited both newspapers and magazines and eventually possessed considerable influence, especially in the South, as editor and contributor of essays and criticism to such journals as the *Southern Literary Gazette, Southern Literary Messenger, Southern Literary Journal, Southern Quarterly Review*, and *Russell's Magazine*. He also contributed to many of the most consequential Northern magazines, including the *Knickerbocker, Democratic Review, Graham's, Harper's New Monthly*, and *Lippincott's*. Some of his best periodical criticism is collected in *Views and Reviews*, but, as Edd W. Parks has noted in *William Gilmore Simms as Literary Critic* (1961), there is also important criticism in prefaces and advertisements to novels and in letters. In the Advertisement to *The Yemassee* in 1835, for example, Simms elaborated on a distinction between the romance and the novel that allowed the writer of the former considerable latitude in the treatment of the possible and the probable; in long critical essays he discoursed learnedly on Cooper's writings in 1842 (and gave his chief American rival every bit of his due), and in 1845 he dealt effectively with "Americanism in Literature"; and in letters in 1842 and thereafter he discussed perceptively the place of realism in fiction and fairly characterized Poe as magazinist, story writer, and poet. Simms's letters have recently assumed their rightful place in any study of his canon as a result of their publication in five volumes (1952–1956), with a sixth supplementary volume.

Simms also wrote a number of plays, including two in blank verse (*Norman Maurice* and *Michael Bonham*), and his view of his own merit as a poet is indicated in a remark in a letter of 24 November 1853 that his "poetical work exhibits the highest phase of the Imaginative faculty which this Country has yet exhibited, and the most philosophical in connection with it." Few, including his friends Paul Hamilton Hayne and Henry Timrod, agreed with him then or subsequently.

Over the years, however, most critics have agreed that Simms's chief contribution was to the novel. This is still largely the case when one considers the size and scope of his accomplishment in the seven books of the Revolutionary Romances (1835–1856) or observes carefully the achievement in such individual works as *The Yemassee, Border Beagles, Katharine Walton, Woodcraft*, or *The Cassique of Kiawah*. But Simms was a significant writer of short fiction, and John C. Guilds maintains in his introduction to *Stories and Tales* (Volume 5 of the Centennial Edition of the Writings) that the "short story or tale" is Simms's "best genre," and the contents of this edition plus the better-known tales of the two volumes of *The Wigwam and the Cabin* clearly show that Simms did indeed make a consequential and varied contribution to short fiction.

Simms's versatility and prolificness, to say nothing of the adverse reaction of Northern readers to his political views during the Civil War and its aftermath, assuredly contributed to the decline in his literary reputation, which reached its nadir with World War II. With, however, studies of C. Hugh Holman in the late 1940's and thereafter, the edition of letters in the 1950's (including especially the critical evaluation of Simms's best work by Donald Davidson), the appraisal of Simms as man of letters by Jay B. Hubbell in *The South in American Literature* in 1954, and the beginning of the publication of the Centennial Edition, Simms's work has received and is continuing to receive the attention it has long merited.

—Rayburn S. Moore

SMITH, Seba. Pseudonym: Major Jack Downing. American. Born in Buckfield, Maine, 14 September 1792; moved with his family to Bridgton, Maine, 1799. Educated at a school in Bridgton; Bowdoin College, Brunswick, Maine, 1815–18, B.A. (honors) 1818. Married Elizabeth Oakes Prince (the writer Elizabeth Oakes Smith) in 1823; five children. Taught school in Portland, Maine, 1818–19; travelled in the South, and in Europe, 1819–20; Assistant Editor, *Eastern Argus*, Portland, 1820–26; Founding Editor, *Portland Courier*, 1829–34 (wrote Downing letters for the paper from 1830); wrote for various periodicals from 1834; moved to New York, 1842; Editor, *Rover*, 1843–45, and Emerson's *United States Magazine*, 1854–59; founded the *Great Republic* magazine, 1859; retired to Patchogue, Long Island, 1860. *Died 29 July 1868.*

PUBLICATIONS

Fiction

The Life and Writings of Major Jack Downing of Downingville. 1833.
Letters Written During the President's Tour "Down East." 1833.
The Select Letters of Major Jack Downing. 1834.
John Smith's Letters, with "Picters" to Match. 1839.
May-Day in New York; or, House-Hunting and Moving. 1845.
Dew-Drops of the Nineteenth Century. 1846.
'Way Down East; or, Portraitures of Yankee Life. 1854.
My Thirty Years Out of the Senate. 1859.
Speech of John Smith, Not Given. 1864.

Verse

Powhalan: A Metrical Romance. 1841.

Other

New Elements of Geometry. 1850.

Reading List: *Smith* by Milton and Patricia Rickels, 1977.

* * *

Jack Downing, the creation of Seba Smith, is the prototype of the Yankee critic and humourist, a racy character set against the rustic and picturesque New England background, yet clever enough to serve as confidant of an American President. This pattern of humour paved the way for such homey critics and philosophers as Sam Slick, Hosea Biglow, and Will Rogers.

Smith launched his Jack Downing in the *Portland Courier*, his own newspaper, the first daily to be issued in Maine, in 1830. Jack takes on the guise of a Yankee adventurer who left his native village of Downingville to trade in Portland. From bartering and bargaining, Jack turned to politics and wrote humorous accounts of his career and partners to the family back home. The Downing letters enjoyed a wide circulation in New England, which encouraged Smith to widen his horizons, so he sent Jack to Washington where he becomes counselor to the President. What poured from his pen was a scathing but humorous satire of Jacksonian Democracy. Singled out for criticism was the horde of job seekers that descended on Washington as well as the folly and disaster of land speculation and the national bank. One of the prime targets for his sarcastic venom was the Mexican War. Jack bitingly remarks to General Pierce: "Uncle Joshua always says, in nine cases out of ten, it costs more to rob an orchard than it would be to buy the apples."

His last series of Downing letters appeared under the title *My Thirty Years Out of the Senate*, a parody of Thomas Hart Benton's *Thirty Years View*. He also wrote a collection of tales on Yankee customs, *'Way Down East*.

—Dominic J. Bisignano

STOWE, Harriet (Elizabeth) Beecher.   American.   Born in Litchfield, Connecticut, 14 June 1811. Educated in the local dame school, and at Hartford, Connecticut Female Seminary, 1824. Married Reverend Calvin Ellis Stowe in 1836 (died. 1886); seven children. Moved with her family to Cincinnati, 1832; contributed sketches to the *Western Monthly Magazine* and *The Mayflower*; moved to Brunswick, Maine, 1850; became ardent abolitionist; full-time writer from 1850; famous and controversial as a writer from publication of *Uncle Tom's Cabin*, 1852; lived in Andover, Massachusetts, then Hartford, Connecticut, and Mandarin, Florida, from 1852; visited England three times, and toured the Continent; a friend of Lady Byron, George Eliot, and Ruskin; contributed to the *Atlantic Monthly*, New York *Independent*, and the *Christian Union*. Died 1 July 1896.

PUBLICATIONS

Collections

   The Writings.   16 vols., 1896.
   Collected Poems, edited by John Michael Moran, Jr.   1967.

Fiction

   Prize Tale: A New England Sketch.   1834.
   The Mayflower: or, Sketches of Scenes and Characters among the Descendants of the Pilgrims.   1843; augmented edition, 1855.
   Uncle Tom's Cabin; or, Life among the Lowly.   1852; edited by Kenneth S. Lynn, 1962.
   Uncle Sam's Emancipation (stories).   1853.
   Dred: A Tale of the Great Dismal Swamp.   1856; as *Nina Gordon*, 1866.
   The Minister's Wooing.   1859.
   Agnes of Sorrento.   1862.
   The Pearl of Orr's Island: A Story of the Coast of Maine.   1862.
   Daisy's First Winter and Other Stories.   1867.
   Oldtown Folks.   1869; edited by Henry F. May, 1966.
   My Wife and I; or, Harry Henderson's History.   1871.

Pink and White Tyranny: A Society Novel. 1871.
Sam Lawson's Oldtown Fireside Stories. 1872.
We and Our Neighbors; or, The Records of an Unfashionable Street. 1875.
Poganuc People: Their Loves and Lives. 1878.

Play

The Christian Slave, from her own novel *Uncle Tom's Cabin.* 1855.

Verse

Religious Poems. 1867.

Other

An Elementary Geography. 1835.
A Key to Uncle Tom's Cabin. 1853.
Sunny Memories of Foreign Lands. 2 vols., 1854.
The Two Altars; or, Two Pictures in One. 1855.
Geography for My Children. 1855.
Our Charley and What to Do with Him. 1858.
A Reply in Behalf of the Women of America. 1863.
The Ravages of a Carpet. 1865.
Stories about Our Dogs. 1865.
House and Home Papers. 1865.
Little Foxes. 1866.
Queer Little People. 1867.
The Chimney-Corner. 1868.
Men of Our Times. 1868.
The American Woman's Home. 1869.
Little Pussy Willow (juvenile). 1870.
Lady Byron Vindicated. 1870.
Woman in Sacred History. 1873; as *Bible Heroines,* 1878.
Palmetto-Leaves. 1873.
Betty's Bright Idea. 1876.
Footsteps of the Master. 1877.
A Dog's Mission. 1881.
Our Famous Women. 1884.

Bibliography: *Stowe: A Bibliography* by Margaret Holbrook Hildreth, 1976.

Reading List: *Life of Stowe from Her Letters and Journals* edited by Charles Edward Stowe, 1889; *Crusader in Crinoline: The Life of Stowe* by Forrest Wilson, 1941; *The Rungless Ladder: Stowe and New England Puritanism* by Charles H. Foster, 1954; *Stowe* by John R. Adams, 1963; *Stowe: The Known and the Unknown* by Edward Wagenknecht, 1965; *The Novels of Stowe* by Alice C. Crozier, 1969; *The Building of "Uncle Tom's Cabin"* by E. Bruce Kirkham, 1977.

*   *   *

Uncle Tom's Cabin, Harriet Beecher Stowe's masterpiece, has been said to have had a "social impact ... on the United States ... greater than that of any book before or since." There is no doubt that it was one of the few books which have changed the climate of public opinion and helped swing the political pendulum. While recent evaluations of the work tend to reveal in it not less but more literary craftsmanship, any critical analysis must consider this novel not so much as a literary production than as an instrument that led to action.

Mrs. Stowe grew up in "a kind of moral heaven, replete with moral oxygen – fully charged with intellectual electricity," and much of that "moral oxygen" and "intellectual electricity" was injected into *Uncle Tom's Cabin*. The guiding principles of self-abnegation, spiritual regeneration, and Christian purpose inculcated in her early training filtered into her writing. Coupled with her own high-minded interest in social reform, they were shaped into a powerful ethical weapon. The author had read of the atrocities of slavery, and, when the Fugitive Slave Law spurred her to action, she was finally metamorphosed into the instrument of the Lord who created an "epic of Negro bondage." This powerful narrative of damnation and salvation, with its bold message that slavery destroys both the master and the slave, electrified the nation. While *Uncle Tom's Cabin* is, on the one hand, a domestic novel, it is also a forceful, vital, original, and daring moral instrument.

Although its characters are sometimes symbols and some of its incidents are stylized, the figures of Simon Legree, Eliza, Mr. St. Clare, Little Eva, and Uncle Tom have joined a parade of unforgettable literary characters that have become part of the national consciousness. The author's reliance upon tact did not preclude her recourse to realism. Just how powerfully Mrs. Stowe's timely propaganda stirred the American conscience is revealed by its publishing history. Within a year of publication its sales topped 300,000, and before the Civil War the figure reached three million. It made its author famous overnight, inspired a spate of anti-*Uncle Tom* novels, and won the praise of such diverse critics as Henry Wadsworth Longfellow and Henry James. According to one reviewer: "The mightiest princes of intellect, as well as those who have scarcely harbored a stray thought ... friends of slavery equally with the haters of that institution ... all ... bend with sweating eagerness over her magic pages." Emerson traced its power to the universality of its message when he commented: "We have seen an American woman write a novel of which a million copies were sold in all languages, and which had one merit, of speaking to the universal heart, and was read with equal interest to three audiences, namely, in the parlor, in the kitchen, and in the nursery of every house." *Uncle Tom's Cabin* still has the power of stirring conflicting emotions in its critics. James Baldwin's attribution of racial prejudice to the novel, for example, has met its effective rebutters. Although the novel is no longer widely read, it is unlikely that it will ever be forgotten.

Mrs. Stowe's earlier work consisted of sentimental and conventional sketches that reflected her belief in the sanctity of the home and woman's place in it. After the success of *Uncle Tom's Cabin* she replied to objectors with *A Key to Uncle Tom's Cabin* and returned to the theme of anti-slavery in *Dred*. Between 1862 and 1884, she produced at least a book a year; most of them consisted of essays on the home, domestic novels, stories of death and redemption, as well as a defense of Lady Byron.

She has recently, and surprisingly, been called "the only major feminine humorist nineteenth-century America produced," an attribution based less upon a sense of the jocular than upon an ear for idiom and an eye for actuality. The books that flowed from her tireless pen often reveal these qualities. They also reveal her dissection of the Calvinist ethic, and despite their sentimentality they provide considerable documentary insight into the moral climate of nineteenth-century New England.

The aptest description of Harriet Beecher Stowe was made by the biographer who dubbed her a "Crusader in Crinoline." For the most part, her crinolines have turned into period pieces, and her crusade has become historic. Yet she helped to document and advance that crusade, and in *Uncle Tom's Cabin* she created a book that shook the world.

—Madeleine B. Stern

TAYLOR, Bayard. American. Born in Kennett Square, Chester County, Pennsylvania, 11 January 1825. Educated at Bolmar's Academy, West Chester, Pennsylvania, 1837–40; Unionville Academy, Pennsylvania, 1842. Married 1) Mary Agnew in 1850 (died, 1850); 2) Marie Hansen in 1857, one daughter. Teacher at Unionville Academy, 1842; apprenticed to the printer of the West Chester *Village Record*, 1842–44; travelled in Europe, as correspondent for the *Saturday Evening Post* and *United States Gazette* of Philadelphia, and the New York *Tribune*, 1844–46; Publisher, *Pioneer* newspaper, Phoenixville, Pennsylvania, 1846–47; Columnist, *Literary World*, New York, 1847–48; Manager, Literary Department, New York *Tribune*, 1848, and covered the California gold rush for the *Tribune*, 1849; travelled in the Middle and Far East, 1851–53, and lectured throughout the United States on his travels, 1854–56; travelled in Europe, 1856–58; settled on a farm, Cedarcroft, near his native village, 1858; served as a correspondent in Washington for the *Tribune*, 1862; Secretary, later Chargé d'Affaires, American Legation, St. Petersburg, Russia, 1862–63; returned to Cedarcroft, and worked on his translation of *Faust*, 1863–70; Non-Resident Professor of German, Cornell University, Ithaca, New York, 1870–77; United States Ambassador to Germany, 1878. *Died 19 December 1878.*

PUBLICATIONS

Collections

> *The Dramatic Works.* 1880.
> *The Poetical Works.* 1880.

Verse

> *Ximena; or, The Battle of Sierra Morena and Other Poems.* 1844.
> *Rhymes of Travel, Ballads, and Poems.* 1849.
> *A Book of Romances, Lyrics, and Songs.* 1851.
> *Poems of the Orient.* 1854.
> *Poems of Home and Travel.* 1855.
> *Poems.* 1856.
> *The Poet's Journal.* 1862.
> *The Poems.* 1864.
> *The Picture of St. John.* 1866.
> *The Golden Wedding: A Masque.* 1868.
> *The Ballad of Abraham Lincoln* (juvenile). 1870.
> *Lars: A Pastoral of Norway.* 1873.
> *Home Pastorals, Ballads, and Lyrics.* 1875.
> *The National Ode.* 1877.

Plays

> *The Masque of the Gods.* 1872.
> *The Prophet.* 1874.
> *Prince Deukalion.* 1878.

Fiction

Hannah Thurston. 1863.
John Godfrey's Fortunes. 1864.
The Story of Kennett. 1866; edited by C. W. La Salle, II, 1973.
Joseph and His Friend. 1870.
Beauty and the Beast, and Tales of Home. 1872.

Other

Views A-Foot; or, Europe Seen with Knapsack and Staff. 1846.
Eldorado; or, Adventures in the Path of Empire. 1850.
A Journey to Central Africa. 1854.
The Lands of the Saracen. 1854.
A Visit to India, China, and Japan in the Year 1853. 1855; revised edition, edited by G.
     F. Pardon, 1860.
Northern Travel. 1857.
Travels in Greece and Russia. 1859.
At Home and Abroad. 2 vols., 1859–62.
Colorado: A Summer Trip. 1867.
By-Ways of Europe. 1869.
A School History of Germany. 1874.
Egypt and Iceland in the Year 1874. 1874.
The Echo Club and Other Literary Diversions. 1876.
Boys of Other Countries: Stories for American Boys. 1876.
Studies in German Literature. 1879.
Critical Essays and Literary Notes, edited by Marie Hansen-Taylor. 1880.
Life and Letters, edited by Marie Hansen-Taylor and H. E. Scudder. 2 vols., 1884.
Unpublished Letters in the Huntington Library, edited by John R. Schultz. 1937.
Correspondence of Taylor and Paul Hamilton Hayne, edited by Charles Duffy. 1945.

Editor, *Hand-Book of Literature and Fine Arts.* 1852.
Editor, *Cyclopedia of Modern Travel.* 1856.
Editor, *Frithiof's Saga,* by Esaias Teghér, traslated by William Lewery Blackley. 1867.
Editor, *Travels in Arabia.* 1871.
Editor, *Japan in Our Day.* 1872.
Editor, *Travels in South Africa.* 1872.
Editor, *The Lake Regions of Central Africa.* 1873.
Editor, *Central Asia.* 1874.
Editor, *Picturesque Europe.* 1877.

Translator, *Faust,* by Goethe. 2 vols., 1870–71; edited by Stuart Atkins, 1972.
Translator, *A Sheaf of Poems,* edited by Mary Taylor Kiliani. 1911.

Reading List: *Tayor* by Albert H. Smyth, 1896 (includes bibliography); *Taylor: Laureate of
the Gilded Age* by Richmond Croom Beatty, 1936; *The Genteel Circle: Taylor and His New
York Friends* by Richard Cary, 1952; *Taylor and German Letters* by John T. Krumpelmann,
1959; *Taylor* by Paul C. Wermuth, 1973.

*   *   *

Although he wished to be remembered for his poetry, Bayard Taylor supported himself by writing travel literature, and it is for these works, as well as his translation of *Faust*, that we remember him today. The titles of his many travel books, most of which were widely read during the nineteenth century, reveal the vast extent of Taylor's travels: *A Journey to Central Africa*, *Lands of the Saracen*, *India, China, and Japan*, *Northern Travel*, *Travels in Greece and Russia*, and *Egypt and Iceland*, among other works too numerous to list here. Ironically, however, Taylor was at his best when writing about his homeland. His book on the California gold rush, *Eldorado*, which he wrote for Horace Greeley's *New York Times*, is one of the earliest and most engaging accounts; and *Colorado*, which he wrote while on a summer trip to the West, is a classic of American overland adventure. Rarely controversial, always factual, and seldom boring, Taylor's books appealed to the sensibilities of a nineteenth-century American audience which was eager to learn more about foreign culture and exotic lands, including the American West.

With the onset of the Civil War, the market for travel literature declined, and, to earn a living, Taylor began writing novels. His models were Dickens and Thackeray, and his plots were overly melodramatic and excessively contrived, but, despite their conventionality, Taylor's novels provide a value insight into the tastes and spirit of the times which demanded felicitous endings, purity from its heroines, and a proper respect for social decorum. They also bridge the gap between the romanticism of the first half of the nineteenth century and the realism of the second. *Hannah Thurston*, for example, is about a bluestocking suffragette turned housewife and mother, who finds true happiness and freedom in the values of the home; and *The Story of Kennett*, with its quaint and descriptive portrayal of life in a rural Pennsylvania town, anticipates the local color movement of the 1870's, 1880's and 1890's.

Taylor's poems, like his travel books and his novels, demonstrate more than a modicum of literary talent but suffer from a self-conscious desire to please. He had an astute ear for music, and his verse is technically quite proficient, but it lacks the universal tensions which make for good poetry. Nonetheless, his most famous poem, "The Bedouin Song," is far from his best; and such poems as "The Summer Camp," "Hylas," "Daughter of Egypt," and "Hassan and His Mare" deserve more recognition than they have received. *The Poet's Journal* and *The Picture of St. John* are especially deserving of attention because they constitute Taylor's attempt to write long narrative verse about his own experiences, vaguely disguised. His most popular collection of poetry, *Poems of the Orient*, displays a refreshing and aesthetically pleasing sense of exoticism. A collected edition of Taylor's poems was published during his lifetime; his masques and closet dramas were published after his death.

Throughout his life, Taylor maintained a genuine admiration for German culture. His second wife was German, and he was for many years non-resident professor of German literature at Cornell University. Taylor's interest in Germany appears in many of his works, but more especially in *Studies in German Literature*, which was for many years one of the best introductions to the field, and in his translation of *Faust*, whose copious scholarly annotations and faithful reproduction of the meter of the original make it to this day one of the finest available translations of Goethe's masterpiece.

—James A. Levernier

TAYLOR, Edward. American. Born in Sketchley, Leicestershire, in 1642. Lost a teaching position in Bagworth, Leicestershire, for failing to subscribe to the Act of Uniformity, 1662; may then have attended Cambridge University; emigrated to Massachusetts Bay Colony, 1668; attended Harvard University, Cambridge, Massachusetts,

B.A. 1671. Married 1) Elizabeth Fitch in 1674 (died, 1689); 2) Ruth Wyllys. Congregational Minister, Westfield, Massachusetts, 1671 until his retirement, 1725. M.A.: Harvard University, 1720. *Died 24 June 1729.*

PUBLICATIONS

Collections

The Poetical Works, edited by Thomas H. Johnson.   1939.
The Poems, edited by Donald E. Stanford.   1960; *Selection*, 1963.

Verse

Metrical History of Christianity (transcript), edited by Donald E. Stanford.   1962.

Other

Christographia (sermons and meditations), edited by Norman S. Grabo.   1962.
The Diary, edited by Francis Murphy.   1964.
Treatise Concerning the Lord's Supper (sermons), edited by Norman S. Grabo.   1966.

Bibliography: *Taylor: An Annotated Bibliography 1668–1970* by Constance J. Gefvert, 1971.

Reading List: *Taylor* by Norman S. Grabo, 1961; *Taylor* by Donald E. Stanford, 1965; *The Will and the Word: The Poetry of Taylor* by William J. Scheick, 1974; *The Example of Taylor* by Karl Keller, 1975.

*   *   *

It should be remembered as we read the poetry of Edward Taylor that he was for over fifty years the village parson of a small New England frontier town, Westfield in western Massachusetts. The ministry was his vocation; poetry was his avocation. The religious experience of the Puritan Calvinist was his abiding concern as a preacher and it was the subject matter of all his extant poems. His library, impressive for its time and place, had many religious books, some of them rare and expensive, but only one volume of verse in English, the poems of Anne Bradstreet. Yet Taylor wrote poetry all of his mature life, and today he is considered the major poet of New England Calvinistic Congregationalism just as Jonathan Edwards, who lived two generations later, is considered its paramount preacher, and this position Taylor has attained in spite of the fact that he published nothing during his life time.

Taylor's reputation as a poet rests on (to quote verbatim his own title page as it appears on his undated manuscript) *Gods Determinations touching his Elect: and The Elects Combat in their Conversion, and Coming up to God in Christ together with the Comfortable Effects thereof* and on his (to quote Taylor's manuscript page again) *Preparatory Meditations before my Approach to the Lords Supper. Chiefly upon the Doctrin preached upon the Day of administration.*

The manuscript of *Gods Determinations* was prepared with particular care and may have been intended for publication, a supposition strengthened by the aim and content of the work. *Gods Determinations* is a series of poems in the form of dramatic dialogues interspersed with narrative and expository passages which explain and justify God's ways in bringing a few selected men ("the elect") to salvation. Its purpose, apparently, was to convert those members of the Puritan community who felt themselves unable to accept full communion in the church because they had not experienced the reception of God's saving grace. Hence a great deal of the poem is taken up with a dramatization of the various ways in which God's grace operates among sinning men.

Gods Determinations opens with a "Preface" which describes the creation in Calvinistic terms. The physical universe as well as all its inhabitants, including man, was created out of nothing by an Omnipotent God who may return it to nothing if he pleases. "The Effects of Mans Apostacy" follows, describing the Fall and the terror of natural man when he finds God his enemy. The tone of the verse and the theology are similar to that of Jonathan Edwards's later famous sermon "Sinners in the Hands of an Angry God." With the third poem, a dialogue between Justice and Mercy, personified attributes of God, the dramatic struggle for the redemption of the elect begins with Justice playing the role of divine avenger who punishes and terrifies man and Mercy playing the role of divine comforter who offers salvation to those who confess their sins and come into the church. Satan and Christ join the struggle and the ensuing action is seen as a series of military engagements in which Satan is eventually defeated by the combined efforts of Justice and Mercy. At the end of the poem the elect are depicted as riding to Glory in Christ's coach.

Much of the poem, in style and content, is "dated." However, Satan's methods of tempting the sinner to abandon hope, methods derived in part from William Ames's *Cases of Conscience*, are subtle and sophisticated, and they reveal an understanding of the psychology of guilt that is still of interest to the modern reader. Also, there are passages written in a vigorous, colloquial, and highly figurative style which are worth noting, particularly the famous query in the opening lines referring to the creation: "Who in this Bowling Alley bowld the Sun?"

The *Preparatory Meditations* is a body of remarkable devotional verse consisting of more than two hundred poems written over a period of more than forty years, from 1682 to 1725. Because of their style, which is reminiscent of the so-called Metaphysical Poets (particularly Herbert but also occasionally Donne, Crashaw, and Vaughan) they have in recent years attracted the attention of scholars, for in the age of Pope he was writing like Donne. But his Meditations are of more than mere historical interest. His recurrent and moving expression of the experience of Saving Grace establishes him as the most important religious poet in American literature and worthy of comparison not only with Donne and Herbert but also with Gerard Manley Hopkins.

The purpose of each Meditation was to prepare the pastor for administering the Lord's Supper, a sacrament by means of which the soul of the participant was united to Christ; therefore a number of the Meditations express the almost mystical exaltation of the union of the human with the divine, as in "The Experience":

> Most strange it was! But yet more strange that shine
> Which filld my Soul then to the brim to spy
> My Nature with thy Nature all Divine
> Together joyn'd in Him thats Thou, and I.

The structure of the poems varies, but more frequently it is three-fold with the opening lines expressing despairing personal awareness of original sin followed by joyful contemplation of Saving Grace made possible through faith in Christ and concluding with the hope that the poet will be one of the elect who will achieve salvation. These poems are in the tradition of the Christian meditative practice of self-examination best exemplified among the Roman Catholics by Loyola, but by the seventeenth-century common among protestant divines such as Richard Baxter, author of *The Saints Everlasting Rest* (1650), a book with which Taylor was probably familiar and which may have influenced his own meditative methods. The meditant fixes his attention on some point of doctrine, analyzes it by means of his understanding, and as a result of comprehending it is moved by feelings of love, hope, joy, etc. The doctrine in Taylor's Meditations is usually stated in a Biblical text which is quoted in the title of the poem, the favorite source of quotation for Taylor being the *Song of Songs* or, as Taylor called it, *Canticles*. Taylor frequently makes use of Christian allegory, symbolism, typology, and a figurative style derived chiefly from the Bible (especially from the *Song of Songs* and *Revelation*) and from Herbert. A widely variant vocabulary is employed with words ranging from the humble life of the farmer – "I'le Wagon Loads of Love, and Glory bring" to abstruse theological terminology. Complicated conceits with terms and images from widely disparate fields of experience are juxtaposed and yoked by violence together in the metaphysical style (as defined by Samuel Johnson). At its best the style is direct and forceful, but at its worst bizarre, over-rhetorical, and rhythmically awkward. Yet in reading the *Preparatory Meditations* as a whole, one gains the impression that they were written by a humble, extremely pious, sincere Puritan for whom the experience of God's grace was profound and overwhelming.

Taylor composed and preached innumerable sermons during his long pastorate but the manuscripts of only a few have survived, the more important being available in *Christographia*, a series of fourteen sermons preached in Westfield from 1701–1703 on the mystery of the union of the divine and human natures of Christ, and in *Treatise Concerning the Lord's Supper* (eight sermons preached in 1694), in which he argues that the Lord's Supper should be confined to the regenerate elect only. These sermons are, then, an attack on the practice of Solomon Stoddard (the grandfather of Jonathan Edwards) who in his Northampton Church was using the sacrament as a converting ordinance and inviting all who led a Christian life to partake. In this as in other matters Taylor expressed the views of the conservative faction of the Congregational Church of New England.

Taylor also wrote a number of occasional poems, the most interesting of which are the charming "Upon a Wasp Child with Cold" and the striking "Upon the Sweeping Flood." He composed a long poem of over twenty thousand lines and of doubtful literary merit on the persecutions and martyrdoms of the Christians from the earliest times through the reign of Queen Mary of England, *Metrical History of Christianity*. He also wrote elegies on his contemporaries, the best being those on his first wife and on Samuel Hooker, pastor of the church of Farmington, Connecticut. But by far his best poetry is to be found in *Gods Determinations* and in the *Preparatory Meditations*.

—Donald E. Stanford

THOMAS, Augustus.   American.   Born in St. Louis, Missouri, 8 January 1857. Educated in local elementary and high schools. Married Lisle Colby in 1890; one son and one daughter. Page boy in the Missouri Legislature, 1868, and in the United States House of Representatives, Washington, D.C., 1870–71; worked in the freight department of a railway company in St. Louis from 1871; Reporter on the *St. Louis Post-Dispatch*, 1885; worked for the *Kansas City Mirror*, 1887–88; began acting and writing for the stage from 1875; moved to New York, 1888, and worked as a theatrical assistant and press agent; full-time playwright after 1891. President, American Dramatists Association, 1906–11; President, National Institute of Arts and Letters, 1914–15; Executive Chairman, Producing Managers Association, and campaigned unsuccessfully for the establishment of a national theatre, 1922–25. Recipient: American Academy of Arts and Letters Gold Medal, 1913. M.A.: Williams College, Williamstown, Massachusetts, 1914; Litt.D.: Columbia University, New York, 1921; LL.D.: University of Missouri, Columbia, 1923. Member, American Academy of Arts and Letters. *Died 16 August 1934.*

PUBLICATIONS

Plays

Alone (produced 1875).
The Big Rise (produced 1882).
A Leaf from the Woods (produced 1883).
A New Year's Call (produced 1883).
Editha's Burglar, from the story by Frances Hodgson Burnett (produced 1883).   1932.
A Man of the World (produced 1883).
Combustion (produced 1884).
The Burglar (produced 1889).
A Proper Impropriety (produced 1889).   1932.
Tit for Tat, with Helen Barry, from a German play (produced 1890; as *A Night's Frolic*, produced 1891).
A Woman of the World (produced 1890).
For Money, with Clay M. Greene (produced 1890).
Afterthoughts (produced 1890).
Reckless Temple (produced 1890).
Alabama (produced 1891).   1898.
Colonel Carter of Cartersville, from the novel by F. Hopkinson Smith (produced 1892).
The Holly-Tree Inn (produced 1892).
Surrender (produced 1892).
In Mizzoura (produced 1893).   1916.
New Blood (produced 1894).
The Music Box (produced 1894).
The Man Upstairs (produced 1895).   1918.
The Capitol, from a story by Opie Read (produced 1895).
Chimmie Fadden, from a story by E. W. Townsend (produced 1896).
The Jucklins (produced 1896).
The Hoosier Doctor (produced 1897).
That Overcoat (produced 1898).
Don't Tell Her Husband (produced 1898; as *The Meddler*, produced 1898).
Colonel George of Mount Vernon (produced 1898).   1931.
Arizona (produced 1899).   1899.
Oliver Goldsmith (produced 1900).   1916.
On the Quiet (produced 1901).
Champagne Charley (produced 1901).
Colorado (produced 1901).
Soldiers of Fortune, from the play by R. H. Davies, from the novel by F. Marion Crawford (produced 1902).
The Earl of Pawtucket (produced 1903).   1917.
The Other Girl (produced 1903).   1917.
Mrs. Leffingwell's Boots (produced 1905).   1916.
Beside the Bonnie Briar Bush, with James MacArthur, from a novel by Ian Maclaren (produced 1905).
The Education of Mr. Pipp, from pictures by Charles Dana Gibson (produced 1905).
Delancey (produced 1905).
The Embassy Ball (produced 1905).
A Constitutional Point (produced 1906).   1932.
The Ranger (produced 1907).
The Member from Ozark (produced 1907).
The Witching Hour (produced 1907).   1916.

The Harvest Moon (produced 1909).   1922.
The Matinee Idol, from the play *His Last Legs* by Bernard (produced 1909).
As a Man Thinks (produced 1911).   1911.
The Model (produced 1912; also produced as *When It Comes Home*).
Mere Man (produced 1912).
At Liberty (produced 1912).
At Bay, with George Scarborough (produced 1913).
Indian Summer (produced 1913).
Three of Hearts (produced 1913).
The Battle Cry, from a novel by Charles N. Buck (produced 1914).   1914.
The Nightingale (produced 1914).   1914.
Rio Grande (produced 1916).
The Copperhead, from the work *The Glory of His Country* by Frederick Landis
    (produced 1918).   1922.
David's Adventures, from a novel (produced 1918).
The Cricket of Palmy Days (as *Palmy Days,* produced 1919).   1929.
Under the Bough (produced 1920; also called *The Blue Devil* and *Speak of the Devil*).
The Tent of Pompey (produced 1920).
Nemesis (produced 1921).   1921.
Still Waters (produced 1925).   1926.

Other plays (for amateurs): *Love Will Find a Way; The Dress Suit.*

Other

The Print of My Remembrance (autobiography).   1922.
Commemorative Tribute to Francis Hopkinson Smith.   1922.

Reading List: *The Wallet of Time* by William Winter, 1913.

*   *   *

Considered by contemporary critics as one of the half-dozen major American dramatists at the turn of the century, Augustus Thomas achieved some success by dramatizing American subjects that would catch the public interest. Like his contemporaries he was a good craftsman who wrote exciting melodramas and farces, generally with a particular actor or actress in mind. During his long career he wrote some 60 plays (including one-act plays and adaptations), organized and managed a professional theatre company, served as Executive Chairman of the Producing Managers Association and tried to develop a sense of self-censorship in the theatre world, was decorated by the French government, and wrote an autobiography, *The Print of My Remembrance,* which remains a useful if biased source for an appreciation of his plays and his theory of playwriting.

    Thomas's playwriting took advantage of such topics of national interest as western regionalism, the labor movement, Washington politics, and new social fads. In *Alabama, In Mizzoura, Arizona,* and *Colorado* he used local scenery and atmosphere to enhance melodramatic plots. Only *Arizona* had any real success on stage. *New Blood* was sympathetic to the problems of laborers in a large manufacturing company. *The Capitol* revealed the influence of financiers on Washington politics and the lobbying practices of the Catholic Church but in a manner that would offend no one. *As a Man Thinks,* an average play on the double moral standard in marriage that interested playwrights and social reformers of this period, is distinguished by one of Thomas's best characters, the Jewish Dr. Seelig, who functions as a raisonneur in the play. *The Copperhead* achieved reasonable success on stage as a realistic picture of the effect of the Civil War on a midwestern town.

Thomas's best known play and probably his most significant work is *The Witching Hour*. Although a conventional melodrama of sentiment and morality, it exploits a popular interest by dramatizing the story of a young man who, under the influence of hypnotism, has killed a man. Beneath the mystery-laden plot there is the deeper idea of the effect of suggestion upon the human mind, but Thomas was seldom thought-provoking. Mainly he entertained with farces such as *The Earl of Pawtucket* and the thrills of the well-made melodrama.

—Walter J. Meserve

THOREAU, Henry David. American. Born in Concord, Massachusetts, 12 July 1817. Educated at the Concord Academy, and at Harvard University, Cambridge, Massachusetts, 1833–37, graduated 1837. Writer from 1835; founded a school with his brother in Concord, 1838, also worked with his father in manufacturing lead pencils; began the walks and studies of nature that became the main occupation of his life, 1839; lived with Emerson, and helped him to edit *The Dial*, 1841–43; lived in a shanty in the woods by Walden Pond, 1845–47; again lived with Emerson, 1847; jailed for refusing to pay taxes, 1847; worked at various odd jobs, including gardening, fence building, and land surveying, also lectured and wrote for various periodicals; visited Canada, 1850, and the Maine woods, 1853, 1857; spent his last years in Concord. *Died 6 May 1862.*

PUBLICATIONS

Collections

> *Complete Works*, edited by Harrison G. O. Blake. 5 vols., 1929.
> *Collected Poems*, edited by Carl Bode. 1943; revised edition, 1964.
> *The Correspondence*, edited by Walter Harding and Carl Bode. 1958.
> *Writings*, edited by William L. Howarth. 1971–
> *Thoreau's Vision: The Major Essays*, edited by Charles R. Anderson. 1973.
> *Selected Works*, edited by Walter Harding. 1975.

Prose

> *A Week on the Concord and Merrimack Rivers.* 1849; edited by Carl Hovde and others, in *Writings*, 1978.
> *Walden; or, Life in the Woods.* 1854; edited by J. Lyndon Shanley, in *Writings*, 1971.
> *Excursions*, edited by Ralph Waldo Emerson. 1863.
> *The Maine Woods.* 1864; edited by Joseph J. Moldenhauer, in *Writings*, 1972.
> *Cape Cod.* 1865.
> *Letters to Various Persons*, edited by Ralph Waldo Emerson. 1865.
> *A Yankee in Canada, with Anti-Slavery and Reform Papers.* 1865; *Reform Papers* edited by Wendell Clark, in *Writings*, 1973.
> *Early Spring in Massachusetts.* 1881; *Summer*, 1884; *Autumn*, 1888; *Winter*, 1892.
> *Miscellanies.* 1894.
> *The Service*, edited by Frank B. Sanborn. 1902.

Sir Walter Raleigh, edited by Henry Aiken Metcalf. 1905.
The First and Last Journeys of Thoreau, edited by Frank B. Sanborn. 2 vols., 1905.
Journals, edited by Bradford Torrey. 14 vols., 1906; edited by Francis H. Allen, 1949;
    Selected Journals edited by Carl Bode, 1967, as *The Best of Thoreau's Journals*, 1971.
The Moon. 1927.
Consciousness at Concord: The Text of Thoreau's Hitherto Lost Journal (1840–1841),
    edited by Perry Miller. 1958.
Literary Notebook, edited by Kenneth Walter Cameron. 1964.
Over Thoreau's Desk: New Correspondence 1838–1861, edited by Kenneth Walter
    Cameron. 1965.
Fact Book, edited by Kenneth Walter Cameron. 2 vols., 1966.
Canadian Notebook, edited by Kenneth Walter Cameron. 1967.

Translator, *The Transmigration of the Seven Brahmans*, edited by Arthur E.
    Christy. 1932.
Translator, *Seven Against Thebes*, by Aeschylus, edited by Leo Max Kaiser. 1960.

Bibliography: *A Bibliography of Thoreau* by Francis H. Allen, 1908; *The Literary Manuscripts of Thoreau* by William L. Howarth, 1974.

Reading List: *The Concord Saunterer* by Reginald Cook, 1940, revised edition, as *Passage to Walden*, 1949; "From Emerson to Thoreau" by F. O. Matthiessen, in *American Renaissance: Art and Expression in the Age of Emerson and Whitman*, 1941; *Thoreau: The Quest and the Classics* by Ethel Seybold, 1951; *The Making of Walden* by J. Lyndon Shanley, 1957; *The Shores of America: Thoreau's Inward Exploration* by Sherman Paul, 1958, and *Thoreau: A Collection of Critical Essays* edited by Paul, 1962; *A Thoreau Handbook*, 1959, and *The Days of Thoreau: A Biography*, 1965, both by Walter Harding; *The Recognition of Thoreau: Selected Criticism since 1848* edited by Wendell Glick, 1969; *Thoreau* by Leon Edel, 1970; *Thoreau as Romantic Naturalist* by James McIntosh, 1974.

*   *   *

Henry David Thoreau is still remembered in his native town of Concord in Massachusetts as a quirky man, and indeed he was, but also as a bold economist. "Most men," he said, "lead lives of quiet desperation," so intent on earning a living that they have no time to live. How much better, he thought, was one day of work and six days at more profitable occupation than six days of labor and one day of rest. Thoreau's work was for a brief period that of school teacher, for a longer time that of a helper in his father's pencil-making business, and latterly that of a surveyor. His occupation was that of an observer and recorder of nature, and of man's proper relation to the world in which he lived. Punning on the correct pronunciation of his name, he called himself a thorough man, and that he was, thoroughly attentive to his daily task of walking, observing, recording, and then painstakingly transcribing into his journals the profits that each day brought. These journals were his storehouse containing materials from which his writings were drawn, and remain a storehouse in which readers today discover quizzical nudgings toward truths.

For to Thoreau truths were not to be captured by declarative frontal attack. They must be warily approached, as any wild thing must be approached, circled cautiously, lest in fear they take flight, or, if sprung on too suddenly become caged in words which inevitably distort. "In wildness," Thoreau announced, "is the preservation of the world." But wildness did not mean wilderness. He was shocked to fear by wind-swept mountain tops, so like primordial chaos. Nature was better with man in it. Thoreau preferred the woodlands, swamplands, and waterways of a man-centered universe. He thought of himself as a "self-appointed inspector of snow-storms and rain-storms," a "surveyor, if not of highways, then of forest paths and across-lots routes," faithfully minding, he said, "my own business."

He had a large sense of drama. He dramatized himself, and he dramatized the world of nature. Though others have been imprisoned for cause of conscience, he is remembered as the one who spent a night in jail for refusal to pay taxes to support a tainted war, and who then wrote an essay in support of "Civil Disobedience" which still remains a handbook for young rebels. When he retired in 1845 to a cabin beside Walden Pond, he chose the 4th of July, the anniversary of America's Declaration of Independence, as the day to take residence there in token of his own independence. He was a supreme egotist, vauntingly unashamed of eccentricities of dress and deportment. His mission was, he said, to crow like Chanticleer, to wake his neighbors up.

He went to his cabin in the woods, not in surly withdrawal from a workaday world. Indeed, he often walked into town, if only to feast on his mother's delicious pies. While officially in residence beside Walden Pond, he took time off for an excursion to Mount Katahdin in Maine. But ordinarily he remained in residence, an eccentric man making daily eccentric pilgrimages around and beyond the still waters of the pond, his evenings spent in recording his daily adventures, culling from them and earlier recordings materials to be made into books or essays. For, like any sensible writer, he sought in his pond-side retreat the quiet and solitude necessary for writing.

While there, again dramatically for exactly two years, two months, and two days, he completed one book and the draft of another. The first was a reminiscent account of a two-week excursion which he and his brother, now deceased, had taken during the summer of 1839, travelling through waterways in a boat of their own construction to the White Mountains in New Hampshire. In composing *A Week on the Concord and Merrimack Rivers*, Thoreau telescoped those two weeks to one and limited himself almost entirely to river adventures. By many, the *Week* is considered Thoreau's most lively book, filled with youthful verve and sombre remembrances, and with observations on men and nature and books, and the livening power of each. "A basket," Thoreau later called it, "of delicate texture," the weaving so fine that, as basket, its strands fall apart to shower a reader with whimsical wisdom and insightful perceptions.

But *A Week* was not well-received when it appeared in 1849. Of an edition of a thousand copies more than seven hundred were returned to him by its publisher unsold. Meanwhile, Thoreau, in residence now in Concord, continued on small excursions, to Cape Cod, again to Maine, but mostly through the outskirts of his native town. He lectured occasionally, but not comfortably nor outstandingly well. He published accounts of his excursions and his essay on civil disobedience, first titled "Resistance to Civil Government." But, if not mostly, most importantly, he puttered over revisions of the second book which had occupied him during his residence beside Walden Pond.

When it appeared in 1854, *Walden; or, Life in the Woods* was better received than *A Week* had been, but the reception was not always enthusiastic, indeed was more than often mocking: who is this humbug, pretending to be a hermit, who has the insolence to tell us how we should live? But no book written in the nineteenth century, except perhaps Karl Marx's *Das Kapital*, has become more of a scripture, a guide, a handbook. Its long first chapter on "Economy" was often reprinted as a tract used by advocates of labor reform on both sides of the Atlantic. Other people built, and still build, secluded small hide-a-ways where work may be done, in art, literature, or contemplation. Many a busy, work-imprisoned person has lived vicariously in an imaginary pond-side retreat of his own. William Butler Yeats is said to have modeled his Innisfree on recollections of *Walden*. W. H. Hudson proclaimed Thoreau "without master or mate ... in the foremost ranks of the prophets."

He condenses his more than two-year residence beside Walden Pond into the four seasons of a single year, joyously through New England's brief summer for twelve chapters, then a single chapter on autumn and three more on winter, an exultant penultimate chapter on spring, moving toward a conclusion which gives final coherence to the cycle, which is not only seasonal but diurnal – day, evening, night, and morning – and which also suggests the ages of man through youth, manhood, old age, death, and finally, with spring and morning, resurrection. Though reprimanding people for work-filled sloth, *Walden* is also a compelling, ecstatic book, a manual of affirmation, confidently asserting in its final sentences, "There is more day to dawn. The Sun is but a morning star."

To most people Thoreau is *Walden*, and *Walden* Thoreau, or, if you wish, thorough. But there was more life to live and record, more excursions to make, more writing to be meticulously done. In his journals he made notes for a Book of the Seasons, which remains in embryo, never put together except by other people who have mined the journals for seasonal lore. When Thoreau died in his mid-fifties, he left sheaves of manuscript as his principal worldly legacy. Most of them have been variously edited by friends or admirers. *Excursions* in 1863 was made up of essays, many of them previously published. *The Maine Woods* in 1864 told of three excursions into the northern wilderness. *Cape Cod* in 1865 and *A Yankee in Canada* in 1866, though not without occasional delicately phrased insights, were, like most of *The Maine Woods*, narratives of travel rather than testaments to an ideal. Thoreau's journals have been published, though not in their entirety, and other people have culled books from them; his letters have been gathered, his poems and translations from the Greek, and his juvenile writings, often neither complete nor completely correct, until in 1971 the Princeton University Press inaugurated a new meticulous edition, now in progress, of his writings.

Thoreau represents many things to many people. To some he is the ultimate nonconformist who brings comfort to those who relish nonconformity in lifestyle or dress. To others, he is an escapist, unhindered by familial responsibilities. Still others suspect that his bachelorhood resulted from fear or distrust of women, or of himself. Naturalists have found him inexpert in identification of species. Ecologists claim him as a pioneer. Civil rebels, from Gandhi to Martin Luther King and beyond, have found him a spark igniting their to action. He was perhaps each of these, but was in total more than the sum of them all. He was a writer, a stylist quite equal to any who in his time or since has managed the flexible complexities of our language. The delicacy of the web that his words construct is too fine to provide the comfort of didacticism. His words fly free to allow each reader to pattern them to dimensions of his own. Everyone, it has been said, gets the Thoreau that he deserves.

—Lewis Leary

THORPE, Thomas Bangs.   American.   Born in Westfield, Massachusetts, 1 March 1815. Educated at Wesleyan University, Middletown, Connecticut, 1833–36. During the Civil War served as Staff Officer to General Butler, in the United States Volunteers, 1862: Colonel. Married. Painter: maintained a studio in Baton Rouge, Louisiana, 1835–53; writer from 1840; edited the Louisiana Whig newspapers, Concordia *Intelligencer*, 1843, New Orleans *Commercial Times*, 1845, New Orleans *Daily Tropic*, 1846, Baton Rouge *Conservator*, 1847, and New Orleans *National*, 1847; moved to New York City, 1853; contributed to numerous periodicals; Co-Proprietor and Co-Editor, *Spirit of the Times*, New York, 1859–60; Surveyor of the Port of New Orleans, 1862–63; City Surveyor of New York, 1865–69, and Chief of the Warehouse Department of the New York Customs House, 1869–78. *Died 20 September 1878.*

PUBLICATIONS

Fiction and Sketches

The Mysteries of the Backwoods; or, Sketches of the Southwest.   1846.
The Hive of the Bee-Hunter: A Repository of Sketches.   1854.
The Master's House: A Tale of Southern Life.   1854.

Other

Our Army on the Rio Grande.   1846.
Our Army at Monterey.   1847.
The Taylor Anecdote Book: Anecdotes and Letters of Zachary Taylor.   1848.
Reminiscences of Charles L. Elliott, Artist.   1868.

Reading List: *Thorpe* by Milton Rickels, 1962.

*   *   *

Thomas Bangs Thorpe, a Northerner who loved the South and lived in Louisiana for many years, is one of the finest writers in the group known as old Southwestern humorists. At his best Thorpe was able to relinquish a formal, educated, fashionable mode of writing for an informal, ungrammatical, humorous view of the old Southwest. Indeed, Thorpe's great talent was his ability to render frontier speech and humor vividly.

In 1839, Thorpe, a portrait painter by trade, achieved national and international attention with his first essay about the frontier. "Tom Owen, The Bee-Hunter" described an eccentric whom Thorpe had met in the backwoods of Louisiana, a man whose primary interest in life was fearlessly pursuing bees and taking their honey. Unfortunately, in this essay Thorpe used a highly literary language, hardly the language of the frontier, and he thereby held himself and his readers at a considerable distance from his subject.

This problem of authorial distance was completely solved, however, in Thorpe's masterpiece "The Big Bear of Arkansas," published in 1841. Although he began this tale with a predominantly formal description of the "heterogeneous" passengers on a Mississippi steamboat and ended it in an equally formal style, Thorpe permitted a rather uncouth passenger to tell a tall tale within this frame. Jim Doggett, an Arkansas frontiersman, speaks throughout most of "The Big Bear" and his language is far from literary. His pronunciation (as suggested by misspellings), the rhythms of his speech, his grammatical errors, the idioms and metaphors he uses are all appropriate to the Western roarer, and form a purposeful, telling contrast to the relatively dull frame style. This contrast is intensified by the exaggerated nature of Jim's frontier humor: Jim reports that in Arkansas beets grow as large as cedar stumps and wild turkeys grow too fat to fly. But the primary exaggeration in this story is not particularly humorous. Doggett says that the big bear seems to raid his farm at will, to have almost supernatural powers, and to loom as large as a "black mist." None of these details sets one laughing. They do, however, suggest that this "creation bar," like Faulkner's bear, is a symbol of a once vast wilderness which itself is doomed. Indeed, Thorpe's bear seems to recognize his inevitable doom and to die, though at Jim's hands, only because "his time come." There is, nevertheless, a joke embedded within this rather melancholy strain. When the bear decides his time has come, he surprises Doggett at a most inopportune moment – the Arkansas hunter is literally caught with his "inexpressibles" down.

Thorpe never equalled this tale. His "second finest frontier story" (according to Milton Rickels), "Bob Herring, The Arkansas Bear Hunter," is certainly of interest. Though Bob Herring is not the ring-tail roarer that Jim Doggett is, he is a realistic frontiersman, and his language is both amusing and authentic. Yet the structure of this story lacks the technical brilliance of "The Big Bear." While "The Big Bear" encloses Jim's yarn within a frame, "Bob Herring" rather awkwardly juxtaposes two bear hunts told from different perspectives. Moreover, the latter story relies extensively upon an imaginative but gentlemanly narrator, and one longs to hear the voice of Bob Herring more pervasively.

Thorpe subsequently published two collections of stories and essays, edited a number of newspapers, wrote a history of the Mexican War, composed a mediocre reform novel, and contributed many articles to national periodicals. But his single most creative product came early in his career and was not to be matched by later works. "The Big Bear of Arkansas" was Thorpe's greatest achievement, one that abetted the rise of realism, dealt with the nature of the frontier, and guaranteed its author a place in American literary history.

—Suzanne Marrs

TIMROD, Henry. American. Born in Charleston, South Carolina, 8 December 1828. Educated at German Friendly Society School and Cotes' Classical School, 1836–40; Franklin College, later University of Georgia, 1845–46; read law in the office of James L. Petigru, Charleston, 1847–49. Served in the Confederate Forces during the Civil War, 1862 (discharged for health reasons, 1862). Married Kate Goodwin in 1864; one son. Schoolmaster and tutor in various Southern plantation families before the outbreak of the Civil War, 1850–61; Assistant Editor, Charleston *Mercury*, 1863; Associate Editor, and part-owner, *South Carolinian*, Columbia, 1864 until 1865 when Sherman's troops sacked the town; Assistant Private Secretary to Governor J. L. Orr, 1867. *Died 7 October 1867.*

PUBLICATIONS

Collections

The Essays, edited by Edd Winfield Parks. 1942.
The Collected Poems: A Variorum Edition, edited by Edd Winfield Parks and Aileen Wells Parks. 1965.

Verse

Poems. 1859.
The Poems, edited by Paul Hamilton Hayne. 1873.
The Uncollected Poems, edited by Guy A. Cardwell. 1942.

Other

The Last Years of Timrod 1864–1867: Including Letters to Paul Hamilton Hayne and Letters about Timrod by William Gilmore Simms, John R. Thompson, John Greenleaf Whittier, and Others, edited by Jay B. Hubbell. 1941.

Reading List: *Timrod* by Edd Winfield Parks, 1964.

*   *   *

Had it not been for the Civil War, Henry Timrod, although the best Southern poet of his time except for Poe, could be almost unknown today. In view of his reputation as chief of the Southern poets of the War – he is characterized in such rebarbative phrases as "Laureate of the Confederacy" and "Harp of the South" – his life and thought are rich in ironies.

There was nothing of the Cavalier about his ancestry, and he was not a zealous propagandist for the region or for slavery. Like a number of other antebellum Southern writers, he was often at odds with his section and its culture; a strain of astrigent candor ran through his excellent essays. Although Charleston was the publishing center of the South, Timrod describes the region as a literary backwater, archaic in taste, unformed in judgment, materialistic, prosaic, uninterested in intellectual and poetic knowledge. He opposed Southernism in literature and emphasized that poetry must belong to the world.

To some of the older generation of Charleston literary men, Timrod seemed extavagantly avant-garde: his principal heroes and models were Wordsworth and Tennyson. His theory and practice were tempered, however, by classicist ideas and habits. He insisted that after inspiration must come artistry; that excessive subjectivity spoils verse; and that poetry must be true and ethical. His apprentice verses show him industriously experimenting in forms and meters, and variant versions of mature poems indicate that he was an assiduous reviser. Sidney Lanier wrongly held that Timrod possessed a dainty artless art but never had time to learn the craft of the poet. His lyricism is most successful when most considered: his verse lacks spontaneity, intensity, and figurative imagination; his ideas and metrics are unoriginal. He was in a large sense an occasional poet whose delight in words and skill with meters could produce simply structured, controlled verses remarkably free of the sentimental verbosity and crudity of form that are characteristic of his Southern contemporaries.

Amative and nature poetry make up the bulk of Timrod's verse, but the critical consensus is right in judging his war poetry, most of which stresses the losses and sorrows of the conflict, to be his best. Most memorable are "Ethno-genesis," "The Cotton Boll," "Carolina," "A Cry to Arms," "Charleston," and his Magnolia Cemetery ode.

Nearly all of Timrod's verses were first published in Southern newspapers and magazines, usually for no pay. *The Southern Literary Messenger*, of Richmond, and *Russell's Magazine*, of Charleston, were the most important of the miscellanies to which he made regular contributions. Friends guaranteed the costs of the one slim volume of his verse that appeared during his lifetime. Posthumous collections more than double the number of poems contained in that first volume.

—Guy A. Cardwell

TOURGÉE, Albion W(inegar). American. Born in Williamsfield, Ohio, 2 May 1838. Educated at Kingsville Academy, Ohio, 1854–59; University of Rochester, New York, 1859–61, B.A. 1862; studied law; admitted to the Ohio bar, 1864. Served in the 27th New York Volunteers, 1861; wounded at the first Battle of Bull Run, 1861; Lieutenant in the 105th Ohio Regiment, 1862–64; prisoner of war, 1863. Married Emma L. Kilbourne in 1863; one daughter. Assistant Principal of a school in Wilson, New York, 1861; taught and wrote for a newspaper in Erie, Pennsylvania, 1864–65; settled in Greensboro, North Carolina, 1865; practised law; entered politics for "carpet-bagger" interests, 1866; founded the *Union Register*, which failed, 1867; delegate to the "carpet-bag" conventions, 1868, 1875; Judge of the Superior Court of North Carolina, 1868–75; writer from 1874; Pension Agent at Raleigh, North Carolina, 1876–78; moved to New York, 1879, and settled in

Mayville, 1881; Editor, *Our Continent*, Philadelphia, 1882–84; regular contributor to the *Daily Inter Ocean*, Chicago, 1885–98; founded *The Basis: A Journal of Citizenship*, Buffalo, New York, 1895–96; United States Consul-General at Bordeaux, 1897 until his death. *Died 21 May 1905.*

PUBLICATIONS

Fiction

Toinette. 1874; as *A Royal Gentleman*, 1881.
Figs and Thistles: A Western Story. 1879.
A Fool's Errand. 1879; revised edition, incorporating *The Invisible Empire*, 1880; edited by John Hope Franklin, 1961.
Bricks Without Straw. 1880; edited by Otto H. Olsen, 1969.
'Zouri's Christmas. 1881.
John Eax and Marmelon; or, The South Without the Shadow. 1882.
Hot Plowshares. 1883.
Button's Inn. 1887.
Black Ice. 1888.
With Gauge and Swallow, Attorneys. 1889.
Murvale Eastmas, Christian Socialist. 1890.
Pactolus Prime. 1890.
'89. 1891.
A Son of Old Harry. 1892.
Out of the Sunset Sea. 1893.
An Outing with the Queen of Hearts. 1894.
The Mortgage on the Hip-Roof House. 1896.
The Man Who Outlived Himself (stories). 1898.

Play

A Fool's Errand, with Steele MacKaye, from the novel by Tourgée, edited by Dean H. Keller. 1969.

Other

The Code of Civil Procedure of North Carolina, with Victor C. Barringer and Will B. Rodman. 1878.
An Appeal to Caesar. 1884.
The Veteran and His Pipe (essays). 1886.
Letters to a King. 1888.
The War of the Standards: Coin and Credit Versus Coin Without Credit. 1896.
The Story of a Thousand, Being a History of the 105th Volunteer Infantry, 1862 to 1865. 1896.
A Civil War Diary, edited by Dean H. Keller. 1965.

Bibliography: "A Checklist of the Writings of Tourgée" by Dean H. Keller, in *Studies in Bibliography 18*, 1965.

Reading List: *Tourgée* by Roy Floyd Dibble, 1921; *Tourgée* by Theodore L. Gross, 1963; *Carpetbagger's Crusade: The Life of Tourgée* by Otto H. Olsen, 1965.

*   *   *

Albion W. Tourgée's views on the art of the novel and his own practice as a novelist carry the unmistakable stamp of his active involvement as a journalist, polemicist, and judge in the political and public issues of the Reconstruction period in the United States. His unreserved preference for historical veracity, content, and social purpose (as implied in his criticism of James) always took precedence over the subtleties of technique and the nuances of character portrayal. Observing no separation between the role of the novelist and that of the historian, he conceived of the novel-form essentially as a frame for "a possible life ... in a true environment," insisting that the test of artistic success was inevitably the consistency with which such a life related to its milieu and to the dominant predispositions of the age. Interestingly enough, such a conviction did not bring him any closer to the writers of a realist and naturalist persuasion whose treatment of human depravity and poverty he found crude and repulsive. His admiration, sometimes carried to uncritical extremes, was for the realism of Cooper's descriptions, for there he found the ideals of love, truth, and purity that were worthy of emulation by the citizen of a New Republic. That he was the author of *The Code of Civil Procedure of North Carolina* and the editor of *The Union Register*, a newspaper firmly committed to radical reformist measures, also accounts for his fascination with such noble ideals.

Tourgée's best novels, *A Fool's Errand*, recounting a carpetbagger's grim struggle to work for the cause of equality and pacificism in the South, and *Bricks Without Straw*, concerned with an uneducated but enlightened black man's attempt to achieve selfhood, amplify and illustrate his prominent fictional themes and moral concerns – the possibility of social amelioration, the problem of vindicating one's cherished beliefs in a hostile society, the responses evoked by the tender and redemptive sentiment of love, sympathy for the Negroes, and the selflessness of the Republican set against the cupidity of the Southern white supremacist intent on denying political and civil rights to the Negro. To these are added a preacher's zeal and intensity, a penchant for melodrama, a forceful style and a penetrating if occasionally biased reading of the political climate in the South in the 1860's and 1870's. Tourgée's commitment to such themes and values places him securely, in Edmund Wilson's incontestable judgment, in the "second category of writers who aim primarily at social history. His narrative has spirit and movement; his insights are brilliantly revealing, and they are expressed with emotional conviction."

The inwardness of the imagination that Tourgée sought to exploit in his later fiction on his return to the North in 1879 produced poor and disappointing results. The absence of concrete historical, political, and social contexts often led him to write sentimental romantic tales abounding with improbable coincidences and permeated by an impractical ethical and religious humanitarianism. Thus, if in *Black Ice* a somnambulist, who has climbed to the top of a snowy mountain in search of her baby's grave, is heroically rescued, in *Button's Inn* the hero, an ex-murderer, is redeemed by conversion to Mormonism. The relative success of *'89*, in which Tourgée returned to his earlier themes in the original Southern setting, showed that he obviously was at ease in the comforts of a familiar environment and that he wrote most competently when called upon to provide a kind of fictional *apologia* of Radical Republicanism.

—Chirantan Kulshrestha

TRUMBULL, John. American. Born in Westbury, Connecticut, 24 April 1750. Educated at Yale University, New Haven, Connecticut (Berkeley Scholar), 1763–70, B.A. 1767, M.A. 1770; studied law in John Adams's law office in Boston, 1773; admitted to the Connecticut Bar, 1773. Married Sarah Hubbard in 1776; seven children. Schoolteacher, Weathersfield, Connecticut, 1770–71; contributed essays (as "The Correspondent") to the *Connecticut Journal*, 1770–73; Tutor at Yale University, 1771–73; practised law in New Haven and Hartford, Connecticut, 1774–1825; Treasurer of Yale University, 1776–82; Member of the Hartford City Council, 1784–93; State's Attorney for Hartford, 1789–95; Member, General Assembly of Connecticut, 1792, 1800–01; Judge, Connecticut Supreme Court, 1801–19, and Supreme Court of Errors, 1808–19. Literary leader of the "Hartford Wits" in the 1780's and 1790's. LL.D.: Yale University, 1818. Member, American Academy of Arts and Sciences, 1791. *Died 11 May 1831.*

PUBLICATIONS

Collections

The Works, edited by Theodore Sizer. 1950; supplement, *The Autobiography*, 1953. *The Satiric Poems*, edited by Edwin T. Bowden. 1962.

Verse

An Elegy on the Death of Mr. Buckingham St. John. 1771. *The Progress of Dulness.* 3 vols., 1772–73. *M'Fingal: A Modern Epic Poem, Canto First.* 1775; *M'Fingal in Four Cantos*, 1782; edited by Benson J. Lossing, 1864. *The Poetical Works.* 2 vols., 1820. *The Anarchiad*, with others, edited by Luther G. Riggs. 1861.

Other

An Essay on the Use and Advantages of the Fine Arts. 1770. *Biographical Sketch of the Character of Governor Trumbull.* 1809.

Reading List: *Trumbull, Connecticut Wit* by Alexander Cowie, 1936 (includes bibliography); *Trumbull* by Victor E. Gimmestad, 1974.

*   *   *

John Trumbull is best remembered as spokesman for the group of writers known as the "Connecticut" or "Hartford Wits." This group, which included Joel Barlow, Timothy Dwight, and David Humphreys, among others, was active during the years following the Revolutionary War. Most of its members, Trumbull included, were educated at Yale and were extremely conservative in their political and literary views. They appreciated Neoclassical decorum, and, from their center at Hartford, Connecticut, they used their literary talent to exert pressure on the nation to stem the rise of Jeffersonian democracy, which they feared, and to create a strong federal government.

A lawyer by profession, Trumbull was also devoted to the arts. He composed verses at the age of four and passed the entrance exam to Yale when he was only seven. He possessed a keen mind and a shrewd wit, which he used to his advantage when he wrote satire. He was a master of the octosyllabic line, and he delighted in writing hudibrastic verse. For poetic models, he emulated the works of Pope, Swift, and Dryden. More concerned with ideas than with emotions, Trumbull valued restraints and disliked emotion. Needless to say, he did not appreciate the Romantics, especially Wordsworth and Coleridge, who he felt placed expression before reason and subjectivity before objectivity.

Trumbull possessed a genuine gift for humor. At his best when writing burlesque or satire, Trumbull found more serious verse difficult to sustain. Like his contemporaries, he considered the ode and the elegy superior in literary merit to satire, and although he frequently tried to write in these forms, his "Ode to Sleep: An Elegy on the Times," and *An Elegy on the Death of Mr. Buckingham St. John* are among his least interesting poems. More engaging is *The Progress of Dullness*, a three part satirical epic, written while Trumbull was studying for his master's degree at Yale, which ridicules outmoded educational practices and which calls for a more useful system of instruction than that which Trumbull experienced as an undergraduate.

His most famous poem, *M'Fingal*, earned Trumbull the title of "Poet of the Revolution." Written in the tradition of Dryden's *Mac Flecknoe*, it is a mock heroic epic about the raucous adventures of a Tory squire named M'Fingal who tries to prevent a group of patriots from giving further support to the Revolutionary War and is himself tarred and feathered in the process. During the Revolutionary War, *M'Fingal* was used to stir up popular sentiment against the British, and it was even printed in England, where its literary merit drew the praise of critics who were impartial enough to disassociate their political allegiances from their critical pronouncements. In America, the popularity of *M'Fingal* continued long after it ceased to be useful as anti-British propaganda. Today it is recognized as one of the finest political verse satires written in America prior to the Civil War.

Trumbull is also remembered for his essays. Like his verse, Trumbull's essays are best when they satirize institutions and events. Favorite among these are education, the clergy, and, of course, the British, whom he never really despised but was always ready to satirize. He patterned his prose style, which is witty and extremely polished, after that of Addison and Steele, whom he very much admired.

—James A. Levernier

TUCKERMAN, Frederick Goddard. American. Born in Boston, Massachusetts, 4 February 1821. Educated at Bishop Hopkins' School, Burlington, Vermont, 1833–37; Harvard College, Cambridge, Massachusetts, 1837–38, and Harvard Law School, Cambridge, 1839–42; admitted to the Suffolk County, Massachusetts Bar, 1844. Married Hannah Lucinda Jones in 1847 (died, 1857); three children. Briefly practised law; retired to Greenfield, Massachusetts, 1847, and lived there for the remainder of his life. *Died 9 May 1873.*

PUBLICATIONS

Collections

The Complete Poems, edited by N. Scott Momaday. 1965.

Verse

Poems. 1860.

Reading List: *Tuckerman* by Samuel A. Golden, 1966.

*   *   *

Because Frederick Goddard Tuckerman's poetry was rescued from near-oblivion only fairly recently, a natural temptation for the critic is to fan the excitement generated by that rescue by overstating the value of the poetry. This temptation should be avoided, for much of Tuckerman's poetry is pedestrian.

Tuckerman's narrative poems are often merely inflated anecdotes. Many poems are maimed by Tuckerman's tepid sermonizing. Sometimes his diction is ornate and tediously archaic, and his syntax awkward, even puzzling. Several sonnets are poorly constructed; the climax is followed by a number of distractingly anti-climactic lines. In his perceptive book on Tuckerman, Samuel A. Golden summarizes part of Tuckerman's world view. For the poet, "man's certainty rests in God." Unfortunately, Tuckerman's expressions of his religious faith are almost always inadequately documented, verbally bland, and so, quite unconvincing.

Nonetheless, the excitement caused by the rediscovery of Tuckerman's work is justified. Five sonnet sequences and "The Cricket" – all inspired by the death, after childbirth, of Tuckerman's wife – represent his finest efforts. Both the content and the form of these poems are, at their best, of a high quality.

In the nineteenth century most American poets regarded nature from a wholly sentimental point of view. Tuckerman tempered his view. As his sonnets make clear, he, too, believed that nature was a part of God's cosmic scheme. Unlike his contemporaries, however, he did not proceed to interpret nature for the benefit of his readers. Instead, he admitted that he did not comprehend the ways of nature. Nor did nature provide Tuckerman with an all-encompassing comfort. "The Cricket" and the sonnets report that he gained solace from nature only after severely qualifying the degree of solace he hoped to gain.

Equally interesting, although Tuckerman – like his Transcendentalist peers – sometimes yearned to merge with nature, he chose to resist this impulse. He also came to realize that it was impossible to fulfill such an impulse. While the Transcendentalists found nature (indeed, the whole universe) to be wondrously like their own personalities, Tuckerman found nature to be quixotic, contradictory, enigmatic, and fundamentally separate from himself.

Finally, in "The Cricket" and the first two sonnet sequences especially, Tuckerman's stylistic weaknesses are far outweighed by many fine phrases, metaphors, and long descriptive passages enhanced by skillful rhythms and rhyming. In "The Cricket," for instance, Tuckerman speaks of dead friends with "faces where but now a gap must be" and of death as the "crowning vacancy." He describes a night of love in terms of "wringing arms . . ./Closed eyes, and kisses that would not let go." His best sonnets also display a superb blending of form and content.

—Robert K. Johnson

TWAIN, Mark. Pseudonym for Samuel Langhorne Clemens. American. Born in Florida, Missouri, 30 November 1835; grew up in Hannibal, Missouri. Married Olivia Langdon in 1870 (died, 1904); one son and three daughters. Printer's apprentice from age 12; helped brother with Hannibal newspapers, 1850–52; worked in St. Louis, New York, Philadelphia, Keokuk, Iowa, and Cincinnati, 1853–57; river pilot's apprentice, on the Mississippi, 1857: licensed as a pilot, 1859; went to Nevada as secretary to his brother, then in the service of the governor, and also worked as a goldminer, 1861; staff member, *Territorial Enterprise*, Virginia City, Nevada, 1862–64; moved to San Francisco, 1864; visited France, Italy, and Palestine, 1867; writer from 1867, lecturer from 1868; Editor, *Buffalo Express*, New York, 1868–71; moved to Hartford, Connecticut, and became associated with the Charles L. Webster Publishing Company, 1884: went bankrupt, 1894 (last debts paid, 1898). M.A.: Yale University, New Haven, Connecticut, 1888; Litt.D.: Yale University, 1901; Oxford University, 1907; LL.D.: University of Missouri, Columbia, 1902. *Died 21 April 1910.*

PUBLICATIONS

Collections

> *Letters*, edited by Albert B. Paine. 2 vols., 1917.
> *The Writings*, edited by Albert B. Paine. 37 vols., 1922–25.
> *The Portable Twain*, edited by Bernard De Voto. 1946.
> *The Complete Short Stories*, edited by Charles Neider. 1957.
> *Selected Shorter Writings*, edited by Walter Blair. 1962.
> *The Complete Novels*, edited by Charles Neider. 2 vols., 1964.
> *Works*, edited by John C. Gerber and others. 1972–

Fiction

> *The Celebrated Jumping Frog of Calaveras County and Other Sketches*, edited by John Paul. 1867.
> *The Innocents Abroad; or, The New Pilgrims' Progress.* 1869.
> *The Innocents at Home.* 1872.
> *The Gilded Age: A Tale of Today*, with Charles Dudley Warner. 1873; *The Adventures of Colonel Sellers, Being Twain's Share of The Gilded Age*, edited by Charles Neider, 1965: complete text, edited by Bryant Morey French, 1972.
> *The Adventures of Tom Sawyer.* 1876.
> *A True Story and the Recent Carnival of Crime.* 1877.
> *Date 1601: Conversation as It Was by the Social Fireside in the Time of the Tudors.* 1880; edited by Franklin J. Meine, 1939.
> *A Tramp Abroad.* 1880.
> *The Prince and the Pauper.* 1881.
> *The Stolen White Elephant etc.* 1882.
> *The Adventures of Huckleberry Finn (Tom Sawyer's Companion).* 1884; edited by Sculley Bradley and others, 1977.
> *A Connecticut Yankee in King Arthur's Court.* 1889; edited by W. N. Otto, 1930.
> *The American Claimant.* 1892.
> *Merry Tales.* 1892.
> *The £1,000,000 Bank-Note and Other New Stories.* 1893.
> *Pudd'nhead Wilson.* 1894; as *The Tragedy of Pudd'nhead Wilson*, 1894; with *Those Extraordinary Twins*, edited by Malcolm Bradbury, 1969.

Tom Sawyer Abroad. 1894.
Tom Sawyer Abroad, Tom Sawyer, Detective, and Other Stories. 1896; as *Tom Sawyer, Detective, and Other Tales,* 1897.
Personal Recollections of Joan of Arc. 1896.
The Man That Corrupted Hadleyburg and Other Stories and Essays. 1900.
A Double Barrelled Detective Story. 1902.
Extracts from Adam's Diary. 1904.
A Dog's Tale. 1904.
The $30,000 Bequest and Other Stories. 1906.
Eve's Diary. 1906.
A Horse's Tale. 1907.
Extract from Captain Stormfield's Visit to Heaven. 1909; revised edition, as *Report from Paradise,* edited by Dixon Wecter, 1952.
The Mysterious Stranger: A Romance. 1916; *Mysterious Stranger Manuscripts* edited by William M. Gibson, 1969.
The Curious Republic of Gondour and Other Whimsical Sketches. 1919.
The Mysterious Stranger and Other Stories. 1922.
A Boy's Adventure. 1928.
The Adventures of Thomas Jefferson Snodgrass, edited by Charles Honce. 1928.
Jim Smiley and His Jumping Frog, edited by Albert B. Paine. 1940.
A Murder, A Mystery, and a Marriage. 1945.
The Complete Humorous Sketches and Tales, edited by Charles Neider. 1961.
Simon Wheeler, Detective, edited by Franklin R. Rogers. 1963.
Twain's Hannibal, Huck, and Tom, edited by Walter Blair. 1969.
Twain's Quarrel with Heaven: Captain Stormfield's Visit to Heaven and Other Sketches, edited by Roy B. Browne. 1970.

Plays

Colonel Sellers (produced 1874; as *The Gilded Age,* produced 1880).
Ah Sin, with Bret Harte (produced 1877). Edited by Frederick Anderson, 1961.
Colonel Sellers as a Scientist, with William Dean Howells (produced 1887). Edited by Walter J. Meserve, in *Complete Plays of Howells,* 1960.
The Quaker City Holy Land Excursion: An Unfinished Play. 1927.

Verse

On the Poetry of Twain, with Selections from His Verse, edited by Arthur L. Scott. 1966.

Other

Twain's (Burlesque) Autobiography and First Romance. 1871.
Memoranda: From the Galaxy. 1871.
Roughing It. 1872; edited by Franklin R. Rogers, in *Works 2,* 1972.
A Curious Dream and Other Sketches. 1872.
Screamers: A Gathering of Scraps of Humour, Delicious Bits, and Short Stories. 1872.
Sketches. 1874.
Sketches, New and Old. 1875.
Old Times on the Mississippi. 1876.
Punch, Brothers, Punch! and Other Sketches. 1878.
An Idle Excursion. 1878.

A Curious Experience. 1881.
Life on the Mississippi. 1883.
Facts for Twain's Memory Builder. 1891.
How to Tell a Story and Other Essays. 1897; revised edition, 1900.
Following the Equator: A Journey Around the World. 1897; as *More Tramps Abroad,* 1897.
The Pains of Lowly Life. 1900.
English as She Is Taught. 1900; revised edition, 1901.
To the Person Sitting in Darkness. 1901.
My Début as a Literary Person, with Other Essays and Stories. 1903.
Twain on Vivisection. 1905(?).
King Leopold's Soliloquy: A Defense of His Congo Rule. 1905: revised edition, 1906.
Editorial Wild Oats. 1905.
What Is Man? 1906.
Christian Science, with Notes Containing Corrections to Date. 1907.
Is Shakespeare Dead? From My Autobiography. 1909.
Speeches, edited by F. A. Nast. 1910; revised edition, 1923.
Queen Victoria's Jubilee. 1910.
Letter to the California Pioneers. 1911.
What Is Man? and Other Essays. 1917.
Europe and Elsewhere. 1923.
Autobiography, edited by Albert B. Paine. 2 vols., 1924.
Sketches of the Sixties by Bret Harte and Mark Twain ... from "The Californian," *1864–67.* 1926.
The Suppressed Chapter of "Following the Equator." 1928.
Twain the Letter Writer, edited by Cyril Clemens. 1932.
Notebook, edited by Albert B. Paine. 1935.
Letters from the Sandwich Islands, Written for the "Sacramento Union," edited by G. Ezra Dane. 1937.
The Washoe Giant in San Francisco, Being Heretofore Uncollected Sketches, edited by Franklin Walker. 1938.
Twain's Western Years, Together with Hitherto Unreprinted Clemens Western Items, by Ivan Benson. 1938.
Letters from Honolulu Written for the "Sacramento Union," edited by Thomas Nickerson. 1939.
Twain in Eruption: Hitherto Unpublished Pages about Men and Events, edited by Bernard De Voto. 1940.
Travels with Mr. Brown, Being Heretofore Uncollected Sketches Written for the San Francisco "Alta California" in 1866 and 1867, edited by Franklin Walker and G. Ezra Dane. 1940.
Republican Letters, edited by Cyril Clemens. 1941.
Letters to Will Brown, edited by Theodore Hornberger. 1941.
Letters in the "Muscatine Journal," edited by Edgar M. Branch. 1942.
Washington in 1868, edited by Cyril Clemens. 1943.
Twain, Business Man, edited by Samuel Charles Webster. 1946.
Letters of Quintus Curtius Snodgrass, edited by Ernest E. Leisy. 1946.
Twain in Three Moods: Three New Items of Twainiana, edited by Dixon Wecter. 1948.
The Love Letters, edited by Dixon Wecter. 1949.
Twain to Mrs. Fairbanks, edited by Dixon Wecter. 1949.
Twain to Uncle Remus, 1881–1885, edited by Thomas H. English. 1953.
Twins of Genius (letters to George Washington Cable), edited by Guy A. Cardwell. 1953.
Mark Twain of the "Enterprise," edited by Henry Nash Smith and Frederick Anderson. 1957.

Traveling with Innocents Abroad: Twain's Original Reports from Europe and the Holy Land, edited by Daniel Morley McKeithan.   1958.
The Autobiography, edited by Charles Neider.   1959.
The Art, Humor, and Humanity of Twain, edited by Minnie M. Brashear and Robert M. Rodney.   1959.
Twain and the Government, edited by Svend Petersen.   1960.
The Twain-Howells Letters 1872–1910, edited by Henry Nash Smith and William M. Gibson.   2 vols., 1960.
Life as I Find It: Essays, Sketches, Tales, and Other Material, edited by Charles Neider.   1961.
The Travels of Twain, edited by Charles Neider.   1961.
Contributions to "The Galaxy," 1868–1871, edited by Bruce R. McElderry.   1961.
Twain on the Art of Writing, edited by Martin B. Fried.   1961.
Letters to Mary, edited by Lewis Leary.   1961.
The Pattern for Twain's "Roughing It": Letters from Nevada by Samuel and Orion Clemens, 1861–1862, edited by Franklin R. Rogers.   1961.
Letters from the Earth, edited by Bernard De Voto.   1962.
Twain on the Damned Human Race, edited by Janet Smith.   1962.
The Complete Essays, edited by Charles Neider.   1963.
Twain's San Francisco, edited by Bernard Taper.   1963.
The Forgotten Writings of Twain, edited by Henry Duskus.   1963.
Letters from Hawaii, edited by A. Grove Day.   1966.
Which Was the Dream? and Other Symbolic Writings of the Later Years, edited by John S. Tuckey.   1967.
The Complete Travel Books, edited by Charles Neider.   1967.
Letters to His Publishers, 1867–1894, edited by Hamlin Hill.   1967.
Clemens of the "Call": Twain in California, edited by Edgar M. Branch.   1969.
Correspondence with Henry Huttleston Rogers, 1893–1909, edited by Lewis Leary.   1969.
Fables of Man, edited by John S. Tuckey.   1973.
What Is Man? and Other Philosophical Writings, edited by Paul Baender, in *Works*.   1973.
Journals and Notebooks, edited by Frederick Anderson and others.   1975–

Translator, *Slovenly Peter (Der Struwwelpeter)*.   1935.

Bibliography: *A Bibliography of the Works of Twain* by Merle Johnson, revised edition, 1935; in *Bibliography of American Literature* by Jacob Blanck, 1957.

Reading List: *Mark Twain: A Biography* by Albert B. Paine, 3 vols., 1912; *Twain: The Man and His Work* by Edward Wagenknecht, 1935, revised edition, 1961, 1967; *Twain: Man and Legend* by De Lancey Ferguson, 1943; *Mark Twain and Huck Finn* by Walter Blair, 1960; *A Casebook on Twain's Wound* edited by Lewis Leary, 1962; *Discussions of Twain* edited by Guy A. Cardwell, 1963; *Mr. Clemens and Mark Twain* by Justin Kaplan, 1966; *Twain: The Fate of Humor* by James M. Cox, 1966; *The Art of Twain* by William M. Gibson, 1976.

*   *   *

Samuel Langhorne Clemens, better known as Mark Twain, remains one of America's most widely read authors. To a great extent his popularity has rested upon his humor. It would be a mistake, however, to think of him simply as a humorist. To do so is to overlook the sharpness of his observation, the trenchancy of his social criticism, the depth of his concern for human suffering, and the clarity and extraordinary beauty of his style.

Story-telling came easily to Mark Twain because he grew up in the little town of Hannibal on the Mississippi river where the telling of "tall tales" was one of the chief pastimes. Even as a boy he developed a reputation for yarnspinning, a reputation he strengthened while a pilot on the Mississippi and a newspaperman in Nevada and California. Before he left California for the East in 1867 he had begun to deliver humorous lectures, a practice that he continued on and off until almost the end of his life. Oral story telling was immensely useful to him as a writer, for it taught him the value of such stylistic elements as point of view, proportion, timing, climax, concreteness, and dialogue that suggests real talk. He learned that the ear can catch much that the eye will miss; before finishing *Huckleberry Finn*, for example, he read it aloud over and over to make sure that it *sounded* right.

It should not be thought, however, that Mark Twain was an untutored genius who became a fine writer simply because he could tell a good tale. To be sure he had only a few years of formal schooling. But he worked in newspaper offices under some of the finest journalists of the time. More importantly he was a steady reader. A limited list of his reading would include American newspaper humor; popular fiction, as well as juvenile fiction; parodies and burlesques; travel books; the novels of such writers as Cervantes and Dickens (whom he admired) and Austen and Scott (whom he did not admire); history, biography, and autobiography; scientific works; and the writings of such persons as Hobbes, Bentham, Paine, Jefferson, Macaulay, Darwin, Carlyle, and especially W. E. H. Lecky. Most of Mark Twain's important works are a blend of his reading and his personal experience given form by his imagination.

Naturally enough he began his literary career by writing humorous sketches for midwestern and western newspapers. These apprentice pieces are derivative, satiric, and often gamy. About the only one that shows Twain's real promise as a literary figure is "The Celebrated Jumping Frog of Calaveras County." Significantly he wrote it for eastern instead of western publication. Van Wyck Brooks has argued that an eastern wife and eastern literary friends stunted Mark Twain's artistic growth, even emasculated it. But most critics agree with Bernard De Voto that Twain would probably have remained little more than a newspaper humorist without the influence of eastern readers and writers. One fact is certain: once Mark Twain began writing for an eastern audience he dropped the gaminess that had characterized his earlier work. Mrs. Clemens has been criticized for being too much of the moral censor, but the facts seem to indicate that Mark Twain censored himself far more than did his wife or any of his friends. Ribald in some of his speeches at men's banquets and in a few works meant only for men readers (e.g., *1601*) he rarely in his major works alludes even to romance between the sexes except in conventional Victorian ways.

Mark Twain continued to write short humorous sketches all through his life. His first longer works were travel books: *Innocents Abroad* and *Roughing It* − followed later by *A Tramp Abroad*, *Life on the Mississippi*, and *Following the Equator*. Actually, the shift from short sketches to travel books was minimal since Twain's travel works were simply series of sketches, tales, and anecdotes strung together by loose chronological threads. Based largely on letters he wrote for the *Alta California*, *Innocents Abroad* relates episodes from a trip Mark Twain took to the Holy Land in 1867. It is not a tightly constructed book but a literary vaudeville show in which the reader's pleasure comes from the variety rather than the cohesion. As narrator, Twain shifts his role back and forth from a superior person (e.g., a gentleman or a teacher) to an inferior person (e.g., a simpleton or a sufferer) with unexpected and hilarious results. The appeal of *Innocents Abroad* lies mainly in its humor, but in its time it also satisfied a growing curiosity in America about foreign lands, and in treating European culture without the customary deference it gave Americans an opportunity to feel less inferior about their own culture. Sold from door to door by agents of the American Publishing Company, a subscription house that published Twain's early books, it was an extraordinary success even though the times were hard.

Roughing It was even more successful and has continued to be one of Twain's best sellers. It is an account of his experiences in Nevada, California, and the Hawaiian Islands from 1861 through 1866. A somewhat more coherent account than *Innocents*, it is still primarily a series of sketches, actual and imagined, salted with old anecdotes and folklore. Although as narrator he again plays a variety of roles for comic effect, there is in *Roughing It* a basic consistency as he shows himself developing from a callow greenhorn to the experienced old-timer. *A Tramp Abroad* recounts a trip with Joseph Twichell, a Hartford minister, through parts of Germany, Switzerland, and Italy in 1878. It also contains such famous set-pieces as "Baker's Blue-Jay Yarn" and "The Awful German Language." *Life on the Mississippi* is the most disconnected of the travel books. The best portion, chapters IV–XVII, was published in seven installments in the *Atlantic Monthly* in 1875 under the title "Old Times on the Mississippi." These chapters offer comic glimpses of Twain's experience as an apprentice pilot. The remainder of the book, sprinkled with many irrelevancies, tells of a trip down and up the Mississippi from New Orleans to St. Paul taken in 1882. *Following the Equator* narrates the story of the around-the-world lecture tour Twain took in 1895–96 with Mrs. Clemens and his daughter Clara in an attempt to recoup some of the fortune he had just lost. Financially the trip was a success, but it was hard on his health and ended in misery when news came to them in England that their oldest daughter, Susy, was dying of meningitis. The book, Mark Twain said, was written to forget.

Mark Twain collaborated with Charles Dudley Warner in writing his first novel, *The Gilded Age*. The work is poorly constructed and in places reads like the worst of sentimental novels, but it contains one of Twain's most memorable characters – Colonel Sellers, the incurable optimist – and some of his finest satire. His attacks on current get-rich-quick schemes and on political corruption were so trenchant that it is hardly an accident that the post Civil War period in America has been called "the gilded age."

Next came the great books about boys. *The Adventures of Tom Sawyer* is his best constructed work since in it Twain manages to keep three narrative strands carefully interwoven: the family complication involving Tom and Aunt Polly; the love story between Tom and Becky; and the murder plot involving Tom, Huck, and Injun Joe. *Tom Sawyer* has been called "an idyll of boyhood," and as such it has never been surpassed. *The Prince and the Pauper*, the story of a mix-up in identity between Edward VI and the ragamuffin Tom Canty, was a happy addition to the children's literature of the time. *Adventures of Huckleberry Finn*, however, was an addition to the world's classics. This picaresque narrative is a modified frame story with Tom Sawyer being the focal center in the first three chapters and the last ten, and Huck and Jim being the center of interest in the middle twenty-nine chapters dealing with the journey down the river on a raft. Episodic in nature, the story nevertheless holds together because of the river, the constant presence of Huck as narrator, and perhaps especially because of Huck's growing awareness of Jim's humanity. The emotional climax of the book occurs where Huck resolves to save Jim from slavery even if he must go to hell for doing so. Many readers believe that the book goes downhill from that point to the end. Despite its humor and picturesque qualities the work is at bottom an unrelenting indictment of Mississippi river society in the 1840's – and of humanity in general at any time. But probably the most notable aspect of *Huckleberry Finn* is its style. Letting Huck tell the story forced Mark Twain to do what he did best: report concrete happenings in colloquial language. The result is what can properly be called folk poetry. It was this colloquial style that caused Ernest Hemingway to say that modern American literature began with *Huckleberry Finn*.

A Connecticut Yankee in King Arthur's Court begins as a spoof of Malory's *Morte Darthur* but quickly turns into an indictment of human tyranny: political, religious, and economic. As the sixth-century "boss," the nineteenth-century Yankee mechanic has one comic experience after another, but the work is essentially social satire, not so much of English history as contemporary industrialized society. The Yankee becomes less and less interesting as Twain uses him increasingly as a mouthpiece for his own views, especially the view that we are all the products of our training. The book is prophetic in its suggestion at the end that technology renders us insensitive to human suffering.

In the last twenty years of his life Twain's work fell off artistically though his political and social concerns continued to expand. In a work of potential greatness, *Pudd'nhead Wilson*, he confronted for the first time the more brutal aspects of slavery. His *Personal Recollections of Joan of Arc* is embarrassingly sentimental but more accurate in depicting the political forces at work than many other biographies of Joan. Shorter pieces attack such aspects of the time as American imperialism, Christian Science, the role of the Western powers in the Boxer Rebellion, King Leopold's treatment of the Congolese, and the lynching of blacks in the Southern states. *The Mysterious Stranger*, a work that Twain started at least three times and never finished, exhibits his philosophy of mechanical determinism and his growing belief that life is only a dream. *What Is Man?*, a dialogue in which an elderly cynic invariably bests a young idealist, argues that man is a machine and that choice is only an illusion. There is no doubt that the pessimism and bitterness, latent in Twain throughout most of his life, finally surfaced in these last twenty years. Financial difficulties and the deaths of his wife and two daughters seemed at times to be more than he could bear. Nevertheless his perceptions remained sharp and his writing controlled. Besides, he was sustained by honors from home and abroad such as no other American writer had ever enjoyed.

Much that Mark Twain wrote was topical and overwrought and is sliding into oblivion. But his best works remain unrivalled in their depiction of the comic and the pathetic in life – and of the inevitable relation between the two. William Dean Howells, Twain's best friend for forty years, composed a fitting epitaph when he wrote that Mark Twain was "sole, incomparable, the Lincoln of our literature."

—John C. Gerber

TYLER, Royall. American. Born in Boston, Massachusetts, 18 July 1757. Educated at Harvard University, Cambridge, Massachusetts, 1772–76, B.A. 1776; also received an honorary B.A. from Yale University, New Haven, Connecticut, 1776; studied law in the office of Francis Dana in Cambridge; admitted to the Massachusetts Bar, 1780. Commanding Major, Independent Company of Boston, in the Continental Army, serving as aide to General Sullivan in the Battle of Rhode Island, 1778; later served as aide to General Benjamin Lincoln and participated in the suppression of Shay's Rebellion, 1787. Married Mary Hunt Palmer in 1794; had at least one son. Practised law in Falmouth, Massachusetts, Portland, Maine, and Braintree, Massachusetts, 1780–85, Boston, 1785–91, and Putney, Vermont, 1791–1801; began writing in 1787; entered literary partnership with Joseph Dennie, as Colon and Spondee, 1794, and contributed satirical verse and prose to various periodicals; served as State's Attorney for Windham County, Vermont, 1794–1801; Assistant Judge, 1801–07, and Chief Justice, 1807–13, of the Supreme Court of Vermont; Professor of Jurisprudence, University of Vermont, 1811–14. Trustee of the University of Vermont, 1802–13. *Died 26 August 1826.*

PUBLICATIONS

Collections

Verse and *Prose*, edited by Marius B. Péladeau.   2 vols., 1968–72.

Plays

The Contrast (produced 1787).   1790; edited by James B. Wilbur, 1920.
May Day in Town; or, New York in an Uproar (produced 1787).
The Georgia Spec; or, Land in the Moon (produced 1797; as *A Good Spec*, produced 1797).
Four Plays (includes *The Island of Barrataria, The Origin of the Feast of Purim, Joseph and His Brethren, The Judgement of Solomon*), edited by Arthur Wallace Peach and George Floyd Newbrough.   1941.

Fiction

The Algerine Captive.   1797.

Verse

The Origin of Evil.   1793.
The Chestnut Tree; or, A Sketch of Brattleboro at the Close of the Twentieth Century.   1824.

Other

The Trial of Cyrus B. Dean.   1808.
The Yankey in London.   1809.
Reports of Cases Argued and Determined in the Supreme Court of Vermont (for 1800–03).   2 vols., 1809–10.
A Book of Forms (law forms).   1845.

Reading List: *Tyler* by G. Thomas Tanselle, 1967.

*   *   *

With the presentation of *The Contrast* in New York City on 16 April 1787, Royall Tyler, identified by the evening's drama critics as "a man of genius," entered the history of American drama, becoming the first known native American writer of comedy to be professionally produced. At a time when the new nation was struggling for identity, Tyler showed his particular genius in his choice of material and the manner of his expression. Creating a typical Yankee character, and generally fostering the "just pride of patriotism" which Washington would later emphasize in his Farewell Address, Tyler wrote a popular play for his time. He was never able to do it again, and perhaps once was enough. He also had other interests to pursue.

Royall Tyler was that inspired person who could combine the joys of literary creation with a professional career, and as a lawyer he eventually rose in his profession to serve as a justice of Vermont's Supreme Court. As a writer, however, he was attracted by all genres. With Joseph Dennie, essayist, critic and editor of the *Port Folio*, he wrote a large number of amusing and satiric essays, sketches, and verses. Signing themselves as "Colon & Spondee" they provided light and topical commentary on society, literature, and politics until 1811. Poetry, particularly in a light and satiric vein, interested Tyler throughout his life. His only novel, an episodic work stimulated by the activity of the Barbary Coast pirates, was *The Algerine Captive*. Other than *The Contrast*, however, he was at his best in the essay or short sketch. The collection called *The Yankey in London* best illustrates his work: a sprightly style, a reverence for America, and a varied subject matter.

It was with *The Contrast* that he gained his reputation as a writer. Although it lacks much of a plot and is a talky play imitative of eighteenth-century British sentimental comedy, it is clearly distinguished by an originality in thought and character. From the prologue – "Exult each patriot heart!" – to the climax all aspects of the play emphasize the new nationalism. Although they may be caricatures, the characters' distinctive qualities delight the reader and viewer. And everywhere there is satire – on fashion, theatre, the English, gossip – superimposed on the *contrast* – a contrast between the people of England and those of America, between affectation and straightforwardness, between city and country, between hypocrisy and sincerity, between foreign fraud and native worth. It was a play well designed to meet the demands and tastes of the new country.

Tyler continued to write more plays, but without great success. *May Day in Town; or, New York in an Uproar* appeared in a New York theatre a month after *The Contrast* but was not repeated. Four of Tyler's plays are published in the *America's Lost Plays* series. *The Island of Barrataria* is based on an episode in *Don Quixote*; the others have biblical sources. Only *The Island of Barrataria* deserves more critical attention than it has received. All, as might be expected of a lawyer, treat concepts of law, government, and justice. For Tyler, however, playwriting was only an avocation, though a pleasant one; he earned his living as a lawyer and justice. For the historian of American letters he is remembered mainly as the author of a single play.

—Walter J. Meserve

VERY, Jones.   American.   Born in Salem, Massachusetts, 28 August 1813; spent much of his childhood at sea with his father, a ship's captain. Educated at Fisk Latin School, Salem, 1832–34; Harvard University, Cambridge, Massachusetts, 1834–36 (Junior and Senior Bowdoin Prize), A.B. 1836; Tutor in Greek at the university and entered the Harvard Divinity School, 1836; forced to resign because of erratic behavior caused by his mystical experiences, 1838. Spent a month in McLean Asylum, Somerville, Massachusetts, 1838; enjoyed the patronage of Emerson, 1838–c. 1840; licensed to preach by the Cambridge Association of Ministers, 1843; held temporary pastorates in Eastport, Maine, and North Beverly, Massachusetts; returned to Salem, 1848, and thereafter lived a retired life with his sisters. *Died 8 May 1880.*

PUBLICATIONS

Collections

Selected Poems, edited by Nathan Lyons.   1966.

Other

Essays and Poems.   1839; revised edition, edited by James Freeman Clarke, as *Poems and Essays,* 1886; edited by Kenneth W. Cameron, as *Poems,* 1965.

Reading List: *Very: Emerson's "Brave Saint"* by William Irving Bartlett, 1942 (includes bibliography); *Very: The Effective Years 1833–1840* by Edwin Gittleman, 1967.

*   *   *

A curious example of single-minded Quietism, Jones Very occupies a special place in 19th-century American poetry. He wrote over 700 poems, most of these produced between 1833 and 1840 – the tumultuous years in which Very resolved his youthful religious doubts and reconciled himself to the eccentricities of his dominating mother and the loss of his sea-captain father. Dramatically realizing the Transcendentalist equation of self-reliance with God-reliance, Very experienced a transfiguring conversion in which he attained a second birth through the agency of the Holy Spirit. True, most of these poems tend to be repetitive, conventional in thought and expression, tedious, oblivious to drama, the play of language, humor, or the ambiguities of human experience. In his best poems, however, Very's voice can be as piercing as a knife-blade. Writing from the perspective of one who knows himself to be the passive instrument of a Higher Will, Very triumphs in lean enunciations of Being rather than explorations of Becoming. Characteristically using mild variations on the form of the Shakespearian sonnet and deeply imbued with the diction and syntax of the Bible, his utterance sometimes rises above its own awkwardness and penchant for bland abstractions to achieve an intense purity of religious awareness. Even though his successful poems are overly dependent on the Christian paradox of total submission as a condition of total fulfillment, the results are unsentimental and wholly persuasive.

His "nature poetry" and his literary essays could perhaps have been written by any gifted young man swept up in the enthusiasm of Channing's Unitarianism and Emerson's *Nature.* But some dozen or so meditational sonnets (e.g., "The Hand and Foot," "The Absent," "Morning," "The Presence," "The Journey," "The Eagles") succeed in translating literally the Transcendentalist exhortations to discover an inner divinity into spiritual declarations of considerable power. At first extravagantly praised by Emerson, Alcott, Margaret Fuller, and

Elizabeth Peabody, Very became something of an embarrassment due to the fanatic rigidity with which he judged all deviations from his way to salvation as well as the monochromatic mediocrity of much of his verse. From 1843 until his death, his literary production was almost entirely restricted to not particularly distinguished sermons.

—Earl Rovit

WALLACE, Lew(is). American. Born in Brookville, Indiana, 10 April 1827; moved with his family to Indianapolis, 1837. Largely self-educated; studied law in his father's office in Indianapolis: admitted to the Indiana bar, 1849. Raised a company, and served as a 2nd Lieutenant in the United States Army Infantry, in the Mexican War, 1846–47; appointed Adjutant General of Indiana at the beginning of the Civil War: served as a Colonel in the 11th Indiana Volunteers; promoted to Brigadier General, 1861, and Major General, 1862; prepared the defense of Cincinnati, 1863; given command of the Middle Division and VIII Army Corps, with headquarters at Baltimore, 1863; fought battle of Monocracy, and saved Washington, D.C. from capture, 1864; member of the court that tried Lincoln's assassins, and President of the court that tried the commandant of the Andersonville prison; mustered out, 1865. Married Susan Arnold Elston in 1852. Edited a free soil paper in Indianapolis, 1848; practiced law in Indianapolis, 1849; moved to Covington, 1850: prosecuting attorney, 1850–53; moved to Crawfordsville, 1853; member of the Indiana State Senate, 1856; returned to Crawfordsville and his law practice after the Civil War; Republican candidate for Congress, for Indiana, 1870; writer from 1870, also an illustrator; Governor of the New Mexico Territory, 1878–81; served as United States Minister to Turkey, 1881–85, then returned to Crawfordsville. *Died 15 February 1905.*

PUBLICATIONS

Fiction

The Fair God; or, The Last of the 'Tzins: A Tale of the Conquest of Mexico.   1873.
Ben-Hur: A Tale of the Christ.   1880.
The Boyhood of Christ.   1888.
The Prince of India: or, Why Constantinople Fell.   1893.

Play

Commodus.   1876.

Verse

The Wooing of Malkatoon, Commodus.   1898.

Other

Life of General Ben Harrison.   1888.
An Autobiography.   2 vols., 1906.

Editor, *Famous Paintings of the World.*   1894.

Reading List: *"Ben-Hur" Wallace* by Irving McKee, 1947.

*   *   *

Though famous in his day as a soldier, governor, lawyer, and diplomat, Lew Wallace is mainly remembered as the author of *Ben-Hur*, one of the three best-selling American novels of the 19th century. Indeed, the novel is known by many who could not name the author. *Ben-Hur* occupies a unique place in American cultural history; subtitled "A Tale of the Christ," it was the first and in some cases the only novel to be read by many puritanical fundamentalists who considered other fiction to be a sinful and idle waste of time. Dramatized in 1899 by William Young, *Ben-Hur* was an immense success for 20 years as a stage spectacle complete with chariot race run on treadmills. The play further broke down puritan inhibitions by introducing many to the theatre, and a colossal 1925 film version accomplished the same thing for the movies. Wallace wrote two other successful historical novels, *The Fair God* and *The Prince of India*; a blank verse drama, *Commodus*; a long narrative poem, *The Wooing of Malkatoon*, about the founder of the Ottoman Empire; a campaign biography of Benjamin Harrison; an account of Fort Donelson for *Battles and Leaders of the Civil War*; and an autobiography completed by his wife after his death in 1905.

Though the reading public considered *Ben-Hur* a supplement to sacred scripture and went to the dramatizations as to a passion play, Wallace was not a churchgoer, and the novel is closer in spirit to Jacobean revenge tragedy than to the New Testament. Wallace claimed, however, that he wrote it in part to refute the agnosticism of Robert Ingersol, and that during its composition he became convinced of the divinity of Jesus. All his novels deal with the clash of religions and cultures: *The Fair God* with the conflict of Aztec and Catholic conquistadors; *The Prince of India* with Moslem and Christian during the fall of Constantinople; and *Ben-Hur* with Jewish, pagan Roman, and Christian. Wallace's heroes are an Aztec prince, a prince of Judea, and a Turkish Sultan – all unusual for a 19th-century Anglo-Saxon to champion. A thorough researcher and a careful stylist, Wallace blended exotic romanticism with realistic detail. Though his own life was as dramatic as any of his fiction, he felt himself in some ways a failure and wrote about the romantic past as an escape from the routine of the law, the army, and political and diplomatic posts.

—Robert E. and Katharine M. Morsberger

WARD, Artemus. Pseudonym for Charles Farrar Browne. American. Born in Waterford, Maine, 26 April 1834. Largely self-educated; learned printer's trade on the *Weekly Democrat*, Lancaster, New Hampshire, 1847–48. Worked as a compositor and reporter on various New England newspapers from 1848, and worked in the printing trade in Boston for three years; writer from 1852; Reporter, then Columnist (as Artemus Ward), *Cleveland Plain Dealer*, 1852–59; member of the staff of *Vanity Fair*, New York, 1859–62; lecturer (performances of selections from his own works) in Boston and New York, 1861, Washington, D.C., 1862, California and Nevada, 1863, New York and Canada, 1864, and London, 1866–67; contributed to *Punch*, London, 1866–67. *Died 6 March 1867.*

PUBLICATIONS

Collections

Selected Works, edited by Albert Jay Nock. 1924.

Prose

Artemus Ward, His Book. 1862.
Artemus Ward, His Travels.   1865.
Artemus Ward among the Fenians.   1866.
Artemus Ward in London and Other Papers.   1867.
Artemus Ward's Lecture, edited by T. W. Robertson and E. P. Hingston.   1869; as
    Artemus Ward's Panorama, 1869.
Letters of Artemus Ward to Charles E. Wilson, 1858–1861.   1900.

Bibliography: in *Bibliography of American Literature* by Jacob Blanck, 1955.

Reading List: *Ward: A Biography and Bibliography* by Don C. Seitz, 1919; *Ward* by James
C. Austin, 1964.

*   *   *

Charles Farrar Browne, better known as Artemus Ward, was a Yankee humorist and a
foremost representative of native American humor. During the decades of the 1850's and
1860's he was so phenomenally popular that he became the national jester of the Civil War
period. He reached national prominence with his Artemus Ward pieces, which first appeared
in his column in the Cleveland *Plain Dealer* in 1858. As editor of *Vanity Fair* (1861–62), he
became the unofficial dean of American humor. Finally, he turned to lecturing and founded
the comic lecture as an enduring American institution.

Browne's literary reputation rests largely on the humor he published in the *Plain Dealer*
and *Vanity Fair.* Basic to his technique in the best of this humor is his use of Artemus Ward,
an old side-showman and rascal, as his alter ego. Using the side-showman's point of view
and colloquial language, Browne commented on a great variety of subjects. The literary
forms which he employed most extensively were the anecdote and the mock letter to the
editor. His favorite humorous device was misspelling, and he used it expertly.

The Artemus Ward pieces generally treat national figures, subjects, and issues; few
significant aspects of mid-nineteenth-century culture escaped his scrutiny. Reformers and
cultists caught his attention early, and he directed some of him most pungent satire at the
fanatics among them. He satirized militant feminists, zealous temperance advocates,
Mormons, Shakers, and proponents of free love; his biggest guns, however, he reserved for
unceasing war on the Abolitionists. A strong northern Democrat, he commented extensively,
too, on the subject of national politics; a strong supporter of the Union, he gave much
attention to the Civil War. During the war he repeatedly attacked Congress, the inept
leadership of the Union Army, draft-dodgers, profiteers, and pseudo-patriots.

Throughout his career Browne expressed freely his socio-economic views, generally those
of the Democratic Party. He was constantly critical of questionable business practices, the
mania for making money, speculation, and the excesses of capitalism in general. The false
ideals of his age he attacked again and again. In a number of his burlesques of the popular
romance, for example, he satirized not only the style of the genre itself, but also the
sentimentality, the questionable values, and superficial moralism which pervaded popular
culture.

Basically burlesques of the serious lyceum lecture, Browne's lectures were pure popular
entertainment. By careful planning and cautious experimentation he succeeded in appealing
to a large segment of the American people, and, at the end of his career, to British audiences
as well. By making comic lecturing both respectable and profitable he paved the way for
Mark Twain and the numerous other literary comedians who followed him. His best and
most famous lecture was "Artemus Ward among the Mormons."

For almost two decades, Charles F. Browne held the attention, affection, and respect of countless Americans, including Abraham Lincoln. Browne not only entertained Americans, but, pleading for sanity, common sense, and moderation, he helped to shape public opinion during a most critical period in American life. Finally, his success abroad helped to bring about a reappraisal by Americans of their native humorists.

—John Q. Reed

WARNER, Charles Dudley. American. Born in Plainsfield, Massachusetts, 12 September 1829; moved with his family to Charlemont, Massachusetts, 1837, and Cazenovia, New York, 1841. Educated at the Oneida Conference Seminary, Cazenovia; Hamilton College, Clinton, New York, B.A. 1851; worked as a railway surveyor in Missouri, 1853–54; joined a friend in business in Philadelphia, 1855; studied law at the University of Pennsylvania, Philadelphia, 1856–58, LL.B. 1858. Married Susan Lee in 1856. Writer from 1851; practiced law in Chicago, 1858–60; moved to Hartford, Connecticut, 1860, and established life-long partnership with Joseph R. Hawley: Assistant Editor to Hawley, 1860, then Editor, 1861–67, of Hawley's *Evening Press*; Editor and Proprietor, with Hawley, of the *Courant* (which consolidated with the *Press*), 1867 until his death; also wrote "The Editor's Drawer," 1884–98, and "The Editor's Study," 1894–98, for *Harper's* magazine; with his brother, George Warner, edited the *Library of the World's Best Literature*, 1896–97. Member, Hartford Park Commission, and Connecticut State Commission on Sculpture; Vice-President, National Prison Association. President, American Social Science Association, and National Institute of Arts and Letters. *Died 20 October 1900.*

PUBLICATIONS

Collections

Complete Writings, edited by Thomas R. Lounsbury.   15 vols., 1904.

Fiction

The Gilded Age: A Tale of Today, with Mark Twain.   1873; edited by Bryant Morey French, 1972.
A Little Journey in the World.   1889.
The Golden House.   1895.
That Fortune.   1899.

Other

My Summer in a Garden.   1871.
Saunterings (travel).   1872.
Backlog Studies.   1873.

Baddeck and That Sort of Thing (travel).   1874.
My Winter on the Nile, Among the Mummies and Moslems.   1876.
In the Levant.   1877.
In the Wilderness.   1878.
Being a Boy.   1878.
Washington Irving (biography).   1881.
Captain John Smith (1579–1631), Sometime Governor of Virginia, and Admiral of New England.   1881.
A Roundabout Journey.   1883.
A Study of Prison Reform.   1886.
Their Pilgrimage.   1887.
On Horseback: A Tour of Virginia, North Carolina, and Tennessee.   1888.
A-Hunting of the Deer and Other Essays.   1888.
Studies in the South and West, with Comments on Canada.   1889.
Our Italy.   1891; as *The American Italy,* 1892.
As We Were Saying.   1891.
As We Go.   1893.
The Relation of Literature to Life.   1896.
The People for Whom Shakespeare Wrote.   1897.
Fashions in Literature and Other Literary and Social Essays and Addresses.   1902.
Charles Dickens: An Appreciation.   1913.

Editor, *The Book of Eloquence.*   1851.
Editor, *The Warner Classics.*   4 vols., 1897.
Editor, *Dictionary of Authors, Ancient and Modern,* and *Synopsis of Books, Ancient and Modern.*   2 vols., 1910.

Reading List: *Warner* by Annie Fields, 1904; *Nook Farm: Mark Twain's Hartford Circle* by Kenneth R. Andrews, 1950.

*   *   *

Charles Dudley Warner was a competent essayist and editor whose high reputation from 1870 to 1900 is matched by an equally undeserved neglect in the present century. About half of his books are pot-boilers, especially the ten travel books that dealt first with Europe and the Near East and later with America. For example, *Our Italy* was subsidized to encourage travel to California. Only through his collaboration with Mark Twain in *The Gilded Age* is Warner known to most readers today. But his 1904 biographer dismissed *The Gilded Age*: "With all its ingenuities and cleverness, the book can hardly be called a literary success." The three novels Warner published from 1889 to 1899 were also passed over without much attention.

But in recent years these novels have been reprinted for their commentary on American society. In the trilogy, a great fortune is built up and finally lost, an indictment of the new American plutocracy which accumulated wealth and sacrificed values. Warner knew the threat posed by the Robber Barons in the period called the "Gilded Age," but he had confidence in the eventual triumph of New England-based morality and middle-class idealism. These novels are the culmination of Warner's observations, and his most serious studies of American society. As fiction they are less notable: Warner was an essayist, not a novelist.

Warner's literary criticism reflects conservative American cultural attitudes at the end of the nineteenth century. His two biographies are workmanlike: *Washington Irving* was his own volume in the "American Men of Letters" series he edited in the 1880's; and *Captain John Smith* was written as a semi-humorous contribution to the abortive "Lives of American Worthies" planned by a rival publisher. With his brother, he edited *The Library of the World's Best Literature,* but they document the literary taste of another day.

Although Warner's literary output was varied, his point of view remained consistent throughout his career. Warner was genial, idealistic, and temperate, a conservative in morals, literary tastes, and business matters. He was a thoroughly professional journalist-literary man, at his natural best in the personal essay. When his modest newspaper pieces collected into *My Summer in a Garden* made a tremendous success, he published the more elaborate *Backlog Studies* and was called a fit successor to Charles Lamb and Washington Irving. *In the Wilderness* and *Their Pilgrimage* are travel books about the Adirondacks and fashionable resorts, but more notable for their essays on manners. *As We Were Saying* and *As We Go* are collections of Warner's *Harper's* essays: American individuality is threatened by materialism and refinement. *Being a Boy* is Warner's nostalgic memories of a farm in the Berkshires in the 1830's. This reminiscence and *My Summer in a Garden* ought to be reprinted: Warner's unpretentious style and mellow mood might charm readers today.

—Clarence A. Glasrud

WARREN, Mercy (née Otis). American. Born in Barnstable, Massachusetts, 14 September 1728; sister of the American political activist James Otis. Educated privately. Married James Warren in 1754; five sons. Settled in Plymouth, Massachusetts, 1754; became active poet and historical apologist for the American cause in the pamphlet war preceding the War of Independence; a friend of John Adams and other American patriots. *Died 19 October 1814.*

PUBLICATIONS

Plays

> *The Adulator.*   1773.
> *The Defeat*, in Boston *Gazette*, 1773.
> *The Group.*   1775.
> *The Sack of Rome* and *The Ladies of Castille*, in *Poems.*   1790.

Verse

> *Poems, Dramatic and Miscellaneous.*   1790.

Other

> *Observations on the New Constitution.*   1788.
> *History of the Rise, Progress, and Termination of the American Revolution.*   3 vols., 1805.
> *A Study in Dissent: The Warren-Gerry Correspondence*, edited by C. Harvey Gardiner.   1968.

Reading List: *Warren* by Alice Brown, 1896; *First Lady of the Revolution: The Life of Warren* by Katharine S. Anthony, 1958.

*   *   *

Under normal circumstances, Mercy Warren would probably have restrained her literary impulse to private correspondence, elegant letters with, now and then, a poem enclosed. By birth and by marriage, however, she was allied to the anti-Tory faction in Massachusetts and, as a matron in her forties, she emerged as a voice in the pamphlet war which preceded America's Revolutionary War for Independence. Unlike her brother, James Otis, whose passionate but closely reasoned pamphlets were so influential in the 1760's, Mrs. Warren chose to write satirical dramatic sketches. In *The Adulateur*, to which some other hand added a high-rhetoric account of the Boston Massacre, *The Defeat*, and *The Group*, she introduced caricatures of her political opponents who, in waspish blank verse, condemned themselves and their colleagues. However interesting as eighteenth-century agitprops, Mrs. Warren's satires are minimally dramatic and have no characters in the complex sense of the word. Since the plays were published anonymously, as so much of the pamphlet literature was, later scholars decided that Mrs. Warren was the author of a number of unsigned satirical plays. *The Blockheads; or, The Affrighted Officers* (1776) and *The Motley Assembly* (1779), are still assigned to her by some editors, but they are so different in tone and style from anything else that she published that it is highly unlikely that she wrote them. One anonymous work, the pamphlet *Observations on the New Constitution*, a vigorous statement of the anti-federalist position in the ratification fight of 1787–88, is now rightly recognized as her work.

Aside from her political writings, Mrs. Warren wrote occasional verse, sometimes satirical, more often philosophic. Written in rhymed couplets, her poems were conventional in sentiment, vocabulary, and imagery, although they often embodied the austere, anti-deist, Christian morality that was so important to Mrs. Warren's life and thought. She wrote two verse tragedies, *The Ladies of Castile* and *The Sack of Rome*, which used historical material with contemporary overtones; like so many minor British plays of the eighteenth century, they substituted declamation for dramatic action. Her *History of the Rise, Progress, and Termination of the American Revolution*, thirty years in the making, is her most lasting work, although it is interesting today not as an objective history but for the "Biographical, Political, and Moral Observations" the title page promises. Her work as a whole is less important as a literary *oeuvre* than as a vehicle which gives the reader a glimpse of a tough-minded American woman who reflected and in some ways transcended the political and social context in which she wrote.

—Gerald Weales

WHEATLEY, Phillis.   American.   Born in Africa, possibly Senegal, c. 1753; sold as a slave to the John Wheatley family in Boston in 1761. Educated in the Wheatley family. Married John Peters, a freed slave, in 1778; three children. Sent to England for her health, 1773, and was received in London society; returned to Boston in the same year to care for Mrs. Wheatley; separated from the Loyalist Wheatleys by the Revolutionary War; thereafter her health deteriorated; died in poverty. *Died 5 December 1784.*

PUBLICATIONS

Collections

Poems (includes letters), edited by Julian D. Mason, Jr.   1966.

Verse

An Elegiac Poem on the Death of George Whitfield.   1770.
To Mrs. Leonard.   1771.
To the Rev. Mr. Pitkin.   1772.
To Thomas Hubbard.   1773.
Poems on Various Subjects, Religious and Moral.   1773.
An Elegy to Mary Moorhead.   1773.
An Elegy to Samuel Cooper.   1784.
Liberty and Peace.   1784.

Reading List: *Wheatley: A Critical Attempt and Bibliography* by Charles Frederick Heartman, 1916; *Bid the Vassal Soar* (on Wheatley and George Moses Horton) by Merle A. Richmond, 1974.

*   *   *

Phillis Wheatley's poetry is characterized by its adherence to form, in particular the heroic couplet, and conformity to neo-classical ritual in language and content. Thematically, she wrote to God's goodness, as opposed to His wrath, and she stressed that salvation is the most important goal in life. Her exposure to history, Classical literature, and myths is obvious in her poetry.

Wheatley's verses were didactic, pious, conventional, and predictable in that she wrote a significant number of occasional poems – for commemorating an event, perhaps, or for lamenting a death. Her tone fits the poems, however, and there is revealed in them a genuine adaptation to the subject-at-hand. She incorporates the Popean politeness into her verses as well as other features of his style – antithesis, the mid-line pause, and apostrophe.

Underneath the instructive tone and religious themes is the note of genuine religious joy based on her salvation from "The land of errors ... those dark abodes." Some critics have argued that Phillis Wheatley lost contact with her blackness; rather, she accomodated her blackness to a form she selected freely to use for expressing herself artistically – the heroic couplet. In all of Phillis Wheatley's poetry there rings an affirmation for life, even when she clearly identifies her race in what seems shame for her past enslavement. Her efforts to project herself away from the individual to the universal was part of the artistic detachment imposed by the form of poetry she loved, and the Puritan world in which she lived and believed. Her total output seems small only if one forgets her origins, her brief life, and the possibility that her husband sold or lost many of her works after her death. From poverty and slavery emerged a remarkable poet who sang "What songs should rise, how constant, how divine!"

—Margaret Perry

WHITMAN, Walt(er).   American.   Born in West Hills, Huntington, Long Island, New York, 31 May 1819. Educated in schools in Brooklyn, New York, 1825–30. Office Boy/Clerk in a lawyer's office, a doctor's office, and, in 1830, a printing office; began newspaper work on the Long Island *Patriot* and *Star*, 1831–34; schoolteacher on Long Island, 1836–41; Founder and Editor, *The Long Islander*, Huntington, 1838; Compositor, *Long Island Democrat*, 1839; worked as a newspaper man in New York, and as editor of the *Aurora, Tatler* and *Democrat*, 1840–46; Editor, Brooklyn *Daily Eagle*, 1846–47; Editor, New Orleans *Crescent*, 1848; Editor, Brooklyn *Freeman* (Free Soil Party paper), 1848–49; gave up newspaper work and, living with his parents, worked as a part-time carpenter while writing verse, 1850–54; free-lance journalist, 1855–62; Editor, Brooklyn *Daily Times*, 1857; served as a nurse in the Civil War, in Washington, D.C., 1862–65; Clerk in the Bureau of Indian Affairs, Washington, 1865; worked in the Attorney-General's Office, Washington, 1865 until he suffered a paralytic stroke, 1873; lived with his brother in Camden, New Jersey; travelled to the Far West and Canada, 1879–80; bought a house in Camden, 1884, and lived there for the remainder of his life. *Died 26 March 1892.*

PUBLICATIONS

Collections

The Collected Writings, edited by Gay Wilson Allen and Sculley Bradley.   1961–
The Complete Poems, edited by Francis Murphy.   1975.

Verse

Leaves of Grass.   1855; revised edition, 1856, 1860, 1867, 1870, 2 vols., 1876, 1881, 1889, 1891, 1897; manuscripts edited by Fredson Bowers, 1955, Harry W. Blodgett, 1959, and Arthur Golden, 2 vols., 1968.
Drum-Taps.   1865; with Sequel to Drum-Taps, 1866.
Poems, edited by W. M. Rossetti.   1868.
Passage to India.   1870.
After All, Not to Create Only.   1871.
As a Strong Bird on Pinions Free.   1872.
November Boughs (includes prose).   1888.
Good-Bye My Fancy.   1891.
Pictures: An Unpublished Poem, edited by Emory Holloway.   1927.

Fiction

Franklin Evans; or, The Inebriate.   1842; edited by Emory Holloway, 1929.
The Half-Breed and Other Stories, edited by Thomas O. Mabbott.   1927.

Other

Democratic Vistas.   1870.
Memoranda During the War.   1875–76.
Specimen Days and Collect.   2 vols., 1882–83; revised edition, as Specimen Days in America, 1887.

Complete Poems and Prose 1855–1888. 1888–89.
Complete Prose. 1892.
Autobiographia. 1892.
In Re Walt Whitman, edited by Horace L. Traubel and others. 1893.
Calamus: Letters, edited by Richard M. Bucke. 1897.
The Wound Dresser (letters), edited by Richard M. Bucke. 1898.
Notes and Fragments, edited by Richard M. Bucke. 1899.
An American Primer, edited by Horace L. Traubel. 1904.
Diary in Canada, edited by William Sloane Kennedy. 1904.
Lafayette in Brooklyn. 1905.
Criticism: An Essay. 1913.
The Gathering of Forces (essays), edited by Cleveland Rogers and John Black. 2 vols., 1920.
Uncollected Poetry and Prose, edited by Emory Holloway. 2 vols., 1921.
Rivulets of Prose: Critical Essays, edited by Carolyn Wells and Alfred F. Goldsmith. 1928.
Whitman's Workshop, edited by Clifton J. Furness. 1928.
A Child's Reminiscence, edited by Thomas O. Mabbott and Rollo G. Silver. 1930.
I Sit and Look Out (essays), edited by Emory Holloway and Vernolian Schwarz. 1932.
Whitman and the Civil War: A Collection of Original Articles and Manuscripts, edited by Charles I. Glicksberg. 1933.
New York Dissected (essays), edited by Emory Holloway and Ralph Adimari. 1936.
Whitman's Backward Glances, edited by Sculley Bradley and John A. Stevenson. 1947.
Faint Clews and Indirections, edited by Clarence Gohdes and Rollo G. Silver. 1949.
Whitman Looks at the Schools, edited by Florence Bernstein Freedman. 1950.
Whitman of the New York Aurora, edited by Joseph Jay Rubin and Charles H. Brown. 1950.
Whitman's Civil War, edited by Walter Lowenfels. 1960.
Whitman's New York: From Manhattan to Montauk (essays), edited by Henry M. Christman. 1963.
Camden Conversations, edited by Walter Teller. 1973.

Bibliography: by Oscar Lovell Triggs, in *Complete Writings 10,* 1902; "Whitman's Journalism: A Bibliography" by William White, in *Walt Whitman Review,* September 1968.

Reading List: *Whitman* by Frederick Schyberg, translated by Evie Allison Allen, 1951; *The Solitary Singer: A Critical Biography,* 1955, revised edition, 1967, and *A Reader's Guide to Whitman,* 1970, both by Gay Wilson Allen; *Whitman Reconsidered,* 1955, and *Whitman,* 1961, both by Richard Chase; *Leaves of Grass One Hundred Years After* edited by Milton Hindus, 1955; *The Evolution of Whitman* by Roger Asselineau, 2 vols., 1960; *The Presence of Whitman* edited by R. W. B. Lewis, 1962; *Whitman: A Collection of Critical Essays* edited by Roy Harvey Pearce, 1962; *A Century of Whitman Criticism* edited by Edwin H. Miller, 1969; *The Foreground of Leaves of Grass* by Floyd Stovall, 1974.

*   *   *

The life and work of Walt Whitman are in some measure a metaphor for America. Whitman began sounding his "barbaric yawp" over the roofs of the world when the youthful United States was a power of little consequence among nations. He was scorned or ignored at first, but gradually his *Leaves of Grass* compelled attention to its democratic message. By the time Whitman died his poetry had become a force to reckon with in the world.

Whitman's considerable apprenticeship as a newspaper writer and editor before 1855 gives no warning of a major poet in the making. His early poetry is undistinguished, and his prose is only competent journalism. But somehow Whitman found his inspiration and his vocation as poet. Emerson was probably the dominant influence, for in his essay "The Poet" he had called for a great American poet: "I look in vain for the poet whom I describe." And he added that "we have yet had no genius in America" who "knew the value of our incomparable materials." Whitman, for his part, later said: "I was simmering, simmering, simmering; Emerson brought me to a boil."

In response to a presentation copy of the first edition of *Leaves of Grass* in 1855 Emerson wrote Whitman: "I find it the most extraordinary piece of wit and wisdom that America has yet contributed ... I greet you at the beginning of a great career." The first edition was a slender volume of 95 pages that Whitman had had to publish himself, but it contained one of the great poems of the English language, the long, untitled poem that later, after revisions and additions, was called "Song of Myself." What Emerson had read when he opened the volume to the beginning of the poetry was

> I celebrate myself,
> And what I assume you shall assume,
> For every atom belonging to me as good belongs to you.

Thus began Whitman's mystic vision of equality, national purpose, and international brotherhood, "hoping to cease not till death," as he added in a line written later. The work did go on as long as he lived, and preparations for the final edition of his lifetime, arranged in the way he wanted his literary executors to print future editions, were in progress at the time he died.

The first edition is the work of the somewhat brash, 36-year-old Brooklyn carpenter-poet. But by the time the third edition appeared in 1860, Whitman had matured and deepened his human sympathies. Also the book had grown from the original 12 poems to 100 and contained the so-called "sex poems" that made Whitman anathema to proper Victorians. These are the "Children of Adam" poems dealing with heterosexual love and the "Calamus" poems treating homosexual affection. Many of them are tender, beautiful poems worth close study. But the most important new poem was "Out of the Cradle Endlessly Rocking," one of Whitman's greatest lyrics. It blends theme, symbol, and reminiscence in a free-verse form that Whitman had absolutely mastered. This edition, moreover, gives us a clear insight into Whitman's growth as a poet. It is an articulated whole, with a beginning, middle, and end, and one can begin to see the shape of *Leaves of Grass* in its final form. The most prominent themes of the third edition are love and death; both appear in the first two editions, but here they take on a tragic significance, and in Whitman's struggle with these themes he becomes a major poet.

Whitman's experiences in Washington as a volunteer nurse and his visits to Virginia battlefields during the Civil War provided the material for *Drum-Taps*, later incorporated into *Leaves of Grass*. This is the best collection of war poetry produced by any American writer on the Civil War. "Come Up from the Fields, Father" and "Vigil Strange I Kept on the Field One Night" are vivid, poignant examples. Shortly after *Drum-Taps* appeared, Lincoln's assassination inspired Whitman's memorable elegy "When Lilacs Last in the Dooryard Bloom'd." This poem employs the symbols of star (Lincoln), lilac (love), and bird (poet's soul) in 16 stanzas of beautiful free verse and begins:

> When lilacs last in the dooryard bloom'd,
> And the great star early droop'd in the western sky in the night,
> I mourn'd, and yet shall mourn with ever-returning spring.

But at the end the poet is reconciled to the loss of the wartime leader. The star, the lilac, and the bird singing in the swamp will remind him annually of "the dead I loved so well."

The fifth edition of *Leaves of Grass* came out in 1870, and in it the main order of the book became settled. It opens with the "Inscriptions," follows with "Starting from Paumanok," and ends with "Songs of Parting." Published as an annex to this edition was another of Whitman's best-known poems, "A Passage to India," a poem in which his vision of universal fraternity is clearly shown. It begins by celebrating the joining of east and west by the transcontinental railroad, the Suez Canal, and the Atlantic cable and goes on to envision these engineering feats as part of "God purpose" for "The people to become brothers and sisters."

An edition of 1881 was to have been brought out by James R. Osgood and Co. of Boston, but the district attorney of Boston threatened prosecution and Whitman was forced to find another publisher. A bolder Philadelphia firm issued the book without incident, for by this time Whitman, "The good gray poet," as his friend William O'Connor had dubbed him during the Washington years, was becoming a national figure and living down the early notoriety. In this edition the poems received their final revisions and titles ("Song of Myself" appears here for the first time) and permanent positions. Whitman continued to write until he died, but later editions print the later poems as annexes.

Although Whitman's poetry is the reason for his literary stature, he also wrote a considerable body of prose. The preface to the 1855 edition is an important statement; also noteworthy is the preface to *As a Strong Bird*. *Democratic Vistas*, however, is his major prose work. It is a collection of essays that are more a glimpse into the future of democracy than an analysis of the present. It tempers Whitman's usual buoyant optimism with a frank admission that the American democracy of 1871 (the period of the Grant Administration and the "Gilded Age") was not perfect. But he did not lose his faith in the ultimate success of the American experiment. Another prose work of interest is the informal autobiography that he published under the title *Specimen Days*.

Whitman is the first American poet to achieve a truly international reputation. Although Baudelaire discovered Poe before anyone ever had heard of Whitman, the Pre-Raphaelites in England soon discovered Whitman, and William Michael Rossetti edited an edition of *Leaves of Grass* in 1868. British interest in Whitman helped to convince Americans that the poet was not a charlatan, and from that modest beginning his reputation has spread like eddies from a rock dropped in still water. Jan Christian Smuts wrote a book on him in 1895, a study of his prosody was published in Italy in 1898, and an important French study appeared in 1908.

Although Whitman claimed he was not interested in technique, the sizable number of extant manuscripts show that he labored over his poems, making many cuts, additions, emendations. The variant readings of successive editions likewise reveal the poet as reviser. His form, however, has given critics trouble over the years. He said: "My form has strictly grown from my purports and facts, and is the analogy of them." His purpose was to present his vision and his experience, and it is not surprising that some readers have seen in his work the raw material of poetry rather than finished poems. The chief structural device is parallelism: repetition of idea, repetition of syntax, repetition of sound. Some 41% of the 10,500 lines of *Leaves of Grass* contain initial reiteration. One notes also that run-on lines are a rarity, and the first person singular is used extensively.

The influences on Whitman's free verse seem to have been public address, the Bible, and music. Not only was Emerson an inspiration in Whitman's finding his vocation as poet, but Emerson's essays, written as lectures, contain many of the same rhetorical devices that Whitman uses. Whitman as a young man wrote speeches and at one time had thought of making a career as a public speaker. The parallelism and coordinate structure of the Bible, which Whitman knew well, also may have influenced his style, though this is hard to document. Finally, the impact of music must be accorded a place in Whitman's development. The repetition of themes, the use of *recitative* and *aria* support Whitman's own statement: "But for the opera I could never have written *Leaves of Grass*."

—James Woodress

WHITTIER, John Greenleaf. American. Born in Haverhill, Massachusetts, 17 December 1807. Educated at local schools; studied art at Haverhill Academy, 1827; teacher there, 1827–28. Editor, various country newspapers, 1826–32; engaged in the anti-slavery campaign as editor of various reform journals and as polemicist, 1833–60; settled at Amesbury, Massachusetts, 1836; after the Civil War lived in semi-retirement, devoting himself to verse. *Died 7 September 1892.*

PUBLICATIONS

Collections

The Writings, edited by Horace E. Scudder.   7 vols., 1888–89; revised edition, 1894.
The Poetical Works, edited by W. Garrett Horder.   1919.
Letters, edited by John B. Pickard.   3 vols., 1977.

Verse

Moll Pitcher.   1831; revised edition, 1840.
Mogg Megone.   1836.
Poems Written During the Progress of the Abolition Question, 1830–1838.   1837.
Poems.   1838.
Moll Pitcher, and The Minstrel Girl.   1840.
Lays of My Home and Other Poems.   1843.
The Song of the Vermonters.   1843.
Miscellaneous Poems.   1844.
Ballads and Other Poems.   1844.
The Stranger in Lowell.   1845.
Voices of Freedom.   1846.
Poems.   1849.
Songs of Labor and Other Poems.   1850.
Poetical Works.   1853.
The Chapel of the Hermits and Other Poems.   1853.
A Sabbath Scene.   1854.
The Panorama and Other Poems.   1856.
The Sycamores.   1857.
The Poetical Works.   2 vols., 1857.
Home Ballads and Other Poems.   1860.
In War Time and Other Poems.   1864.
National Lyrics.   1865.
Snow-Bound: A Winter Idyl.   1866.
The Tent on the Beach and Other Poems.   1867.
Among the Hills and Other Poems.   1869.
Poetical Works.   2 vols., 1870.
Ballads of New England.   1870.
Miriam and Other Poems.   1871.
The Pennsylvania Pilgrim and Other Poems.   1872.
Hazel-Blossoms.   1875.
Mabel Martin: A Harvest Idyl.   1876.
Favorite Poems.   1877.
The Vision of Echard and Other Poems.   1878.

The King's Missive and Other Poems. 1881.
The Bay of Seven Islands and Other Poems. 1883.
Early Poems. 1885.
Saint Gregory's Guest and Recent Poems. 1886.
Poems of Nature. 1886.
Narrative and Legendary Poems. 1888.
At Sundown. 1890.
Legends and Lyrics. 1890.
A Legend of the Lake. 1893.
The Demon Lady. 1894.

Other

Legends of New England. 1831.
Justice and Expediency. 1833.
Narrative of James Williams. 1838.
The Supernaturalism of New England. 1847; edited by Edward Wagenknecht, 1969.
Leaves from Margaret Smith's Journal. 1849.
Old Portraits and Modern Sketches. 1850.
Literary Recreations and Miscellanies. 1854.
Prose Works. 2 vols., 1866.
Works. 1874.
Complete Works. 1876.
Whittier on Writers and Writing: The Uncollected Critical Writings, edited by Edwin Cady and Harry Hayden Clark. 1950.

Editor, *The Journal of John Woolman.* 1872.
Editor, *Child Life: A Collection of Poems.* 1873.
Editor, *Child Life in Prose.* 1874.
Editor, *Songs of Three Centuries.* 1876; revised edition, 1877.

Bibliography: *A Bibliography of Whittier* by Thomas F. Currier, 1937.

Reading List: *Life and Letters of Whittier* by Samuel T. Pickard, 1894, revised edition, 2 vols., 1907; *Whittier: Bard of Freedom* by Whitman Bennett, 1941; *Whittier: Friend of Man* by John A. Pollard, 1949; *Whittier* by Lewis Leary, 1961; *Whittier: An Introduction and Interpretation* by John B. Pickard, 1961; *Whittier: A Portrait in Paradox* by Edward Wagenknecht, 1967; *Whittier's Poetry: An Appraisal and a Selection* by Robert Penn Warren, 1971; *Life of Whittier* by William J. Linton, 1972.

*   *   *

In the "Proem," a poem which introduced his collected works, John Greenleaf Whittier scrutinized his life and poetic achievement in these lines:

> The rigor of a frozen clime,
> The harshness of an untaught ear,
>   The jarring words of one whose rhyme
>   Beat often Labor's hurried time,
> Or Duty's rugged march, through storm and strife,
>   are here.

The honesty of these sparse lines is characteristic. Reared as a poor farm boy in a non-conformist Quaker faith, he had little education and was primarily a sectional romantic poet in his early years. Fortunately his enlistment in the abolitionist cause in 1833 converted the aspiring young lyricist into a radical propagandist, politician, and part-time editor whose verses championed the rights of slaves and democratic principles. The twenty years of abolitionist work reforged Whittier's vapid sentimentalism into a powerful weapon for the oppressed and strengthened his regard for moral action. By the 1850's Whittier's reform work was over, and in his remaining years his writing showed him as a religious humanist, striving for moral perfection and inner spirituality rather than social and political reform.

Like most of the "schoolroom" poets, Longfellow, Lowell, Holmes, and others, Whittier's themes were few and limited: the value of domestic emotions, the innocence of childhood, the necessity of social equality, and the nobility of ethical action. However, unlike these other popular poets, Whittier drew upon his native roots for inspiration. In his best poems Whittier displayed a mastery of local color techniques, a competent use of rural imagery, and the everyday language of the Merrimack farmer. His instinctive handling of native materials conveyed his inner love for the environment that molded, and his understanding of the traditions that inspired, him. Still his poetry suffered from the diffusion and sentimentality inherent in the tradition of public rhetoric in which he wrote. Perhaps no other established nineteenth-century American poet wrote so much poor verse, but the miracle is that by the most exacting poetical standards his best remains so good.

Aside from a few nature poems like "The Last Walk in Autumn," an occasional Abolitionist poem like "Ichabod," and selections from his religious poems, Whittier's ballads and genre pieces represent his finest poetical achievement. They contain some of the best examples of native folklore written in America. His ballads, especially, express his lifelong interest in colonial history, the Quakers, local legends, and folk superstitions; and they are remarkably true to the graphic realism and dramatic intensity of traditional folk balladry. His best ballads take incidents like a skipper who had betrayed his own townspeople, a witch who prophesied death, or the terrifying actions of specter warriors, bed-rocks them with exact physical detail, and then concentrates on the dramatic moment of conflict. "Telling the Bees" skillfully handles a local superstition with childlike detail to hide the chilling reality of nature's destruction; "The Garrison of Cape Ann," "The Palatine," and "The King's Missive" rework historical incidents; "Amy Wentworth," "The Countess," and "The Witch of Wenham" narrate pastoral romances; while the often-parodied "Barbara Frietchie" was accepted by a war-wearied nation as an expression of their personal conviction that the Union must be preserved. Whittier's finest ballad, "Skipper Ireson's Ride," was based on an old Marblehead song about women tarring and feathering a fishingboat captain. The ballad opens *in medias res*, plunging directly into the wild tumult and chaos of mob action as the skipper is pushed through Marblehead. Finally Ireson cries out his remorse, and with "half scorn, half pity" the women free him. The final refrain changes "Old" Floyd Ireson to "Poor" Floyd Ireson and becomes a mournful dirge forever accusing and dooming Ireson, besides emphasizing the hollowness of the women's revenge.

Similarly, Whittier's genre poems elevated the ordinary details of Essex County life into a universal expression of boyhood innocence, agrarian simplicity, and pastoral romance that caught the pathos and beauty of a dying rural tradition. In poems like "Maud Muller," "In School-Days," "Among the Hills," and "Memories," Whittier idealized and typified the district school days, the harvest-filled autumn days, and the barefoot-boy days to capture the romantic aspirations of a responsive American public. "Cobbler Keezar's Vision," "Abraham Davenport," "To My Old Schoolmaster," and others contain some of Whittier's best rustic anecdotes as well as realistic and humorous sketches of the Yankee character. Whittier's particular skill in recreating the past is seen most fully in his one sustained triumph, *Snow-Bound*. In this poem Whittier expresses the value of family affections by the symbolic development of a fire-snow contrast and by the skillful interweaving of present reality with past memories. His artistic handling of structure, careful development of the fire image, and graphic depiction of the family and outside visitors make this a minor masterpiece of nineteenth-century poetry. In this poem Whittier captured the essence of the New England mind and placed himself in the direct line of American expression that stretches from Anne Bradstreet to Robert Frost.

Although Whittier's poems fall far short of the poetic imagination and philosophical depth of major American poets such as Whitman, Poe, Dickinson, and Emerson, his verses exhibit more spiritual illumination and downright "grit" than the polished verses of Longfellow and the other minor poets. Despite the severe criticism of his poetry in the twentieth century, Whittier's place in American literature seems secure. He will continue to be read and enjoyed as long as people respond to their traditions and demand honest expression of their fundamental democratic and religious feelings.

—John B. Pickard

WIGGLESWORTH, Michael. American. Born in England, probably in Yorkshire, 18 October 1631; emigrated with his parents to the Massachusetts Bay Colony, 1638. Educated at Harvard University, Cambridge, Massachusetts, graduated 1651. Married 1) Mary Reyner in 1655 (died, 1659), one daughter; 2) Martha Mudge in 1679 (died, 1690), six children; 3) Sybil Sparhawk Avery in 1691, one son. Fellow and Tutor at Harvard University, 1652–54; ordained to the ministry of the Puritan Church, 1656, and thereafter served as Minister to the church at Malden, Massachusetts; also studied and practised medicine; Fellow at Harvard University, 1697–1705. *Died 27 May 1705.*

PUBLICATIONS

Collections

The Day of Doom with Other Poems, edited by Kenneth B. Murdock. 1929.

Verse

The Day of Doom. 1662(?); revised edition, 1666.
Meat Out of the Eater. 1670; revised edition, with *Riddles Unriddled,* 1689.
Riddles Unriddled: or, Christian Paradoxes. 1689.

Other

The Diary, edited by Edmund S. Morgan. 1965.

Reading List: *Sketch of the Life of Wigglesworth, with a Fragment of His Autobiography, Some of His Letters, and a Catalogue of His Library* by John W. Dean, 1863, revised edition, 1871; *No Featherbed to Heaven: A Biography of Wigglesworth* by Richard H. Crowder, 1962.

*   *   *

Michael Wigglesworth's first major publication, *The Day of Doom* – a best-seller for a century – was a jeremiad of 224 eight-line stanzas presenting in vivid detail the Calvinist notion of the events of the Final Judgment. The writer's purpose was not to write fine poetry but to provide uncomplicated facts in easy rhyme. For generations children recited from memory the entire poem, which devotes a few stanzas to the rewards of the saved but many more to the pleas, sentencing, and punishment of the damned. In the same volume with *The Day of Doom* Wigglesworth published several other poems setting forth Puritan doctrine, pleading with the reader to turn from wickedness and avoid everlasting punishment (e.g., "A Short Discourse on Eternity" and "Vanity of Vanities"), verses couched in sermonic phrases, jogging along in well-worn meters without much variety. The imagery, already familiar to his church-going readers, was nevertheless vigorously pictorial as the poet strove to convert the sinners.

Another jeremiad, "God's Controversy with New-England," showed the reader that because of the general evil-doing of the colonists God was right in inflicting illness and drought on the region. The verse forms here change from ballad structure ("fourteeners") to six-line iambics to quatrains as Wigglesworth pleads the cause for spiritual renewal.

The other large work he called *Meat Out of the Eater*, a series of ten meditations and "A Conclusion Hortatory" demonstrating "the Necessity, End, and Usefulness of Afflictions." "Riddles Unriddled," clusters of verses constituting nine paradoxes, uses a little more variety in verse form in an attempt to fit structure to meaning. For example, the first paradox, "Light in Darkness," consists of ten "Songs," some in the form of medieval debates. The poet moves from ballad form in one "Song" to six-syllable lines in couplet rhyme in another. The other paradoxes likewise are composed of a number of separate poems, illustrating such themes as "Strength in Weakness" and "In Confinement Liberty."

In a twelve-year span (1662–1673) – during a period when he was physically too weak to preach from his Malden pulpit – Wigglesworth wrote nearly all his extant poetry, and in a surprising variety of forms: lyric, dramatic, narrative, descriptive, didactic and hortatory, and autobiographical. Though not a major poet, he made a serious contribution to Puritan Calvinist doctrine, preserving in not unreadable verse the ideas that his readers were hearing from the pulpit Sunday after Sunday.

Wigglesworth's *Diary* was edited by Edmund S. Morgan. He transcribed and made available to modern readers the frequent passages in shorthand. The *Diary* fully discloses the poet's constant struggle with his conscience, his soul warring against powerful drives inside his frail flesh. A couple of college orations (including "The Praise of Eloquence") have been preserved and are sometimes anthologized. Written in "plain style," they are obviously class assignments discussing the elements of effective oratory.

—Richard H. Crowder

WILLIS, Nathaniel Parker. American. Born in Portland, Maine, 20 January 1806. Educated at Boston Latin School; Phillips Academy, Andover, Massachusetts; Yale University, New Haven, Connecticut, graduated 1827. Married 1) Mary Stace in 1835 (died, 1845); 2) Cornelia Grinnell in 1846, three daughters and two sons. Became known as a writer while still an undergraduate; edited 2 issues of *The Legendary*, 1828, and an annual *The Token*, 1829; Founding Editor, *American Monthly Magazine*, Boston, 1829–31; settled in New York, 1831; lived in Europe, as Foreign Correspondent for the *New York Mirror*, edited by George Pope Morris, 1831–36; returned to New York, and continued to travel and write for the *Mirror*, 1836–39; with D. T. O. Porter, Founding Editor of the *Corsair*, New York,

1839; Proprietor and Editor, with Morris, of the weekly *New Mirror*, subsequently the daily *Evening Mirror*, 1840–45; visited Europe, 1845, then returned to New York and joined Morris as editor and proprietor of his *National Press*, which they renamed the *Home Journal*, 1846–64, as sole owner and editor, 1864–67; settled at Idlewild, a country seat on the Hudson, 1853. *Died 20 January 1867.*

PUBLICATIONS

Collections

    Prose Writings, edited by Henry A. Beers.   1885.
    Poetical Works.   1888.

Fiction

    Inklings of Adventure.   1836.
    Loiterings of Travel.   1840.
    Romance of Travel (stories).   1840.
    Dashes at Life with a Free Pencil.   1845.
    People I Have Met (stories).   1850.
    Life Here and There (stories).   1850.
    Fun-Jottings; or, Laughs I Have Taken a Pen To (stories).   1853.
    Paul Fane; or, Parts of a Life Else Untold.   1857.

Plays

    Bianca Visconti; or, The Heart Overtasked (produced 1837).   1839.
    Tortesa; or, The Usurer Matched (produced 1839).   1839.

Verse

    Sketches.   1827.
    Fugitive Poetry.   1829.
    Poem Delivered Before the Society of the United Brothers, with Other Poems.   1831.
    Melanie and Other Poems.   1835.
    The Sacred Poems.   1843.
    Poems of Passion.   1843.
    The Lady Jane and Other Poems.   1843.
    Poems Sacred, Passionate, and Humorous.   1845; revised edition, 1849.
    Poems of Early and After Years.   1848.

Other

    Pencillings by the Way.   3 vols., 1835; revised edition, 1844; reprinted in part as *Summer Cruise in the Mediterranean,* 1853.
    A l'Abri; or, The Tent Pitched.   1839; revised edition, as *Letters from under a Bridge, and Poems,* 1840.

American Scenery, drawings by W. H. Bartlett.   2 vols., 1840.
Canadian Scenery Illustrated, drawings by W. H. Bartlett.   2 vols., 1842.
The Scenery and Antiquities of Ireland, with J. Stirling Coyne, drawings by W. H.
   Bartlett.   2 vols., 1842.
Lectures on Fashion.   1844.
Rural Letters and Other Records of Thought at Leisure.   1849.
Hurry-Graphs; or, Sketches of Scenery, Celebrities, and Society.   1851.
Memoranda of the Life of Jenny Lind.   1853.
Health Trip to the Tropics.   1853.
Famous Persons and Famous Places.   1854.
Out-Doors at Idlewild.   1855.
The Rag-Bag: A Collection of Ephemera.   1855.
The Convalescent.   1859.

Editor, *The Legendary*.   1828.
Editor, *Trenton Falls, Picturesque and Descriptive*.   1851.

Reading List: *Willis* by Henry A. Beers, 1885 (includes bibliography); *The World of Washington Irving* by Van Wyck Brooks, 1944; *Willis* by Cortland P. Auser, 1969.

*   *   *

Nathaniel Parker Willis was in his day the most famous recorder of the details of social life and customs in America. In a sense, he was to his age what Tom Wolfe is to ours, but he was, in a way that Wolfe is not, sympathetic to most of the signs of status that he found around him – the resorts, homes, clothes, and so forth.

Willis seldom dealt with old established families. He generally concerned himself with the newly rich in search of the means through which they could express their status. He provided them with newspaper and magazine columns describing exactly the things they wanted to know and collected his observations in a series of volumes that were quite popular at the time. His books about fashionable life can be divided into three categories: (1) books dealing with fashionable life abroad (a subject of endless fascination for newly rich Americans who, as a measure of their recently acquired status, adopted European standards, customs, and even diction – although few such people had crossed the Atlantic), (2) books concerning fashionable life in America, especially in New York and in such watering-places as Saratoga Springs, New York, and (3), most significantly, books detailing rural, middle-class life. *Pencillings by the Way* is an excellent account of his observations abroad, and *Hurry-Graphs* is typical of his volumes on life in America. His books on rural life include *A l'Abri*, *Out-Doors at Idlewild*, and *The Convalescent* and are of major importance to social as well as cultural historians as three of the earliest and most influential expressions of middle-class obsession with rural and suburban life. Willis, together with the essayist and landscape gardener Andrew Jackson Downing, was among the first to popularize this way of life in America. He also worked with the picturesque painter W. H. Bartlett.

Willis was also a poet (albeit a minor one), a playwright, a novelist, and a short story writer. His short stories, such as those collected in *Dashes at Life with a Free Pencil*, have from time to time attracted critical attention, and his novel *Paul Fane* has been considered a forerunner of Henry James's international novels, but it was as a journalist, critics generally agree, that he was most successful. In particular, it is his documents of fashionable life for which he should be remembered.

—Edward Halsey Foster

WISTER, Owen. American. Born in Germantown, Philadelphia, Pennsylvania, 14 July 1860. Educated at schools in Switzerland and England; Germantown Academy; St. Paul's School, Concord, New Hampshire, 1873–78; Harvard University, Cambridge, Massachusetts, 1878–82, B.A. (summa cum laude) in music 1882; studied music in Europe, 1882–84, then studied at the Harvard Law School, 1885–88, LL.B. 1888; admitted to the Pennsylvania bar, 1889. Married his second cousin Mary Channing Wister in 1898 (died, 1913); three sons and three daughters. Practised law in Philadelphia, 1889–91; thereafter a full-time writer; settled in Charleston, South Carolina, 1902. Overseer, Harvard University, 1912–18, 1919–25. Fellow, American Academy of Arts and Letters. Honorary Member, Société des Lettres, Paris; Honorary Fellow, Royal Society of Literature, London. *Died 21 July 1938.*

PUBLICATIONS

Fiction

The New Swiss Family Robinson. 1882.
The Dragon of Wantley. 1892.
Red Men and White (stories). 1895.
Lin McLean. 1897.
The Jimmyjohn Boss and Other Stories. 1900.
The Virginian: A Horseman of the Plains. 1902.
Philosophy 4: A Story of Harvard University. 1903.
Lady Baltimore. 1906.
How Doth the Simple Spelling Bee. 1907.
Mother. 1907.
Members of the Family. 1911.
When West Was West. 1928.

Verse

Done in the Open, illustrated by Frederic Remington. 1902.
Musk-Ox, Bison, Sheep, and Goat, with Caspar W. Whitney and George Bird Grinnell. 1904.
Indispensable Information for Infants. 1921.

Other

Ulysses S. Grant. 1900.
The Seven Ages of Washington: A Biography. 1907.
The Pentecost of Calamity (essay). 1918.
A Straight Deal; or, An Ancient Grudge (essay). 1920.
Neighbors Henceforth. 1922.
Watch Your Thirst: A Dry Opera in Three Acts. 1923.
Roosevelt: The Story of a Friendship, 1880–1919. 1930.
The Writings. 11 vols., 1928.
Wister Out West: His Journals and Letters, edited by Fanny Kemble Wister. 1958.

Reading List: *The Eastern Establishment and the Western Experience: The West of Frederic Remington, Theodore Roosevelt, and Wister* by G. Edward White, 1968; *Wister* by Richard W. Etulain, 1973.

*   *   *

Although he never gave himself fully to the American West, the West was the making of Owen Wister as a man and as a writer. Born into an aristocratic Philadelphia family, educated in eastern schools and abroad, Wister initially sought a career in music. His practical father encouraged a business career, then law. Uncertain of himself, Wister took the advice of his physician in 1885 and went to Wyoming for the summer. Then and in succeeding summers in the West, he found health, and a frontier and cowboy milieu that he knew was about to end and deserved to be put into fiction. Wister saw great romantic possibilities in the cowboy, known to fiction only in dime novels.

Wister had published a burlesque of *Swiss Family Robinson* the year he graduated from Harvard. Shortly thereafter he and a cousin wrote a novel, but he took the advice of William Dean Howells, who found the book too bold, and did not submit it for publication. Wister's instinct was for the actual and the concrete, and he might have been a better writer had he not acquiesced repeatedly to the genteel tradition. The habit of writing ingrained, he kept detailed journal entries on his Western summers – the factual basis for many of his stories. The journals, published twenty years after Wister's death, are well worth reading.

In 1891 Wister wrote "Hank's Woman," his first Western story. *Harper's* accepted it and encouraged Wister to write about the West. His stories were full of local color interest when the local color movement was still important in American literature. *Red Men and White*, his first short story collection, was published in 1896, followed by *Lin McLean*. The cowboy McLean gave some unity to the book, but it is hardly a novel. *The Virginian*, the novel that is Wister's most important achievement, was likewise based on earlier published stories. It, too, has problems of point of view. The Eastern tenderfoot who arrives in Wyoming and "grows up" there could not possibly know all the material he relates. The novel's structure is episodic. The contrast of East and West, however, gave embodiment to Wister's sense of the romantic possibility of the cowpuncher, possibilities that became legion in Western novels and movies. Wister's hero is a natural aristocrat who is capable of showing his inner fiber in a land with its own rules for law and order. Wister was not particularly interested in portraying the inside of ranch life; rather he wished to show his hero grow and adjust to the closing frontier, proving himself worthy of the aristocratic Molly Stark Wood of Vermont who has come to Wyoming to teach school.

However attractive the West might be for summer hunting and adventure, Wister became increasingly pulled to the East and to Europe, and to the South. He had moved to Charleston, South Carolina, in 1902, where the southern aristocratic codes were congenial to Wister's temperament. *Lady Baltimore* is Wister's Jamesian comedy of manners. The Jamesian narrator comes from the North to Kings Port (Charleston) to engage in genealogical research. The love story he narrates, and plays a part in, enables Wister to juxtapose culture against culture. The novel is pleasant reading, convincing in its portrayal of Southern attitudes of the time, and indicative of the reservations Wister had about the cruder West. Thereafter, Wister wrote other stories about the West, but he ceased to visit it, and by the time of World War I his main concern was his family, Europe, and politics.

—Joseph M. Flora

WOOLSON, Constance Fenimore. American. Born in Claremont, New Hampshire, 5 March 1840; while still an infant moved with her family to Cleveland. Educated at Miss Hayden's School, Cleveland, and the Cleveland Seminary; Madame Chegary's School, New York City, graduated 1858. Returned to the family home in Cleveland, 1858; writer from 1862, full-time writer from 1869; lived in the Carolinas and Florida, 1873–79; wrote criticism for the *Atlantic Monthly*, Boston, 1877–79; lived in Europe after 1879, in England, 1883–86, Florence, 1887–89, Oxford, 1891–93, and Venice, 1893–94. *Died 24 January 1894.*

PUBLICATIONS

Collections

(Selection), edited by Claire Benedict. 1932.

Fiction

The Old Stone House (juvenile). 1872.
Castle Nowhere: Lake Country Sketches. 1875.
Rodman the Keeper: Southern Sketches. 1880.
For the Major. 1883.
Anne. 1883.
East Angels. 1886.
Jupiter Lights. 1889.
Horace Chase. 1894.
The Front Yard and Other Italian Stories. 1895.
Dorothy and Other Italian Stories. 1896.

Verse

Two Women: 1862. 1877.

Other

Mentone, Cairo, and Corfu. 1895.

Reading List: *Woolson: Literary Pioneer* by John D. Kern, 1934; *Woolson* by Rayburn S. Moore, 1963.

*   *   *

Although Constance Fenimore Woolson contributed verse to the magazines and published a long poem, wrote a children's story, and collected some of her travel sketches for a volume that appeared posthumously, she was best known in her own day as a writer of fiction, and to one Boston critic at least as the "novelist laureate" of America. Such a characterization is likely to strike present readers as a bit off the mark, but in the late nineteenth century her stories and novels struck many reviewers and critics, including Henry James, as an important contribution to literature.

Even present readers must concede that Woolson made a contribution to the short fiction of her period. Her best stories — "The Lady of Little Fishing," "Rodman the Keeper," "King David," "The Front Yard," and "A Transplanted Boy," among others — demonstrate her capacity to deal with scenes as varied as the Great Lakes country, the South, and Europe and with universally valid characters. She was not an innovator in technique, but her best tales suggest that she was mindful of the work of George Eliot, Turgenev, and Henry James.

As a novelist she was less successful. Though the scenes and characters are, as in the short stories, handled ably, the structure of her novels (except *Horace Chase*) seems episodic and infrequently functional. This weakness in structure is ironically pointed up by her success with *For the Major*, her only novella, a minor classic in many ways, and her most successful sustained piece of fiction. Still, each novel has its individual merits and *East Angels*, as James maintained in *Harper's Weekly* in 1887, "is a performance which does Miss Woolson the highest honour."

Her best work belongs to the development of realism in America, as regards both local color and the psychological analysis of character, and it offers, as I have noted in *Constance Fenimore Woolson*, "a sympathetic understanding and treatment of character in authentic surroundings by one whose vision was broad enough and whose insight was deep enough to include not only her own country but Europe as well."

—Rayburn S. Moore

NOTES ON CONTRIBUTORS

ASHLEY, Leonard R. N.   Professor of English, Brooklyn College, City University of New York. Author of *Colley Cibber*, 1965; *19th-Century British Drama*, 1967; *Authorship and Evidence: A Study of Attribution and the Renaissance Drama*, 1968; *History of the Short Story*, 1968; *George Peele: The Man and His Work*, 1970. Editor of the *Enriched Classics* series, several anthologies of fiction and drama, and a number of facsimile editions. **Essay:** Henry Wheeler Shaw.

AUSTIN, James C.   Professor of English Language and Literature, Southern Illinois University, Edwardsville. Author of *Fields of the Atlantic Monthly*, 1953; *Artemus Ward*, 1964; *Petroleum V. Nasby*, 1965; *Bill Arp*, 1970; *Popular Literature in America*, 1972, and of many articles on American literature, humor, and dialect; also author of the words and lyrics for four musical shows. **Essay:** Petroleum V. Nasby.

BELLMAN, Samuel Irving.   Professor of English, California State Polytechnic University, Pomona. Author of *Marjorie Kinnan Rawlings*, 1974, and articles on Hawthorne and other writers. **Essay:** Edwin Markham.

BENNETT, George N.   Professor of English, Vanderbilt University, Nashville, Tennessee. Author of *The Realism of William Dean Howells, 1889–1920*, 1973. **Essay:** William Dean Howells.

BISIGNANO, Dominic J.   Associate Professor of English, Indiana University-Purdue University, Indianapolis. **Essays:** Hannah Foster; Seba Smith.

BLACKALL, Jean Frantz.   Professor of English, Cornell Univeristy, Ithaca, New York. Author of *Jamesian Ambiguity and The Sacred Fount*, 1966, and of articles on Harold Frederic and Charlotte Brontë in *PMLA, Markham Review, Notes and Queries, Journal of Narrative Techniques*, and *Journal of English and Germanic Philology*. **Essay:** Harold Frederic.

BOWDEN, Mary Weatherspoon.   Co-ordinator of a scholarly edition of Freneau's works. Author of *Philip Freneau*, 1976, and of articles on Washington Irving. **Essay:** Philip Freneau.

BURCHELL, R. A.   Lecturer in American History and Institutions, University of Manchester. Author of *Westward Expansion*, 1975, "American Immigration in the Nineteenth and Twentieth Centuries" in *History of the United States*, edited by W. P. Adams, 1977, and of articles in *Journal of American Studies, California Historical Quarterly*, and *Southern California Quarterly*. **Essay:** Helen Hunt Jackson.

CARDWELL, Guy A.   Professor of English Emeritus, Washington University, St. Louis. Author of *Twins of Genius*, 1953, *Der Amerikanische Roman*, 1954, *Charleston Periodicals*, 1960, and of articles, poems, and stories in periodicals. Editor of *The Uncollected Poems of Henry Timrod*, 1942; *Readings from the Americas*, 1947; *Discussions of Mark Twain*, 1963; *Life on the Mississippi*, by Twain, 1968. **Essay:** Henry Timrod.

COHEN, Hennig.   John Welsh Centennial Professor of History and Literature, University of Pennsylvania, Philadelphia. Former Editor of *American Quarterly* and President of the Melville Society. Author of *The South Carolina Gazette, 1953,* and *The Parade of Heroes: Legendary Figures in American Lore* (with Tristram Potter Coffin), 1978. Editor or Co-Editor of *The Battle Pieces, 1963, Selected Poems,* 1964, and *White Jacket,* 1967, all by Melville; *Humor of the Old Southwest,* 1964; *Folklore in America,* 1966; *The American Culture,* 1968; *Landmarks in American Writing,* 1969; *Folklore from the Working Folk of America,* 1973; *The Indians and Their Captives,* 1977. **Essay:** Herman Melville.

COLLINS, William J.   Member of the English Department, University of California, Davis. Free-lance music critic and the author of a forthcoming book on Maria Callas and Renata Tebaldi. **Essay:** Stephen Collins Foster.

CROWDER, Richard H.   Professor Emeritus of English, Purdue University, Lafayette, Indiana. Fulbright Lecturer, University of Bordeaux, 1963–65. Author of *Those Innocent Years* (on James Whitcomb Riley), 1957, *No Featherbed to Heaven: Michael Wigglesworth,* 1962, and *Carl Sandburg,* 1964. Joint Editor, *Frontiers of American Culture,* 1968. **Essay:** Michael Wigglesworth.

CURRENT-GARCIA, Eugene.   Professor of American Literature, Auburn University, Alabama. Editor of *Southern Humanities Review.* Author of *American Short Stories, 1952, What Is the Short Story?,* 1962, and *Realism and Romanticism in Fiction,* 1962 (all with W. R. Patrick), and of *O. Henry: A Critical Study,* 1965, and *Shem, Ham, and Japheth: The Papers of W. O. Tuggle,* 1973. **Essay:** Anna Cora Mowatt.

DAHL, Curtis.   Samuel Valentine Cole Professor of English, Wheaton College, Norton, Massachusetts. Author of *Robert Montgomery Bird,* 1966, and of articles on William Cullen Bryant, Edward Bulwer-Lytton, and Benjamin Disraeli. **Essay:** William Cullen Bryant.

DUUS, Louise.   Lecturer in American Studies, Douglass College, Rutgers University, New Brunswick, New Jersey. **Essay:** Rebecca Harding Davis.

EICHELBERGER, Clayton L.   Professor of American Literature, University of Texas, Arlington; Editor of *American Literary Realism.* Author of *A Guide to Critical Reviews of United States Fiction, 1870–1910,* 2 vols., 1971–73, *William Dean Howells: A Research Bibliography,* 1976, and *Harper's Lost Reviews: The Literary Notes by Laurence Hutton, John Kendrick Bangs, and Others,* 1976. **Essay:** Richard Harding Davis.

FANNING, Charles.   Assistant Professor of English, Bridgewater State College, Massachusetts. Author of *Finley Peter Dunne and Mr. Dooley: The Chicago Years,* 1978, and of articles on Dunne, the Chicago Irish, and Robert Lowell. Editor of *Mr. Dooley and the Chicago Irish: An Anthology,* 1976. **Essay:** Finley Peter Dunne.

FLETCHER, Ian.   Reader in English Literature, University of Reading, Berkshire. Author of plays and verse, and of *Walter Pater,* 1959 (revised, 1970); *A Catalogue of Imagist Poets,* 1966; *Beaumont and Fletcher,* 1967; *Meredith Now,* 1971; *Swinburne,* 1972. Editor of anthologies of verse and drama, and of works by Lionel Johnson, Victor Plarr, and John Gray. **Essays:** Fitz-James O'Brien; Edgar Saltus.

FLORA, Joseph M.   Professor of English, University of North Carolina, Chapel Hill. Author of *Vardis Fisher,* 1965, *William Ernest Henley,* 1974, and *Frederick Manfred,* 1974. Editor of *The Cream of the Jest* by James Branch Cabell, 1975, and *A Biographical Guide to Southern Literature* (with R. A. Bain and Louis D. Rubin, Jr.), 1978. **Essay:** Owen Wister.

FOSTER, Edward Halsey. Associate Professor and Director of the American Studies Program, Stevens Institute of Technology, Hoboken, New Jersey. Author of *Catharine Maria Sedgwick,* 1974; *The Civilized Wilderness,* 1975; *Josiah Gregg and Lewis Hector Garrard,* 1977; *Susan and Anna Warner,* 1978; and of articles on American literature and American studies. Editor of *Hoboken: A Collection of Essays* (with Geoffrey W. Clark), 1976. **Essays:** Richard Henry Dana, Jr.; Fitz-Greene Halleck; Donald Grant Mitchell; Catharine Maria Sedgwick; Nathaniel Parker Willis.

FRENCH, Warren. Professor of English and Director of the Center for American Studies, Indiana University-Purdue University, Indianapolis; Member of the Editorial Board, *American Literature* and *Twentieth-Century Literature;* series editor for Twayne publishers. Author of *John Steinbeck,* 1961; *Frank Norris,* 1962; *J. D. Salinger,* 1963; *A Companion to "The Grapes of Wrath,"* 1963; *The Social Novel at the End of an Era,* 1966; and a series on American fiction, poetry, and drama, *The Thirties,* 1967, *The Forties,* 1968, *The Fifties,* 1971, and *The Twenties,* 1975. **Essays:** Timothy Shay Arthur; Joseph Holt Ingraham.

GABIN, Jane S. Teaching Assistant in English, University of North Carolina, Chapel Hill. Author of an article on Dudley Buck; has directed a recital of the music and poetry of Sidney Lanier. **Essays:** Richard Hovey; Sidney Lanier.

GERBER, John C. Chairman of the Department of English, State University of New York, Albany; Member of the Editorial Board, *Resources for American Literary Study.* Formerly Chairman of the Department of English, University of Iowa. Author of *Factual Prose* (with Walter Blair), 1945; *Literature,* 1948; *Writers Resource Book,* 1953; and other works on writing and speaking. Editor of *Twentieth-Century Interpretations of "The Scarlet Letter,"* 1968, and *Studies in Huckleberry Finn,* 1971; General Editor of the Iowa-California edition of the works of Mark Twain. **Essays:** Ralph Waldo Emerson; Mark Twain.

GITENSTEIN, Barbara. Assistant Professor of English, Central Missouri State University, Warrensburg. Author of articles on Nathaniel Hawthorne and Isaac Bashevis Singer in *The Comparatist* and *Yiddish.* **Essay:** Abraham Cahan.

GLASRUD, Clarence A. Professor of English Emeritus, Moorhead State University, Minnesota; Advisory Editor, *Studies in American Fiction;* Member of the Board of Publications, Norwegian-American Historical Association. Author of *Hjalmar Hjorth Boyesen: A Biographical and Critical Study,* 1963. Editor of *The Age of Anxiety,* 1960. **Essays:** H. H. Boyesen; F. Marion Crawford; Oliver Wendell Holmes; Charles Dudley Warner.

HIGGINS, William. Member of the Department of English, Western Carolina University, Cullowhee, North Carolina. **Essays:** Robert Herrick; Joseph Kirkland.

HITCHCOCK, Bert. Associate Professor and Head of the Department of English, Auburn University, Alabama; member of the bibliography committee, Society for the Study of Southern Literature. Author of "Whitman: The Pedagogue as Poet," in *Walt Whitman Review,* 1974. **Essay:** S. Weir Mitchell.

HOFFMAN, Daniel. Professor of English, University of Pennsylvania, Philadelphia. Author of several books of verse, the most recent being *Able Was I Ere I Saw Elba,* 1977, and of critical works including *The Poetry of Stephen Crane,* 1957; *Form and Fable in American Fiction,* 1961; *Poe Poe Poe Poe Poe Poe Poe,* 1972; *Barbarous Knowledge: Myth in the Poetry of Yeats, Graves, and Muir,* 1973. Editor of anthologies and of works by Crane and Robert Frost. **Essays:** Stephen Crane; Washington Irving; Edgar Allan Poe.

HUDSPETH, Robert N.   Associate Professor of English, Pennsylvania State University, University Park. Author of *Ellery Channing*, 1973. Currently editing the letters of Margaret Fuller. **Essay:** William Ellery Channing.

INGE, M. Thomas.   Professor and Chairman of the Department of English, Virginia Commonwealth University, Richmond; Founding Editor of *Resources for American Literary Study* and *American Humor*. Author of *Donald Davidson: An Essay and a Bibliography*, 1965, and *Davidson*, 1971 (both with T. D. Young). Editor of works by George Washington Harris and William Faulkner, and of *Agrarianism in American Literature*, 1969; *The Black Experience*, 1969; *Studies in Light in August*, 1971; *Ellen Glasgow: Centennial Essays*, 1975. **Essay:** George Washington Harris.

JOHNSON, Robert K.   Professor of English, Suffolk University, Boston. Author of articles on Richard Wilbur, Wallace Stevens, T. S. Eliot, and William Carlos Williams. **Essay:** Frederick Goddard Tuckerman.

JOYNER, Nancy C.   Member of the Department of English, Western Carolina University, Cullowhee, North Carolina. **Essay:** Susanna Rowson.

KELLNER, Bruce.   Associate Professor of English, Millersville State College, Pennsylvania. Author of *Carl Van Vechten and the Irreverent Decades*, 1968; *The Wormwood Poems of Thomas Kinsella*, 1972; *The Poet as Translator*, 1973; *Alfred Kazin's Exquisites: An Excavation*, 1975. Editor of *Selected Writings of Van Vechten about Negro Arts and Letters*, 1978. **Essays:** Henry Blake Fuller; Henry Wadsworth Longfellow.

KING, Kimball.   Member of the Department of English, University of North Carolina, Chapel Hill. **Essays:** George Washington Cable; Augustus Baldwin Longstreet; Thomas Nelson Page.

KUHN, John G.   Professor of English and Director of Theatre, Rosemont College, Pennsylvania. Author of an article in *Walt Whitman Review*, 1962, poems in *Denver Quarterly*, 1973, and a play, *Statu(t)es Like Cartoons*, produced 1976. **Essays:** James Nelson Barker; William Dunlap.

KULSHRESTHA, Chirantan.   Reader in English, University of Hyderabad, India. Author of *The Saul Bellow Estate*, 1976; *Bellow: The Problem of Affirmation*, 1978; chapters in *Considerations*, edited by Meenakshi Mukherjee, 1977, and *Through the Eyes of the World: International Essays in American Literature*, edited by Bruce A. Lohof, 1978; and articles in *Chicago Review, American Review, Quest, Indian Literature*, and other periodicals. Editor of *Not by Politics Alone!* (with V. V. John), 1978. **Essay:** Albion W. Tourgée.

LEARY, Lewis.   Kenan Professor of English, University of North Carolina, Chapel Hill. Author of *Idiomatic Mistakes in English*, 1932; *That Rascal Freneau: A Study in Literary Failure*, 1941; *The Literary Career of Nathaniel Tucker*, 1951; *Mark Twain*, 1960; *Twain's Letters to Mary*, 1961; *John Greenleaf Whittier*, 1962; *Washington Irving*, 1963; *Norman Douglas*, 1967; *Southern Excursions*, 1971; *Faulkner of Yoknapatawpha County*, 1973; *Soundings: Some Early American Writers*, 1975; *American Literature: A Study and Research Guide*, 1976. Editor of works by Freneau and Twain, and several collections of essays. **Essay:** Henry David Thoreau.

LEVERNIER, James A.   Assistant Professor of English, University of Arkansas, Little Rock. Contributor to *ESQ: A Journal of the American Renaissance, Research Studies, The Markham Review, Explicator*, and other periodicals. Editor of *An Essay for the Recording of Illustrious Providences* by Increase Mather, 1977, and *The Indians and Their Captives* (with

Hennig Cohen), 1977. **Essays:** Ebenezer Cooke; Louise Imogen Guiney; Charles Fenno Hoffman; Francis Hopkinson; Joaquin Miller; Bayard Taylor; John Trumbull.

LOHOF, Bruce A.   Associate Professor and Chairman of the Department of History, University of Miami; Joint Editor of the *Indian Journal of American Studies,* and member of the editorial board of *Journal of Popular Culture.* Former Senior Fulbright-Hays Scholar and Director of the American Studies Research Centre, Hyderabad, India. Author of articles for *Social Studies Bulletin, Industrial Archaeology, Centennial Review,* and other periodicals, and of papers for the American Studies Association and the Popular Culture Association. **Essays:** Horatio Alger; George Henry Boker; Margaret Deland; Timothy Dwight; Edward Eggleston.

LONGEST, George C.   Associate Professor and Assistant to the Chairman of the Department of English, Virginia Commonwealth University, Richmond. Author of *Three Virginia Writers: Mary Johnston, Thomas Nelson Page, and Amélie Rives Troubetzkoy,* 1978, and of many articles and reviews. **Essays:** James Lane Allen; Joseph G. Baldwin; Bret Harte; Johnson Jones Hooper.

MARRS, Suzanne.   Assistant Professor of English, State University of New York, Oswego. **Essay:** Thomas Bangs Thorpe.

MESERVE, Walter J.   Professor of Theatre and Drama, Indiana University, Bloomington. Author of *An Outline of American Drama,* 1965, *Robert Sherwood: Reluctant Moralist,* 1970, and *An Emerging Entertainment: The Drama of the American People to 1828,* 1977. Editor of *The Complete Plays of W. D. Howells,* 1960; *Discussions of Modern American Drama,* 1966; *American Satiric Comedies,* 1969; *Modern Dramas from Communist China,* 1970; *The Rise of Silas Lapham* by W. D. Howells, 1971; *Studies in "Death of a Salesman,"* 1972; *Modern Literature from China,* 1974. **Essays:** Robert Montgomery Bird; Augustin Daly; Clyde Fitch; Edward Harrigan; Bronson Howard; Langdon Mitchell; John Howard Payne; Augustus Thomas; Royall Tyler.

MILLER, Jordan Y.   Chairman of the Department of English, University of Rhode Island, Kingston. Exchange Professor, University of East Anglia, Norwich, 1977. Author of *Eugene O'Neill and the American Critic,* 1962; *Maxwell Anderson: Gifted Technician,* 1967; *Eugene O'Neill,* 1968; *The War Play Comes of Age,* 1969; *Expressionism: The Wasteland Enacted,* 1974; *The Other O'Neill,* 1974. Editor of *American Dramatic Literature,* 1961, *Playwright's Progress,* 1965, and *Twentieth-Century Interpretations of "A Streetcar Named Desire,"* 1971. **Essay:** James A. Herne.

MONTEIRO, George.   Professor of English, Brown University, Providence, Rhode Island. Editor of *Henry James and John Hay: The Record of a Friendship,* 1965; *Poems* by Emily Dickinson, 1967; *The Scarlet Letter* by Hawthorne (with Hyatt H. Waggoner), 1968; *The Poetical Works of Longfellow,* 1975. **Essay:** John Hay.

MOORE, Jack B.   Professor of English, University of South Florida, Tampa. Author of *The Literature of Early America,* 1968; *The Literature of the American Renaissance,* 1969; *Guide to "Idylls of the King,"* 1969; *Maxwell Bodenheim,* 1970; *The Literature of the American Realistic Period,* 1971; *Guide to "Last of the Mohicans,"* 1971. **Essay:** Ignatius Donnelly.

MOORE, Rayburn S.   Professor of English and Chairman, Division of Language and Literature, University of Georgia, Athens; Member of the Editorial Board, *Georgia Review.* Author of *Constance Fenimore Woolson,* 1963, *Paul Hamilton Hayne,* 1972, and many articles and reviews. Editor of *The Major and Selected Short Stories of Woolson,* 1967.

Essays: Thomas Holley Chivers; John Esten Cooke; Paul Hamilton Hayne; William Gilmore Simms; Constance Fenimore Woolson.

MORSBERGER, Katharine M. Feature Writer, Pitzer College, Claremont, California. Author of articles on Nathaniel Hawthorne, Lew Wallace, and John Steinbeck. **Essay** (with Robert E. Morsberger): Lew Wallace.

MORSBERGER, Robert E. Professor and Chairman of the Department of English, California State Polytechnic University, Pomona. Author of *James Thurber,* 1964; *Commonsense Grammar and Style,* 1965; *Swordplay and the Elizabethan and Jacobean Stage,* 1974; and of articles on Lew Wallace. Editor of *Viva Zapata!* by John Steinbeck, 1975. **Essay** (with Katharine M. Morsberger): Lew Wallace.

O'DONNELL, Thomas F. Professor of English, State University of New York, Brockport. Author of *Harold Frederic* (with Hoyt C. Franchere), 1961, and of articles on American writers, especially those of New York State, for *American Transcendental Quarterly* and other periodicals. Joint Editor of *A Bibliography of Harold Frederic,* 1975, and editor of works by Frederic, James Kirke Paulding, and Adriaen Van Der Donck. **Essays:** Anne Bradstreet; Joseph Rodman Drake; James Kirke Paulding.

PERKINS, Barbara M. Director of Writing Improvement, Humanities Program, Eastern Michigan University, Ypsilanti. **Essay:** John William De Forest.

PERKINS, George. Professor of English, Eastern Michigan University, Ypsilanti. Author or editor of *Writing Clear Prose,* 1964; *Varieties of Prose,* 1966; *The Theory of the American Novel,* 1970; *Realistic American Short Fiction,* 1972; *American Poetic Theory,* 1972; *The American Tradition in Literature* (with others), fourth edition, 1974. **Essays:** Nathaniel Hawthorne; Henry James.

PERRY, Margaret. Assistant Director for Reader Services, University of Rochester Libraries, New York; Contributing Editor, *Afro-American in New York Life and History.* Author of *A Bio-Bibliography of Countée P. Cullen,* 1971, *Silence to the Drums: A Survey of the Literature of the Harlem Renaissance,* 1976, and of several short stories published in periodicals. **Essay:** Phillis Wheatley.

PICKARD, John B. Associate Professor of English, University of Florida, Gainesville. Author of *Whittier: An Introduction and Interpretation,* 1961, and *Emily Dickinson,* 1967. Editor of *Legends of New England* by Whittier, 1965, and *The Letters of Whittier,* 3 vols., 1975. **Essays:** James Russell Lowell; John Greenleaf Whittier.

REED, John Q. Chairman of the Department of English, Pittsburg State University, Kansas. Author of *Benjamin Penhallow Shillaber,* 1972, and of articles on Artemus Ward, Henry James, Faulkner, and Twain, in *American Literature, Midcontinent American Studies Journal, Encyclopaedia Britannica, Civil War History,* and *Midwest Quarterly.* **Essay:** Artemus Ward.

REEVES, James. Author of more than 50 books, including verse (*Collected Poems,* 1974), plays, and books for children; critical works include *The Critical Sense,* 1956, *Understanding Poetry,* 1965, *Commitment to Poetry,* 1969, *Inside Poetry* (with Martin Seymour-Smith), 1970, and *The Reputation and Writings of Alexander Pope,* 1976. Editor of many collections and anthologies, and of works by D. H. Lawrence, Donne, Clare, Hopkins, Robert Browning, Dickinson, Coleridge, Graves, Swift, Johnson, Marvell, Gray, Whitman, and others; translator of fairy tales. Died, 1978. **Essay:** Emily Dickinson.

REILLY, John M. Associate Professor of English, State University of New York, Albany; Advisory Editor, *Obsidian: Black Literature in Review*, and *Melus*. Author of the bibliographical essay on Richard Wright in *Black American Writers* and of articles on Wright and other Afro-American writers, and on detective fiction, in *Colorado Quarterly*, *Phylon*, *CLA Journal*, *Journal of Black Studies*, *Armchair Detective*, *Journal of Popular Culture*, and other periodicals. Editor of *Twentieth-Century Interpretations of "Invisible Man"*, 1970, *Richard Wright: The Critical Reception*, 1978, and of the reference book *Detective and Crime Writers*, 1980. **Essay:** William Wells Brown.

RENDER, Sylvia Lyons. Specialist in Afro-American History and Culture, Manuscript Division, Library of Congress, Washington, D.C. Author of the introduction to Charles Waddell Chesnutt's *The Marrow of Tradition*, 1969, and of articles in *Encyclopaedia Britannica*, *CLA Journal*, *North Carolina Folklore*, and *Tennessee Folklore Society Bulletin*. Editor of *The Short Fiction of Chesnutt*, 1974. **Essay:** Charles Waddell Chesnutt.

RINGE, Donald A. Professor of English, University of Kentucky, Lexington. Author of *James Fenimore Cooper*, 1962, *Charles Brockden Brown*, 1966, and *The Pictorial Mode: Space and Time in the Art of Bryant, Irving, and Cooper*, 1971. Member of the Editorial Board for *The Writings of James Fenimore Cooper*. **Essays:** Hugh Henry Brackenridge; Charles Brockden Brown; James Fenimore Cooper; John Pendleton Kennedy; John Neal.

ROVIT, Earl. Professor of English, City College of New York. Author of *Herald to Chaos: The Novels of Elizabeth Madox Roberts*, 1960; *Ernest Hemingway*, 1963; *The Player King*, 1965; *Saul Bellow*, 1967; *A Far Cry*, 1967; *Crossings*, 1973. **Essays:** Henry Adams; Jones Very.

SEELYE, Catherine. Free-lance writer. **Essay:** Eugene Field.

SEYERSTED, Per. Professor of American Literature and Director of the American Institute, University of Oslo; Chairman of the Nordic Association for American Studies. Author of *Gilgamesj*, 1967, and *Kate Chopin: A Critical Biography*, 1969. Editor of *The Complete Works of Kate Chopin*, 1969. **Essay:** Kate Chopin.

SHARMA, J. N. Academic Associate, American Studies Research Centre, Hyderabad. **Essay:** Ambrose Bierce.

SHUCARD, Alan R. Associate Professor of English, University of Wisconsin-Parkside, Kenosha. Author of two books of verse – *The Gordon Bog*, 1970, and *The Louse on the Head of the Lord*, 1972. **Essay:** Paul Laurence Dunbar.

SMITH, Stan. Lecturer in English, University of Dundee, Scotland. Author of the forthcoming book *A Superfluous Man* (on Edward Thomas), and of articles on modern literature for *Critical Quarterly*, *Literature and History*, *Irish University Review*, *Scottish International Review*, and other periodicals. **Essay:** Lafcadio Hearn.

STAGG, Louis Charles. Professor of English, Memphis State University, Tennessee; Member of the Executive Committee, Tennessee Philological Association. Author of *Index to Poe's Critical Vocabulary*, 1966; *Index to the Figurative Language in the Tragedies of Webster, Jonson, Heywood, Chapman, Marston, Tourneur, and Middleton*, 7 vols., 1967–70, revised edition, as *Index to the Figurative Language of the Tragedies of Shakespeare's Chief 17th-Century Contemporaries*, 1977. **Essay:** William Gillette.

STANFORD, Donald E. Professor of English, Louisiana State University, Baton Rouge; Editor of *The Southern Review*. Author of *New England Earth*, 1941, and *The Traveler*,

1955. Editor of *The Poems of Edward Taylor*, 1960; *Nine Essays in Modern Literature*, 1965; *Selected Poems of Robert Bridges*, 1974; *Selected Poems of S. Foster Damon*, 1974. **Essay:** Edward Taylor.

STERN, Madeleine B. Free-lance Writer; Partner in Leona Rostenberg-Rare Books, New York. Author of *Louisa May Alcott*, 1950; *Imprints on History: Book Publishers and American Frontiers*, 1956; *We the Women: Career Firsts of 19th-Century America*, 1963; *Heads and Headlines: The Phrenological Fowlers*, 1971; *Old and Rare: Thirty Years in the Book Business* (with Leona Rostenberg), 1975, and of several biographies for adults and for children. Editor of *Women on the Move*, 1972; *The Victoria Woodhull Reader*, 1974; and *Louisa's Wonder Book*, 1975, *Behind a Mask*, 1975, and *Plots and Counterplots*, 1976, all by Louisa May Alcott. **Essays:** Louisa May Alcott; Mary Noailles Murfree; Harriet Beecher Stowe.

THWAITE, Ann. Free-lance Writer; Contributing Editor of *Cricket* magazine. Author of 15 books for children, the most recent being *Chatterbox*, 1978, and of *Waiting for the Party: The Life of Frances Hodgson Burnett*, 1974; currently working on a book on Edmund Gosse. Editor of the *Allsorts* series for children and of *My Oxford*, 1977. **Essay:** Frances Hodgson Burnett.

WALSH, George. Publisher and Free-lance Writer. **Essay:** Joel Chandler Harris.

WEALES, Gerald. Professor of English, University of Pennsylvania, Philadelphia; Drama Critic for *The Reporter* and *Commonweal*. Author of *Religion in Modern English Drama*, 1961; *American Drama since World War II*, 1962; *A Play and Its Parts*, 1964; *The Jumping-Off Place: American Drama in the 1960's*, 1969; *Clifford Odets*, 1971. Editor of *The Complete Plays of William Wycherley*, 1966, and, with Robert J. Nelson, of the collections *Enclosure*, 1975, and *Revolution*, 1975. **Essays:** James Whitcomb Riley; Mercy Warren.

WESTBROOK, P. D. Professor of English, State University of New York, Albany. Author of *Acres of Flint: Writers of Rural New England*, 1951; *Biography of an Island*, 1958; *The Greatness of Man: An Essay on Dostoevsky and Whitman*, 1961; *Mary Ellen Chase*, 1966; *Mary Wilkins Freeman*, 1967. **Essays:** Edward Bellamy; Mary E. Wilkins Freeman; Sarah Orne Jewett.

WOODRESS, James. Professor of English, University of California, Davis; Editor of *American Literary Scholarship*. Author of *Howells and Italy*, 1952; *Booth Tarkington*, 1955; *A Yankee's Odyssey: The Life of Joel Barlow*, 1958; *Willa Cather: Her Life and Art*, 1970; *American Fiction 1900–1950*, 1974. Editor of *Voices from America's Past* (with Richard Morris), 1961, and *Eight American Authors*, 1971. **Essays:** Joel Barlow; Hamlin Garland; E. W. Howe; Frank Norris; Walt Whitman.